The Tennessee Williams Encyclopedia

The Tennessee Williams Encyclopedia

Edited by Philip C. Kolin

Greenwood Press
Westport, Connecticut • London

Library of Congress Cataloging-in-Publication Data

The Tennessee Williams encyclopedia / edited by Philip C. Kolin.
    p.   cm.
    Includes bibliographical references and index.
    ISBN 0–313–32101–9 (alk. paper)
    1. Williams, Tennessee, 1911–1983—Encyclopedias.   2. Dramatists, American—20th century—
Biography—Encyclopedias.
    PS3545.I5365Z459   2004
    812'.54—dc22   2003059583

British Library Cataloguing in Publication Data is available.

Library of Congress Catalog Card Number: 2003059583
ISBN: 0–313–32101–9

First published in 2004

Greenwood Press, 88 Post Road West, Westport, CT 06881
An imprint of Greenwood Publishing Group, Inc.
www.greenwood.com

Printed in the United States of America

The paper used in this book complies with the
Permanent Paper Standard issued by the National
Information Standards Organization (Z39.48–1984).

10   9   8   7   6   5   4   3   2   1

For Maureen, my wife and partner in all things.

Contents

Preface

The name and accomplishments of Tennessee Williams are synonymous with twentieth-century theater. For over a half century (from the 1930s to the early 1980s) Williams wrote plays that transformed stages and amazed audiences around the world. He made major contributions to the theater in the way that characters are expressed, ideas about sexuality and desire are conveyed, and sets are represented. Williams helped to define desire. Plays like *The Glass Menagerie*, *A Streetcar Named Desire*, and *Cat on a Hot Tin Roof* are icons of American culture that quickly ascended into classic status. *A Streetcar Named Desire*, for example, has been voted the most significant twentieth-century drama by the American Theatre Critics Association and selected as one of the top 50 American films of all time by the American Film Institute. A list of characters from Williams's works reads like a who's who of roles in American drama, presenting a litany of some of the most well-known, colorful, and imaginative characters in the theater— Amanda Wingfield, Blanche DuBois, Stanley Kowalski, Alma Winemiller, Serafina Delle Rose, Kilroy, Brick and Maggie Pollit, Big Daddy, Chance Wayne, Princess Kosmonopolis, Val Xavier, Lady, and the Reverend T. Lawrence Shannon.

Williams's canon is one of the most extensive of any modern playwright. He wrote at least 70 plays, including many one-acts, two novels, five collections of stories, two volumes of poems, a group of finely honed essays, memoirs, letters, journals, and haunting paintings of people and scenes. New or rediscovered plays continue to be uncovered; since 1995, at least four of them have been published for the first time—*Not about Nightingales*, *Spring Storm*, *Stairs to the Roof*, and *Fugitive Kind*. In addition to being an experimenter with theatrical forms, and a spokesperson for the underdog, the fugitive, and the artist, Williams is a cultural hero, in part thanks to the many film and teleplay adaptations of his works known worldwide.

Despite Williams's immense body of work and contributions to the theater, there has been no general encyclopedia of his life and works as there is for Eugene O'Neill. Admittedly, there are numerous biographies and critical books and articles, and even a

Guide to Williams's scholarship. To fill this gap, *The Tennessee Williams Encyclopedia* offers in one convenient, concise, and authoritative volume over 150 detailed entries essential to understanding Williams's life and work. The *Encyclopedia*

- identifies major figures in Williams's life
- supplies a succinct biography of the playwright
- summarizes and concisely interprets Williams's plays and their characters, plots, and themes, as well as his stories, poems, essays, and journals
- provides essential background information about sources and publications
- gives brief histories of the performances of his plays, citing influential directors, actors, producers, and designers
- surveys important film adaptations and how they differ from the plays

AUDIENCE

The Tennessee Williams Encyclopedia will benefit a variety of readers, including public, academic, and school librarians; teachers of drama, theater, film studies, and American literature; students and the general reader; film enthusiasts and theatergoers; directors, designers, and actors at little, community, and regional theaters; and Williams's researchers as well. In short, anyone looking for clear and concise information to understand and appreciate Williams's vast canon should find the *Encyclopedia* a welcome reference work.

MAJOR FEATURES OF THE BOOK

The Tennessee Williams Encyclopedia offers these features for the reader:

1. Entries have been written by many of the leading Tennessee Williams authorities in America and abroad, thus making *The Tennessee Williams Encyclopedia* an authoritative and val-uable reference work. As a rule, entries have been assigned to scholars who are recognized as leading editors and/or critics on the individual topic(s) because they have already published significant work in the area. For example, Albert Devlin, who coedited *The Selected Letters of Tennessee Williams*, supplies the entry on Williams's correspondence; Margaret Thornton, who has edited Williams's *Journals* for Yale University Press, has contributed the entry on the journals; George Crandell, who published *Tennessee Williams: A Descriptive Bibliography*, prepared the entry on texts; Allean Hale, an editor of many of Williams's early apprentice plays, wrote the entries for most of these works; Brenda Murphy, who has published extensively on Williams's theater and government, has written the entry on politics. Editors of two Williams journals, Robert Bray of the *Tennessee Williams Annual Review* and Janet Haedicke of the *Tennessee Williams Literary Journal*, have also contributed several entries. Nicholas Moschovakis, who edited the New Directions volume on Williams's poetry, did the entry on poetry. Among other contributors are scholars whose books bear directly on their entries: Jacqueline O'Connor on madness; Annette Saddik on Williams's late plays and his reputation vis-à-vis Pinter and Beckett; Philip Kolin on *Small Craft Warnings* and other late plays, and on *A Streetcar Named Desire*, cowritten with Maureen Curley; John Clum on gender and sexuality; Leonard Leff on Hollywood; Felicia Hardison Londré on Williams's biography; and Gene Phillips on film adaptations.

2. *The Tennessee Williams Encyclopedia* is the most up-to-date reference work on Williams, including entries on all periods and genres of Williams's work, ranging from the early apprentice plays of the 1930s to his later and less frequently performed plays of the 1960s to the 1980s. Entries supply factual information as well as provide concise critical commentary, introducing and explaining Williams's plots, sources, symbols, characters, sets, and ideas. Some longer entries are really essays on his key concepts, themes, ideas, and techniques.

3. Most entries conclude with a list of further reading to assist readers in locating related information pertinent to the topic of the entry.

4. Helpful cross-references have been included throughout *The Tennessee Williams Encyclopedia* in two ways to assist readers looking for additional or collateral information: first, as boldfaced items within an entry and, second, when appropriate, in a list of related entries introduced by "See also" at the end of an entry.

5. Entries are alphabetically arranged under clearly recognizable headwords for quick reference. A topical listing of entry names, the "Guide to Related Topics," lists them under broad subject headings. A general index provides more detailed access to the *Encyclopedia*'s contents.

6. A detailed chronology lists key Williams's accomplishments and associations.

7. A classified bibliography of primary sources, Williams's works, and a bibliography of secondary sources of scholarship, biography, and criticism can be found at the end of the *Encyclopedia*.

SCOPE AND CONTENT

In light of Williams's extensive canon and seemingly endless friendships and associations, it would be impossible to claim that *The Tennessee Williams Encyclopedia* is comprehensive. That would take five or six volumes. In fact, Lyle Leverich's magisterial first volume on the life of Williams—*Tom: The Unknown Tennessee Williams* (New York: Crown, 1995)—covers only the years 1911 to 1945 and is over 600 pages long; and the second projected volume by John Lahr promises to be equally long or longer. The overriding goal of the *Encyclopedia* is to include only the most essential information on Williams and his work. The entries here provide essential, basic information to help readers understand the context and performance of a Williams's work and the

contours of his life into which it fits. *The Tennessee Williams Encyclopedia* contains, in general, four types of entries: on individuals, on places, on works, and on concepts.

Individuals

Judging by Williams's lifelong travels, extensive writings, and the productions of his plays worldwide, his influence in the theater, film, and the world of the arts, plus his boundless energy, it seems as if he knew everyone in the post–World War II theater. Clearly, not everyone who worked with or on a Williams's play could have been included in *The Tennessee Williams Encyclopedia*, and the goal has been to give readers only the most essential information to answer their questions, to better understand Williams's work, and to put it in a theatrical context. An especially good starting point is the succinct but valuable biography on the playwright included in the *Encyclopedia*.

Not every director, actor, costumer, or sceneographer could have been included. The criteria for inclusion are that the individual had to be of enormous importance to Williams himself and/or occupy a key role of influence on a production and/or reception/interpretation of Williams's work. Sometimes a major director or actor may not be listed in a separate entry, but his or her accomplishments are included under several relevant different entries. For example, Laurence Olivier can be found under entries on "*A Streetcar Named Desire*," "Vivien Leigh" (whom he directed in the British premiere of the play), "*Cat on a Hot Tin Roof*," and "Film Adaptations" for his portrayal of Big Daddy.

Essential biographical data—where, how, why, and when the individual was important to and for Williams—is given in each entry. Factual details include birth/death dates, titles of works, and the origin and significance of the person's relationship with Williams. Focusing directly on or illuminating that relationship, entries exclude details that do not precisely relate to the playwright. Entries also provide focus on Williams's family members who surface or are shadowed in so many of his works: for example, his mother; his sister Rose; his grandfather, the Reverend Walter Dakin; and his father, Cornelius. Individuals who played a major role in Williams's formative years include Williams's teachers, Edward Charles Mabie and Erwin Piscator; directors and early encouragers of his art, including Willard Holland and Lyle Saxon; Williams's "homo/lectual friends" as well as his lovers, such as Eloi Bordelon, Kip Kiernan, Frank Merlo, and Pancho Rodriguez y Gonzales; and his literary sparring partners—Clark Mills (McBurney) and Paul Bigelow. Williams's favorite publisher, James Laughlin, his longtime agent and friend, Audrey Wood, and even his dreaded psychiatrist, Lawrence Kubie, qualify for separate entries.

The Tennessee Williams Encyclopedia emphasizes, too, the theater community who helped Williams realize production of his work, the Mummers and the Group Theater; directors such as Elia Kazan and George Keathley; sceneographer Jo Mielziner; actors who were also Williams's friends—Hugh Cronym, Jessica Tandy, Vivien Leigh, Marlon Brando, Maureen Stapleton, Eli Wallach, Karl Malden, Kim Hunter, and so on. Also worthy of inclusion are those creative artists who had a love-hate relationship with Williams, such as Tallulah Bankhead, Truman Capote, and Gore Vidal. An entry goes to Williams's self-proclaimed executor, Maria Britneva (Lady St. Just). Readers will also find a range of authors who influenced Williams, including Anton Chekhov, Thomas Mann, D.H. Lawrence, Hart Crane, and Samuel Beckett, as well as writers whom he influenced—Edward Albee, William Inge, and Lanford Wilson.

Places

Tennessee Williams was a world traveler, going down and up the crossroads of desire wherever his imagination led him. Appropriately, readers will find entries on major geographic locations where Williams lived, worked, wrote about, and/or mythologized. The criterion for the inclusion of places in *The Tennessee Williams Encyclopedia* is that it had to be all of the above. Although Williams visited and enjoyed Tangiers, for example, it has been excluded since it does not meet all of the above criteria. A major entry on New Orleans, Williams's spiritual home, provides an especially informative literary tour of Williams's famous haunts, residences, and symbolic settings in his plays and fiction found in the various neighborhoods of the city. The entry on Clarksdale, Mississippi, defines and illustrates the importance of this Delta town in Williams's life and work. Key West was a major Williams's retreat—his official address—and a source of inspiration. The entry on St. Louis documents Williams's connection, biographically and imaginatively, to the city he loathed as "St. Pollution." Surprisingly, although Williams is considered a playwright with literary roots in the South, more than 30 of his works—plays and stories—were set in St. Louis, according to Allean Hale.

Works

The largest number of entries in *The Tennessee Williams Encyclopedia* are devoted to Williams's works, including all of the genres in which he wrote—plays, full-length and one-acts, stories, poems, essays, memoirs, journals, even paintings. Separate entries go to every full-length play, from his leftist, socialist works from the 1930s (*Not about Nightingales*, *Fugitive Kind*) to the once-disesteemed canon of the 1960s and 1970s that is now being more regularly performed, studied, and revitalized—*The Gnädiges Fräulein*, *Small Craft Warnings*, *The Two-Character Play*, *Clothes for a Summer Hotel*. The longest entries, of course, are reserved for the most frequently read and performed Williams's plays, for example, *The Glass Menagerie*, *A Streetcar Named Desire*, *Summer and Smoke*, *The Rose Tattoo*, *Cat on a Hot Tin Roof*, *Sweet Bird of Youth*, *The Night of the Iguana*, *Orpheus Descending*. These entries are organized to give readers information about date of composition and date of first performance; relationship to an earlier or later Williams's work(s); influences that affected Williams's composition; characters—the importance of their names, symbolic presence; symbols—Williams's, stock in trade; plot—how it evolved and what analogues and structural parallels it offers; setting; and a brief production history.

Williams's one-act plays also receive attentive coverage in the *Encyclopedia* but are not always listed individually. Instead, many of them are discussed under the heading of the original collection in which they appeared—for example, *American Blues*, or *Twenty-seven Wagons Full of Cotton and Other One-Act Plays*. Usually, only the later one-act plays receive an individual entry—for example, *Lifeboat Drill*, *A Perfect Analysis Given by a Parrot*, *The Remarkable Rooming-House of Mme. Le Monde*. Because Williams's poems are too numerous to list individually, they are also productively grouped and interpreted in the entry "Poems." The history and artistic significance of nearly 20 adaptations of Williams's films are concisely organized under "Film Adaptations." The exceptions, however, are *Baby Doll* and *Stopped Rocking and Other Stories* since Williams wrote these screenplays himself rather than collaborating with or turning them over to a screenwriter.

Williams's poetry, journals, correspondence, and memoirs each have entries. The characters in Tennessee Williams's work are not given individual entries but are discussed in entries for the play or story in which they appear.

Concepts

Longer entries on key ideas, themes, ideologies, and Williams's techniques/dramaturgy are a vital part, perhaps the heart, of *The Tennessee Williams Encyclopedia*. The inclusion of these concepts was based on their overwhelming importance in helping readers understand the shaping influences and ideas that recur in Williams's works. Providing foundational insights, these entries include "Plastic Theater," "Music," "Mythology," "Race," "Gender and Sexuality," "Art," "Politics," "Religion," "Madness," and "Southern Culture and Literature." Each is an essay giving precise background information, clear definitions, identifications of relevant titles and works, and pertinent examples drawn from across the Williams canon. In fact, these conceptual entries are both a synthesis of contemporary scholarly commentary on Williams and a synoptic guide for readers—pulling together much information to offer an excellent overview of Williams's themes, ideologies, and thought. Like the entries on individuals, places, and works, each of those on concepts is essential to learning about Williams's life and theater.

Acknowledgments

Editing a large reference book such as *The Tennessee Williams Encyclopedia* happily brings many debts, and I am honored to acknowledge them here. First off, I thank my contributors for their participation, enthusiasm, and endurance. Coordinating the efforts of 56 contributors has taught me gratitude and patience. I owe a special debt of thanks to Thomas Keith for his help in securing several photos from New Directions, Williams's publisher, included in the *Encyclopedia*. I also thank Allean Hale for her characteristic kindness in answering my frequent questions about dates, people, and influences in Williams's life, and Rick Kramer for his expert help in proofreading.

I am grateful to the administration of the University of Southern Mississippi for its continued support of and appreciation for my work. In particular, I thank the Chair of the English Department, Dr. Angela Ball, for her help, encouragement, and, most of all, her friendship. My thanks go to the research assistants who have worked with me over the last three years, the gestation period of the *Encyclopedia*—Kate McKean, Marcus Weekley, and Micah Stack. To Micah, I record an additional thank you for his assistance in preparing the index for the *Encyclopedia*.

I thank my editors at Greenwood, Dr. George Butler and Anne Thompson, for their help and continued faith in me and this project. Anne deserves extra kudos for the developmental work she did on the *Encyclopedia*, including helping me locate photos to accompany many of the entries.

I have been blessed by the love and care of an extended family that includes Margie and Al Parish, Sister Carmelita Stinn, S.F.C.C., Deacon Ralph and Mary Torrelli, and Abbot Cletus Meigher, O.S.B.

To my children—Kristin, Eric, and Theresa—and to my grandchildren—Evan Philip and Megan Elise—I say thanks for your love. For Kristin I add a father's gratitude for her research assistance for yet another one of "Dad's projects." My wife Maureen, the light of my life, has been a gift from God.

Alphabetical List of Entries

Alphabetical List of Entries

Guide to Related Topics

Below is a list of entries from this *Encyclopedia*, arranged by broad topic. Also see the index for more detailed access to terms.

Awards, Collections, and Festivals

Awards and Honours
Tennessee Williams/New Orleans Literary Festival
Todd, Fred W., Tennessee Williams Collection

Culture, Politics, Religion, and Social Issues

Art
Drugs
Gender and Sexuality
Group Theatre
Kazan, Elia
Madness
Mummers
Music
New School for Social Research
Odets, Clifford
Politics
Race
Religion

Family and Early History

Alpha Tau Omega
Clarksdale, Mississippi
Collected Stories
Dakin, Rosina Maria Francesca Otte
Dakin, Walter Edwin
Holland, Willard
Kramer, Hazel
Mabie, Edward Charles
Mills (McBurney), Clark
Mythology
Poems
Southern Culture and Literature
St. Louis
Williams, Cornelius Coffin
Williams, Edwina Estelle Dakin
Williams, Rose Isabel
Williams, Thomas Lanier, III ("Tennessee")
Williams, Walter Dakin

Guide to Related Topics

People

Albee, Edward
Bankhead, Tallulah
Beckett, Samuel
Benton, Thomas Hart
Bigelow, Paul
Bordelon, Eloi
Bowles, Paul Frederic
Brando, Marlon
Brecht, Bertolt
Britneva, Maria (Lady St. Just)
Capote, Truman
Cerf, Bennett
Chekhov, Anton
Crane, Hart
Cronyn, Hume
Dakin, Rosina Maria Francesca Otte
Dakin, Walter Edwin
Dowling, Eddie
Faulkner, William
Gonzales, Pancho Rodriguez y
Hall, Sir Peter
Holland, Willard
Hunter, Kim
Inge, William
Jones, Margaret (Margo) Virginia
Kazan, Elia
Keathley, George
Kiernan, Kip
Kramer, Hazel
Kubie, Lawrence
Langner, Lawrence
Laughlin, James
Lawrence, D.H.
Leigh, Vivien
Lindsay, Vachel
Lorca, Federico García
Mabie, Edward Charles
Magnani, Anna
Malden, Karl
Mann, Thomas

McCullers, Carson
Merlo, Frank
Mielziner, Jo
Miller, Arthur
Mills (McBurney), Clark
Mishima, Yukio
Nazimova, Alla
Odets, Clifford
O'Neill, Eugene Gladstone
Parrott, Jim
Pinter, Harold
Piscator, Erwin
Saroyan, William
Saxon, Lyle
Selznick, Irene
Stapleton, Maureen
Tandy, Jessica
Taylor, Laurette
Thacher, Molly Day
Vaccaro, Marion Black
Vidal, Gore
Wallach, Eli
Williams, Cornelius Coffin
Williams, Edwina Estelle Dakin
Williams, Rose Isabel
Williams, Thomas Lanier, III ("Tennessee")
Williams, Walter Dakin
Wilson, Lanford
Windham, Donald
Wood, Audrey

Places

Clarksdale, Mississippi
Hollywood
Key West
New Orleans
St. Louis

Theater and Films

Albee, Edward
Bankhead, Tallulah

Beckett, Samuel

Brando, Marlon

Brecht, Bertolt

Britneva, Maria (Lady St. Just)

Chekhov, Anton

Dowling, Eddie

Film Adaptations

Group Theatre

Hall, Sir Peter

Holland, Willard

Hunter, Kim

Inge, William

Jones, Margaret (Margo) Virginia

Kazan, Elia

Keathley, George

Langner, Lawrence

Leigh, Vivien

Lorca, Federico García

Mabie, Edward Charles

Magnani, Anna

Malden, Karl

Mielziner, Jo

Miller, Arthur

Mishima, Yukio

Mummers

Nazimova, Alla

New School for Social Research

Odets, Clifford

O'Neill, Eugene Gladstone

Pinter, Harold

Piscator, Erwin

Plastic Theater

Selznick, Irene

Stapleton, Maureen

Tandy, Jessica

Taylor, Laurette

Thacher, Molly Day

Wallach, Eli

Wilson, Lanford

Windham, Donald

Wood, Audrey

Works*

American Blues

At Liberty

Baby Doll

Battle of Angels

Cairo! Shanghai! Bombay!

Camino Real

Candles to the Sun

Cat on a Hot Tin Roof

The Chalky White Substance

Clothes for a Summer Hotel

Collected Stories

Confessional

Correspondence

The Eccentricities of a Nightingale

Film Adaptations

The Frosted Glass Coffin

Fugitive Kind

The Glass Menagerie

The Gnädiges Fräulein

A House Not Meant to Stand

I Can't Imagine Tomorrow

In the Bar of a Tokyo Hotel

I Rise in Flame, Cried the Phoenix

Journals

Kingdom of Earth (The Seven Descents of Myrtle)

Kirche, Kutchen, und Kinder

Lifeboat Drill

A Lovely Sunday for Creve Coeur

Manuscript Collections

Me, Vasha!

Memoirs

The Milk Train Doesn't Stop Here Anymore

Moise and the World of Reason

---

*This is not a complete list of Williams's works but rather a list of works for which there are entries in the *Encyclopedia*. For a more complete list, see "Bibliography of Primary Sources" at the back of this book.

Guide to Related Topics

Chronology

1909

Rose Isabel Williams, Tennessee's sister, is born on 17 November

1911

Thomas Lanier Williams III is born on 26 March in Columbus, Mississippi

1911–1918

Rose, Tom, and mother Edwina live with her parents, Walter and Rosina Dakin, in Cleveland, Mississippi, while father Cornelius Coffin Williams works as a traveling salesman

1918

Walter Dakin Williams, Tennessee's brother, is born on 21 February; Williams's family moves to St. Louis, where Cornelius Williams becomes branch manager at International Shoe Company

1924

First story, "Isolated," appears in Ben Blewitt Jr. High School newspaper

1928

First story for which Williams was paid, "The Vengeance of Nitocris," is published in *Weird Tales*

1929

Enters University of Missouri in September and joins Alpha Tau Omega (ATO) fraternity

1930–1931

Enters Mahon literary contest at the University of Missouri in fiction, drama, and prose, but highest award Williams receives is third place

1932

Father withdraws Williams from university for failing ROTC; Williams starts work as a clerk at International Shoe Company

1935

First production of a Williams play—*Cairo! Shanghai! Bombay!*—in a backyard Memphis garden with amateur actors

1936

Enrolls at Washington University; writes the one-act play *Twenty-seven Wagons Full of Cotton*

1937

Two leftist plays, *Candles to the Sun* and *Fugitive Kind*, staged by the Mummers, an amateur theater group in St. Louis; transfers to University of Iowa to study playwriting

1938

Graduates from the University of Iowa with a degree in English; writes *Not about Nightingales*, another socialist protest play about a prison revolt

1939

Monumental year in Williams's career: first time to sign his name "Tennessee" Williams for a short story, "The Field of Blue Children," in *Story Magazine*; receives award for *American Blues* from Group Theatre; wins a $1,000 grant from Rockefeller Foundation; meets Audrey Wood, his longtime agent; has possibly his first homosexual experience in French Quarter

1940

Studies playwriting with John Gassner at the New School for Social Research; *Battle of Angels* has disastrous premiere in Boston in December

1941–1942

Travels to Key West, New Orleans, and New York; has first of four cataract operations; collaborates on *You Touched Me!* with Donald Windham

1943

Works for MGM as screenwriter where he writes *The Gentleman Caller*, which later becomes *The Glass Menagerie*

1944

National Institute of Arts and Letters awards Williams $1,000 for *Battle of Angels*; Margo Jones of Dallas directs *The Purification*; *The Glass Menagerie* premieres in Chicago on 26 December; reviewer Claudia Cassidy urges theatergoers to see the masterpiece

1945

Three Williams plays are performed—*Stairs to the Roof* opens in March at the Pasadena Playhouse; *The Glass Menagerie* opens on Broadway for 561 performances and wins New York Drama Critics Circle Award; *You Touched Me!* opens in New York; publishes book *Twenty-seven Wagons Full of Cotton and Other One-Act Plays by Tennessee Williams*

1947–1948

A Streetcar Named Desire comes to New York for 855 performances and wins Williams his first Pulitzer Prize as well as a New York Drama Critics Circle Award and the Donaldson Award; directed by Elia Kazan, who will also direct *Camino Real*, *Baby Doll*, *Cat on a Hot Tin Roof*, and *Sweet Bird of Youth*; *Summer and Smoke* premieres in Dallas and opens on Broadway later in 1948; *One Arm and Other Stories* published; meets longtime lover and companion Frank Merlo

1949

A Streetcar Named Desire, directed by Laurence Olivier and starring his wife Vivien Leigh, premieres in London

1950

Williams's novel *The Roman Spring of Mrs. Stone* is published; Warner Brothers releases film version of *The Glass Menagerie*, the first of Williams's plays to be adapted for the screen

1951

The Rose Tattoo opens in New York for 306 performances; Warner Brothers' acclaimed film of *A Streetcar Named Desire* is released with the original theater cast except for Vivien Leigh, who replaced Jessica Tandy as Blanche

1952

Williams is elected to the National Institute of Arts and Letters

1953

Camino Real opens in New York but closes after only 60 performances

1954

Hard Candy: A Book of Stories is published

1955

Cat on a Hot Tin Roof premieres on 24 March in New York and earns Williams his second Pulitzer Prize

1956

One of Williams's most controversial works—the film *Baby Doll* for which he wrote the screenplay—is released; condemned by Cardinal Spellman of New York; first collection of poems, *In the Winter of Cities*, is published

1957

Orpheus Descending opens in New York for 68 performances

1958

Garden District (*Suddenly Last Summer* and *Something Unspoken*) opens off-Broadway; film of *Cat on a Hot Tin Roof* is released

1959

Sweet Bird of Youth opens in New York on 10 March for 95 performances; screen version of *Suddenly Last Summer* is released

1960

Period of Adjustment, a comedy, opens in New York on 10 November for 132 performances; film version of *Orpheus Descending*—titled *The Fugitive Kind*—is released

1961

The Night of the Iguana premieres in New York on 28 December and runs for 316 performances

1962

The Milk Train Doesn't Stop Here Anymore premieres at the Spoleto Festival on 16 July; films of *Sweet Bird of Youth* and *Period of Adjustment* are released

1963

The Milk Train Doesn't Stop Here Anymore opens in New York on 16 January and runs for 69 performances

1964

Highly successful film of *The Night of the Iguana* is released

1966

Slapstick Tragedy (*The Mutilated* and *The Gnädiges Fräulein*) closes in New York after only seven performances; *The Knightly Quest*, a novella and stories, is published

1967

First version of *The Two-Character Play* (later *Out Cry*) opens in London on 12 December

1968

Seven Descents of Myrtle (later *Kingdom of Earth*) opens on 27 March for 29 performances; the film of *The Milk Train Doesn't Stop Here Anymore*—called *Boom!*—is released

1969

Baptized a Roman Catholic by Father Joseph LeRoy, a Jesuit priest, in Key West; *In the Bar of a Tokyo Hotel* opens in New York on 11 May for 23 performances; Williams is admitted to Barnes Hospital in St. Louis by brother Dakin for alcohol and drug detoxification

1970

Dragon Country: A Book of Plays is published; Williams appears on *The David Frost Show* and publicly admits his homosexuality

Chronology

1971

Out Cry, the revised *The Two-Character Play*, opens on 2 July in Chicago

1972

Small Craft Warnings opens off-Broadway on 2 April and moves to Broadway in June for 200 performances; Williams plays the role of Doc, the only time he acted in a professional production of one of his plays

1973

Revised version of *Out Cry* premieres in New York on 1 March for 13 performances

1974

The Latter Days of a Celebrated Soubrette, a revision of *The Gnädiges Fräulein*, premieres off-Broadway for only one performance; *Eight Mortal Ladies Possessed: A Book of Stories* is published

1975

Highly controversial and explicit *Memoirs* and *Moise and the World of Reason*, Williams's second novel, are published; *The Red Devil Battery Sign* is staged in Boston and then New York

1976

This Is (An Entertainment) premieres on 16 January at American Conservatory Theatre in San Francisco

1977

Androgyne, Mon Amour, Williams's second collection of poetry, is published; *Vieux Carré* opens on 11 May in New York for only 11 performances

1979

A Lovely Sunday for Creve Coeur opens in New York on 10 January for 36 performances; Williams's postmodern and camp play *Kirche, Kutchen, und Kinder* ("Church,

Kitchen, and Children") plays at the Jean Cocteau Repertory in New York

1980

Will Mr. Merriwether Return from Memphis? premieres at the Tennessee Williams Performing Arts Center in Key West on 24 January; *Clothes for a Summer Hotel* opens on 26 March

1981

Two of Williams's plays premiere—*A House Not Meant to Stand* at the Goodman Theatre in Chicago on 24 August and *Something Cloudy, Something Clear* at the Jean Cocteau Repertory in New York, the last of his plays to be professionally produced while Williams is alive

1982

Receives honorary doctorate from Harvard University

1983

Dies by choking on a medicine bottle cap at the Hotel Elysee (Elysian Fields!) on 24 February in New York; memorial service takes place at St. Louis Cathedral in New Orleans but Williams is buried in St. Louis

1984

Stopped Rocking and Other Screenplays is published

1985

Collected Stories—with an introduction by Gore Vidal—is published

1996

The Notebook of Trigorin opens at the Cincinnati Playhouse in the Park on 5 September

1998

Not about Nightingales premieres at the Royal National Theatre in London on 5

March and then moves to Houston and to New York; *Streetcar* opera, scored by Andre Previn, premieres 19 September at San Francisco Opera Company

2000

Stairs to the Roof, unperformed since 1945, is staged at the Krannert Center for Performing Arts at the University of Illinois in November; Volume 1 of *The Selected Letters of Tennessee Williams* is published

2003

Hartford (Connecticut) Stage features *8 by Tenn* including three previously unproduced one-act plays and five others that have been infrequently staged

2004

Williams Revival at Kennedy Center for the Performing Arts in Washington, D.C., in April

A

Albee, Edward (1928–). A three-time Pulitzer Prize–winning playwright, Edward Albee has often voiced a special affection for Tennessee Williams. Albee quotes famous lines twice from *A Streetcar Named Desire* in *Who's Afraid of Virginia Woolf?* (1962), once about a poker night and again as George intones the haunting lines: "Flores, flores para los muertos. Flores." When asked why he chose to echo Williams, Albee, who teaches playwriting at the University of Houston, replied, "It was a joke. I was very fond of Tennessee and admired his work. I thought he would enjoy hearing his lines coming from the mouths of Martha and George." Additionally, Albee drew inspiration from another Williams play—the long speech in *Garden District* for the model of Jerry's narrative in *The Zoo Story*, beginning, "I've been to the zoo . . ."

There are many reasons for Albee's affinity for Williams. Both are indebted to **Chekhov** and the ironies of his plays. Both frequently depict a hostile universe in which isolation can only be relieved by sanctuary—whether through death, the creation of a more acceptable reality, the harboring em-brace of a significant partner, or total immersion in fantasy. Albee and Williams look for a way to hold off a malevolent and threatening world. Though approaching their material differently, Albee and Williams are experimenters, using a variety of theatrical forms. Albee's plays range variously from the realistic to the absurd, but an air of menace hovers over his characters. In plays ranging from such early one-acts as *The Zoo Story* and *The American Dream* to the full-length *Who's Afraid of Virginia Woolf?*, *A Delicate Balance*, *All Over*, and the more contemporary *Three Tall Women* and *The Goat: or Who Is Sylvia?*, Albee's characters, like Williams's, exist in a state of continual crisis, seeking desperately to provide insulation against an encroaching reality or desperately searching for escape from a loveless world. Ultimately, the work of both playwrights depends on the incisiveness and clarity of language. That medium is a scalpel with which Albee dissects contemporary society and reveals its crippled inhabitants, while Williams's evocation of the lyrical results from his deep empathy for the lost and the injured. A key idea in Albee's work, reflected in Williams's plays as well, is the need to bond in love-hate relationships rather than face a life of solitary existence. Solitude is unendurable in Williams, as it is in Albee. With both playwrights, characters hover in a "delicate balance" on that tightrope perched precariously between sanity and madness. Accordingly, Albee and Williams write about the emotionally and psychologically distressed. Despite the fact that many of Williams's plays shock with violence, rape, cannibalism, castration, and drug addiction, he maintains, however, a deep empathy with his damaged characters. Both playwrights also reveal a similar debilitating view of American life and deal with the consequences of escape from its pain by immersion in a more comforting world of illusion.

Illusion is a major theme in Albee and Williams. George and Martha's construction of a fantasy child and the destruction of that fiction in *Who's Afraid of Virginia Woolf?* offers an intriguing parallel to Laura's world of glass. In a rage, Tom attempts to destroy Laura's menagerie to force his sister to return to a world of reality she regards as hostile. The feat is echoed in George's destruction of his and Martha's imaginary child. In *A Streetcar Named Desire*, Blanche bears an equal need to immerse herself in a delusion of the Old South where she can find comfort and escape, just as Zelda seeks refuge in the asylum in Williams's *Clothes for a Summer Hotel*. This same tendency to create an avenue of escape is found in Albee's *The Zoo Story*, in which Peter creates a small, insular world where he can be tranquil, temporary as it may be, until he is forced to accept a shattering reality. In Albee's plays, illusion is destroyed so that the characters can adjust to a new reality, while in Williams's plays, the choice is more frequently for illusion or death. Zelda's cry in *Clothes for a Summer Hotel* aptly articulates

Williams's predominant theme of the need for a safe harbor. The fantasy refuge for Albee's Martha, however, is consciously destroyed by George who knows both the danger and the solace of the sanctuary they have conceived. He is equally aware that, ultimately, survival means the acceptance of reality and the necessary destruction of illusion, no matter how comforting the latter may be. Albee thus joins Williams in using Strindbergian life lies around which to build some of the major dramas of the twentieth century.

Further Reading

Kolin, Philip C. *Conversations with Edward Albee*. Jackson: University Press of Mississippi, 1988.

Sidney Berger

Alpha Tau Omega. The fraternity that Williams pledged at the University of Missouri in 1931 was Alpha Tau Omega (ATO). His membership was no doubt engineered by his father **Cornelius** who had relatives in ATO and who saw a fraternity as a manly organization for his son to join. Williams's early letters are filled with events at the fraternity house, from dress codes (white shirts were worn at dinner) to social events and even a raid on "Greektown" by revenue agents in 1932. An athletic Williams represented ATO at a cross-country meet. His college writing may have been further encouraged by being an ATO; Coleman Scott Ware, an English instructor, lived in the ATO house. Undoubtedly, Williams's experiences as an ATO brother influenced many of his later works. Several of Williams's characters were modeled after his ATO brothers. Jim Conor was the source for Jim O'Connor in *The Glass Menagerie*, and Williams's roommate Harold Mitchell turned into Mitch in *A Streetcar Named Desire*. Another ATO fraternity brother, Jack Bud Pollitt, the "Bull of the Ball," was the impetus for Brick in *Cat on a Hot Tin Roof.* And Blanche's most illustrious, if elusive, beau in *A Streetcar Named Desire* is Shep Huntleigh, who presented her with his ATO pin.

Further Reading

Hale, Allean. "How a Tiger Became the Cat." *Tennessee Williams Literary Journal* 2.1 (Winter 1990–1991): 33–38.
Leverich, Lyle. *Tom: The Unknown Tennessee Williams.* New York: Crown, 1995.

Philip C. Kolin

American Blues. *American Blues* (1939, 1948) began as three sketches that Williams submitted to the **Group Theatre** under that umbrella title to suggest that together they constituted a full-length play. For this Williams received a special award of $100 in 1939. After the success of *The Glass Menagerie* and *A Streetcar Named Desire*, Dramatists Play Service published an acting edition of the original three pieces— *Moony's Kid Don't Cry, The Dark Room,* and *The Case of the Crushed Petunias*— along with two others, *The Unsatisfactory Supper* and *Ten Blocks on the Camino Real*, all collected under the title *American Blues: Five Short Plays by Tennessee Williams.* A "Publisher's Note" indicates that Williams had wanted to withhold the "early and immature" *Case of the Crushed Petunias* but was persuaded that the public would surely recognize its special, "lighter" merits.

Moony's Kid Don't Cry began as a one-act titled *Hot Milk at Three in the Morning,* which Williams wrote in 1931 for a play competition at the University of Missouri and in which Lyle Leverich sees the influence of **Eugene O'Neill's** *Before Breakfast.* Moony is a restless backwoodsman trapped in a factory job, a cramped apartment, and marriage, with a month-old baby. While his thin, ailing wife Jane prepares hot milk to help him get back to sleep, he rhapsodizes about the stars, sky, wind, and river of the North Woods. Her dialogue, in contrast, is anchored in the mundane: diapers, illness, money. She reproaches him for his extravagant purchase of a hobbyhorse for the infant and calls him a fool. Moony takes his axe and opens the door, declaring that he will cut his own way through the world alone. But as he hesitates on the threshold, Jane fetches his "property" to take with him; she places the blanket-wrapped baby in his arms and leaves the room. Succumbing to the responsibility of fatherhood, Moony realizes his escape must be through whatever freedoms he can make possible for his kid.

The Dark Room is a conversation between a spinsterish social worker and an Italian American whose husband cannot work and whose elder sons have left home. Mrs. Pocciotti continues doing her household chores as she stoically answers questions about her teenage daughter Tina, who has spent the last six months secluded in her darkened room. The gradual revelation of the girl's story serves as the narrative through-line: her boyfriend's parents forced him to marry a German girl; lately the boyfriend Max has been bringing Tina food and is the only one she allows into the dark room. Tina is always naked and is clearly pregnant. Thematically, *The Dark Room* touches upon issues of social class difference and ethnic prejudice. The symbolism of the offstage dark room linked to the unseen Tina portrays women and their sexuality as something to be hidden away.

The Case of the Crushed Petunias, written in 1941, is dedicated "to the talent and charm of Miss Helen Hayes." Miss Dorothy Simple, a 26-year-old maiden reports to the police that during the night someone with size 11D shoes had crushed the double rows of petunias surrounding her shop. The first customer of the day is a man with size 11D shoes, whose clumsiness occasions some physical comedy. He confesses to having crushed the petunias because Miss Simple had been using them to barricade her heart against life. He offers a packet of seeds as restitution. She is shocked at the thought of growing wild roses from the seeds, but he gradually succeeds in convincing her to leave an ordered existence behind rows of petunias and her Boston state of mind and to meet him that night on Highway No. 77, "where roots have cleft the rocks and made them crumble," a phrase that adumbrates the violets breaking the rocks in *Camino Real*. Miss Simple agrees to meet him. Her change of heart—a new readiness to defy convention in Primanproper, Massachusetts—leads to her dropping the case against the petunia crusher. Asking the police officer for directions to Highway No. 77, she is warned that people do outrageous things there and can never return to Primanproper. But Dorothy bids her old life good-bye.

All three plays of the original *American Blues* collection explore themes of confinement and liberation. The cramped apartment, the economic burden of marriage and family, the prejudices that stigmatize and isolate individuals on the basis of ethnicity or social class, the rigid social conventions of a puritanical mind-set—all restrict and limit the freedom of self-expression. Moony wants to find himself again through a return to nature but channels the yearning into a gift for his child. Tina's retreat to the dark room may be simultaneously a socially constructed prison and a hideaway where passion can be unleashed. And Miss Simple gives up her ordered existence to venture into the unknown. The "blues" are a yearning for space in which the personality can expand.

The Long Stay Cut Short, or, The Unsatisfactory Supper uses characters and plot elements that would reappear in the later one-act *Twenty-seven Wagons Full of Cotton* (1945), in the movie *Baby Doll* (1956), and in the full-length play *Tiger Tail* (1978). A twilight storm is brewing when the "large and indolent" Baby Doll comes out on the porch of the Mississippi frame house, followed by her husband Archie Lee. They complain about Aunt Rose's having undercooked the mess of greens they had for supper. Then the delicate elderly aunt comes out to cut roses before the wind blows them away. She tries to be ingratiating, but the young couple become irritated with her. After she wanders off, they discuss which other relatives might take her in, because, as Archie claims, the old lady "[has] out-stayed her welcome," Aunt Rose returns, eager to show them the "poems of nature" she has gathered, and while she is apprehensive about their dissatisfaction with the supper, she expresses her trust in Jesus and confidence that when it is her time to go, a wind will carry her up like roses. Archie Lee declares that he will transfer her to someone else's house the next morning. Changes in the lighting and sound herald a twister. While Archie Lee and Baby Doll hurry to the cellar, Aunt Rose refuses to go with them, and as the wind and darkness swirl around her, she sinks to her knees, releases her armload of roses to the wind, and is blown toward the rosebush. The character of Aunt Rose disappears from later workings of this material when the focus shifts to Baby Doll's sexuality, yet aspects of the maiden aunt whose poetic or spiritual qualities place her at odds with the vulgar or provincial environment in which she is trapped appear in other early one-acts such as *Portrait of a Madonna* and in full-length plays, as exemplified by Aunt Nonnie in *Sweet Bird of Youth*.

Ten Blocks on the Camino Real, subtitled *A Fantasy*, is a short version of what would become the full-length *Camino Real* (1953). Most of the characters and plot devices of the later play are already in place here, but without the extravagant poetic flights of the later work. The big-hearted American, Kilroy, finds himself at the end of his resources in this nameless town where the indigent are coldheartedly dispatched before they can come in contact with the privileged. Death is represented by two white-uniformed Streetcleaners, announced by a weird piping sound when they come to take corpses to the laboratory. Kilroy's tryst with the Gypsy's daughter Esmeralda ends in disappointment, and the Street-cleaners soon come for him. While his body is dissected and his solid gold heart extracted, the Madrecita keens for him and all such unfortunates. On a note of hope, however, Kilroy's spirit meets the weatherbeaten old knight, Don Quixote, who will help him find a way out. Meanwhile, Marguerite Gautier offers to share her room with the evicted Jacques Casanova. A little gesture of human compassion counterbalances all the suffering inflicted by social inequities.

The five one-acts in *American Blues* are rarely performed today, yet they thematically adumbrate Williams's mature work and reveal an early phase in the creative development that would quickly arc into genius.

Further Reading

Hale, Allean. "Early Williams: The Making of a Playwright." In *The Cambridge Companion to Tennessee Williams*, ed. Matthew C. Roudané. Cambridge: Cambridge University Press, 1997. 11–28.

Leverich, Lyle. *Tom: The Unknown Tennessee Williams*. New York: Crown, 1995.

Felicia Hardison Londré

Art. Many of the plays of Tennessee Williams demonstrate his acquaintance with specific paintings or painters and suggest that he used a visual image for his work. His most famous drama, *A Streetcar Named Desire*, first titled *The Poker Night*, was specifically based on Van Gogh's painting *The Night Cafe* with its "lurid nocturnal brilliance." Where Van Gogh centered his painting on a green billiard table lit by a hanging lamp of citron yellow, Williams substitutes a kitchen table and reverses the colors. Van Gogh wrote that he was trying to express "the terrible passions of humanity" in blood red and green. Williams describes his poker players as men "as coarse and direct and powerful as the primary colors." Later, artist **Thomas Hart Benton** merged both descriptions in his painting of the poker night scene. Van Gogh's sunflowers became a motif of Williams's **The Two-Character Play**. In **The Glass Menagerie** Williams calls for Laura to be lighted with "a pristine clarity such as light used in early religious portraits of female saints or Madonnas" and mentions El Greco. In **Orpheus Descending** a crisis evolves around Vee's primitive painting. A stone sculpture of an angel is the central metaphor of **Summer and Smoke**. The dressmaker's dummies in **The Rose Tattoo** clearly evolved from De Chirico's mannequins, as early scripts indicate, and their tortured positions were meant to symbolize Serafina's frustration. The fact that Sebastian in **Suddenly Last Summer** evidently refers to the painting of St. Sebastian by Sodoma carries its own load of meaning.

Williams's wide acquaintance with art and his increasing sophistication are evidenced by the range of his references, from the pre-Raphaelites to the abstract painters, impressionism to surrealism. In his late play **The Gnädiges Fräulein**, Molly and Polly might have been drawn by Toulouse Lautrec, but the piece as a whole has the cartoonish pop-art quality of a Lichenstein or Warhol. With **In the Bar of a Tokyo Hotel**, 1969, he constructed an entire play around art images that, being oriental, were seldom understood. His stage diagram as pictured in the Dramatists Play Service edition is a semicircle with a cyclorama that "should be a perfect half-circle." Small round tables are the only stage furniture, and each character is shown seated in a circle of light. The constant light-dark emphasis suggests the Taoist principle of yin and yang, represented by a black and white circle whose opposite halves must be in balance to create the whole person. In the play Miriam confronts Mark with the possibility that they are two sides of the same person—the artist tied to the animal. Even the action of the play is circular, ending as it began, with Miriam seated in her circle of light. The "large round decorative symbol" that hangs behind the bar projects the mandala, the circular diagram that has spiritual significance in Buddhist philosophy. So the play, interpreted through its art images, takes on a religious rather than secular meaning.

In addition to using art images as keys to his paintings, Williams aptly used painters as subjects. The painter protagonist of *In the Bar of a Tokyo Hotel* who seeks the source of light itself obviously refers to Jackson Pollock. *Will Mr. Merriwether Return from Memphis?* brings the ghost of Vincent Van Gogh on stage. The namesake figure of the novel *Moise and the World of Reason* is a painter. Williams knew and learned from many artists; the sculptor Tony Smith was a long-term friend, as was Fritz Bultman, both of whom had studied at the New Bauhaus in Chicago. In 1941 and 1942 when Williams summered at Provincetown, Bultman introduced him to Hans Hofmann, who taught there. Later, Williams tried his hand at art criticism, writing "An Appreciation" of Hans Hofmann that compared him in vision to Euclid and Einstein and placed him

philosophically as an interpreter of the atomic age.

Williams himself was an enthusiastic painter, delighting in the use of vivid color. The art collection at the Humanities Research Center in Texas has a small oil painting of sea and palm trees that they date as painted by Williams at age 17. He seems to have taken his first art lessons in California from the mother of his friend **Jim Parrott**, who had been a Works Progress Administration (WPA) art instructor. He wrote from Laguna Beach in 1939 that he was becoming quite an artist, having completed about a dozen landscapes and portraits in oil. After he moved to **Key West** in 1949, painting became his serious hobby. On demand, he began to sell his paintings, for prices ranging from $2,000 to $3,500. His Key West friend David Wolkowsky has one of the most complete collections of his paintings. In 1986 the Key West Art and Historical Society mounted an exhibit called "Interpretations of the Literary Works of Tennessee Williams," showing more than a dozen examples of his work, along with the work of other painters inspired by Williams. His paintings varied in quality and would perhaps best be described as "naïf." Most of Williams's canvases not in private hands were purchased after his death by the Rare Book and Manuscripts Library of Columbia University, New York, and are still in crates. See also **Manuscript Collections**.

Further Reading

Hale, Allean. "*In the Bar of a Tokyo Hotel*: Breaking the Code." *In Magical Muse: Millennial Essays on Tennessee Williams*, ed. Ralph F. Voss. Tuscaloosa: University of Alabama Press, 2002. 147–162.
———. "Of Prostitutes, Artists and Ears." *Southern Quarterly* 39.1 (Fall 1990): 32–45.
Hjerter, Kathleen. "Tennessee Williams." In

Doubly Gifted: The Author as Visual Artist. New York: Harry M. Abrams, 1986. 140.

Parker, Brian. "Tennessee Williams and the Legends of St. Sebastian." *University of Toronto Quarterly* 69.3 (Summer 2000): 634–659.

Plumley, William. "Tennessee Williams's Graphic Art: 'Two on a Party.' " *Mississippi Quarterly* 39.4 (Fall 1995): 789–805.

Ruckel, Terri Smith. "*Ut Pictura, Ut Poesis Pictura*: The Painterly Texture of Tennessee Williams's *In The Bar of a Tokyo Hotel*." In *The Undiscovered Country: The Later Plays of Tennessee Williams*, ed. Philip C. Kolin. New York: Lang, 2002. 80–92.

Allean Hale

At Liberty. An early one-act play, *At Liberty* was first published along with *This Property Is Condemned* in William Kozlenko's *American Scenes* under the heading "Landscapes with Figures (Two Mississippi Plays)" (New York: John Day, 1941) and, with slight revisions, reprinted in Betty Smith's anthology, *25 Non-Royalty One-Act Plays for All-Girl Casts* (New York: Greenberg, 1942). *At Liberty* has yet to be included in any Williams anthologies, though it is an instructive compilation of many of his later characters, themes, and landscapes.

Set in the Delta, with references to such well-known Williams places as the Delta Panters Hotel and Blue Mountain, *At Liberty* finds a mother waiting for her daughter's return from a date at 2:30 A.M. on a rainy September night. When the daughter, Gloria Bessie La Green (whom the mother calls by her less glamorous middle name of Bessie) returns, she and her mother quarrel, in some of Williams's most acrimonious dialogue, about Gloria's health, marital plans, and career dreams. Coming back to Blue Mountain from a failed career in show business, Gloria despises this southern community that stays up only to wait for death. Restless and bitter, Gloria rejects her mother's choice for a husband—the staid Vernon (a name Williams will use for a weak man in *Summer and Smoke*)—and reminisces about a man she did love, Red Allison, who lost both his legs and his life falling off a freight car. Gloria hopes for success from an ad she placed describing herself as 27, skilled as an ingenue, and "at liberty." Worried about her daughter's health (Gloria's lung x-rays are not good), the mother rebukes her for being "full of misrepresentation" in the ad. At 32, in bad health, and looking like "death at a masquerade party," Gloria, according to her mother, needs to settle down. Both women feel that their dreams have been dashed.

At Liberty looks forward to a host of Williams's fading, doomed women—most notably Blanche in *A Streetcar Named Desire* or Camille in *Camino Real*—but also rebels like Carol Cutrere in *Battle of Angels* and failing movie stars such as the Princess in *Sweet Bird of Youth* or Jimmie, the would-be star in Williams's short story "Interval" (1945). *At Liberty* also finds Williams adroitly using setting, clothes symbolism (Gloria's lining in her cape is "rotten"), and situation to present a mother/child conflict that would be the basis for *The Glass Menagerie, The Rose Tattoo*, and *Suddenly Last Summer*. Red anticipates the vulnerable, absent young men in Williams, such as Skipper in *Cat on a Hot Tin Roof*. Like Gloria, too, the budding playwright star lied about his age by three years in his quest for the fame of a career in theater. Aptly, Lyle Leverich titles chapter 22 of his biography of Williams during the period from January to August 1942 as "At Liberty."

Further Reading

Leverich, Lyle. *Tom: The Unknown Tennessee Williams.* New York: Crown, 1995.

Philip C. Kolin

Awards and Honors. Williams won his first literary prize, $5, at age 16 for a "personal experience" letter on the question "Can a Good Wife Be a Good Sport?" in a national contest sponsored by *Smart Set* magazine. In 1936 he won his first drama prize with "The Magic Tower" in the Webster Groves, Missouri, one-act play contest that included production. In 1939 *American Blues*, his collection of four one-act plays, won a special award of $100 in the **Group Theatre** contest in New York and got the attention of **Audrey Wood**, who became his agent. After that, many honors and awards followed, including a Rockefeller Fellowship (1940), a grant from the National Institute of Arts and Letters (1943), the Sidney Howard Memorial Award for *The Glass Menagerie* (1945), New York Drama Critics Circle Awards for *The Glass Menagerie* (1945), for *A Streetcar Named Desire* (1948), for *Cat on a Hot Tin Roof* (1955), and for *The*

Night of the Iguana (1962), which also won the Tony Award. He won the Pulitzer Prize for *A Streetcar Named Desire* (1948) and for *Cat on a Hot Tin Roof.* Subsequent honors included the Brandeis University Creative Arts Medal in Theater (1965), the National Institute of Arts and Letters Gold Medal for Drama (1969), the National Theatre Conference Annual Award (1972), the Centennial Medal of the Cathedral Church of St. John the Divine (1973), and the Medal of Honor for Literature by the National Arts Club (1975). Inducted into the Theatre Hall of Fame (1979), Williams was given the presidential arts achievement award at the Kennedy Center (1979) and the Medal of Freedom presented by President Jimmy Carter in 1980. He received honorary doctoral degrees from the University of Missouri (1969) and from Harvard College (1982), among others. He was nominated for the Nobel Prize.

Further Reading

Leavitt, Richard Freeman, ed. *The World of Tennessee Williams.* New York: Putnam, 1978.

Allean Hale

B

Baby Doll. *Baby Doll* (1956) was one of Tennessee Williams's most controversial films. With Tennessee Williams writing the screenplay, *Baby Doll* was intended exclusively for film and was only later rewritten as the much less successful play *Tiger Tail*. Like so many of Williams's other works, *Baby Doll* grew out of several shorter plays—*Twenty-seven Wagons Full of Cotton* and *The Long Stay Cut Short, or The Unsatisfactory Supper*. Williams saw *Baby Doll* as a comedy, but because of extensive revisions made by director **Elia Kazan**, the film carries a strong social message. *Baby Doll* starred **Karl Malden** as Archie Lee Meighan (Mitch in *A Streetcar Named Desire*), Carroll Baker as Baby Doll (who later starred in a film on Jean Harlow), **Eli Wallach** as Silva Vacarro, and Mildred Dunnock as Baby Doll's Aunt Rose Comfort. *Baby Doll* was filmed in Benoit, in the Mississippi Delta, within 40 miles of where Tennessee Williams grew up.

Portraying a woman used as commodity/barter, the film traces Baby Doll McCorkle's descent from being valuable and treated with respect to a woman who wears and responds to dark-skinned Sicilian Vacarro who brings out her emerging sexuality. Shot in black and white, *Baby Doll* reflected Kazan's intense sense of realism to express psychological states and a fervent commitment to civil rights. Yet Kazan was also sensitive to the poetry in Williams's script.

Baby Doll provoked much controversy, spearheaded by the Legion of Decency and New York's Cardinal Spellman, who, in the age of religious and social censorship, denounced the film as immoral because of its strong sexual content, dialogue, and costuming. *Baby Doll* continues to be controversial because of Kazan's cinematic techniques and commentary on racial tensions and civil rights in the 1950s. The score by Kenyon Hopkins foregrounds the **music** of the Mississippi Delta (gospel, blues, and jazz), expressing lament, protest, and loss.

Baby Doll is a straightforward script, blending the southern Gothic and the medieval fabliaux. Baby Doll McCorkle promises to consummate her marriage to cotton gin owner Archie on her twentieth birthday, provided he gives her a household of furniture. Under financial pressure, Archie also

9

must confront losing business to the new Syndicate Plantation Gin, represented by Silva Vacarro. To get the upper hand, Archie sets the new gin on fire, but events turn against him. The furniture is repossessed, and Vacarro woos Baby Doll to get her to sign an affidavit against her husband. He also pretends to give Archie business, sends him on a wild goose chase to Memphis, and tries to seduce Baby Doll. At the end of a fateful meal, Archie attempts to kill Vacarro and is hauled off to jail, leaving Baby Doll and her Aunt Rose Comfort to look toward tomorrow.

Baby Doll is saturated with Tennessee Williams's familiar cast of characters and themes. Archie Meighan, like Jabe in **Orpheus Descending**, is the foolish, vindictive *senex* cuckolded by his young wife Baby Doll, a sexual tease and mocker. Archie is loud, buffoonish, the man of prejudice and backwardness. Like his house and business, Archie is crumbling, falling apart. Malden's appearance suggests Archie's desperation and loss of esteem. Sweaty, going bald, dressed in overalls, hectic, and sneaking swigs of bootlegged liquor, Malden's Archie is foolishly dangerous and easily duped. Archie fights a new technological environment where the Syndicate Plantation and Gin managed by Vacarro threatens his business, reputation, and wife. Sexually impotent, Archie is mocked in scenes with the doctor and nurse, the townspeople, and his black retainers and by Vacarro. Archie burns the Syndicate Gin and depends on his community to whitewash his crimes. In the end, he loses Baby Doll, his house, his furniture, his status in the white community, and his freedom and is ignominiously taken off to jail by the town marshal.

Blonde and sensual, Carroll Baker's Baby Doll is a Lolita figure. She wears her trademark baby doll pajamas, sleeps in a crib,

and provocatively sucks her thumb. In one of the key cinematic symbols, Baby Doll shares her crib with an exhausted yet victorious Vacarro. She repeatedly elicits and suffers from different responses from the male gaze—for example, leering whistles from townspeople including the druggist, the gin laborers, Archie's workers, Archie himself, and Vacarro. Both vulnerable because of and yet in control of her sexual prowess, Baby Doll is at the mercy of the men from whom she seeks protection—her father who gives her in marriage to Archie even though she is unprepared, her husband who uses her to entertain Vacarro, and Vacarro himself who manipulates her to convict Archie.

Both baby and woman, she vacillates in the film between handling food like a baby and sucking liquids—Coke, water, pot-licker (all with sexual relish)—and flirtatiously eating pecans, the ubiquitous confectionary of the South. Baby Doll fears and is attracted to Vacarro's overtly sexual advances—talking, touching, stroking, riding a pony with its sadomasochistic implications, standing by as he suggestively pumps the water from the old well on Archie's land, as well as playing hide and seek with Vacarro in the rafters of Archie's house that ends in her submission, signing an affidavit naming Archie as the arsonist who destroyed Vacarro's gin.

Vacarro is the outsider, the underdog, the Sicilian (**Frank Merlo**'s kin) who always won Tennessee Williams's sympathy. Perfectly cast in this film role as the Sicilian Vacarro, Wallach plays the younger, wily, darker suitor whose touch (hands, lips, or body language) sharply contrasts with Archie's deficient courtship modeling. A shrewd businessman who easily outsmarts Archie, Vacarro uses the law that Archie claims to live by to manipulate and destroy him. Always dressed in black, politically and sexually aligning him with the black char-

Carroll Baker, Karl Malden, and Eli Wallach in the 1956 film *Baby Doll*. Springer/Photofest.

acters who in song and humor mock Archie, Vacarro uses his sexuality successfully to court Baby Doll while at the same time relying on his business acumen to establish the Syndicate Plantation Gin.

Aunt Rose Comfort, played by Mildred Dunnock (who appeared as Aunt Nonnie, another comforting aunt, in **Sweet Bird of Youth**), is a highly symbolic figure in the Williams canon—the visiting spinster relative, the old woman who has been jilted and hurt, the decaying porch maiden. She is yet another talismanic rose (the name of Tennessee Williams's beloved sister, **Rose Isabel**) associated with sweetness, tenderness, yet possessing an innocence that is too vulnerable. She is the epitome of southern family kindness, yet she has not received any from Archie or Baby Doll. Rather, she is the victim of male inhospitality and is unable to nurture anyone. Aunt Rose is present at the spoiled dinner of pot liquor at the end of the film, the true dissolution of the relationship between Baby Doll and Archie. The broken banquet in *Baby Doll* demands comparison with Blanche's fated birthday supper in *A Streetcar Named Desire* or the disastrous dinner in **The Glass Menagerie**. Like Baby Doll, Aunt Rose has few belongings. Her favorite food is candy, symbolizing her plight for kindness, and she visits the hospital to snitch chocolate candy from the dying patients who are past care. Aunt Rose and Baby Doll's feminine intimacy contrasts with Vacarro's male aggressiveness, though Aunt Rose is genuinely saddened when Vacarro leaves.

Baby Doll is a tribute to Williams and Kazan's collaborative effort. Sixty years later, the film is still both entertaining and instructive, offering insights into marriage, family, community, loss, and freedom with a combination of humor, pathos, and social commentary. Far from being only a sexual tease, Baby Doll McCorckle survives male adversity and may be admitted into the ranks of such strong Williams heroines as Maggie in *Cat on a Hot Tin Roof* and Catherine Venerable in *Suddenly Last Summer*. See also **Race**.

Further Reading

Baker, Carroll. *Baby Doll: An Autobiography.* New York: Arbor House, 1983.

Kolin, Philip C. "Civil Rights and the Black Presence in *Baby Doll.*" *Film and Literature Quarterly* 24 (1996): 1–11.

Phillips, Gene D. *The Films of Tennessee Williams.* Philadelphia: Arts Alliance, 1980.

Tischler, Nancy M. *Tennessee Williams: Rebellious Puritan.* New York: Citadel Press, 1961.

Maureen Curley

Bankhead, Tallulah (1903–1968). Tallulah Bankhead was a famous actress with whom Tennessee Williams had a love-hate relationship. Williams saw Bankhead on stage, perhaps for the first time, in *The Little Foxes* (1939). The daughter of Alabama politician William Brockman Bankhead, the Speaker of the House of Representatives, Tallulah was a convent-educated teenager who, winning a hometown beauty contest, chose mammon over God. She was talented—no question. She was also bawdy, outspoken, and quick-witted. Like many men, many of them gay, Williams was drawn to her; in the next 20 years their paths (and swords) would cross several times.

Williams and Bankhead met several years after *Foxes*. She was appearing in a play on Cape Cod, and he had just finished *Battle of Angels* and was euphoric to learn that the Theatre Guild hoped to interest her in his drama. Not only was she the antithesis of the prim women he so disliked, but her glamour and reputation would act as box-office magnets. Although she agreed to read the script, she apparently never responded, and the producers cast Miriam Hopkins as Lady.

As Williams noted in his *Memoirs*, Bankhead was a nonstop conversationalist; when nature called, she would continue talking and drag the dramatist into the bathroom with her. Williams admired her frankness and her composure; he also liked her free and easy ways, he said—code words for her broadmindedness (and more) toward gays and lesbians. She "performed" femininity and reminded her audience, as Williams did in his best plays, that gender was a social construction.

In early 1956 Bankhead starred in the first major revival of *A Streetcar Named Desire*. Seeing the production during tryouts in Florida, Williams criticized her Blanche, calling it the worst he had seen. A brouhaha ensued. His open letter of apology, published in the *New York Times* (4 March 1956), was at once candy-coated and insincere, as the actress herself understood and his later cutting remarks about her confirmed. When the curtain rose in New York in mid-February 1956, the critics weighed in. Some attacked Bankhead because she refused to acknowledge **Jessica Tandy** and **Vivien Leigh** as lodestars for Blanche and because, as one reviewer noted, she had turned a serious drama into "A Streetcar Named Tallulah."

More supported her, however. Like Blanche, she was as southern as grits, and indeed the southern woman's accent, bearing, and tenacity were writ large in her portrayal. Blanche DuBois invites a critique of gender and class; unearthing it, Bankhead prepared the way for future productions that accented it.

Bankhead's association with Williams ended in 1964, with her performance of Flora Goforth in **The Milk Train Doesn't Stop Here Anymore.** Her notices were worse than the worst ones for *A Streetcar Named Desire.* Williams ascribed her failure to liquor and pills but also noted that the cheering of the gay audience at the first New York preview affected her and the press's reaction to her. (Gays had reportedly had a similar effect on *A Streetcar Named Desire* in 1956.) Bankhead, according to *Newsweek,* was now more act than actress; her performance of femininity, on stage and off, had become a parody of itself. *Milk Train* ran for four performances. Four years later, Bankhead died. See also **Gender and Sexuality.**

Further Reading

Israel, Lee. *Miss Tallulah Bankhead*. New York: Putnam's, 1972.

Williams, Tennessee. *Memoirs*. New York: Doubleday, 1975.

Leonard J. Leff

Battle of Angels. Williams's first professionally staged play, *Battle of Angels,* opened at the Wilbur Theatre in Boston on 30 December 1940 in a Theatre Guild production directed by Margaret Webster and starring Miriam Hopkins as Myra. The play incurred the scorn, if not the wrath, of audiences and reviewers, resulting in its closing on 11 January 1941 after the Boston City Council called for censorship. Williams received a $500 advance from the Theatre Guild to rewrite the play before its New York production. In May, he submitted a new version but to no avail, as plans for a Broadway opening were abandoned; in fact, the Guild sent out letters to its subscribers apologizing for ever including the play in its repertoire. *Battle of Angels* was first published in 1945 in *Pharos,* a magazine distributed by Williams's publisher, New Directions; the first two issues, which were to be the only issues, contained the script as well as an essay by the playwright, "The History of a Play (with Parentheses)."

The devastation that Williams experienced upon his first foray into professional theater is evident in the essay's tracing of his initiation as an inexperienced, not yet 38-year-old playwright. Shocked upon returning from Mexico to read that *Battle of Angels* was being produced, Williams flew to New York for the rehearsals of a script that he had considered a first draft. The five weeks of rehearsal left Williams feeling ill-equipped and the cast unprepared; for example, three actors were cast as Val, the musical score was scuttled at the dress rehearsal, the final scene was desperately and futilely rewritten the night before opening. The Boston audience, having first been offended by the combination of religious with sexual symbols, stampeded out of the theater when the smoke-pots produced excessively in the fire scene, filling the stage and choking actors and audience.

Williams pledged that the play would appear again, without the published Prologue and Epilogue, which he regarded as defensive additions spawned by memories of the Boston premiere. The framing of the play involves scenes in a southern small-town store converted to a museum commemorating the violence that occurred there a year before and presided over by a black Conjure Man. As Act One opens, two local women gossip as they prepare a homecoming buffet for the terminally ill store owner, Jabe Torrance, who is returning with his wife Myra from a

Memphis hospital. Myra first hires and then seduces Val, a sexually magnetic drifter in a snakeskin jacket brought into the store by Vee Talbott, the Sheriff's wife and religious visionary. Her vision of Val as Jesus, the portrait of which becomes a feature of the museum, sent the first palpable shock waves through the Boston theater; this response, in turn, shocked the playwright since he viewed his character, Valentine Xavier, as indeed Christ-like and his play as a moral battle between light and darkness. Val's spurning of Cassandra Whiteside, the profligate daughter of the town's oldest family and prophetess of his doom, attests to a quest for the uncorrupted. Val becomes, however, the victim of a mob; fueled by accusations of rape by a Woman from Waco, he is lynched after Myra has been fatally shot by her husband and the store set afire. The Prologue attests to Val's mythic status as we learn that Cassandra has committed suicide and Vee lost her mind, leaving the Conjure Man to guard the snakeskin jacket.

A revival of *Battle of Angels* was staged by the Circle Repertory Company in New York in 1974. By that time, however, Williams had delivered on his pledge to resurrect this play in another version: The radically revised and retitled **Orpheus Descending** appeared in 1957.

Further Reading

Barringer, Milly S. "*Battle of Angels*: Margaret Webster Directs Tennessee Williams." *Journal of American Drama and Theatre* 4 (Winter 1992): 63–77.

Hale, Allean. "Early Williams: The Making of a Playwright." In *The Cambridge Companion to Tennessee Williams*, ed. Matthew C. Roudané. Cambridge: Cambridge University Press, 1997. 11–28.

Quirino, Leonard. "Tennessee Williams' Persistent 'Battle of Angels.'" *Modern Drama* 11 (1968): 27–39.

Janet V. Haedicke

Beckett, Samuel (1906–1989). Samuel Beckett was an Irish playwright and novelist closely associated with the antirealistic theater of the absurd, a type of drama that aims to illustrate the futility of human existence. Williams was an admirer of Beckett's work and in fact helped to make it known in the United States. Beckett's most famous play, *Waiting for Godot*, premiered the same year as Williams's highly experimental **Camino Real** (1953). Beckett's plays present situations that portray human life as absurd, devoid of any higher meaning or purpose, and focus on the impossibility of human communication. Like Beckett's works, many of Williams's later plays of the 1960s and 1970s such as **I Can't Imagine Tomorrow** (1966, 1970), **In the Bar of a Tokyo Hotel** (1969, 1970), and **The Two-Character Play/Out Cry** (first version performed 1967) defy realistic expectation of character, plot, action, and language in an attempt to raise central questions about the nature of reality and the role that language plays in its representation.

Along the same lines as plays such as Beckett's *Waiting for Godot* and *Endgame*, Williams's later work focuses on the concept that language is the medium through which reality is constructed and defined rather than directly expressed. The typical situation presented in these plays involves characters who are trying to escape from a language that is neither an accurate nor a satisfying expression of their thoughts and desires. Yet the realization that language, however flawed, is the only means of constructing their reality and being traps them into the endless need to continue speaking. A simultaneous frustration with and dependence on dialogue creates the tension in both Beckett and Williams's later plays. In *The Two-Character Play*, most obviously, Williams was aiming for a more Beckettian kind of drama, one that actively challenges orthodox notions of plot, representation, and the construction of meaning.

Williams's deliberate movement away from the long, poetic speeches of his earlier plays to a more minimalist dialogue characteristic of Beckett's works, as well as his diminished reliance on the realistic conventions of narrative plot and psychologically complex characters, was often misunderstood by the critical establishment as a failure to live up to the standards of his earlier style, or as a desperate attempt to stay current through ineffectual imitation of avant-garde playwrights, such as Beckett, **Edward Albee**, and **Harold Pinter**. Williams's anti-realistic plays of the later period, however, generally stand on their own as sound and original experiments that fuse his talent for the poetic nuances of language with Beckett's sense of linguistic and dramatic irony.

Further Reading

Saddik, Annette. *The Politics of Reputation: The Critical Reception of Tennessee Williams' Later Plays*. Madison, NJ: Fairleigh Dickinson University Press, 1999.

Annette J. Saddik

Benton, Thomas Hart (1889–1975). A leader of the American regionalist movement in art in the 1930s, Thomas Hart Benton painted murals depicting common everyday scenes of Midwestern life. Louis B. Mayer commissioned Benton to paint *Poker Night* (from *A Streetcar Named Desire*) as a Christmas gift for his daughter, *A Streetcar Named Desire*'s producer **Irene Selznick**, in 1948. An interpretation of *A Streetcar Named Desire*'s third scene, "The Poker Night," the egg tempera and oil image captured the dangerously charged atmosphere in the Kowalskis' squalid Elysian Fields apartment as Stanley, Mitch, Pablo, and Steve drink, fight, and play poker while Blanche, barely clad in a see-through blue slip, admires her image in a mirror and Stella hides behind a chair.

After the painting had been completed, *Look* magazine asked Tennessee Williams to convince **Jessica Tandy** to pose for a promotional photograph replicating Benton's painting. But Williams worried when he wrote to Tandy that she would hesitate due to Blanche's attire in the painting—a garment far more revealing than Tandy's costumes in the production. Tandy's objection to the plan was not based on prudish modesty; instead, she rejected the idea because she felt Benton's painting would mislead future audiences about the salaciousness of the production and because she believed the painting portrayed Stanley's point of view at the expense of Blanche's. Eventually, Williams, a painter himself who continued to admire many aspects of *Poker Night*, concurred with Tandy's astute evaluation.

Benton's image, used on the cover of the first Signet paperback edition of *A Streetcar Named Desire*, accurately conveys the spirit and tensions of Williams's play despite the controversy over the painting. Blanche's scale dwarfs the rest of the figures in the scene. Her larger-than-life presence in the image's foreground, slightly off-center, indicates her disruption of the normal functioning of the domestic space. The figures in *Poker Night*, painted in Benton's signature style, seem to have been freed from the normal physical laws governing the movement of the human body. The male figures including Stanley and Mitch are ready to erupt into a brawl over the poker game and/or the sight of Blanche, while the female figure of Blanche languorously ponders her image in a mirror while Stella cowers in the shadow of this erotic image seemingly in anticipation of the violence she will endure from Stanley before the scene's end. The painting unfurls in a fluidity akin to the music of the French

Quarter that might be rolling in through the apartment's open windows. The lurid colors of the scene bathe the image in the colored lights similar to those that Stanley would like to get going as soon as Blanche is driven from his apartment. Finally, Benton's strong use of light, particularly in his brash illumination of Blanche, gives the image an unmistakable quality of theatricality and air of artificiality. Though, as Tandy argued, Benton objectifies Blanche (a criticism levied against his depiction of the female figures in many of his works) and tips the scale of visual power sharply in Stanley's favor, he also renders *A Streetcar Named Desire*'s clashing sensuality and violence, artifice and reality, in eloquent visual form.

Further Reading

Adams, Henry. *Thomas Hart Benton: An American Original*. New York: Knopf, 1989.

Leslie Atkins Durham

Bigelow, Paul (1905–1988). Paul Bigelow was a close friend of Williams and a member of his homosocial group in the 1940s that included Jordan Massee (Bigelow's partner) and **Donald Windham**. Williams dedicated *The Roman Spring of Mrs. Stone* to Bigelow with these words: "With ten years of affection to Paul." Slightly older than Williams, Bigelow was also a playwright who was well read and a southerner, and served as Williams's guardian and confidant. In his letters to Bigelow, whom he met in 1940, Williams shared news about his sexual escapades with various "intimates," his dread of abstinence, and his ambitions as a playwright. Not surprisingly, when writing to Williams about Bigelow, **Audrey Wood** called him "that remarkable friend of yours." Williams's "Poem for Paul," written in 1941, was eventually incorporated into the caroler's lyrics in *The Mutilated* (1976).

Williams's friendship with Bigelow had many dimensions. Bigelow nursed Williams, encouraged him in his writing, and even assisted him with those domestic details— laundry, finding checks, making appointments—that overwhelmed Tennessee. When Williams was recuperating from an illness, he stayed in Bigelow's apartment in New York. He also visited Bigelow on St. Simon's Island in Georgia during the summer of 1941, and for a much longer time, they shared an upstairs apartment in Bigelow's hometown of Macon, Georgia.

In 1942, Audrey Wood hired Bigelow to help Williams finish *You Touched Me!* As a friend to both Williams and Windham, as well as a respected writer, Bigelow could navigate the troubled waters between the two. Bigelow was not so much a collaborator, as Windham had been, but an editor who helped, even prompted, Williams to make the changes in setting mandated by John Gassner of the Theatre Guild, essential for the play's acceptance and production. While Williams did not find all of Bigelow's suggestions to his liking, Bigelow did succeed in getting *You Touched Me!* in shape. See also **Group Theatre**.

Further Reading

Devlin, Albert J., and Nancy M. Tischler, eds. *The Selected Letters of Tennessee Williams, Volume 1—1920–1945*. New York: New Directions, 2000.

Leverich, Lyle. *Tom: The Unknown Tennessee Williams*. New York: Crown, 1995.

Philip C. Kolin

Bordelon, Eloi (1919–1985). Eloi (pronounced "*Ell-wah*") Bordelon was one of Tennessee Williams's early lovers whom he met at the **New Orleans** Athletic Club in autumn 1941. Letters to **Paul Bigelow** during this period describe Williams's intimate and tempestuous relationship with Bordelon, a Creole descended from one of the oldest families in the city. Bordelon rented a room at 722 Toulouse Street, the French Quarter rooming house that serves as the setting for *Vieux Carré*. Williams had roomed there in 1939, during his first period in New Orleans, and he stayed there again with Bordelon frequently between September and November of 1941. He often received mail at the Toulouse Street address.

His relationship with Bordelon ended violently, according to Williams, who claimed that the young man was jealous of his attentions to other men. In a letter to Charles Criswell, Williams reported that Bordelon subsequently locked him out of the room and refused to relinquish his belongings, including a typewriter that Williams had borrowed from Criswell. Claiming that he spoke to Williams in the years after their parting, Bordelon told friends that Williams called him in 1948 asking for his gumbo recipe.

Bordelon, a painter, appears in fictionalized form as a tubercular young man who seduces the protagonist in "The Angel in the Alcove," the short story that prefigures *Vieux Carré*; for the play, Williams created another version of Bordelon, this time an older man. Also, Williams used the name "Eloi" for the young man, and "Bordelon" for the name of the unseen female boarder, in *Auto-Da-Fé*, a short play set in New Orleans. See also *Twenty-seven Wagons Full of Cotton and Other One-Act Plays*.

Further Reading

Holditch, Kenneth, and Richard Freeman Leavitt. *Tennessee Williams and the South*. Jackson: University Press of Mississippi, 2002.
Leverich, Lyle. *Tom: The Unknown Tennessee Williams*. New York: Crown, 1995.

Jacqueline O'Connor

Bowles, Paul Frederic (1917–1973). A longtime associate of Tennessee Williams, Paul Bowles was a writer, musical composer, and expatriate. His wife, Jane (1917–1973), was also a writer. At Williams's request, Bowles composed the background music for *The Glass Menagerie, Summer and Smoke, Sweet Bird of Youth*, and *The Milk Train Doesn't Stop Here Anymore*. He and his wife Jane, both bisexuals, shared a house together and at times led quite separate personal lives. Williams's friendship with Paul and Jane Bowles was one of the most enduring of his life. Williams often highly praised their work and even considered Jane, whose play *Two Serious Ladies* and short stories gained her serious attention, a major writer of the twentieth century.

Even though Bowles made trips back to the United States from time to time, he spent most of his adulthood in Tangier. He first went there with Aaron Copeland to study musical composition. After meeting Paul and Jane in Acapulco in 1940, Williams traveled with them and visited them several times in Tangier. He encouraged Jane, who suffered from physical and mental illness, to pursue her writing. Williams also visited with other prominent writers in Tangier, including André Gide and the Cypriot writer Mohamed Choukri, who reported on a visit Williams made to Tangier in 1973.

Although Bowles was interested in poetry in his youth, he was discouraged from being a poet by Gertrude Stein and did not pursue a career as an author until he was in his late twenties. He was well-read in existentialist philosophy and literature—as his fiction suggests—and wrote musical compositions, short stories, novels, and travel literature. Also a translator, Bowles's fiction examines the human condition in a way similar to Albert Camus, the French existentialist novelist, and he translated Jean-Paul Sartre's play *No Exit* into English in 1946. Bowles's first novel, *The Sheltering Sky*, takes place in the Sahara, and his other sometimes shocking (with violence and loneliness as central motifs) works include *The Delicate Prey and Other Stories*, a collection of short fiction, which Williams reviewed in the *New York Times* in 1949. Typical of Williams, he wrote hyperbolic reviews of his friends' (both Jane's and Paul's) works.

An interview with Bowles in 1968, shedding light on his friendship with Williams and their collaboration on his plays, originally appeared in Mike Steen's *A Look at Tennessee Williams* and is reprinted in *Conversations with Paul Bowles*. See also **Music**.

Further Reading

Caponi, Gena Dagel. *Conversations with Paul Bowles*. Jackson: University Press of Mississippi, 1993.

Choukri, Mohamed. *Tennessee Williams in Tangier*. Trans. Paul Bowles. Santa Barbara, CA: Cadmus, 1979.

Green, Michelle. *The Dream at the End of the World: Paul Bowles and the Literary Renegades in Tangier*. New York: HarperCollins, 1991.

Spoto, Donald. *The Kindness of Strangers: The Life of Tennessee Williams*. Boston: Little, Brown, 1985.

Steen, Mike. *A Look at Tennessee Williams*. New York: Hawthorn, 1969.

Dean Shackelford

Brando, Marlon (1924–). Method-trained actor Marlon Brando is best known for his portrayal of brutish Stanley Kowalski in both the original stage (1947) and film (1951) versions of ***A Streetcar Named Desire***. In Stanley, Tennessee Williams created a complicated figure of postwar energy and masculinity—sensual, boyish, and violent—whom Brando brought to life. His splendid physique was accentuated when costume designer Lucinda Ballard dressed him for the role in tight T-shirts, dyed faded red and slightly torn, and blue jeans that she altered to hug his body. The look transformed American casual fashion, and the performance influenced the development of American film by creating a new kind of male protagonist, one whose sexual desirability depended upon the presence of both toughness and vulnerability in a slightly feminine and very physical package. Brando collaborated with Williams and with director **Elia Kazan** to create a compelling dramatic character, and every actor who has played Stanley since Brando has had to reckon with this complex characterization of Williams's most virile creation.

Born in Omaha, Nebraska, Brando arrived in New York City in 1943 to attend **Erwin Piscator**'s Dramatic Workshop at the **New School for Social Research**; among the faculty at the time was Stella Adler, a veteran of the **Group Theatre** who served as both teacher and mentor to Brando. Cast in *I Remember Mama* in 1944, he was noticed by actors and audiences for his easy naturalness and depth while playing timid immigrant son Nels.

Brando and Williams first met in the summer of 1945 in Provincetown, Massachusetts; two years later they met again in the popular beach town when the actor visited Williams to read for *A Streetcar Named Desire*. Brando impressed Williams with his audition and won the part, already having endeared himself to the playwright's friends by making emergency plumbing and electricity repairs to the cottage they rented. Brando stayed with *A Streetcar Named Desire* from its premiere in December 1947 until May 1949 when he was replaced by Anthony Quinn. Starring in the 1951 Warner Brothers film version, also directed by Kazan, Brando was only one of the four principal actors who did not win the Oscar, though the film received twelve Academy Award nominations and four awards.

Brando practiced an intense acting style that was intuitive and inward; through improvisations and bits of stage business, Brando always left his mark on a role and never more so than in his realization of Stanley Kowalski. In guiding Brando to create Stanley, director Kazan took advantage of the actor's facility with props to demonstrate Stanley's intense need for physical pleasure. Brando's Stanley exhibits his oral fixation by putting cigarettes, beer, cold cuts, even his own greasy fingers into his mouth, and he demonstrates his attachment to objects by fingering and caressing things of pleasure with an intense possessiveness. Brando's Stanley became a figure of grasping consumption, exuding the raw energy that fuels such cravings while embodying a new age of American consumerism.

Ironically, after having created one of the most memorable and influential dramatic portrayals of twentieth-century drama, Brando abandoned theater for film. Williams wanted him to play Val Xavier, the itinerant musician with a guitar and a trademark snakeskin jacket, in the 1957 Broadway production of *Orpheus Descending*, but Brando refused. He did agree, however, to play Val in the film version, retitled *The Fugitive Kind* (1960), costarring Anna Magnani, Joanne Woodward, and **Maureen Stapleton**. Brando believed that Val's underwritten role paled in comparison to Magnani's character, Lady Torrance, and throughout the shooting Brando and Magnani battled for control of the set and of the film. Despite the abundance of talent among the group of Oscar-winning Williams veterans, *The Fugitive Kind* received negative reviews and became the first film in which Brando starred that lost money.

Personal tragedy and professional missteps have marked Brando's later years, but his best performances still testify to a unique talent that personified an age, an acting style, and Williams's attitudes toward mid-century masculinity. See also **Film Adaptations**; *Orpheus Descending*; *A Streetcar Named Desire*.

Further Reading

Bosworth, Patricia. *Marlon Brando*. New York: Penguin Putnam, 2001.

Brando, Marlon. *Songs My Mother Taught Me*. New York: Knopf, 1994.

Gronbeck-Tedesco, John. "Ambiguity and Performance in the Plays of Tennessee Williams." *Mississippi Quarterly* 48 (Fall 1995): 735–749.

Manso, Peter. *Brando: The Biography*. New York: Hyperion, 1994.

Murphy, Brenda. *Tennessee Williams and Elia Kazan: A Collaboration in the Theatre*. Cambridge: Cambridge University Press, 1992.

Jacqueline O'Connor

Brecht, Bertolt (1898–1956). German playwright Bertolt Brecht's epic theater conventions and politics influenced the young Tom Williams greatly. Williams's proletarian leanings and focus on social problems in the 1930s and 1940s made him a willing student of Brecht's own antifascist philosophy. Williams became familiar with Brecht's epic theater at Washington University through Professor Otto Heller, **Clark Mills** (**McBurney**), and director Willard Holland and his experimental theater group, the **Mummers of St. Louis**, and later at the University of Iowa through Professor **Edward Charles Mabie** (protagonist of the "Iowa Renaissance" movement and Midwestern director of the Works Progress Administration [WPA]). Brecht's impressionistic style had been used by Thornton Wilder since 1931 and thus was available to Williams through American theater, too. The hallmarks of Brecht's work also surface in Williams's, such as the disillusioning of an audience through suggestive stage design and projections; cinematic and musical effects; and provocative comments *ad spectatores* by a stage manager (*Spielleiter*). Williams adapted Brecht's anti-illusionistic distancing devices such as the chorus, projections, montage, flashbacks, and symbolic setting in **Candles to the Sun** and in **Not about Nightingales** (where the jail symbolized the microcosm of society). Highly relevant, too, Williams's characters bear comparison with Brecht's epic figures, for example, Birmingham Red in *Candles to the Sun* (based on the real Jack Conroy, the "American Gorkey") and Tom Wingfield in **The Glass Menagerie**. Williams's own psychosocial **"Plastic Theater"** exhibits many Brechtian techniques.

In January 1940, Williams joined the Dramatic Workshop at the **New School for Social Research** and studied under **Erwin Piscator**, Brecht's partner at the Berlin Volksbühne, and John Gassner, head of the Theatre Guild's Playwriting Department. There he learned firsthand Brecht's ideology of agitprop, including antifascist propaganda, social engagement, and didactic enlightenment. Williams hailed Brecht's *Mutter Courage und ihre Kinder* (*Mother Courage and Her Children*) in a 1941 English translation by Hoffmann R. Hays (who tried in vain to organize a Broadway production) as "the greatest of modern plays, a work that I think affirms the only kind of essential human dignity and decency." *Mother Courage* supplied Williams with the prototype for "Big Mama" figures. In **Battle of Angels**, Williams had modernized the Orpheus myth and incorporated a sociocritical, antiracist, and highly political message, but Piscator misunderstood it as "a Fascist play" full of evil, selfish rednecks, and instead demanded a "didactic sermon on social injustice."

Though Williams was never introduced to Brecht, who escaped Nazi Germany in 1942, the two playwrights might have met in **Hollywood** where Brecht collaborated with Fritz Lang. Fellow emigré and poet Ferdinand Reyner introduced Brecht to **Audrey Wood** (Williams's agent) and Williams's plays. After attending a Playhouse Theatre performance of *The Glass Menagerie* in June 1945, Brecht praised Laurette Taylor as the ideal Mother Courage but disliked Williams's play, calling it apolitical and offering too much psychology and too little politics. Unfortunately, Brecht staged *The Glass Menagerie* as a parody of the decadent American dream with the Berliner Ensemble in 1950, starring Helene Weigle as Amanda. In 1946 Brecht considered casting longtime Williams director **Elia Kazan** as a performer for his drama on the inquisition, *Galileo Galilei*, just before Kazan was to appear before the McCarthy hearings. Although Brecht watched the last rehearsals of Berthold Viertel's translation of **A Streetcar Named Desire**, premiering on 10 May 1950 at Berlin Schloßparktheater, he left no comment on the play's first German production by Heinz Hilbert at the Zurich Schauspielhaus on 10 November 1949. Although Brecht was never a big fan of Williams's plays (on 10 October 1954 he wrote a letter to Gustav Rudolf Sellner, manager of the Landestheater Darmstadt, sending his apologies that he could not come to a performance of **Camino Real**, which premiered on 6 November 1954, based on Viertel's translation), Williams unquestionably learned a great deal from the German playwright. Even though Williams claimed no great knowledge of political and social dialectics, it was Brecht who helped shape the theatrical expressions of his political ideas.

Further Reading

Ley-Piscator, Maria. *The Piscator Experiment: The Political Theatre*. New York: Heinemann, 1967.

Thomas Molzahn

Britneva, Maria (Lady St. Just) (1921–1994). For 35 years one of Tennessee Williams's closest friends, Maria Britneva was a strong presence in Williams's intimate circle. She was flamboyant, candid to a fault, and fiercely partisan on Williams's behalf. Her published collection of Williams's letters, *Five O'Clock Angel*, gives one of the most animated pictures of Williams's daily life. She remained by his side through the vicissitudes of a long association. After his death, she made herself a controversial administrator-executor of his affairs and works.

Born in Leningrad to Alexander Vladimirovitch Britneva and Mary Britneva, she, her mother (a writer and translator), and her sister left Russia in 1922 for England, where they, like many émigrés, faced poverty and loss of social position. She trained as a dancer, and then as an actor, but alienated one of London's important theatrical producers, H.M. Tennent. Britneva met Tennessee Williams at a party on 11 June 1948 at John Gielgud's, for whom she had worked as a sort of personal assistant. She and Williams quickly bonded, and over the years he supported her career as an actress and occasionally lobbied directors on her behalf for acting parts. However, he did not overestimate her talent. She appeared in only small roles in four productions of his works between 1951 and 1977 and her Blanche DuBois in the *A Streetcar Named Desire* in March 1955 at the Actors' Playhouse in New York was uncelebrated. She was married to Peter Grenfell, Lord St. Just, from 1956 until his death in 1984.

A frequent traveling companion, Britneva was expected to carry out some of Williams's unpleasant tasks, leaving him free to appear uninvolved. Britneva's sharp tongue often sparred on Williams's behalf, allowing him to avoid confrontation, which he loathed. On the downside, Britneva was used to saying whatever she thought, and she spoke her mind to Williams, as well as to everyone else. Williams's personal life operated at a continually high emotional temperature, and Britneva matched it. For example, **Dakin Williams** considers, as does biographer John Lahr, the possibility that Britneva was behind Williams's firing his longtime agent **Audrey Wood** in 1971. Whether or not Britneva and Wood ever fought (Wood denied it), it is not inconceivable that Britneva fed Williams's suspicion that Wood did not support his more recent work. Dakin Williams claimed Britneva once tried to kill him by pushing him off a catwalk.

Five O'Clock Angel, published in 1990, primarily contains letters from Williams to Britneva, since he apparently did not save many of her letters. In this redacted collection, she fills in the gaps with notes written in the third person, some inside quotation marks and some not. These notes give her narrative a feel of authority and objectivity it may not entirely deserve. In any case, from the first, Williams's letters to her sound the themes that echo through his life, among them financial confusion; misplaced objects; fears and anxieties; missed appointments; real or imagined illness; ceaseless travel; addictions; constant hard work; the irritating demands of celebrity; insecurity about reviews; and tumultuous relationships, with numerous highly charged scenes that could come out of, or go into, a Tennessee Williams play. *Five O'Clock Angel* also suggests her quarrels with Williams. For long periods of time there are few letters, particularly between 1963, when **Frank Merlo** died, and 1970. Yet Britneva spent a week with Williams only months before he died. In his will he named her co-trustee of the **Rose Williams Trust**, established to provide for his sister Rose after his death. By all accounts, Britneva helped take good care of Rose.

Abetted in part by the vagueness of Williams's will and exact wishes, she took on the role of Williams's literary executor, a role for which she had not been named. (Ironically, Williams mentions her only briefly in his *Memoirs*.) She claimed authority to determine whether or not particular plays could be produced or published, and by force of will she inserted herself into such issues as authorized versions (a complicated situation, since Williams rewrote so frequently) and casting. She alienated scholars by severely restricting access to Williams's unpublished papers (held primarily by Harvard University and the University of Texas) and made the work of biographers difficult or impossible, a situation that only began to correct itself after her death, when several of Williams's apprentice plays (e.g., *Not about Nightingales* and *Spring Storm*) were published by New Directions.

Scholars credit Britneva as a likely inspiration for traits in several of Williams's characters. Williams wrote that he put her high-spirited nature into Maggie in *Cat on a Hot Tin Roof* and the Countess in *This Is (An Entertainment)*, which originally bore the continued title *for Maria St. Just*. However, according to Philip Kolin, Britneva may be the model for the murderous landlady in the grotesque *The Remarkable Rooming-House of Mme. Le Monde* (published 1984) and the mysterious Mona in Williams's last short story, "The Negative" (1982), who drives the central character to his death. Williams's later writings show the stresses, and even the apprehensions, involved in his long and emotional relationship. See also **Correspondence; Texts; Wood, Audrey.**

Further Reading

Kolin, Philip C. "*The Remarkable Rooming-House of Mme. Le Monde*: Tennessee Williams's Little Shop of Comic Horrors." *Tennessee Williams Annual Review* 4 (2001): 39–48.

Lahr, John. "The Lady and Tennessee." *The New Yorker* 19 December 1994: 77–96.

St. Just, Maria. *Five O'Clock Angel: Letters of Tennessee Williams to Maria St. Just, 1948–1982*. New York: Knopf, 1990.

Williams, Dakin, and Shepherd Mead. *Tennessee Williams: An Intimate Biography*. New York: Arbor House, 1983.

Kirk Woodward

C

Cairo! Shanghai! Bombay! This short play has the honor of being the first produced play of Tennessee Williams. A light comedy in four scenes, the play was staged by The Garden Players in Memphis in Mrs. Rosebrough's backyard on 12 July 1935 and directed by Arthur B. Scharff. Williams was so thrilled by having an audience for his work that he credited *Cairo!* with his entrance into playwriting. Regrettably, the play has never been published; the Harry Ransom Humanities Research Center at the University of Texas does have a manuscript copy, however. While recuperating from an illness at his maternal grandparents' home in Memphis, Williams met Bernice Dorothy Shapiro, who lived near the Dakins and who convinced the young Tom to write the play with her. *Cairo!* also marks Williams's first collaborative work. Shapiro contributed a wordy prologue (cut in production) and an epilogue. The play also marks Williams's first (unprofessional) acting role, taking the part of a blind man with a dog and tin can for donations. Set in an unnamed seaport, *Cairo!* finds two sailors out on the town to pick up girls. One of the sailors meets a girl named Aileen, who is jilted on her way to the altar as the sailor leaves without her, making her one of Williams's early front "porch maidens." The presence of sailors in this early play is also significant, since Williams would later include them in *The Glass Menagerie*, *A Streetcar Named Desire*, *The Rose Tattoo*, and *Something Cloudy, Something Clear*.

Further Reading

Devlin, Albert J., and Nancy Tischler, eds. *The Selected Letters of Tennessee Williams, Volume 1—1920–1945*. New York: New Directions, 2000.
Leverich, Lyle. *Tom: The Unknown Tennessee Williams*. New York: Crown, 1995.

Philip C. Kolin

Camino Real. A highly experimental play pleading for the triumph of a romantic attitude about life over brutalizing reality, *Camino Real* is one of Williams's most ambitious and boldly symbolic dramas. *Camino Real* met with critical and commercial apathy in its original Broadway production directed by **Elia Kazan**, a situation resulting as

Scene from the original 1953 Broadway production of *Camino Real* with Jo Van Fleet (center). Photo by Alfredo Valente, used courtesy of New Directions Publishing Corp.

much from its startling theatrical innovations as from its complex subject matter and literary ambitions. Historical crosscurrents are imagined within Williams's rich literary sensibility, intermingling some of literature's most memorable characters—Cervantes's Don Quixote, Dumas's Marguerite Gautier, Proust's Baron de Charlus—within a phantasmagoric world woven from disparate elements of Spanish folklore, traditional Christianity, and Williams's own fertile imagination. *Camino Real* premiered on 19 March 1953 at the Martin Beck Theatre to

predominantly negative critical response. Walter Kerr, for example, condemned it as the worst play written by the best playwright of his era, although a few critics did admire its ambitions and genuine novelty. A strong cast including **Eli Wallach**, Jo Van Fleet, Hurd Hatfield, Frank Silvera, Barbara Baxley, Jennie Goldstein, and Joseph Anthony could not keep the play running beyond a mere 60 performances.

Among Williams's least realistic works, *Camino Real*, like **The Glass Menagerie** and **A Streetcar Named Desire**, presents poetic glimpses of autobiography expressed in the attitudes of its main character, Kilroy, the mythical All-American G.I. In the play, Kilroy arrives in a strange land where the privileged and powerful mingle with the poor and weak, all residing in a landscape at once a vaguely South American plaza and, at the same time, an imaginary netherworld of beggars, rogues, and the debased and discarded of the world. This literary Skid Row is revealed in 18 scenes (or "blocks") on the Camino Real where the cynical Gutman, a character inspired by Sydney Greenstreet's screen characters from the Fat Man of *The Maltese Falcon* to the unscrupulous blackmarketeer of *Casablanca*, narrates encounters in which Kilroy, with his heart of gold (who has pawned his boxing gloves to come to the Camino Real), encounters a Gypsy and her daughter, Esmeralda, as well as the various characters from literary history ruminating on their various human dilemmas. Redemption is among the play's themes, as the characters struggle to defeat their own demons, the harshness of their world, the decay of their bodies, the bruises to their souls, and death itself.

The play touchingly and, at times, disturbingly, aptly illuminates Williams's recurrent themes of the need for a romanticized attitude toward life, despite its inevitable corrupting influences, and his belief in the basic human yearnings for love, compassion, and personal freedom. Williams's own ambitious dramatic experimentation is mirrored by Lord Byron's memorable proclamation to "make voyages." Voyaging into distinctly new dramatic terrain, as he would consistently attempt throughout the remainder of his career (although, perhaps, never as boldly), Williams passionately defended *Camino Real* to critics who condemned its innovations. The play's symbolism was dismissed by some critics, while others praised it, and many identified a dizzying array of

influences on Williams in the creation of *Camino Real*, from Dante, **Chekhov**, Kafka, Wedekind, Strindberg, and Eliot to Wilder, **Lawrence, Brecht, O'Neill**, Sartre, **Beckett**, the art of Escher, and such memorable soldier-of-fortune films as the aforementioned *Casablanca*. Another significant influence was the time period in which the play was written. The corrupt society and deceptive characters of *Camino Real* mirror the harsh political realities of the United States in the early 1950s, from the growing materialism and conformity of the era to the communist "witch hunts" of the politically opportunistic Wisconsin Senator Joseph McCarthy. Williams almost certainly viewed McCarthy's crusade, which also targeted liberals and homosexuals, as a corruption of individual freedom, powerfully influencing him in the creation of this unique play as his characters all struggle for some sort of liberation. Several critics judged *Camino Real* to be a failure because its first production was a commercial flop, even though this view has been challenged by new revivals and recent criticism that address the subtle dissection of American politics surrounding the play and its vivid exploration of recurring themes to emerge in Williams's entire body of work.

Camino Real resulted from a long gestation period beginning in 1946 when Williams completed a one-act version, *Ten Blocks on the Camino Real*, and published it in **American Blues** in 1948. After Elia Kazan directed a scene from this version at New York's Actors Studio, Williams was encouraged by Kazan and others to expand it. He completed a full-length treatment in January 1952, increasing the "10 blocks" of the original version to 16 and simplifying its title to *Camino Real*. Kazan regarded the play as Williams's finest, but he was outnumbered by those puzzled by its challenging literary and theatrical devices, from its episodic structure and dislocation from any genuine place or reality of time to its mixture of characters from all corners of the world of literature. *Camino Real* offers a vision of a surreal and harshly decadent world (in which garbage men appear frequently to collect bodies of the dead and Esmeralda's virginity is magically restored) redeemed by the faint but necessary possibility of the prevailing of the sensitive and poetic spirit over the brutal and coarse. The central metaphor of violets breaking through the seemingly impenetrable rocks of a mountain underscores Williams's hope for the unleashing of compassion for the world's most fragile beings and the valuing of the beautiful and poetic. *Camino Real*'s grotesque imagery and striking theatricalism, seen in Williams's use of cascading symbols, a fractured sense of time, and a bold blending of comic and tragic elements, tended to obscure the subtle optimism of its themes and delicacy of its lyrical language. Williams frequently indulged his taste for the grotesque in such later works as **Suddenly Last Summer, The Milk Train Doesn't Stop Here Anymore**, and **Kingdom of Earth**, but these do not as vividly provide the hope for survival of the poetic spirit that is the soul of *Camino Real*.

The play's central strength may be found in Williams's deep affection for many of *Camino Real*'s characters (characters like Gutman and the Generalisimo excluded), many of whom gallantly face life's suffering with spirits that may, at times, seem corrupt or broken but retain, on some level, a fundamental optimism. Like the habitués of Harry Hope's saloon in Eugene O'Neill's *The Iceman Cometh*, the characters of *Camino Real* survive only by clinging, however tenuously, to their hope. Rootless and displaced wanderers in an incomprehensible world (cut off, as they are, from their original literary home), the characters float through a confusing environment seen most vividly in Kilroy's kaleidoscopic journeying through the bizarre, carnivalesque world of the play, reminiscent of a fascist-run state of a Latin American dictatorship. Attempting to create iconic characters in a nonrealistic play, Williams only fueled the critical controversy, but some critics admiringly tracked distinct categories of characterization among these archetypes, including (1) decadents (Marguerite, Casanova, Baron De Charlus), (2) outcasts (the play's numerous bums and drunks), (3) idealists (Don Quixote, Kilroy, Lord Byron), and (4) oppressive state figures (the garbagemen). Williams's ability to explore these aspects of humanity in the play's netherworld of arrested time was appreciated by as many critics as those who rejected it.

The stage as a realm of suspended time fascinated Williams, who rarely manipulated it as boldly as he did in *Camino Real*. The conflation of bits of various eras and cultures is one of the play's strengths, despite the confusion it has sometimes caused critics and audiences. *Camino Real*'s voluptuous symbolism begins with its title meaning either "royal road" or "real road," with an ambiguity fully intended by Williams who also puns on real (real/reel to capture the cinematic quality of the script). Williams passionately believed symbols to be the essential language of the stage, although some critics charge Williams with employing them in place of action, which, they believe, leads to an oversimplification of complex concepts.

Despite the critical and commercial disappointment of the original production, *Camino Real* has been widely and frequently produced. Among the earliest European productions were three German stagings—Darmstadt (1954), Bochum (1955), and Hanover (1959)—all of which met with mixed reviews. Similar response greeted the 8 April 1957 British premiere at London's

Phoenix Theatre, under the direction of **Peter Hall** and featuring Denholm Elliott as Kilroy. A 1960 American revival directed by José Quintero at New York's Circle in the Square had a respectable run, but did little to improve the play's critical history in the United States. A well-produced television adaption of *Camino Real* was broadcast on 7 October 1966 by the NET Playhouse, based on Williams's one-act version, *Ten Blocks on the Camino Real*. Some critics found it superior to the Broadway version and praised cast members including Albert Dekker, Lotte Lenya, Hurd Hatfield, Carrie Nye, Janet Margolin, and a young Martin Sheen. The Forum production inspired a major New York revival at the Vivian Beaumont Theatre beginning 8 January 1970 with a stellar cast that included Al Pacino, **Jessica Tandy**, Jean-Pierre Aumont, and Philip Bosco, but again critics were largely apathetic. The first major revival of *Camino Real* in decades was staged in June 1997 by the Royal Shakespeare Company (a first-ever RSC production of a Williams play) at their Swan Theatre in Stratford-upon-Avon. Under the direction of Steven Pimlott, and featuring Peter Egan and Susannah York, it continued *Camino Real*'s controversial critical history.

Further Reading

Atkinson, Brooks. "*Camino Real*: New Play by Tennessee Williams Offers Personal Conception of Life Today." *New York Times* 29 March 1953, sec. 2: 1.

Balakian, Jan. "*Camino Real*: Williams's Allegory about the Fifties." In *The Cambridge Companion to Tennessee Williams*, ed. Matthew C. Roudané. Cambridge: Cambridge University Press, 1997. 67–94.

Bradley, Frank. "Two Transient Plays: A *Streetcar Named Desire* and *Camino Real*." In *Tennessee Williams: A Casebook*, ed. Robert E Gross. New York: Routledge, 2002. 51–62.

"*Camino Real* (1953)." In *The Critical Response to Tennessee Williams*, ed. George Crandell. 107–117. Westport, CT: Greenwood, 1996.

Cless, Downing. "Alienation and Contradiction in *Camino Real*: A Convergence of Williams and Brecht." *Theatre Journal* 35 (March 1983): 41–50.

Coakley, James. "Time and Tide on the *Camino Real*." In *Tennessee Williams: A Tribute*, ed. Jac Tharpe. Jackson: University Press of Mississippi, 1977. 232–236.

Jenckes, Norma. " 'Let's Face the Music and Dance': Resurgent Romanticism in Tennessee Williams's *Camino Real* and *Clothes for a Summer Hotel*." In *The Undiscovered Country: The Later Plays of Tennessee Williams*, ed. Philip C. Kolin. New York: Lang, 2002. 181–193.

Kerr, Walter. "*Camino Real*." *New York Herald Tribune* 20 March 1953: 12.

Parker, Brian. "A Developmental Stemma for Drafts and Revisions of Tennessee Williams's *Camino Real*." *Modern Drama* 39 (Summer 1996): 331–341.

———. "Documentary Sources for *Camino Real*." *Tennessee Williams Annual Review* 1 (1998): 41–51.

Turner, Diane E. "The Mythic Vision in Tennessee Williams's *Camino Real*." In *Tennessee Williams: A Tribute*, ed. Jac Tharpe. Jackson: University Press of Mississippi, 1977. 237–251.

Williams, Tennessee. "On the *Camino Real*." *New York Times* 15 March 1953, sec. 2: 1, 3.

Wolf, Morris Philip. "Casanova's Portmanteau: *Camino Real* and Recurring Communication Patterns of Tennessee Williams." In *Tennessee Williams: A Tribute*, ed. Jac Tharpe. Jackson: University Press of Mississippi, 1977. 252–276.

James Fisher

Candles to the Sun. Written in the summer of 1935, *Candles* was produced by the **Mummers** on 18–20 March 1937 when Williams was a senior at Washington University.

Directed by **Willard Holland,** who took one of the parts, *Candles to the Sun* was the first full-length Williams play staged by the small St. Louis troupe who would later do *Fugitive Kind*. Like that play, *Candles to the Sun* was ambitious, with 10 scenes and 17 characters, and crowded with impassioned depression-era social protests. Reviewing *Candles to the Sun*, Colvin McPherson, the drama critic for the St. Louis *Post-Dispatch*, praised Williams for his "unusual promise" and, identifying an early Williams hallmark, observed that "theatrical fireworks there are a-plenty."

About a coal miners strike, *Candles to the Sun* is set in the Red Hills country of Alabama where Bram, the coal miner, and his wife Hester eek out a dreary living totally dependent on the Comstock Mining Company. Even though Hester resolves that their son John will not go down into the mines, he is forced to and is killed, leaving his son Joal for Hester to raise. Joal, too, dies in the mines when his grandfather Bram insists that he work in the poorly shored fifth level on his first day. Further pain visits Bram's house when he evicts his daughter Star for staying out all night with a miner. Into this fray comes Birmingham Red (played by Holland), a strike agitator who uses Joal's death to mobilize the miners. But Red is murdered, Star becomes a prostitute, and her brother Luke is also consigned to a perilous life in the mines. Claiming that the ending is one of "mingled sadness and exaltation," Williams has the miners sing "Solidarity Forever."

Candles to the Sun reveals the socialist-leaning Williams capturing the pulse of the times. Though he had never been in a coal mine, Williams's work in *Candles to the Sun* may have been influenced by his St. Louis acquaintance Jack Conroy, the editor of the proletariat magazine *The Anvil*, who had been a miner. Moreover, strikers in St. Louis sang "Solidarity Forever," a famous communist anthem of the times.

Affirming the rights of the workers, Williams, in *Candles to the Sun*, fights against the oppression of a cruel system, supports the idealism of the young (Luke, Joal), and laments the sexual degeneracy of a poor woman, themes that would illuminate his later, more mature works. In 1938, *Candles to the Sun* was rejected in a Dramatist Guild contest Williams had entered as being too filled with propaganda. Though it was dismissed as "labor melodrama" by the Guild, *Candles to the Sun* showed Williams's talent in writing realistic dialogue and in creating believable and sympathetic characters.

Further Reading

Devlin, Albert J., and Nancy Tischler, eds. *The Selected Letters of Tennessee Williams, Volume 1—1920–1945*. New York: New Directions, 2000.

Hale, Allean. "Early Williams: The Making of a Playwright." In *The Cambridge Companion to Tennessee Williams*, ed. Matthew C. Roudané. Cambridge: Cambridge University Press, 1997. 11–28.

[McPherson, Colvin.] "Mummers Present Play by St. Louisian." St. Louis *Post-Dispatch* 19 March 1937.

Philip C. Kolin

Capote, Truman (1924–1984). A novelist most famous for *In Cold Blood*, Truman Capote was a Williams friend turned vituperative foe. When he was first introduced to Capote, their attraction to each other as writers and as friends was completely positive. Both were southerners, gay, and full of mischief. They met in 1948, in the wake of the publication of Capote's *Other Voices, Other Rooms*. Describing Capote as an excellent companion, Williams praised his sense of humor and his satire. Their high-jinks together are renowned. They appeared in tandem on W.H. Auden's doorstep in Italy but were refused an audience, and they also traveled from London to New York on the *Queen Mary*, making a sport of raiding the first-class corridors to switch the pairs of shoes set outside each door for polishing. Stories of their drinking escapades include Capote's breaking into Williams's New York apartment through the transom and getting caught by "the Bo-Peep squad," as they called female officers of the law, who inquired about Williams's sleeping pills but conceded that the few Seconals he had did not warrant a drug bust.

Yet their friendship withered. Williams became jealous over the attention Capote received in **Key West,** where Williams had been the leading celebrity. To make things worse, Capote enthusiastically played the role of darling to the Key West community, as George Plimpton pointed out. Williams became furious at Capote's mocking imitations of **Margo Jones**'s remark to the cast of *Summer and Smoke* that the play was the work of a dying writer. In a letter to **Donald Windham**, Williams pointedly skewered Capote for his haughty assaults. Their fighting, accordingly, became even more public. In 1975–1976, *Esquire* printed excerpts from Capote's as yet unpublished *Answered Prayers*, which included a vicious portrait of a character unmistakably patterned after Williams. Williams retaliated. Headlines in a 2 February 1977 edition of the New York *Daily News* read "Truman and Tennessee Try on Some Suits" (Smith 10). Capote sued Williams for $5 million over his statement in an interview that "someone else" was writing Capote's manuscript *Answered Prayers* (Windham 123). Williams continued to make other disparaging remarks about Capote, especially regarding his high pitched, squeaking voice. Neither man would ever relinquish the role of most wronged by the other. Despite the initial exuberance of their friendship, then, the end of it was dramatically and sadly final. At a party in 1982, Williams asked Capote when he thought they would see each other again. "In Paradise," was Capote's reply (qtd. in Hayman 237).

Further Reading

Hayman, Ronald. *Tennessee Williams: Everyone Else Is an Audience.* New Haven, CT: Yale University Press, 1993.

Leverich, Lyle. *Tom: The Unknown Tennessee Williams.* New York: Crown, 1995.

Plimpton, George. *Truman Capote: In Which Various Friends, Enemies, Acquaintances, and Detractors Recall His Turbulent Career.* New York: Anchor, 1997.

Rader, Dotson. "The Art of Theatre V: Tennessee Williams." *Paris Review* 81 (Fall 1981): 145–184.

Smith, Liz. "Truman and Tennessee Try on Some Suits." New York *Daily News* 2 February 1977: 10.

Windham, Donald. *Lost Friendships: A Memoir of Truman Capote, Tennessee Williams and Others.* New York: Morrow, 1987.

Susan Swartwout

Cat on a Hot Tin Roof. Awarded both the Drama Critics' Circle Award and the Pulitzer Prize for Drama, *Cat on a Hot Tin Roof* (1955) ranks along with **The Glass Menagerie** (1944) and **A Streetcar Named Desire** (1947) as one of the three best dramas by Tennessee Williams and, likewise, one of the best American plays of the twentieth century. Of his major works, Williams preferred *Cat on a Hot Tin Roof* to the others, first because the play observes Aristotle's dictum in *The Poetics* that a tragedy have unity of time and place as well as magnitude of theme; and second because Williams believed that he had outdone himself in creating the crude but eloquent character Big Daddy.

Initially shocked by the play's "vulgar"

language and confused by the playwright's oblique references to homosexuality, audiences nevertheless flocked to see *Cat on a Hot Tin Roof*. The reviewers' response was likewise divided between moral outrage and respectful admiration. In time, however, critics acceded to the popular assessment, reluctantly acknowledging the greatness of Williams's creation. Opening at the Morosco Theater on 24 March 1955, *Cat on a Hot Tin Roof* played on Broadway for 694 performances. Directed by **Elia Kazan**, the original Broadway cast starred Burl Ives (Big Daddy), Barbara Bel Geddes (Maggie), Ben Gazzara (Brick), and Mildred Dunnock (Big Mama). Praise for the cast was almost uniformly positive. **Jo Mielziner**, who had previously collaborated with Williams and Kazan on *A Streetcar Named Desire*, designed the set. A 1958 film version of the play, directed by Richard Brooks, was just as much a popular success. Starring Burl Ives again as Big Daddy, the film garnered six Academy Award nominations and propelled Elizabeth Taylor (Maggie) and Paul Newman (Brick) into stardom. Although Williams benefited financially from the film's success (it grossed more than $10 million in the United States), he disliked the film because the **Hollywood** version of the story lacked the purity of the play and because he had never imagined Elizabeth Taylor in the role of Maggie. Critics have noted, too, that the film version departs significantly from the original play in deleting all references to Brick's sexual identity; instead, Brick is depicted as immature and unable to face responsibility. *Cat on a Hot Tin Roof* has since been broadcast on television. On 6 December 1976, NBC presented Laurence Olivier as Big Daddy, Natalie Wood as Maggie, and Robert Wagner as Brick. A second television broadcast aired on Showtime on 19 August 1984. This production starred

Burl Ives and Barbara Bel Geddes in the 1955 Broadway production of *Cat on a Hot Tin Roof*. Photo by Arthur Zinn, used courtesy of New Directions Publishing Corp.

Jessica Lange (Maggie), Rip Torn (Big Daddy), and Tommy Lee Jones (Brick).

By the time of the play's first major revival in 1974 (at the American Shakespeare Theatre in Stratford, Connecticut, and then at the ANTA Theatre in New York), Big Daddy's coarse language and Brick's alleged homosexuality were no longer subjects for censorship or critical controversy. The New York production, which featured Fred Gwynne as Big Daddy, Elizabeth Ashley as Maggie, and Keir Dullea as Brick, opened on 24 September 1974. By then, many had forgotten that in England, in 1958, the Lord Chamberlain had banned the public performance of *Cat on a Hot Tin Roof* because of its homosexual content (instead, it played to a private-club audience at the Comedy Theatre on 30 January 1958). With the exception of this private engagement, it was not until 30 years later that the general public actually saw *Cat on a Hot Tin Roof* performed largely as Williams had originally written it.

Prior to the Broadway production, director Elia Kazan had suggested changes to the third act of the script that Williams agreed to incorporate. Audiences in 1955 thus saw the revised or "Broadway" version of the play. When *Cat on a Hot Tin Roof* was published, however, Williams chose to include both the original and the revised third act (as it was played on Broadway), with a note of explanation about the two versions. According to Williams, Kazan recommended three significant changes: (1) that Big Daddy reappear in the third act (in the original version, he exits at the conclusion of the second act and never returns); (2) that Brick undergo a transformation as a result of his excoriating interview with Big Daddy in act two; and (3) that Maggie be made more sympathetic to the audience. Although Williams claims to have embraced only the third of these suggestions wholeheartedly, he nevertheless revised the script according to Kazan's wishes. The phenomenal success of the Broadway production seemed to confirm Kazan's judgment, but critics have long since debated the merits of the rival third acts.

Actually, the two published versions of *Cat on a Hot Tin Roof* point to a more widespread phenomenon revealed by the examination of Williams's published and unpublished work. A compulsive writer, Williams repeatedly revised his work, even after it had been produced or published. As a result, one published version of a Tennessee Williams play may differ from another edition of the same work published at a later time. The "acting edition" of *Cat on a Hot Tin Roof*, for example, published in 1958 by the Dramatists Play Service, includes revisions to the text that do not appear in the 1955 New Directions edition. For the 1974

production at the American Shakespeare Theatre, Williams wrote yet another version of the third act, a hybrid of the first two. As in the Broadway version, Big Daddy returns to the stage in the third act. Published in a new edition by New Directions in 1975, the revised *Cat on a Hot Tin Roof* incorporates 140 substantive changes to the text, among them expansions of the text, brief cuts, changes to dialogue, and alterations to stage directions. This version includes, for example, an elephant joke that Williams withdrew from the 1955 Broadway production because of objections from censors.

Not until 1988, then, at the Lyttelton Theatre in London and again in 1990 at the **Eugene O'Neill** Theatre in New York, did large audiences see *Cat on a Hot Tin Roof* performed with much of the original third act restored. Howard Davies directed both the British and the American revivals. At the London production, which opened on 17 February 1988, the cast featured Eric Porter (Big Daddy), Lindsay Duncan (Maggie), and Ian Charleson (Brick). In New York, on 21 March 1990, the play starred Charles Durning (Big Daddy), Kathleen Turner (Maggie), and Daniel Hugh Kelly (Brick). The positive critical response to these performances gave credence to the long-held belief that Williams's first instincts had been right. Since then many critics have viewed Kazan's shaping influence on Williams less positively and have suggested more strongly that Williams compromised his artistic integrity by revising *Cat on a Hot Tin Roof* to meet Kazan's demands.

Recognizing in Big Daddy a character both powerful and unique in American drama, Elia Kazan felt justified in recommending to Williams that Big Daddy be brought back on stage in the third act. Indeed, characterization is one of Williams's great strengths in *Cat on a Hot Tin Roof*. All of the characters, most notably Big

Daddy, Maggie "the Cat," and Brick, are the blended product of Williams's personal memories and fertile genius. Scholars have identified relatives, friends, and personal acquaintances as well as the playwright himself as prototypes for characters in the play. Big Daddy, as played by Burl Ives, resembles in physical appearance and dress a man named Jordan Massee, Sr., the father of Jordan Massee, Jr., with whom Williams vacationed in the summer of 1941. Brick Pollitt is a composite figure, similar to both childhood acquaintances of Williams and a fellow student at the University of Missouri. According to Williams, Maggie's personality resembles that of his friend, **Maria Britneva (Lady St. Just)**, but scholars have also pointed out similarities to a Mississippi woman that Williams once met. Observers searching for biographical parallels see in both Maggie and Brick the warring sides of Williams's own split personality. In the crucible of Williams's fiery imagination all of these people have been transformed into some of the most unforgettable characters ever to appear on stage. In a 1952 short story, "Three Players of a Summer Game," Williams first tells a version of the legend that in the spring of 1954 he would begin to revise in dramatic form as *Cat on a Hot Tin Roof*. In this process, he would add Big Daddy to the cast of characters, regarded by many as the best male character in the Williams canon.

Set on a plantation in the Mississippi Delta, *Cat on a Hot Tin Roof* takes place on Big Daddy's sixty-fifth birthday. Ordinarily a day of celebration, the event is overshadowed by a report that Big Daddy is dying of cancer, tragic news that is concealed from the victim. The impending death of the family patriarch prompts Gooper, the elder son, to vie for a share of the inheritance, knowing Big Daddy's preference for the younger brother, Brick. The alcoholic Brick,

however, prefers to drink his life away rather than compete for the family fortune. Brick suffers from a variety of psychological and physical maladies (including a broken ankle), brought about when Skipper, Brick's best friend, confesses his love to Brick. Brick's subsequent rejection of his friend's amorous advance leads to Skipper's death (by drinking too much) and portends Brick's own demise. Brick's wife, Maggie, is determined, however, to reconcile Brick to his father and likewise to her by luring him back into bed with her, there to produce an heir. Even before she succeeds, Maggie publicly declares she's pregnant, a lie that Big Daddy accepts as true (in the Broadway version). The announcement, although derided by Gooper and his wife Mae, nevertheless reestablishes Brick as heir to the Mississippi plantation and guarantees Maggie's financial security. At the conclusion of the play, it remains only for Maggie to make the lie come true.

Cat on a Hot Tin Roof abandons the episodic structure that characterizes earlier plays such as *The Glass Menagerie* and *A Streetcar Named Desire* for a form that is both classic and contemporary. The play observes the classical unities of time and place at the same time that it makes plot subordinate to characterization. Some reviewers, who fault the play for having no plot, describe it as a series of confessional monologues, pointing especially to Maggie's extended speeches in the first act and Big Daddy's in the second. At the same time, other critics have argued that *Cat on a Hot Tin Roof* advances too many plots and therefore lacks focus. As these observers have pointed out, *Cat on a Hot Tin Roof* is a story about a troubled marriage (Maggie and Brick's); it is also a tale about a father and son unable to communicate with one another (Brick and Big Daddy); likewise, it's a story about idealized friendship or homosexual desire (Brick and Skipper); and moreover, it dramatizes feuding brothers competing for a share of an inheritance (Brick and Gooper). However one describes the plot, *Cat on a Hot Tin Roof* is a play about characters in relationship and in conflict with one another.

The strength of these characterizations and the dynamic relationships among them make *Cat on a Hot Tin Roof* a fascinating study. Many of the early critical responses to the play focus on Big Daddy's character as an image of power, assertiveness, and masculine virility. A larger-than-life character, he represents the virtues and vices of southern patriarchal society. Given his commanding presence on stage, his absence from the third act in the original printed version of the play and his reappearance in the Broadway revision have prompted considerable debate. To some critics, his return in the third act serves no purpose. To other critics, Big Daddy's return is a sign of transformation and redemption. While in the second act, Big Daddy refuses to acknowledge the inevitability of death and rages against the dying of the light, in the third act he accepts what must be. He also sees the reconciliation of Brick and Maggie as the means to sustaining the life that he can no longer hold on to. Their reunion thus becomes a sign of hope for new life—to be delivered by Maggie with the birth of a new child. By acknowledging, even without concrete evidence, that Maggie has life in her body, that she is expecting a child, Big Daddy lends support to Maggie's leading role as the life force of the play. In more recent studies, Big Daddy has been seen as an intermediary character in a line of homosexual descent extending from Jack Straw and Peter Ochello to Brick. In similar studies, Big Daddy is viewed as someone who by tolerating homosexual love takes a broader-than-normal view of human nature, thus motivating Brick

in particular and society in general to emulate his model behavior.

Even while Williams took great pride in the creation of Big Daddy, he thought of *Cat on a Hot Tin Roof* as Maggie's play. She is the "Cat" of the title, and her fiery passion, whether for sex or for success, ignites the action of the play. While others about her are dying or have resigned themselves to death, Maggie is a life force whose determination to succeed brings about both reconciliation and redemption. Hers is the psychological victory at the end of the play that reunites the father with the prodigal son. Meanwhile, the elder son, Gooper, is left to reflect upon his life of dutiful service. Often seen as a mediator, Maggie serves as a link between the living (Brick) and the dead (Skipper), just as she embraces the extremes in human nature—both the animal and the spiritual. As an intermediary, she also serves to break down barriers that inhibit honest communication. Likewise viewed as a redemptive spirit, she is frequently linked with mythical figures who share with her the powers of fertility and regeneration, among them Artemis, Aphrodite, and Phaedra.

Initially viewed as the play's weakest link because of his peripheral role in the action, Brick has since become the focus of many critical discussions if not the center of attention. From the beginning, the "mystery" of his character has been a point of contention. A minority of critics argue that Williams evaded the issue of Brick's sexual identity. By far the larger group contends that Brick simply can't acknowledge his homosexuality because he accepts society's condemnation of it. He is, like the society in which he lives, unwilling to confront the truth. If the mystery of Brick's character is one source of dissatisfaction among critics, then his miraculous transformation (in the Broadway version of the play) is another. In the revision, Brick emerges from his passive state to defend Maggie's lie (about her pregnancy) as the truth. Many view the change in character as unmotivated, while almost all agree that the transformation takes place much too quickly to be believed.

More recent studies of Brick's character emphasize his centrality. He is the one figure around whom much of the action revolves and likewise the person in relationship to whom each of the other characters is defined. Even more important, Brick's malady, defined as narcissism in one study, serves as a metaphor for a range of symptoms that characterize society as a whole and threaten the health and psychic well-being of the American people. In *Cat on a Hot Tin Roof*, the Pollitt family is a reflection of American culture as it is or may become in the future. In this context, Brick's narcissism reflects a society characterized by self-interested individuals, people largely indifferent to the needs of others, and a culture—in its pursuit of immediate gratification—unwittingly intent upon self-destruction. Almost all critics agree that Brick faces a moral crisis in his life and that he must come to terms with life in a mendacious society, his sexual identity, and the prospect of death—his father's and his own.

Other characters, though less central to the action of the play, contribute significantly to the dynamic relationships that Williams depicts in *Cat on a Hot Tin Roof*. Big Mama is frequently characterized in contrast with Big Daddy or Maggie. On the Pollitt plantation, a microcosm of southern patriarchal society, Big Mama plays a subordinate role to Big Daddy. Even in his absence (as in the original third act of the play), Big Mama lacks the power and strength of character to enforce his will (having, it seems, none of her own) and so appears more comic than authoritative. Similar to Maggie, Big Mama may also been seen as a represen-

tative of frustrated love. Unlike Maggie, however, she lacks the emotional resources to change her unfortunate situation.

Because Skipper never appears on stage in *Cat on a Hot Tin Roof*, he is often neglected in discussions of important characters in the play, but he nevertheless functions as a significant motivating figure. He is the source of Brick's grief and provides the key to understanding the emotional and psychological state of Brick's character. When Skipper confesses his love to Brick, he shatters Brick's fantasy of ideal friendship. As a result, Brick's own secure heterosexual self-image is challenged. Brick thus suffers a narcissistic injury that threatens his cohesive image of himself that subsequently motivates Brick's narcissistic or destructive rage against himself and others. Skipper serves another important function as well, one that has only recently been discussed in criticism of *Cat on a Hot Tin Roof*. As he is characterized by others on stage, his figure emerges (like that of Allan Grey in *A Streetcar Named Desire*) for others to see. Without putting a gay character on stage, Williams nevertheless succeeds in painting a portrait in words of the gay male subject. Other characters in the play function to provide comic relief and social commentary. Gooper and Mae, along with their growing family of "no-neck monster" children, occupy the lowest rung on the social ladder, epitomizing the worst in people who aspire to material wealth and social prominence.

For Williams, the mendacity that underlies affluent society is the theme that unites the play's action. Finding support for Williams's claim, subsequent commentators have amplified the theme to include the problem of communication and likewise the conflict between truth and illusion. Still other critics single out the elemental struggle between the destructive powers of death and the affirmative powers of life as an important theme.

From this perspective, Maggie's triumph at the end of the play, signaled by the presence of life in her body, guarantees Brick's redemption from a state of moral paralysis and likewise assures the continuation of the line of succession from Big Daddy, through Brick, to Brick's child. Critics who focus on Brick's mysterious character often suggest that homosexuality is a theme. From this point of view, *Cat on a Hot Tin Roof* employs coded language to achieve more subversive aims, expressing, in contrast with the homophobic discourse of the 1950s, a muted plea for social tolerance.

The major themes of the play are accentuated by obvious symbols. The bed that dominates the set of the play signifies the troubled marriage between Brick and Maggie and suggests, as Big Mama reiterates, that sex is the source of the trouble between them. It is also a reminder of Straw and Ochello, the homosexual couple who once shared it. As one critic argues, their relationship represents an ideal that cannot be achieved by the heterosexual couples in *Cat on a Hot Tin Roof*. The image of the cat in the title links Maggie with heat and passion, while Brick's broken ankle is a sign of his spiritual woundedness. An entertainment center and a plentiful supply of liquor are indicators that the characters desire to escape from an often painful reality. The Mississippi plantation is a symbol of patriarchal society and is associated with wealth, power, and prestige.

Along with **Arthur Miller**'s *Death of a Salesman* (1949) and **Eugene O'Neill**'s *A Long Day's Journey into Night* (1956), *Cat on a Hot Tin Roof* is a significant contribution to the genre of modern domestic tragedy. In Williams's play, ordinary and contemporary problems—mendacity, alcoholism, fatal illness—are magnified for closer scrutiny and raised from the level of private concern to that of public awareness.

In this process, Williams leaves behind a legacy of enduring characters: Big Daddy, Maggie "the Cat," and Brick Pollitt. Almost always lauded as a romantic lyricist, Williams reveals in *Cat on a Hot Tin Roof* that he also possesses a rare talent for psychological realism. In addition, he demonstrates a realist's ear for the coarse vocabulary and repetitious diction of common people to which Williams ascribes a kind of crude eloquence. Although the social and political climate in America has changed considerably since *Cat on a Hot Tin Roof* debuted in 1955 (hush-hush attitudes toward cancer and homosexuality have since moderated), the play's subversive message, articulated then in convert discourse, continues to remind audiences about the precariousness of individual freedom and the limits of tolerance. Combining the best of Williams's realistic and romantic talents, *Cat on a Hot Tin Roof* ranks among the best of his major plays. For its changeable endings and for its daring but ambiguous treatment of homosexuality, *Cat on a Hot Tin Roof* remains Tennessee Williams's most controversial play. See also **Collected Stories**; **Mythology**.

Further Reading

Clum, John M. "*Something Cloudy, Something Clear*: Homophobic Discourse in Tennessee Williams." *South Atlantic Quarterly* 88 (1989): 161–179.

Crandell, George W. " 'Echo Spring': Reflecting the Gaze of Narcissus in Tennessee Williams's *Cat on a Hot Tin Roof*." *Modern Drama* 42 (1999): 427–441.

Murphy, Brenda. "Brick Pollitt Agonistes: The Game in 'Three Players of a Summer Game' and *Cat on a Hot Tin Roof*." *Southern Quarterly* 38 (1999): 36–44.

Parker, Brian. "A Preliminary Stemma for Drafts and Revisions of Tennessee Williams's *Cat on a Hot Tin Roof*." *Papers of the Bibliographical Society of America* 90 (1996): 475–496.

Price, Marian. "*Cat on a Hot Tin Roof*: The Uneasy Marriage of Success and Idealism." *Modern Drama* 38 (1995): 324–335.

Shackelford, Dean. "The Truth That Must Be Told: Gay Subjectivity, Homophobia, and Social History in *Cat on a Hot Tin Roof*." *Tennessee Williams Annual Review* 1 (1998): 103–118.

George W. Crandell

Cerf, Bennett (1898–1971). Bennett Cerf was the publisher of Random House whose influence Williams sought as he started his professional career in the 1940s. The publisher of **O'Neill** and **Faulkner**, Random House offered Williams the publicity and prestige he craved. Courting Cerf in 1940, in the hopes he would publish *Battle of Angels*, Williams took advantage of Cerf's influence to convince Miriam Hopkins to play Myra in *Battle of Angels* and also urged Cerf to obtain the blessing for *Battle of Angels* from critic George Jean Nathan. But because of *Battle of Angel*'s failure on stage, Random House did not publish the play, which, however, was subsequently printed in *Pharos*, the magazine of New Directions' publisher **James Laughlin**.

Unknown to Williams's agent, **Audrey Wood**, Tennessee Williams did sign a contract in 1945 with Cerf for Random House to publish *The Glass Menagerie*, and he gave Cerf the right to publish his next work as well. For this, Williams received an advance of $100, and the Random House first edition of *Menagerie* came out in 5,000 copies on 31 July 1945. However, because of his loyalty to Laughlin at New Directions and his "sympathy for the writers in that group and what they stand for" (Devlin and Tischler 560), Williams prevailed on Cerf to cancel Random House's right to his next work, which would have been *A Streetcar Named Desire*. According to Williams, "I want no part of any commercial publisher now or ever" (in a letter to Laughlin, 11 March 1945; Devlin and Tischler 552). New Directions thus became Williams's exclusive publisher, with the exception of his **Memoirs** released by Doubleday, the small Albondocani Press issue of *The Remarkable Rooming-House of Mme. Le Monde* (1984) in a limited edition, the Sylvester and Orphanos issue of *It Happened the Day the Sun Rose*, and several other small presses.

Further Reading

Devlin, Albert J., and Nancy Tischler, eds. *The Selected Letters of Tennessee Williams, Volume 1—1920–1945*. New York: New Directions, 2000.
Leverich, Lyle. *Tom: The Unknown Tennessee Williams*. New York: Crown, 1995.

Philip C. Kolin

The Chalky White Substance. A one-act Williams play first published in *Anteaus* (Spring 1991), *The Chalky White Substance* is regarded by Linda Dorff as part of a trilogy of Williams apocalyptical dramas including **The Red Devil Battery Sign** and *The Lingering Hour*. *The Chalky White Substance* depicts two male lovers struggling through physical, emotional, and spiritual devastation in a postnuclear, fallen world where individuals have lost faith in God. Mark and Luke, the play's main characters, contend with a world destroyed and now covered with the powder of crushed bones, which (symbolically and literally) eminate from the body of the dead God. In this barren landscape, water rations are strictly enforced by a dictatorial, Big Brother–like regime. As if the challenge of seeking air and water in a world hostile to life were not enough, Mark and Luke also battle fear, loneliness, mistrust, and faithlessness, well-known Tennessee Williams maladies.

The play opens with Luke (age 20), dressed in a monk's robe, waiting for an evening rendezvous with Mark (age 28). Watching his lover waiting, Mark advances and then ruminates with Luke about the world's condition: its lack of food and water, the purpose of protectors (prisonlike guardians exploiting commoners sexually), and the fragility and declining numbers of females due to the chalky white substance. After Luke confides in Mark about his illegal personal habits of cleansing himself from a hidden well prior to their nightly meetings, Mark turns Luke in for this private act of loving abundance. Like Judas Iscariot, Mark uses Luke's love against him and betrays him to the authorities in return for a reward. Only in *The Chalky White Substance*, there is no resurrection, no salvation. God died "endlessly long ago."

Williams's play, and the world Mark and Luke inhabit, as Philip C. Kolin notes, is filled with God (His dead body at least), though ironically devoid of a living God. Mark and Luke, whose names suggest the Gospel writers in the New Testament, represent two very different disciples on a spiritual quest. Motivated by cynicism and greed, Mark has given up on faith and morality; he selfishly mocks Luke's desire to call out for God's salvation. Contrasting with Mark's faithlessness, Williams's Luke, like the biblical Luke, wants to heal himself and others through love, in a dying and nearly barren world. With the exception of Luke's love for Mark, though, Williams offers no solution to the problems caused by a self-destructive, world-decimating society. As in many of Williams's works, love (sexual or otherwise) is meant to redeem characters but, paradoxically, leaves them more vulnerable and hopeless, as befalls Luke in the powdery universe of *The Chalky White Substance*. See also **Politics**.

Further Reading

Dorff, Linda. "Babylon Now: Tennessee Williams's Apocalypses." *Yale Theater* 29.3 (1999): 115–123.

Kolin, Philip C. "The Existential Nightmare in Tennessee Williams's *The Chalky White Substance*." *Notes on Contemporary Literature* 23 (January 1993): 8–11.

J. Marcus Weekley

Chekhov, Anton (1860–1904). A Russian playwright and short story writer, Anton Chekhov exerted boundless influence on Williams. Among the various writers who shaped Williams's craft, Chekhov takes precedence. C.W.E. Bigsby rightfully hails him as "Williams's favourite playwright" (41). Chekhov's reputation is essentially based on four plays—*The Sea Gull* (1896), *Uncle Vanya* (1899), *Three Sisters* (1901), and *The Cherry Orchard* (1904)—and a collection of finely honed stories. Williams first read Chekhov in the summer of 1934 in **St. Louis** and several years later wrote a term paper on Chekhov's art for a drama class at Washington University. In 1981, he adapted *Sea Gull* in his play **The Notebook of Trigorin** (published in 1997). Significantly, when the young writer (a model of the youthful Williams) in Williams's short play *Lady of Larkspur Lotion* is asked to identify himself by an irate landlady, he replies, "Anton Pavlovich Chekhov," showing how closely Williams identified with the Russian dramatist.

In Chekhov, Williams encountered a literary sensibility in many ways similar to his own. He learned from the Russian author about creating melancholy, character-driven dramas that explore the intimacies of the psyche in subtle, highly symbolic ways. In particular, Williams admired the delicacy of Chekhov's writing and his creation of character. In fact, the dislocation of characters who are caught between their memories (or fantasies) of a beautiful dying past and a harsher present reality is central to the work of both writers. Like Chekhov, Williams created effects and conveyed themes through lyrical language and a probing of character, demonstrating a strong sympathy for the sensitive and artistic sensibilities within the human persona. The longing for the triumph of the romantic, lyrical, and sensitive spirit over the disillusionments and disappointments of real life link Williams and Chekhov; both acknowledge that such a triumph is unlikely, yet profess that human beings can survive and live together only through a romanticized view of the world and a great compassion for mutual struggles.

The influence of Chekhov's plays on Williams stems from *The Glass Menagerie*, a play of delicate, frustrated dreams, and poetic language reminiscent of Chekhov's works. Demanding comparison with *The Glass Menagerie*, too, is Chekhov's *Sea Gull* with its emotional fragility, struggles of a fledgling writer, the deeply troubled Constantine Treplev, and his strained relationship with a domineering mother. This same Chekhovian influence can be identified in numerous other Williams plays over the years. *A Streetcar Named Desire* echoes *The Cherry Orchard* in many significant ways. Both plays explore the decaying upper class that can preserve the past only by mythologizing it and who are in a struggle with a new, uneducated, rising bourgeoisie. Relevantly, Blanche DuBois's name (white wood) in *A Streetcar Named Desire* may evoke Madame Ranevsky's endangered orchard. With the passing of the old order, both Williams and Chekhov also lament the dissolution of courtesy and culture. According to Alice Griffin, *Cat on a Hot Tin Roof*, with its psychodrama, lack of communication, and lev-

els of deception/irony, merits the honor of being "the most Chekhovian of his plays" (144). *Small Craft Warnings*, with its endless talk and shattered lives, also evokes Chekhov. And Bruce J. Mann affirms that that "final line" of *Vieux Carré* "echoes the ending of *The Cherry Orchard*," since as Williams's "younger self leaves to launch his career, his older self must remain behind [like the old retainer Firs], entombed, to await death" (143).

Ultimately, while Williams revered Chekhov, he invented his own dramatic world built on overt sexuality and harsh violence quite removed from Chekhov's (and his director Constantine Stanislavsky's) Moscow Art Theatre.

Further Reading

Bigsby, C.W.E. *Modern American Drama, 1945–2000*. Cambridge: Cambridge University Press, 2000.

Callow, Philip. *Chekhov, the Hidden Ground*. New York: Ivan R. Dee, 1998.

Griffin, Alice. *Understanding Tennessee Williams*. Columbia: University of South Carolina Press, 1995.

Gunn, Drewey Wayne. " 'More Than Just a Little Chekhovian': *The Seagull* as a Source for the Characters in *The Glass Menagerie*." *Modern Drama* 33 (September 1990): 313–321.

Mann, Bruce J. "Memories and Muses: *Vieux Carré* and *Something Cloudy, Something Clear*." In *Tennessee Williams: A Casebook*, ed. Robert F. Gross. New York: Routledge, 2002. 139–152.

Quintus, John Allen. "The Loss of Dear Things: Chekhov and Williams in Perspective." *English Language Notes* 18 (March 1981): 201–206.

James Fisher

Clarksdale, Mississippi. A town in the Mississippi Delta about 80 miles due south of Memphis, Clarksdale played a shaping influence on Williams's life and work. A significant part of his early childhood was spent in Clarksdale with his maternal grandparents, the Reverend **Walter Edwin** and **Rosina Otte Dakin**, at the rectory of St. George's Episcopal Church. Williams began school in Clarksdale, recuperated from diphtheria there, and was nurtured by a loving black maid named Ozzie. In 1918, when Williams was only eight, his father moved the family to **St. Louis**, but Williams went back to Clarksdale for another part of his grammar school education (1920–1921) until he returned to St. Louis, a move he dreaded because it took him away from the comfort and love of his grandparents. He briefly returned to Clarksdale in 1928 to accompany his grandfather on a tour of Europe with members of his parish.

Williams used this Delta town and its environs (Friar's Point, Lyon, Tutwiler) for the settings and characters in many of his plays. Clarksdale symbolized the paradoxical mythos of the South for Williams, idyllically expressed through Amanda's Blue Mountain in *The Glass Menagerie* but painfully recast as the hellish underworld of Two River County in *Battle of Angels* and *Orpheus Descending*. He also fictionalized Clarksdale and the Delta through such places as Port Tyler in *Spring Storm* (1937), Mistah Charlie's ("the last of the Delta drummers") territory in *Last of My Solid Gold Watches* (1940), and Glorious Hill, the home of "the Nightingale of the Delta," Alma Winemiller, in *Summer and Smoke*. The wealthy Cutrer family, whose mansion is a literary landmark in Clarksdale, figure prominently in *Battle of Angels* and *Orpheus Descending*. Williams also fashioned Moon Lake, a place of romance and death in *Summer and Smoke* and *A Streetcar Named Desire*, from a casino in Luling (Dundee), Mississippi, less than 20

miles from Clarksdale. In *Cat on a Hot Tin Roof*, the Delta becomes a baronial estate, a rich inheritance over which Big Daddy's children fight. The Delta plantation in *Kingdom of Earth* (1967) is endangered by the rising floodwaters of the Mississippi. Several of Williams's stories also have Clarksdale and Delta settings, for example, "Resemblance between a Violin Case and a Coffin."

In addition to geography, some Clarksdale residents found their way into Williams's canon. The prominent Cutrers are presented in *Battle of Angels* and *Orpheus Descending* through the characters of David and his rebellious sister Carol. Blanche Clark Cutrer may have been a model for Blanche DuBois. A Clarksdale boyhood friend, E.D. Perry, had a sister (Mary Edmunds) whose nickname Williams's immortalized in his 1956 screenplay *Baby Doll*, set in Benoit, Mississippi, north of Clarksdale. Two more Clarksdale boys became the models for Brick Pollitt in *Cat on a Hot Tin Roof*—Albert "Buck" Gotcher and John Wesley Clark.

The ethnography of Clarksdale—as much as its topography and residents—infused Williams's works. The birthplace of the blues, Clarksdale gave the youthful Thomas Lanier Williams invaluable memories about the culture and the sounds of the Delta. Val Xavier (in *Battle of Angels* and *Orpheus Descending*) honors the great blues artist Bessie Smith. The "blue piano" in *A Streetcar Named Desire* recalls the Delta musical form, and the musical arrangements in *Baby Doll* are also authentic blues. Williams's sympathetic representation of black characters doubtless, too, has its roots in his Clarksdale experiences.

The Mississippi Delta Tennessee Williams Festival is held each year in Clarksdale commemorating the influence this region had on his life and work. See also *Twenty-seven*

Wagons Full of Cotton and Other One-Act Plays; Southern Culture and Literature.

Further Reading

Leverich, Lyle. *Tom: The Unknown Tennessee Williams*. New York: Crown, 1995.

Philip C. Kolin

Clothes for a Summer Hotel. *Clothes for a Summer Hotel* was the last of Tennessee Williams's plays to come to Broadway in his lifetime, premiering at the Cort Theatre on 26 March 1980. Drawing chiefly upon Nancy Milford's *Zelda* and Hemingway's *A Moveable Feast* as primary sources, and influenced by Swedish playwright August Strindberg, Williams labeled *Clothes for a Summer Hotel* "a ghost play," replete with a cast of long-dead characters keenly aware of their respective fates and doomed to play out pivotal moments of their lives. A fusion of past, present, and future resembling *Camino Real* in its blurring of time and reality, *Clothes* dramatizes a one-day visit by F. Scott Fitzgerald to his wife Zelda at Highland Hospital, a sanitarium on a windy, desolate hilltop near Asheville, North Carolina, where she perished in a fire in 1948.

Told by her physician that Zelda has recovered from her long bout with madness, Scott has left sunny California without a change of clothes suitable for the cold of North Carolina (hence Williams's enigmatic title). He finds, however, a still-delusional and combative Zelda; she blames her descent into madness on her estranged husband, who had earlier denied her a career as a novelist by demanding that she assume only the role of author's wife.

Williams's characterizations of Scott and Zelda are culminations of two archetypes that haunt his plays: the artist and the faded Southern Belle. Like Tom Wingfield of *The Glass Menagerie* and the Writer in *Vieux Carré*, Scott is a tormented creator who struggles to make his art and yet survive in a world that measures artistic success by its commerciality. Zelda is a representation of Williams's schizophrenic sister **Rose Williams**, also embodied by Laura, Blanche, and Catherine of *Suddenly Last Summer*—the inherently pure women destroyed by a corrupting and hostile environment. Williams's portrayal of the hostile relationship of Scott and Zelda (and Brick and Maggie, Stanley and Stella, and others) owes much to **D.H. Lawrence**, another of Williams's major influences, whose works depict marriage and male/female partnerships as war.

To explain Zelda's madness, Williams employs dreamlike flashbacks in which locale changes as swiftly as the shifting of memories to transport Scott and Zelda as glamorous expatriates to "Jazz Age" 1920s France. Scott has turned to alcohol to fuel his creativity and to tune out his wife's demands for a writing career of her own, compelling Zelda to turn to a French aviator (whose occupation suggests a means for transcendence) to satisfy the physical and emotional needs not met by her distant and competitive husband. Scott is violent and abusive, and Zelda loses grip on reality as her lover refuses to liberate her from what she perceives to be a life of inconsequentiality, shaped by a husband envious of her own literary talent. Throughout the flashbacks, Williams weaves in prominent historical figures important to the Fitzgeralds, including Gerald and Sara Murphy (the American socialites to whom Scott dedicated *Tender Is the Night*) and Ernest Hemingway. The two rival writers share an intriguing confrontation in which Scott's sexuality is called into question.

Ultimately, of course, there is no reconciliation, and Zelda and Scott come to an understanding that they have each served to destroy the other. The play ends as it began, in the 1940s, as the iron gates of Highland confine Zelda to further insulin treatments (and to her eminent immolation). Claiming sole ownership of her identity and exhorting Scott to stop using her as inspiration for his literary creations, she exorcises Scott, leaving him a lonely ghost silently pondering the wreckage of their partnership.

Fire is a dominant thematic element in *Clothes for a Summer Hotel*, not only as the force that claimed Zelda Fitzgerald's life but also as a metaphor for the passions that consumed both her and her husband. Throughout the play, Zelda acknowledges her death, asserting that she is not a salamander, a mythic creature that can survive fire (she is, however, a Cassandra, prophesying for deaf ears). Red, symbolizing fire, also enflames Williams's script: the asylum is painted a dark red, a bush with fiery red leaves that Zelda cannot bear to look at dominates one corner of the stage, and the asylum's windows reflect the oranges and reds of sunset at the end of the play. Fire, as a metaphor and a manifestation of internal chaos, rages in many of Williams's other works, including the one-acts *Twenty-seven Wagons Full of Cotton*; *Auto-da-Fé*; *The Rose Tattoo*; *Orpheus Descending*; and *I Rise in Flame, Cried the Phoenix*, which concerns the final moments of D.H. Lawrence. Scholarship has also focused on the inherent romanticism and antirealistic qualities in *Clothes*.

But perhaps the most profound thematic element in the play is that of confinement, also prominent in many of Williams's other plays, including *The Two-Character Play/ Out Cry* (1973), in which two actors and the characters they play are trapped in their roles and are locked in a theater, and *Not about Nightingales* (1939), set in a prison. Certainly the physical asylum confines Zelda (and shuts out Scott), but other powerful bonds constrain them, including prescribed gender roles, their passionate artistic impulses, alcoholism, and fame. The psychic confinements of Zelda and Scott also tormented Williams, forcing him in 1969 into an involuntary confinement at Barnes Hospital in **St. Louis**.

Directed by José Quintero, the Broadway production of **Clothes for a Summer Hotel** starred Kenneth Haigh as Scott and perennial Williams leading lady Geraldine Page as Zelda. Critics were not kind, finding the play pedantic, bleak, and superfluous and suggesting that Williams had lost the poetic quality of his earlier works. The Broadway production closed after 15 performances; the script was first published in 1981. Recent productions of *Clothes for a Summer Hotel* include a 1989 staging at the Williamstown Theatre Festival and a 1995 off-Broadway production at the York Theatre. In 1998, the play was produced by the Thomas Wolfe Festival in Asheville, North Carolina, during which a plaque honoring the memory of Zelda Fitzgerald was unveiled by her granddaughter at the site of Highland Hospital. See also **Madness**.

Further Reading

Adler, Thomas P. "When Ghosts Supplant Memories: Tennessee Williams's *Clothes for a Summer Hotel*." *Southern Literary Journal* 19.2 (Spring 1987): 5–19.

Crandell, George W. " 'I Can't Imagine Tomorrow': Tennessee Williams and the Representations of Time in *Clothes for a Summer Hotel*." In *The Undiscovered Country: The Later Plays of Tennessee Williams*, ed. Philip C. Kolin. New York: Lang, 2002. 168–180.

Dorff, Linda. "Collapsing Resurrection Mythologies: Theatricalist Discourses of Fire and Ash in *Clothes for a Summer Hotel*." In *Tennessee Williams: A Casebook*, ed. Robert F. Gross. New York: Routledge, 2002. 153–172.

Jenckes, Norma. " 'Let's Face the Music and Dance': Resurgent Romanticism in Tennessee Williams's *Camino Real* and *Clothes for a Summer Hotel.*" In *The Undiscovered Country: The Later Plays of Tennessee Williams*, ed. Philip C. Kolin. New York: Lang, 2002. 181–193.

W. Douglas Powers

Collected Stories. The *Collected Stories* (1985) represents a chronological compilation of titles from Tennessee Williams's four short story collections: *One Arm and Other Stories* (1948), *Hard Candy and Other Stories* (1954), *The Knightly Quest: A Novella and Four Short Stories* (1967), and *Eight Mortal Ladies Possessed: A Book of Stories* (1974), as well as previously uncollected stories appearing in such magazines as *Esquire* and *The New Yorker*. In addition, New Directions added 9 unpublished stories, bringing the total number to 50 (the preface, titled "The Man in the Overstuffed Chair," is also a short story). In his introduction to the volume, **Gore Vidal** called the *Collected Stories* "the true memoir of Tennessee Williams" and contends that they may serve as an autobiographical guide. As is the case in most of Williams's writing, the parallels between life and art are obvious, although the transformation of actual events into stories inevitably results in departures from the reality of the factual world.

The stories cover 50 years of Williams's writing, from 1928 to 1978, but the collection may not be regarded as exhaustive, as additional unpublished stories have surfaced since the volume's 1985 publication; and some stories, such as "Isolated" (written and published when Williams was 13) and "The Negative" (written in 1982, shortly before his death), were not added to the collection.

Many of the stories serve as the organic seeds of future one-act and full-length plays. For example, "Twenty-seven Wagons Full of Cotton" (along with a one-act play titled

"The Unsatisfactory Supper") was expanded into the 1956 screenplay *Baby Doll* as well as the 1977 play *Tiger Tail.* "Portrait of a Girl in Glass" would eventually evolve into *The Glass Menagerie* (1944). "The Night of the Iguana" underwent a radical evolution to become the 1961 play of the same title, and "Three Players of a Summer Game" served as the basis for a very different *Cat on a Hot Tin Roof.* "Man Bring This Up Road" found dramatic form in *The Milk Train Doesn't Stop Here Anymore* (1962). "The Kingdom of Earth," first published in 1954, premiered under the title *The Seven Descents of Myrtle* in 1968 and reverted to the short story title *The Kingdom of Earth* for the 1975 and subsequent productions. "The Angel in the Alcove" would be expanded into the full-length *Vieux Carré*, but Williams actually began the play before writing the short story. Although these stories serve as the bases of future one-act and full-length plays, as well as screenplays ("One Arm" is an example of the latter), it is misleading to view these stories only as blueprints for his later works, for we must remember that Williams wrote stories before he ever turned to drama. He started writing stories in junior high school, and he continued to craft short fiction until his death in 1983. Williams occasionally worked on the same play and story simultaneously (as with "Portrait of a Girl in Glass" and *The Glass Menagerie*), and in other cases, it is impossible to determine whether Williams himself recognized the dramatic possibilities of a particular story as he was composing it. He usually worked from strong and indelible images, and the stronger the image, the more he shaped and nurtured it. His own composing process was anything but methodical and sequential, and although the glosses in his collected letters and journals are very helpful in determining the sequence of Williams's writing, any attempt to declare definitively his scheme for development seems precarious.

Some of Williams's most emotionally compelling stories are biographically inspired. The majority of the author's childhood and young adulthood were painful years, and through his fiction, we readers can fully sense his apprehensions and anxieties. Whether he is reliving the horrible death of his beloved grandmother (**Rosina Dakin**) in "Grand" or describing his sister's (**Rose Williams**) steady progression into schizophrenia in "Portrait of a Girl in Glass," these stories doubtless served as catharsis for the troubled Williams, allowing him to shape life's pain into art. Another sketch relating to Williams's youth, "The Man in the Overstuffed Chair" reassesses the tortured relationship between Williams and his father **Cornelius Coffin Williams** from the perspective of Tennessee's adulthood. Pitying Cornelius more than hating him, Williams became more tolerant of his father's indiscretions. "The Resemblance between a Violin Case and a Coffin" exquisitely addresses Williams's formation of sexual identity and may be read as a case study of prepubescent homosexual longing and the concomitant confusion involved with the discovery. The story is also a beautiful testimony to Williams's love for his sister Rose. Another piece that has been largely overlooked is "Completed," which demonstrates Williams's practice of combining autobiographical facts with his poetic imagination in order to produce a haunting portrait of a troubled young woman. The story centers on Rosemary McCool, a pathologically shy girl (Rose) with a forceful mother (Edwina), who experiences her first menstruation at the age of 20. Another story inspired from personal experience, titled "The Interval," is based very loosely on Williams's first trip to **Hollywood**, California in 1939 and

also serves as a commentary on the illusory world of the movie industry.

Williams claimed that **Anton Chekhov** influenced his development as a storywriter as well as a dramatist, and in some of the more subtle psychological portraits, such as "The Accent of a Coming Foot," the influence seems palpable. In other stories, such as "The Field of Blue Children," "Oriflamme," and "The Vine," the flesh-and-blood tactility of **D.H. Lawrence** reigns. But the collection is so rich and diverse as to defy any direct comparisons with the legacy of any specific stylist. With the incredible range, stylistic richness, and variety of the collection, which move from Gothic fantasy ("The Vengeance of Nitocris") to late postmodern ("The Killer Chicken and the Closet Queen"), Williams demonstrates that had he never written plays, he would probably be among the great American short story writers of the twentieth century.

The 50 years of his short stories reveal a variety of genres, such as allegories, confessionals, character studies, fantasies, reveries, and psychological studies, as well as other kinds of stories, but no clear chronological pattern is evident. Almost all the stories reflect Williams's masterful attention to setting, whether they be actual or symbolic locales. As with his drama, Williams positions most of his stories either in **St. Louis**, the Mississippi Delta, or **New Orleans**. For example, "The Man in the Overstuffed Chair" and "Portrait of a Girl in Glass" are set in St. Louis. "Big Black," "The Resemblance between a Violin Case and a Coffin," and "Three Players of a Summer Game" take place in and around **Clarksdale, Mississippi**. "One Arm," "The Yellow Bird," "The Angel in the Alcove," and "In Memory of an Aristocrat" all unfold in New Orleans. However, many of the stories are set in places other than these three chief locales for most of Williams's fiction and drama, such as Hollywood for "The Interval," Thebes for "The Vengeance of Nitocris," Manhattan for "Two on a Party," and central Europe for "A Recluse and His Guest." But Williams's short fiction cannot be said to be uniformly rooted in any one region; there appears no constant, ubiquitous backdrop such as Flannery O'Connor's Christ-haunted Georgia backwaters or Eudora Welty's Mississippi Delta. Ultimately, the stories stubbornly resist any attempt at uniform groupings by place or technique, yet nearly all are set in familiar Williams territory—the locale of the heart.

Williams's narrative skill helps shape the success of his fiction as well as his plays. Only one fourth of the stories are told in first person, and almost all of these are from personal reminiscence, such as "The Resemblance between a Violin Case and a Coffin" or "In Memory of an Aristocrat." The voice of the remaining 38 stories is seldom uniform and never repetitive. At times, in stories such as "Three Players of a Summer Game" the narrator seems detached and ironic; with other stories, such as "The Mysteries of the Joy Rio," the voice is intimate and inextricable, escorting the reader to sights and sounds beyond the usual privileges of the casual observer, well into the realm of voyeurism, as George Crandell maintains. However a Williams story is told, the narrator always seems in control of the subject matter and tone. Whether the story is about cruising ("Two on a Party"), disease—possibly AIDS, as Philip C. Kolin speculates ("Mother Yaws"), failed romance ("The Field of Blue Children"), sexual repression ("The Night of the Iguana"), or cold war politics ("The Knightly Quest"), the pitch and timbre of the narrator's voice are usually flawless. In only a few stories, such as "Ten Minute Stop" or "Something by Tolstoi," does the reader find Williams struggling with establishing a convincing voice.

If there is one leitmotif to be found among these stories of incredible range and scope, it may be Williams's idea of "incompleteness," a void occurring in those characters who lack something in their own constitutions or in their relationships. The collection is filled with a panoply of societal and sexual misfits who constantly swim against the common current of humanity. Williams directly addresses this idea of incompleteness in several of the stories, and his recurring use of the theme may help readers to characterize this obstinately diverse collection of short stories. Broadly defined, this incompleteness may be seen as an inability to satisfy desire in relationships, whether they be familial, conjugal, or spiritual. Many of these stories transmit an overwhelming feeling of loss and regret for what could have been—or, to use Blanche DuBois's words, what "*ought* to be." Desire often leads to unrequited fulfillment, which, in turn, leads to incompleteness. "The Mysteries of the Joy Rio," "The Inventory at Fontana Bella," and "The Knightly Quest" all illustrate this concern. Williams's characters often seem befuddled and distraught as they attempt to superimpose the ideal upon the real. As with the characters in E.A. Robinson's fiction, Williams's characters often seem displaced from time, community, and self.

A classic example of incompleteness in the form of sexual repression and thwarted desire may be found in "Big Black," one of Williams's most carefully crafted early stories. This "Idyll," written when Williams was only about 20 years old, chronicles the thoughts of a mythic road gang worker named Big Black who attempts to ravish a white girl as she bathes in a nearby river. He restrains himself by reacting to his own ugliness and viewing himself from the perspective of the terrified young girl. Written some two years before the release of the film *King*

Kong (as Philip C. Kolin notes), this beauty and the beast parable is actually more about the self-repulsion that results from the way others look at Big Black, which becomes his looking-glass self. With this story Williams raises questions about racial issues some 20 years before the civil rights movement forced a reassessment of the stereotypical images of black males.

Another story involving sexual desire and the black exotic other is "Desire and the Black Masseur," one of Williams's most richly textured and complex stories from the collection and one that has consequently received more scholarly attention than any other story. David Savran offers one of the most detailed interpretations of this key Williams story. The piece is fascinating on several levels: as an anatomy of a sadomasochistic fetish, as an allegory of racial conflict, and as a study of the psychodynamics of mutual desire. In the case of Burns and the masseur, atonement equals completeness, and "an air of completion" is realized only after Burns is tortured and literally consumed by the giant.

"One Arm," another story of frustrated desire and incompletion, was one of Williams's own favorites. He even wrote a screenplay of the story that was considered but eventually rejected for production by **Marlon Brando**. What begins as a story of a deformed hustler evolves into a study of unreciprocated love, psychological transference, and incompleteness as Oliver recounts the many love letters and the Lutheran minister confronts his own emerging sexual compulsions as he attempts to "heal" Oliver. Other stories dealing directly with this theme of incompletion include "The Vine," a lover's tale that reflects the influence of D.H. Lawrence, and "The Malediction," a strange boarding-house story about a man named Lucia, his cat, and his attempt to find happiness with a pitiful landlady. In addition,

"Oriflamme," "The Field of Blue Children," and "The Poet," as well as scores of other stories, deal at least marginally if not directly with unrequited love, loss, and regret—all components of incompleteness.

Although David Savran, Dennis Vannatta, Philip C. Kolin, George Crandell, and John Clum, among others, have written noteworthy analyses of Williams's short fiction, as a whole the collection merits even more attention. For example, "A Lady's Beaded Bag," published in *The Columns* when Williams was just 19 years old, has not received any commentary. This brief but fascinating tale about a "dumpster diver" who finds a purse and returns it to its owner survives as an early example of Williams's exquisite sense of irony that he would continue to develop throughout his writing. Further, "A Lady's Beaded Bag" demonstrates a writer still in his teens who could pack explosive issues of loneliness, social inequity, and hope into a narrative of fewer than four pages in length. Other uncelebrated stories include "Sand," a brief sketch of an elderly couple attempting to come to terms with senility; "The Yellow Bird," an occasionally anthologized story offering parallels with Alma Winemiller in *Summer and Smoke*; "The Poet," sounding with reverberations of Sebastian's death in *Suddenly Last Summer*; and "The Coming of Something to the Widow Holly," giving us a tale of magical realism set in Williams's beloved French Quarter.

From his earliest beginnings as a writer to his last works, Williams devoted a considerable amount of his artistic energy to his short fiction. He realized, about the time that Tom Williams changed to Tennessee Williams, that writing and having his plays produced would inevitably result in far greater rewards than the slow, laborious process of sending in stories to magazines. Hence, playwriting assumed a primacy in his life that he would never abandon. However, the *Collected Stories* demonstrates his lifelong devotion to the craft of short fiction and serves to remind us of his protean gifts across fiction as well as drama. See also **Politics; Race.**

Further Reading

Crandell, George. "Peeping Tom: Voyeurism, Taboo, and Truth in the World of Tennessee Williams's Short Fiction." *Southern Quarterly* 38 (Fall 1999): 28–35.

Kolin, Philip. "It's Not Life with Auntie Mame: Tennessee Williams's 'Completed.' " *Tennessee Williams Literary Journal* 5 (Spring 2003): 80–83.

———. "Tennessee Williams, 'Mother Yaws,' and AIDS." *Popular Culture Review* 13 (January 2002): 63–68.

———. "Tennessee Williams's 'Big Black: A Mississippi Idyll' and Race Relations, 1932." *RE: Arts & Letters (REAL)* 20 (1995).

———. "Tennessee Williams's 'Interval': MGM and Beyond." *Southern Quarterly* 38 (Fall 1999): 21–27.

———. "Vulnerable Intimacies in Tennessee Williams's 'Happy August Tenth.' " *Notes on Contemporary Literature* 32 (November 2002): 4–6.

Saddik, Annette. "The (Un)Represented Fragmentation of the Body in Tennessee Williams's 'Desire and the Black Masseur' and 'Suddenly Last Summer.' " *Modern Drama* 41 (Fall 1998): 347–354.

Savran, David. *Communists, Cowboys, and Queens: The Politics of Masculinity in the Work of Arthur Miller and Tennessee Williams.* Minneapolis: University of Minnesota Press, 1992.

Vannatta, Dennis. *Tennessee Williams: A Study of the Short Fiction.* Boston: Twayne, 1988.

Robert Bray

Confessional. *Confessional,* a play in one act, was written in 1967 and first staged in July 1971 during the Maine Theatre Arts Festival in Bar Harbor. It appeared on the same playbill with *I Can't Imagine Tomorrow.* Local reviewers found in both plays a compassionate treatment of emotions and needs common to all people. William E. Hunt, who directed both of these productions, was reportedly slated to direct the off-Broadway premiere of *Confessional* in early 1972 with Helena Carroll playing the lead. But there is no evidence the one-act had even a brief New York run. Rather, an expanded two-act version titled *Small Craft Warnings*, with Helena Carroll in the lead role, briefly appeared at the Truck and Warehouse Theatre in early April 1972. Except for slight differences in the opening scenes, which introduce a motif of personal betrayals, both plays overlap considerably. In *Confessional,* Leona dominates the opening scene raging about Violet's betrayal of their friendship with her own parasitic boyfriend Bill, while in *Small Craft Warnings* the vulgarity of Williams's dramatic world is heightened and the catalog of betrayals amplified to include misogyny, professional ethical turpitude, mean-spiritedness, and rank ingratitude.

The setting of *Confessional* is that of a seedy waterfront bar in a small northern California town, patronized by the kind of human flotsam that one associates with such a locale and establishment. An evening of drinking among the regulars of Monk's Bar and two strangers degenerates into verbal aggression, threats of brawls, and painful, self-revelatory soliloquies. These "confessions" account for the play's title and its technique—nine spot-lit confessions confided directly to the audience by eight of the play's characters. These set speeches, because of the play's length, bypass the unfolding of dramatic tensions from which a play's action normally develops. Because they largely account for the play's action, these confessions lend to the play the quality of being a gallery of character portraits. By play's end, characters have either acquiesced to disillusionment, accepted the cramped circumstances of their lives, or succeeded in sustaining the illusions that they desperately believe will impart to their lives a measure of meaning. Gathering at Monk's Bar to find connection or community, they soon reveal the emptiness of their gregariousness when they blatantly betray one another or misguidedly allow the demands of the flesh to overrule their need for a larger life. The gallery includes the barfly Violet; her boyfriend Steve; Bill, Leona's unfaithful boyfriend; and Leona. Monk's other regulars are no less freakish. Doc, an incompetent, disbarred physician who drunkenly interprets in an evening star the promise of delivering a new Messiah at the Treasure Island Trailer Park, turns fugitive after he bungles a delivery in which neither baby nor mother survive. Monk later gives Violet refuge from the night.

There are two strangers who visit Monk's in *Confessional*—the Young Man who confesses to the erosion of spirit and hope that accompanies his homosexuality and the Boy from Iowa who, recently initiated into homosexuality and caught between guilt and desire, can only anticipate a future of loneliness. Unlike the message of many of his other plays where sex is liberating, here sex is oppressive and emotionally barren. Though they do not want the life they have, these characters do not know what they need. Ultimately, they are like Val Xavier in *Orpheus Descending* who laments that he is sentenced to loneliness.

It is in this world of vulgarity, misfits, and failures that Leona, an itinerant beautician, becomes the play's ostensible heroine. But unlike the other characters whose lives have come to a standstill and who are frozen in their isolation and self-loathing, Leona, at play's end, will continue her search to satisfy an unsatisfied need. Her constancy of spirit allows her to accept change. In the face of betrayals—Violet's and Steve's mutual infidelity—and loss—the death of a brother, a homosexual violinist—and homelessness, she retains a capacity to express tenderness, extend sympathy, and in the person of the Boy from Iowa, offer shelter to the emotionally needy and vulnerable.

In contrast to its boisterous opening, *Confessional* closes on a quiet note. Leona's dignified acceptance of loneliness is impressive as she prepares to leave the world of Monk's Bar and expresses her readiness to meet the road before her clearheaded. With this ending, albeit a muted affirmation, *Confessional* distinguishes itself from many of Williams's unrelentingly pessimistic plays that follow in the 1970s. See also *Small Craft Warnings*.

Further Reading

Funk, Lewis. "One from Tennessee, One from Tom." *New York Times* 19 December 1971: 3+.

Kolin, Philip C. " 'having lost the ability to say: "My God!" ' The Theology of Tennessee Williams's *Small Craft Warnings*." In *The Undiscovered Country: The Later Plays of Tennessee Williams*, ed. Philip C. Kolin. New York: Lang, 2002. 107–124.

Newell, Robert H. "Two Tennessee Williams Plays Premiere at M[ount] D[esert] I[sland] High School." *Bangor* [Maine] *Daily News* 20 August 1971: 4.

"700 Turn Out to Attend Tennessee Williams Premieres." *Bar Harbor Times* [Maine] 26 August 1971: 16.

Arthur Wrobel

Correspondence. Tennessee Williams was a voluminous letter-writer. Four volumes of Williams's correspondence represent his achievements: *Tennessee Williams' Letters to Donald Windam, 1940–1965* (New York: Holt, 1977); *Five O'Clock Angel: Letters of Tennessee Williams to Maria St.*

Just, 1948–1982 (New York: Knopf, 1990); *The Selected Letters of Tennessee Williams, Volume 1—1920–1945* (New York: New Directions, 2000); and Peggy Fox and Thomas Keith, eds., *Tennessee Williams and James Laughlin: Selected Letters* (New York: W.W. Norton, forthcoming). In all, these collections bring to print some 700 letters, notes, and telegrams written by Williams from 1920 until his death in 1983.

Considered comparatively, these volumes present Williams from different perspectives of intimacy and vary widely in kind and degree. **Donald Windham** and Maria St. Just (see **Maria Britneva**), as was true of nearly all of Williams's close friends, were by turns admired and criticized, trusted and suspected, embraced and rejected. Traces of this unsettling dynamic can be found in the apparatus of both collections: Windham minutely analyzes the motives of his mercurial friend in what often amounts to editorial acts of self-defense, while St. Just is intent upon confirming her guardianship of the fragile Williams's ego and career. If only by virtue of its diverse range of correspondents, volume 1 of *The Selected Letters* helps to relieve the intensely personal and self-regardful editing of the preceding volumes by placing Williams in a more complicated and varied field of relations. Williams's correspondence with his New Directions publisher, **James Laughlin**, also gives us invaluable information about this key relationship. Containing approximately 220 letters, this collection sheds light on the 40-year friendship between Williams and Laughlin, as well as chronicling Williams's input into the published editions of his works and his relationship to the publishing world at large.

Together these collections offer a superb view of Williams as a resourceful, adaptive writer of letters that he used both to entertain his correspondents and to conduct literary and theater business. A gay referent is woven into many of the Windham letters, at times (as in #20 in volume 1, July 1942) with a sensual zest that is intended to regale the recipient and contribute, comically, to the record of sexual performance. With Maria St. Just, the emphasis falls more heavily upon the speech, gestures, motives, and foibles of family, friends, lovers, and luminaries such as **Truman Capote** and **Carson McCullers**—all of whom are cast in a vanity fair and made to perform as caricatures. In volume 1 of *The Selected Letters*, more than one third of the correspondence is directed to Williams's immediate and extended family, and thus his tone and subject matter are more rigorously censored or controlled. Rhetorical control is also evident in Williams's correspondence with his agent **Audrey Wood** (the most frequent recipient of the letters in volume 1 of *The Selected Letters*), which is intended to create a portrait of the artist as an earnest young man, beset by artistic self-doubt and the accompanying "blue devils" of fear and depression. With gay friends such as **Paul Bigelow**, another frequent correspondent in volume 1, Williams writes colloquially and sexually to give salt or ginger to his correspondence.

The cumulative effect of the four collections of letters is to cast Williams in a multifaceted personal-professional drama. He was engaged in a ceaseless production and modification of various roles—son, brother, grandson, student, traveler, friend, satirist, outsider, homosexual, and always the tireless writer and seeker of fame. Through the familial focus of *The Selected Letters*, readers can follow a long-running saga whose effect is to lay a deep foundation for Williams's domestic theater and for the role that his tragic sister **Rose Williams** played in it. Letter #8 is addressed to Rose in 1927 at the time of her informal debut in Knoxville, Tennessee, where her Aunt "Belle" was socially prominent. Rose's failed courting in a southern city and the "frivolities" of her bath and boudoir, portentous to "Tom" Williams in the aftermath of her departure, anticipate with uncanny precision both the argument and the intimate feminine imagery of *A Streetcar Named Desire* (1947). It was not until March 1945, in letter #327, that "Tennessee" Williams revealed the composition of *A Streetcar Named Desire* to his agent Audrey Wood, but its impetus had long lain in this early family letter, suggesting a seamless imaginative relation between the two compositions.

Donald Windham's collection is sparsely annotated, but its apparatus is supported by a journal that Windham had kept for many years and that has proven useful in dating the letters that Williams frequently mailed without such information. Maria St. Just's apparatus is more elaborate and more puzzling, consisting as it does of a companion narrative that is part quoted journal or diary, part stitching and transition. Volume 1 of *The Selected Letters* is fully annotated with a wide array of sources including Williams's **journals**.

Tennessee Williams's letters appear to be far less numerous than the four volumes of George Bernard Shaw's edited letters by Dan Laurence, nor do they possess Shaw's wide-ranging intellectual and social attention. As business correspondence, the Williams letters are consistently less detailed and informed than those of **Eugene O'Neill**, edited by Travis Bogard and Jackson Bryer. **D.H. Lawrence**, Tennessee Williams's model letter-writer, was more far ranging in the philosophical, cultural, and aesthetic pronouncements regularly issued to friends and literary associates. But what Williams created in his correspondence is something more personal and perhaps more limited in scope by virtue of its essentially lyrical character. The Williams letters record the slowly advancing knowledge and control of the writer's dramatic craft, informed by strong familial and religious forces. They also implicitly record Williams living a literary life far less centrally located than many of his distinguished peers. He kept no close company with **Faulkner**, Hemingway, **O'Neill**, William Carlos Williams, Allen Tate, Robert Penn Warren, or Katherine Anne Porter but found literary society instead on the talented margins, as his friendship and correspondence with **Paul Bowles** and his wife Jane Bowles, Christopher Isherwood, and Carson Mc-Cullers may suggest.

For all of the busy communication to be inferred from his correspondence, Williams chiefly valued his mornings alone in the studio before his Olivetti typewriter. This testimony was written to Maria St. Just following the success of *Cat on a Hot Tin Roof* in 1955, but it was also the discipline of less auspicious periods, as many early letters attest. Williams's correspondence creates an intensely realized literary life, one whose integrity and resolve were severely tested by the great events of the first half of the twentieth century—economic depression and world war—and whose conclusion was marred by the critical malice and the ingratitude of Broadway. While his letters seldom expand upon works in progress, they are invariably—inescapably—about writing: the times of indolence and the waiting for vision, the physical act and the exhaustion that followed, the "levitation" of a play in production, the retreat from Broadway to Mexico or Provincetown or **Key West**.

It was from Key West, in a letter to Carson McCullers, that Williams revealed most clearly the artistic event that correspondence often became for him: "It is a soft grey rustling muttering sort of rainy afternoon with Frank gone from the house and the town and Grandfather dozing on the front room couch and me mixing a sad and lonely martini now and then and making a few ineffectual pecks at the typewriter" (7 April 1951). These lines suggest, perhaps, that a play is about to begin, a Chekhovian one with Tennessee Williams cast as his own designer, director, and of course, the artist-actor in the house.

Further Reading

Tischler, Nancy M. "Letters to a Friend, Third Edition." *Mississippi Quarterly* 39 (Winter 1996–1997): 167–174.

Albert J. Devlin

Crane, Hart (1899–1932). Hart Crane, the poet, was one of the most important influences on Williams's emotional life after his sister, his parents, and his grandparents. In fact, Crane was arguably the person most important to his artistic development. Other literary models, such as **D.H. Lawrence** and **Anton Chekhov**, were in many ways more directly relevant to Williams's themes and style. In Crane, however, Williams saw not only a source of poetic inspiration but also a man whose life and tragic fate prefigured his own.

Williams discovered Crane's poetry through **Clark Mills (McBurney)** in the later 1930s, several years after Crane's suicide and the publication of his *Collected Poems*. The process of absorbing Crane's work affected Williams profoundly. For the rest of his life, but especially during the earlier 1940s, Williams would quote and allude to Crane's poems—in his own verse, in his plays (and their epigraphs), and in his **correspondence**. He was especially prone to seize on phrases from the poems that evoked loss, transience, torment, and self-destructive passion.

Another book that made a comparable impression on Williams was Philip Horton's biography of Crane, published in 1937. As Gilbert Debusscher has shown, Williams identified so closely with what he learned about Crane that he came to understand his own life—as well as those of the sensitive and imaginative characters, often wandering or sexually straying, who are usually the most sympathetic figures in his plays—through the details of Crane's biography. Foremost among these biographical facts were Crane's homosexuality and his fraught relations with his mother. Others included Crane's father's disapproval of poetry as a vocation, Crane's nomadic and fugitive lifestyle, his impetuous temperament, his hypochondriacal tendencies, and his real mental illness. Williams thought himself fated to succumb to encroaching dementia, just as Crane had, according to a letter written by **Paul Bigelow** in August 1942 (quoted in Leverich 460).

The frontispiece to the 1933 edition of Crane's poems was a black-and-white reproduction of a portrait by David Siqueiros, who had painted the poet with closed eyes. According to Horton, this was because of Siqueiros's inability to paint the strikingly desperate expression of Crane with his eyes open. Williams, who knew the portrait, would allude to this story in *The Night of the Iguana*, as well as in his short play about Crane and his mother, *Steps Must Be Gentle*. Horton also reported an episode in which Crane shredded the same picture with a razor, an image that typifies the artist's inner struggle and impulse toward self-immolation.

In the spring of 1953 Williams was reading Crane's letters, which had appeared the previous year. In 1965, he read Crane's poetry aloud on a recording, for which he also wrote revealing sleeve notes. As Debusscher has observed, Crane served Williams as a guide to the reading and rereading of other American authors. Thus, in some undated verses ("As I stood") that have recently been published as an epigraph to Williams's *Collected Poems*, Williams addressed Crane as the leader of a trio of literary divinities that also included Walt Whitman and Edgar Allan Poe; a fourth presence in the poem is that of Herman Melville.

Writing in his journal (see **Journals**) on a lonely night in the fall of 1941, having sought solace in a recently purchased *Pocket Book of Verse*, Williams affirmed his belief that Crane loomed larger than all other poets—comparing his supremacy to Chekhov's in the field of prose writing and praying for inspiration from both men. Again, in a preface published in 1944, Williams claimed to have discarded the baggage of all literary influences save Crane's. He even confessed to a preference of Crane over T.S. Eliot, calling Crane the artistic peer of William Shakespeare, John Keats, and Whitman. Williams's *Steps Must Be Gentle: A Dramatic Reading for Two Performers* (1980) is a dialogue between Crane and his mother. Crane's presence is also to be found in *Suddenly Last Summer* in the absent, gay poet Sebastian Venable.

Williams's directions for his own burial, which were disregarded on his death in 1983, called for the disposal of his body from a small boat offshore from Key West, near the spot where Hart Crane had jumped to his death from a steamer 51 years earlier.

Further Reading

Crane, Hart. *The Collected Poems of Hart Crane.* Ed. Waldo Frank. New York: Liveright, 1933.

Debusscher, Gilbert. " 'Minting Their Separate Wills': Tennessee Williams and Hart Crane." *Modern Drama* 26 (December 1983): 455–476.

Gross, Robert F. "Consuming Hart: Sublimity and Gay Poetics in *Suddenly Last Summer.*" *Theatre Journal* 47 (March 1995): 229–51.

Horton, Philip. *Hart Crane: The Life of an American Poet.* New York: Norton, 1937.

Leverich, Lyle. *Tom: The Unknown Tennessee Williams.* New York: Crown, 1995.

Williams, Tennessee. "As I stood in my room tonight . . ." In *The Collected Poems of Tennessee Williams*, ed. David Roessel and Nicholas Moschovakis. New York: New Directions, 2002. viii.

———. "Preface to My Poems." In his *Where I Live: Selected Essays*, ed. Christine R. Day and Bob Woods. New York: New Directions, 1978. 1–6.

———. *Tennessee Williams Reads Hart Crane.* Sleeve notes to LP record. Caedmon TC 1206, 1965.

Nicholas R. Moschovakis

Cronyn, Hume (1911–2003). An actor and director, Hume Cronyn and his wife **Jessica Tandy** frequently worked on stage and screen in plays by Tennessee Williams. Cronyn was instrumental in having Tandy be the first Blanche. When he directed her as Lucretia Collins in Williams's one-act drama *Portrait of a Madonna*, in January 1947 at Los Angeles' Actors Laboratory Theatre, Williams and director **Elia Kazan** on seeing Tandy's performance abandoned their plans to pursue Katharine Cornell or **Tallulah Bankhead** for the role and instead offered it to the relatively unknown Tandy. *Portrait of a Madonna*, which depicts Lucretia's descent into madness after she has a hallucinatory vision of a former beau, seemed to Cronyn an embryonic version of *A Streetcar Named Desire*. Tandy appeared in a television production of *Portrait of a Madonna* again under Cronyn's direction, in 1948, on the heels of her triumph as Blanche.

Following the Actors Laboratory Theatre production of *Portrait*, Cronyn found himself peripherally involved in the *A Streetcar Named Desire* production. In his memoir *A Terrible Liar*, Cronyn recalls urging Williams that the play needed trimming, but when Williams suggested that Cronyn try making the cuts himself, Cronyn failed to find any in Williams's tightly constructed drama. The Cronyns collaborated again on an evening of scenes from Williams's plays, called *Many Faces of Love*, which they first performed on tour and then at Minneapo-lis's Guthrie Theatre and the Seattle Repertory Theatre in late 1975. They later performed this "concert recital" on television.

Further Reading

Cronyn, Hume. *A Terrible Liar: A Memoir*. New York: Morrow, 1991.
Leverich, Lyle. *Tom: The Unknown Tennessee Williams*. New York: Crown, 1995.

James Fisher

D

Dakin, Rosina Maria Francesca Otte
(1863–1944). Rosina Dakin was Williams's
beloved maternal grandmother whom he
memorialized in his 1964 story "Grand," included in *Collected Stories*. Though born to
German Lutheran parents, she attended a
Catholic convent in Cincinnati. She married
Walter Dakin, Williams's grandfather, in
Maryville, Ohio (her hometown) in 1883
and for over 60 years was devoted to her
family. She had a powerful and loving influence on her grandson Tom and the rest of
the Williams family. She often visited her
only child, daughter **Edwina**, to help with
the children, to offer financial help, and to
calm the troubled Williams family caught in
the fury of **Cornelius Williams**'s rage. According to Tennessee, she cast a "spell of
peace" over the household. Like her kindly
husband, she was exceedingly generous to
her grandson, giving him spending and living money and later paying his college tuition at Washington University in 1936 from
the money she had earned from giving music
(piano) lessons. A frugal and magnanimous
woman, Rosina Dakin denied herself clothes
and even health care so she could give her
more indulgent husband and her grandchildren the luxuries they could not have otherwise afforded. "Grand was all we knew of
God in our lives" ("Grand"), said her playwright grandson.

Williams was a frequent visitor to his
Grand's house, being raised in her Columbus
and **Clarksdale** parsonages and returning to
Mississippi in 1920 and coming to his
grandparents in 1935 when they lived in
Clayton, Missouri, to recover from a mental
and physical breakdown following his dismissal from the Continental Shoe Factory.
Her kindness contrasted with the detractions
of his father Cornelius.

Williams learned much from Grand. A
graduate of the Cincinnati Conservatory of
Music, she taught him and his sister **Rose**
piano and violin lessons, and as Williams
said in a 5 April 1943 letter to Horton
Foote, he was absorbed in "my grandparents' reminiscences." Williams's letters to
and about his Grand reflected the radiance
that she brought into his life. Along with his
sister, Rosina Dakin provided yet another

compelling reason for the powerful and continuing mythologies of the rose throughout Williams's canon.

Further Reading

Devlin, Albert J., and Nancy Tischler, eds. *The Selected Letters of Tennessee Williams, Vol. 1—1920–1945*. New York: New Directions, 2000.

Philip C. Kolin

Dakin, Walter Edwin (1857–1955). Tennessee Williams's maternal grandfather, Walter Dakin, was born in Harveysburg, Ohio. The fact that the Dakins could trace their lineage back to the Normans, who fought under William the Conqueror, was of more importance to Walter Dakin's only daughter (Tennessee's mother) than it was to anyone else. After graduation from business school, he returned to Ohio, worked as an accountant in Marysville, and married **Rosina Otte** (see **Rosina Dakin**) when he was 26 and she was 20. Their only daughter, Edwina Estelle Dakin (see **Edwina Williams**), was born in August 1884.

After a career as a superintendent of public schools and a college teacher, Dakin entered the Episcopal Theological School at the University of the South in 1895. He was ordained a priest in the Episcopal Church, and over the next 35 years, he served at Episcopal churches in Springfield and Cleveland Ohio; Nashville, Tennessee; and Church Hill, Port Gibson, Columbus, Canton, and **Clarksdale, Mississippi**. In 1915 he became rector at St. George's Episcopal Church in Clarksdale, where he stayed until his retirement in Memphis in 1931, but he often returned to Clarksdale.

The Reverend Dakin and his wife became surrogate parents to their grandchildren, Tom and Rose, who lived with them and their mother while Edwina's husband—Cor-

nelius **Coffin Williams**—traveled the countryside selling men's clothing. His youngest grandson, **Dakin Williams**, bore his grandfather's surname. Tom accompanied the Reverend Dakin on calls throughout Coahoma and Tunica counties, absorbing his grandfather's stories and forming a bond of friendship and love. Thanks to his grandfather's well-stocked library and love of the classics, which the Reverend Dakin fondly recited, Williams was exposed as a child to the works of Homer, Milton, Shakespeare, Charles Dickens, Sir Walter Scott, Edgar Allan Poe, and many others. Williams returned to Clarksdale to live with his grandparents later for over a year. They comforted and protected him from the contempt of his father, who had nicknamed him "Miss Nancy."

In 1928, when Williams was 17, he traveled to Europe with his grandfather, who escorted a church group traveling aboard the USS *Homeric* to see Paris, Marseilles, Nice, Monte Carlo, Naples, Rome, Milan, Florence, Venice, Cologne, and Amsterdam. Thanks to Reverend Dakin, Williams saw *Les Folies Bergere*, the Ritz, the Louvre, Versailles, and the Rhine. The Reverend Dakin was a *bon vivant* who enjoyed life's pleasures including literature, art, music, fine wines, Manhattan cocktails, gourmet meals, and trips to New York, **Key West**, and **New Orleans**. In the Reverend Dakin's retirement, his grandson Tom always had a room waiting for him at his various residences.

As an innocent and gullible old man, Reverend Dakin was once conned out of $5,000 his wife had carefully saved in government bonds. It was such a painful experience that it was never to be spoken of. Watching his wife's health degenerate as he grew weaker with age, he rented out his house in Memphis and moved into the St. Louis home owned by his daughter Edwina and her husband Cornelius, who had nothing but contempt for the old man. In fact, Tennessee Williams found visits home so painful that he made them as short as possible. After the death of his wife in 1944, the Reverend Dakin frequently traveled in the States and abroad with his grandson and often stayed in Key West with Edwina as housekeeper. She was always a trial for him, as her lectures and Puritanism got on his nerves but he enjoyed his grandson's friends and loved the good life that Tom was willing to share with him.

His family paid loving tribute to their father and grandfather. Williams modeled Nonno, the "ninety-seven years *young*" poet of *The Night of the Iguana*, after his grandfather, and Edwina, in *Remember Me to Tom*, acknowledges the kindness and intellect of her father. Most lasting, however, was the Reverend Dakin's influence on his grandson's highly symbolic and mythic plays, which no doubt grew from the Dakins' library and literary tastes, which Williams treasured.

Further Reading

Devlin, Albert J., and Nancy Tischler, eds. *The Selected Letters of Tennessee Williams, Volume 1—1920–1945*. New York: New Directions, 2000.

Leverich, Lyle. *Tom: The Unknown Tennessee Williams*. New York: Crown, 1995.

Williams, Edwina Dakin. *Remember Me to Tom*. New York: Putnam, 1963.

Colby H. Kullman

Dowling, Eddie (1889–1976). Eddie Dowling was the director—with an assist from **Margo Jones**—and costar of *The Glass Menagerie*. Dowling was born Joseph Nelson Goucher in 1889 and began his long career in the musical theater, later both acting in and directing works by **William Saroyan** before **Audrey Wood** sent him the script of *The Glass Menagerie*, in which he would play Tom Wingfield, the narrator and authorial character. Although he was too old for the part (49), Williams thought him "a great actor." Feeling that his role could stand enhancing, and that the play could benefit from some humor, Dowling and New York theater critic George Jean Nathan conceived adding a drunk scene. Williams totally rewrote the scene for the completed play, in which it became the only moment that Tom and Laura had on stage alone together. In his *Memoirs*, Williams concluded, "I honestly think that it did the play little harm," while Dowling preferred to think that it "made" the play "good." As a director, Dowling was concerned that some of the dramatist's nonrealistic technical innovations were too costly, and so the original Broadway production jettisoned the legends and images that were to have been projected on a wall of the apartment set. But Dowling failed to convince Williams that the play should be given a happy ending. As an actor, Dowling was prone to ad-lib; and **Laurette Taylor**, who played Amanda, found his performances unnecessarily mannered.

Further Reading

Leverich, Lyle. *Tom: The Unknown Tennessee Williams*. New York: Crown, 1995.

Thomas P. Adler

Drugs. Drugs played a significant role in the life and works of Tennessee Williams. His plays and fiction reflect his knowledge and involvement with drugs and the drug culture of the 1930s to the 1980s. In fact, Williams's allusions to drugs increased as his canon expanded, documenting his increased dependency on them and their influence in his work. The relative risk of Williams's drug use was magnified by his combining drugs with large amounts of alcohol. Although Williams increasingly referred to street drugs in his later fiction, there is no record of his using drugs such as hashish or heroine.

Williams's **Memoirs** fully documents his use and abuse of prescription drugs, including sedatives, amphetamines, and antipsychotic drugs such as Mellaril (to treat behavioral disorders), Ritalin (a stimulant), and Miltown (to treat anxiety and tension). The sedative Seconal, a barbiturate, may have been Williams's drug of choice, dating from 1948; he frequently referred to "pinks" or "pinkies," alluding to the color of Seconal tablets and capsules. Seconal was found in the toxicology reports at his autopsy. Other sedatives ingested by Williams were Nembutal, a barbiturate, and Doriden, an addictive barbiturate substitute to treat insomnia. He openly admitted injecting amphetamines during the 1960s, his "Stoned Decade," as he called it.

In 1969, Williams was committed to Barnes Hospital in St. Louis for his dependency on amphetamines, barbiturates, and alcohol. Although he was in a detox program during his hospitalization, he plotted to obtain drugs and asked for specific items of clothing to be brought to the hospital in the hopes of discovering secreted drugs in the pockets. Even while Williams earned a hospital pass, he visited a physician's office under a pseudonym to obtain a prescription for Seconal but was only marginally successful. Ironically, Williams claimed he was a traveling salesman who had left home without his medications; shades of his father Cornelius followed him. The street-wise physician prescribed Williams only three Seconal tablets, despite his elaborate ruse.

Many of Williams's works directly mention or relate to drugs. *Cat on a Hot Tin Roof* (1955), for example, refers to Amytal, a barbiturate, and to morphine, an opiate. Amytal was prescribed to treat Brick's growing dependence on alcohol, and morphine was given to Big Daddy to cope with the pain of his cancer. *Sweet Bird of Youth* (1959) alludes to a variety of other drugs, including veiled references to Seconal, pot (marijuana), and hashish. Both Princess Kosmonopolis and Chance chased pills with vodka. In the film version of *Sweet Bird of Youth* we often see the Princess clutching a bottle with the Smirnov red label on it. The Princess also mailed Moroccan hashish to herself in America to escape the penalties of smuggling drugs through customs.

The history of Williams's drug use goes back to his lesser known early plays. *Not about Nightingales* (1938) included the use of phenobarbital and weed (marijuana). Mrs. Bristol calmed her palpitations with phenobarbital, and Queen confessed to smoking "weed." Williams's one-act play "Twenty-seven Wagons Full of Cotton" in *Twenty-seven Wagons Full of Cotton* (1945) alludes to paregoric, which carried over to his 1956 screenplay *Baby Doll*, based on the one-act play. Flora (later Baby Doll) took paregoric to cope with a nervous condition. In *Summer and Smoke* (1948), Alma Winemiller's little white tablets (sleeping pills), prescribed by Dr. John Buchanan to treat her anxiety, were probably Amytal, or amobarital, a barbiturate with a calming effect that induced sleep. The one-act play "Camino Real" (1948) included Marguerite's smoking opium and "kif" (hashish) in Ahmed's café in Block Seven of *Camino Real*. In *The Rose Tattoo* (1951). Serafina delle Rose was widowed because of her late husband's fatal drug running on the Mississippi Gulf Coast. Williams, moreover, incorporated subliminal references to Seconal in *The Red Devil Battery Sign*, a street term for the substance.

Not only do these works allude to drugs, so do many others in the canon. In *The Glass Menagerie* (1945), Tom threatens to go to opium dens. Though the strongest drug mentioned in *A Streetcar Named De-*

sire (1947) is aspirin, Blanche DuBois is frequently intoxicated by liquor. *Orpheus Descending* (1958) employs a mix of drugs, using drug slang such as *weed*, *grass* (marijuana), *luminal* (phenobarbital), and *bennies* (amphetamines). Val Xavier proclaimed that marijuana was a part of his past, and Lady used luminal to help her sleep. Her frenetic behavior is compared to the effects of bennies and strong coffee. Jabe Torrance, her revengeful husband, needed morphine injections to alleviate the pain of terminal cancer. Written during Williams's "Stoned Decade" of the 1960s, in *The Milk Train Doesn't Stop Here Anymore* (1964), morphine, pep pills, tranquilizers, codeine, adrenaline, and emperin (an analgesic) pepper the script. Perhaps his most drug-dependent theatrical character, Mrs. Goforth washed down pep pills and tranquilizers with brandy, received injections of morphine and adrenaline, and numbered codeine and emperin in her personal pharmacopoeia. The Fräulein in *The Gnädiges Fräulein* (1966) used a Mary Jane cigarette (marijuana). Even more blatantly, the bar scene in *In the Bar of a Tokyo Hotel* (1969) finds Miriam filling a pipe with Panama Red (marijuana).

In 1972, Williams developed *One Arm* (stories from the 1950s) as a film play with numerous references to the drug culture, including dexedrine, bennies, and speed (amphetamines). A sign and declaration of Williams's own use of drugs, he played Doc, a longtime drug-using physician who used a combination of brandy and Benzedrine to steady himself before delivering a baby, in *Small Craft Warnings*. *Vieux Carré* (1979) is filled with allusion to the drug culture of the French Quarter of New Orleans, circa 1938–1939, including paraphernalia (needle, pillbox), street drugs (grass, marijuana), and prescription drugs (sleeping pills). In 1980, in *A Lovely Sunday for Creve Coeur*, adapted from the screenplay *All Gaul Is Divided* (1955), Williams repeatedly inserted mebaral, a barbiturate used to treat anxiety. *Loss of a Teardrop Diamond* (1980), which Williams hoped to adapt to a film, was suffused with opiates and sleeping medications.

But Williams's fiction (four collections of stories, two novellas, and one novel, *Moise and the World of Reason*), even more than the plays, document his wide-ranging knowledge of the drug culture. Williams's references to drugs and drug culture broadened and increased over time. In the early short stories, drug references included morphia ("The Mysteries of the Joy Rio," 1941); barbital and sedatives ("One Arm," 1945); and belladonna and benzedrine (*The Roman Spring of Mrs. Stone*, 1950). As street drugs became more imbedded in popular culture, Williams imbedded these drugs in his fiction. In "The Knightly Quest" (1966) he included hallucinogenic mushrooms; LSD (lysergic acid diethylamide) and grass (marijuana) appeared in "Sabbatha and Solitude" (1973), while quaaludes are found in "The Killer Chicken and the Closet Queen" (1977). Several Williams characters are developed through descriptions of their drug use. In "Night of the Iguana," Miss Jelkes and the older writer discuss Seconal and barbital, respectively, and explained the relative merits of these drugs. In "The Angel in the Alcove" (1943), Mrs. Wayne's reaction to the smell of food is compared to the effects of drugs on an addict. In "Competed" (1973), Aunt Ella's withdrawal from the world is enhanced by nightly doses of morphine. Williams chronicled the risky combinations of drug abusers in "Das Wasswe Ist Kalt" (1979), as he described Barbara's attempt to sleep by combining generous doses of codeine, Valium, and Nembutal. But unquestionably, the Williams work that described the drug culture most graphically is *Moise and the World of Reason*. The novel introduced "blackbirds" and "white crosses," street terms for amphetamines, as well as numerous references again to Seconal and Nembutal (barbiturates) and LSD. The novel's notable narrator, a young male writer from Alabama, compares his introduction to the homosexual culture of New York City to drug addiction. An addict's reaction to the first effects of a powerful drug is equated with the reaction of rats freezing.

Williams's abuse of drugs surely contributed to his revolutionary, radical experimentation in the theater, such as **The Two-Character Play** and *In the Bar of a Tokyo Hotel* and played a part in creating some of his most outrageous characters, for example, the Gnädiges Fräulein. Although later critics charge that Williams was "zoned out," he nonetheless produced a large, impressive body of work while under the steady influence of drugs washed down with booze.

Further Reading

Lux, Mary F. "Tenn among the Lotus-Eaters: Drugs in the Life and Fiction of Tennessee Williams." *Southern Quarterly* 38 (1999): 117–123.

St. Just, Maria. *Five O'Clock Angel: Letters of Tennessee Williams to Maria St. Just, 1948–1982*. New York: Knopf, 1990.

Mary Frances Lux

E

The Eccentricities of a Nightingale. A Williams play written between 1951 and 1964, *The Eccentricities of a Nightingale* has the same major themes and symbols, dramaturgy, and provenance as **Summer and Smoke**, from which it evolved. After the Broadway failure of *Summer and Smoke*, Williams, who often declared his special affection for the character of Alma Winemiller, could not let the play die, and he began rewriting it in Rome in 1951. The new script was *The Eccentricities of a Nightingale*, the story of a lonely spinster, Alma, whose desire for the love of young Doctor John Buchanan next door leads her to do something against her morals and to follow her fantasies, just as in *Summer and Smoke*. Dealing with Williams's frequent themes of longing, alienation, and unrealized dreams, *The Eccentricities of a Nightingale* is tragically romantic.

Despite the obvious similarities between *Summer and Smoke* and *The Eccentricities of a Nightingale*, however, Williams considered *Eccentricities* a new play rather than a revision of the earlier one. Admittedly, significant differences exist between the two plays, the most salient being the absence of the senior Dr. Buchanan, Nellie Ewell, and Rosa and Papa Gonzales but with the addition of Mrs. Buchanan. Moreover, there is no stabbing or shooting, and the Moon Lake Casino episode has been replaced with a visit to a cheap hotel. Dr. John is less amoral and tempestuous in *The Eccentricities of a Nightingale* than in *Summer and Smoke* and more controlled by his mother than his counterpart is influenced by his father; Alma becomes less proper and prim and more peculiar.

The shift from the remote elder Dr. Buchanan of *Summer and Smoke* to the dominating, emasculating Mrs. Buchanan may mirror Williams's change in attitude toward his parents. In his youth, Williams hated his father, **Cornelius Coffin Williams**, and adored his mother, **Edwina**, but the playwright asserted that shortly before the death of his father in 1957, he learned not to hate him and began to understand, even love him. The playwright also began to blame Edwina for his sister **Rose**'s lobotomy, leaving her a helpless invalid.

The influence of Williams's psychoanalyst,

David Selby and Betsy Palmer in the 1976 Broadway production of *The Eccentricities of a Nightingale*. Springer/ Photofest.

Lawrence Kubie, is also manifested in the reworking of *Summer and Smoke* into *The Eccentricities of a Nightingale*. Though Williams asserts that he began the new play in 1951 (he tried to substitute it for the script that was in rehearsal for the London premiere of *Summer and Smoke*), he certainly continued to dwell on it during his years of psychoanalysis, and the completed script, which dates from 1961, illustrates the new-found Freudian outlook. In *The Eccentricities of a Nightingale*, Mrs. Buchanan has assumed the function of representing the social establishment of Glorious Hill, Missis-

sippi, that the elder Dr. Buchanan had served in *Summer and Smoke*, but the domineering, disagreeable, and somewhat foolish Mrs. Buchanan does double duty in *Eccentricities* as one of the "heavies," along with Mrs. Winemiller, who has also changed for the worse. Instead of having a cold and distant father, John confronts a controlling mother, and Mrs. Winemiller has been transformed from a childlike personality into a potentially destructive one. Young Dr. John is no longer the undisciplined pagan that suggested Williams's image of his own father. All the violence of *Summer and Smoke* has been excised—almost in direct response to Dr. Kubie's treatment.

The Eccentricities of a Nightingale premiered on 25 June 1964, with Edie Adams as Alma opposite Alan Mixon's John, at the Tappan Zee Playhouse, Nyack, New York, a production that is often omitted from histories of the play. Later productions in the 1960s took the title "premiere," ignoring the actual Tappan Zee debut. While Mariruth Campbell, the critic for the local *Rockland County Journal-News*, found the play wonderful, Norman Nadel of the *World-Telegram and Sun*, the only New York City paper to review it, found the show pale and melodramatic in comparison with *Summer and Smoke*.

A local revival by the Theatre Society of Long Island at the Mineola Theatre (14–28 May 1968) starred the original Stella Kowalski, Kim Hunter, as Alma, opposite Ed Flanders as John and James Broderick as the Reverend Winemiller, with director, Edwin Sherin, who later staged the Broadway production. The Public Broadcasting Service's *Theatre in America* presented *The Eccentricities of a Nightingale* starring Blythe Danner and Frank Langella for "Great Performances" on 16 June 1976. Then a production of Buffalo's Studio Arena Theatre (8 October–6 November 1976) starring Betsy Palmer and David Selby moved to Broadway's Morosco Theatre on 23 November 1976.

Further Reading

Clum, John M. "From *Summer and Smoke* to *The Eccentricities of a Nightingale*: The Evolution of the Queer Alma." *Modern Drama* 39.1 (Spring 1996): 31–50.

Kramer, Richard. "The Lost Premiere of Tennessee Williams's *Eccentricities of a Nightingale*." *Journal of American Drama and Theatre* 11.2 (Spring 1999): 42–59.

Williams, Tennessee. "I Have Rewritten a Play for Artistic Purity." *New York Times* 21 November 1976, sec. 2: 1, 5.

———. "Let Me Hang It All Out." *New York Times* 4 March 1973, sec. 2: 1, 3.

———. *Memoirs*. New York: Bantam, 1975.

Richard E. Kramer

F

Faulkner, William (1897–1962). William Faulkner was Williams's fellow Mississippian who created his mythical Yoknapatawpha County in short stories and novels including *The Sound and the Fury* (1929), *As I Lay Dying* (1930), *Absalom, Absalom!* (1936), *The Hamlet* (1940), and *Go Down Moses* (1942). Both Faulkner and Williams mined early impressions of southern scenes and myths to develop characters and settings. Faulkner spent most of his life in Oxford, about a hundred miles from Williams's birthplace in Columbus and from his grandparents' home in **Clarksdale** in north Mississippi. Both writers witnessed the social and economic changes in classes during the early decades of the twentieth century and incorporated these materials into their art. Each of them examined the dreams and realities of the dwindling plantation culture, the increasing political and commercial power of the working classes, the expectations and failings in family relationships, the rigidity of local Protestant ideologies, and frustrations of romantic idealism. Neither Williams nor Faulkner avoided the sex and violence that accompanied such realities. While Williams risked portrayals of homosexuality, Faulkner more fully braved and developed issues of race in such novels as *Light in August* (1932) and *Intruder in the Dust* (1948). Both writers found inspiration in the city of **New Orleans**, Williams's spiritual home and the setting for several of his works, including **A Streetcar Named Desire**, and Faulkner's locale for scenes and settings in *Pylon* (1935) and *Wild Palms* (1939). Faulkner, too, spent time in **Hollywood** writing scripts for the movie studios, working on such titles as *The Southerner* (1945) and *The Land of the Pharaohs* (1955). During the 1950s and early 1960s, Williams's screenplays fared much better than Hollywood's versions of Faulkner's fiction, such as *The Sound and the Fury* starring Yul Brynner. When publicists pushed Faulkner to help promote that movie by writing stories about the film, the frustrated author allegedly told them to get Tennessee Williams to do it.

Ironically, Faulkner and Williams met each other only briefly through a mutual acquaintance, Jean Stein, with whom Faulkner had become involved and had worked on the Philadelphia production of **Cat on a Hot Tin**

Roof. After the opening there in March 1955, she and Faulkner joined a table where Williams and friends including **Carson McCullers**, Christopher Isherwood, and **Gore Vidal** had gathered. In September of the same year, Williams attended a restaurant dinner party Stein had arranged to entertain William Faulkner when he stopped in Paris during a tour for the State Department. In his *Memoirs* and interviews, Williams talked briefly of his encounters with Faulkner, who typically remained quiet and did not engage in animated conversation. Williams surmised that the married Faulkner may have felt embarrassed in the company of a young woman not his wife.

Only brief comments about each other's work appear on record. In one interview, Williams gave Faulkner credit for reviving "Southern Gothic," a phrase used in the commentary of both writers. Williams mentioned only one Faulkner title, "A Rose for Emily." In turn, when Faulkner served as a resident writer at the University of Virginia in 1957, he praised *Camino Real* as Williams's best and most poetic drama. In Williams's expressionistic play, his subjects and techniques correspond at times with those in Faulkner's *A Fable* (1954), a complex and poetic novel for which Faulkner won a Pulitzer Prize. But Faulkner did criticize Williams's emphasis in *Cat on a Hot Tin Roof* because he considered Big Daddy's story of more interest than his son Brick's dilemma. Faulkner's last novel, *The Reivers*, was published the month before his death in 1962, and one year after the Broadway premiere of *The Night of the Iguana*. Williams saluted Faulkner in a 1979 interview as a southern gentleman and "an honest man." Each writer had developed a unique voice to create experimental, lyrical, and monumental works of art, yet both had mythologized their home state of Mississippi.

Further Reading

Blau, Herbert. "Readymade Desire." In *Confronting Tennessee Williams's "A Streetcar Named Desire": Essays in Critical Pluralism*, ed. Philip C. Kolin. Westport, CT: Greenwood, 1993. 19–25.

Blotner, Joseph. *Faulkner: A Biography*. 2 vols. New York: Random House, 1974.

Linda Elkins McDaniel

Film Adaptations. For the popular audience Williams is well known through the film adaptations of his plays. Fifteen screen adaptations of Williams's works were produced between 1950 and 1970, with a remake of *The Glass Menagerie* in 1987. Williams wrote the screenplays for *Baby Doll* in 1956 and *Boom!* (based on *The Milk Train Doesn't Stop Here Anymore*) in 1968 and was variously involved with those for *The Glass Menagerie* (1950), *A Streetcar Named Desire* (1951), *The Rose Tattoo* (1955), and *The Fugitive Kind* (based on *Orpheus Descending* in 1960). The other adaptations were done by diverse writers.

The Glass Menagerie was the first Williams's play to be filmed. Though he is credited as coauthor of the screenplay of Irving Rapper's 1950 film adaptation, Williams contributed only a few scenes. To avoid box-office poison, the studio imposed a happy ending when, after the gentleman caller (Kirk Douglas) walks out on Laura (Jane Wyman), she introduces her mother (Gertrude Lawrence) to a new gentleman caller. Williams said that the happy ending represented a complete reversal of the intent of his play and infuriated him. In Hollywood fashion, Jim literally sweeps Laura off her feet in the dinner sequence by dancing with her to the music that intrudes into the Wingfield living room from the Paradise Dance Hall, and his attempt to bring the glamour of the outside world, which Paradise represents, to Laura was at least artfully done.

In addition to confining to Hollywood conventions, over the years censorship mandated many changes in Williams's films and, as a consequence, marred the artistry of his work. Many of Williams's films were made when the screen did not enjoy the same freedom that the theater did. Themes and situations that Williams treated frankly on stage were a source of controversy when these same elements found their way into film, for example, homosexuality, violence, and sexuality. The screenplay for *A Streetcar Named Desire* (1951), which Williams collaborated on with Oscar Saul, for example, contained significant alterations from the play because of insistent censorship. Joseph Ignatius Breen, the film industry's censor, made two key demands, among many—references to Blanche's late husband's homosexuality were to be obscured, and Stanley's rape of Blanche could not go unpunished. Allusions to Allan Grey's homosexuality thus had to be veiled in the film, a deplorable change for Williams. Director **Elia Kazan** depicted Stanley's (Marlon Brando) rape of Blanche (**Vivien Leigh**) with artistic indirection by cutting from the image of Stanley holding Blanche's body, seen in a mirror in Scene Eleven, to a streetcleaner's hose in the gutter outside, just as a blast of water gushes forth and dwindles to a trickle in Scene Twelve. Moreover, to show Stanley's punishment for his lust, Williams revised the ending to suggest that Stella was leaving Stanley by having her flee upstairs to a neighbor's flat, confiding in her newborn infant, "We're not going back there. Not this time. We're never going back," a shrewdly ambiguous way to end the movie, since the mature viewer might realize that Stella's resolution to leave Stanley was nothing more than the emotional outburst of the moment. Yet neither Williams nor Kazan was satisfied with this compromise ending. Despite such changes to Williams's script, Vivien Leigh,

Karl Malden (Mitch), and **Kim Hunter** (Stella) won Academy Awards for the film. Brando, ironically, did not.

In 1993, a restored version of the *Streetcar Named Desire* film (the "Director's Cut") was released to theaters and then on videocassette, containing four minutes of censored footage cut from the film just before its release in 1951. These excisions included shots emphasizing Stella's passion for Stanley, which were deemed to be too carnal, such as her slinking downstairs to be reunited with Stanley at the end of Scene Three. Studying these two versions, Leonard Leff fears that the 1993 restored *Streetcar Named Desire* may erase the 1951 film, leading to a loss of cinema history. He stresses: "Multiple editions destabilize texts: they expose the myriad forces and collaborations that lie behind them to 'create' their own versions" (36).

For the popular film version of *The Rose Tattoo* (1955), directed by Daniel Mann, who had also directed the play, and photographed by James Wong Howe, who won an Oscar, Williams collaborated on the script with screenwriter Hal Kanter. **Anna Magnani** also won an Oscar for *The Rose Tattoo* (1955) for her portrayal of Serafina Delle Rose, and Burt Lancaster (Alvaro) turned in a comedy-filled performance. Coming to films from the stage, Mann's theatrical background enabled him to elicit strong performances from these actors. James Wong Howe's camera caught the bright sunlight of the outdoor setting, representing the warm, exuberant vitality of the Sicilian villagers. Williams and his co-adapter enhanced the storyline by adding a player piano in Serafina's living room that closely associated Serafina with her dead husband Rosario. The piano bursts into a joyous rendition of the lighthearted song "The Sheik of Araby" at the least provocation, recalling the gaiety of Serafina's cherished relationship with Rosa-

Tennessee Williams in 1955, when he was working on a screenplay. Photo © A.H. Berger, used courtesy of New Directions Publishing Corp.

rio. At the close of the film, when she accepts Alvaro, the hunky truck driver, as the replacement of Rosario, she turns on the piano to play the tune now in honor of her new mate.

Different versions of *Cat on a Hot Tin Roof* exist, including very different endings. Writer-director Richard Brooks filmed a commercially successful *Cat on a Hot Tin Roof* in 1958, which he coscripted with James Poe. Staying as close as possible to Williams's text, Brooks had to contend with censorship problems, as Kazan did. In Williams's play, Brick, a latent homosexual who suffers from impotence, jeopardizes his marriage because he is still in love with his former football chum, Skipper. When Skipper phones Brick at last to confess his feelings for him, Brick cruelly hangs up, precipitating Skipper's suicide. Yet in Brooks's film, Big Daddy (Burl Ives) does not brand Brick (Paul Newman) a homosexual because of his involvement with Skipper, but accuses his son of being an immature and irresponsible

38-year-old who refuses to relinquish adolescence. Although the suggestion of Brick's latent homosexuality is still present, Brooks ruled it out as the decisive factor in Brick's relationship with Skipper and his alienation from Maggie (Elizabeth Taylor). Judith Anderson played Big Mama, and Madeline Sherwood was Mae. Given the taboos that existed in the film industry in the 1950s, Brooks consciously adapted *Cat on a Hot Tin Roof* to the screen. He began *Cat on a Hot Tin Roof* with a scene not in Williams's play but with one that was suggested in the dialogue. Drunkenly trying to recapture his long-lost days as an athlete, Brick jumps hurdles in a dark, deserted stadium, lit only by his car's headlights. An imaginary crowd roars its approval as Brick stumbles and breaks his leg, spending the rest of the film on crutches, symbolizing the emotional crutch he uses to get through life; that is, his attempts to relive his past days of glory. Newman, Taylor, and cinematographer William Daniels were nominated for Academy Awards, and the film was nominated as best film of the year. Curiously enough, Burl Ives was not nominated for his portrayal of Big Daddy even though his performance in the film at certain moments surpasses any previous work Ives did in any movie.

Two teleplays of *Cat on a Hot Tin Roof* demand comparison with Brooks's film version. Laurence Olivier gave a superb performance as Big Daddy, a southern feudal lord, in the 1976 NBC TV version of *Cat on a Hot Tin Roof*, which he also directed. The first TV broadcast of *Cat on a Hot Tin Roof*, this teleplay was based on the 1974 staging of the play by the American Shakespeare Festival. Capturing the gruff and imposing patriarch that Williams created, Olivier rightly dominated *Cat on a Hot Tin Roof* just as Burl Ives's portrayal of Big Daddy did in the original Broadway production and the film. Natalie Wood and Robert Wagner

Katharine Hepburn in the film of *Suddenly, Last Summer*, 1959. Springer/Photofest.

played Maggie and Brick much more explicitly than Newman and Taylor in the Brooks film. The second *Cat on a Hot Tin Roof* teleplay was aired on Showtime on 19 August 1984, starring Rip Torn as Big Daddy, with Jessica Lang as Maggie and Tommy Lee Jones as Brick. Torn's southern accent was very difficult to understand, and Jones's Brick was far more sheepish than Newman's.

In 1959, novelist-screenwriter **Gore Vidal** adapted *Suddenly Last Summer* for director Joseph L. Manckiewicz, with Elizabeth Taylor as Catherine, Montgomery Clift as Dr. Cukrowicz, and Katherine Hepburn as Mrs. Veneable. This film treated homosexuality far more frankly than ever before on the screen because the subject was crucial to the plot and the cause of Sebastian's gory murder. For these reasons, the censor allowed it. Sebastian is killed and eaten by the young cannibals with whom he had engaged in sexual encounters. The film received the industry's official seal of approval after only minor changes in Vidal's script. In Williams's play, Sebastian's horrible death is described in an impassioned monologue by his cousin Catherine, who witnessed the incident. But in the film Sebastian's murder is depicted through a flashback narrated by Catherine. Vidal found Mankiewicz's direction of the movie "generally good," though he deplored "the literal rendering of the ending" through the flashback. Mankiewicz, however, wanted to emphasize Sebastian's hideous death by depicting it on screen to justify treating such lurid material. Interestingly, Sebastian is only a phantom in Williams's play, yet in the film he appears but never speaks, nor is his face seen. Mankiewicz's *Suddenly Last Summer* was a breakthrough film that dealt with homosexuality with integrity, presenting the officially prohibited subject in a way neither *A Streetcar Named Desire* nor *Cat on a Hot Tin Roof* could have done.

Summer and Smoke (1961), the next Williams play adapted for the screen, was directed by Peter Glenville, who had earlier staged the play in London. Geraldine Page played spinster Alma Winemiller, who nurtures an unrequited love for the suave John Buchanan, the town rebel dashingly portrayed by Laurence Harvey. As in Williams's play, the film is punctuated with verbal references to the smoke of the title, including Alma's declaration that she is suffocating. Glenville symbolically complemented the verbal imagery by surrounding Alma with smoke from burning autumn leaves, a wonderfully apt metaphor for her dwindling hopes for love. Page excelled as an inhibited young woman confined in a small town, rebeling against her Puritan heritage. At one point, Alma dons a plumed hat as a symbol of the French cavaliers' blood that runs in her veins, competing with her Puritan heritage, to visualize why she is attracted to the cavalier John Buchanan. The genius of Page's controlled performance captured Alma's spirit as well as her inhibitions. Her touching portrayal marked the film as a work of seamless art about a broken heart. Thanks to Elmer Bernstein's atmospheric score, *Summer and Smoke* was also praised as a piece of chamber music.

Sweet Bird of Youth (1962) reunited Richard Brooks with Paul Newman, who played Chance Wayne, a Hollywood drifter escorting Alexandra Del Lago, an aging star (Geraldine Page), back to his hometown of St. Cloud. There he is confronted by Boss Finley (Ed Begley), the vengeful father of the girl whom he had seduced, Heavenly (Shirley Knight). Both Newman and Page reprised their roles from the Broadway premiere. To show Chance's reluctance to face the truth of his past, Brooks inserted flashbacks of him when he was younger, for example, diving into a swimming pool. Shot in slow motion, the flashbacks show Chance, for one lingering moment, floating through the air as if he were the very incarnation of the "Sweet Bird of Youth" of the title. Yet the image also suggests, ironically, that the "Sweet Bird of Youth" has inevitably flown away from the aging Chance. Modifying the harsh ending of Williams's play, where Chance is castrated, Brooks had Chance attacked by Boss Finley's son and his henchmen who batter his face, his meal ticket. Though Hollywood insisted on a future for the couple—at the final fade-out Chance leaves town with Heavenly on his arm—Williams's message about the inevitable loss of youth, and the futility of trying to prolong it, still came through. Ed Begley won an Oscar as the blustering, tyrannical Boss Finley, but the most memorable performance was given by Geraldine Page, who swaggers as Alexandra with hauteur and style.

The same year *Period of Adjustment* was filmed by director George Roy Hill, who had also directed the play on Broadway, with the screenplay written by Isobel Lennart. Newlyweds George Haverstick (Timothy Hutton) and Isabel (Jane Fonda) try to adjust to their first period of marital discord. They visit George's bitter, married friend played by Tony Franciosa. Fonda stands out as a scatterbrained daddy's girl who finds herself married to a mate who suffers from insecurity and inadequacy. In the end, they are reconciled and ready to face the future together. *Period of Adjustment* remains an uninspired version of Williams's domestic comedy.

Unquestionably, the best film of a Williams play in the 1960s was *The Night of the Iguana* (1964), directed by John Huston, who coauthored the script with Anthony Veiller. Trying to be faithful to Williams's play, Houston even had Williams touch up the screenplay when he visited the set. The film begins with an American, Reverend T. Lawrence Shannon (Richard Burton), a defrocked Episcopal clergyman, conducting a bus tour throughout Mexico as "a man of God on vacation." Shannon delivers a busload of Texas tourists to the tawdry Costa Verde Hotel, run by Maxine Faulk (Ava Gardner, in an impeccable performance). Most of the exteriors were shot on location in a peninsula just south of Puerto Vallarta, Mexico. Significantly, Huston carried over into the film much of Williams's verbal and physical imagery from the play. Most impressively, Huston used Williams's chief symbol, the iguana, and showed it being captured by some Mexican boys, who tie it under the hotel porch to fatten it up for the table. As symbolic parallel to the captive iguana tied underneath the porch, Shannon is entangled in a number of unresolved emotional problems. He has reached the end of his rope—literally and spiritually. But the most pronounced parallel between the captive iguana and Shannon occurs when Shannon is tied down—almost sewn into—in a hammock until his suicidal impulse subsides, one of the most powerful moments in Huston's film. Shannon gets through his dark night of the soul mostly with the help of Hannah Jelkes (Deborah Kerr), who teaches him that he should leave the past behind and get on with his life. In Huston's film, that life will be with the blowzy Maxine who asks him to stay with her as co-proprietor of the ramshackle hotel. Shannon thus ministers to the lonesome, flawed human beings—common in Williams's plays and films—who have taken refuge from the world in Maxine's wilderness outpost. Overall, Huston's *Night of the Iguana* is a genuinely cinematic film, a valid adaptation of Williams's work.

Two of Williams's later plays have been unsuccessfully adapted to film in the 1970s. Williams himself adapted *The Milk Train Doesn't Stop Here Anymore* for director Joseph Losey. Starring in her third Williams film, Elizabeth Taylor plays Flora Goforth, the dying dowager who lives on a Mediterranean island and takes as her last love Chris Flanders (Richard Burton), an itinerant poet who has earned the title of "Angel of Death" because he calls on ladies to prepare them to face death with resignation. Despite their star appearances, Losey's film was dismissed as a pretentious comment about the acceptance of mortality. *The Last of the Mobile Hot-Shots* (1976), directed by Sidney Lumet and adapted from Williams's **Kingdom of Earth (The Seven Descents of Myrtle)** by Gore Vidal, fared no better with the critics and with the public than did *Boom!* Jeb (James Coburn), a deathly ill southerner, marries a floozy, Myrtle (Lynn Redgrave), to have an heir to inherit his mother's estate. She falls for his black half brother, "the wood's colt" Chicken (Robert Hooks). The two men contend for the woman while the

dilapidated homestead they fight for is threatened by a summer storm (a familiar Williams's symbol) that turns into a raging flood. Jeb, the levee, and the film all finally collapse. An off-center adaptation of a slapstick tragedy, *The Last of the Mobile Hot-shots* (a line about Myrtle's past) is still noteworthy because of the performances of the three leads and also because of James Wong Howe's naturalistic cinematography.

A televised version of *The Glass Menagerie* (1987) by Paul Newman, who faithfully used Williams's script as his screenplay, demands comparison with the 1950 version. Joanne Woodward, his wife, appeared as Amanda, John Malkovich as Tom, and Karen Allen as Laura. Because Newman and Woodward had done the play so remarkably well in regional theater before making the film, they were well prepared for its transformation into cinema. Needless to say, there was no new Gentleman Caller waiting in the wings to replace Jim in Laura's life at the final fade-out, as in the 1950 adaptation of the play. Malkovich turned in a powerful performance as a disillusioned and angry son who still conveyed his sorrowful tenderness for his mother and sister. After Tom's departure, the audience sadly realizes that Laura will remain at home with her mother while her brother searches for success in a world forever alien to them.

Williams's plays merit our applause as extraordinary drama. However, the film versions, such as Newman's *The Glass Menagerie*, share enough of the tone, power, and intent of Williams's original plays to be considered valid, even superior, adaptations. See also **Baby Doll**; **Hollywood**; **Kazan, Elia.**

Further Reading

Baer, William, ed. *Elia Kazan: Interviews*. Jackson: University Press of Mississippi, 2000.

Hirsch, Foster. "The Films of Tennessee Williams." *Cinema* 8.2 (Spring 1977): 2–8.

Kolin, Philip. "*A Streetcar Named Desire* in Other Media." In *Williams: "A Streetcar Named Desire."* Plays in Production. Cambridge: Cambridge University Press, 2000. 149–174.

Leff, Leonard. "And Transfer to Cemeteries: *The Streetcars Named Desire.*" *Film Quarterly* 55.3 (Spring 2002): 29–37.

———, and Jerold Simmons. "Tennessee Williams." In *The Dame in the Kimono: Hollywood and Censorship.* Rev. ed. Lexington: University Press of Kentucky, 2001. 177–183.

Palmer, Burton. "Hollywood in Crisis: Tennessee Williams and the Evolution of the Adult Film." In *The Cambridge Companion to Tennessee Williams*, ed. Matthew C. Roudané. Cambridge: Cambridge University Press, 1997. 204–231.

Phillips, Gene D. *The Films of Tennessee Williams.* Philadelphia: Arts Alliance, 1980.

———. "Tennessee Williams's Forgotten Film: *The Last of the Mobile Hot-Shots* as a Screen Version of *The Seven Descents of Myrtle.*" In *The Undiscovered Country: The Later Plays of Tennessee Williams*, ed. Philip C. Kolin. New York: Lang, 2002. 80–92.

Tischler, Nancy. " 'Tiger—Tiger!' Blanche's Rape on Screen." In *Magical Muse: Millennial Essays on Tennessee Williams*, ed. Ralph F. Voss. Tuscaloosa: University of Alabama Press, 2002. 50–69.

Gene D. Phillips, S.J.

The Frosted Glass Coffin. *The Frosted Glass Coffin*, a one-act play from 1970, is one of Williams's sardonic depictions of old age and encroaching death and deserves comparison with his other geriatric plays **Lifeboat Drill** and **This Is the Peaceable Kingdom**. It premiered at the **Key West** Waterfront Playhouse on 1 May 1970 and subsequently was performed at the Atlanta Alliance Theatre on 11 February 1980 and

the Goodman Theatre in Chicago from 8–23 November 1980.

With parts for six characters—Mr. One, Two, Three, Betsey (Mr. One's wife), and Mr. and Mrs. Kelsey—*The Frosted Glass Coffin* is set in a cheap retirement home, ironically named the Ponce de Leon, in downtown Miami under a "zinc white" light resembling "frosted glass." One, Two, and Three complain about the rising prices at Dixie Mammy's, the budget restaurant across the street, and also about Dixie herself, an old black woman who rings her bell too early in the morning. Grumpy old men grumble about women outliving men and speculate that wives buy rat poisoning to speed their husbands' demise. These *senex* figures, one of them a former mayor, also satirize an old woman, Mrs. Walker, who is always first in line at Dixie's but who once passed out and had to be taken away in an ambulance. Their captious banter is followed by the tragic events befalling Mr. and Mrs. Kelsey, also guests at the hotel. After Mrs. Kelsey dies, her husband loses his strength and even his mind, thinking she is still alive, causing the other residents to arrange to have him taken away to a nursing home in Fort Lauderdale. But at the end of the play, as Dixie's bell stops and the zinc light gets brighter, Mr. Kelsey opens his mouth to scream in horror and pain.

Despite its geriatric humor, *The Frosted Glass Coffin* contains Williams's lament over an uncaring world that busies itself in trivialities, statistics, and mean-spiritedness. Within this otherwise satiric play, Williams incorporates several tragic symbols of death, including Dixie Mammy as a sexton tolling the bell for the departed, the white light suggesting the numbing void from losing a loved one, and the existential howl of Mr. Kelsey's grief. As he did in **The Milk Train Doesn't Stop Here Anymore**, or **The Night** *of the Iguana*, Williams here again fuses the comic and the elegaic.

Further Reading

Kolin, Philip C. "Williams's *The Frosted Glass Coffin*." *The Explicator* 59 (Fall 2000): 44–46.

Philip C. Kolin

Fugitive Kind. *Fugitive Kind*, written in 1937 when Williams was 26, had its only production by the St. Louis **Mummers** on 30 November and 6 December of that year. The Mummers, an activist theater group, were a primary influence on Williams's becoming a playwright, having produced his first long play, **Candles to the Sun**, in March 1937. When reviews were enthusiastic, they pressed him to write a second play, but *Fugitive Kind*, the same year, was less well received. The *St. Louis Globe-Democrat* of 1 December compared its "sordid realism" to *Tobacco Road* and judged it stronger in theme than plot. Colin McPherson of the *Post-Dispatch* also found it plotless, though noted its "wealth of colorful characters." Reed Hynds in the *Star-Times* found it stimulating and vivid and praised its "first-rate theatrical craftmanship," comparing its author to Sidney Howard and Maxwell Anderson. He predicted that "Thomas Lanier Williams is a playwright to watch." All complained that the ending was inconclusive; indeed, all his life Williams would have trouble ending his plays.

The key influence on *Fugitive Kind* was the movies, a resource seldom used by American playwrights before Williams. Specifically, the Maxwell Anderson film *Winterset*, with its unforgettable shot of Brooklyn bridge, inspired Williams to adapt his local setting of Eads bridge on the St. Louis waterfront to a similar plot and characters: the Jewish immigrant father, his rebellious son, the naive daughter, and a mysterious stranger on a quest for justice who arouses her love. Their sudden affair promises each escape from a constrained life but ends in tragedy in Anderson's play; the film has a happy ending. As in *Winterset*, *Fugitive Kind* involves a gangster shootout.

A third influence may have been a 1933 novel by Jack Conroy, *The Disinherited*, called the most representative work on the Great Depression. Its title and portrayal of homeless characters may have inspired Williams to set his play in a flophouse and to introduce some 30 transients who tell their stories, incidentally displaying the playwright's early gift for characterization. He had met Conroy, editor of *The Anvil, the Magazine of Proletarian Fiction*, through **Clark Mills (McBurney)**, his college friend, who was an editor of the magazine in 1935 and had briefly been drawn into the radical group of writers and artists on the Works Progress Administration (WPA) to whom Conroy was mentor. Mills himself influenced Williams's play, which was written in Clark's basement where the two set up a "literary factory" in the summer of 1937 and exchanged ideas. Clark's poem "The White Winter" inspired the snowy background that became the chief symbol of Williams's play, along with the cathedral bells, both suggesting purification. In opposition was the red light at the foot of the steps where the final carnage takes place. Williams also introduced symbolic names: "Glory" and "Leo" both have religious meaning.

Fugitive Kind is significant as a veritable index to Williams's later work, in its basic character of the outsider, victim of an unjust society, its theme of escape, its revelation of Williams's gift for dialogue, its introduction of the "aria," which would become typical of his dramas, its use of music as motif, and especially in using himself and his sister as characters. *Fugitive Kind* introduced a technique Williams would employ in future dramas of splitting one character, usually himself, into opposites. Leo, the poetic young writer who rebels against rules and is dismissed from college, acts out Williams's own history, although he was taken from school for flunking journalism, not distributing radical pamphlets. Tex, the traveling minstrel, represents the outside world the youthful playwright longed for; Terry, the romantic hero, bets his life on escape as Williams was too timid to do. The play demonstrates the innovations Williams would bring to theater, writing in cinematic scenes instead of acts, discarding realistic props and backgrounds for expressionistic lighting and music. *Fugitive Kind* is also significant as the creative basis for **Battle of Angels** (1940), his first professional production, which became **Orpheus Descending** and premiered on Broadway in 1957. Here Tex of *Fugitive Kind*, with his guitar, developed into the traveling minstrel Val of *Orpheus Descending*, while Glory of the early play, shown older and tougher but still vulnerable, suggested Myra of *Orpheus Descending*. The 1960 film *The Fugitive Kind* relates to *Orpheus Descending* rather than to the early play. See also **Candles to the Sun**; **Not about Nightingales.**

Further Reading

Conroy, Jack. *The Disinherited*. 2nd ed. New York: Hill and Wang, 1963.

Hale, Allean. "A Playwright to Watch." Introduction to *Fugitive Kind* by Tennessee Williams, ed. Allean Hale. New York: New Directions, 2001. xi–xxi.

Winterset. Film produced by Pandro S. Berman for RKO as adapted from the play by Maxwell Anderson by Alfred Santell. With Burgess Meredith and Margo Jones.

Allean Hale

G

Garden District. See *Suddenly Last Summer.*

Gender and Sexuality. The details of Williams's sexual life are well known. He claimed that he did not have a homosexual experience until his late twenties but after that enjoyed the kindness of many strangers. While his letters from the 1940s record a happily promiscuous sex life, one of his later autobiographical projections, Quentin in *Small Craft Warnings*, laments the obsessive quality of his middle-aged sexual exploits as an addiction devoid of real feeling. Williams died in the bedroom of a New York hotel suite with the last in a long series of paid companions who was too drugged out to hear his choking sounds.

There were only two serious relationships in his life, and they were all doomed in a way that appealed to Williams's dark, romantic imagination. His affair with his first love, bisexual dancer **Kip Kiernan,** was the raw material for his play *Something Cloudy, Something Clear* (published 1995). Kip left Williams for a conventional marriage and died young of a brain tumor. Williams's one

lengthy relationship was with **Frank Merlo,** a working-class Italian American whom Williams met in 1948. The devoted Merlo was the inspiration for *The Rose Tatoo* (1951). While those close to Williams felt that Merlo was a salutary, stabilizing force in his life, the writer's psychoanalysis in the late 1950s and his increasing addiction to liquor and drugs led to Williams breaking off their relationship. After Merlo's death from lung cancer in 1963, Williams's guilt and grief made him even more unstable.

In many ways, Tennessee Williams encapsulates the problems of writing about a gay artist before gay liberation allowed writers to be more open about their sexuality and to express that openness in their works. Williams's career began at a time when the Broadway Theatre was exceedingly timid about any serious representation of the lives of homosexual characters. Between the Wales Padlock Act in 1928, created in response to the perceived threat of plays about homosexuality, the political and social climate of World War II, and the repressive climate of the cold war era during which, as critics David Savran and Robert J. Corber have noted, homosexuality was equated with treason, writers like Williams were discouraged from publicly admitting their sexual orientation or expressing their sexuality in their work. Nonetheless, Williams came of age in New York City in a vibrant gay artistic subculture, and in the period after World War II, a tradition of gay writing began in the United States with the publication of works like **Gore Vidal**'s *The City and the Pillar* (1948), Christopher Isherwood's *The World at Evening* (1954), and James Baldwin's *Giovanni's Room* (1955). Their success suggests that there was a significant gay, if closeted, readership for these works. The double standard of policed silence in the legitimate theater and a new openness in poetry and fiction is reflected in Williams's own work. In the 1940s and 1950s, he wrote a number of short stories that are classics of gay fiction and in which Williams's own themes and obsessions are developed in ways more daring than we see in his plays. Williams's best poetry depicts the spiritual distance that can exist between two men in a bedroom. At the same time, while seeming cautious to us now, Williams's plays, which during this period had no homosexual characters on stage, insistently and courageously raise the subject of homosexuality.

Williams's own homosexuality was never deemed politically correct. Throughout his career, conservative critics denounced him and his work as immoral and corrupt. In the early 1960s he and his successful gay colleagues, **Edward Albee** and **William Inge**, were viciously attacked by the critics of the *New York Times* and other journals for the homosexual themes and characters in their plays. The nastiness hastened Inge's and Williams's personal and professional destruction. Ostensibly liberal critics claimed that Williams's female characters were nothing but men in drag (would one say that of the creations of a heterosexual like Shaw or Ib-

Tennessee Williams, 1963. Photo by London Service Co., used courtesy of New Directions Publishing Corp.

sen?), as if a gay writer were incapable of writing characters who were authentically masculine or feminine because, as a homosexual, he was supposedly incapable of being authentically either. Though he was "out" in the preliberation sense of sexually active and open about his homosexuality with friends and colleagues, some of the first generation of post-Stonewall gay critics attacked Williams for not coming out publicly. By then, drink and drugs had robbed Williams of the artistic control he once had, and his kiss-and-tell *Memoirs* (1975) is sloppy and part fabrication. His later self-portraits in the play *Small Craft Warnings* (1972) and the novel *Moise and the World of Reason* (1975) offer portraits of sad, jaded gay men for whom love is impossible and sex no longer meaningful. It is better to look at the more controlled, consistent, if dark vision of

73

sexuality and homosexuality offered in his earlier works; for now we can see how Williams pushed the envelope of homosexual representation in a particularly repressive period.

Throughout his career, Williams acknowledged two principal artistic influences: **D.H. Lawrence** and **Hart Crane**. Williams believed he and Lawrence shared similar backgrounds (sickly childhoods, unsympathetic fathers) and a similar philosophy: the centrality of sexual desire in human experience. More important was the powerful identification Williams felt with the gay poet Hart Crane. Williams not only used Crane's verse in the titles and epigraphs to his plays (e.g., *Summer and Smoke* and *A Streetcar Named Desire*) but identified with Crane's Dionysian, obsessive hunger for rough trade and his ultimate suicide. Williams's most artistically vivid portrayals of gay experience were of the dark side—furtive sexual encounters, male prostitution, and in the story "Desire and the Black Masseur" (1945), literal consumption of the flesh. Like Crane, Williams's shadowy gay presences, Mr. Burns ("Desire and the Black Masseur"), Allan Grey (*A Streetcar Named Desire*) and Skipper (*Cat on a Hot Tin Roof*), also commit suicide.

Many of the stories that center on homosexual characters were written in the 1940s at the same time Williams was writing his first classics—*The Glass Menagerie* and *A Streetcar Named Desire*. Like the latter, they are set in **New Orleans**. Still making peace with his own sexuality, Williams created a gallery of fascinating doomed men whose experiences define the nexus of desire and death that fascinated Williams. They also define his religion of the flesh in opposition to traditional Christianity, which, for him, denied the truth of the body and its hungers. When, in "One Arm" (1945), Oliver Winemiller, the beautiful boxer-turned-hustler, one of the first of Williams's hustler saints, waits in prison to be executed for murder, he is visited by a young, sexually repressed Lutheran minister, already on medication for "a little functional trouble of the heart." Obsessed by a newspaper picture of Oliver, the minister tries to save his soul. Oliver knows that the sublimation the minister offers is "bullshit" and offers the minister the physical experience he craves, from which the cleric runs in terror. Oliver dies with the letters of his many johns wedged between his legs. Facing death, he comes to understand the longing and affection his clients offered. Anthony Burns in "Desire and the Black Masseur" received both sexual release and atonement for his supposed sins at the hands of a giant black masseur. Out of the nexus of atonement and vengeance came a kind of love. When the masseur was fired because Burns's cries of pain/pleasure became too loud, he took Burns to his house in the black section of town where, during Easter week, Burns's cries mixed with those of the hell and brimstone services across the street. When Burns is finally battered to death, his masseur, in a parody of the Eucharist, consumes his corpse. The fulfillment of desire is death. Christianity offers a pale symbolic approximation of the Dionysian sacrifice at the heart of real passion. While Williams celebrates the ecstatic connection between these two men, he is also aware that it stems from fundamental human malaises: sexual guilt and racial hatred.

The links between sexual hunger and food, sex and death, are also at the heart of the story "Hard Candy" (1953). Aging, ill Mr. Krupper dies in the upper reaches of an ornate movie theater while enjoying the sexual favors of a beautiful, hungry young Latino he has paid with candy and a handful of quarters. Sex and eating are combined in the image of hard candy, which is also a sexual pun. Mr. Krupper died on his knees in what seemed to be "an attitude of prayer."

Williams develops these themes in *Suddenly Last Summer* (1958) in which the effete poet Sebastian, named after the saint whose life and martyrdom have been the subjects of the work of many gay artists and writers, is killed and eaten by the destitute Mexican boys he has paid for sex. Sebastian's sexual desire is described as hunger, and the connection of feeding and desire is linked to Sebastian's vision of God as birds of prey devouring the baby turtles as they rush toward the sea on the Galapagos Islands. His death is consonant with his own vision: The human birds of prey feed on his corpse as he sexually feasted on their bodies.

In "Desire and the Black Masseur," "Hard Candy," and *Suddenly Last Summer*, sexual desire is projected onto men who are racially or ethnically different as it is projected onto embodiments of youth. Mortality is always terrifying in Williams's work, and men and women stave off their fear of aging through sex with beautiful adolescent boys or young men. Pederasty is part of the worship of youth.

Though Sebastian Venable is the central character in *Suddenly Last Summer*, he never appears. Like all of the gay characters in Williams's major plays, he is dead when the action of the play begins but still an object of obsession for the surviving characters. To some extent, one can judge the cultural importance and perceived danger of the gay ghosts that haunt Williams's major plays by the fact that, with the exception of Sebastian, they were bowdlerized from the film versions of the plays in which they are discussed, rendering the narratives relatively unintelligible; for Sebastian and the dead gay men who obsess the central characters of *A Streetcar Named Desire* (1947) and *Cat on a Hot Tin Roof* (1955) are the moral centers of those plays.

In *A Streetcar Named Desire*, Blanche DuBois is haunted by the memory of her husband, Allan Grey, a young poet whom Blanche adored and worshiped. She was aware that Allan wanted her to save him from something for which her southern background didn't have a name—homosexuality—and from which no one could "save" him. Blanche's sister Stella does have a word for Allan—"degenerate," a common term for homosexuals at the time the play was written and a phrase Williams used to describe himself. In a letter he jokingly described himself as "[agent] **Audrey Wood**'s degenerate playwright." Shortly after Blanche accidentally walked into a room in which Allan and an older man were having sex, she exposed and rejected him on the dance floor of the Moon Lake Casino. In response to this public rejection, Allan shot himself. Blanche's fixation on this moment is shown in her hearing the Varsouviana, the song she and Allan danced to when she made her denunciation. Only the memory of the ensuing gunshot silences the song. Her obsession is also shown in her attraction to teenage boys, which causes the loss of her teaching position and creates the dire economic circumstances that brings her to Elysian Fields. Humiliating and rejecting Allan is the one act for which Blanche cannot forgive herself. She says to Stanley: "I hurt him the way you would like to hurt me"; and in a sense, Stanley's exposure and destruction of Blanche is poetic justice for her part in Allan's death.

Blanche herself is a figure for transgressive sexuality. In love with a gay man and unabashedly promiscuous, Blanche understands that "the opposite of death is desire." Sex for her is a way of affirming life in the face of disease and mortality. She describes her nocturnal visits from the soldiers, before she was declared "off limits," in terms of empowerment. Stanley's exposure and rape of Blanche is the destruction of a sexual outsider he cannot control. In this light, one reading of *A Streetcar Named Desire* is the destruction by an animalistic heterosexual male of the sexual other who could as easily be a closeted, if flamboyant, gay man as a woman. Moreover, *A Streetcar Named Desire* contains elements that would be hallmarks of gay drama: ironic presentation of normative relationships (the camp final tableau of Stella, Stanley and their child), flamboyant theatricality, its consciousness of the performativity of gender (Blanche's assumption of various feminine roles) and the slipperiness of language, and playfulness within scenes of impending entrapment and destruction.

A Streetcar Named Desire was also one of the first successful Broadway plays to allow a sympathetic female character to voice her sexual desire shamelessly. It was also one of the first Broadway plays to eroticize its central male character. Stanley Kowalski is a brute, but he is also sexy. In Williams's work it is the man who is the object of the gaze and of sexual desire, not the woman. Without being able to name it, this eroticization of the beautiful, sexy male was no doubt one of the shocking, supposedly immoral aspects of Williams's work that so outraged conservative, homophobic critics.

Williams had not had a major commercial success in the seven years between *A Streetcar Named Desire* and *Cat on a Hot Tin Roof*, and was eager for a hit. What empowered him to go further than he had previously with the themes of homosexual love and homophobia was probably the success of Robert Anderson's *Tea and Sympathy* (1953), about a sensitive young man branded falsely with homosexuality at a New England boarding school. There it is not the guitar playing boy who would rather spend time with women but the seemingly "normal" man's man, the housemaster, who is the latent homosexual. *Tea and Sympathy* proved that questioning current norms of masculinity and hinting at the scandalous subject of homosexuality could be potent at the box office. Williams, with more experience of homosexual desire and homophobia than Anderson had, could take these ideas and make of them a classic that remains powerful.

Cat on a Hot Tin Roof is the most conventionally realistic play among Williams's major works that makes the memories of the homosexual characters who haunt the bedroom in which the play is set all the more powerful. The setting is the former bedroom of a devoted gay couple, Jack Straw and Peter Ochello, once owners of the plantation whose ownership is the crux of the play's action. The principal furnishing is the giant, ornate bed Straw and Ochello once shared and that represents the only happy marriage the play offers. Big Daddy tells his son Brick that when Straw died, Peter Ochello stopped eating and soon died. Ochello willed the estate to its overseer, Big Daddy Pollitt who years before as a penniless young man arrived at Straw and Ochello's door and asked for a job. Now Big Daddy has inoperable cancer, and the battle is on between his daughter-in-laws as to who will inherit Straw and Ochello's legacy, the "twenty-eight thousand acres of the richest land this side of the valley Nile": Mae's husband Gooper, the eldest son who has done all the right things (become a lawyer, married into society, and sired six children), or Maggie's spouse, the feckless drunkard, Brick, who refuses to sleep with his wife. Brick, beautiful but profoundly unhappy, is Big Daddy's favored son precisely because he hasn't feigned devotion he didn't feel.

The memory of Brick's best friend, Skipper, keeps him and his wife apart. For Brick, his friendship with Skipper was his primary relationship, not his marriage, but he lives in terror that anyone will see his "pure" relationship with Skipper as "dirty." Maggie, who understands what Brick cannot accept, challenged Skipper to admit his love for Brick, then out of frustration and loneliness went to bed with Skipper, whose inability to perform sexually led him to realize the true nature of his feelings for Brick. Unable to face his sexual orientation, Skipper drank himself to death. Since then Brick has blamed Maggie for Skipper's death, but it was not Maggie's challenge to his manhood but Brick's rejection of their friendship that destroyed him. When Skipper phoned Brick and confessed his love, Brick hung up on him and never spoke to him again. When the play opens, Brick, like Skipper, has taken to the bottle. As in *A Streetcar Named Desire*, betrayal and rejection of a homosexual are the actions that haunt the central character. Brick rejected Skipper because the society in which he was educated, the jock–frat boy culture of Old Miss, taught him only loathing and derogatory language for what Skipper felt for him (and what he may have felt for Skipper), but Big Daddy, the heir of Straw and Ochello, tries to silence Brick's expressions of homophobia. While Brick could never bring himself to have sex with his friend, he definitely is what psychologists in the 1950s would label a "latent homosexual."

Recent London revivals, particularly the 1988 Royal National Theater production directed by Howard Davies with Ian Charleson as Brick and the 2001 production, directed by Anthony Page with Brendan Fraser, offered a Brick who clearly was tortured over his love for and loss of Skipper and for whom marriage to Maggie was a necessary compromise for the appearance of normality. At the end, Brick will sire the child he and Maggie need to ensure their inheritance. Brick admires Maggie's strength of will.

Moreover, he will never have the courage to defy his and others' homophobia. But the legacy he will inherit is best represented by the bed Jack Straw and Peter Ochello shared. Other than Baron Charlus in the fantasia **Camino Real**, Brick is the closest Williams comes to putting a homosexual character on stage during the 1950s, but it is only his denial of the possibility of complete love for Skipper, which his wife Maggie attributes to his "ass-aching" Puritanism, that made him acceptable for audiences of 1955.

Of course, the homosexual is only one version of the sexual outsider at the heart of Williams's plays. The women seeking sexual freedom and empowerment and the straight men who, like Val Xavier in *Orpheus Descending* or Chance Wayne in *Sweet Bird of Youth*, are destroyed for offering a patriarchal society an alternative view of masculinity are more central than the gay characters because they are visible, present.

One does not look to Williams's work for positive gay role models any more than one looks to him for uncomplicated, happy heterosexuals. His "blue devils," his anxieties, idées fixes, and the view he affords from the brink of madness make him a unique writer. Moreover, Williams's principal theme was the impossibility of true intimacy of any kind set against the dreams men and women have of a meaningful emotional and spiritual connection. "Intimacies with strangers" is all one can expect. While that pessimistic belief may have had its origins in his particular experience as a gay man in the pre-Stonewall era, and in his own idiosyncrasies, his work convinces us, while we experience it, of its universality. Nonetheless, one does not fully understand or appreciate Tennessee Williams's major work until one grasps the ways in which his homosexuality informs his poems, fiction, and drama. See also *Collected Stories*; Mythology; Politics.

Further Reading

Clum, John M. "From *Summer and Smoke* to *The Eccentricities of a Nightingale*: The Evolution of the Queer Alma." *Modern Drama* 39.1 (Spring 1996): 31–50.

———. "The Sacrificial Stud and the Fugitive Female in *Suddenly Last Summer, Orpheus Descending*, and *Sweet Bird of Youth*." In *The Cambridge Companion to Tennessee Williams*, ed. Matthew C. Roudané. Cambridge: Cambridge University Press, 1997. 128–146.

———. *Still Acting Gay: Male Homosexuality in Modern Drama*. New York: St. Martin's–Palgrave, 2000.

Savran, David. *Communists, Cowboys, and Queers: The Politics of Masculinity in the Work of Arthur Miller and Tennessee Williams*. Minneapolis: University of Minnesota Press, 1992.

Sinfield, Alan. *Out on Stage: Lesbian and Gay Theatre in the Twentieth Century*. New Haven, CT: Yale University Press, 1999.

John M. Clum

The Glass Menagerie. *The Glass Menagerie* (1945) was the play that launched Tennessee Williams's career. After a shaky pre-Broadway run in Chicago that was saved only by the persistent exhortations of newspaper reviewers and columnists who urged theatergoers to see the play and made it a modest success, it opened in New York on 31 March 1945 at the Playhouse Theatre. There were 24 curtain calls on opening night, and virtually overnight Williams went from obscurity to being the subject of feature stories about him in *Time* and *Life* magazines. Within two weeks of its opening, *The Glass Menagerie* was voted the year's best play by the New York Drama Critics' Circle, and it later won the Donaldson Award and the Sidney Howard Memorial Award.

Referred to in the script as a memory play, *The Glass Menagerie* is the most directly autobiographical of Williams's plays. Williams even said it was his most painful work. The play is based on events of 1932–1935 in his life when he worked at the International Shoe Company (Continental Shoemakers in the play) in St. Louis during the day and wrote poems and short stories at night. He lived in a small apartment with his older sister **Rose**, his younger brother **Dakin**, and his parents, **Edwina and Cornelius**, the latter of whom formerly was a salesman who traveled a great deal. The Wingfield family mirrors Williams's own. Significantly, *The Glass Menagerie* is set in the city Williams loathed ("Saint Pollution," he called it) and reflects the alienation he felt in the cold, urban North to which his parents moved from the idyllic southern community of **Clarksdale, Mississippi,** the home of his beloved grandparents. St. Louis is a dark, dreadful place from which people try unsuccessfully to escape. In fact, one of the most symbolic pieces of the play's stage design is the fire escape to which Tom Wingfield flees to smoke and to get away from the trap laid for him by his mother Amanda and his sister Laura. But such escapes in *The Glass Menagerie* are short-lived, as Williams himself found out.

The personal trials of the Wingfield family unfold against the larger social and political upheaval of the Depression and an encroaching world war. The sharp realities of the 1930s serve as a counterpoint to the Wingfields' dashed hopes and dependencies. The millions of people who were hungry, out of work, and desperate are unseen players in the stark world of St. Louis. The Paradise Dance Hall across the alley from the Wingfield apartment offers an illusive and ultimately futile hope for happiness. The depression-era problems confronting St. Louis and America are situated against the backdrop of the storm clouds gathering in

Europe before World War II, further intensifying the sense of angst and despondency in the Wingfield family. Woven into Williams's memory play are references to Hitler tricking British prime minister Neville Chamberlain out of freedom for Czechoslovakia, the fascists, the bombing of Guernica in Spain, and finally, the uncertain times of late 1944, the closing days of the war, where the play ends. Memory and recent history coalesce in *The Glass Menagerie*.

The sources for *The Glass Menagerie* are diverse, rich, and immediate. Many individuals and places from Williams's St. Louis past resurface in the play. As Allean Hale claims, "*The Glass Menagerie* belongs wholly to St. Louis. It's his least disguised work" (611). The Williams's apartment building on Enright, the movies, the high school, Rubicam's Business College, and the warehouse all are actual St. Louis sites. Chekhov's *The Sea Gull* has been identified as a source for *The Glass Menagerie*. Earlier versions of the play include a short story, "Portrait of a Girl in Glass," and "The Gentleman Caller," a play that Williams unsuccessfully converted into a screenplay during his brief time working at MGM in 1943. As a number of critics have pointed out, the genesis of *The Glass Menagerie* as a film-script probably led to the play's use of cinematic techniques and devices—both overtly in the use of the screen on which images and titles for scenes are periodically projected and more generally in its employment of music and dim lighting and in its fractured time scheme, appropriate for a memory play moving freely between past (the 1930s) and present (1944–1945). These expressionistic techniques, combined with Williams's cinematic interests, foreshadow the style of many later Williams plays, which show him to be one of the most cinematic playwrights on the American stage.

The Glass Menagerie is narrated in the present by Tom Wingfield (Thomas Lanier Williams) who tells us of the events in the past that precipitated his leaving the St. Louis apartment he shared with his mother and sister to join the Merchant Marines. Tom thus serves a dual role in the play—he is a character (and for many readers the play's leading character) as well as the narrator through whose consciousness, memory, and history the events are ordered, interpreted, and synthesized. His point of view is pivotal in understanding what happened and why. Tom Wingfield suffers from problems that fueled Williams's own guilt, such as leaving his sister Rose, who eventually underwent a prefrontal lobotomy. Like his character Tom, Tennessee Williams adopted numerous costumes/disguises, as his letters from the 1930s and 1940s to his family amply attest. Moreover, Tom Wingfield is a frustrated writer (he is derisively known as Shakespeare at the shoe warehouse) and a traveler, just like his creator.

These events from Tom's memory, which form the action of the play, center around Amanda's attempts to find a husband for Laura, crippled by a childhood illness that has left one leg shorter than the other and in a brace. Laura in many ways calls to mind Williams's sister Rose. Amanda, whose husband abandoned his family some years before and whose smiling portrait as a World War I doughboy hangs in the living room, was once a popular Southern Belle pursued by many suitors. She now tries to help support her family by selling magazine subscriptions over the telephone, capitalizing on her membership in and contacts from the DAR (Daughters of the American Revolution) but to no avail. Tom hates his job at the local shoe factory and escapes by going to the movies, by writing, and by planning to join the Merchant Marines. At the end of the play he is dressed as a sailor. Laura, as a result of her crippled condition, is painfully

Laura (Tracey Ellis) receives her first gentleman caller (Jim Birdsall) in this scene from the Missouri Repertory Theatre's production of *The Glass Menagerie*. Used by permission of the Missouri Repertory Theatre.

shy and takes refuge in her phonograph records and her collection of glass animals.

Amanda discovers that Laura has dropped out of the typing and shorthand courses she had enrolled her at business college because she had become so nervous her first day there that she had thrown up in front of her classmates. Instead, every day when she was supposedly in class, she has been visiting the zoo, walking in the park, or going to the movies. Realizing that Laura will not be able to support herself, Amanda prevails on Tom to find a suitor for his sister among his co-workers at the shoe factory. Tom brings Jim O'Connor to dinner one evening amidst a great fanfare that includes extensive redecorating of the apartment and Amanda putting on a dress that she wore to greet her

gentlemen callers, vicariously being the young lady who is again the center of a man's attention. Unbeknownst to Amanda and Tom, Jim and Laura were in high school together, and she had a crush on him (their yearbook, which she still treasures, is called *The Torch*) but was far too reserved to approach him. When Laura recognizes who her brother's friend is, she is too upset and nervous to come to the dinner table and must go into the living room and lie down.

After dinner, Jim comes in to speak with Laura, and she reminds him of their earlier acquaintance. She speaks glowingly of his high school performance in *The Pirates of Penzance*, the Gilbert and Sullivan operetta. He obviously has a much dimmer memory of her than Laura does of him, but he does recall, as she does, that he called her "Blue Roses," an ominous (and sickly) inversion of the red roses symbolizing romance, because when he asked her why she had been absent from school and she told him that she had pleurosis, he thought she'd said "Blue Roses." Gradually, as the two reminisce, her shyness evaporates, and he admits to her that he hasn't realized very much of the potential promised by his popularity in high school. She in turn admits that she dropped out of high school, and he urges her to have more self-confidence, telling her that, in high school, he never noticed that she was crippled. She shows him her glass animal collection, especially her favorite, a unicorn; and when they clumsily dance to music from the Paradise Dance Hall, they bump into a table and the unicorn falls, breaking off its horn. Impulsively, as Jim assures Laura that she is unique and pretty, he kisses her; but he immediately draws back, apologizing and explaining that he won't be calling on her again because he is engaged to be married. After he leaves, Amanda comforts Laura as Tom explains to the audience that, shortly after the events of the play, he was fired from his job and traveled around the world trying in vain to forget the memory of his sister.

The Glass Menagerie introduced characters, themes, and techniques that would reappear in many of Williams's later plays. Tom and Laura Wingfield are among the first of his fragile poetic dreamers who are out of step with the practical realities of an often cruel world. Laura's failure to graduate from high school and to succeed at the business college and Tom's loss of his job because, as he explains to us, he is caught writing a poem on the lid of a shoebox are the manifestations of their inability to cope with the real world. Tom fails to pay the power bill, indicating his lack of concern for practicalities, and thereby casts the apartment and its guest into darkness. In their capacity as failed dreamers, Laura and Tom prefigure such later Williams characters as Blanche in *A Streetcar Named Desire*, Alma in *Summer and Smoke*, and Marguerite and Jacques in *Camino Real*, and they also foreshadow the brother and sister pairs who appear in later Williams works such as *The Two-Character Play*.

The real strength of Williams's plays, however, lies in their ambivalence about the encounter between these two worlds. In *The Glass Menagerie*, this ambivalence is apparent in the figure of Amanda, who, in a sense, lives in both the world of reality and in the world of illusion. Her position in the world of reality is most apparent in her understanding that she must sell subscriptions to trashy magazines over the telephone in order to provide for her family. And it is glaringly apparent in her wanting Tom to get ahead in a career. Her romantic side flowers in her memories of her southern girlhood and in her refusal to acknowledge that Laura is handicapped. This ambivalence is both complicated and made more acceptable because her responses are typical of a mother's atti-

tude toward her children. Amanda's over-protectiveness and overbearing personality can be seen either as indications that she is a tyrannical witch or that her motives are good but her methods are flawed. Because she is caught between the two worlds of the play and because she has been played by some of the greatest actors of the American theater, Amanda has often been regarded as the play's central character and has elicited a myriad of contradictory responses from critics. Marc Robinson sees her as "suffocating" (36), and Robert Jones calls her "pathetic" (212); but Delma E. Presley seems closer to a balanced appraisal in observing that Amanda reflects "the extremely complex nature of human love" (39). She may be a shrewish harridan who nags her children over proper ways to eat, to dress, and to socialize; yet Amanda can also be applauded as a devoted mother whose solicitude reminds readers of the hardships of single-parent households today.

Jim O'Connor, in turn, represents one of Williams's first depictions of the practical, real world. His abandonment of Laura at the end of the play shows how the world treats eccentric romantics—roughly and insensitively. Jim is also the symbol of the new world of technology; he goes to night school to study electronics and television engineering. He is enthusiastic about what he believes is his budding career in the world of commerce, which is beyond reach or acceptance by Laura, by Amanda, and even by Jim himself. He is filled with unrealized ambition that Williams satirizes through his narcissism (Jim foolishly checks his looks in a mirror), his aging all-American boy image, and in his less-than-prestigious position at the warehouse. When he stretches to admire his own shadow in the darkened Wingfield living room, we see how self-impressed he is. Too self-assured, Jim has no idea of how much pain and disappointment he brings to the Wingfield household. He is not the long-awaited gentleman caller who will be Laura's savior. Instead, as Philip C. Kolin argues, he is in a line of Williams's unsuitable suitors, including Mitch in *A Streetcar Named Desire*, and, more comically, Alvaro in **The Rose Tattoo**, whose own sexuality is far from manly and powerful. In his stalwart commitment to realism and antiromanticism, Jim resembles Stanley in *A Streetcar Named Desire*, John in *Summer and Smoke*, and Gutman in *Camino Real*.

The ambivalence of Williams's drama can also be seen in the play's climactic scene between Laura and Jim. He is drawn in by her innocence and openness, attributes Jim obviously is not accustomed to experiencing in his world. And his act of kissing her is an unpremeditated, impulsive one that indicates the power of Laura's world to have an impact on his defenses; but just as surely his reaction after the kiss testifies to how incapable the real world is of accepting the tenderness and sensitivity offered by its poets and dreamers. Like so many of Williams's other plays, *The Glass Menagerie* also ends ambivalently. Because the playwright very deliberately does not let us hear what is being said by Laura and Amanda as they converse behind Tom's closing speech to the audience, we are left with two very different, competing responses—the fear that Laura has been devastated forever by her encounter with Jim or the hope that his encouragement has in fact made her more capable of facing the world outside her apartment.

There is little doubt that Williams's own personal sympathies lay with the Lauras, Toms, and Blanches of the world. Sharply departing from critical tradition, Stephanie Hammer argues that Laura is not Rose Williams but the playwright himself, "the hysterical, withdrawn, secretly desirous, feminine crippled artist" (45). The undeniable achievement of his plays is that he also

saw the impossibility of escaping from the reality that Jim and Stanley Kowalski represent. Just as Tom cannot escape the memory of Laura by joining the Merchant Marines, none of Williams's damaged misfits can truly find happiness in a world that does not understand or appreciate them. That fact, however, does not diminish in any way their importance in that world for Williams.

The symbolism in *The Glass Menagerie* complements character and plot. The glass unicorn, undeniably the most important symbol in the play, is a harbinger of the many beautifully crafted and carefully integrated symbols that appear in Williams's works. The unicorn is rich in psychological and sexual meaning. It represents Laura's illusions, her dreams, her vulnerability. When the unicorn loses his horn as Laura dances with Jim, the tiny animal will, as she notes, feel more comfortable with the other horses and will seem less "freakish." On one level, this is an indication that Laura will feel more comfortable as a result of her time with Jim and has been made to feel less freakish like the unicorn who, in losing his horn, will look like all the other horses in Laura's collection. Since unicorn horns were supposed to be aphrodisiacs, the symbolic rupture can be regarded as a sexual awakening for Laura. But the symbol has received other, less benevolent interpretations. The encounter with Jim shatters Laura's innocence (her uniqueness), just as it did the unicorn's horn, and leaves her broken. In this view, the symbol represents a loss, a severing of one part of the body from another, as in Rose Williams's prefrontal lobotomy in 1943. Georges Sarotte, in fact, reads the broken unicorn as Laura's castration (144), and Constantine Starvou sees it as a loss of "one of the surrogate objects of her erotic fantasies" (29). The unicorn, we must also remember, is a mythical beast that never really exists, just as Laura's hope for happiness and marriage with Jim will never materialize. The ambivalence of Williams's symbol here can be compared to the ending of *A Streetcar Named Desire*. There we are permitted to believe that Blanche has been irreparably damaged by Stanley's rape or that she finds hope in imagining that the doctor who is taking her to the asylum is an old beau come to rescue her.

But many other symbols in *The Glass Menagerie* show the collision of private and public worlds, symbols that energize Williams's **Plastic Theater** and his desire to show the fluidity of experience and consciousness. Music, magic, and commerce are a few of the areas from which Williams drew his symbols in the play. Still many others are rooted in religion and point to the promise or the impossibility of salvation. Ironically, Amanda brings out a broken candelabrum from the Church of the Heavenly Rest (a real church in Blue Mountain where she grew up) at the ill-fated dinner. Candles (and flickering light through glass) are the perfect objective correlative (to use T.S. Eliot's phrase) for Williams's play of collapsing and changing times, places, and desires. The dinner itself has been seen as a symbolic, ironic Annunciation (there is no happy news about the coming of new life into Laura's shattered world) as well as a broken Holy Communion service.

The performance history of *The Glass Menagerie* features the work of some of American's greatest actors. The Broadway premiere ran for 563 performances with a cast headed by **Laurette Taylor** as Amanda Wingfield, in a performance that many regarded at the time—and still do—as one of the finest and most memorable in the history of the American theater. **Eddie Dowling** played Tom and directed the production as well, while Julie Haydon was Laura, and Anthony Ross was Jim, the Gentleman Caller. A 1948 London production starred Helen Hayes as Amanda, a role she would reprise in a 1956 Broadway revival. A twenty-fifth anniversary presentation in 1970 starred **Maureen Stapleton** as Amanda; and in 1983, British director John Dexter's New York production featured **Jessica Tandy** as Amanda and Amanda Plummer as Laura and was the first Broadway version to use Williams's screen projections—which had been in the published play but had been omitted from most previous productions. A 1994 revival starred Julie Harris as Amanda.

Black theater companies have an illustrious history of staging *The Glass Menagerie*, radicalizing the script and thereby opening it to powerful, new interpretations. They have explored in original and challenging ways the social implications of the absent father and Laura's physical problems as a trope for racial discrimination. A 1965 revival at the Karamu House Theatre in Cleveland cast black actors as the Wingfield family and a white performer as the Gentleman Caller. All-black casts staged the play in 1989 at Arena Stage in Washington, D.C. (with Ruby Dee as Amanda) and in 1991 at San Francisco's Lorraine Hansberry Theatre.

The Glass Menagerie was the first Williams play to be turned into a film (1950), directed by Irving Rapper and starring Gertrude Lawrence as Amanda, Jane Wyman as Laura, and Kirk Douglas as the Gentleman Caller. Replacing Williams's script with a happy ending (Laura looking forward to more gentlemen callers) was for Williams the "worst" adaptation of his work. Much more successful were the two televised versions of *The Glass Menagerie*—the 16 December 1973 teleplay starring Katharine Hepburn as Amanda, Sam Waterston as Tom, Michael Moriarity as Jim, and Joanna Miles as Laura and the highly acclaimed 1987 version, directed by Paul Newman, with Joanne Woodward as Amanda, Karen Allen as Laura, and a sensitive but strong John Malkovich as

Tom. Like *A Streetcar Named Desire, The Glass Menagerie* is a staple in American and world theater. See also **Film Adaptations; Hollywood.**

Further Reading

Bigsby, C.W.E. "Entering *The Glass Menagerie.*" In *The Cambridge Companion to Tennessee Williams*, ed. Matthew C. Roudané. Cambridge: Cambridge University Press, 1997. 29–44.

Bloom, Harold, ed. *Tennessee Williams's "The Glass Menagerie."* New York: Chelsea, 1988.

Hale, Allean. "Tennessee Williams's St. Louis Blues." *Mississippi Quarterly* 48 (1995): 609–626.

Hammer, Stephanie B., " 'That Quiet Little Play': Bourgeois Tragedy, Female Impersonation, and a Portrait of the Artist in *The Glass Menagerie.*" In *Tennessee Williams: A Casebook*, ed. Robert F. Gross. New York: Routledge, 2002. 33–50.

Jones, Robert Emmet. "Tennessee Williams's Early Heroines." *Modern Drama* 2 (1959): 211–219.

Kolin, Philip C. "Black and Multi-Racial Productions of *The Glass Menagerie.*" *Journal of Dramatic Theory and Criticism* 9 (Spring 1995): 97–128.

———. "The Family of Mitch: (Un)Suitable Suitors in Tennessee Williams." In *The Magical Muse: Millennial Essays on Tennessee Williams*, ed. Ralph F. Voss. Tuscaloosa: University of Alabama Press, 2002. 131–146.

Parker, R.B. *Twentieth-Century Interpretations of "The Glass Menagerie."* Englewood Cliffs, NJ: Prentice-Hall, 1983.

Presley, Delma E. *"The Glass Menagerie": An American Memory.* Boston: Twayne, 1990.

Robinson, Marc. "Tennessee Williams." In his *The Other American Drama.* Cambridge: Cambridge University Press, 1994. 29–59.

Sarotte, Georges-Michel. "Fluidity and Differentiation in Three Plays by Tennessee Williams." In *Staging Preference: Cultural Pluralism in American Theatre and Drama*, ed. Marc Maufort. New York: Lang, 1995. 141–156.

Starvou, Constantine N. "The Neurotic Heroine in Tennessee Williams." *Literature and Psychology* 5.2 (1995): 26–34.

Jackson R. Bryer

The Gnädiges Fräulein. *The Gnädiges Fräulein* is a one-act play that together with *The Mutilated* comprises Williams's *Slapstick Tragedy* (1996). *Fräulein* was originally published in *Esquire* (August 1965) and then included in *Dragon Country* (1969). Characteristic of Williams, he rewrote this one-act play as *Later Days of a Celebrated Soubrette*, which was produced in 1974. *The Gnädiges Fräulein* chronicles the downfall of a once-famous singer, now a permanent resident at a questionable beachfront rooming house in Cocalooney Key, Florida.

To pay for her upkeep the Gnädiges Fräulein ("Gracious Lady" or "Gracious Miss" in German) is ordered to bring the proprietor, Molly, three fish a day. But the Fräulein has to battle the local cocaloonies (large pelicans) for her day's catch. Struggling with these birds, she has her legs covered with blood, loses her hair, and is blinded in both eyes. She resembles a freakish clown. The birds pursue her even into the see-through walls of Molly's rooming house. In her earlier European career, the Fräulein was jilted by a "Viennese dandy" named Toivo, with whom she worked in a circus act with a trained seal who caught fish. Alienating the seal, the dandy, and her audience, she positioned herself between the dandy and the seal, catching the fish herself. Her sad fate in *The Gnädiges Fräulein* is now narrated by Molly before Polly, the society editor at the *Cocaloony Gazette*, from whom Molly seeks a complimentary write-up for her rooming house. Both women lust after another boarding house guest, the blond Indian Joe, who resembles a **Hollywood** Indian in his war cries and brandishing tomahawk. Ironically, this Indian want-to-be whistles "The Indian Love Call."

For almost 35 years after its premiere, critics ignored or denigrated *Fräulein*. Richard Gilman labeled it a "witless arbitrary farce," and John McCarten dismissed it "as too outlandishly horrible to be talented." When taken seriously, the play has often been read as a parable on the cruel fate befalling Williams himself in the theater. A chief architect of this biographical interpretation, Harold Clurman explicated *Fräulein* as follows: "The vindictive cocaloony represented the critics, the public are the permanent transients at Molly's boarding house, Polly stands for certain elements of a complacent yet malicious press, Molly represents those who manage the theater and playwrights, and the Fräulein who loses her sight is none other than the playwright, who suffered loss of sight because of a cataract."

But in the last few years *Fräulein* gained new life as critics turned away from an exclusively autobiographical reading to study the play in terms of other traditions, other discourses. Taking a cue from Williams's own description of the play as "vaudeville, burlesque, slapstick, with a dash of pop art," critics approached *Fräulein* not as failed realism but as emerging from the art forms of the 1960s that elucidate Williams's other post–*Night of the Iguana* work. Allean Hale, for instance, examined *The Gnädiges Fräulein* in light of the pop art of the 1960s—the work of artists like Andy Warhol or Ray Lichtenstein (both of whom Williams knew)—and Williams's own achievements as an artist, too (see **Art**). Also exploring the play through popular art—the animated cartoon—Linda Dorff labeled *Fräulein* as one of Williams's "outrageous" plays in which he used irony, parody, and satire against the

"theatre-as-world," the very medium in which he launched his career in the 1940s. Through distorted cartoon imagery Williams's challenges conventional, realistic drama in this antimimetic camp play. Also judging the play from the perspectives of the 1960s, Philip C. Kolin argues that Williams incorporated Alfred Hitchcock's 1963 film *The Birds* as "submerged ideological, visual and aural text" expressing "the lunacy and dread of nuclear attack in the 1960's" (6). Hitchcock's crows, like Williams's cocaloonies, are metaphors for missiles. The identity of its eponymous character—the Fräulein—has also radically changed. She is seen as performer/artist who is grotesquely undone/undercut in mockery. Exploring the Fräulein in terms of Artaud's theater of cruelty, emphasizing pain and isolation, Annette Saddik claims she is "trapped into performing failed and absurd representations of herself." For Una Chaudhuri, the Fräulein carries on Williams's postmodern attack of identity itself. Destabilizing the binary categories of human/animal, the Fräulein expresses what it means in "becoming animal." She is on the edge of Williams's world of humanity and routinely performs like an animal to survive her journey "into otherness."

A vital theme in Williams's theater of mutilation and spectacle in *The Gnädiges Fräulein* is the breakdown of language. There is no stable, authoritative voice in *The Gnädiges Fräulein*. In fact, this black comedy blasts audiences with squawks, screams, howls, guttural noise, grunts, and banter. The Fräulein utters only "AHHHHHH," or simply screams. The cocaloony squawks a menacing monosyllable "AWK," expressing the schizophrenia and fury of the Fräulein's existence. Indian Joe also sticks to one-syllable utterances—"How," "Pow," "Ugh." The topsy-turvy world of uncertainties that *The Gnädiges Fräulein* represents defies rational communication and expresses only

Broadway premiere of *The Gnädiges Fräulein* at the Longacre Theatre, 22 February 1966, with Zoe Caldwell as Polly, Kate Reid as Molly, and Art Ostrin as the Cocaloony. Photo by Friedman-Abeles. Billy Rose Theatre Collection, The New York Public Library for the Performing Arts, Astor, Lenox and Tilden Foundations.

primal fears. Even Polly and Molly's dialogue is uncaring, devoid of compassion or poetry.

Fräulein premiered on Broadway on 22 February 1966 but closed after only seven performances. Directed by Alan Schneider, who directed *Who's Afraid of Virginia Woolf?* in 1962, the production starred Zoe Caldwell as Polly, Kate Reid as Molly, Margaret Leighton as the Fräulein, and James Olson as Indian Joe. For the next 30 years or so, the play was seldom staged. Martin Denton estimated that the play received not more than 20 New York performances from 1966 to 1999. From 24 September through 9 October 1999, though, Theatre Ten Thousand performed *Fräulein*, directed by Arnold Barkus, at the Ohio Theatre in New York. In 2000, *Fräulein* was staged at the Krennert Center at the University of Illinois in a powerful and appreciative revival.

Further Reading

Chaudhuri, Una. "AWK! Extremity, Animality, and the Aesthetic of Awkwardness in Tennessee Williams's *The Gnädiges Fräulein*."

In *The Undiscovered Country: The Later Plays of Tennessee Williams*, ed. Philip C. Kolin. New York: Lang, 2002. 54–67.

Clurman, Harold. "Theatre." *Nation* 14 March 1966: 309.

Denton, Martin. www.NYtheatre.com/NYtheatre/Gnadiges.htm. 25 September 1999.

Dorff, Linda. "Theatricalist Cartoons Tennessee Williams's Late 'Outrageous' Plays." *Tennessee Williams Annual Review* 2 (1999): 13–33.

Gilman, Richard. "Glass Menagerie." *Newsweek* 7 March 1966: 90.

Hale, Allean. "*The Gnädiges Fräulein*: Tennessee Williams's Clown Show." In *The Undiscovered Country: The Later Plays of Tennessee Williams*, ed. Philip C. Kolin. New York: Lang, 2002. 40–53.

Kolin, Philip C. " 'a play about terrible birds': Tennessee Williams's *The Gnädiges Fräulein* and Alfred Hitchcock's *The Birds*." *South Atlantic Review* 66 (Winter 2001): 1–22.

McCarten, John. "The Out and the Abstract." *New York Journal American* 23 February 1966: 17.

Saddik, Annette. " 'The Inexpressible Regret of All Her Regrets': Tennessee Williams's Later Plays as Artaudian Theatre of Cruelty." In *The Undiscovered Country: The Later Plays of Tennessee Williams*, ed. Philip C. Kolin. New York: Lang, 2002. 5–24.

Philip C. Kolin

Gonzales, Pancho Rodriguez y (1920–1993).

Pancho Rodriguez y Gonzales was born in **New Orleans** and lived with Tennessee Williams at 632 Rue St. Peter in the French Quarter in the 1940s when Williams was writing *A Streetcar Named Desire*. In fact, Pablo Gonzales in *A Streetcar Named Desire* may have been influenced by Williams's relationship with Pancho, given the similarities between the two. It's more than coincidental that they shared the same surname, Gonzales. Pancho and Pablo were both Mexicans who had reputations for fighting. Pancho's tempestuous rows with Williams may have been the cause of their separation. Yet Williams kept in touch with Pancho over the years. A photo of the two, possibly taken in the early 1970s, shows Williams seated, wearing a sombrero, with a graying but distinguished Pancho Gonzales standing behind him. In an undated letter to Pancho from the 1940s, Williams likened his former partner to a "Spanish grandee" and gave Pancho his gratitude for dispelling the loneliness he felt while writing *A Streetcar Named Desire*. Given the presence of Hispanic characters in Williams's plays named "Gonzales," Pancho continued to play an important role in Williams's artistic life, for example, the knife-wielding Papa Gonzales in **Summer and Smoke** and the Mexican Pablo Gonzales with whom the old Emil Kroger fell in love in "The Mysteries of Joy Rio" (See **Collected Stories**). The Hispanic world, especially Mexico, contributed much to Williams's romantic vision and his theater of danger and desire. Pancho Gonzales was a vital part of that world.

Further Reading

De Salvo, Joseph J. Interview by author. Owner, Faulkner House Bookstore, Pirate's Alley, New Orleans, March 29, 2003. Information on photo of Gonzales and Williams courtesy of Joseph DeSalvo.

Holditch, Kenneth, and Richard Freeman Leavitt. *Tennessee Williams and the South*. Jackson: University Press of Mississippi, 2002.

Philip C. Kolin

Group Theatre.

The Group Theatre, formed in 1931 as an offshoot of the Theatre Guild and arguably the most famous and successful producer in its day of new plays in the United States, awarded Williams $100 in 1939 for his **American Blues**, his collection of one-act plays, submitted under the name "Tennessee." It was Williams's first recognition by a professional, nationally prominent theater company and the first official use of the name he adopted and by which he was to become world famous. To meet the contest requirements of being under 25, Williams, having disguised his identity for the submission, also gave his birthdate as 1914 instead of 1911. The winner of the new-play contest was Ramon Noya, the Group having decided to award only one $500 prize. But **Molly Day Thacher**, the Group's playreader, and the other judges, director and Group cofounder Harold Clurman and playwright Irwin Shaw, had been so impressed with *American Blues* that Thacher convinced the Group's treasurer, Kermit Bloomgarden, to make a special award to the young writer. The *New York Times* announcement of the award effectively transformed Tom Williams, a 28-year-old poet from **St. Louis**, into the 25-year-old playwright from **New Orleans** named Tennessee Williams.

Williams garnered other immediate repercussions of the contest as well—money, time to work, and a boost to his confidence. Most important, it led him to New York and the professional theater where Thacher introduced his writing to **Audrey Wood**, who became his longtime agent and friend. Through Thacher, he also began an association with her husband, **Elia Kazan**, and other members of the Group became significant figures in his career: Kazan directed six of Williams's plays (*A Streetcar Named Desire*, 1947; *Camino Real*, 1953; *Cat on a Hot Tin Roof*, 1955; *Orpheus Descending*, 1957; *Sweet Bird of Youth*, 1959; *Period of Adjustment*, 1960) and two of his films (*A Streetcar Named Desire*, 1951; *Baby Doll*, 1956), and Cheryl Crawford, another Group cofounder, produced four Williams productions (*The Rose Tattoo*, 1950; *Camino Real*;

Sweet Bird of Youth; *Period of Adjustment*). Clurman had appointed Thacher head of the Group's new-play department, and she actively sought out and nurtured talented unknown writers like Williams. At meetings at the Group, for example, Thacher guided Williams through the first draft of an early version of **Battle of Angels**, and she, Kazan, and Robert Lewis all tried to interest Clurman in the script. Before the dissolution of the company, Williams harbored hopes that Clurman would stage *Battle of Angels* there. Energized by his newfound acceptance, Williams was already developing early versions of *A Streetcar Named Desire* and began modeling Stanley Kowalski for Group actor Jules (later John) Garfield. In addition, because Crawford, Clurman, and Lee Strasberg, the remaining founding triumvirate, had all been employees there, Williams had an entrée at the Theatre Guild, the powerful commercial New York producing house that eventually mounted *Battle of Angels* (1940), his first professional production. (Theresa Helburn, who, as executive director of the Guild, was the prime mover in its decision to produce *Battle of Angels*, also had a close association with the Group Theatre.)

During its life, the Group Theatre left a stamp on the American stage that endures in the acting, directing, and playwriting the world recognizes as the American style in theater and film of the mid-twentieth century, including, significantly, the works of Williams. Indeed, cultural analysts such as Brenda Murphy conclude that together, Williams and Kazan, along with their frequent designer **Jo Mielziner**, defined the American style of film and theater of the era. The names of Group Theatre members and associates are a roll call of preeminent actors, directors, dramatists, producers, and teachers, many of whom had a profound impact on Williams's plays. Many were trained at the Actors Studio—founded by Group members Crawford, Lewis, and Kazan. Through Kazan and Crawford, then, came access to Actors Studio members like **Marlon Brando, Kim Hunter,** Geraldine Page, **Eli Wallach,** and **Karl Malden** who created indelible stage and film incarnations of Williams characters. Artistically, the Group Theatre was devoted to the theories of Konstantin Stanislavsky (See **Chekhov, Anton**) and the company's actors and directors trained in the Group's own studio. Strasberg eventually became the sole acting instructor and developed what became known as the Method, an acting style renowned for its intensity of emotion and private feeling, its naturalism, its psychological veracity, and its visceral and earthy energy. These characteristics were, not surprisingly, also hallmarks of Williams's seminal works, especially on film, as embodied in the the acting talents of Brando, Malden, Page, and Wallach.

The Group, however, had a political and social agenda, too, and produced plays that were socially conscious without being overtly propagandistic. Members of the Group were of course, famously left wing, even comprising a communist cell for which they were investigated by the House Committee on Un-American Activities during the McCarthy era in the early 1950's. On a less concrete level, therefore, the Group's most enduring influence on Williams, who was certainly hospitable to the ways of serious, socially conscious drama, was his association with its playwrights, especially **Clifford Odets**, who may have been the Group's social conscience. Odets was a model for the young Williams; and his earliest scripts, before he came to New York, bear the unmistakable stamp of the social activist. Years after the Group Theatre had disbanded, Harold Clurman praised Williams and other young writers for sustaining its social concerns. With a change of Williams name and a $100 recognition of his promise in 1939, the Group Theatre lit the fuse that led to the explosion on the world stage five years later of the author of some of the world's most enduring dramas and characters. See also **Politics**.

Further Reading

Clurman, Harold. *The Fervent Years*. New York: Hill and Wang, 1966.

Devlin, Albert J., and Nancy Tischler, eds. *The Selected Letters of Tennessee Williams, Volume 1—1920–1945*. New York: New Directions, 2000.

Gronbeck-Tedesco, John L. "Absence and the Actor's Body: Marlon Brando's Performance in *A Streetcar Named Desire* on Stage and in Film." *Studies in American Drama—1945–Present* 8.2 (1993): 115–126.

Kirby, Michael, ed. "The Group Theatre." (Special issue.) *The Drama Review* 28.4 (Winter 1984).

Smith, Wendy. *Real Life Drama: The Group Theatre and America, 1931–1940*. New York: Grove Weidenfeld, 1990.

Richard E. Kramer

H

Hall, Sir Peter (1930–). Sir Peter Hall, a British theater director, has been a leading interpreter of Williams's works since 1957, when he directed the London premiere of *Camino Real* at the Phoenix Theatre. Two years before, Hall had made his name with the first English-language production of **Samuel Beckett**'s *Waiting for Godot* and with *Camino Real*, and secured his reputation for uncompromising experimentation. In 1958, he followed up this success with the British premiere of *Cat on a Hot Tin Roof* at the Comedy Theatre, though the play had to be produced under club conditions (and not officially open to the public) because public licensing was forbidden by the Lord Chamberlain (whose office was eventually abolished in 1968). By making it private and thus not subject to regular licensing regulations, the theater could get around censorship. Hall has noted that "homosexuality was an unmentionable secret even in the mid-20th century," and so *Cat on a Hot Tin Roof* "had to be preformed in clubs, because the play implied homosexuality might exist."

Hall's engagement with Williams's work was minimal through the 1960s, 1970s, and 1980s, the time he served as artistic director at Britain's two great, publicly funded theater institutions, the Royal Shakespeare Company (1961–1968) and the National Theatre (1971–1988). Hall seems to have felt it inappropriate to pursue his interest in Williams's work while at the helm of these theaters, but since returning to the commercial theater, after leaving the National, he has been responsible for a number of major Williams revivals. His 1988 production of *Orpheus Descending* starred Vanessa Redgrave and proved so successful in London that it transferred to a Broadway run in 1989 and was filmed for television in 1990. This film provides a considerably more faithful rendition of the play than the 1960 movie *The Fugitive Kind* (though it lacks a central presence as charismatic as Marlon Brando's). Hall's production, full of eerie lighting and supernatural portents, adopted a tone of southern Gothic grotesquerie that emphasized the play theatrically rather than attempting to "iron it out" as naturalism.

Yet this extravagance was balanced by real emotional subtlety in the central performances.

Much the same was true of Hall's 1991 London production of *The Rose Tattoo*, featuring Julie Walters, which presented an unsettling mix of minutely observed details and overly theatrical gestures, while surprising audiences with its emphasis on the play's comedic qualities. In 1997, Hall mounted a star-studded revival of *A Streetcar Named Desire* in which **Hollywood** actress Jessica Lange gave a critically acclaimed performance as Blanche. However, Hall's plans to follow this up in 1998 with a West End version of *Cat on a Hot Tin Roof*, in which pop star Madonna would star as Maggie, eventually came to nothing.

Further Reading

King, Kimball. "The Rebirth of *Orpheus Descending*." *The Tennessee Williams Journal* 1.2 (1989–90): 18–30.

Stephen J. Bottoms

Holland, Willard (1908–1963). The director of the **Mummers**, the experimental semiprofessional theater group in **St. Louis**, Willard Holland helped to launch Williams's career. Under Holland's guidance, the Mummers staged the first two full-length Williams's plays—*Candles to the Sun* in March 1937 and *Fugitive Kind* in December of the same year. Holland was immediately attracted to these two Williams plays because of their strong themes of social protest against capitalism, the political agenda that the leftist-leaning Mummers shared with the **Group Theatre**. As **Elia Kazan** would do 10 years later, Holland heavily influenced William's scripts by asking Williams to modify characters and revise the endings of these plays. In fact, Holland even played one of the major roles in *Fugitive Kind*, offering his sympathetic interpretation.

Williams's letters are full of appreciation for Holland's interest in his work, and he confided in the Mummers director about his career plans and ambitions. Williams's friendship with and mentoring by Holland contrasted sharply with the rejection he suffered from Professor **Edward Charles Mabie** at the University of Iowa, where Williams was studying when he first sent a script to Holland. Holland had written to Mabie in support of admitting Williams to the theater program and even sent him notices about the success of the two plays the Mummers produced, but to no avail. Mabie never endorsed Williams and denied him a scholarship when he did enroll. But Holland's commitment to Williams continued when Holland temporarily left the Mummers to work in **Hollywood** as an actor. Yet he was not able to place any of Williams's early plays, including *Spring Storm* and *Not about Nightingales*, as screenplays. In the meantime the Mummers fired and then rehired Holland as a director, but he finally left the theater troupe in 1938 to return to Hollywood and work as a dialogue coach for University Studios and, for a time, was a part of the Pasadena Playhouse.

Though he was unable to help the aspiring Williams outside the theater precincts of St. Louis, Holland nevertheless played a profound role in Williams's career, and the fact that he was instrumental in bringing Williams before a theater audience no doubt assisted Williams in securing **Audrey Wood** as an agent and in winning a Rockefeller grant. See also **Williams, Thomas Lanier, III ("Tennessee")**.

Further Reading

Devlin, Albert J., and Nancy Tischler, eds. *The Selected Letters of Tennessee Williams,*

Volume 1—1920–1945. New York: New Directions, 2000.

Philip C. Kolin

Hollywood. Hollywood had biographical and literary significance for Tennessee Williams. He first visited Hollywood in 1939 with his friend **Jim Parrott**. He stayed in cheap lodgings in the city, then moved on to a potato ranch where he earned his keep shoveling manure. It was good experience, he wrote, if he were ever to return to the West Coast as a writer. Four years later, **Audrey Wood** sold Metro-Goldwyn-Mayer a package of talent that included Williams, designer Lem Ayers, and choreographer Eugene Loring. The then-unknown Williams's salary was $250. Take the money and run, Williams heard day in, day out, in the MGM commissary. Some of the cynics, despite themselves, had learned something from writing screenplays. Less so Williams. Scenario writing was architecture, and this was not Williams's strong suit.

Southern California nonetheless was important to Williams in other ways. He was living frugally; his transportation was a motor scooter, and his home was a small flat in Santa Monica, above a municipal recreational area known as "muscle beach." It was noisy but eye appealing. The desires that beefcake swimmers aroused Williams could satisfy easily; especially in wartime, southern California was a cruiser's paradise. Williams claimed to be lonely at various periods of his life, including his semester in Hollywood. Had the movies been located in New Jersey, or Detroit, or even **St. Louis**, where the gay population was less coherent and less visible, his sense of isolation might have been worse.

MGM had bought Williams's services for seven years, the industry standard. Every six months, however, the studio had the option to cancel a contract, so Williams, at first, was conscientious. Pandro Berman, his supervisor, assigned him a script for Lana Turner. Her recent picture *Slightly Dangerous* had been a moneymaker, and *Marriage Is a Private Affair* (Williams's assignment) was seen as a way to extend her fame. But Williams found the story improbable. Moreover, he found it difficult to write a character, like Turner's, that had no interior life. MGM itself soon lost interest in the project. Louis B. Mayer's empire was a congenial enough place to write, however, and soon Williams was hard at work on a screen adaptation of *The Gentleman Caller* (see **Film Adaptations**; *The Glass Menagerie.*)

Audrey Wood was dubious. She also cautioned Williams to exercise restraint in what he showed and sold to the studio, since the sale could compromise any theatrical potential the work might have. *Gentleman Caller*, as Williams then conceived it, was a long script that, he thought, would work better on screen than stage. He envisioned Teresa Wright as Amanda—a superb choice, as anyone who had seen her luminous as Charlie Newton in Alfred Hitchcock's *Shadow of a Doubt* (1942) could attest. Williams sent the script forward, but MGM declined; Wood must have been relieved.

Soon enough Williams was taking long lunch hours, then days off when he wrote at home or cruised the Palisades for sex. By 1 July MGM supervisor Lillie Messinger had removed him from the Turner project and assigned him to Arthur Freed's administrative unit. Williams thought that he, Loring, and Ayers were going to work with Aaron Copland on a movie short of *Billy the Kid*. Like the Lana Turner project, it too foundered. In early August 1943, MGM laid Williams off. Less than two months later, the studio failed to pick up his option. The pink slip wrote *fini* to his history as a writer-for-hire in Hollywood.

Williams's plays bore little resemblance to mainstream American films in 1945. In fact, one cornerstone of the postwar American theater was its rebellion against Hollywood's devotion to the well-made play. Williams's plays constituted a new theatrical experience; they were delicate fabrics woven of poetic imagery and long speeches, closed-in spaces, and little action. They were, in other words, improbable Hollywood vehicles. By the late 1940s, however, film producers were looking for something different to tear audiences away from their television sets and drive them back into the theaters. Producers like Jerry Wald and Charles K. Feldman chose *The Glass Menagerie* and *A Streetcar Named Desire* not only because they had been Broadway and road-show hits but because their characters were so psychologically rich. Williams was not altogether pleased with the result, but the movie monied producers and their successors helped to make him rich.

Further Reading

Leverich, Lyle. *Tom: The Unknown Tennessee Williams*. New York: Crown, 1995.

Phillips, Gene D. *The Films of Tennessee Williams*. Philadelphia: Arts Alliance, 1980.

Leonard J. Leff

A House Not Meant to Stand. *A House Not Meant to Stand* (1982), Williams's last new play to be produced during his lifetime, is based on *Some Problems for the Moose Lodge*, a one-act that premiered in 1980. *A House Not Meant to Stand (A Gothic Comedy)* was developed twice as a full-length comedy at Chicago's Goodman Theatre—first in their studio theater in April 1981, directed by Gary Tucker, and then the final version under the direction of Andre Ernott in April 1982 on the Goodman's main stage, all produced by the Goodman's artistic director, Gregory Mosher. *A House Not Meant to Stand* is one of the few full-length comedies in the Williams canon and one of two full-length Williams plays written in "real time." During its limited run the play was reasonably well received by a few local critics but was not reviewed outside Chicago.

A House Not Meant to Stand is the story of Cornelius and Bella McCorkle of Pascagoola [*sic*], Mississippi, a late-middle-aged couple who return home one midnight from the Memphis funeral of their older son Chips who was gay and died of a nonspecified illness, probably related to alcoholism. The McCorkles' daughter Joanie has recently been admitted to an insane asylum, and their younger son Charlie, out of work again, is upstairs having sex with his pregnant, born-again Christian girlfriend as the McCorkles enter.

Bella is in mourning for Chips, but it is clear that she has long been in a state of mild confusion; when she can manage to focus on anything, it is her desire for all three of her children to return home to her and be together as the loving family she believes they once were. It is her haze that shields Bella from the constant verbal abuse of her defeated and insensitive husband. Cornelius is trying to find Bella's family inheritance, an enormous amount of cash she had hidden somewhere in their home—the location of which she has, in fact, forgotten. As the play progresses, Cornelius's attempts to find the money are interrupted by a series of eccentric characters whose visits to the McCorkle residence increase the chaos in a house already filled with turmoil. The ghost of their son Chips appears to Bella and tells her the location of the money, after which she slips deeper into her private world until "spirits," representing her three grown children as young children, appear to her, and Bella, having found the moment she so desperately sought, dies.

The set for the McCorkle house is so dilapidated that it is shocking and serves as the
central metaphor for the decay of the characters and the society in which they live. The
extreme condition of the collapsing house is
also a practical device that is used to propel
much of the comedy as well as the pathos—
the narrow concerns of the characters, especially Cornelius, often seem ridiculous in
the context of the unlivable house.

Bella McCorkle is obsessed with a past
long since impossible for her to find, and so
she has retreated into a world of her own.
In spite of her preoccupation with the past
and her lack of a secure grasp on reality,
Bella is a significant variation on the Williams faded Southern Belle, especially in her
disregard for her personal appearance, her
unqualified love for her children, and her
particular sense of grace and modesty. While
there are certain potentially comic elements
to Bella's character, notably her physical
weight, she stands out among the characters
in *A House Not Meant to Stand* as a sympathetic figure. Bella follows an internal
plotline unknown and unseen by the other
characters—the "ghosts" in *A House Not
Meant to Stand* do not belong to the total
world of the play, only Bella's world; they
are parts of Bella's broken heart reassem-
bling itself, finding her a way to ultimately
let go of her sorrow.

Not incidentally named after Williams's
own father, **Cornelius Coffin Williams**, Cornelius is unique among Williams's major
male characters. Obsessed with money and
power far beyond his grasp, Cornelius shows
none of the sexual potency, self-awareness,
or dignity of Stanley Kowalski, Reverend
Shannon, or Big Daddy, respectively. Cornelius is in many ways a fictional interpretation of Williams's own father, and by the
1980s Williams was able to draw his father
as a comic menace rather than the intensely
painful figure he was in life—it is Cornelius's

self-centeredness that provides much of the
play's humor. Cornelius also presents insight
into many of the personal problems Williams faced with the onset of old age, and
the character is as fascinated as he is disturbed by his failing health and the battery
of medications he takes.

In *A House Not Meant to Stand*, Williams
was addressing not only the decay of the
American dream but also his own mortality.
Theatrical elements of *A House Not Meant
to Stand* such as the use of ghosts, camp humor, characters who talk to the audience,
and a lack of any significant realism in the
traditional sense are consistent with many
of his plays that were written, or surfaced,
late in Williams's life such as *Clothes for a
Summer Hotel*; *Vieux Carré*; *Something
Cloudy, Something Clear*; *Will Mr. Merriwether Return from Memphis?*; and *This Is
(An Entertainment)*.

Further Reading

Goodman Theatre. Theater program for *A House
Not Meant to Stand*, Chicago, April 1982.
Williams, Tennessee. *A House Not Meant to
Stand: A Gothic Comedy*. Unpublished
manuscript (typescript with revisions, in
two acts, 102 pp., "April 27, 1982"). Chi-
cago and New York: Goodman Theater
Collection, New Directions Files.

Thomas Keith

Hunter, Kim (1922–2002). Kim Hunter is
best remembered for creating the role of
Stella in the Broadway premiere and Warner
Brothers film of *A Streetcar Named Desire*.
Born Janet Cole, Hunter was a founding
member of Actors Studio. Her first professional role was in the 1939 Miami production of *Penny Wise*, and her screen debut
came in 1943 in *The Seventh Victim*, where
she played an ingenue. But her most memorable and significant role was her sexually
charged portrayal of Stella in *A Streetcar*

Named Desire in 1947, for which she won an Academy Award for Best Supporting Actress for her passionate reprise of the role in the 1951 *A Streetcar Named Desire* film. Hunter was cast for the part of Stella by **Irene Selznick**, the producer for *A Streetcar Named Desire* and like **Marlon Brando**'s Stanley, she left her indelible mark on the role. Director **Elia Kazan** immediately recognized Hunter's talent, and his views about the spine of the character, expressed in his *Notebook on A Streetcar Named Desire*, perfectly fused with Hunter's own interpretation of the role.

Hunter's Stella was a loving, gentle, intensely sexual woman torn between mixed loyalties for her sister and her husband. She exuded innocence, trust, and devotion as Stella, Blanche's younger sister, but also displayed an unswerving passion for reality. Unlike Blanche, Hunter's Stella was able to adjust and adapt to Stanley's sleazy **New Orleans** with its Dionysian frenzy, bars, fights, and music. Hunter's interpretation of Stella's life with Stanley was notable for an almost narcotized acceptance of the wild passion of New Orleans that contrasted with the culture and refinement she had experienced growing up at Belle Reve, the lost DuBois estate. The love scenes Hunter had with Brando's Stanley sizzled with the intense physical pleasure of the couple's relationship—kisses, hugs, love slaps, and sexual roughhousing. Hunter and Brando were in each other's passions at pivotal moments in the script, most notably when Brando falls at her knees at the end of Scene Three as she comes down the stairs from her neighbor Eunice's apartment. The spatial symbolism of Hunter's entrance embodied Stanley's desire to pull Stella down from the Belle Reve columns. Hunter was also able to present Stella's warm domestic earthiness in Scene Four when Blanche finds her in bed after Stanley's lovemaking.

But displaying yet another side of Stella's character, Hunter flashed Stella's anger at Stanley in Scene Eight, Blanche's failed birthday party, because of his cruel behavior. She also captured Stella's profound guilt in the last scene as Blanche is sent to the asylum. Ultimately, Hunter in the Broadway production left audiences absolutely certain of her allegiance to Stanley and their new baby. Hunter's Stella as the nurturing but indolent pregnant wife differed from later interpretations of the role, notably by Beverly D'Angelo who lacked Hunter's combination of innocence and feistiness in the 1984 ABC teleplay of *A Streetcar Named Desire*.

Hunter continued working in film, theater, and television for six decades until her death. Her work in television led to two Emmy nominations. A liberal Democrat and civil rights activist, Hunter herself was blacklisted (unlike Kazan) in the early 1950s, but her career resumed in 1956. She portrayed Dr. Zira in the 1968 film *Planet of the Apes* and continued the role for the sequels in 1970 and 1971.

Further Reading

Kolin, Philip C. *Williams: "A Streetcar Named Desire."* Plays in Production. Cambridge: Cambridge University Press, 2000.

Mary Frances Lux

I

I Can't Imagine Tomorrow. A one-act play of Williams's later period (1961–1983), *I Can't Imagine Tomorrow* was first published in his collection of shorter plays, *Dragon Country* (1970). Much like the other plays in *Dragon Country*, *I Can't Imagine Tomorrow* tends to depart from the very articulate poetic discourses that earned Williams his early reputation in favor of a dramatic form that focused on the silences and gaps in language and undermined orthodox functions of plot and character development. The play deals with the theme of pathological human dependence expressed through a fragmented dialogue that illustrates a symbiotic relationship between the two characters, a woman and a man identified respectively as "One" and "Two."

I Can't Imagine Tomorrow presents a linguistic reality that is rapidly deteriorating toward a silence that the characters both desire and resist, and much like the plays of **Samuel Beckett** or **Harold Pinter**, the dialogue serves to further the action and save the characters from silence rather than to communicate a determinate meaning. At the center of *I Can't Imagine Tomorrow* is the threat of confinement, both literal physical confinement and confinement within the linguistic prison that drives the action with no movement toward rational expression. Characters One and Two repeat the same empty routine together every evening to pass time and to divert their attention away from the fear of silence, death, and change. This routine is the foundation of their relationship, and the characters' situation rapidly approaches a Beckettian world of decay, mutual dependence, repetition, and frustration. The fear of change is so strong in this play that Two, a junior-high school teacher, has been unable to meet his classes for a week. Two's paralyzing fear stems mainly from a pervasive existential dread with no known origin or rational cause other than simply being alive. But when he attempts to see a therapist for his problem he cannot get past the receptionist. Significantly, he can barely complete sentences by himself throughout the play, and it is only One's prompting that furthers the dialogue, as she struggles to resist the eventual breakdown into silence.

While One mentally and emotionally appears to be the stronger of the two characters, physically she is breaking down just as Two is breaking down linguistically. Two is approaching the symbolic silence that will free him from the prison of repetition and language, madness, while One is moving toward the alternative—death. She can no longer eat and can barely climb the stairs by herself. One needs Two for physical survival, just as he needs her for emotional survival, but as she is dying she encourages Two to form new acquaintances, something he is both unable and unwilling to do. *I Can't Imagine Tomorrow* ends with One falling asleep on the landing of the stairs she started to climb as Two remains to comfort her.

Even though communication is breaking down in this play, One still retains the ability and the desire to express herself in language, while Two finds expression difficult, speaking very little and mostly in incomplete sentences. These characters can, therefore, be seen as representing a transition from the desire for logical expression through language in Williams's earlier plays and toward the breakdown of linguistic expression that he sought to represent in his later works. In later plays such as *In the Bar of a Tokyo Hotel* or *The Two-Character Play* Williams used repetition, silence, and incomplete sentences to focus attention on the limitations and performative action of language as opposed to its rational meaning.

Largely ignored by critics until recently, conventional criticism of *I Can't Imagine Tomorrow* has focused primarily on its apparently autobiographical roots, reading the two characters either as a representation of a divided Williams struggling with his own fears of death and isolation or as a reproduction of the relationship between Williams and **Frank Merlo**, his lover of nearly 15 years. Although *I Can't Imagine Tomorrow* is written for a man and a woman, a 1989 production by the Mason Gross School of the Arts (at the Levin Theater in New Bruns-

wick, New Jersey) innovatively endorsed an autobiographical reading by casting two men as One and Two, encouraging audiences to focus on Williams's relationship with Merlo. While an autobiographical reading is feasible, dismissing the play as excessively personal ignores its autonomy as an art form and the crucial linguistic subtleties that Williams explores. As such, *I Can't Imagine Tomorrow* is a pivotal work in Williams's movement from realism to a minimalist, antirealistic exploration of a private world of fear, panic, alienation, and death.

Further Reading

Phillips, Jerold A. "Imagining *I Can't Imagine Tomorrow.*" *Tennessee Williams Review* 3.2 (1982): 27–29.
Saddik, Annette. *The Politics of Reputation: The Critical Reception of Tennessee Williams' Later Plays.* Madison, NJ: Fairleigh Dickinson University Press, 1999.

Annette J. Saddik

Inge, William (1913–1973). A successful American playwright of the 1950s, William Inge wrote for the **St. Louis** *Star Times* when, in late 1944, he met Tennessee Williams who was in St. Louis to visit his mother. Inge interviewed Williams, and they discovered many common interests: they were about the same age, both loved drama, both were ambitious, and they eventually learned each was gay. After seeing *The Glass Menagerie* in Chicago in 1944, Inge confessed his own ambition to write plays, and Williams encouraged him. In fact, Williams played a substantial role in helping Inge launch his own career, which was clearly influenced by Williams's themes and characters, especially his female characters.

Inge grew up in Independence, Kansas in a nervous matriarchy similar to that of Williams's youth. His father was a traveling salesman who drank and philandered while away from home; his mother was a high-strung housewife who drew her son smotheringly close. The young Inge recited pieces at ladies' clubs and performed in school plays and was generally different from most boys. The repressively anxious sexual climate of his home and community probably caused Inge's lifelong concealment of his homosexuality. Unlike Williams, however, Inge never felt free and confident enough to come out of the closet.

Inge graduated from the University of Kansas, later earned an M.A., and then taught at Stephens College in Columbia, Missouri, before moving to St. Louis. Shortly after meeting Williams, Inge resumed teaching at Washington University. Though struggling with alcoholism and depression, he was inspired by *The Glass Menagerie* and wrote *Farther Off from Heaven*, also an autobiographical play, which was produced by Williams's friend **Margo Jones** in Dallas in 1947. Inge also drew on his remembrances of small-town Kansas people and places in *Front Porch*, his second play, which was locally produced in 1948 and would later become *Picnic*. Williams introduced Inge to his agent, **Audrey Wood**, who helped Inge place his next play, *Come Back, Little Sheba*, on Broadway in 1950, earning Inge accolades as the year's "most promising" playwright. Like Williams, Inge created memorable characters, particularly women. Lola in *Come Back, Little Sheba* and Madge in *Picnic* are, like many of Williams's heroines, caught up in destructive romantic illusions. Many observers considered Inge and Williams friendly competitors. While Williams explored his southern roots, Inge drew on his small-town Kansas background in *Picnic*, which won the Pulitzer Prize in 1953, and in *Bus Stop*, produced in 1955. *The Dark at the Top of the Stairs* (1957) was Inge's fourth consecutive successful Broadway play, and he dedicated it to Williams,

who wrote the introduction for the Random House publication of the play. Their friendship cooled, however, because Williams, whose **Camino Real** and **Orpheus Descending** failed at the same time Inge's *Picnic* and *Dark* succeeded, was jealous of Inge's popularity, further enhanced by highly successful film versions of his plays. *Picnic* starred William Holden and Kim Novack in a box office success.

Despite success, happiness eluded Inge, who constantly felt the pressures of writing, concealing his sexuality, and coping with his alcoholism. Like Williams, he entered psychoanalysis but was devastated when his fifth Broadway play, *A Loss of Roses* (1959), became his first failure. Having invested so much of his self-esteem in the success of his work, Inge was poorly prepared for the vicious rejection that often occurs in America's celebrity culture, a viciousness that Williams endured better. Sadly, Inge's sixth New York play *Natural Affection* also failed, and *New Yorker* critic Edith Oliver surely struck a nerve when she claimed that with this play Inge seemed to be trying to be a "junior varsity Tennessee Williams," probably a reference to such powerful Williams scenes as the castration in **Sweet Bird of Youth**.

Inge's career rallied in 1961 when he won an Academy Award for his original screenplay *Splendor in the Grass*, in which he collaborated with **Elia Kazan**, who had also worked closely with Williams. But Inge's unsuccessful attempts on Broadway and in **Hollywood** left him depressed and suicidal. Having lost his stage and screen audiences, Inge published two novels, but they were essentially ignored.

Further Reading

Oliver, Edith. "The Theatre." *The New Yorker* 9 February 1963: 66.

Voss, Ralph F. *A Life of William Inge: The*

Strains of Triumph. Lawrence: University Press of Kansas, 1989.
———. "Tennessee Williams and Williams Inge: Friends, Rivals, Great American Playwrights." *Tennessee Williams Literary Journal* 4 (Fall 1999): 9–19.

Ralph F. Voss

In the Bar of a Tokyo Hotel. Williams's late, one-act play *In the Bar of a Tokyo Hotel* was published and premiered in 1969 during the playwright's "Stoned Age." Sophisticated, experimental, and characterized by fragmented language, this short, avant-garde drama rendered Williams's new perception of reality and his need to escape from dialogue. Herbert Machiz directed the premiere of *In the Bar of a Tokyo Hotel* at New York City's Eastside Playhouse on 11 May 1969 in an ill-fated production starring Anne Meacham as Miriam and Donald Madden as Mark; Jon Lee portrayed the Barman, and Lester Rawlins starred as Leonard. Following the play's opening performances, *Time* magazine, which had been chronically antagonistic to Williams, announced that *In the Bar of a Tokyo Hotel* deserved a coroner's report more than a critical review. After 22 previews and 25 performances, the play closed to a barrage of harsh criticism on 1 June, less than a month after opening. Immediately following this "monumental failure," Williams left New York for Tokyo, accompanied by Meacham, and from Tokyo, he entered Barnes Hospital in **St. Louis** to receive treatment for drug and alcohol addiction. Ten years after *In the Bar of a Tokyo Hotel's* first demise, director Eve Adamson and New York's Jean Cocteau Repertory Theatre at Williams's request tried to revive the play, but the production, which opened on 20 April 1979 and closed by 10 June, was relatively ignored by critics and audiences alike.

Typically described as Williams's dark portrait of an artist, *In the Bar of a Tokyo Hotel* consists of one act divided into two parts. All the action takes place in the small tropical bar of an unnamed Japanese hotel—the play's solitary and sparsely furnished set was a marked departure from Williams's earlier, more elaborate sets. The sparse plot deals with the mental collapse and subsequent death of American artist Mark Conley, a brilliant painter who has "discovered color" and just broken through to "a new style." Gifted yet possessed, Conley has submerged his life into his art, a fate shared by other artists in Williams's works, like Van Gogh in ***Will Mr. Merriwether Return from Memphis?*** and, of course, by Williams himself (see **Art**). Accompanying Mark on his working holiday is Miriam, his tragic, sex-starved wife who occupies rooms—but little else—with her aphasic husband. To satisfy her sexual cravings that Mark no longer meets, Miriam has resorted to sleeping around, and most of the play's action focuses either on her attempt to seduce the barman or on her articulated plans of suicide. All the while, a naked Mark crawls around in his room, smearing paint on a canvas nailed to the floor, perhaps Williams's comment on Jackson Pollock. The only other character is Leonard, Mark's homosexual agent from New York. At Miriam's request, Leonard arrives at the Tokyo hotel so that he may escort Mark back to New York. Miriam's plans, seemingly echoes of Williams's own fears, are to have Mark committed to a mental hospital so that she can salvage what's left of her life. Unexpectedly, Mark dies, leaving Miriam free to go her own way, though at the end of *In the Bar of a Tokyo Hotel* she stands at center stage, frozen in a spotlight, repeating that she has no plans and nowhere to go.

In the Bar of a Tokyo Hotel was irreversibly new for audiences and critics who could not identify with or accept the daring and

Donald Madden and Anne Meacham in *In the Bar of a Tokyo Hotel*, 1969. Springer/Photofest.

highly experimental side of Williams's art. Unlike Williams's early work, which had become collectively a part of the symbolic American imagination, his new play seemed a betrayal and motivated critics to bemoan his artistic decline. Though *In the Bar of a Tokyo Hotel* was abstract and metaphysical, it did signal Williams's new style exploring the emptiness of speech—a style that sharply contrasted with Williams's signature lyricism. Yet he intentionally turned to other dramatic traditions, especially Noh drama stemming from Zen and known for its minimally decorated sets, its anemic plot development, and its frozen "action" poses filled with symbolic meaning. Noh drama, the opposite of Western drama, is typically performed by one or two principal players

whose intentions are philosophically didactic. Identifying these traits, Allean Hale concludes that *In the Bar of a Tokyo Hotel* was simply alien to Western expectations and so evoked criticism rather than informed respect.

In the Bar of a Tokyo Hotel can be read as the metaphor of the artist consumed by his masterpiece. Hale concludes, for example, that the play's experimental dialogue is coded with elusive references to Taoist philosophy and Christian symbols not easily expressed in production, though intriguingly present as physical text. Annette Saddick, on the other hand, sees the truncated lines and fragmented sentences in *In the Bar of a Tokyo Hotel* as a representation of experience itself as fragmented and cyclical. Through the broken lines and syntax in *In the Bar of a Tokyo Hotel*, Williams confronts the elusiveness and existential void of postmodernism. His syntax mirrors the unreliability of language and the obstacles besetting the postmodern subject, abundantly represented in Williams's later career, including **Something Cloudy, Something Clear**. The minimalist dialogue of *In the Bar of a Tokyo Hotel* is also found in **I Can't Imagine Tomorrow, Lifeboat Drill, The Two-Character Play, Now the Cats with Jewelled Claws**, and **Clothes for a Summer Hotel**. In brief, in *In the Bar of a Tokyo Hotel*, Williams questioned the very nature of reality and truth and moved away from the realism and lyrical symbolism of his earlier plays.

In the Bar of a Tokyo Hotel can also be read in light of Williams's own paintings, showing how his experiments on canvas compare with those in the theater. *In the Bar of a Tokyo Hotel*, in fact, becomes a performance of Williams's own painted words and images. Three Williams paintings—*Many Moons Ago, The Faith of Gatsby's Last Summer*, and *On ne peut pas comprendre toujours* in particular—illuminate the similarities between *In the Bar of a Tokyo Hotel*'s performed dialogue and the impressionistic images he painted on canvas.

Further Reading

Hale, Allean. "*In the Bar of a Tokyo Hotel*: Breaking the Code." In *Magical Muse: Millennial Essays on Tennessee Williams*, ed. Ralph F. Voss. Tuscaloosa: University of Alabama Press, 2002. 147–162.

———. "The Secret Script of Tennessee Williams." *Southern Review* 27.2 (1991): 363–376.

Ruckel, Terri Smith. "*Ut Pictura Poesis, Ut Poesis Pictura*: The Painterly Texture of Tennessee Williams's *In the Bar of a Tokyo Hotel*." In *The Undiscovered Country: The Later Plays of Tennessee Williams*, ed. Philip C. Kolin. New York: Lang, 2002. 80–92.

Saddik, Annette. *The Politics of Reputation: The Critical Reception of Tennessee Williams' Later Plays*. Madison, NJ: Fairleigh Dickinson University Press, 1999.

Terri Smith Ruckel

I Rise in Flame, Cried the Phoenix. *I Rise in Flame, Cried the Phoenix*, Tennessee Williams's rarely produced one-act play imagining the death of writer **D.H. Lawrence**, is his tribute to a man whom he greatly admired and, perhaps, even emulated. Lawrence deeply influenced Williams's earliest works, *Battle of Angels* (1940) and its later manifestations, *The Purification* (1941) and **You Touched Me!** (1942; coauthored with **Donald Windham**), but also continued through *A Streetcar Named Desire* (1947) and *Kingdom of Earth (The Seven Descents of Myrtle)* (1968). Though Williams's themes and style may have obscured Lawrence's influence as Williams matured, he frequently cited Lawrence as a kindred spirit important to his development as a writer. In his 1939 correspondence with Frieda Lawrence, the writer's widow, and

Williams's agent, **Audrey Wood**, he discussed plans to write a full-length play about Lawrence's first meeting with Frieda von Richthofen Weekley and end with Lawrence's death. But Williams abandoned the idea of making it a full-length work and settled instead for the one-act play, *I Rise in Flame*, which was published by New Directions in 1951. Williams did not expect the play to be staged, although it has had a modest production history. *I Rise in Flame* is not particularly dramatic; it is more elegy than drama, more reflection than conflict, more poem than dialogue. It is a lyrical chamber piece by an otherwise operatic writer.

As the play begins, a dying Lawrence is seen reclining in a sun porch on the French Riviera under a banner of a phoenix emerging from a nest of flame. He awaits the arrival of a friend, Bertha, who has gone to London at his behest to monitor an exhibition of his paintings. Lawrence's unexpected foray into the fine arts has shocked the British public at the same time his notorious novel *Lady Chatterly's Lover* remains banned. Williams attempts to express both the pain and joy of the artist who knows his work to be groundbreaking and significant but who has yet to succeed in persuading critics and his audience. There is tension between the virginal Bertha, who obviously loves Lawrence, and Lawrence's powerful wife Frieda, who, despite the frictions in their relationship, values the freedom and honestly that has characterized their lives. Prior to Bertha's arrival, Lawrence and Frieda do verbal combat, described by the real Frieda Lawrence in her published note on the play as "the eternal antagonism and attraction between man and woman." Vacillating between harsh insults and loving gestures, Lawrence and Frieda ruminate on their relationship, its connection to his literary accomplishment, and the nature of death. He also reflects on his life as an artist and as a man loving but showing mastery over a woman. Lawrence insists that he wants no one with him at the moment of his imminent death. When he is suddenly gripped by a hemorrhage, he springs from the sun porch as the conflicted Frieda restrains Bertha from going to his assistance. As the curtain falls, Lawrence cries out for Frieda, who rushes to his side. But Lawrence, the phoenix/artist, will rise again through his works.

I Rise in Flame, Cried the Phoenix explores themes of sexuality and the human body central to Williams's work, and, like Lawrence, he strove to unravel the inherent contradictions between the spiritual and the terrestrial, the soul and the flesh, and the imaginary and the real. For Williams, Lawrence felt the "mystery and power of sex" that met resistance from a prudish society, a struggle he himself faced. Thus in *I Rise in Flame, Cried the Phoenix*, Williams examines a writer whose work had thematic connection with his own, especially one who challenges the expectations and perceptions of his audience. *I Rise in Flame, Cried the Phoenix* has as much to say about Williams's creative frustrations as about Lawrence's. In his introductory note to the play, Williams describes Lawrence's work as "probably the greatest modern monument to the dark roots of creation," an apt assessment of Williams's canon as well.

I Rise in Flame, Cried the Phoenix was first produced on 14 April 1959 at New York's Theatre de Lys as part of the ANTA Matinee Theatre Series. Directed by Tom Brennan, the production featured Alfred Ryder (Lawrence), Viveca Lindfors (Frieda), and Nan Martin (Bertha). It received respectful reviews, and Ryder again played Lawrence (with Jo Van Fleet as Frieda) in a February 1961 television production on PBS's *Play of the Week* series, along with four other Williams one-act plays. *I Rise in Flame, Cried the Phoenix* had its first British production at London's Basement Theatre on 2 April 1971, and an operatic version by Thomas J. Flannigan, Jr., originally composed in 1959, was produced at New York's Golden Fleece on 7 February 1980.

Further Reading

Debusscher, Gilbert. "Creative Rewriting: European and American Influences on the Drama of Tennessee Williams." In *The Cambridge Companion to Tennessee Williams*, ed. Matthew C. Roudané. Cambridge: Cambridge University Press, 1997. 167–188.

Dorff, Linda. "Collapsing Resurrection Mythologies: Theatrical Discourses of Fire and Ash in *Clothes for a Summer Hotel*." In *Tennessee Williams: A Casebook*, ed. Robert F. Gross. New York: Routledge, 2002. 153–172.

Tischler, Nancy M. *Tennessee Williams: Rebellious Puritan*. New York: Citadel Press, 1961.

James Fisher

J

Jones, Margaret (Margo) Virginia (1911–1955). Margo Jones was a major theater innovator whose dedication to new plays, regional repertory theater, and theater-in-the-round exerted profound influence on the reception of Williams's work and American theater in general. With Tennessee Williams she shared a southern upbringing, an extensive appreciation for European art and culture, and a commitment to the Little Theatre Movement. Both tried to get Broadway theater to embrace the experimentation in a broader range of literary and theater styles.

Jones's first contact with Williams came in 1943 through **Audrey Wood**, the playwright's agent, from whom Jones had asked for some promising scripts. Among those that Wood sent were Williams's *The Purification*, a one-act play written in verse, and *You Touched Me!*, which he coauthored with **Donald Windham**, based on a short story with the same title by **D.H. Lawrence**. Williams and Jones communicated about *You Touched Me!* during the spring of 1943, while the playwright was working for MGM and Jones was at the Pasadena Playhouse; they also conferred about *The Purification*

and *The Gentleman Caller*, which eventually became *The Glass Menagerie*. In late summer of the same year, *You Touched Me!* opened at the Cleveland Playhouse. Frederick McConnell succeeded Jones because he disapproved of Jones's more generative approach to staging. When Williams and Wood saw the production in Cleveland, he expressed his debt to Jones's aggressive perseverance and artistic skill. The play then opened at the Pasadena Playhouse on 29 November. In both Cleveland and Pasadena, *You Touched Me!* received enthusiastic reviews that provided encouragement for the production of *The Purification*, which opened at the Pasadena Playhouse in July 1944 under Jones's direction. Both plays gave audiences an introduction to and insight into Williams's stylistic and thematic range.

As Jones was nearing her long-standing goal of establishing a regional theater in Dallas, **Eddie Dowling** asked her to be the assistant director for *The Glass Menagerie*. Williams had prevailed on Dowling to hire Jones. Moreover, Dowling's decision to play Tom Wingfield required another director with an intimate knowledge of the playwright's intentions to supplement his own. Jones cast Anthony Ross in the role of Williams's Gentleman Caller, Jim O'Connor, and helped to shape his poignant scene with Julie Haydon (Laura). She opposed George Jean Nathan (Haydon's partner) and Eddie Dowling, both of whom wanted the *Glass Menagerie* to include a clownish drunk scene, and thus agreed with Williams on the inappropriateness of the change in his script. The success of Williams's play gave Jones more directorial opportunities on Broadway before returning to Dallas to establish her own theater.

Jones's credibility and artistic stature through her association with Williams's plays culminated in the opening of her Theatre '47, the first of several incarnations (the names changing with the year) of her Dallas regional theater project. Jones claimed it as the first professional arena theater in the country, which she later described in her book *Theatre-in-the-Round* (1951). Her first season included William Inge's first play, *Further Off from Heaven* (later to become *Dark at the Top of the Stairs*) and Williams's **Summer and Smoke**, which Jones became intent upon moving to Broadway, where it opened on 6 October 1948. Williams's play garnered strong recommendations from theatre critics Brooks Atkinson and Joseph Wood Krutch, whose support proved prophetic, but the reviews were mixed. After the initial failure of Jones's production, her friendship with Williams seemed to cool, but in 1954, in her own Theatre '54, Jones again directed Williams's *The Purification* in a double bill with Jean Giraudoux's *The Apollo of Bellac*.

The Purification was to be Jones's last production of a Williams play. She died accidentally in Dallas on 24 July 1955. Her Dallas theater, which began partially on the strength of her connection to Williams, closed in 1959. Between 1947 and 1955, roughly 70 percent of the plays Jones produced were world premieres. In addition to her influence on the early career of Williams, Inge, and other important American playwrights, Jones's legacy includes the establishment of regional theaters and advocacy of theater-in-the-round productions. See also **Twenty-seven Wagons Full of Cotton and Other One-Act Plays**.

Further Reading

Hewitt, Barnard. *Theatre USA, 1668–1957*. New York: McGraw-Hill, 1959.

Jones, Margo. *Theatre-in-the-Round*. New York: Rinehart, 1951.

Sheehy, Helen. *Margo: The Life and Theatre of Margo Jones*. Dallas: Southern Methodist University Press, 1989.

Tischler, Nancy M. *Tennessee Williams: Rebellious Puritan*. New York: Citadel Press, 1961.

John Gronbeck-Tedesco

Journals. The journals of Tennessee Williams span the years 1936 to 1981, the period a few weeks before Williams's twenty-fifth birthday to almost two years before his death at age 71 in February 1983. Unlike his **correspondence**, where he modulated his tone and style to suit the recipient, the journals reveal Williams's authentic voice—genuine and unadorned—writing to himself about himself. The journal entries are relatively consistent in their continuity but do include a 21-year gap, from 1958 to 1979.

In the numerous, unremarkable-looking notebooks, Williams recorded his daily thoughts and emotions. Much of his writing is casual, spontaneous, and at times confessional. The entries, ranging from a few sentences to several pages, cover his early apprenticeship as he finished college and set out on his own to **New Orleans**, the West Coast, New York, and **Key West**. After his success with *The Glass Menagerie* and *A Streetcar Named Desire*, Williams gained financial freedom and traveled extensively in the late 1940s and the 1950s, spending summers in places like Rome and Barcelona. On these travels he was rarely without a journal, and he recorded his daily life and relationships with individuals such as his lover **Frank Merlo** and friend **Paul Bowles**.

The journals provide rare insights into Williams's voice and how it changed over the decades. He begins the journals with a voice that is innocent, earnest, and at times melodramatic. For example, he contemplates suicide but decides to go swimming at the country club instead. He records his health, often colored with hypochondria, and he reveals his fears of social inadequacy, anxiety, loneliness, constant restlessness, and panicky feelings of extinction. After he leaves home, his instinct for survival, his growing sphere of experience, his sexual indoctrination, shape this innocent voice into one that is harder, savvier, more worldly. By the end of the journals, Williams, depleted by an addiction to drugs and alcohol and debilitated by the lack of success of his late plays, is tired, discouraged, and morose. In his last journal entry he wonders: "where do I [go] from here?"

The journals offer clues, especially in the early years, about Williams's creative apprenticeship. He comments on poets and writers he admires: **Hart Crane**—"the biggest of them all"; **Chekhov**—"above all the prose writers"; **D.H. Lawrence**—"I read from his letters and conceived a strong impulse to write a play about him"; August Strindberg—"his unfailing fire to strike out profiles of life"; **Faulkner**—"by distortion, by outrageous exaggeration he seems to get an effect closer to reality"; Tom Wolfe—*You Can't Go Home Again* has the "stamp of genius on it"; Emily Dickinson—"love her"; and perhaps, most surprisingly, Hem-

ingway, whose "great quality, aside from his prose style, is this fearless expression of brute nature."

In these early years, Williams refers to manuscripts he is working on, stories about popular subjects such as gangsters, melodramatic tales with dying heroines, and sophomoric tales of sexual awakenings. He writes "This Spring" similar in style and theme to **Saroyan**'s remarkable "The Daring Young Man on the Flying Trapeze." He looks at Grant Wood's painting *American Gothic* and writes a play of the same name from the perspective of the expressionless couple whom he depicts as the parents of a bank-robbing son, a Clyde Barrow figure. Influenced by Crane's poetry, he attempts a modernist poem, "Middlewest."

The journals significantly document the moment Williams began to understand his own voice. He speaks in the spring of 1939 about wanting to write a play that would be more autobiographical, simple, and direct, but it would not be long before he began working on *The Glass Menagerie*. The annotations in the journals shed light on the constant reworking of several variants of a manuscript that would evolve into *The Glass Menagerie*. Williams began the short story "Portrait of a Girl in Glass" in February 1941 and over the next two years worked on several plays and stories including, "The Spinning Song," "A Daughter of the American Revolution," and "Blue Roses and the Polar Star." Williams would borrow pieces of each of these for *The Glass Menagerie*. In May 1943, he then began a play, *The Gentleman Caller*, based on "Portrait of a Girl in Glass," attempted a number of endings, and returned to his short story for a brief period before turning back to the play that would emerge as *The Glass Menagerie*. The process of shifting scenes, borrowing bits from one piece for another, returning to the short story as the basis for a play, illustrate the nonlinear way in which he worked and revised.

The journals also give glimpses into what Williams chose from his life and fitted with twists and turns into his fiction. Echoes of situations and sentiments he experiences are found in his fiction. Sometimes the distance between an experience or contact and appropriation spanned decades. For example, as a college student, Williams wrote about feeling embarrassed when a girl's pocketbook is stolen. In his short story "Two on a Party," written over a decade later, Williams's character Billy experiences the same feelings of guilt when Cora loses her diamond earrings. Many of the people Williams mentions appear either as characters or as names in his work—Kroger, Hatcher, Gallaway, Kramer, O'Connor, Mitchell, Jelkes, Trinket—the list goes on.

No figure would appear more in his writing than his sister Rose. And the journals reveal the strong bond between Williams and Rose, who was just 16 months older and who suffered from schizophrenia. The journals record the last year she remained at home before being committed to institutions where she would spend the rest of her life. Williams's concerns about his sister appear randomly in his journals. Unable to save her, he turns to his writing and mentions several manuscripts based on Rose, such as "The Spinning Song" and "The Four Leaf Clover."

Of the dreams Williams records in his journals, none are more revealing than those about his sister. He dreams about missing a bus that his sister is on. He manages to stop the bus, but the case containing his manuscripts is not on it. He dreams of seeing his sister in a cream-colored dress, and then discovers he is wearing the same dress. He tries to sit down between two tables, but they are wedged so tightly together that he cannot breathe. In another account, he dreams of being entertained by a wealthy old lady who reads his journal and has her maid put it in the incinerator from where he has to rescue it twice.

The journals also reveal that despite the tremendous success of his work, Williams began to doubt his artistic abilities. In the early 1950s, he confesses to having serious difficulty writing. Exhausted, he recognized the need to rest, but addicted, he knew he could not face one day without the few hours of escape work provided. He struggled with his dilemma, admitting that he could not "recover any nervous stability" until he was able to "work freely again" and that he could not work freely until he recovered a nervous stability.

By the mid-1950s, Williams's journal had begun to diminish, in part because of his dependence on alcohol and drugs. The journals record his progressive addiction, which begins as early as 1936 when he is drinking so much coffee that he experiences heart palpitations. In order to sleep he needs to take sleeping pills. By 1957 he records having consumed, in one day, six mixed drinks, including two scotches and one daiquiri, six glasses of wine, two Seconals, and two other tranquilizers. The journals stop in September 1958, and in the second-to-last entry, Williams describes himself as feeling "like death."

Williams resumes his journal in late spring 1979 in a journal titled "Mes Cahiers Noirs," written in a style that is part confessional and part evaluative. Whether journals for this 21-year gap will eventually surface is unclear. In 1962 Williams wrote to a friend that he abandoned the practice of keeping a journal in the 1950s. In "Mes Cahiers Noirs," which is more of a reflective essay than a record of daily activity, Williams looks back over the past decades and reevaluates his relationships with various friends and business associates, and he ponders the causes of his demise as an artist.

The journals were Williams's companion and last refuge, and he understood that they captured an illusive quality of life. He would return to them from time to time. They talked to him in a comforting way, for, as he noted, "the past gets lost so completely." See also **Drugs;** *The Glass Menagerie.*

Further Reading

Devlin, Albert J., and Nancy Tischler, eds. *The Selected Letters of Tennessee Williams, Volume 1—1920–1945.* New York: New Directions, 2000.

Margaret Bradham Thornton

K

Kazan, Elia (1909–2003). Born Elias Kazanjoglou, Elia Kazan, Williams's most important director, was involved with the productions and even development of many Williams plays, including the Broadway premiere of *A Streetcar Named Desire* in 1947. When Williams entered *American Blues* in the **Group Theatre**'s new-play contest in 1938, however, Kazan, known to his colleagues as "Gadge" or "Gadget," was already a full-fledged member of the company. His wife, **Molly Day Thacher**, was the Group's playreader and oversaw the contest that first brought Williams to the Group and New York. Over his career, Kazan directed six Williams plays (*A Streetcar Named Desire*; *Camino Real*, 1953; *Cat on a Hot Tin Roof*, 1955; *Orpheus Descending*, 1957; *Sweet Bird of Youth*, 1959; *Period of Adjustment*, 1960) and two films (*A Streetcar Named Desire*, 1951; *Baby Doll*, 1956). Brenda Murphy even argues that Kazan was Williams's collaborator, especially on *Cat on a Hot Tin Roof*, though not all Williams scholars agree with this assertion.

Kazan began as a member of the Group's acting company, appearing in a several plays by **Clifford Odets**, including *Waiting for Lefty*. He began directing, applying the Group's techniques as he had learned them as an actor from Stella Adler, Robert Lewis, and Lee Strasberg and went on to become one of the most successful and influential U.S. directors of mid-twentieth-century stage and film, though he rarely directed after 1964. After the Group disbanded in 1941, Kazan, Cheryl Crawford, and Lewis founded the Actors Studio (1947) in order to perpetuate the theatrical style of the Group. This cradle of the American Method style of naturalistic acting, based on the teachings of Konstantin Stanislavsky, the father of modern Western acting, produced many actors who appeared brilliantly in stage and film productions of Williams's works: **Marlon Brando**, Ben Gazzara, **Eli Wallach, Maureen Stapleton, Kim Hunter**, Mildred Dunnock, **Karl Malden**, and Geraldine Page.

Impressed with Kazan's direction of **Arthur Miller**'s *All My Sons* earlier in 1947, Williams had asked producer **Irene Selznick** to hire him to direct *A Streetcar Named Desire*. Williams's agent, **Audrey Wood**, whose husband and partner, William Liebling, rep-

Elia Kazan, right, directing Karl Malden and Vivien Leigh in the film version of *A Streetcar Named Desire*, 1951. Springer/Photofest.

resented Kazan, recounts that Kazan was reluctant to take the job, turning it down at first. In rehearsals for *A Streetcar Named Desire*, Williams was generally passive, responding to Kazan's suggestions and requests with the necessary, minor changes but otherwise only observing. In his "Notebook for *A Streetcar Named Desire*," sections of which have been published in various volumes, Kazan recorded his work on the play and his thoughts and questions during the rehearsals. The notebook, which was not intended for public consumption, reveals the director's private probing to understand and realize *A Streetcar Named Desire* and his analysis of the characters' lives—their spines—both before and during the events of the play.

Kazan's influence was sweeping. With Williams, he selected the producers and made casting decisions, but beginning with *The Rose Tattoo*, Williams also sent Kazan early drafts of his scripts for the director's responses and suggestions. From that point until the association dissolved, Kazan collaborated with Williams not only in staging but in developing the texts themselves. Kazan exerted his influence on how the play would be shaped with respect to his own vision of its meaning. He also incorporated his own theatrical influences, which included film, Stanislavsky, and Russian avant-garde directors Vsevolod Meyerhold and Evgeny Vakhtangov. Kazan's suggestions were detailed and extensive, though he did not write any of the words in the scripts—Williams was unquestionably the sole author of the prose. The plays were nonetheless collaborative efforts, and their successes were the responsibility of Kazan as much as of Williams himself. Kazan believed that the director should bring out the personality and intentions of the writer more strongly and plainly than is revealed in the script. He brought Williams's dramas to life on the stage—and later on film. It is notable, for instance, that both *A Streetcar Named Desire* and *Cat on a Hot Tin Roof* won Pulitzer Prizes, a literary award for the plays' texts, and recognitions like the New York Drama Critics' Circle Award (*Cat on a Hot Tin Roof* was also nominated for a Tony), given for production as much as writing.

Kazan was renowned for creating highly emotional, intense, and naturalistic productions in keeping with his understanding of Stanislavskian acting and the Method followed by the Actors Studio. But he also added the nonrealistic elements in *A Streetcar Named Desire* and *Camino Real*, although these were readily apparent in Williams's pre-Kazan scripts such as *The Glass Menagerie* and *Summer and Smoke*. Kazan, credited with the vibrant sexuality in his productions, also found in Williams an abundant supply or creativity to work with. Kazan's unique talent, though, was judgment of acting talent and his ability to direct actors. The emblematic performances of so many of the actors in the Williams plays and films Kazan directed—Brando, Kim Hunter, **Jessica Tandy**, Geraldine Page, Eli Wallach, Burl Ives, Mildred Dunnock, Paul Newman, Carroll Baker, Maureen Stapleton—were as much due to the director's astute casting and sensitive individual coaching as Williams's

writing. (Kazan's *A Streetcar Named Desire* film, for example, won performing Oscars for three of its cast members.)

Critics like Arthur Knight argued that Kazan humanized Williams's characters so that audiences accepted them more readily than they would have the harsher, less forgivable portraits Williams had originally composed, among others, Stanley in *A Streetcar Named Desire*, Chance in *Sweet Bird of Youth*, or Big Daddy in *Cat on a Hot Tin Roof*. Kazan also removed some of Williams's characteristic antisocial zest. Brando's signature performance in *A Streetcar Named Desire*, both on stage and in the film, for instance, is often said to have been skewed by Kazan in Stanley's favor, softening his brutality and making him a more appealing figure to audiences than Williams intended, and thus taking the sympathy away from Blanche. The changes Williams made in his first version of *Cat on a Hot Tin Roof* at Kazan's insistence—bringing Big Daddy back into the play in the third act, making Maggie a more appealing character, and changing the end of act three so that the sexually troubled Brick decides to return to his wife's bed—altered or obscured the play's original meaning, though such change unquestionably generated a commercial Broadway, and later cinematic, hit. Murphy asserts that some critics labeled Kazan's influence the intrusion of commercial standards into the artistic realm, while others chastised Williams for compromising his own intentions.

The collaboration between Williams and Kazan was immensely productive; however, it was just as fraught with tension and suspicion. Though Kazan directed several more Williams plays afterward, the relationship began to deteriorate seriously during the rehearsals of *Cat on a Hot Tin Roof*. Williams had begun to resent Kazan's intrusions and increasingly resisted his recommendations, believing that Kazan was forcing him to make unwanted adjustments. Williams continued to esteem Kazan—he still spoke admiringly of the director years later—and credited him with the successes of many of his plays, but the trust diminished, and, ultimately, Williams was unwilling to fight the constant duel for control. After *Period of Adjustment*, the astonishingly productive and successful 13-year collaboration between Williams, one of America's greatest playwrights, and Kazan, one of the theater's most talented directors, dissolved. Beyond the success of individual productions, however, Williams, Kazan, and **Jo Mielziner**, who designed several Williams-Kazan productions (*A Streetcar Named Desire*, *Cat on a Hot Tin Roof*, *Sweet Bird of Youth*, and *Period of Adjustment*), defined the American style of theater in the 1950s. Kazan's papers have been given to Wesleyan University.

Further Reading

Hewes, Henry. "The Boundaries of Tennessee." *Saturday Review* 29 December 1956: 23–24.

Jones, David Richard. "Elia Kazan and *A Streetcar Named Desire*: A Director at Work." In *Great Directors at Work: Stanislavsky, Brecht, Kazan, Brook*. Berkeley: University of California Press, 1986. 138–199.

Kazan, Elia. *Elia Kazan: A Life*. New York: Knopf, 1988.

———. "Notebook for *A Streetcar Named Desire*." In *Twentieth-Century Interpretations of "A Streetcar Named Desire": A Collection of Critical Essays*, ed. Jordan Y. Miller. Englewood Cliffs, NJ: Prentice-Hall, 1971.

Knight, Arthur. "SR Goes to the Movies: The Williams-Kazan Axis." *Saturday Review* 29 December 1956: 22–23.

Murphy, Brenda. *Tennessee Williams and Elia Kazan: A Collaboration in the Theatre*. Cambridge: Cambridge University Press, 1992.

Pauly, Thomas H. *An American Odyssey: Elia Kazan and American Culture*. Philadelphia: Temple University Press, 1983.

Richard E. Kramer

Keathley, George (1925–). George Keathley directed plays by Tennessee Williams at each of the major theaters with which he was associated as producer or artistic director. In 1950 he founded the Studio M Playhouse in a remodeled garage in Coral Gables, Florida. Among the hundred or so plays he produced and directed during his six years there was the world premiere of **Sweet Bird of Youth**. Keathley had asked his friend Williams for a new play to premiere, and Williams gave him the one-act *The Enemy: Time*, which had been written in 1952 but not produced. During rehearsals, Williams began frantically revising, inundating director and cast with new pages every day, with the result that a full-length *Sweet Bird of Youth* opened at Keathley's playhouse on 16 April 1956.

The first of Keathley's four major productions of **The Glass Menagerie** starred Helen Hayes, who was the driving force behind the creation of the Theatre Guild American Repertory Company that would take three American plays on a State Department–sponsored 15-week tour of Europe and the Middle East, followed by a 13-week Latin American tour. Keathley later directed the 20th anniversary production of *The Glass Menagerie* at the Paper Mill Playhouse in Milburn, New Jersey, and moved to the Brooks Atkinson theatre on Broadway on 4 May 1965. **Maureen Stapleton** (Amanda), Piper Laurie (Laura), George Grizzard (Tom), and Pat Hingle (Gentleman Caller) earned the respect of critics who had seen the memorable original production, while Keathley's direction was praised for its sensitivity, perceptiveness, and honest comic values. The cast gave a command performance at the White House. Later in the run,

Jo Van Fleet replaced Stapleton, Farley Granger replaced Grizzard, Hal Holbrook replaced Pat Hingle, and Carol Rossen replaced Piper Laurie. Keathley again directed *The Glass Menagerie* in 1987 at Missouri Repertory Theatre, Kansas City, where Ann Hillary played Amanda.

At Chicago's Ivanhoe Theatre from 1968 to 1980, Keathley staged the premiere of *Out Cry* (opened 8 July 1971), the first revision of *The Two-Character Play* under the new title. Keathley's strong direction was instrumental in emphasizing the dramatic through-line of the multilayered action, as well as helping Williams through a difficult time in his personal life. Keathley's staging of *The Rose Tattoo* at the Ivanhoe starred Rita Moreno (who also starred in *West Side Story*), who won the Jefferson Award for Best Artist. In 1978, Keathley directed *The Night of the Iguana* at the Goodman Theatre in Chicago in a cast that featured Barbara Rush and Ruth Roman.

Other Tennessee Williams plays that Keathley directed include *A Streetcar Named Desire*, starring Julie Harris, and at Missouri Repertory Theatre in 1996, and *Cat on a Hot Tin Roof* with Marco Barricelli as Brick and Kenneth Albers as Big Daddy in 1996.

Further Reading

Hayman, Ronald. *Tennessee Williams: Everyone Else Is an Audience.* New Haven, CT: Yale University Press, 1993.
Wood, Audrey, with Max Wilk. *Represented by Audrey Wood.* Garden City, NY: Doubleday, 1981.

Felicia Hardison Londré

Key West. The last and most southern of the Florida Keys, Key West was one of Williams's haunts for over 40 years and listed as his official residence from 1950 when he purchased a house, and later added a swimming pool in the backyard, on Duncan Street. Visiting Key West in February 1941 to recuperate from cataract surgery, Williams was immediately enchanted with the Key, calling it the "most fantastic" place in America, even "more colorful" than **New Orleans**. He first stayed at the Trade Winds, owned by Cora Black, the mother of Williams's longtime friend **Marion Black Vaccaro**. An avid swimmer and beachcomber, Williams found the social/sexual and literary climate of Key West stimulating and inspiring. He frequented local trysting places such as Sloppy Joe's Bar and the Starlight Gambling Casino that attracted the ubiquitously randy sailors and soldiers, whom Williams zestfully pursued, as did the local B girls.

In addition to its nightlife, Key West had a vibrant reputation as a writer's and artists' colony. Hemingway worked on his novels in Key West in the 1930s, and Williams even met one of his wives there, as well as James Leo Hertiley, who wrote *Midnight Cowboy*, and philosopher John Dewey. In fact, it became the most conducive spot for Williams to write; he finished *A Streetcar Named Desire* at La Concha Hotel. Williams also painted in Key West (see **Art**). Over the years he (and his lover **Frank Merlo**) entertained a chorus of celebrities, artists, family members (Williams frequently brought his grandfather to Key West), theater people (**Sir Peter Hall** and his wife and director Frank Corsaro) at their home on Duncan Street. Sadly, in early April 1979, Williams was the victim of a mugging in Key West.

Though Key West itself did not play the role New Orleans had in Williams's work, he did use its landscapes—literal and metaphoric—to create Cacaloony Key, Florida, "the Southernmost" Key in *The Gnädiges Fräulein* (1966). In this play, part of the *Slapstick Tragedy*, the docks, the pelicans in their search for fish prey, Molly's battered rooming house, and the bizarre character of Indian Joe surely must have reminded Williams of Key West sights and sounds. Interestingly enough, the film adaptation of *The Rose Tattoo*, ostensibly set on the Mississippi Gulf Coast between Mobile and New Orleans, was filmed on Duncan Street in Key West.

Key West is also the home of the Key West Theatre Festival where several of Williams's play received their world premiere, including *Will Mr. Merriwether Return from Memphis?*

Further Reading

Bellavance-Johnson, Marsha. *Tennessee Williams in Key West and Miami*. Ketchum, ID: The Computer Lab, 1989.

Leavitt, Richard Freeman. *The World of Tennessee Williams*. New York: Putnam, 1978.

Leverich, Lyle. *Tom: The Unknown Tennessee Williams*. New York: Crown, 1995.

Williams, Tennessee. "Homage to Key West." In *Where I Live: Selected Essays*, ed. Christine R. Day and Bob Woods. New York: New Directions, 1978.

Philip C. Kolin

Kiernan, Kip (1918–1944). Born Bernard Dubowsky, Kip Kiernan was Williams's first great love, whom he met through his friend Joseph Hazan during the summer of 1940 in Provincetown, Cape Cod, when he was preparing *Battle of Angels* for production. Hazan studied with Kiernan at the School of American Ballet in New York, and on first seeing the young man, Williams was immediately struck by his dancer's body. Kip was also an artist's model. A Canadian alien, Kiernan changed his name from Dubowsky to escape the draft.

Williams's love affair with Kip was intensely personal but short-lived, pulsing from mid-June through mid-August 1940. Williams shared a house with Kip and Hazan on Captain Jack's Wharf and graphically described his sexual exhilaration with Kip in his *Memoirs*, journals, and letters to such gay friends as **Donald Windham**. A bisexual, Kip had met a girl who convinced him that if he stayed any longer in a homoerotic relationship, he would turn into a homosexual. Williams was devastated when the relationship suddenly ended and in a bitter letter "bequeath[ed] to Kip the female vagina" (Devlin and Tischler 369). Williams saw Kip several times after their breakup, once in June 1941 to watch him dance the role of Saturn in "The Golden Fleece, an Alchemistic Fantasy," with music by Alex North, the composer who would write the **music** for *A Streetcar Named Desire*, and then again shortly before Kip's death of a brain tumor in 1944.

Some 40 years later, in 1981, Williams used the events of that summer of 1940 to create *Something Cloudy, Something Clear*, premiering at the Jean Cocteau Repertory Company in New York, where Kip (and his fictitious sister Clare) became central characters in Williams's postmodern memory play. Examining those events from this distance, Williams fused past and present, compressing time and space. But an older Williams (called August in *Something Cloudy, Something Clear*) pays the price for his memories. Williams portrays himself as reveling in the more brutal side of his sexual nature; and any lyrical rapport between Kip and August has vanished. Kip is memorialized as a "saintly Nijinskyesque icon . . . [who] wears virginal white and tirelessly rehearses" his dance routines on the beach and emerges as "spiritually wounded" from the affair (Rich C3). Williams transmuted experience to preserve Kip as angelic. He thus blends into Laura in *The Glass Menagerie* and ultimately into **Rose**, Williams's sister. Kip's (c)overt presence in the Williams canon demands comparison with the many young, innocent men who flicker brightly but fade too soon—Allan Grey in *A Street-*

car Named Desire, Skipper in *Cat on a Hot Tin Roof*, and Haley in *Small Craft Warnings*.

Further Reading

Devlin, Albert J., and Nancy Tischler, eds. *The Selected Letters of Tennessee Williams, Volume 1—1920–1945*. New York: New Directions, 2000.

Kolin, Philip. "*Something Cloudy, Something Clear*: Tennessee Williams's Postmodern Memory Play." *Journal of Dramatic Theory and Criticism* 12 (Spring 1998): 35–56.

Leverich, Lyle. *Tom: The Unknown Tennessee Williams*. New York: Crown, 1995.

Rich, Frank. "Memories Distilled." *New York Times* 11 September 1981: C3.

Philip C. Kolin

Kingdom of Earth (The Seven Descents of Myrtle). The *Kingdom of Earth* (1968) is the only work by Williams in which a person of color—Chicken Ravenstock—plays a major role (see **Race**). The only other two characters on stage are the transvestite Lot, Chicken's white half brother, and a floozy Myrtle whom Lot marries and brings back to the Delta plantation to disinherit Chicken. *Kingdom of Earth* has often been seen as a parody of Williams's earlier work where Chicken is judged as a muddled hybrid of either Orpheus or Stanley Kowalski. *Kingdom of Earth* has also been seen as an exploration of Williams's own homosexuality through the character of Lot or of his "nostalgia" for the lost southern heritage (see **Southern Culture and Literature**). *Kingdom of Earth* belongs to the collection of Williams's Delta plays, like **Battle of Angels**, **Orpheus Descending**, *Baby Doll*, and *Cat on a Hot Tin Roof*. It symbolizes local landmarks—towns, casinos, the Great River—and captures the struggles of the resident against nature and the tyranny of prejudice and parochialism.

Williams first conceived the idea behind *Kingdom of Earth* from a short story included in both *Hard Candy* and *The Knightly Quest* (see **Collected Stories**). He converted his short story into a one-act play, which was published in the February 1967 issue of *Esquire*. By March 1968, he had expanded this one-act play into a seven-act version titled *The Seven Descents of Myrtle*, which enjoyed a brief run on Broadway. The title refers to the structured fate of the only woman character on stage in the play. Williams continued to revise the play and then renamed it *Kingdom of Earth* before it was published by New Directions in 1968. His most significant revision was to change Chicken's racial identity from Cherokee Indian to "mixed" African descent.

As *Kingdom of Earth* opens, Chicken's white neighbors insist he should abandon his home as the floodwaters of the Mississippi rise. Chicken is determined to survive this flood, but later that night, a sick and vengeful Lot arrives with his new wife, Myrtle, whom he met and married on a TV show. Chicken informs Myrtle that Lot is dying from tuberculosis and has married her only to cheat him out of his inheritance. After Mr. Ravenstock's death, Lot's mother forced Chicken to leave rather than have him associated with her son. After her death, when Lot became ill and discovered that he couldn't run the farm, he convinced Chicken to return. Lot signed a document to the effect that Chicken would inherit the farm after his death as long as he took care of things. Now, the dying Lot married Myrtle to disinherit Chicken. As Lot's physical condition disintegrates, he retires from the gilted parlor to his mother's bedroom and begins to slowly put on her clothes. When Lot sends Myrtle down to get Chicken drunk and reclaim this "deed," Chicken convinces her that Lot will never be able to save her from the impending flood and he is her only chance to survive. Realizing that she has more in common with the sexual Chicken than the effeminate Lot, she performs fellatio on Chicken, who informs her of his colored blood. At first disgusted, Myrtle decides to stay while Lot, in full women's attire, goes to Miss Lottie's parlor before dying. As the play ends, Myrtle and Chicken discuss the possibility of their having children before the action is interrupted by the flood.

Chicken has been harshly judged as the ravisher of culture and art by several critics. Both Adler and Kalson reject the sexual in *Kingdom of Earth* as a sterile and cynical, a definite turn from sex as a "saving grace" in other of Williams's plays. Londré regards *Kingdom of Earth* as a dichotomy of flesh and spirit, while Phillips sees it as a confrontation between Lot's cold rationalism and Chicken's destructive sexuality. Judith Thompson, however, sees *Kingdom of Earth* as the affirmation of the natural world—regardless of its corruption—over the romantic. Kolin interrogates the postcolonial aspects of *Kingdom of Earth*, including the destabilization of the southern economy and the racial stereotypes it is founded upon. As the "Other," the outsider, and vulgar, Chicken is nonetheless the ironic savior Myrtle has been waiting for. His sexual victory might represent the emergence of a new "breed" of man, as Kolin maintains.

Myrtle's character is judged in light of her maternal nature, her role as wife to both Lot and Chicken, and her sexuality. Most critics agree that her maternity leads her to marry the childlike Lot, while her sexuality and desire for survival draw her to Chicken. Through her act of fellatio on Chicken, Myrtle can be viewed as either a submissive victim or the mother of a new race of color-liberated men. Her symbolic name, suggesting both fertility and artistic immortality, points to a much more laudatory role

for her than most critics in the past have been willing to concede.

Lot has most often been seen as sick and treacherous. He is a tubercular transvestite who dresses in his mother's clothes and plays the Southern aristocrat in her parlor. He is not above lying and cheating to disinherit his half brother Chicken. Derounian, in fact, points to Lot as a parody of impotent aestheticism. In several ways, Lot's morbid connection to his deceased mother looks back to the power of the dead mother in **O'Neill**'s *Desire under the Elms*. Yet Michael Schiavi reads Lot in light of "effeminancy presentational credibility" (106) and on "integrated subjecthood that far transcends lazy or periodic writing" (109).

Kingdom of Earth is rich in religious and sexual symbolism. Thompson points out the obvious biblical parallels to Noah and the Flood, Lot's disobedient wife, and the promise of inheriting the kingdom. The farmhouse itself is one of the most obvious symbolic elements, separating the two racial spheres: Lot reigns in his parlor of gentility, while Chicken controls the shadowy, alienated realm of the kitchen. The floodwaters can be viewed as bringing death or rebirth to the Delta which itself has been interpreted as either a wasteland or a new world.

Ultimately, *Kingdom of Earth* has been labeled as a flawed play. Kalson and Derounian stamp it as an artistic failure. Phillips, however, judges it as a work of imagination and intensity. Chicken's status in the play poses a big problem. As Kolin points out, the audience is asked a most perplexing set of questions: Should he be viewed as a savior or a beast, a sexual deviant or the progenitor of a new race? The ending of the play is just as problematic. Kalson sees it as offering a false optimism for a future engendered by Chicken and Myrtle, while Kolin prizes it as the affirmation of a new "de-colonialized" future. Beyond dispute, though, *Kingdom of*

Earth provides insight into Williams's liberal racial attitudes and further established him as a political commentator on the sociopolitical history of the South.

Kolin offers the fullest history of *Kingdom of Earth* in production. The New York premiere opened at the Ethel Barrymore Theatre and ran only for 29 performances, with José Quintero directing Harry Guardino as Chicken, Estelle Parsons as Myrtle, and Brian Bedford as Lot. Critics objected to the "unrealized" script, the lack of direction, the faulty staging, and Guardino's "fake" tan and command of grammar in the role of an uneducated outcast. The London premiere at the New Vic (1978) starred another white actor, Peter Postlethwaite, as Chicken who was also criticized for his difficulty in conveying a "Deep South accent" and his "bronzed farmhand" appearance. A 1991 production by the Boston Post Road Stage, directed by James Luse, cast a Hispanic actor—Ramiro Carrillo—in the role of Chicken. **Gore Vidal** wrote the screenplay for *Last of the Mobile Hot Shots*, which was directed by Sidney Lumet and starred Robert Hooks as Chicken, Lynn Redgrave as Myrtle, and James Coburn as Job (Lot).

Further Reading

Adler, Thomas P. "Two Plays for Puritans." *Tennessee Williams Newsletter* 1.1 (Spring 1979): 5–7.

Derounian, Kathryn Zabelle. " 'The Kingdom of Earth' and *Kingdom of Earth (The Seven Descents of Myrtle)*: Tennessee Williams's Parody." *University of Mississippi Studies in English* 4 (1983): 150–158.

Kalson, Albert E. "Tennessee Williams' *Kingdom of Earth*: A Sterile Promontory." *Drama and Theatre* [Purdue University] 8 (Winter 1969–1970): 90–93.

Kolin, Philip. "Sleeping with Caliban: The Politics of Race in Tennessee Williams's *Kingdom of Earth.*" *Studies in American Drama, 1945–Present* 8.2 (1993): 140–162.

Londré, Felicia Hardison. *Tennessee Williams.* New York: Ungar, 1979.

Phillips, Jerrold A. "*Kingdom of Earth*: Some Approaches." In *Tennessee Williams: A Tribute*, ed. Jac Tharpe. Jackson: University Press of Mississippi, 1977. 349–353.

Schiavi, Michael R. "Effeminacy in the *Kingdom*: Tennessee Williams and Stunted Spectatorship." *Tennessee Williams Annual Review* 2 (1999): 99–113.

Thompson, Judith J. *Tennessee Williams' Plays: Memory, Myth, and Symbol.* Rev. ed. New York: Lang, 2002.

Tuma, Mirko. "Williams Revision Opens at McCarter." *News Tribune* [Woodbridge, NJ] 4 March 1975.

Deana Holifield

Kirche, Kutchen, und Kinder (1979) (German for "Church, Kitchen, and Children") is Tennessee Williams's 1979 fragmentary and metadramatic experimental play in which he created outrageous metaphors and symbols of the mind for the stage. Not yet published (a typescript is found at Morris Library of the University of Delaware), *Kirche, Kutchen, und Kinder* was produced Off-Off-Broadway as a work-in-progress by the Jean Cocteau Repertory at the Bouwerie Lane Theatre from September 1979 through January 1980 and directed by Eve Adamson, one of Williams's favorite directors. Its subtitle, "An Outrage for the Stage," suggests that this bawdy farce—a collage of biographical and literary references—is best seen as a postmodern travesty of modern dramas such as Ibsen's *Nora*, Peter Handke's *Offending the Audience*, or Allen Ayckbourn's *Living Together*. Williams also borrowed freely from Artaud's "Theatre of Cruelty" and **Samuel Beckett**. As a contemporary commentary on the gay movement, *Kirche, Kutchen, und Kinder* can be seen as an animated cartoon full of blasphemous clichés and parodies of the Holy American Family, based on Williams's homoerotic life. *Kirche, Kutchen, und Kinder* with its egregious overacting, can also profitably be seen in light of queer theory.

The central character is the Man, a "voluntarily" retired male prostitute in tight pants, gaudy T-shirts, and a studded belt who "though he can still manage to do somersaults, [but] pretends to be confined to a wheelchair." He is writing his memoirs in the Kirche, a secluded room where a young spinster, Miss Rose (with echoes of Williams's sister **Rose**), enters periodically to accompany his soliloquies on the organ. His wife, the Woman, is a pert, frumpy, axe-swinging hausfrau who spends most of her time in the Kutchen cooking crullers and speaks with a Katzenjammer dialect. The Kinder—their children, an adolescent boy and girl dressed in kiddy clothes—have left kindergarten after 15 years and are taught by the Man to become hustlers. But his lessons fail since the Kinder give up their virginity for true love instead of for money, as the Man instructed them not to do. The grotesque bestiary of *Kirche, Kutchen, und Kinder* is completed by the Woman's father, a Dickensian villain and Lutheran minister who is abnormally tall, wears a stovepipe hat and a vampirelike coat, and carries an oversized Bible and an umbrella to hit his daughter. He also uses the umbrella to rape (on stage!) a 99-year-old hag, Fraülein Haussmitzenschlogger (originally played by drag actor Harris Berlinsky).

The church (Kirche), supposedly located in Manhattan's Soho district, is the play's principal *mise-en-scène*, a symbolic refuge for both body and soul. This space, dominated by a surrealistic-looking pipe organ, is alternatively a compartment for the psyche, a "chambered nautilus," a "sanctuary" for private thoughts and fantasies dedicated to Priapus, and a practical arena for interior monologues about the harmful effects of time (symbolized by an artificial giant daisy that grows on stage). As if satirizing his own renowned expressionistic devices and scenery in his plays of the 1940s, Williams frames the Kirche with three walls, each painted in a different primary color matching each of the protagonist's varying moods. Lights flash and a huge daisy moves, reflecting the psychic disturbances of the characters, most notably the Man who defends himself by rushing to his wheelchair whenever light flashes to preserve his reclusive existence and to avoid sexual relations with his wife. All in all, *Kirche, Kutchen, und Kinder* seems a grim self-parody of Williams's romantic comedy *Period of Adjustment* as well as an attempt to satirize those sacrosanct norms and values of the American establishment from which he was estranged.

With heavy irony, Williams intended the alliterative title to suggest the "Katzenjammer" cartoon, where an ill-bred and sloppy housewife speaks a German American dialect. The actual, original German phrase, "kinder, küche, kirche," was used to define a woman's role in society (e.g., praying in church, cooking in the kitchen, and raising children), totally denying her liberation from these matriarchal roles. **Gore Vidal** comments on Williams's (often faulty) use of German phrases throughout his work for sarcasm, for example, Estelle Hohengarten in *The Rose Tattoo* (inspired by his **Mummers** colleague, Albert Hohengarten), the "Lorelei" steamer from *Not about Nightingales*, or grammatically incorrect sentences as "Ich kommen!" in "Das Wasser ist kalt." Though Williams's German may have been off, his satiric thrust in *Kirche, Kutchen und Kinder* seemed to be right on target, skewering what is artificial and mercenary in America.

Further Reading

Dorff, Linda. "Theatricalist Cartoons: Tennessee Williams's Late, 'Outrageous' Plays." *Tennessee Williams Annual Review* 2 (1999): 13–33.

Thomas Molzahn

Kramer, Hazel (1913–1951). Hazel Kramer was Tennessee Williams's closest and best friend in his teenage years after his sister **Rose** and the only woman to whom, at the age of 18, he proposed marriage. He christened her the "love of his life" during this formative period of his life. The red-headed Hazel lived a block away from the Williamses in **St. Louis** with her grandparents, Emil J. and Emma Kramer, and her mother Florence, a flashy divorcée. Like **Edwina Dakin Williams**, Florence was a possessive mother but not nearly as inhibited socially. Emil Kramer worked at the International Shoe Company, along with **Cornelius Williams**, but he held a much higher position. The Kramers were also more prominent in St Louis social circles than were the Williamses.

Hazel and Tennessee went steady, going to dances, river cruises on the Mississippi, and to movies, his passion. They had many friends in common, most notably Esmeralda Mayes, to whom Williams also confided his heart. Williams regarded Hazel almost as a sister and grew even closer to her when Rose left St. Louis in 1925 for Vicksburg. Though Williams's relationship with Hazel was close emotionally, it was not sexually. When she rejected his offer of marriage, he was crushed, but her grandparents and the Williamses were delighted, each family thinking that their offspring was too good for the other. Moreover, Edwina disapproved of

Hazel's mother, while Cornelius rebuked his son's courting behavior, branding it as weak and sentimental. Williams was to write some juvenilia over his loss of Hazel, including the poem "Madrigal," lamenting that she went out of his life with the spring, and in a 1937 poem, "Letter to an Old Love," Hazel in fact scurries away "on graceful feet."

Hazel Kramer was not Williams's only girlfriend. He dated several others and was serious about Bette Reitz, who dumped him for a more masculine type. But Hazel's importance as a female confidante and an early lost love may be reflected in the heartbreaks so many Williams men suffer—Mitch in *A Streetcar Named Desire* or Chance Wayne in *Sweet Bird of Youth*.

Further Reading

Leverich, Lyle. *Tom: The Unknown Tennessee Williams*. New York: Crown, 1995.

Philip C. Kolin

Kubie, Lawrence (1896–1973). Among the first American-trained psychoanalysts, Lawrence Kubie was one of the profession's leading spokesmen and well-known practitioners when Williams came to him for treatment in 1957. Kubie's clientele included some of the era's most famous and glamorous figures, including **William Inge**, Moss Hart, Laura Z. Hobson, and Charles Jackson. Inge, Hart, and Jackson were homosexuals, and treating gay men was one of Kubie's specialties. In 1942, as a member of the National Research Council's Committee on Neuropsychiatry working for the U.S. Department of Defense, Kubie formulated the regulation that defined and identified homosexuals for purposes of excluding them from military service. It's most unlikely that Kubie's gay clients were aware of this, although some of them no doubt sought him out in order to be "cured."

Although Kubie held prominent positions in psychiatric circles (he was the long-term president of the New York Psychoanalytic Society beginning in 1939), he was an unorthodox and an independent thinker. He was one of the first to call for the audio and, later, video recording of psychiatric sessions and, toward the end of his career, for the complete overhaul of the sequence of psychiatric and psychoanalytic training. A prolific writer, he published hundreds of articles, including several on the nature of creativity. During World War II, he was instrumental in rescuing hundreds of European psychoanalysts and seeing that they found housing and employment in America.

Unlike conventional analysts who rarely comment on their patient's remarks, Kubie was known to voice his opinions in his sessions. Williams, who found Kubie's personality to be overbearing and intimidating, wrote his mother **Edwina** that Kubie had accused him of writing cheap melodramas. According to Williams, Kubie urged him to give up homosexuality and writing (at least for a time). While Williams did neither, he did temporarily move out of the New York townhouse he shared with **Frank Merlo** and into his own apartment.

Williams wrote *Suddenly Last Summer* while seeing Kubie in 1957 and 1958. The character of Dr. Cukrowicz, a neurosurgeon who performs lobotomies, may well have been inspired by Kubie, who, unusual for psychoanalysts of the time, was deeply interested in neurosurgery and the role of the temporal cortex in memory and personality. Cukrowicz's nickname is "Dr. Sugar," and it is this character, Dr. Sugar/Kubie, whom Catharine hopes will save her from the lobotomy demanded by her Aunt Violet.

Williams offered several reasons for breaking off his analysis with Kubie after a year. Among them were Kubie's fearsome personality, which, Williams said, reminded him too much of his late father **Cornelius**; the expense of five sessions a week; and the impossibility of taking him seriously after he suggested Williams give up writing and homosexuality.

Further Reading

Brody, Eugene B. "Symbol and Neurosis: Selected Papers of Lawrence S. Kubie." *Psychological Issues* 11.4 (1978): 1–40.

Glover, Edward. "In Honor of Lawrence Kubie." Special issue of *Journal of Nervous and Mental Disease* 149.1 (1969): 5–18.

Paller, Michael. "The Couch and Tennessee." *Tennessee Williams Annual Review* 3 (2000): 37–55.

Michael Paller

L

Langner, Lawrence (1890–1962). Lawrence Langner, who founded the Theatre Guild, produced with Theresa Helburn Williams's *Battle of Angels* on 30 December 1940 in Boston to a full house, but the play was unsuccessful, and the run closed early and disastrously. But Williams's association with Langner and the Theatre Guild continued, in his memory if nowhere else, with Langner's unflattering appearance in *Something Cloudy, Something Clear* in 1981 under the pseudonym of Maurice Fiddler.

Langner was a naturalized citizen who emigrated from South Wales to New York in the early 1900s. Drawing a handsome income from his career in patent law, Langner had the funds and the contacts necessary to form the Washington Square Players, which evolved into the Theatre Guild in 1919, and it was to this group that Williams's agent, **Audrey Wood**, brought *Battle of Angels*. Enjoying a reputation as a founder of art theater, Langner searched for writers who had artistic genius, and he saw that in Williams's work. In 1940, the Theatre Guild agreed to stage *Battle of Angels*, and Langner became powerfully involved in Williams's life. Lang-

ner's influence is documented in Williams's correspondence to him. By June of that year, their relationship was close enough for Langner to invite Williams to use a small house on his property in Weston, Connecticut, to revise his script. Langner also offered Williams help on editing *Battle of Angels*, introductions to stars, and essential financial backing.

Battle of Angels was scheduled to open in New Haven in December, but the premiere was moved to Boston, which was a fateful mistake, since both the language and conflating religious and sexual imagery infuriated staid Boston audiences. The Boston theater critics made sure *Battle of Angels* had a short run because of its unconventional staging, bold subject matter, and unsuccessful use of props. Langner stopped the production and gave Williams a $100 advance on possible future royalties, telling him to rewrite the script. Williams's revision, however, was judged even more harshly by Langner, which angered Williams and contributed to his determination to succeed with this play 17 years later in the production of *Orpheus Descending*.

Nonetheless, Langner provided Williams with his first, painful lesson on the cruel realities of commercial play production. The sacrifice of art for the sake of commercial success never suited Williams, who had the last word by portraying Langner as the manipulative, controlling, and ruthless producer, Maurice Fiddler.

Further Reading

Adamson, Eve. Introduction to *Something Cloudy, Something Clear* by Tennessee Williams. New York: New Directions, 1996.

Devlin, Albert J., and Nancy Tischler, eds. *The Selected Letters of Tennessee Williams, Volume 1—1920–1945*. New York: New Directions, 2000.

Leverich, Lyle. *Tom: The Unknown Tennessee Williams*. New York: Crown, 1995.

Williams, Tennessee. *Memoirs*. Garden City, NY: Doubleday, 1976.

Jean Rhodes

Laughlin, James (1914–1997). Founder of New Directions Publishing, which was Williams's publisher, James Laughlin was born in Pittsburgh, an heir to the Jones & Laughlin steel fortune. Laughlin was a student at Harvard in 1935 when he took a leave of absence and went to Paris to work for Gertrude Stein. Later that year he went to Rapollo, Italy, to study poetry with Ezra Pound, who dismissed Laughlin's desire to be a poet and suggested that Laughlin become a publisher instead.

In 1936 Laughlin started New Directions, which went on to be the most successful independent American publishing house of its size in the twentieth century. With a strong belief in modernist and avant-garde writers as well as a passion for American writing, Laughlin became the publisher (often the first or only American publisher) for Apollinaire, Djuna Barnes, Bei Dao, Borges, **Paul Bowles, Brecht**, Kay Boyle, Camus, Céline, Creeley, Cocteau, Corso, Robert Duncan, Shusaku Endo, Ferlinghetti, **Lorca**, Hawkes, Hesse, Isherwood, Alfred Jarry, Joyce, Kafka, Denise Levertov, Henry Miller, Thomas Merton, Michaux, **Mishima**, Nabakov, Neruda, Kenneth Patchen, Octavio Paz, Ezra Pound, Kenneth Rexroth, Rilke, Rimbaud, Sartre, Delmore Schwartz, W.G. Sebald, Dylan Thomas, Vittorini, Nathanael West, Tennessee Williams, and William Carlos Williams, among dozens of others. New Directions also brought back into print neglected classics by Sherwood Anderson, F. Scott Fitzgerald, E.M. Forster, **William Faulkner**, Henry Green, **William Saroyan**, Muriel Spark, and Robert Penn Warren.

As it turned out, Pound's assessment of Laughlin's poetry was premature—Laughlin kept writing for 60 years and became a talented and critically acclaimed poet in his own right, producing over a dozen books of poetry and memoirs.

As a publisher Laughlin was always on the lookout for new and unknown talent, and when he met the young Tennessee Williams at a party thrown by Lincoln Kirsten in New York in 1942, the two men had an instant rapport—they shared a passion for the poetry of **Hart Crane**—which turned into a friendship that lasted for 40 years until Williams's death in 1983. Williams promptly sent Laughlin a group of poems that New Directions published as part of an anthology, *Five Young American Poets, 1944*. New Directions then brought out Williams's first book, a special edition of *Battle of Angels*, and then a volume of Williams's early one-acts, *Twenty-seven Wagons Full of Cotton*. After fulfilling an obligation to Random House, which published the first edition of *The Glass Menagerie*, Williams declared his loyalty to Laughlin in letters to Random House editor **Bennett Cerf** and Williams's agent **Audrey Wood**, and that loyalty never waned. Laughlin in turn never wavered in his loyalty to Williams, and New Directions eventually published over 50 Williams titles, nearly all of his plays, poetry (see **Poems**), fiction, and **correspondence**.

Laughlin attended the premiere of every major Williams play from *The Glass Menagerie* to *Clothes for a Summer Hotel* and kept up with Williams's theatrical life over those years, no matter how well or poorly Williams's work was being critically received. Williams agreed with Laughlin that New Directions should publish reading editions, not performance scripts, of Williams's plays. Laughlin appreciated and supported Williams's propensity for rewrites, sometimes years after the publication of a play, and so instead of only publishing scripts of initial performances, Laughlin encouraged Williams to make the alterations, adding or deleting material, to his plays until he felt they had taken the form he wanted published for posterity. This led to corrections in the published versions of most of the full-length Williams plays, as well as the publication of two endings for *Cat On a Hot Tin Roof*, a somewhat different version of the same play published in the 1970s, the different editions of *The Two-Character Play* and its evolution into the play *Out Cry*, as well as editions of *The Milk Train Doesn't Stop Here Anymore*, *Kingdom of Earth*, *The Red Devil Battery Sign*, and *Clothes for a Summer Hotel* wherein Williams was able to include material he felt was essential to the completeness of the respective plays that had been removed during rehearsals, often due to the constraints of commercial theater.

By the 1950s the in-house editing of Williams's work was done by Laughlin's trusted office manager and senior editor Robert MacGregor. Frederick L. Martin took over for MacGregor for a few years after MacGregor's death in 1974, and since 1976,

Peggy L. Fox has been Tennessee Williams's editor at New Directions.

As long as he lived, Laughlin was involved in every aspect of publishing Williams's works, from jacket designs to editorial decisions. Outside of Williams's unique relationships with director Elia Kazan, producer Cheryl Crawford, and agent Audrey Wood, Laughlin was the only mentor Williams looked to for serious and personal criticism of his writing. They kept up a correspondence over the course of their 40-year friendship that reveals their mutual respect and shared love of poetry. Laughlin was a champion of Williams's poetry and, year after year, coaxed, exhorted, and encouraged Williams to keep writing poetry along with the plays. For Williams, who saw himself as poet first and playwright second, this was loyalty and support for which he was always grateful. A month before his death Williams wrote a tribute for a National Arts Club ceremony honoring Laughlin in which he hailed their personal friendship and professional relationship as the most enduring of his life.

Further Reading

Fox, Peggy, and Thomas Keith. *Tennessee Williams and James Laughlin: Selected Letters.* New York: W.W. Norton, forthcoming.

Gussow, Mel. "James Laughlin, Publisher with Bold Tastes, Dies at 83." *New York Times* 14 November 1997: D19.

Thomas Keith

Lawrence, D.H. (1885–1930). D[avid] H[erbert] Lawrence and Frieda Lawrence (1879–1956) figure prominently in Williams's work. He had a lifelong admiration for D.H. Lawrence's writing that he frequently expressed in his plays and in his short stories. Williams acknowledged Lawrence, along with **Anton Chekhov**, as one of the most important influences on his writing. Among Lawrence's must influential works was his highly autobiographical novel *Sons and Lovers*, published in 1913, not long before Lawrence met Frieda von Richthofen Weekley. Their relationship was passionate and turbulent, supplying Lawrence with considerable inspiration for his writings, including the novel *The Rainbow* (1915), with its controversially frank sexuality and liberal use of four-letter words. Lawrence's experience connected with Williams's, whose plays were similarly steeped in representations of sexuality previously unseen in American drama.

Lawrence's death in 1930 precluded any meeting with Williams, although he later became acquainted with Frieda after writing to her in 1938 to praise her husband's writing and to point out the broad similarities between his life and Lawrence's. As a nomadic and restless writer, Williams seemed to be seeking validation from Frieda as Lawrence's surrogate. He visited Frieda at her home in Taos, New Mexico, where he was taken ill and hospitalized for abdominal surgery. When Williams recovered, Frieda drove him to her mountain ranch and offered him a small piece of her property on which to build a house, but Williams did not accept the offer.

The similarities between Lawrence and Williams in their lives and in their work elucidate Williams's art. Despite their ill health as children and domineering mothers, Lawrence and Williams were sexually repressed in their formative years and had early relationships with virginal childhood sweethearts. Each worked for a time in stifling factory conditions before finding themselves as artists. Both explored sexuality (the erotic and the sensual), the conflict between reality and imagination (often expressed symbolically), and the life of the flesh (realized in the passions of well-drawn women characters) and the realm of the spiritual. Both writers met with resistance from bourgeois values and fought against accepted literary traditions. Despite having profound insecurities about their gifts as writers, Lawrence, like his student Williams, persevered through personal and professional obstacles. As Williams biographer Lyle Leverich described it, he was attracted to Lawrence's view of the "sensual as spiritual" and his image of the liberated spirit of the artist.

Lawrence enters the Williams canon in several ways. In 1939, Williams dedicated his poem "Cried the Fox" to Lawrence's memory, as he did with his early play *Battle of Angels* (1941), writing that Lawrence was a "flame that fought and prevailed over darkness." Williams mocked his own mother's horrified reaction to Lawrence's novels when, in *The Glass Menagerie*, Amanda Wingfield (Edwina Dakin Williams) condemned "that insane Mr. Lawrence" in front of her son, the aspiring writer Tom Wingfield, Williams's dramatic alter ego. Williams's one-act play, *The Case of the Crushed Petunias* (1941), was inspired, in part, by Lawrence's story "The Fox." Williams and **Donald Windham's *You Touched Me!*** is also based on a Lawrence short story. Williams's most direct paeon to Lawrence's indomitable spirit is his lyrical one-act play ***I Rise in Flame, Cried the Phoenix*** (1941), depicting the last moments of Lawrence's life, an idea Williams may have been interested in for years. In fact, Williams had initially planned a full-length play about Lawrence, tentatively titled *The Long Affair*, opening with Lawrence's first meeting with Frieda and ending, as the one-act does, with Lawrence's death. Williams occasionally returned to this project but eventually abandoned the idea of making it a full-length play, settling instead for the one-act *I Rise in Flame, Cried the Phoenix*. Especially important, many Lawrentian men are prototypes for such sensual, animalistic Williams characters as Stanley in *A Streetcar*

Named Desire, Vaccaro in *Baby Doll*, and Chicken Ravenstock in *Kingdom of Earth*, thus inscribing and enshrining Lawrence's views in some of Williams's most notable works.

Further Reading

Burgess, Anthony. *Flame into Being: The Life and Work of D.H. Lawrence*. New York: Morrow, 1985.

Devlin, Albert J., and Nancy Tischler, eds. *The Selected Letters of Tennessee Williams, Volume 1—1920–1945*. New York: New Directions, 2000.

Dorff, Linda. "Collapsing Resurrection Mythologies: Theatricalist Discourses of Fire and Ash in *Clothes for a Summer Hotel*." In *Tennessee Williams: A Casebook*, ed. Robert F. Gross. New York: Routledge, 2002. 153–172.

Fedder, Norman. *The Influence of D.H. Lawrence on Tennessee Williams*. The Hague: Mouton, 1966.

Fernihough, Anne, ed. *The Cambridge Companion to D.H. Lawrence*. New York: Cambridge University Press, 2001.

———. *D.H. Lawrence: Aesthetics and Ideology*. New York: Oxford University Press, 2001.

Leverich, Lyle. *Tom: The Unknown Tennessee Williams*. New York: Crown, 1995.

Tischler, Nancy. *Tennessee Williams: Rebellious Puritan*. New York: Citadel Press, 1961.

James Fisher

Leigh, Vivien (1913–1967). Vivien Leigh was a British actress whose international reputation is based on her film roles as two famous fictional females, each representing a version of the southern woman: Scarlett O'Hara and Blanche DuBois. Leigh, at the time an unknown in **Hollywood**, landed the coveted role of Scarlett in *Gone with the Wind* (1939) despite fierce competition from a score of Hollywood leading ladies. Replacing **Jessica Tandy** as Blanche in the film of *A Streetcar Named Desire* (1951), Leigh was the only actor who had not starred in the original 1947 Broadway production. However, she was playing Blanche in the London premiere of *A Streetcar Named Desire*, directed by her husband Laurence Olivier, when the film was being cast. Leigh was chosen over Tandy because producers believed that her work in *Gone with the Wind* would help to insure *A Streetcar Named Desire*'s box-office success, and with a salary of $100,000, she became the highest-paid British screen actor of the time. Leigh earned Oscars for both film roles, a remarkable feat considering that poor health limited her to fewer than 20 films throughout her entire career.

Leigh brought a delicate fragility to the role of Blanche but combined it with an undercurrent of wild sexuality that brought out the beast in **Marlon Brando**'s animalistic Stanley. Costume designer Lucinda Ballard dressed Leigh in frilly, dated clothes that emphasized Blanche's advancing age and her failure to keep pace with the changing times. Leigh's British refinement clashed with Brando's coarseness onscreen and off, and the two used their differences to fuel the conflict between the genteel Southern Belle and the working-class king. Leigh's talent relied upon a thoughtful perfectionism, and director **Elia Kazan** saw in her a greater determination to succeed than he had ever seen in any other actress. However, the ways she created character were out of sync with the Method training of the other actors, so Kazan was forced to redirect the strained, even artificial mannerisms that she had attributed to Blanche under Olivier's direction. As rehearsals for the film proceeded, a more complex Blanche emerged as Leigh adopted a more naturalistic and psychological acting style. Her earlier portrayal of Scarlett O'Hara contributed to the success of this performance as well, for audiences were already convinced that she typified the Southern Belle.

Playing Blanche was an extremely demanding part both physically and mentally, and it took an immense toll on her; Leigh claimed that the role pushed her over the edge into madness, and in the years immediately following *A Streetcar Named Desire*, her mental health deteriorated, and she underwent several hospitalizations and electroshock therapy.

In one of her final films, she once again played a tormented Williams heroine, the title character in ***The Roman Spring of Mrs. Stone*** (1961). Based on Williams's 1950 novella and costarring Warren Beatty, the film tells the story of Karen Stone, a lonely widow who travels to Rome and becomes involved with a young gigolo. It was the first film for director José Quintero, who had directed several of Williams's plays on stage. Pale painted backdrops of the famed city and a stylized apartment setting done in frosty blue were used effectively to suggest the emotional frigidity and the isolation of Mrs. Stone. As Leigh's Karen returns to life, however, the sets become more beige and brown; even Leigh's blonde wig takes on the warmer tones of the changed surroundings as her character softens under the influence of physical pleasure. In this film, Leigh's refinement and her remarkable but now fading beauty combine to embody the paradox of the proper widow drifting into a sordid relationship with the handsome gigolo who despises her. While not as frantic or as fragile as her Blanche, Leigh's depiction of Williams's heroine nonetheless conveys the life of quiet desperation reminiscent of his other characters, such as Alma Winemiller from ***Summer and Smoke***. Williams claimed that *The Roman Spring of Mrs. Stone* was his favorite of the many film adaptations of his work, and he considered it a fine example of both Leigh's and Quintero's talents.

Further Reading

Kolin, Philip. "Olivier to Williams: An Introduction." *Missouri Review* 13.3 (1991): 143–57.

———. *Williams: "A Streetcar Named Desire."* Plays in Production. Cambridge: Cambridge University Press, 2000.

Molt, Cynthia Marylee. *Vivien Leigh: A Bio-bibliography*. Westport, CT: Greenwood, 1992.

Walker, Alexander. *Vivien: The Life of Vivien Leigh*. New York: Weidenfeld and Nicolson, 1987.

Jacqueline O'Connor

Lifeboat Drill (1979). *Lifeboat Drill* is Williams's one-act black comedy about two octogenarians, Mr. and Mrs. E. Long Taske, who repeatedly miss lifeboat drills and even their destination while sailing on board the *Queen Elizabeth II*. Premiering on 12 December 1979 at the New York Ensemble Theatre's "Invitational," an evening of one-act plays, *Lifeboat Drill* starred John Wardell and B. Constance Barry. A more recent production, hilariously staged, starred Dick Cavett. Though the New York reviewers quickly dismissed this play as farce, slapstick, or plain vaudeville, *Lifeboat Drill* fits generically with Williams's **Now the Cats with Jewelled Claws** and the **Frosted Glass Coffin** (another play about geriatric fears and tempers) as absurdist dramas similar to **Samuel Beckett**'s *Happy Days* and Eugene Ionesco's *The Chairs*.

Suffering from almost every malady of old age, the Taskes appear in their first-class stateroom sitting next to each other in twin beds. Dressed in flannel pajamas over which are their unfastened lifejackets, they try to communicate with each other but fail miserably. Everywhere "meaning is off," which explains both the subject and the style of this "tragicomedy," as Williams labeled *Lifeboat Drill*. Mr. Taske is the inept, henpecked husband, and she is a harridan, the feisty wife found across the Williams canon. Comically, Mr. Taske falls between the two beds, fumbling around to locate a copy of the directions on how to use their lifejackets. He mistakenly puts in his wife's dentures, while without them she blurts out nonsense syllables. Their conversation is filled with banalities in disconnected dialogue. Mrs. Taske fears the male steward is trying to take advantage of her sexually and threatens to complain to her friend Emerald Cunard, whom her husband reminds her has been dead for 25 years. The offended wife drops the names of her friends in London society and menaces her husband with a divorce. The central comic event of the play, though, comes as she issues orders on how he needs to put on his jacket, which only flummoxes him. Equally foolish, Mrs. Taske blows the whistle at the wrong place and at the wrong time. Like their conversation, the Taskes travel in circles, missing objects, drills, and people in their lives.

As in Williams's other works, *Lifeboat Drill* affords audiences insight and sensitivity into the playwright's psyche. The septuagenerian Williams here writes about characters whose age is close to his own, a fact that may embody a fretful self-fulfilling prophecy, turning *Lifeboat Drill* into an autobiographical *memento mori* on stage. Williams no doubt saw the Taskes as the senescent abyss toward which he might well be falling someday himself. Moreover, much of Williams's biography is linked to sea voyages, such as the one represented in *Lifeboat Drill*. The peripatetic Williams relished sea cruises, having taken them often throughout his long career, and so he may have had firsthand experience of some of the events depicted in this late one-act play.

But *Lifeboat Drill* is a much more sophisticated piece of Williams's dramaturgy than just his travelogue or the senescent fable the

reviewers labeled it. In set and word, Williams's play absurdly dismantles the ways in which communication is frustrated. *Lifeboat Drill* in fact subverts any attempt to valorize the two most conventional questions of dramaturgy—"Who's talking?" and "What is being said?" Words are exchanged but answers are withheld. And even in this short, late play, Williams found appropriate symbols—dentures, eyeglasses, and a whistle—to emphasize the woes of failed, emfeebled communication.

Further Reading

Kolin, Philip C. "Lost in a Sea of Words: Tennessee Williams's *Lifeboat Drill*." *Mississippi Quarterly* 53 (Winter 1999–2000): 57–66.
Saddik, Annette. *The Politics of Reputation: The Critical Reception of Tennessee Williams' Later Plays*. Madison, NJ: Fairleigh Dickinson University Press, 1999.

Philip C. Kolin

Lindsay, Vachel [Nicholas] (1879–1931). Vachel Lindsay was a poet from Springfield, Illinois, author of "General Booth Enters Heaven" and "The Congo," whom Williams admired and about whom he had hoped to write a play in 1939, a crucial year in Williams's own development as an artist. Williams found much in Lindsay's life to celebrate and to mourn. Lindsay had a harsh father and a mother who indulged her son in the arts, as Williams did. Williams knew much about Lindsay from following the life of **St. Louis** romantic poet Sara Teasdale, a close friend of Lindsay's, and from reading Edgar Lee Master's biography *Vachel Lindsay: A Poet in America* (1935).

The kinship between the two men as artists was inspiring to the young Tom. Like Lindsay, Williams, in the late 1930s saw himself as a vagabond artist trying to promote his work, as Lindsay once did going door to door selling his poems. Even more important, Lindsay engaged in a battle against "the tyranny of . . . [the] times" (176), as Williams saw himself doing confronting the "problem of the poet or creative artist in American or any other capitalistic state" (Devlin and Tischler 176). Williams wrote to Wood that he was working on a play on Lindsay's life and his ghastly suicide (he swallowed Lysol)—tentatively titled *Dead Planet, the Moon*—to submit it with his application for a Rockefeller Fellowship. Lindsay provided an excellent model for the "psychological drama" Williams hoped to write. But the play never materialized, in part because Williams ultimately found too many "grotesque elements" to have to confront. But his interest in the lives of artists continued as evidenced in **I Rise in Flame, Cried the Phoenix**, his play on **D.H. Lawrence**. Nancy Tischler suggests that Lindsay's legacy as the fugitive artist surfaces in Williams's creation of Val Xavier and Carol Cutrere in **Battle of Angels/Orpheus Descending**.

Further Reading

Devlin, Albert J. "The Year 1939: Becoming Tennessee Williams." In *Magical Muse: Millennial Essays on Tennessee Williams*, ed. Ralph F. Voss. Tuscaloosa: University of Alabama Press, 2002. 35–49.

———, and Nancy M. Tischler, eds. *The Selected Letters of Tennessee Williams, Volume 1—1920–1945*. New York: New Directions, 2000. 176.

Tischler, Nancy. "Tennessee Williams: Vagabond Poet." *Tennessee Williams Annual Review* 1 (1998): 73–80.

Philip C. Kolin

Lorca, Federico García (1898–1936).

Federico García Lorca was a leading poet and dramatist of the twentieth century. Since his death at the hands of the Franquist forces during the Spanish Civil War, he has become the subject of an ever-growing body of research. Lorca's influence on Williams comes through Lorca's *Blood Wedding* (1933), *Yerma* (1934), and *The House of Bernarda Alba* (1936). The use of poetic language within the context of hard-edged social realities struck a respondent chord in Williams, whose early Broadway successes employed similar juxtapositions.

But the similarities between Lorca and Tennessee Williams are as striking as the differences. Both occupied precarious positions inside and outside the mainstream; both seemed to have had ambivalent feelings about their fame, each wanting it but on his own terms; and both were persecuted for their homosexuality. Lorca and Williams excelled in writing women's roles. Each created several complex mother characters who combine a number of contrasting qualities in suffocating social systems driven by traditional norms. Amanda in **The Glass Menagerie**, Bernada in *The House of Bernada Alba*, and the Mother in *Blood Wedding* exhibit a strength that—however ironically—works against them and those they love. Each assumes or insists upon a value system that is antiquated and at odds with the world that her children must face.

Williams and Lorca also wrote roles for women whose haunting vulnerability leads to problems these characters can neither articulate nor surmount. For example, Laura's fragility in *The Glass Menagerie* leads her to identify explicitly with the glass figurines in her collection; Yerma's (in Lorca's play) deep frustration from a passionless marriage and childless future often explodes into a desperation that leads her to a violence at once reminiscent of and more extreme than Blanche's confessed violence toward Allan Grey (her first husband) in **A Streetcar Named Desire**. And Serafina Delle Rose's memory and yearning for passionate love in

Williams's *The Rose Tattoo* brings her close to a comic parody of Yerma.

Sexuality, especially in relation to gender and power, is a pervasive subject in both Lorca and Williams. Whereas in *Blood Wedding* and *The House of Bernarda Alba*, Lorca viewed the tensions of sexual desire as the products of clearly defined institutional pressures, Williams—in *A Streetcar Named Desire, The Rose Tattoo,* and *Summer and Smoke*—viewed such tensions more generally as proceeding from the contradictions in American culture and not from any particularly well-defined institutions. In Lorca's major plays, women achieve or lose power by the way they manage their own desires and/or the desires of other women, but in Williams's plays, women must strive for power by managing the desires of men.

Williams and Lorca shared a selective reliance on some of the tendencies of the Symbolist movement, including a highly charged poetic language that combined intense compression with dense imagery, the use of complex symbolic processes (synecdoche, metonymy, metaphor, etc.), emphasis on suggestion rather than traditional exposition, and the use of hidden or ambiguous motivations that required a good deal of inference by the audience. In Williams's work, these Symbolist characteristics frequently mingled with realistic elements, whereas in Lorca, they were blended with surrealism or with structures reminiscent of classical Greek drama. A major legacy of both authors was a dramaturgy that was formally congruent with what became the aesthetic norms of high modernism but within a context of their own liberal politics. See also **Politics.**

Further Reading

Gibson, Ian. *Federico García Lorca*. London and Boston: Faber and Faber, 1989.

Piasecki, Andrew. *File on Lorca*. London: Methuen, 1991.

Stainton, Leslie. *Lorca: A Dream of Life*. New York: Farrar, Straus, Giroux, 1999.

John Gronbeck-Tedesco

A Lovely Sunday for Creve Coeur. *A Lovely Sunday for Creve Coeur* was written in about 1975 but set in the 1930s. In this play, Williams returns to the **St. Louis** setting of **The Glass Menagerie** and other early plays. Based on *All Gaul Is Divided* (see **Stopped Rocking and Other Screenplays**), a screenplay Williams wrote in the 1950s but said he had forgotten, *A Lovely Sunday for Creve Coeur* is the dramatist's only full-length play with an all-female cast. Its chief theme, according to Williams, is loneliness. But it is a loneliness, the play's dramaturgy suggests, that is as much existential anxiety as social isolation. The play, too, is about the need to go on (to Creve Coeur, or heartbreak, if necessary) even when going on seems to be impossible.

The characters, four single women who are no longer young, prepare or just wait for something to happen on one ordinary hot Sunday. Dotty dreams of a phone call and an offer of marriage from Ralph, the principal of the high school where she teaches. Bodey, her eccentric German American roommate, prepares the regular Sunday picnic for Creve Coeur amusement park (on a lake outside St. Louis), where she hopes her fat, unromantic but hardworking twin brother Buddy will propose to Dotty. Helena, a fellow-teacher, tries to persuade Dotty to share an upscale apartment and elegant female lifestyle with her. Sophie Gluck, a mentally disturbed neighbor whose mother has just died, seeks company and comfort from Bodey. At the end of the play Dotty learns of Ralph's engagement and, recovering quickly from her own heartbreak, chooses to follow Bodey to see Buddy and Creve Coeur. The play's conflict, both literal

Helena (Felicity LaFortune, seated) Bodey (Sonja Lanzener, center), and Sophie (Heather Robinson, far right) in the Alliance Theatre production of *A Lovely Sunday for Creve Coeur*. Photo by Jonathan Burnette. Courtesy of Alliance Theatre Company, Atlanta, Georgia.

and symbolic, lies in Bodey and Helena's farcical struggle for Dotty's allegiance and its mild suspense in the (inevitable) choice that Dotty finally makes.

Despite renewed interest in Williams's later plays, criticism of *A Lovely Sunday for Creve Coeur* has been sparse. Critics have dismissed the play as an uninteresting return to a realistic style in which Williams was no longer interested, as Annette Saddik suggests; or they have focused on Williams's recapitulation of themes and characters from his earlier work, especially the play's parodic relation to *A Streetcar Named Desire*, with Dotty as a comic Southern Belle, disappointed in love but more resilient than Blanche in getting on with her life, following

Judith Thompson's reading. A more promising line of approach, as the play's recent successful productions have demonstrated, emphasizes, as Linda Dorff has, the comically grotesque elements that align *A Lovely Sunday for Creve Coeur* with Williams's other experimental plays of the 1960s and 1970s.

In *A Lovely Sunday for Creve Coeur* Williams combines the Chekhovian psychological realism of his early, most popular plays, such as *The Glass Menagerie* and *A Streetcar Named Desire*, with the grotesque, absurdist style he developed in plays of the 1960s, such as *The Gnädiges Fräulein* and *In the Bar of a Tokyo Hotel*. In particular, Williams combines in *A Lovely Sunday for Creve Coeur*

129

the ordinary and the monstrously bizarre in the manner of Ionesco. The four female characters are all credibly motivated and sympathetic in their various efforts to avoid loneliness and despair through marriage, family, companionship, or a more elegant lifestyle. They spend their time, as might characters in a **Chekhov** play, in the ordinary pursuits of cooking, eating, drinking, talking, planning; and they recur constantly to the subjects closest to their hearts: the expected phone call, food, being alone, and the absent icons Ralph, Buddy, Helena's rich cousin Dee Dee, and Sophie's dead mother.

The women are also, however, with the partial exception of Dotty, caricatures, as their names and personal attributes emphasize. Bodey Bodenhafer, who speaks in convoluted Germanic sentences and covers her hearing aid with an enormous paper flower, is large, cowlike, nurturing, and in her desire for nieces and nephews from Dotty's marriage with her brother, life-affirming. Helena Brookmire, slim, elegantly dressed, and sarcastic, looks and moves like a predatory bird; she insinuates herself into Bodey's apartment like an intrusive snake (Bodey says she speaks with a hiss) as she attempts to win Dotty for herself. Even more comically grotesque is the hysterical neighbor Sophie Gluck, whose name, ironically, connotes wisdom and good luck. If Bodey and Helena's competition for Dotty's future structures *A Lovely Sunday for Creve Coeur* and gives it a mythic resonance, Sophie is the play's keynote character. Bearing some resemblance to the comic but disturbing title character of Williams's earlier "slapstick tragedy" *The Gnädiges Fräulein*, Sophie looks like a demented but suffering saint. She speaks a shrill hybrid of German and English, makes unhappy noises, shuffles, dribbles, suffers from an attack of diarrhea, and obsessively expresses her terror of being alone in the supposedly haunted apartment

where her mother died. Sophie embodies and enacts the loneliness and degradation that all of the women fear, providing the audience with a glimpse of the abyss that underlies the ordinariness of their daily routines. Williams's characterization of Sophie, in particular, underscores the absurdist orientation of his dramaturgy.

Like the characters, the set of *A Lovely Sunday for Creve Coeur*, Bodey's apartment, is both realistic and fantastic. The apartment is at once grounded in the familiarity of a depressing lower-middle-class St. Louis neighborhood and alarmingly distorted. The glaring light that comes through the huge windows, the clashing purple, orange, and yellow colors and loud patterns, and the clutter of decorative objects testify to Bodey's attempt to make her surroundings cheerful and, in effect, an extension of her personality. The garish decor also makes the apartment a fitting location for the numerous farcical yet humiliating accidents that befall its inhabitants. Bodey, for example, is repeatedly spattered with hot fat as she fries chicken for the picnic, Helena is sprinkled with baking soda, and worst of all, Sophie is afflicted with diarrhea (brought on by hot coffee), after which she floods Dotty's bathroom. Throughout the play, too, cacophonous noises combine with the overpowering visual effect of the apartment in assaulting the audience's senses. Such noises as Dotty's exaggerated panting while she does her exercises, Bodey's screeching hearing aid, Helena's satiric laughter, and Sophie's choric wailing and moaning about her unhappy existence are typical of Williams's experiments with unusual and startling sound effects in his later plays (for example, the ugly cries of the cocaloony birds in *The Gnädiges Fräulein*). Both visually and aurally Bodey's apartment creates a sense of oppressive confinement that underscores the limited lives and opportunities of the four women.

Only Dotty seems to have any choice at all, though the choice she finally makes among the options represented by the other three women has been a foregone conclusion from the beginning. Dotty is by her own admission a woman who must have a man to feel fulfilled in life. Thus when the hoped-for gentleman caller, unsurprisingly, disappoints (as he does in many other Williams's plays, notably *The Glass Menagerie*), a substitute savior becomes necessary. Bodey's single-minded preparation of the Creve Coeur picnic reminds the audience throughout the play of the inevitability of Buddy. But *A Lovely Sunday for Creve Coeur* ends on an ambiguous note. Understanding that she must make the best of things by settling for Buddy, Dotty rejects Helena and sets off for Creve Coeur, assuring Sophie that she will be back before dark. At this point, however, the lights dim out. The play's final visual effect undermines the guarded optimism of Dotty's choice, suggesting that happiness is illusory.

The play was first performed in its original one-act version as *Creve Coeur* at the Spoleto Festival in Charleston, South Carolina, in 1978. Williams's retitled two-act revision had its premiere at the Hudson Guild Theatre in New York in 1979. Apart from its London premiere at the Old Red Lion in Islington in 1986, the play was rarely staged for the next 20 years. Recent successful productions by Northlight Theatre, Skokie (Chicago) in 1998, Chain Lightning at the Connelly Theatre, New York, in 1999, and the Alliance Theatre Company in Atlanta in 2001 testify to renewed interest in the work and have demonstrated the viability and indeed the necessity of emphasizing in production the play's comic grotesque elements, in accordance with Williams's own preference in comments he made on the play's earliest productions (Bilowit).

Further Reading

Bilowit, Ira J. "Roundtable: Tennessee Williams, Craig Anderson, and T.E. Kalem Talk about *Creve Coeur*." In *Conversations with Tennessee Williams*, ed. Albert J. Devlin. Jackson: University Press of Mississippi, 1986. 308–317.

Dorff, Linda. "Theatricalist Cartoons: Tennessee Williams's Late 'Outrageous' Plays." *Tennessee Williams Annual Review* 2 (1999): 13–33.

Foster, Verna. "Waiting for Buddy, or Just Going on in *A Lovely Sunday for Creve Coeur*." In *The Undiscovered Country: The Later Plays of Tennessee Williams*, ed. Philp C. Kolin. New York: Lang, 2002. 155–167.

Free, William S. "Williams in the Seventies." In *Tennessee Williams: A Tribute*, ed. Jac Tharpe. Jackson: University Press of Mississippi, 1977. 815–828.

Saddik, Annette. *The Politics of Reputation: The Critical Reception of Tennessee Williams' Later Plays*. Madison, NJ: Fairleigh Dickinson University Press, 1999.

Thompson, Judith J. *Tennessee Williams' Plays: Memory, Myth, and Symbol*. Rev. ed. New York: Lang, 2002.

Verna Foster

M

Mabie, Edward Charles (1892–1956). Edward Charles Mabie was Williams's playwriting teacher (1937–1938) and chairman of the Theater Department at the University of Iowa. An extremely demanding professor (nicknamed "the Boss"), Mabie insisted that his students become experienced in all aspects of theater. As a result, Williams was required to work on sets (including one for a play Mabie himself directed, *First Lady*), to sell tickets, and to write plays. Taking Mabie's playwriting seminar in the summer of 1938, Williams wrote **Spring Storm** (originally titled *April Is the Cruellest Month*), but this play, like Williams's other work at Iowa, was not well received by Mabie, who dismissed it with these words, "Well, we all have to paint our nudes," referring to Williams's portraits of intimacy in the play. Mabie, who was an arch conservative, was not sympathetic toward Williams's dramatic style or his bohemian lifestyle. A former director of the Midwest WPA (Works Progress Administration) Federal Theatre Project, Mabie believed theater needed to make an overt political statement and had Williams's class write plays like those in the WPA's "living newspapers," based on subjects snatched from the headlines of the day. Williams's psychological examination of character was too introspective for Mabie's taste. Mabie would neither recommend Williams for a Rockefeller Grant nor allow one of his plays to be staged at Iowa. Ironically, Mabie's great passion was to identify and to nurture budding playwrights, yet Tom Williams's work merited only his disapproval.

Further Reading

Leverich, Lyle. *Tom: The Unknown Tennessee Williams*. New York: Crown, 1995.

Philip C. Kolin

Madness. Known for creating psychologically complex characters, Tennessee Williams had a profound interest in exploring mental instability and its consequences, motivated in part by his personal and family history. In 1937, his older sister Rose suffered a mental breakdown and was hospitalized; she spent the rest of her life confined to a mental institution or under private care, and her treatment regimes included insulin therapy and, eventually, a lobotomy. Williams therefore related madness to confinement, for as he had seen in the case of his sister, the two are connected; in his *Memoirs* he acknowledged that confinement was his biggest fear. His response to this fear created in him an obsessive desire to keep moving, and throughout his adult life he moved from one hotel or apartment to another and from one city to another on the wings of anxiety. Through it all, he used his writing as an act of resistance, convinced that it was the one habit that might protect him from the forces that had claimed his sister. He believed that if he did not write, he would go mad.

Ultimately, he could not exempt himself, however. As was the case for many of the characters he created, his own mental instability was prompted by drug and alcohol abuse, and in 1969, the final year of a decade he referred to as his "Stoned Age," he admitted himself voluntarily to the psychiatric ward of Barnes Hospital in St. Louis, where he underwent treatment for drug and alcohol withdrawal. Never again could he see himself exempt from the forces that had claimed his sister. Williams himself sought care from psychoanalyst **Lawrence Kubie** and portrayed other doctors, such as Dr. Cukrowicz, who wants to perform a lobotomy in *Suddenly Last Summer*, as dangerous.

In his work, the obsession with madness appeared in a variety of forms throughout his career. As early as 1937, the year Rose was institutionalized, Williams included a mentally disturbed figure in his dramatic cast of characters: Abel White, an unbalanced pyromaniac obsessed with young women, appears that year in the play *Fugitive Kind*, produced by the **Mummers** in **St. Louis**. Although White has only a minor part in the action, he represents a character type that Williams would return to as madness and its many manifestations came to dominate his works and the characters who suffered from mental illness took center stage. Manifested in behavior that ranges from extreme nervousness to obsession and hysteria, Williams's representations of madness emphasized the grotesque yet nonetheless human elements of the individual psyche. His mad characters are often depicted sympathetically, even as their actions are implicitly or explicitly ostracized or punished.

A number of short plays written during the 1930s and 1940s feature characters suffering from delusions, depression, or delirium. Lucretia Collins, the aging spinster of "Portrait of a Madonna," the title character in "Hello from Bertha, and "The Lady of Larkspur Lotion" (see *Twenty-seven Wagons Full of Cotton and Other One-Act Plays*) are all destitute women who fantasize about former or nonexistent lovers; as they become increasingly lost in their illusions, they are threatened with eviction, confinement, or both. The Little Man from "The Strangest Kind of Romance" also loses his rented room when he suffers a breakdown from the pressures of factory work and is confined for mental observation.

The connection between destitution and institutionalization is carefully constructed in *A Streetcar Named Desire* (1947), which contains one of the most terrifying and developed examinations of the descent into madness that Williams ever charted. Blanche DuBois exhibits nervous behavior early in the play, but her mental deterioration escalates when the truth about her former life, including her inability to support herself, is revealed. After being raped by Stanley, she is taken away by a doctor and nurse who arrive with straitjacket in hand, her removal witnessed by the entire community of characters.

Williams uses the mental institution as a stage setting that both literally and figuratively constitutes madness as a reason, or even an excuse, for confinement and punishment. Although the stage version of *Suddenly Last Summer* (1958) was set in a garden in **New Orleans**'s Garden District, the play involved the struggle between Catharine Venable and her aunt over whether the younger woman should be transferred from a private hospital to a state institution where she may be lobotomized. In preparing the screenplay for the film version (1959), cowriters Williams and **Gore Vidal** even moved some of the action to the state hospital; besides making the issue of confinement a visual component of the work, these scenes typify **Hollywood**'s depiction of the madhouse as a snake pit populated by hideous and lascivious freaks.

Williams's characters often narrate a memory of instability and commitment, either a family member's or their own. Alma Winemiller from *Summer and Smoke* (1948) suffers from a nervous disorder inherited from her mother, while Shannon from *The Night of the Iguana* (1961) has been a resident of the "Casa de Locos," and his involuntary confinement to the hammock on stage recalls that time. Actors Felice and Clare of *The Two-Character Play/Out Cry* (1973) bear witness to the insanity they have inherited from their father; their confinement takes place in a locked theater in which they have been abandoned by their company. In order to ward off madness, they retreat into the fiction of an autobiographical play modeled on their lives. Here Williams uses a brother/sister configuration that recalls his own relationship to Rose as he explores the connections between creativity and madness. *In the Bar of a Tokyo Hotel* (1969), another play from this period, also features an artist's mental and physical breakdown: Mark, who often speaks in fragments and exhibits the signs of what may be a brain tumor, dies on stage near the end of the play.

Madness and aging are connected in such late plays as *Clothes for a Summer Hotel* (1980) and *A House Not Meant to Stand* (1982). In the former work, which Williams called a "ghost play," an ailing F. Scott Fitzgerald visits his wife Zelda at the Highland Hospital in Asheville, North Carolina; these real-life figures, the darlings of the Jazz Age, meet at the asylum where Zelda spent her final years before dying in a fire, and scenes from their marriage are played out with actors who double as their friends and the asylum attendants. The play proposes that Zelda's writing talents were sacrificed to further Scott's career, thus providing another opportunity for Williams to explore the connections between creativity and madness. In *A House Not Meant to Stand*, the last new play produced before Williams's death in 1983, he returns once more to the brother/sister theme, where one is about to be committed, and the other becomes a victim of alcoholism.

Several critical studies of Williams's use of madness have explored deeper implications of its place in his canon. William Kleb discusses madness in *A Streetcar Named Desire*, for example, as a way of interrogating postwar constructions of sexuality and difference, while Anne Fleche argues that madness and desire are employed in that work to test the limits of theatrical realism. However, Williams's nondramatic works demonstrate that his explorations of madness were not limited to his plays; as part of her study of what she calls his late "grotesque" work, Linda Dorff argues convincingly for his affinity with the "mad" romantics as demonstrated in his exegetical poetry. (See **Drugs; Poems**).

Further Reading

Dorff, Linda. " 'I prefer the mad ones': Tennessee Williams's Grotesque-Lyric Exegetical Poems." *Southern Quarterly* 38.1 (1999): 81–93.

Fleche, Ann. *Mimetic Disillusion: Eugene O'Neill, Tennessee Williams, and U.S. Dramatic Realism.* Tuscoloosa: University of Alabama Press, 1997.

Kleb, William. "Marginalia: *A Streetcar Named Desire*, Williams, and Foucault." In *Confronting Tennessee Williams's "A Streetcar Named Desire": Essays in Cultural Pluralism*, ed. Philip C. Kolin. Westport, CT: Greenwood, 1993. 27–43.

O'Connor, Jacqueline. *Dementia Dramatized: Madness in the Plays of Tennessee Williams.* Bowling Green, OH: Bowling Green State University Popular Press, 1997.

Jacqueline O'Connor

Magnani, Anna (1908–1973). Anna Magnani starred in two film versions of plays by Williams, *The Rose Tattoo* (1955) and *The Fugitive Kind* (1960) (see **Orpheus Descending**). Williams wrote *The Rose Tattoo* especially for her. From their first meeting in Rome in 1948, Williams counted Magnani among his best friends and referred to her warmly in numerous interviews. Her free-spirited personality inspired the emotional range and intensity of the character of Serafina in *The Rose Tattoo*, and Williams had his heart set on her for the role on Broadway in 1950. But Magnani, however, felt that her English was not good enough for live performance, so the stage role went to **Maureen Stapleton**. For the film, Magnani worked from a script with English and Italian on facing pages. **Frank Merlo**, Williams's longtime lover, coached her during a transatlantic voyage to New York, so that she was letter perfect by the time they docked. Magnani often clashed with her costar Burt Lancaster, and her fight scene with Virginia Grey (playing Estelle Hohengarten) resulted in two fractured ribs for Gray. While the film gar-

nered mixed reviews, Magnani earned enthusiastic accolades for her overpowering performance. She won both the Academy Award and the New York Film Critics' Award for best actress.

In *The Fugitive Kind*, based on Williams's play *Orpheus Descending*, Magnani played Lady Torrance opposite **Marlon Brando**'s Val Xavier. Again, she learned her lines as letter-perfect equivalences for meanings that she mentally registered in Italian. However, Brando could never say a line exactly as it was written, often ad-libbing or embellishing the words with nonverbal sounds; thus Magnani rarely got the cue word for which she was listening. Various people who were on the set recalled tensions between the two stars. She had come to the film eager to work with Brando, perhaps even bent on sexual conquest. When Brando did not respond, Magnani apparently became self-conscious about her age and her looks, and perhaps this reaction accounted for her relatively subdued performance.

Both Williams's films starring Magnani were subject to the motion pictures' Production Code, which was in effect until 1966. Williams felt that his original material was bowdlerized in the screenplays, and he respected Magnani for an artistry that could not be reduced by **Hollywood**'s constraints. Her earthiness, passion, and personal magnetism defied definition in moral terms; thus she might be said to have embodied authorial intention on film. This surely figured in Williams's assessment of her (reported by Don Ross) as "the greatest living actress" (Devlin 42). See also **Film Adaptations**.

Further Reading

"Anna Magnani Lifted Int'l Stature of Italo Films, Dies in Rome at 65." *New York Times* 3 October 1973.

Crowther, Bosley. Rev. of *The Fugitive Kind*, dir.

Malden, Karl

Sidney Lumet. *New York Times* 15 April 1960: 13.

Crowther, Bosley. Rev. of *The Rose Tattoo*, dir. Daniel Mann. *New York Times* 13 December 1955: 55.

Devlin, Albert J., ed. *Conversations with Tennessee Williams*. Jackson: University Press of Mississippi, 1986.

Leavitt, Richard F., ed. *The World of Tennessee Williams*. New York: Putnam, 1978.

Yacowar, Maurice. *Tennessee Williams & Film*. New York: Ungar, 1977.

Felicia Hardison Londré

Malden, Karl (1914–   ). Karl Malden is the actor who played Mitch in *A Streetcar Named Desire* (both in the 1947 play and in the 1951 film) and Archie Lee Meighan in *Baby Doll*. He had held blue-collar jobs as a steel mill worker and truck driver, not unlike Mitch's work, before attending the Goodman Dramatic School in Chicago and then becoming a member of the Actors Studio, which had its roots in the **Group Theatre**. In New York, he met **Marlon Brando** and appeared with him in *Truckline Café*. But his big break, like Brando's, came with *A Streetcar Named Desire*. Under **Elia Kazan**'s direction, Malden developed the role of Mitch for which he won an Academy Award for Best Supporting Actor.

With his large frame, gruff voice, and uncourtly appearance, Malden made the perfect Mitch. He captured Mitch as the unsuitable suitor—ill at ease, funny faced, gawky, and self-effacing. Malden also projected Mitch's suppressed sexuality—the mama's boy whose own masculinity is called into question by Stanley Kowalski and his friends. Malden's Mitch was a lumbering beau who swayed like a bear listening to the music coming from Blanche's radio in Scene 3 of *A Streetcar Named Desire* and who is shamefacedly rebuffed by the prudish-acting Blanche in Scene 6. Yet Malden also released

Mitch's pent-up fury when he attempts to rape her in Scene 9 but is frightened away by Blanche's hysterical cries for help. Malden also superbly portrayed the pathos and dejection Mitch felt as Blanche is ushered off stage to the asylum.

In *Baby Doll* (1956), Malden played the middle-aged Mississippi redneck Archie Lee who lusts after Baby Doll, his bride who is half his age and who denies him sex. Again, Malden melded with the role that Williams created and that Kazan once again brilliantly directed. Like Mitch, Archie Lee is an egregiously unsuitable suitor but without Mitch's redeeming honesty. Malden comically portrayed Archie as a lecherous voyeur (he peeks through a hole in the wall to watch Carroll Baker's Baby Doll take a bath), an inevitable cuckold, and a bigot and butt of community humor. Malden played the spine of Archie's character as a foolish, blustering plotter who is easily unnerved and thwarted by **Eli Wallach**'s Vacarro. In fact, Kazan powerfully used Malden's comic genius to cast Archie as the gullible dupe of the other; the Sicilian Vacarro and the black characters mock Archie behind his back as well as openly. Malden's portrayal of these two roles became the standard by which other actors' interpretations have been measured. See also **Race**.

Further Reading

Corliss, Richard. "*A Streetcar Named Desire* and *Baby Doll*." *Film Comment* 4 (Summer 1968): 44–47.

Murphy, Brenda. *Tennessee Williams and Elia Kazan: A Collaboration in the Theatre*. Cambridge: Cambridge University Press, 1992.

Phillip, Gene. D. *The Film of Tennessee Williams*. Philadelphia: Art Alliance, 1980.

Yacowar, Maurice. *Tennessee Williams and Film*. New York: Ungar, 1977.

Philip C. Kolin

Mann, Thomas (1875–1955). Thomas Mann was the Nobel Prize–winning German author who served as an icon of German culture for expatriates in the United States. Williams became familiar with Mann's work in 1935 through his friend **Clark Mills (McBurney)** and also through Professor Otto Heller, a German-born philologist at Washington University in **St. Louis** where Williams studied. Although Mann was highly appreciated by **O'Neill**, Fitzgerald, Hemingway, and **Faulkner** (who called him "the foremost literary artist of the time") and was a close friend of Sinclair Lewis, Mann held a special place for the young generation of intellectuals and poets in the 1930s such as Mills, Howard Nemerov, Guy Stern, **Donald Windham**, and Williams. As a friend of director Alvin Johnson, Mann was in touch with the **New School for Social Research** where Williams took a seminar on playwriting in 1939. Williams in fact met Mann at his residence in Pacific Palisades in August 1943 through fellow MGM screenwriter Christopher Isherwood. At this meeting, Mann may have learned about Williams's *Gentleman Caller* (see **Film Adaptations; Hollywood**) from Isherwood or from the playwright himself.

Mann's influence can be seen in Williams's fiction and plays. Williams's early reading of Mann's novellas *Tonio Kröger* (1903) and *Der Tod in Venedig* (1912) may have led to his using these symbolic names in his own fiction. The telling name of Tonio Kroger is split between the character Emiel Kroger in Williams's "The Mysteries of Joy Rio" (see *Collected Stories*) and "Tonio," the title and character in Williams's late story of the same name. Mann's "Aschenbach" and "Tadzio," representing rational Apollonian (German) north and a sensual Dionysic (Latin) south, embody the conflict of the two cultural spheres and the incompatibility of love and life in Mann and Williams. Incorporating Plato and Nietzsche, Mann disguised and sublimated his original (homo)erotic desires while Williams clearly wrote them into his work. Williams's embodiment of sexual desire (in *The Roman Spring of Mrs. Stone* and *The Milk Train Doesn't Stop Here Anymore*) may, ironically, paraphrase Mann's *Death in Venice*. Aschenbach's pederastic cruising might be seen as analogous to Karen Stone's need for young giglos. The battle between eros (desire) and thanatos (death) is an existential longing for youth and beauty common to Mann's novel and to Williams's novella. Significantly, Williams, like Mann, chose a decadent Italian environment in which to situate this conflict. Finally, Williams may have borrowed elements from *Death in Venice* in *Suddenly Last Summer*, especially in shaping the identity and name of Sebastian Venable, the erased homosexual character.

Thomas Molzahn

Manuscript Collections. The location and scope of Tennessee Williams's manuscripts are essential to understanding the playwright and his work. Such manuscripts document how Williams extensively reworked all his plays and also explored in poetry and prose form themes that dominated his dramatic work.

The bulk of Williams's personal papers are housed at three libraries—the Harry Ransom Humanities Research Center at the University of Texas at Austin; the Harvard Theatre Collection; and Columbia University. Other significant collections of manuscripts are housed at the University of Delaware, the Historic **New Orleans** Collection, Harvard University's Houghton Library, and the University of California at Los Angeles. Smaller groups of Williams manuscripts can also be found at Princeton University Library's Theatre Division and the University of Virginia. Descriptions are provided through the Web sites listed at the end of this entry.

The Tennessee Williams collection at the Harry Ransom Humanities Research Center at the University of Texas at Austin was built from four major acquisitions in the 1960s, with smaller amounts of material added over the years. The nucleus of the collection began with Williams's own papers, given to the Ransom Center by the playwright between 1962 and 1969. These materials document his early career thoroughly (especially for *The Glass Menagerie* and *A Streetcar Named Desire*) and include over 1,000 separately titled plays, short stories and poems, correspondence, and newspaper clippings. In 1964, the Center expanded the collection with the purchase of the correspondence between Williams and his agent, **Audrey Wood**. In 1965, the Center further acquired valuable manuscripts, including Williams's first full-length play, *Candles to the Sun*, from Andreas Brown, now owner of the Gotham Book Mart in New York City. Brown's materials also included a complete run of Williams's publications, and Brown's own correspondence, notes, and drafts from his work on Williams's bibliography. Williams Family papers were also acquired in 1965 from his mother, **Edwina Estelle Dakin Williams**, including original manuscripts and works of art by Williams, over 700 letters, scrapbooks, personal memorabilia, and 650 photographs of the Williams family, Williams himself, and his friends and acquaintances.

The Collection documents Tennessee Williams's life, work, family, and friends from 1880 to 1993 and is organized into four series: Works, 1925–1982, Correspondence, 1880–1980, Williams Family, 1892–1969, and Works by Others, 1940–1993. The Works series constitutes over two thirds of the Williams Collection. While the dates of the collection span from 1880 to 1993, the focus is from the mid-1930s to the mid-1970s. Related collections include the papers of Audrey Wood, Williams's agent from 1939 until the 1970s, and the papers of stage manager Robert Downing and actress **Laurette Taylor**.

The Harvard Theatre Collection received most of its Tennessee Williams manuscripts as a bequest from Williams but has also added individual items through purchases. The collection includes manuscripts, preliminary drafts, annotated copies, contracts, diaries, and letters. The Theatre Collection also includes several archives of correspondence with Williams, some additional annotated typescripts, an extensive collection of photographs, and a self-portrait, all acquired separately. Also very important, the Houghton Library at Harvard University contains the archive of New Directions, Williams's primary publisher, which includes important Williams-related material and a few manuscript works by Williams, notably three draft versions of *Cat on a Hot Tin Roof* (see **Laughlin, James**).

In the two decades spanning 1970 to 1990 Columbia University's Rare Book and Manuscript Library purchased a substantial number of play scripts, production material, photographs, and correspondence by and relating to Tennessee Williams. The largest part of Columbia's present collection, however, consists of material found in Tennessee Williams's Key West home at the time of his death. It was acquired in 1994 from the Tennessee Williams Estate. The collection dates from 1942 to 1982, with a few earlier items present. Manuscripts of such Williams plays as *A House Not Meant to Stand* and *The Two-Character Play* date primarily from the 1960s to 1982. The collection is organized in six series—Correspondence; Works; Personal; Works by Other Authors; Photographs; and Audiotapes—and contains notes, diaries, drafts, rewrites, scripts, type-scripts, programs, flyers, ads, newspaper and magazine clippings, art work, tapes, note-books, awards, photographs, and realia.

The Tennessee Williams Collection at the University of Delaware, spanning from 1939 to 1990, consists of manuscripts of plays, poems, essays, and other work, photographs of the writer and play productions, pro-grams and playbills, correspondence related to his play scripts, articles about Williams or his work, and theatrical and film ephemera. The collection was formed from various ac-quisitions, including those originally belong-ing to the private collector Norman Unger, acquired in 1980. There is also a separate collection of Tennessee Williams manuscript poems and materials related to *The Rose Tattoo* gathered by stage manager Ralph Delauney.

In 2001 the Historic New Orleans Collec-tion acquired what was perhaps the finest collection of Tennessee Williams books and manuscripts still in private hands. Collected over a period of 45 years by Fred Todd, a librarian, and long available to scholars at Mr. Todd's San Antonio residence, the col-lection has now gone "home" to the city most closely associated with Tennessee Wil-liams. Among the highlights of the collection are rewrites for *The Glass Menagerie* and *A Streetcar Named Desire*, notes on filming *The Rose Tattoo*, an operatic version of *Summer and Smoke*, the correspondence of **Marion Black Vacarro**, and **Elia Kazan**'s notes and queries on a copy of the script for *Baby Doll*.

In 1970, the University of California, Los Angeles, Library purchased from Tennessee Williams a small collection of manuscripts spanning the years from 1930 to 1970. In-cluded were manuscripts of several of Wil-liams's published and unpublished plays, play fragments, short stories, screen scenar-ios, and poetry. The collection also includes transcripts of early versions of *Sweet Bird of Youth* and *The Night of the Iguana* and un-corrected proofs and galleys of Gilbert Max-well's book *Tennessee Williams and Friends* (1965). See also **Correspondence; Journals; Texts.**

Further Reading

Columbia University. Available online at http://www.columbia.edu/cu/libraries/indiv/rare/guides/Williams/

Harry Ransom Humanities Research Center, University of Texas at Austin. Available on-line at http://www.hrc.utexas.edu/fa/hrc findingaids.html

Harvard Theatre Collection, Harvard University. Available online at http://hcl.harvard.edu/houghton/departments/htc/theatre.html

Historic New Orleans Collection, New Orleans, LA. Available online at http://www.hnoc.org/

Houghton Library, Harvard University. Available online at http://oasis.harvard.edu/hou.html

UCLA Library, Department of Special Collec-tions, Manuscript Division, Los Angeles, CA. Available online at http://www.oac.cdlib.org:80/dynaweb/ead/ucla/mss/willi 492/@Generic_BookView;cs=default;ts=default

University of Delaware, Newark, DE. Available online at http://www.lib.udel.edu/ud/spec/findaids/williams_t/willtenn.htm

Cathy Henderson

McCullers, Carson (1917–1967). A Geor-gia-born novelist, short story writer, and playwright, Carson McCullers was a close friend of Williams. Williams met McCullers during the summer of 1946 after he read her novels *The Heart Is a Lonely Hunter*, *Re-flections in a Golden Eye*, and *The Member of the Wedding* and was impressed by the dramatic potential and emotional honesty of McCullers's work. He invited her to join him on Nantucket for the summer. In response to their shared southern heritage, similar aesthetic sensibilities, and common emotional vulnerabilities, the two writers immediately formed a strong bond. From their first meeting in 1946 until McCullers's death in 1967, the two writers provided each other with constant emotional support, artistic inspiration, and critical encouragement.

Williams saw in McCullers a reflection of his sister **Rose**, institutionalized for most of her life, and saw his friendship with McCullers as a second chance at having a siblinglike relationship with a like-minded friend, free of the guilt he felt for not having rescued Rose from the emotional minefield that was their childhood home. Williams called Carson and Rose his "two dear sisters, lion-hearted."

McCullers found in Williams the ideal companion with whom to form the "we of me" that, like her character Frankie Adams longed for in *The Member of the Wedding*, she had searched for unsuccessfully throughout her life. While Williams was not the first, nor the last, of the persons McCullers thought could complete her, he was the artist in whom she saw the greatest potential for emotional fulfillment. When McCullers was debilitated by a series of strokes (brought on by a misdiagnosed and untreated case of childhood rheumatic fever), Williams often served, especially through his letters from abroad, as an emissary from the broader literary world to McCullers at her home in Nyack, New York.

McCullers wrote about meeting Williams and the importance of their friendship in her posthumously published autobiography *Illumination and Night Glare*. Williams recalled the summer the two writers spent on Nantucket as well as the significance of his friendship with McCullers in his *Memoirs*, where he remembered McCullers through the prism of three painful exits they shared—the first, the experience of the opening night of his play *Summer and Smoke* and its negative reception by the critics; the second, their escape from Dylan Thomas's birthday party, where they both felt unjustly treated by the guest of honor; and the third, another theatrical premiere in which their friendship and mutual support would prove necessary, the critically disastrous opening night of McCullers's play *The Square Root of Wonderful*. The mutual support McCullers and Williams provided for each other during these trying times is characteristic of the relationship the two writers shared.

More personal and emotional than literary, McCullers and Williams's relationship was characterized more by total devotion, encouragement, and acceptance and less by literary influence. A list of direct literary influence between McCullers and Williams is brief. He declared that the character Maxine Faulk from *The Night of the Iguana* was based on McCullers; that his nickname for McCullers, "Sisterwoman," was used as a character's name in *Cat on a Hot Tin Roof*; and the father of McCullers's cousin, Jordan Massee, was the inspiration for the character Big Daddy in *Cat on a Hot Tin Roof*. Williams's influence on details in McCullers's work is equally short. McCullers supposedly based the character Judge Clane, from her final novel *Clock without Hands*, on Williams's maternal grandfather, Reverend **Walter Edwin Dakin**. Williams and McCullers's relationship also may have been reflected in Williams's *The Two-Character Play*, though the primary kinship here is between the playwright and his sister Rose.

Williams contributed significant critical responses to McCullers's work through his introduction to a 1950 reissue of McCullers's *Reflections in a Golden Eye* that provided an aesthetic and philosophical defense of the novel. Williams also wrote a major, positive review of McCullers's final novel *Clock without Hands* and a forward to Virginia Spencer Carr's *The Lonely Hunter: A Biography of Carson McCullers.*

Further Reading

Carr, Virginia Spencer. *The Lonely Hunter: A Biography of Carson McCullers.* Garden City, NY: Doubleday, 1975.
"Exotic Birds of a Feather: Carson McCullers and Tennessee Williams: A Panel." *Tennessee Williams Annual Review* 3 (2000): 69–90.
McCullers, Carson. *Illumination and Night Glare: The Unfinished Autobiography of Carson McCullers.* Madison: University of Wisconsin Press, 1998.
Spoto, Donald. *The Kindness of Strangers: The Life of Tennessee Williams.* Boston: Little, Brown, 1985.
Williams, Tennessee. *Memoirs.* Garden City, NY: Doubleday, 1975.

Carlos L. Dews

Me, Vasha! *Me, Vasha!* is a one-act play that Williams wrote in 1937 for a Techniques of Modern Drama course taught by Professor G.B. Carson at Washington University in **St. Louis**. Like most of Williams's works, this short play has an interesting history biographically and in performance. Williams originally submitted the play for the contest at the end of Carson's course, but when he won only an honorable mention, Williams became angry and then depressed; his grades plummeted as a result. But *Me, Vasha!* later was adapted (and considerably shortened to seven minutes) by **Willard Holland** of the **Mummers** for his *March of Time* radio series, where it was presented under the title of "Men Who March." Ultimately, Williams revised the play, re-entitling it *Death Is the Drummer*, and sent it to **Audrey Wood** in the hopes of having it produced professionally.

An antiwar story, *Me, Vasha!* is based on the life of Sir Basil Zaharoff, a notorious munitions dealer who sold armaments to both sides during World War I. Characteristically, though, Williams's interest was focused more on the mad princess who married the arms dealer but who is close friends with a poet. In lurid detail, Williams recounts what happens when the jealous husband finds out about the poet whom he arranges to be sent to the front, where he is shot in the head. In a vision, the princess sees the poet-friend come to her bedside, asking her to revenge his death. As she kills her husband, he kisses the bottom of her garment in a loving gesture. A woman gone mad like the princess became the subject of many of Williams's later plays—*Hello from Bertha, Portrait of a Madonna*, **A Streetcar Named Desire**, **The Two-Character Play**, and **Clothes for a Summer Hotel**. In 1937, though, Williams wrote about madness firsthand, due to the mental breakdown of his sister **Rose** and from experiencing his own bouts with depression, which he picturesquely labeled "Blue Devils."

Further Reading

Leverich, Lyle. *Tom: The Unknown Tennessee Williams.* New York: Crown, 1995.

Philip C. Kolin

Memoirs. *Memoirs*, published in 1975, attracted a great deal of negative attention because of Williams's scandalous self-revelations. A mixture of fiction and fact, *Memoirs* reveals Williams's explicit sexual recollections of his "impure" life, revealing his no-holds-barred sentiments toward a wide range of people, places, and events. Prepublication interviews aroused national interest as well as horrific hearsay. Williams's illustrated and "undisguised self-revelation" was offered to the public in a limited as well as a trade edition and was designated by Doubleday as a Book-of-the-Month Club selection. *Memoirs* skyrocketed to the bestseller list; on one afternoon alone, Williams broke Doubleday records when he signed and sold more than 800 copies in a New York bookstore.

Despite *Memoirs*'s immediate popularity, critics disdained its sensationalism, faulting Williams's sexual exposé as a source of disgust and pity. Most significantly, they were outraged that Williams seemingly disregarded discussion about his own plays. Though *Memoirs* sidesteps reflections on the American theater, Williams's elegiac confessions are at times fearfully honest and, with reservations, might be read as a gloss on his plays. He does usefully discuss, though not at great length, his writing process, production details, and anecdotal information on a majority of the plays he wrote up to *Memoirs*, including *The Glass Menagerie, A Streetcar Named Desire*, as well as *Suddenly Last Summer* and *The Night of the Iguana*. He names *Cat on a Hot Tin Roof* his favorite play and calls *The Two-Character Play* the last objective of his life in theater. He admits *Camino Real* "may have been flawed, [but] it surpassed its flaws"; *Orpheus Descending* has "lyric eloquence"; and *The Milk Train Doesn't Stop Here Anymore* is "a work of art manqué." Williams also provides inside information about his professional and sometimes personal relationships with **Elia Kazan, Maria Britneva (Lady St. Just), Audrey Wood, Marlon Brando**, producer David Merrick, and others.

Unfortunately, Williams's attitudes toward family, God, and writing are overshadowed by his sexual transgressions, seen as violations of acceptable public behavior. Williams flaunted his numerous homosexual trysts, drug addictions, prima donna temper tantrums, and even his unfaithfulness to his dying lover, **Frank Merlo**. Rightfully, Williams lavishes a great deal of time remembering Merlo, his longtime companion, and

disproportionately spends two lines on composer Leonard Bernstein. Then he devotes two pages to anonymous all-male parties where he learned how to "follow." Williams is colorfully candid on a host of political and literary figures, seeing Fidel Castro as "a gentleman," Hemingway as charming, Jean-Paul Satre as "polite," but Dylan Thomas as rude, and Thornton Wilder as having a mortician's smile. Of course, Williams's autobiography is full of opinions on the **Dakins**, his maternal grandparents, and offers an intimate portrait of himself as a child while reminiscing about **Edwina Williams** and his sister **Rose**, demanding comparison with his mother's and brother's recollections of him in their respective autobiographies (Edwina's *Remember Me to Tom* and **Dakin Williams**'s *Tennessee Williams: An Intimate Biography*).

Memoirs can be viewed from a variety of perspectives. It might be read traditionally as an Augustinian-styled confessional, an *Apologia Pro Vita Sua*, in which Williams defends his homosexuality and his resistance to homophobic assaults. Appropriately, Williams called for a "New Morality" in *Memoirs* to revolutionize the world toward pluralistic acceptance of the Other. In retrospect, *Memoirs* appear less sensational and more innovative. Today *Memoirs* seems as if Williams were writing a postmodern autobiography, consistent with his theatrical experiments in the 1960s and 1970s. His lack of chronological orderliness, his seemingly disorganized and incoherent narrative, breaks between past and present, and conflating past and present typify a postmodern style, image, and narrative strategy. In this light, Williams's incoherence and inaccuracies can be subsumed as an inevitable consequence of his quintessential uncertainty. Ultimately, *Memoirs* can be seen as a text functioning just outside the parameters of autobiography. Read as meta-biography,

Memoirs is Williams's quasi-fictional attempt to (de)construct his own identity.

Further Reading

Cooke, M.G. "The Hero in Autobiography." *Yale Review* 65 (1976): 587–591.

Lehmann-Haupt, Christopher. "Love Songs of a Crocodile." *New York Times* 1 November 1975: 35.

Pagan, Nicholas. *Rethinking Literary Biography: A Postmodern Approach to Tennessee Williams*. Rutherford, NJ: Fairleigh Dickinson University Press, 1993.

Richardson, Jack. "Unaffected Recollections: *Memoirs*." *New York Times Book Review* 2 November 1975: 42.

Ruckel, Terri Smith. " 'A giggling, silly, bitchy, voluptuary': Tennessee Williams's *Memoirs* as *Apologia Pro Vita Sua*." *Southern Quarterly* 38 (Fall 1999): 94–103.

Spoto, Donald. *The Kindness of Strangers: The Life of Tennessee Williams*. Boston: Little, Brown, 1985.

Williams, Tennessee. "Born Forty Years Too Soon." *Vogue* (November 1975): 193–195, 232–238.

———. "Survival Notes: A Journal." *Esquire* (September 1972): D1.

Terri Smith Ruckel

Merlo, Frank (1929–1963). Frank Merlo was one of Williams's closest friends and a long-time companion/lover. Williams met Merlo, a handsome, Sicilian-American World War II veteran, in Provincetown in the summer of 1947. At the time, Williams was contemplating ending his turbulent relationship with **Pancho Rodriguez y Gonzales**. Merlo, who had a gift for attracting well-known writers (**Gore Vidal** notes that he also had been the lover of journalist Joseph Alsop), was living, not too happily, with lyricist John LaTouche. After a romantic night together, Williams and Merlo parted company. In October 1948, Williams ran into Merlo on a New York street. Williams and Merlo quickly set up housekeeping together, and Merlo was his constant companion for over a decade after that.

In many ways Williams and Merlo are an example of opposites attracting. Merlo was a northern, working-class man, second-generation Sicilian, definitely "straight looking and acting," and plain speaking, the opposite of the southern, effete Williams. The differences between Williams and Merlo were not merely physical or cultural. While Williams in his life and work was driven to a nomadic existence, Merlo provided constancy, stability, and security. Frank took care of all the quotidian details of Williams's life. While Williams's shyness and insecurity made socializing difficult, Merlo's easygoing charm drew people to him. While the exigencies of Williams's career took them to New York and Los Angeles and Williams's urge to keep moving kept them traveling quite a bit, the center of their domestic life was **Key West**, where Williams bought a house with a pool for his daily swims. There Merlo became such a popular figure that he was called "the Mayor of Key West." For Williams, Merlo was friend, lover, amanuensis, and protector. He more than earned the regular salary Williams paid him to take care of all the practical details of the playwright's life.

For a decade, the life of Williams and Merlo seemed relatively secure. Williams was exceptionally productive between *A Streetcar Named Desire* in 1947 and *Cat on a Hot Tin Roof* in 1956, and if none of the intervening plays matched the critical or commercial success of *A Streetcar Named Desire*, they were, nonetheless, regarded as the work of a major writer. They were sold to **Hollywood** and made Williams a household name and a relatively wealthy man. His 1951 play *The Rose Tattoo* was dedicated to Merlo and Sicily, Merlo's ancestral home. While not one of the playwright's more successful works, it is one of his lightest and one of the rare Williams plays with a happy ending. Williams called *The Rose Tattoo* "my love play to the world," demonstrating his own personal happiness and, rare for him, faith in the possibility of love, if, characteristically, a love built almost exclusively on sexual attraction. Merlo was assigned a percentage of the royalties to *The Rose Tattoo* and **Camino Real,** two works written during the happiest years of their relationship. However, there was constant tension. Merlo wanted a stable, monogamous life, and Williams was disinclined to give up his promiscuity.

If most chronicles are consistent about the beginning and middle of the relationship of Tennessee Williams and Frank Merlo, they differ somewhat on the end. When his father died in 1957, Williams began intensive psychoanalysis, which, typically for the time, led him into a negative exploration of his sexuality and his relationship with Merlo. The analysis led Williams deeper into a cycle of alcohol, **drugs**, and sexual promiscuity, which strained his relationship with the steadfast Merlo, whose frustration could be expressed in violence. Finally, in 1961, Williams broke with Merlo, but he kept him on salary and allowed him to stay in the Key West home he so loved. Shortly thereafter, Merlo, a heavy smoker, contracted lung cancer. Williams, guilt-ridden over deserting his "little horse," Merlo's nickname, stayed with him during his final months and visited him regularly at Memorial Hospital, where Merlo died in September 1963. Merlo's death sent Williams into an even deeper cycle of depression and self-destruction. The playwright whose work is a vivid argument against the possibility of lasting love and a celebration of intense sexual connections was tortured by his inability to maintain his relationship with Merlo and that he wasn't there for his friend during his illness. Frank Merlo gave Williams his last and longest loving relationship. Without the stability Merlo brought to Williams's life, the playwright seemed incapable of coherence in his writing or his life. See also **Kubie, Lawrence.**

Further Reading

Gronbeck-Tedesco, John. "On *The Rose Tattoo*." In *Tennessee Williams: A Casebook*, ed. Robert F. Gross. New York: Routledge, 2002. 63–78.

Spoto, Donald. *The Kindness of Strangers: The Life of Tennessee Williams*. Boston: Little, Brown, 1985.

John M. Clum

Mielziner, Jo (1901–1976). Jo Mielziner was a leading designer of many Williams's plays. One of the most prolific and important sceneographers of the twentieth century, Mielziner, with Lee Simonson and Robert Edmond Jones, helped usher onto U.S. stages the principles of the new stage craft. Mielziner's influence is particularly evident in the production histories of plays such as Maxwell Anderson's *Winterset* (1935), Williams's **A Streetcar Named Desire** (1947) and **Summer and Smoke** (1948), **Arthur Miller**'s *Death of a Salesman* (1949), and Rodgers and Hammerstein's *The King and I* (1951). Subsequent designers considered many of Mielziner's decisions definitive and retained parts of his scenography in their own settings and lighting for later productions of their plays.

Mielziner's working principles, derived in part from European practice, connected smoothly to Williams's aesthetic: (1) The playwright's use of strong metaphors found its parallel in Mielziner's regard for the space as a suggestive metaphor for the text; (2) the manneristic style of movement and posture that characterized the productions of *A Streetcar Named Desire* and *Summer and Smoke* was understood and enhanced by Mielziner's playing horizontal and vertical lines against and with the actor's movement and position; (3) Mielziner's light and moveable scrims changed one space into another almost instantly as if space were fluid and malleable, thus allowing the setting for Williams's plays to be altered quickly without breaking the crucial rhythms of the words and scenic action; (4) mood, understood as the spiritual or inner quality of a scene, occupied a major position in Mielziner's designs, which corresponded with Williams's concern for mood in scenes, such as Laura's meeting with the gentleman caller in *The Glass Menagerie* or the rape scene in *A Streetcar Named Desire*; (5) Mielziner's continually altering the relative intensities of individual lighting instruments guided an audience's concentration even while illuminating more than one section of the stage, making it possible to visualize scenic arrangements or characters even while emphasizing others. Chance Wayne in **Sweet Bird of Youth** (1959), for example, could deliver his final monologue while other pieces of the setting could remain hauntingly aglow; (6) Mielziner's emphasis on suggestion and abstraction aligned his work with Williams's own preference for synecdoche and metonymy.

Jo Mielziner. Springer/Photofest.

The Glass Menagerie (1945) provided Mielziner's first opportunity to collaborate with Williams. Many of the designer's images employed contrast between the heavy darkness and garish light of the alleyways around the tenement and the intermittent luminescence of the Wingfield apartment. Mielziner developed the psychological interiority of the characters by fashioning the walls out of transparent scrims that let the gaze of the audience pierce the inner spaces the characters inhabited. In his collaboration with **Elia Kazan** and Williams on *A Streetcar Named Desire*, Mielziner again used translucent scrim walls to symbolize seeing through barriers into private lives. Along with the scrims, he used lighting techniques that moved the audience's attention from one part of the stage to another in an instant or revealed two or more parts of the setting simultaneously. Similarly, Mielziner and director **Margo Jones** interpreted *Summer and Smoke* (1948) through a scenic leitmotif made up of broken lattice work to convey brittleness and vulnerability. Incomplete pieces of heavier structures mingled with the light lattice to create a surrounding environment that was broken, discontinuous, and threatening to the more delicate objects.

In *Cat on a Hot Tin Roof* (1955), Mielziner used a fluid space with only the most necessary set pieces to create the impression of stolid opulence and excess. Designer, director, and playwright had become deft collaborators so that the set seemed to function as another character interacting with

145

the human characters. Williams wrote the action to be performed in one space and in a running time that was the same as the time of the action. Mielziner experimented with a modified thrust stage partially to accommodate Big Daddy's elephant speech, which the playwright wanted delivered almost directly to the audience. The result was a deep playing space that allowed the actors proximity to or distance from the audience.

Mielziner was not completely satisfied with his work on *Sweet Bird of Youth* and confessed that he and Kazan failed to include cinematic images in the play as Williams wished. Mielziner's designs featured even more emptiness and sparseness in the foreground than in *Cat on a Hot Tin Roof*. His backgrounds for the play were rendered in striking, unrealistic colors that made it difficult to judge depth and caused the playing space to seem suspended in a dream world, where somber shadows and dark silhouettes brought the world back to brutish reality.

Mielziner continued his work with Williams in 1963 when he designed *The Milk Train Doesn't Stop Here Anymore*. Setting aside elaborately wrought collaborations between light and multiple surfaces, Mielziner relied even more than usual on synecdoche. The play's Italian villa became a series of interiors and exteriors connoted by colors on the cyclorama and a few set pieces that suggested an entire decor. Sets and lights created the sense of a separate world that, instead of representing the real physical world by means of similarity, invoked reality by creating parallels to it. The stage as an analogue to reality pushed *The Milk Train Doesn't Stop Here Anymore* into allegory and contrasted with the more realistic performances of the actors.

Jo Mielziner's preferred aesthetic magic merged nicely with Williams's. Influenced by art movements in early-twentieth-century Europe—especially symbolism and impressionism—Mielziner demonstrated his artistic kinship with Williams. Mielziner's settings and Williams's plays might be viewed as a "conversation" between these two artists constructing plays based on similar artistic theatrical assumptions.

Further Reading

Christian, Jonathan. "Jo Mielziner Stage Designs." <http://www.wfu.edu/Academic departments/Theatre/resources/mielzinerf/ mielmain.htm> [accessed December 28, 2001].

Kolin, Philip C. *Williams: "A Streetcar Named Desire."* Plays in Production. Cambridge: Cambridge University Press, 2000.

Mielziner, Jo. *Designing for the Theatre: A Memoir and a Portfolio.* New York: Atheneum, 1965.

Murphy, Brenda. *Tennessee Williams and Elia Kazan: A Collaboration in the Theatre.* Cambridge: Cambridge University Press, 1992.

Smith, Harry. "Tennessee Williams and Jo Mielziner: The Memory Plays." *Theatre Survey* 23.2 (1982): 223–235.

John Gronbeck-Tedesco

The Milk Train Doesn't Stop Here Anymore. *The Milk Train Doesn't Stop Here Anymore*, written in 1962, is a dramatic adaptation of Tennessee Williams's short story "Man Bring This Up Road," first published in *Mademoiselle* in 1959. Like many of Williams's later works, this play was criticized for its lack of conventional dramatic action and conflict. *The Milk Train Doesn't Stop Here Anymore*, especially in its later rewrite, was influenced by Asian philosophy and theatrical tradition. Several critics, notably Allean Hale and Michael Paller, have cited audiences' unfamiliarity with Zen and Asian theatrical tradition as a cause of the play's poor reception.

The action of the play, in six scenes over two acts, spans the last two days in the life of Flora "Sissy" Goforth, a dying, wealthy American widow ensconced on a mountaintop on Italy's "Divina Costiera" overlooking the Mediterranean. Mrs. Goforth is visited by Christopher Flanders, a 35-year-old, itinerant, no-longer-promising American poet and translator of Hindu texts, who finds and gives comfort in the company of wealthy women at the end of their lives.

After its first production in 1963, Williams rewrote the play as his longtime companion **Frank Merlo** was dying of lung cancer. Biographer Donald Spoto characterizes the rewrites for the revival as an effort to come to terms with the inevitability of death. Aspects of Williams's life, personality, and his relationship to his public image also surface in both Mrs. Goforth, the drug-addled, aging, frightened bon vivant, and Christopher Flanders, a poet past his prime. Furthermore, the play acknowledges and references its own autobiographical qualities by having Mrs. Goforth dictate her autobiography throughout.

An early version of *The Milk Train Doesn't Stop Here Anymore* was produced by the Spoleto Festival of Two Worlds in July 1962. After some rewrites, it opened on Broadway on 16 January 1963 and ran for 69 performances, closing in March of that year. After more rewrites, another version was produced in Virginia in September 1963 and opened on Broadway in a new production on 1 January 1964, playing for only two previews and five performances. The changes made by the playwright between the play's two Broadway openings included the addition of two "attendants" who comment on the action and function as Kabuki stagehands, unseen by the other characters on stage. The revisions shaped a less naturalistic, more Asian-influenced work, that was more appropriate to Williams's conception of the piece as an allegory, as he described his intention in his introduction to the revised text. In his study of the play's relationship to Noh drama, Michael Paller notes that the plot parallels that of classic Noh plays, in which a traveling priest offers salvation to a stranger.

Mrs. Goforth spends much of her time dictating her memoirs to her young female secretary, Blackie, recounting and reliving the glories and terrors of her transformation from carnival stripper to a woman who achieved international renown for her beauty, and married four times, but only once (the last time) for love. Chris Flanders, dubbed "the Angel of Death" in aging aristocratic circles, believes that he can give Mrs. Goforth, in her final days, a form of enlightenment he has offered to his other hostesses. Intending to take him on as a lover, Mrs. Goforth has less spiritual plans for Flanders. The struggle to control their relationship, paralleling Mrs. Goforth's struggle with her own decline, shapes the plot. Williams also penned a comic scene in which Mrs. Goforth trades barbs with the vampirelike Vera Ridgeway Condotti, known as the Witch of Capri, a fellow doyenne, who tries to abscond with Mrs. Goforth's houseguest.

Much critical reaction has focused on the spiritual concerns of the play. Like St. Christopher, the "Christ Bearer," and as reinforced by the association of his last name with Flanders field, the visitor brings not only salvation from loneliness and fear but salvation from life itself. In Williams's 1959 short story, the visiting poet is named Jimmy Dobyne, he is not an "Angel of Death," and Mrs. Goforth remains living. By the second Broadway production, the poet, now named Christopher Flanders, is identified with death, and Mrs. Goforth dies before the end of the play. While Christopher offers Mrs. Goforth the salvation of acceptance, Sissy

Goforth is a coward, a "sissy," fearful of death and attached to her earthly possessions and memories. In an earlier version of the script, Christopher Flanders leaves the still-living Mrs. Goforth at the end of the play, and Mrs. Goforth asks Blackie to call him back as he has affected her in a way she did not think was still possible. In that version, Flanders offered a salvation that allowed Flora to break through her greed and acquisitiveness to accept the affection of another human being. In the final version of the play, Flanders offers a total salvation that will allow Flora to break through life itself.

The difference between these two endings reflects not only the effect of Frank Merlo's illness (Williams's long-time lover) but an increased influence of Asian philosophy on the play. Allean Hale cites Williams's visits to **Yuko Mishima**, a Zen writer, during a trip to Japan in 1960, to explain the Noh influence on Williams. Hale traces Mishimo's influence in various ways, including the use of the sea as a symbolic representation of death. Building on Hale's observations, Michael Paller also identifies the Zen influence in the play's treatment of life and death, noting that while Mrs. Goforth despairs that she found no meaning when she visited the pyramids, Flanders urges her to accept the absence of meaning.

Christopher Flanders's spiritual altruism is suspect, as he has made a profession of being a houseguest. This ambiguity regarding his motivation is highlighted when the audience and Mrs. Goforth overhear him telling lies, both comforting and self-justifying, to the spinster daughter of a newly deceased client. His motivation seems even more complex when he describes his caring for someone as a way that he himself can feel protected. With many of the qualities found in Val Xavier and Chance Wayne, Flanders is, at one time, a shaman, an artist, a lost soul, and a gigolo.

Interestingly, Flanders and Mrs. Goforth do not address each other in person until the fifth scene of the play, until which time Mrs. Goforth communicates with him through the secretary, Blackie. The flirtatious banter between Blackie and Christopher, as Blackie settles him into a cupid-decorated Pink Villa in Scene Two, offers the conventional prospect of Blackie being delivered from her oppressive employment by the handsome stranger. Viewed as the story of a young couple's life-affirming happiness being threatened by a frightened, declining, but somehow sympathetic, older woman, the plot parallels that of *A Streetcar Named Desire*. However, the extended scene between Mrs. Goforth and her visiting neighbor, The Witch of Capri, interrupts the development of an expected relationship between Christopher and Blackie.

In her relationship to the past, and fear of the future, Mrs. Goforth is related to Blanche DuBois in *A Streetcar Named Desire*, Maggie in **Cat on a Hot Tin Roof**, Princess Kosmonopolis in **Sweet Bird of Youth**, and even Amanda in **The Glass Menagerie**. However, while all these characters long for their more carnal pasts, Flora is a far less sympathetic character than they are. Michael Paller points out that it is her earthly, passionate past, all she claims to have left, that Sissy must overcome in order to be redeemed. It is not surprising that an audience is less than sympathetic toward a character whose existence is the antagonist.

The Milk Train Doesn't Stop Here Anymore abounds in symbols. In one of many self-referential moments that support the frank theatricality of the play, Blackie tells Christopher that everything on Mrs. Goforth's property is symbolic. The "Divina Costiera" of the setting is also the coast separating the earthly from the divine for the dying Flora. The recurring "boom" of the waves below signals the vastness and impenetrability of the life process. Flanders's repetition of the sound, the act of a poet giving voice to his perception, becomes a call to accept, or at least acknowledge, the impenetrability of life and death. The sea itself, into which things are thrown, and Mrs. Goforth almost falls, is the great source and end of life. The coast, like the beach at the Encantadas described by Mrs. Venable in *Suddenly Last Summer*, marks the place where life begins and ends—and where one might see God.

In the prologue added for the second Broadway version of *The Milk Train Doesn't Stop Here Anymore*, the stage assistants raise a flag emblazoned with a golden griffin, a creature they describe as a monster made up of equal parts lion and eagle, a tidy introduction to the character of Flora Goforth, whom Blackie later identifies as a monster. Christopher later describes a griffin as being almost capable of defeating death. Mrs. Goforth's rings, which she wears to keep them from being stolen, and finally surrenders to Christopher, represent the "loot" with which she has surrounded her heart, hurting her when her would-be comforter holds her hand too tightly. In another bit of overt symbolism, the "Saint Christopher" of the play comes bearing not Christ but a mobile named "The Earth Is a Wheel in a Great Big Gambling Casino," an embodiment of the message of acceptance and release he hopes to share with Mrs. Goforth. This symbolism is very apparent and works on a conscious level throughout the play. In another self-referential moment, the text itself acknowledges its symbolic blatancy, as the attendants make their last exit, declining to make another "obvious statement."

A lack of sympathy for Mrs. Goforth seems to have been a major handicap for the play according to reviewers. The *New York Times* reviews of the play's first Broadway run and of a 1987 revival both complain that the productions lacked a sympathetic center. This lack of a sympathetic "heart," identified as Mrs. Goforth's spiritual ailment, has also been a problem for the play in production. Williams, however, saw the character of Flora Goforth as a key to the play's future, writing in his *Memoirs* that the role would be valued by older female stars trying to maintain their careers and public images.

Another point of exchange between the play and its context includes the casting of **Tallulah Bankhead** in the lead role for the second Broadway run. Bankhead had a large homosexual following and was playing a character whose nickname, it is reported in an earlier version of the script, was given her by gay chorus boys. Another celebrated public figure, and friend of the playwright, associated with the work was **Paul Bowles**, mentioned in the 1959 short story as a contemporary celebrity and later hired to compose **music** for the play's first Broadway production.

In the film adaptation, *Boom!*, the casting capitalized on the stormy romance between Elizabeth Taylor and Richard Burton, who played Mrs. Goforth and Christopher Flanders. Maurice Yacowar, in his study of *Boom!*, discusses a shot featuring Mrs. Goforth's large diamond ring as referencing Burton's much celebrated habit of buying expensive jewelry for Taylor. Noel Coward's turn as the Witch of Capri, played as a man in the film, may also be seen as a campy nod to Coward's image as a fading homosexual *bon vivant* with an acerbic wit.

A 1994 production at the Glasgow Citizens Company featured Rupert Everett, in drag, in the role of Mrs. Goforth, further reinforcing "Sissy," Mrs. Goforth's nickname, as a derogatory term for an effeminate male, and capitalizing on Everett's public persona. Among the most personal of Williams's works, the play is as disjointed as Flora's dictation, and perhaps as unfathomable as Williams's life, or the "boom" of a great sea. See also *Collected Stories*.

Further Reading

Devlin, Albert J., ed. *Conversations with Tennessee Williams*. Jackson: University Press of Mississippi, 1986.

Fayard, Jeanne. "Meeting with Tennessee Williams." In *Conversations with Tennessee Williams*, ed. Albert J. Devlin. Jackson: University Press of Mississippi, 1986. 108–112.

Gross, Robert F. "Tracing Lines of Flight in *Summer and Smoke* and *The Milk Train Doesn't Stop Here Anymore*." In *Tennessee Williams: A Casebook*, ed. Robert F. Gross. New York: Routledge, 2002. 91–106.

Gruen, John. "Tennessee Williams." In *Conversations with Tennessee Williams*, ed. Albert J. Devlin. Jackson: University Press of Mississippi, 1986. 112–123.

Hale, Allean. "Tennessee's Long Trip." *Missouri Review* 7 (1984): 201–212.

Kolin, Philip C., ed. *The Undiscovered Country: The Later Plays of Tennessee Williams*. New York: Lang, 2002.

Paller, Michael. "The Day on Which a Woman Dies: *The Milk Train Doesn't Stop Here Anymore* and Nō Theatre." In *The Undiscovered Country: The Later Plays of Tennessee Williams*, ed. Philip C. Kolin. New York: Lang, 2002. 25–39.

Spoto, Donald. *The Kindness of Strangers: The Life of Tennessee Williams*. Boston: Little, Brown, 1995.

Weales, Gerald. "Tennessee Williams' Achievements in The Sixties." In *Tennessee Williams: A Collection of Critical Essays*, ed. Stephen Stanton. Englewood Cliffs, NJ: Prentice Hall, 1977. 61–70.

Williams, Tennessee. *Memoirs*. Garden City, NY: Doubleday, 1975.

Yacowar, Maurice. *Tennessee Williams and Film*. New York: Ungar, 1977.

Francis X. Kuhn

Miller, Arthur (1915–). Born in 1915 in New York City to immigrant parents, Arthur Miller is a major American playwright often compared with Williams and, along with **Eugene O'Neill**, is often cited as one of America's three most important playwrights. The lives and works of Williams and Miller often intersect. Both owe a great deal to **Elia Kazan** for his masterful direction for their early success as playwrights. Kazan directed *All My Sons* (1945) and *Death of a Salesman* (1949), perhaps Miller's best-known plays, and between them he directed *A Streetcar Named Desire* (1947). In 1951 Kazan chose to work with Miller on a film of *All My Sons* rather than direct Williams's *The Rose Tattoo*, which initiated the first significant conflict between Kazan and Williams.

Williams and Miller were both instrumental in bringing Expressionism to the American stage with *The Glass Menagerie* and *Death of a Salesman*. Williams saw himself as a social writer, considering Miller a polemicist. In an important study, addressing the relationship between the two playwrights' images of men and masculinity, David Savran's *Communists, Cowboys, and Queers* argues that Williams is much more ambiguous, radical, and subversive than Miller, who often uses binary oppositions. Even though both playwrights address father-son relationships and the social construction of gender relations, Miller's male characters seem more conventional in their masculinity, caught up within a traditional system of binary oppositions between masculinity and femininity.

Both Miller and Williams were against McCarthyism. When Miller was denied a passport to attend a performance of *The Crucible* in Belgium in 1951, he was investigated as a communist by the State Department and asked to appear before the House Un-American Activities Committee to identify others sympathetic to communism. Supporting Miller, Williams wrote a rousing letter to the State Department, arguing that America's reputation abroad would be adversely damaged if its artists were to face censorship in the West. Unlike Kazan, Williams refused to give names of communist sympathizers. *Camino Real*, one of Williams's most controversial and experimental works from the early 1950s, denounced McCarthyism as did Miller's *The Crucible*, a thinly veiled allegory about the Salem witch trials that simultaneously blasted McCarthy's witch hunts for communists. Some critics have also seen elements of McCarthyism in the paranoia surrounding Brick in **Cat on a Hot Tin Roof**.

Williams's important essay "The Timeless World of a Play" (reprinted in **Where I Live**) focuses on Willy Loman from *Death of a Salesman*, often cited as the quintessential modern tragic hero threatened by a loss of human dignity. Arguing that even though the audience would probably not be patient with Willy in real life, Williams nonetheless suggests that a tragedy humanizes even those with whom we least identify because a play exists outside of time. It is larger than life. Williams's essay demands comparison with Miller's manifesto, "Tragedy and the Common Man," which explains and defends his conception of Willie as a tragic hero.

Both Miller and Williams also made enormous contributions to film by having their plays adapted for the screen. Williams's influence on the film industry, however, may have been more profound than that of Miller, who was predominantly a social realist

and less popular with film audiences. Though Williams valued film as an art form more and was much more concerned that adaptations of his works be made into artistic achievements, he and Miller both brought the innovations of their theaters to a larger (film) audience.

In sum, both playwrights, though different in orientation and impact, held the other in great respect. Miller considered Williams a major figure in American letters and was sympathetic to the closeted nature of Williams's plays dealing with homosexuality in a repressive era. Williams's respect for Miller was equally sincere and significant. See also **Politics**.

Further Reading

Palmer, R. Barton. "Hollywood in Crisis: Tennessee Williams and the Evolution of the Adult Film." In *The Cambridge Companion to Tennessee Williams*, ed. Matthew C. Roudané. Cambridge: Cambridge University Press, 1997. 204–231.

Saravan, David. *Communists, Cowboys, and Queers: The Politics of Masculinity in the Work of Arthur Miller and Tennessee Williams*. Minneapolis: University of Minnesota Press, 1992.

Dean Shackelford

Mills (McBurney), Clark (1913–1986). Clark Mills (McBurney) was one of Williams's closest friends and mentor in 1936–1937 when he attended Washington University, between the time he left the University of Missouri and the time he enrolled at the University of Iowa. Lyle Leverich claims that Mills was "one of the most important influences on Tom Williams's life and in the career of Tennessee Williams" (155). Like Williams, Mills lived in Clayton, Missouri, a suburb of St. Louis; he was a graduate student in French at Washington University when Williams was an undergraduate studying literature. The two bonded as good friends because of their love of poetry and their own aspirations as writers. It was Mills who introduced Williams to **Hart Crane**, Rimbaud, and Rilke. Both were members of a small intellectual group at the university devoted to literature and were part of what they called the St. Louis Poets Workshop. Indefatigable in their reading, Mills and Williams set up what Williams called "the literary factory" in Mills's basement and later at **Edwina Dakin Williams**'s house where they read each other's work and sought publishers for their verse. Mills, an editor of Washington University's *Anvil*, had published widely in contemporary magazines (under the name Clark Mills) and had won first place in 1937 in a contest sponsored by *College Verse*. Mills's poem "The White Winter" can be found at the beginning of Allean Hale's edition of *Fugitive Kind* (New Directions, 2001). A keen observer of Williams's writing ability and devotion, Mills heard the voice of the poet in Williams's plays and frequently commented on Williams's "fanatical" writing.

Mills left Washington University in 1937 to study and travel in France and became an instructor in French at Cornell. The two men met in St. Louis one more time in the summer before Mills went to Cornell and several times later. Williams's early letters and **journals** are laced with fond remembrances of Mills and hailed him as "one of the most promising younger poets" in a story about him titled "Return to Dust." See also **St. Louis**.

Further Reading

Leverich, Lyle. *Tom: The Unknown Tennessee Williams*. New York: Crown, 1995.

Philip C. Kolin

Mishima, Yukio (1925–1970). The pseudonym for Hiraoka Kimitake, Yukio Mishima was a prolific and celebrated Japanese novelist, poet, essayist, and playwright who was a close friend of Williams and an important influence on his later work. Williams and Mishima met in New York in the summer of 1957, leading to a 13-year friendship. They first met when Williams approached Mishima on the street to invite him to a party. They were formally introduced a week later through their mutual publisher, **James Laughlin** at New Directions, when Mishima was discussing the forthcoming American publication of his first novel, *Confessions of a Mask* (1949; trans. 1958). Mishima then introduced Williams to his *Five Modern Noh Plays*, a form of Japanese theater that impressed Williams and led him to experiment with new forms in his own writing. The two considered themselves "soul mates," and although he was married, Mishima shared Williams's homosexual preference. In 1959, Williams traveled to Tokyo to visit Mishima and learn more about the Japanese Noh and Kabuki theater. The two writers were interviewed by international television hookup in 1960 on the CBS broadcast of Edward R. Murrow's *Small World* and discussed love and violence in modern drama. Both Williams and Mishima were at some point candidates for the Nobel Prize, although neither won it.

Mishima's influence on Williams is well documented. Allean Hale discovered a "secret" Noh play that Williams wrote as a tribute to Mishima, *The Day on Which the Artist Dies (An Occidental Noh Play)*, an early forecast of *In the Bar of a Tokyo Hotel* (1969), found in a box of original drafts sold by Williams to the University of California at Los Angeles in 1970 and which is dated 1960. It is dedicated to "Yukio Mishima in token of long friendship and much admiration." After his visit to Tokyo, Williams seemed to have changed the title to *The Day on Which a Man Dies* and revised his secret script, as Scene Two especially relates to Kabuki in its staging and presents a character called "The Oriental," a law student from Imperial University (as Mishima had been) who performs as stage assistant, chorus, and narrator. "The Oriental" delivers the monologue that divulges the play's final action, explaining that this is the day when the character "The Man" will kill himself. Williams apparently never showed his script to Mishima. Hale also notes that Williams apparently influenced Mishima's work in return, as Williams's leading lady in *Suddenly Last Summer* became Mishima's lead in *The Lady of Aoi*. In *Suddenly Last Summer*, too, the predatory homosexual cannibalized by the young men he consumed sexually can be compared to the sailor who is vivisected by young boys in Mishima's *Sailor Who Fell from Grace*. Finally, Mishima's *Leper King* and Williams's *In the Bar of a Tokyo Hotel* explore the idea of the artist consumed by his final masterpiece.

The two men met for the last time in Tokyo on 1 October 1970. Six weeks later, Mishima committed ritual suicide at the age of 45, performing a Japanese rite involving disembowelment and decapitation known as *seppuku* or *hara-kiri*. Critics have long read an obsession with suicide as an erotic act in Mishima's work, and many regard his death as a political protest against modern Japanese weakness. Just after Mishima's death, Williams revised the script of *The Day on Which a Man Dies*, changing the dedication to "In Memory of Yukio Mishima, with great respect for his art." Neither the 1960 nor the 1970 version of the play has ever been performed. Williams wrote in his *Memoirs* that Mishima's suicide was performed not only because of political concern about the collapse of the old traditions in Japan but because Mishima felt he had completed his major work as an artist.

In 2000, the lesbian-feminist troupe Split Britches, along with Asian American performance artist Stacy Makishi, presented *Salad of the Bad Café*, a postmodern cabaret inspired by **Carson McCullers**'s novel *The Ballad of the Sad Cafe*, on the lives of Williams and Mishima.

Further Reading

Hale, Allean. "The Secret Script of Tennessee Williams." *Southern Review* 27.2 (1991): 363–375.

Murrow, Edward R. "Interview with Tennessee Williams, Yukio Mishima, and Dilys Powell." In *Conversations with Tennessee Williams*, ed. Albert J. Devlin. Jackson: University Press of Mississippi, 1986. 69–77.

Stokes, Henry Scott. *The Life and Death of Yukio Mishima*. New York: Cooper Square, 2000.

Tischler, Nancy M. "Romantic Textures in Tennessee Williams's Plays and Short Stories." In *The Cambridge Companion to Tennessee Williams*, ed. Matthew C. Roudané. Cambridge: Cambridge University Press, 1997. 147–166.

Annette J. Saddik

Moise and the World of Reason. *Moise and the World of Reason*, a Williams novel published in 1975, signals a radical departure from the techniques of his previous fiction. He manipulates his text through the use of unconventional narrative strategies, freehanded intertextuality, and nonstandard sentence structure and punctuation. Williams's plot, setting, and character are just as unconventional as his writing technique. Readers would be hard-pressed to outline a traditional plot, and the young narrator, who confesses early on that he is a failed writer, operates within a world of artistic personalities centered around Moise (pronounced Mō-ease), the aging painter-mentor. Most of the action takes place in the shoddy art and warehouse district of New

York City. The fictitious author, who is clearly Williams himself, reveals what readers ordinarily are not privy to: the struggle an author goes through in the act of creating, the pain of rejection—both professional and personal—and the private world of a colony of artists.

Williams's manipulation of text is highly effective and convincing. Commentary interspersed throughout the novel takes the form of short, ironic interjections or lengthy expositions. Williams's technique results in a shift in voice from the public author to the private writer. When listening to the voice of the private writer, we strain over the Bon Ami box while he composes the very work we are reading; hearing with him the ticking clock in his dour room on the dock of the Hudson River, we fall into his state of dejection when he abandons the notebooks and scribbles his thoughts on rejection slips from publishers. When the public author emerges, we spring forward with the narrative voice, and the story advances.

The novel closes as it opens, in the home of Moise. In the final section, the dejected writer comes to her for inspiration and sits with his Blue Jay notebook open waiting for the profundities that he hopes she will share. There are frequent shifts in voice that move readers from one perspective to another: now observing the dialogue between Moise and the writer, now being made privy to the private thoughts inside the writer's head. It is Williams's intent to portray this writer as transporting actual experience to pages within his text with little or no alteration. The duration of time within the novel is incredibly short; all the action takes place within a 24-hour span, but Williams plays with the concept of time in true postmodern fashion. The characters introduced in this brief period take on special significance for readers who had ample incentive to become familiar with Williams's life story. The novel

was published in 1975, closely behind the appearance of his *Memoirs*.

There is really no mystery in determining the origin and symbolism of the characters in the novel. For instance, Moise states that the old playwright is the aged version of the young writer: he is, in effect, the image of the future. When the elderly playwright visits the writer's abode—breaking in on him in the act of writing—he appears as the spectral presence of Williams himself, defying the boundaries of time and reality. The private writer takes flight from this apparition, and readers are taken with him up the stairs to the roof of the warehouse. Under the vast expanse of a star-lit sky, he tackles metaphysical questions, but his indulgence in existential angst does not last, for, in the end, he reclaims meaning by returning to Moise. He discovers that the vehicle used to deliver art becomes art itself, validating Williams's attempt to bring readers into his world through a self-reflexive narrator/author whose reality is sometimes beyond reason. Hence the title of the novel.

Moise reveals Williams's deliberate strategy, commonly employed by postmodern writers, to expose the chaos of modern existence through a blatant disregard of form and order. Williams's success with this technique results in the emergence of a new, self-imposed order that ignores old systems of belief and creates a unique worldview. We are told how the title was decided upon and given glimpses into his prized Blue Jay notebooks as he is composing the very story we are reading. In using this technique, the act of writing about writing, Williams deconstructs his own novel.

Williams further fractures traditional prose form in *Moise* by incorporating other postmodern devices. He manipulates sentence structure through countless unfinished sentences, sometimes with trailing ellipses, sometimes dangling without ending punctuation pointing to wordless, white spaces on the page, all implying unspoken meaning. Through this deliberate stylistic sabotage, Williams invites play and interaction between readers and the text, leaving it up to readers to finish sentences and search for meaning. His use of intertextuality unfolds in frequent allusions to writers, living and dead, such as Samuel Taylor Coleridge, John Steinbeck, **Jane Bowles**, Gertrude Stein, and Alice B. Toklas. Williams also intersperses real celebrities with fictitious ones and rewrites part of his autobiography in the creation of a grandfather who wrote screenplays. Blending the real and imagined in the pages of this text calls into question the thin line between fiction and life, asking us to deconstruct our perception of traditional form and explore the artist's role in the creative process.

Many readers have regarded *Moise* as the product of a Williams stupefied by alcohol and strung out on **drugs**, but it can profitably be read as autobiography, testifying to the fragmentation of the psyche—serving, as some would maintain, as a record of Williams's postbreakdown period in which he was submerged in a debilitating state of anxiety and apprehension over a world where the border between reason and unreason was increasingly blurred. *Moise* demands comparison with *The Glass Menagerie* and *Something Cloudy, Something Clear* as Williams's memory texts.

Further Reading

Barth, John. "The Literature of Exhaustion." In *Narrative/Theory*, ed. David H. Richter. White Plains, NY: Longman, 1996. 77–86.

Bray, Robert. "Moise and the Man in the Fur Coat." *Southern Quarterly* 12 (1999): 58–70.

Hassan, Ihab. "Toward a Concept of Postmodernism." In *The Postmodern Turn*. Columbus: Ohio State University Press, 1987. 84–96.

Savran, David. *Communists, Cowboys, and Queers: The Politics of Masculinity in the Work of Arthur Miller and Tennessee Williams*. Minneapolis: University of Minnesota Press, 1992.

Robert Bray and Jean Rhodes

Mummers. The Mummers was a semi-professional theater group in **St. Louis** that staged two of Tennessee Williams's early full-length dramas—*Candles to the Sun* on 18 March 1937 and *Fugitive Kind* on 1 December 1937—in addition to a curtain opener *Headlines* (shortened from a much longer work) for Irwin Shaw's antiwar play *Bury the Dead* on 11 November 1936. Devoted to a theater of social protest in a time of great economic distress, the Mummers' goal was to stage hard-hitting plays that caught the revolutionary fervor of the times. Under the directorship of **Willard Holland** (1908–1963), who went on to become a dialogue coach for Universal Studios and a reporter, the Mummers performed such plays as Sinclair Lewis's *It Can't Happen Here* and George Bernard Shaw's *Arms and the Man*.

Holland worked closely with Williams, through extensive rewriting and revising, for both *Candles to the Sun* and *Fugitive Kind*. These plays were exactly the types of scripts Holland and the Mummers wanted to promote—*Candles to the Sun* dramatized the plight of Alabama coal miners who went on strike in the face of economic deprivation and threats to their human dignity, while *Fugitive Kind*, set in a St. Louis flophouse, localized national hardships in the 1930s through the lives of an assorted cast of misfits not unlike those characters who would populate Williams's later plays. The violence and cinematic flow of these early works done for the Mummers were to become

Williams's hallmarks. Holland vigorously helped Williams's career by praising his talents and urging reviews of his plays in the local press. Reviewing *Fugitive Kind*, Reed Hynds of the *St. Louis Star-Times*, for example, concluded that "Thomas Lanier Williams is a playwright to watch."

Because of the Mummers, the 25-year-old Williams received an enthusiastic boost at a crucial time in his fledgling career. The Mummers were as right for Williams as he was for them; they were hospitable to and even increased his antifascist politics and his rebellious, romantic spirit. To show their appreciation of Williams, he was asked to be an honorary member of this experimental theater group, and Holland proudly announced on the playbill for *Fugitive Kind* that the younger Tom Williams was "their own playwright" and that "the play justifies the Mummers's conviction that Mr. Williams has an important contribution to make to the American stage in the field of realistic drama."

Further Reading

Hale, Allean. Introduction to *The Fugitive Kind* by Tennessee Williams, ed. Allean Hale. New York: New Directions, 2001.
Leverich, Lyle. *Tom: The Unknown Tennessee Williams*. New York: Crown, 1995.

Philip C. Kolin

Music. Music was a major influence on Williams's life and work. As a child, he took piano and violin lessons from his maternal grandmother **Rosina Dakin** and danced with his sister Rose to popular music played on their old Victrola; as a young man setting out for **New Orleans**, he took with him a wind-up phonograph as well as his portable typewriter; when he left New Orleans for California, the phonograph and a guitar went with him; and when he moved on to New Mexico, he wore his guitar on a rope around his neck. From his earliest efforts as a playwright, Williams recognized the signifying potential and emotional power of music as an element of drama. Music was an integral aspect of Williams's dramaturgy throughout his canon, where incidental music by such composers as **Paul Bowles**, Alex North, David Diamond, and Ned Rorem, a wide range of preexisting music, and a lyrical treatment of sound effects combined to achieve a variety of dramatic effects. In addition to Williams's incorporation of music into his plays, a number of his songs, among them "Heavenly Grass" from *Orpheus Descending*, have been recorded independently, some of his poems have been set to music, and several of his plays, including *A Streetcar Named Desire* (1999) and *Orpheus Descending* (1995), have been adapted into operas (see also *A Streetcar Named Desire* as Opera).

The Glass Menagerie was Williams's first major success as a playwright, and in his production notes on the play, he signaled his commitment to exploring nonrealistic techniques, including the use of music, in order to represent reality more accurately than he felt was possible within the confines of realism. These production notes read as a manifesto for Williams's future career, and the importance of music in his early "memory play" anticipates many of its functions in his later works. Within the flashback scenes of *The Glass Menagerie*, the dance tunes that drift across the alley to the Wingfields' apartment from the Paradise Dance Hall establish the historical moment to which the narrator Tom is returning and later provide the Gentleman Caller Jim O'Connor with an occasion to ask the shy and delicate Laura Wingfield to dance. At the same time, the music from the Paradise helps to set Laura apart from the world outside the Wingfield apartment, so that whereas Tom suggests that nights spent dancing to "hot swing music" and making love in the alley offer couples compensation for their otherwise uneventful lives, his discussion with his mother Amanda of his sister Laura's difference from other girls is underscored by an ominous-sounding tango. Laura's difference is further clarified by her tendency to retreat, at difficult and painful moments, to the old Victrola left behind by her father when he abandoned the family, and the "faraway, scratchy"–sounding records she plays on the Victrola relate aurally to the haunting incidental music that is associated with her throughout the play. As his production notes reveal again, Williams wanted this incidental music to provide "emotional emphasis" in certain scenes but also to connect the flashback scenes to Tom's present reality as narrator and to endow the play as a whole with the quality of nostalgia. This nostalgia is the play's unifying tone, despite occasional ironic moments such as when a phrase of the hymn "Ave Maria" represents Tom's sense of Amanda's self-dramatization in her role as his long-suffering mother.

The integral and complex use of music in *The Glass Menagerie* continues in *A Streetcar Named Desire*. Incidental jazz and blues music emanating from a local bar, together with the intermittent cries of a street vendor selling "red hots" and the screeches of an alley cat, help to represent and define the New Orleans setting, dominated by Stanley, as well as Blanche's loneliness and separateness from the world into which she has entered. When Blanche is left alone after Mitch refuses to marry her, for example, "[t]he distant piano is slow and blue," whereas when she is raped by Stanley, we hear a hot blues trumpet. The ambient New Orleans music and related neighborhood sounds contrast with the leitmotif of a delicate, old-fashioned, faraway-sounding "Varsouviana" heard only by Blanche and that haunts her

as an aural trace of her lost innocence and gentility, becoming more pervasive and distorted as the play progresses toward its tragic conclusion. This expressionistic use of music to reveal Blanche's increasingly desperate and fragile state of mind extends, during the rape scene, to the "inhuman jungle voices" that suggest her subjective experience of a savagely brutal world. Earlier, Williams's counterpointing of Stanley's ruthless exposure of Blanche's sexual past with her blithely ignorant bathtub rendition of the ironically appropriate popular song "Paper Moon" served to heighten her pathos.

The use of music to establish time and place, suggest mood, forward dramatic action, define character, express theme, and achieve poetic unity, as exemplified in *The Glass Menagerie* and *A Streetcar Named Desire*, extends to and is further developed in many other of Williams plays. In **The Eccentricities of a Nightingale**, for example, Alma's singing is suggestive of her impossible yet nonetheless beautiful ideal of disembodied feeling, whereas in *Orpheus Descending*, music functions as a metaphor for the spirit of life that conventional society seeks to stifle and kill. This life spirit is exemplified not only in Val Xavier, the guitar player who reawakens Lady Torrance from the living death of her marriage to Jabe just as the mythical musician Orpheus retrieved his wife Eurydice from the underworld, but also in the Dionysian figure of Lady's murdered father, an Italian mandolin player who served wine to lovers who came to tryst in his orchard. As for Val Xavier, with his "wild beauty," warm blood, and snakeskin jacket, when he plays the hymnlike ballad "Heavenly Grass" on a guitar inscribed by such blues greats as Leadbelly and Bessie Smith, he may bring to mind the young Elvis Presley, who began his recording career with Sun Records in Memphis in 1954, three years before the premiere of *Orpheus Descending*.

On a different note, in *The Rose Tattoo*, Williams's production notes call for the play to begin with a song by a Sicilian folk-musician that is then resumed at each major division of the play and completed at the end, thus containing the plot within a balladlike structure. This folkloric quality is enhanced through the intermittent bleating of a goat, an ancient symbol of primal desire, while the bacchic nature of such desire is suggested through percussive sounds such as the timpani that accompanies Alvaro's first entrance and a child's banging of improvised cymbals as Alvaro chases the goat around Serafina's yard. In *Suddenly Last Summer*, the crude percussion instruments of the band of naked children who consume their sexual exploiter Sebastian Venable are a human equivalent to the wild and ravenous bird-cries heard earlier during Mrs. Venable's account of how her son's witnessing of an attack on hatchling sea turtles by flesh-eating birds confirmed his belief in a savage god presiding over a predatory universe barely concealed under the veneer of civilization.

Further instances of Williams's musical treatment of sound effects include the measured beating of Jabe's cane that signifies death's approach in *Orpheus Descending*, the dry gourd that serves as a death rattle in *Camino Real*, and the clock that marks time's irrevocable passage in *Sweet Bird of Youth*, where the fleeting cries of gulls and the wind sighing in the palms also suggest the same painful truth of lost youth and innocence. Williams used the wind in *Summer and Smoke* as well, where it implies the unbridgeable gulf between Alma and John, and in *Camino Real*, where it is associated with the great unknown of Terra Incognita. A cacophonous blast of "cries of pain and pleasure" and fragments of song, followed by the call of a clarinet, suggest the uncertain future that awaits the young writer as he leaves his New Orleans rooming house for California at the end of *Vieux Carré*.

Finally, Williams's dialogue is generally characterized by a lyrical quality and cadence that is perhaps most evident in the great "aria"-like speeches of such characters as Blanche DuBois, Alma Winemiller, and Maggie the Cat. This distinctively musical quality of speech, combined with Williams's accomplished use of music and sound effects, contributed immeasurably to the emotional and poetic power of his drama and its impact on the stage.

Further Reading

Crandell, George W. "Music." In his *Tennessee Williams: A Descriptive Bibliography*. Pittsburgh: University of Pittsburgh Press, 1995. 553–557.

McCraw, Harry W. "Tennessee Williams, Film, Music, Alex North: An Interview with Luigi Zaninelli." *Mississippi Quarterly* 48.4 (Fall 1995): 763–775.

Williams, Tennessee. Interview with Cecil Brown. In *Conversations with Tennessee Williams*, ed. Albert J. Devlin. Jackson: University Press of Mississippi, 1986. 251–283.

———. Production Notes. *The Glass Menagerie*. In *Tennessee Williams: Plays 1937–1955*. Ed. Mel Gussow and Kenneth Holditch. New York: Library of America, 2000. 395–397.

Penny Farfan

The Mutilated. A companion piece to *The Gnädiges Fräulein*, *The Mutilated* was produced on 22 February 1966 at the Longacre Theatre in New York as part of a double bill titled *Slapstick Tragedy*. Probably better suited to off-Broadway audiences, the one-act play received neither critical nor public acclaim, closing after a run of only seven performances.

The Mutilated underscores Williams's compassion for society's misfits, conveying the belief that all human beings have their mutilations—whether these wounds are physical, emotional, or psychological. Set in a seedy section of the French Quarter, the play focuses on a pair of alcoholic prostitutes: Trinket Dugan, who feels mutilated after undergoing a mastectomy, and Celeste Delacroix Griffin, who has been arrested for shoplifting and is threatened with homelessness. After Celeste humiliates Trinket publicly, the two women clash bitterly (and sometimes comically) until they manage to renew their friendship on Christmas Eve, experiencing a mystical redemption when the Virgin Mary makes her presence felt in Trinket's fleabag hotel room.

Although *The Mutilated* has been interpreted as an autobiographical allegory (i.e., a portrait of the tormented artist), its primary significance lies in its experimental form, as Williams strove in the 1960s to break from the constraints of realism and to embrace a new alternative theater. The author's nonrealistic technique is revealed in the play's *mise-en-scène*, which, according to the production notes, should resemble a delicate Japanese line drawing, possessing an abstract, "spidery" quality. This nonrealistic style is reinforced by Williams's dialogue (which includes rapidly overlapping speech and direct addresses to the audience) and by the use of a Greek chorus—a group of carolers who sing repeatedly of the possibility of miracles—even for the dispossessed and the mutilated. Williams also includes two characters who are clearly more symbolic than realistic: the Bird-Girl (based on an actual Quarter resident, Ruthie the Duck Girl)—a freak-show attraction representing human degradation—and Jack in Black—a dark-clad, singing cowboy who personifies death.

As the title *Slapstick Tragedy* suggests, *The Mutilated* offers a combination of humor and poignancy, portraying its female derelicts as both laughable and pathetic. The slapstick element of the drama derives largely from the prolonged "catfight" between the two hookers, who insult each other in an outrageous, childlike manner. The play's resolution—emphasizing reconciliation, faith in human survival, and the promise of resurrection—is also typical of the seriocomic mode. Yet Williams's drama is still a tragedy because it accentuates the price that these hapless prostitutes must pay in order to survive. In all probability, Trinket and Celeste will remain alcoholic and loveless, forced to endure continued mutilations from their fellow human beings. Moreover, the two women will have to ultimately confront the funereal figure of Jack in Black, who, at the end of the play, grants Williams's characters only a temporary reprieve.

With the production of *Slapstick Tragedy*, critics began to accuse Williams of self-plagiarism, of recycling familiar themes and characters from his previous dramas. Reviewers saw Trinket and Celeste as pale imitations of other wounded women in Williams's plays, particularly Blanche DuBois in **A Streetcar Named Desire** and Alma Winemiller in **Summer and Smoke**. Harold Clurman was one of few critics to appreciate Williams's experimental form and to understand that in identifying with the misfits of the world, the playwright was really offering a caustic variation of an old theme.

Although scholars have generally neglected *The Mutilated*, several have called attention to the play's experimental style. June Bennett Larsen argues that *The Mutilated* reflects a symbolist aesthetic, pointing to Williams's preoccupation with death, his interest in the duality of flesh and spirit, and his desire to create an antirealistic theater by offering a mixture of dramatic forms. Larsen also maintains that Williams differs from the symbolists because of his penchant for grotesque humor and his optimistic belief in resurrection. In a more recent discussion of *The*

159

Mutilated, Ruby Cohn similarly accentuates the play's nonrealistic features—its dialogue, its symbolic characters, and its mystical epiphany—noting that the experimentation of Williams's later plays often tends toward the Gothic and/or the grotesque. On the whole, however, most critics have shown more interest in the play's absurdist companion piece, *The Gnädiges Fräulein*.

Further Reading

Clurman, Harold. "Theatre: Slapstick Tragedy." *Nation* 14 March 1966: 309. Reprinted in *The Critical Response to Tennessee Williams*, ed. George W. Crandell. Westport, CT: Greenwood, 1996. 220–222.

Cohn, Ruby. "Tennessee Williams: The Last Two Decades." In *The Cambridge Companion to Tennessee Williams*, ed. Matthew C. Roudané. Cambridge: Cambridge University Press, 1997. 232–243.

Larsen, June Bennett. "Tennessee Williams: Optimistic Symbolist." In *Tennessee Williams: A Tribute*, ed. Jac Tharpe. Jackson: University Press of Mississippi, 1977. 413–428.

Susan Koprince

Mythology. Tennessee Williams made frequent use of classical myths. His formal education in classics began in high school with the study of Latin, and his interest in Latin literature is evident in such works as his poem *Ave atque Vale* and his screenplay *All Gaul Is Divided*, which takes its title from the beginning of Julius Caesar's *Gallic War* (*Gallia est omnis divisa* . . .). Williams also enrolled in a course on classical Greek in 1937 at the University of Washington, but at the time he made a poor showing in most of his classes, including Greek. Despite this academic failure, he maintained an interest in Greek myth and cult throughout much of his life. The titles of some of his plays, for example, **Orpheus Descending** and **I Rise in**

Flame, Cried the Phoenix, reflect the influence of popular stories from antiquity. Such mythical figures as Psyche, Daphne, and Narcissus played a central role in shaping his characters. To portray the darker instincts of modern humanity, he also drew upon the rituals of Greco-Roman cult that expressed the irrational, violent forces of nature or upon such strange cultic figures as the Great Mother Goddess, Attis, and Adonis.

But it is Dionysus, the Greek god who encompassed both the violence of death and the regeneration of life, who seems to have held a special place in Williams's thinking. The descriptions of the violent death of Val Xavier in *Orpheus Descending* and of Sebastian Venable in **Suddenly Last Summer** evoke the horror of the Dionysian rituals of the *sparagmos*, in which an animal was torn asunder by devotees of the god, or the *omophagia*, in which raw flesh was consumed by frenzied initiates. Yet Williams also saw the beauty of rebirth as also inherent in the Dionysian impulse and sought to explore it.

Judith J. Thompson notes that in **The Glass Menagerie** (1944) Williams combined classical models with the typologies of the Christian tradition. Laura's name evokes the laurel and its association with the myth of Apollo. Her arrested sexuality parallels the story of Daphne, who sought to preserve her virginity, resisted the advances of Apollo, and was transformed into the laurel tree. Amanda, on the other hand, embodies the conflict between the innocence of Eden and the sexual attraction of the goddess Aphrodite. As Laura's mother, she is reminiscent of the "Sorrowful Mother" (*Mater Dolorosa*) of Christian tradition and of the Great Mother Goddess of ancient pagan ritual. These contradictory typologies elevate the climatic scene of the play to an amalgamation of the pagan rituals of fertility and initiation, Christian communion, and the rites of courtship.

In *A Streetcar Named Desire* (1947), Williams drew upon a wide range of female figures of classical antiquity to portray Blanche DuBois. Her contradictory roles as temptress and queen of the French Quarter particularly show the influence of Shakespeare's treatment of Cleopatra as strumpet and majestic queen of the Nile, as Philip C. Kolin maintains. Blanche's dignified stature in the midst of her tragic degradation also evokes the role of Persephone as queen of the underworld. Her descent into insanity takes place in Elysian Fields, the quarter of New Orleans named for the abode of the dead in classical antiquity. Blanche's description of her first encounter with Allan Grey recalls the story of Eros and Psyche, whose sudden awakening to love ended in the tragic loss of her lover. Blanche's inability to convince Stella of her sexual violation by Stanley Kowalski suggests the story of Philomela, who was silenced by having her tongue removed so she could not report her seduction by her brother-in-law Tereus.

Noteworthy, too, is the contest between Blanche and Stanley, which parallels the struggle between Dionysus and Pentheus, king of Thebes, in Euripides's *Bacchae*. Stanley embodies the instinctive forces of nature and the sensual impulses of Dionysus, while Blanche, like Pentheus, denies the need to fulfill irrational passions, seeks to restrain nature, and refuses to embrace the liberating power of Dionysus. The king's rejection of the god as a barbaric deity unworthy of recognition also seems to parallel Blanche's scorn for Stanley as bestial and primitive. The action in both plays also hinges upon a *peripeteia*, or reversal of fortune. Pentheus becomes the pursued instead of the hunter, is driven mad, and suffers dismemberment at the hands of his mother and other Bacchantic revelers. Blanche likewise undergoes a reversal of fortune, is pursued by a harsh Dionysian hunter, and suffers a psychic dis-

memberment. Stanley Kowalski's French Quarter has been seen as a ghoulish underworld with many echoes of Hades by Leonard Quirino.

Diane E. Turner argues that *Camino Real* (1953) is an extensive parody of ancient cult traditions and mythic patterns. The complex structure of the play unfolds through the dream of Don Quixote and follows the stages of a heroic quest that transforms Kilroy from a young American athlete into a cult figure. He suffers abuse as a scapegoat, becomes a ritual lover, endures death and dismemberment, and is reborn as a hero-god in a series of events that parody the mythic themes of fertility, sacrifice, death, and resurrection. The women he encounters along the way are figures drawn from pagan and Christian traditions. La Madrecita, who aids Kilroy in the first stage of his journey, is a composite of the Great Mother, the goddess Demeter, and the Virgin Mary. She appears to represent an amalgamation of the ancient traditions of the cycle of sacrifice, death, and rebirth. Esmeralda, who is adorned with emerald snakes over her breasts, calls to mind the ancient Mediterranean snake goddess and evokes primitive rites of fertility.

The Dionysian impulse is a benign force in *The Rose Tatoo*. Hugh Dickinson observes that the play is indebted to the story in Petronius' *Satyricon* about a widow who is enticed by a lover to begin life anew after having been excessively devoted to the memory of her husband. Williams's plot, of course, does not fully depend upon the ancient folktale. Instead, it develops a reenactment of the Dionysian cycle of death and rebirth. As Judith Thompson notes, the unfaithful husband, Rosario delle Rose, is the embodiment of Dionysian passion and, like the god, suffers a violent death. His occupation as a driver of a banana truck conjures phallic images and strengthens the connection with Dionysus, portrayed in antiquity with fruit to symbolize fertility. Rosario's widow, Serafina, on the other hand, attempts to elevate her husband's impulses to an idealized, monogamous romance. Her own relationship with Alvaro, however, divests her of illusions and frees her from social constraints so that she can forgive her husband's infidelities and accept her own natural instincts.

For Peter Hays, *Sweet Bird of Youth* (1956) can be read in light of the story of Adonis, the handsome youth who attracted the attention of Aphrodite. According to this myth, the hero died from a wound in the groin by a wild boar, but through the intervention of the goddess returned to life every spring. Thus Adonis became a popular figure of cult whose resurrection served as a pagan symbol of annual fertility and rebirth. Set on the Gulf Coast, *Sweet Bird of Youth* alludes to the ancient cult by recreating the mysterious atmosphere of the eastern Mediterranean. Chance Wayne and Princess Kosmonopolis correspond to Adonis and Aphrodite, although Williams conflates the classical models and themes with typologies from other traditions. In particular, Chance's self-sacrifice in the play evokes both the ritual mutilation of cult and Christ's sacrifice as an act of redemption. The most apparent connection between Adonis and Chance is that, like the hero, Chance suffers castration. Williams's treatment of the classical model is ironic, however, for Chance embodies the ravages of time rather than the eternal youthfulness of the cult figure.

Multiple typologies also shape *Cat on a Hot Tin Roof.* As the play's most complex character, Brick has numerous connections with classical treatments of love. His friendship with Skipper reflects Plato's myth about ideal love as the fulfillment of a spiritual union between males, while his protracted grief over his role in the death of his friend recalls the story of Hyacinthus, who was accidentally killed and was mourned by his lover Apollo. Brick's abstinence from sexual relations with Maggie also suggests that he might be read as a counterpart to Hippolytus, who was destroyed because he refused to acknowledge Aphrodite and her claims upon human nature. Further, the reference in the play to "Echo Spring," the name of the liquor cabinet over which Brick's obsesses, alludes to the mythical pool of Narcissus, who was captivated with his own reflection and was cursed with the inability to love anyone other than himself as punishment for spurning Echo's affections. Maggie is a contradictory figure in the role of a wife-mother, encompassing both the harsh cruelty typical of Artemis in classical myth and the loving protection of Aphrodite. Together, Brick and Maggie seem to reenact the archetypal pattern of the death and resurrection of a god as it is found in the Egyptian story of Osiris's destruction at the hands of his brother and his restoration to life by his wife, Isis.

Orpheus Descending (1957) is Williams's fullest adaptation of the myth of Orpheus, who descended with his lyre into the house of Hades to prevail upon the god of the dead for the return of his wife Eurydice. By glancing backward, however, the hero violated the conditions of her return, and Eurydice disappeared among the shades forever. Inconsolable, he wandered until he was killed and dismembered in a bacchantic frenzy by a group of Maenads. Williams grafted the classical material upon an earlier play, *Battle of Angels*, where the characters are associated with multiple symbols and images. Yet the myth of Orpheus brings clarity to the roles of the two main characters. The protagonist, Val Xavier, is the counterpart of Orpheus, and his guitar identifies him as a musician much in the same way as the lyre in the Orpheus myth. As a modern hero, he descends into the hell of a provincial southern town and attempts to rescue Lady Torrance. Val thus appears as a savior figure in the mode of the Orphic-Christian conceptions, although, like Orpheus, he is unable to accomplish the rescue from the underworld, and his death by blowtorch is every bit as horrific as the classical hero's demise. In late antiquity, Orpheus was seen as a pagan counterpart to Christ. Ironically, in *Battle/Orpheus* he fails as savior, however. Lady Torrance, on the other hand, does not so neatly fit the mythical Eurydice because she refuses to abandon her hell and prevents Val from escaping before it is too late. Her enactment of an idyllic memory of youthful love expands Williams's plot beyond the classical story and conflicts with Val's heroic role.

Williams's darkest picture of the Dionysian spirit is found in *Suddenly Last Summer* (1958). Sebastian Venable's gruesome death by being torn apart and cannibalized by a mob of young men recalls the sinister aspects of Dionysian cult. The picture is rendered even more bizarre by an irreconcilable conflation of the Dionysian elements with the Christian tradition and other orgiastic cults from pagan antiquity. Sebastian's dismemberment ironically suggests the martyrdom of the Christian Saint Sebastian and, at the same time, the Phrygian cult of Cybele, the Great Mother Goddess of antiquity, and her consort, Attis. The **music** attending the murder resembles the beating drums and clashing cymbals of the worship of Cybele and evokes the particular ceremony of the Day of Blood, when the cult priests castrated themselves to the accompaniment of frantic rhythms. Thus Sebastian's death becomes a mysterious, barbaric ritual.

Because Williams's plays are saturated with diverse myths, he might be seen as a modern American mythographer who drew upon the typologies of the classical tradition to shape his characters and, to a lesser degree, his plots. Appropriately, the well-known PBS program (1994) on Williams's life and work was titled "Tennessee Williams: Orpheus of the American Stage."

Further Reading

Dickinson, Hugh. *Myth on the Modern Stage*. Urbana: University of Illinois Press, 1969.

Frye, Northrop. "Archetypal Criticism: Theory of Myths." In his *Anatomy of Criticism: Four Essays*. Princeton, NJ: Princeton University Press, 1957. 131–239.

Hays, Peter L. "Tennessee Williams's Use of Myth in *Sweet Bird of Youth*." *Educational Theatre Journal* 18 (October 1966): 255–258.

Kolin, Philip C. "Cleopatra of the Nile and Blanche DuBois of the French Quarter: *Antony and Cleopatra* and *A Streetcar Named Desire*." *Shakespeare Bulletin* 11 (Winter 1993): 25–27.

Quirino, Leonard. "The Cards Indicate a Voyage on *A Streetcar Named Desire*." In *Tennessee Williams: A Tribute*, ed. Jac Tharpe. Jackson: University Press of Mississippi, 1977. 77–96.

Thompson, Judith J. *Tennessee Williams' Plays: Memory, Myth, and Symbol*. Rev. ed. New York: Lang, 2002.

Turner, Diane E. "The Mythic Vision in Tennessee Williams' *Camino Real*." In *Tennessee Williams: A Tribute*, ed. Jac Tharpe. Jackson: University Press of Mississippi, 1977. 237–251.

Mark Edward Clark

N

Nazimova, Alla (1879–1945). Born Mariam Edez Adelaida Leventon, a famous Russian actress Alla Nazimova, had a profound influence on Williams. In February 1936, his professional life involved typing, filing, dusting shoes in sample rooms, and hauling cases from Continental Shoemakers to the J.C. Penney store in **St. Louis**. An evening at the American Theater in St. Louis that same month gave his life new energy and focus. He attended what he claimed to be his first professional theater performance. Watching from the "peanut gallery," he saw Nazimova as Mrs. Alving in Henrik Ibsen's *Ghosts*. Her performance was so powerful that Williams could not remain in his seat and listened to it from the lobby. Williams claimed this experience as being instrumental in his decision to become a playwright.

Significantly, too, as Lyle Leverich points out, **Eugene O'Neill** himself had been moved by Nazimova's performance of Ibsen almost 30 years earlier. She eventually took the role of Christine in the Theatre Guild's production of O'Neill's *Mourning Becomes Electra* in 1936. An apprentice with Stanislavsky at the Moscow Art Theatre in 1899, she came to America in 1905 and in 1906 signed a contract with Lee Shubert to star in Ibsen's *Hedda Gabler*, *The Wild Duck*, *The Master Builder*, and *A Doll's House*.

Further Reading

Lambert, Gavin. *Nazimova: A Biography*. New York: Knopf, 1997.
Leverich, Lyle. *Tom: The Unknown Tennessee Williams*. New York: Crown, 1995.

Mark Cave

New Orleans. New Orleans was Williams's sure refuge in a lifelong flight from the familial restraints of his youth and, later, from loneliness and himself. He declared that if he ever had a home, it was New Orleans, that almost half of his work was done there, and that no other place provided him with more artistic material. Besides **Hollywood**, the Delta, and **Key West**, the Crescent City became the foremost symbolic place in his life and work.

On 26 December 1938 he fled **St. Louis** and a family situation that had become increasingly unbearable. Yearning for a place where he could find the freedom necessary for his bursting creativity, he went to New Orleans. He hoped that here he could find a job in the Works Progress Administration (WPA) Writer's Project and that the Federal Theatre Project might be interested in his work in progress. He was opening a new chapter in his life, a change that also required a new name. Consequently, on his journey to New Orleans, when he stopped briefly for a night at his grandparents' in Memphis, he started to use his nom de plume "Tennessee" for the first time in sending his plays to a **Group Theatre** contest in New York. He stayed his first night in New Orleans in a squalid hotel off Lee Circle, checked into a small hotel at 431 Royal Street the next day, and after a week moved to a rooming house at 722 Toulouse Street, where he signed in as "Tennessee Williams, writer."

From the very beginning, he found the city's eroticism both shocking and fascinating. The inhibitions of his puritanical nature and education and the confinement of his life in St. Louis contrasted dramatically with the moral laissez-faire of the French Quarter, and this clash became one of the central subjects of his work. However, New Orleans could not really set him free. Though he had physically escaped St. Louis and his family, they haunted his imagination, and often he recreated them in his works, transposing them to the New Orleans of his mind.

Soon after his arrival in the city, he rejoiced in his journal (see **Journals**): this was the place he was made for. Soon, however, he was lonesome and destitute, and his hopes of a future with the WPA were also shattered. Since he sensed that the hedonism of the French Quarter threatened to paralyze his creativity, he left the city on 20 February 1939, joining a new friend on a journey to the West Coast. This first stay in New Orleans was most crucial in his development as a writer, because in these few weeks he gathered material for later use in his plays.

When he fled from the disastrous off-Broadway premiere of *Battle of Angels* (30 December 1940) in Boston, his final sanctuary after an erratic flight was, again, New Orleans. Although he felt that the city had failed him before, it was here that he hoped to overcome his writer's block. On 11 September 1941 he checked into a rooming house at 1124 St. Charles Avenue but soon moved into the Quarter, first to 708 Toulouse, in late September to 538 Royal, and on 24 October for apparently only one night to an unidentified windowless, roach-infested "cubicle" that inspired "The Lady of Larkspur Lotion." He left New Orleans for St. Louis on 2 November 1941.

This second period in the Crescent City was very different from the first. After confessing his homosexuality as much as was possible in those guarded days, he seems to have been driven by his passion to "cruise" rather than to write. His restless life in what he called "homosociety" provided him with many plot ideas and the dominant character in his writings: the hypersensitive outcast. He was now concluding his New Orleans apprenticeship in bohemianism. When he came back to the city for a brief stop in December (staying at 722 Dumaine Street), New Orleans had changed to wartime sobriety, and now Williams devoted himself more to his work than to the bars. His third New Orleans period followed in 1945–1946: when he moved into the Pontchartrain Hotel on St. Charles Avenue, and then, on 1 January 1946, transferred to 710 Orleans Avenue. Later that year he stayed at 632 St. Peter Street, where he worked on *Summer and Smoke* and his most famous New Orleans play, *A Streetcar Named Desire*.

After these three relatively extended periods in the city, he would return frequently, but only for short visits. Nonetheless, New

Orleans had become the spiritual home for Williams, the homeless itinerant; it was here that in his later years he would try to find relaxation, if not inspiration. In "The Angel in the Alcove" the autobiographical narrator states that whenever he felt a psychic wound, a loss, or a failure, he would return to New Orleans for a time of recession and new energy. New Orleans was the place where Williams felt he belonged. He called it his favorite city and said that he had spent his happiest years there.

There is evidence that Williams repeatedly returned to New Orleans in the 1950s and later. In 1962 he purchased the townhouse at 1014 Dumaine Street but did not move there until early 1972. It was here that he hoped to die. But on his last stay in the city (January 1983), he prepared for the sale of the house with a leaseback provision for the second-floor apartment. After his death in New York a few weeks later, he was not buried in New Orleans but in St. Louis. But the city he had immortalized in many of his works gave him a memorial service on 19 March 1983 at St. Louis Cathedral at Jackson Square immediately behind the French Market at the Mississippi River.

In his canon, New Orleans is not a monolithic metropolis but is divided into discrete neighborhoods. There is the French Quarter, with its seedy bars and cheap rooming houses run by inquisitive and bossy spinsters. This is the neighborhood of Williams's apprenticeship to bohemianism, during which he recreated a number of autobiographical stories and plays, symbolic of exotic and erotic decadence. In these texts he describes his homosexual initiation during his first New Orleans period at 722 Toulouse Street ("The Angel in the Alcove") and his puritanical shock at the Quarter's erotic freedom. In "Auto-Da-Fé" (see *Twenty-seven Wagons Full of Cotton and Other One-Act Plays*), Eloi is so disgusted by the

corruption of the Quarter (and himself) that he starts a purifying fire. Like the Lutheran minister in "One Arm," Williams was torn between moral inhibition and sexual passion, and like the female protagonist in "The Yellow Bird," he escaped from the restrictions of his family to the promiscuous freedom of New Orleans. The most extended and openly autobiographical play about Williams's first months in the Quarter is *Vieux Carré*. It takes up motifs from "The Lady of Larkspur Lotion," where he introduced one of his bossy landladies, who rents rat holes at extortionate rates, and an old spinster, who is unable to face reality. The bohemians in *The Mutilated* are also based on persons Williams met in the Quarter during his first stay there; it is a Christmas carol for the agonized and wounded, the deformed, and fugitives—including Trinket Dugan and Celeste Delacroix Griffin whose symbolic names ironically point to the sacred and profane in the Crescent City. "The Coming of Something to the Widow Holly" describes the riotous and destructive behavior of extravagant roomers and the landlady's fairy-tale resurrection through the promise of erotic love. In "Lord Byron's Love Letter," two old spinsters are so destitute that they have to make a living out of showing a questionable letter to gullible tourists from the North. Thus, the French Quarter in Williams's canon is the symbolic sanctuary for the defeated and mutilated who have lost their innocent illusions (as in the poem "Mornings on Bourbon Street") and are victimized by frauds (as in the poem "Crepe-de-Chine").

Life in Williams's symbolic French Quarter is threatened from two very different neighborhoods. To the one side is the fashionable Garden District with a closed, upper middle class living on memories and what Williams called "mendacity." If the central image for Williams's French Quarter was the roach-infested cubicle in a shabby rooming house, the dominant symbol in his mythic Garden District of **Suddenly Last Summer** was the tropical jungle where pretentious and "predatory" ladies like Violet Venable forge fate. The play depicts the unscrupulous violence, intrigue, and duplicity with which they defend their facade of propriety. Although set in Meridian, Mississippi, **Something Unspoken** is also a Garden District play, because it, too, exposes the vanity of a class and presents older women who suppress secrets and leave "something unspoken." This similarity was stressed when in 1958 the two plays were billed together under the collective title *Garden District*. While the French Quarter plays present a sanctuary for the victimized and recreate Williams's education in bohemianism, the Garden District plays present the world of the victimizers and, in a way, dramatize Williams's traumatic years with his family in St. Louis. Mrs. Venable and Mrs. Holly of *Suddenly Last Summer* are recreations of his socially ambitious mother, **Edwina Williams**; the play metaphorically explains why Williams rejected his family's "Garden District" life of privilege, money, and social position.

At the other end of his symbolic French Quarter is the bustling and multiethnic neighborhood of *A Streetcar Named Desire*, Faubourg Marigny. Although Williams envisioned it to be geographically still on the Quarter side of Esplande Avenue (despite the Elysian Fields Avenue address), it is a completely different world. For the mutilated pariahs of the French Quarter it is as destructive as the Garden District. Just as in *Vieux Carré* the rooming house at 722 Toulouse Street is used as a universal symbol of "all the cheap rooming houses of the world," the neighborhood where Stella and Stan start a new family is symbolic of an energetic vivacity that springs up amid decay. Blanche, both bossy and helpless, rep-

resents the pretence and duplicity of the old Garden District as well as the psychic mutilation of the French Quarter. Even in her dress she parades in a facade of whiteness, incongruous in this world of trenchant realism, and will inevitably be stripped away by the hoodlum vitality of this modern neighborhood where the Kowalskis hold sway. Williams seems to have realized the symbolism of these New Orleans neighborhoods only gradually; early drafts of *A Streetcar Named Desire* were set in St. Louis, Chicago, and Atlanta. The New Orleans setting is dynamic in **Elia Kazan**'s film version of the play, which creates a paradoxically claustrophobic and Dionysian French Quarter environment. In contrast, the screen adaptation of *Suddenly Last Summer* transforms the enclosed New Orleans garden into a symbol of civilized savagery.

Even in plays not set in New Orleans, the Crescent City is symbolically present because its neighborhoods and the characters inhabiting them are universal in Williams's work and in humanity at large. The duality of the tourist's New Orleans, where Canal Street stereotypically separates the daytime reality of commercialism from the "exotic unreality" of the nighthawks' Quarter, diversifies into a universe where the playwright's numerous alter egos finally, though briefly, take center stage in the moments of their defeat. His sensitive creativity has transformed the microcosm of New Orleans as he experienced it during his stays into a drama of human anguish. See also **Poems**.

Further Reading

Barranger, Milly S. "New Orleans as Theatrical Image in Plays by Tennessee Williams." *Southern Quarterly* 23 (1985): 38–54.

Ciment, Michael. *Kazan on Kazan*. New York: V. King, 1974.

Holditch, Kenneth. "The Last Frontier of Bohemia: Tennessee Williams in New Orleans,

1938–1983." *Southern Quarterly* 23 (1985): 1–37.

———. "South toward Freedom: Tennessee Williams." In *Literary New Orleans: Essays and Meditations*, ed. Richard S. Kennedy. Baton Rouge: Louisiana State University Press, 1992. 61–75.

———. "Tennessee Williams in New Orleans." In *Magical Muse: Millennial Essays on Tennessee Williams*, ed. Ralph F. Voss. Tuscaloosa: University of Alabama Press, 2002. 193–202.

Leavitt, Richard Freeman. *The World of Tennessee Williams*. New York: Putnam, 1978.

Richardson, Thomas. "The City of Day and the City of Night: New Orleans and the Exotic Unreality of Tennessee Williams." In *Tennessee Williams: A Tribute*, ed. Jac Tharpe. Jackson: University Press of Mississippi, 1977. 631–646.

Jürgen C. Wolter

New School for Social Research. The New School for Social Research, a New York institute renowned for challenging conventional academic practice, launched the Dramatic Workshop under the directorship of **Erwin Piscator** on 15 January 1940. The Workshop was sponsored by **Eddie Dowling** (who would coproduce, codirect, and star in *The Glass Menagerie*), Elmer Rice, Robert E. Sherwood, S.N. Behrman, George S. Kaufman, Clifton Fadiman, Sinclair Lewis, Oscar Levant, Paul Muni, the Theatre Guild, and the **Group Theatre**. A young Tennessee Williams enrolled in the Playwrights' Seminar in that first semester at the behest of **Audrey Wood**. Looking out for her client's theatrical education and his introduction to the business of theater, Wood had arranged a $1,000 Rockefeller grant to pay for the course. Williams also saw opportunity: The chairs of the Seminar were Theresa Helburn, an active producer of the Theatre Guild, and John Gassner, its principal playreader. He hoped to interest them

in *Battle of Angels*, his first commercial effort. (The Theatre Guild did present *Battle of Angels*, but it closed after a disastrous opening.)

In the Seminar students were expected to produce one script during the term, and sessions were devoted to analyses of the students' work and current productions; "collaborators" who met with the students included playwrights S.N. Behrman, Marc Connelly, **Clifford Odets**, Elmer Rice, Robert E. Sherwood and the director Harold Clurman. Among Williams's fellow Seminar participants was **Arthur Miller**; other Dramatic Workshop students included African American playwright Abram Hill, actor John Randolph, and Phyllis Thaxter.

In addition to the Seminar, all students were required to attend Barrett H. Clark's "The American Drama in Our Times." Among those who gave these informal talks were Maxwell Anderson, Clurman, Dowling, Lillian Hellman, Robert Edmond Jones, **Lawrence Langner**, Maria Ley (Mrs. Piscator), **Edward Charles Mabie** (Williams's old professor from the University of Iowa), and Monty Woolley. Further, Piscator ran the New School's Studio Theatre, where he presented productions with professional actors in major roles and students both on stage and behind the scenes. In May 1942, Piscator presented his adaptation of Tolstoy's *War and Peace* at the Studio Theatre, and Williams was among his young assistants. The director's expressionistic techniques and his use of film and projections no doubt influenced Williams's work, particularly *The Glass Menagerie*, which employed a character-narrator in the same vein as Piscator had used Pierre Besuchov. In 1942, after Williams's *Battle of Angels* has failed in its commercial production, Piscator expressed interest in mounting it at the Studio, but the script ultimately would not meet Piscator's "epic theatre" requirements. On the other hand, student productions of Williams short plays *The Long Goodbye* and *This Property Is Condemned* were presented by the Workshop in February 1941 and June 1942, respectively. By the time Williams left at the end of the spring term on 15 June 1940, the New School had given him contacts, influences, and exposure to his new milieu (as well as one subsistence job in 1942, doing publicity for the Studio Theatre). See Also **Stapleton, Maureen.**

Further Reading

Devlin, Albert J., and Nancy Tischler, eds. *The Selected Letters of Tennessee Williams, Volume 1—1920–1945.* New York: New Directions, 2000.

Leverich, Lyle. *Tom: The Unknown Tennessee Williams.* New York: Crown, 1995.

Ley-Piscator, Maria. *The Piscator Experiment: The Political Theatre.* New York: Heinemann, 1967.

Rutkoff, Peter M. *New School: A History of the New School for Social Research.* New York: Free Press, 1986.

Willett, John. *The Theatre of Erwin Piscator: Half a Century of Politics in the Theatre.* London: Methuen, 1978.

Richard E. Kramer

The Night of the Iguana. *The Night of the Iguana*, which opened on Broadway in 1961, holds the dubious distinction of being Tennessee Williams's last great critical and commercial success, as many critics began writing Williams's artistic obituaries in the years following the play's initial run. *The Night of the Iguana* is indeed a hard act to follow. In many respects his most ambitious play, *The Night of the Iguana* is at once cosmic and intimate, slapstick and sublime. As with most of Williams's work, this play reflects not only autobiographical elements from the past but also reveals the turmoil of Williams's life during the actual composing

process. He turned his full attention to *The Night of the Iguana* shortly after a period of psychotherapy in 1957 with Dr. **Lawrence Kubie,** again plunging himself into his work to stave off the "blue devils." In *The Night of the Iguana* he sought order in his writing that he could not achieve through analysis. The Reverend T. Lawrence Shannon's "therapy session" with Hannah Jelkes confronts many of the issues Williams was facing in what he called one of his "desperate periods." But during these periods, he observed, we are "most alive." Aptly, Foster Hirsch called *The Night of the Iguana* one of Williams's "confession dramas." In this context, *The Night of the Iguana* also looks back to another Williams's self-portrait—Blanche DuBois in *A Streetcar Named Desire.* In fact, Williams claimed that with Shannon he "was drawing a male equivalent of a Blanche DuBois." Like Blanche, Shannon feels desperately isolated and seeks refuge.

The Night of the Iguana was the result of a long, multifarious evolution, from a short story to a one-act play to the full-length work. In 1940, Williams, on the rebound from an intense affair with dancer **Kip Kiernan,** journeyed to Mexico to seek consolation in his writing and languish in a warmer, exotic climate. After visiting Mexico City, Williams next went to Acapulco and on to the Hotel Costa Verde, the locale that would serve as the setting for all versions of *The Night of the Iguana.* Williams met Jean Paul Sartre there, and the two spent long hours in conversation discussing, among other topics, suicide. The distillation of this experience shows up in the short story and also in the play when Shannon talks about intentionally drowning himself.

While on the veranda of the hotel during his visit, Williams began composing Nonno's poem found in *The Night of the Iguana* as well as the short story, which is considerably different from the playscript versions.

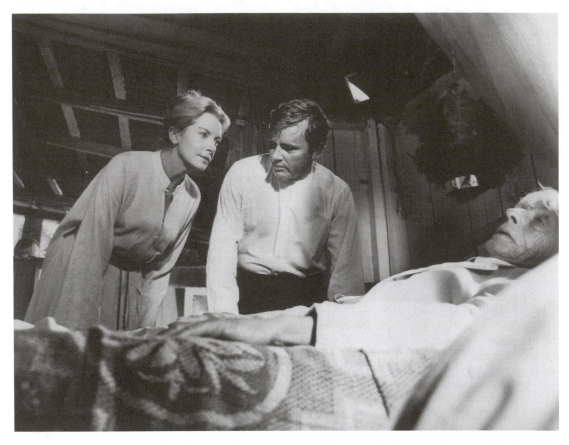

Deborah Kerr and Richard Burton visit the bedside of a dying Cyril Delevanti in this scene from the 1962 film of *The Night of the Iguana*. Springer/Photofest.

Williams shelved the story and finished it in 1948, but *Harper's Bazaar* found it too salacious and rejected it. He began reworking the material into play form under the working title *Quebrada*, or "The Cliff." Williams then revised and expanded the work into a lengthy one-act that was submitted to Spoleto, Italy, in 1959. After later tryouts at the Coconut Grove in Coral Gables and in other cities, *The Night of the Iguana* moved to the Royale Theatre on Broadway, where it ran for 316 performances. Although *The Night of the Iguana* received mixed reviews, it earned Williams his fourth Drama Critics' Circle Award. The Broadway run featured Margaret Leighton as Hannah, Patrick O'Neal as Shannon, Bette Davis (who was eventually replaced by Shelley Winters) as Maxine, and Alan Webb as Nonno. The London premiere followed in February 1962 at the Ashcroft Theatre and later at the Savoy (1965). In the 1990s, major revivals opened in London (Lyttelton Theatre, 1992) and at New York's Criterion Center Stage Right (1996).

In *The Night of the Iguana*, as elsewhere, Williams concentrates on character and dialogue rather than plot. Shannon arrives at the Hotel Costa Verde after he has hit rock bottom in his personal and clerical life. Once a respected Episcopalian priest, he has been defrocked for "fornication and heresy" and has been thrown out of his church in Virginia. Now the guide for Blake Tours, Shannon engages in a personal quest clearly at odds with the itinerary desired by the ladies of whom he is in charge. Maxine, who runs the Hotel Costa Verde, has her own agenda, as she has designs on him to satisfy her considerable sexual appetite. Hannah's arrival puts on hold Maxine's plan, and thus the contest for Shannon's body and soul begins to take shape between these two women who represent the spiritual (Hannah) and the carnal (Maxine). As in the forest settings of Nathaniel Hawthorne's fictions, Williams's wild tropical coast becomes a place for moral choice, far removed from institutional and conventional societal regulations.

Despite the tropical decay of Williams's setting, references to death and suicide, psychological destitution, and haunting burdens of the past, *The Night of the Iguana* stands as one of Williams's most affirmative plays. In a battle between forces of life and death, vitality triumphs, and in terms of Williams's perennial struggle with the inexorable burden of the past, *The Night of the Iguana* is a play about turning to the future—however limited or uncertain that future might be. Each major character in *The Night of the Iguana* is liberated from past burdens. Shannon achieves reintegration into the present by rejecting his misguided responsibilities as a priest and trying to find meaning in the present (and future). Only after his "therapy" with Hannah, in which he is forced to confront his past, does he achieve peace. Considering his physical and emotional baggage when he first climbs up the hill to the hotel, his transformation is no small accomplishment. In resolving neither to return to the ministry nor to rebel against his mother and God, Shannon's decision to stay with Maxine rids him of a futile, self-destructive

battle to regain his collar and in turn enables him to achieve companionship based on a healthy sexuality and fruitful compassion.

Maxine also confronts the past and her dissatisfaction with Fred, her deceased husband, as a lover. In Act One she remains haunted by his echo from an adjoining hill. By the play's end she looks forward to sexual satisfaction with Shannon. The aged Nonno, Jonathan Coffin, himself a symbol of the past as the oldest living poet, finally reaches the one great artistic goal of his life—finishing his magnificent poem. Hannah, the only major character whose future remains absolutely uncertain as the play closes, does not anguish over what lies ahead. When Shannon asks her what she will do after her grandfather Nonno dies, she stresses her adaptability and capacity for adjusting to difficult circumstances. Although Hannah seems weary and lonely, her determination and strength will carry her through her present transition, for she is one of Williams's most well-adjusted characters. Even the iguana is set free in the play, and it is no accident that Williams chooses to free it instead of to fry it. He clearly saw the roped iguana as a metaphor for Shannon, as human hands and ropes constrict the freedom of both. The iguana, like the characters, achieves freedom from torture and pain and deliverance noticeably absent in most other works by Williams. Shannon's stripping off his collar and his eventual extrication from the hammock where he is tied symbolizes that he has achieved freedom as well. Despite its somewhat optimistic ending though, *The Night of the Iguana* raises almost as many questions as it answers. Is Shannon's quest for God satisfied by the revelation of the God of thunder and lightning at the end of Act Two? Has Shannon successfully confronted his "spook" or merely driven it further into the dark shadows of the forest/mind? And in this morality play, where flesh struggles with spirit, how, if at all, are these dichotomies finally resolved?

With the exceptions of *A Streetcar Named Desire* and *Summer and Smoke*, few of Williams's plays contain such incongruous ingredients as *The Night of the Iguana*. In an interview around the time of *The Night of the Iguana*'s premiere, Williams believed that this might be his final play, and perhaps he sought to pack all his uncertainties into one cosmic, multidimensional drama. What is noticeably lacking in this long play, however, is plot. Williams achieves structure instead through a series of long monologues between Hannah and Shannon, and the tension achieved from these lengthy exchanges substitutes for any real dramatic actions on stage. As a result, *The Night of the Iguana* has sometimes been criticized for being too long and static. Williams, however, realized that his audiences might suffer from fatigue and sought to relieve some of the ponderous dialogue with characteristic bits of humor—ambitious, satiric, and absurd. He achieves this through subtle exchanges between Hannah and Shannon but also through Maxine's libidinous gusto, the subplot involving Charlotte Goodall and Miss Fellowes, and the periodic entrances by the Germans visiting Mexico and cheering Hitler's blitz on the radio. In placing these porcine Nazis (their skin shrivels in the heat of the day) in the middle of the more serious stage business between Hannah and Shannon, Williams includes grotesque and animated comic relief he more fully exploited in such later plays as *The Gnädiges Fräulein*, *The Mutilated*, and *This Is (An Entertainment)*. Although some readers may question the inclusion of the Nazis, Williams's juxtaposition of their cartoonish antics with their glee over the human tragedy associated with the tragedy over London demonstrates how easily human compassion can surrender to reckless

sadism and therefore serves as another testimony of Williams's social consciousness.

While *The Night of the Iguana* is set at Maxine's hotel, there is a constant psychic journey from the beginning to the end of the play in Shannon's quest for faith, hope, and love (see **Religion**). *The Night of the Iguana* is, after all, a play about a fallen pilgrim seeking peace and understanding and what he must relinquish in order to achieve them. Shannon must abandon egoism and be reintegrated into the physical and moral universe with which he has never felt comfortable. The quest for Shannon began when he sought God in the Episcopal Church. However, when God is merely revealed as a "senile delinquent," Shannon's disappointment turns to outrage, and he rejects this Old Testament God in favor of his Blake's Tour of the "underworld." Shannon's journey to Costa Verde brings him back to an almost primeval site of naturalistic wonder, a neutral site that affords a place for moral choice. The Hotel Costa Verde becomes a "fantastic" site as opposed to the pressures and regulations of the "realistic" world of obligation and responsibility Shannon faced daily with his Virginia congregation. Shannon's visit to Mexico—like Williams's in the 1940s—is thus a rite of passage to the world of tropical beauty and the forces of nature—a place where the concept of God makes itself much more apparent than behind the pulpit in Pleasant Valley, Virginia. The physical isolation and sheer beauty of the Pacific coast offer Shannon an opportunity to recalibrate his psychic space, a ritual that he has performed before but must reenact, this time with the aid of a fellow voyager in the realm of truth—Hannah.

Once the force of God is revealed in the *King Lear*-like thunderstorm, Shannon moves from viewing the sea as an opportunity for suicide to embracing Nonno's view of it as the "cradle of life." Fittingly, Shannon and Maxine descend the hill to renew their sexual relationship baptized by the warm tropical waters of Costa Verde—whereas earlier the "long swim to China" was how Shannon planned to end his life. Moreover, the revelation of God as Nature is completely different from what Sebastian Venable observes in the Encantadas in *Suddenly Last Summer*. For Sebastian, God is seen as a devouring, horrific force, dark and unrelenting, an unmerciful God. For Shannon, God is a "giant white bird attacking the hilltop of the Costa Verde," but the "attack" is merely one of an assault on the senses, or the awful presentation of the deity through "convulsions of light." Shannon's God is not merely predatory or destructive; on the contrary, the storm brings rain—nourishment to the tropical forest that surrounds them. Paradoxically, in both cases (Shannon's and Sebastian's) the revelation of God is actually a reflection of the self. For Sebastian, the esthete devoured by his own ego, God is a voracious consumer; for Shannon, God is the turbulence that overpowers all. With Hannah's guidance, this recognition leads Shannon to contemplate how an external, naturalistic God may be approximated within the temple of his own soul.

Hannah, who becomes Shannon's spiritual "tour guide," has a presence that is nearly unique in the Williams canon. She is a woman of refined nature, confident and assertive, even though she carries her own emotional baggage. As she works through her therapy session with Shannon in the hammock, she envelopes the former priest in an Eastern sense of calm that has apparently evaded him all his life. Hers is a luminous presence that exudes inner serenity, an unemotional acceptance of her fate, and a sensitivity to others' sufferings. In addition, she is about as nonjudgmental as a person can be, and her tolerance of others' indiscretions and mistakes renders her almost saintlike.

Whereas Maxine's solution for Shannon's peace of mind consists of a rum-coco and a good roll in the hay, Hannah concentrates on healing Shannon's spiritual wounds. She exhorts Shannon to confront the "spook" and deal with his self-absorption by reaching out to others. Hannah's "sketch" of Shannon forces him to see himself as he really is, and her insistence on the efficacy of human communication—one of the most persistent themes in the Williams canon—leads Shannon to the realization that only by reaching out to others with small, simple acts of grace can he extinguish the existential dread that torments his psyche.

As with *Suddenly Last Summer*, Williams invests *The Night of the Iguana* with a good dose of Jungian vocabulary and theory, perhaps gained as a result of his sessions with psychoanalyst Lawrence Kubie. Jung believed that the "shadow" exists in all of us as the accumulation of those unpleasant aspects of our personalities that remain hidden. In *The Night of the Iguana* this "shadow self" may be identified with the "spook" that torments Shannon and is the source of Shannon's neuroses as well as his cruelty toward others. When he hurls objects at the "spook" and tries to drive it further into the forest—that is, repress it more deeply into his unconscious—his evasion only contributes to the shadow's determination to surface. Hannah describes her own contests with her shadowy side and urges Shannon toward self-scrutiny. This same dichotomy plagued Williams all his life, of course, and he never seemed able to reconcile the two. At the end, we are left to wonder whether Shannon will be more successful than Williams in his quest for unifying this divided self. With *The Night of the Iguana* Williams has written a psychodrama that serves as a contemporary morality play in which salvation is not always easily accessible or acceptable.

Further Reading

Embrey, Glenn. "The Subterranean World of *The Night of the Iguana*." In *Tennessee Williams: A Tribute*, ed. Jac Tharpe. Jackson: University Press of Mississippi, 1977. 325–340.

Hirsch, Foster. *A Portrait of the Artist: The Plays of Tennessee Williams*. Port Washington, NY: Kennikat, 1979.

Leverich, Lyle. *Tom: The Unknown Tennessee Williams*. New York: Crown, 1995.

Levin, Lindy. "Shadow into Light: A Jungian Analysis of *The Night of the Iguana*." *Tennessee Williams Annual Review* 2 (1999): 87–98.

Matthews, Kevin. "The Evolution of *The Night of the Iguana*: Three Symbols in the Manuscript Record." *Library Chronicle of the University of Texas* 25.2 (1994): 67–89.

"Studs Turkel Talks with Tennessee." In *Conversations with Tennessee Williams*, ed. Albert J. Devlin. Jackson: University Press of Mississippi, 1986.

Thompson, Judith J. *Tennessee Williams' Plays: Memory, Myth, and Symbol*. Rev. ed. New York: Lang, 2002.

Williams, Tennessee. "A Summer of Discovery." In *Where I Live: Selected Essays by Tennessee Williams*, ed. Christine R. Day and Bob Woods. New York: New Directions, 1978. 137–147.

Robert Bray

"The Night Was Full of Hours." "The Night Was Full of Hours" is a short story Williams wrote in 1973 in **New Orleans** and revised in 1978, but it was published for the first time in *French Quarter Fiction* (2003). A postmodern haziness infuses this indelibly autobiographical story where the 62-year-old Williams is both author and character, merging present nightmares with past dreams. Framed by Williams's reactions to an interviewer labeling him "the loneliest man on God's green earth," "The Night Was Full of Hours" follows Williams's thoughts on a sleepless, postmidnight watch in his house on Rue Dumaine in the French Quarter. He takes readers through his nightly rituals toward sleep, which rarely came before dawn. **Drugs**, hot tubs, sitting before his Smith-Corona portable typewriter ("his enemy and his lover" [367]) to write—nothing brings Williams sleep. Cataloging the numerous drugs he ingests, Williams recollects happier times when his big brass bed was not a grave but filled with lovers, either now-dead ones like **Frank Merlo**, or Victor, who currently shares the house with Williams but leaves at night to cruise for warm flesh in the Quarter. Far too old and vulnerable for such prowling, Williams fantasizes about finding a youth who will take away the loneliness the interviewer so rightly identified. Totally self-reflective, "The Night Was Full of Hours" records Williams's stream of consciousness strained through paragraphing that denies conventions. Paragraph indentations come in the middle of sentences without regard for logical division or punctuation and are sometimes only a line or two long, characteristic of Williams's narcotized insomnia. Consistent, though, is Williams's love of the French Quarter whose pleasures are now beyond his grasp.

Further Reading

Williams, Tennessee. "The Night Was Full of Hours." In *French Quarter Fiction: The Newest Stories of America's Oldest Bohemia*, ed. Joshua Clark. New Orleans: Light of New Orleans Publishing, 2003. 365–368.

Philip C. Kolin

Not about Nightingales. Written in 1938, *Not about Nightingales* premiered 60 years later at the Royal National Theatre, London, on 5 March 1998, with an Anglo-American cast directed by Trevor Nunn. A coproduction with the Moving Theatre of

Vanessa and Corin Redgrave and the Alley Theatre of Houston, it had its U.S. premiere in Houston on 5 June 1998. A New York production followed on 25 February 1999 at Circle in the Square. The play led the Tony nominations that June, with six nominations, and won for Best Set Design. It also won four Drama Desk awards for Outstanding Director, Set Design, Lighting Design, and Sound Design. It had productions in Cologne, Germany, on 24 September 1998, and in Helsinki, Finland, on 30 September 2001, and has been translated into German, Japanese, and Finnish.

Not about Nightingales was the 27-year-old Tom Williams's response to a prison scandal of August 1938 in Holmesburg, Pennsylvania, when four inmates on a hunger strike were locked in a steam cell with radiators turned up to maximum heat and found roasted alive. The play shows the influence of the Federal Theatre social drama of the Works Progress Administration (WPA) that Williams had encountered as a recent student in playwriting at the university of Iowa and their "living newspaper" style of using headlines and projections. Also influenced by the prison movies of the 1930s, in particular *The Big House*, *Not about Nightingales* is written in 22 fluid scenes, with quick dissolves, the most cinematic of any Williams play. It reflects his practical experience with the St. Louis **Mummers**, a radical theater group who had produced his two preceding proletarian plays.

Here Canary Jim, the Warden's trusty, despised as a stool pigeon by the other inmates, especially Butch, the lead prisoner, actually plans to disclose conditions in the prison when he gets his forthcoming parole. Into the situation comes Eva, the Warden's new secretary, who falls in love with Jim but must walk a tightrope between keeping her job and accepting her boss's advances. When Butch calls a hunger strike and the Warden condemns the strikers to the dreaded steam cell, the "Klondike," Jim tries to intervene and the Warden retracts his parole. Determined to help Jim escape, Eva gives in to the Warden's seduction, on condition that he sign Jim's release. When Jim and Butch join forces to free the prisoners, all hunt down the Warden and beat him to death. As state troopers arrive, Jim jumps from the prison window into the moat below, his fate uncertain.

The play is significant in changing critical opinion of Tennessee Williams after 60 years. It drew more than 150 reviews in London and U.S. papers, most of which heralded the discovery of a "new" Williams. "One of the most remarkable theatrical discoveries of the last quarter century," declared the London *Evening Standard* of 6 March 1998; "a world premiere of tremendous importance" (*The Spectator*, 11 March 1998); "a hard-hitting violent argument for penal reform" (*Theatre Record*, 11 March 1998); "*Not about Nightingales* proves that Williams . . . was always a radical writer on the side of the oppressed" (*The Guardian*, 6 March 1998).

As in all of Williams's early plays—and a prediction of his later ones—the theme is escape. A key symbol of the play is the cage in which all the characters find themselves, represented scenically by the prison bars. In opposition is Keats's "To A Nightingale," symbolizing the poetic yearnings of Jim, the would-be writer. The name of the passing pleasure boat, *The Lorelei*, suggests the lure of the outside world closed to the prisoners and perhaps also warns of Jim's possible fate. The set, in uniform gray from the newspaper headline projections to the American flag, suggests the drab world of the prison. Jim, the mordant idealist, a victim of circumstance in an unfair society, predicts a typical Williams hero. Jim is a self-taught intellectual who reads Keats but is interested in social reform. Eva, although she shows considerable spunk, is the generic girl of Williams's early plays (perhaps a portrait of his sister **Rose**), imprisoned in her situation and looking for love. The Warden is the villain of the melodrama, who appears in later form as Boss Finley in *Sweet Bird of Youth*. Butch, the gangster-tough stereotype, is individualized by his tender reminiscences of Goldie, his dance-hall sweetheart. The other prisoners, a diverse ethnic mix, demonstrate the playwright's early gift for characterization and dialogue. The plot conflict is resolved by Jim's transformation from stool pigeon to hero, when he joins Butch to lead the prisoners' revolt and punishment of the Warden. Although justice is served in the brutal resolution of the plot, the future of Jim and Eva's romance is left ambiguous. Ambiguous endings would become characteristic of the playwright.

Further Reading

Canby, Vincent. " 'Nightingales' Sings of Williams's Promise." *New York Times* 7 March 1999, "Theater": 10.

Hale, Allean. "A Call for Justice." Introduction to *Not about Nightingales* by Tennessee Williams. New York: New Directions, 1998. xiii–xxii.

———. "*Not about Nightingales*: Tennessee Williams as Social Activist." *Modern Drama* 42 (Fall 1999): 346–362.

Simon, John. "*Not about Nightingales*." *New York Magazine* 15 March 1999, "Theater."

Allean Hale

The Notebook of Trigorin. The Notebook of Trigorin, Tennessee Williams's free adaptation of **Anton Chekhov**'s *The Sea Gull* (1896), presents a rare collaboration of two dramatic masters whose highly individual styles were, on many levels, complementary. Williams had long hoped to direct *The Sea Gull*, a work he considered the greatest of modern plays. He never did, but he did have the opportunity to adapt the play. Williams brought his singular lyrical skills to the task of refashioning *The Sea Gull* into another play entirely. *The Notebook of Trigorin* rests on the multiple strengths of the original in the areas of plot, theme, and character but is also a unique dramatic creation. *The Notebook of Trigorin* does not supersede *The Sea Gull*; it stands beside it. Borrowing key elements from Chekhov, it refracts them through the vision of a writer of similar poetic sensitivities, but with a more liberated sensibility and a penchant for unrestrained emotion.

Williams's lifelong fascination with *The Sea Gull* centered on the personal connections he made with Constantine Treplev and Boris Trigorin, the play's two central male characters. Constantine's fragility, his struggles as a fledgling writer, and his tragically strained relationship with a difficult mother drew Williams to the play as a young man, but as he aged, he increasingly related to Trigorin's world weariness, imagining in Trigorin the sexual experimentation and ambivalence about life and the value of art he himself had experienced.

Critics who attacked Williams's liberties with Chekhov certainly have plenty of ammunition in this adaptation. On close examination, Williams's changes and additions generally succeed in enhancing the original through his efforts to bring the subliminal life of its characters closer to the surface, even when, as in the case of expanding Trigorin's persona, that subliminal life is a wholly original invention on Williams's part. Among Williams's changes the introduction of a bisexual history for Trigorin is most controversial. This jaded writer privately doubts his ability as an artist and blunts his anxieties and boredom through sexual promiscuity. He turns to a pursuit of the naive Nina as a distraction from the emasculating dominance Arkadina holds over him. Williams changes this catalytic but decidedly secondary character solely by deciding that Trigorin is troubled by his sexual attraction to men, demonstrated first by erotic encounters with a servant, and later through his admission of past relationships in new scenes with Arkadina and Nina.

Williams's expansion of Trigorin's persona links him to several characters in Williams's own works whose sexuality is central to their personal struggles. When Arkadina confronts Trigorin over his philandering, he not only admits his bisexual nature but speaks with regret about the tragic death of a former male lover. Trigorin's interest in Nina is partly a matter of jealousy—he envies the purity of Constantine's feelings for her and the tremulous enthusiasm the younger man has for creating "new forms." Undoubtedly, Trigorin also feels uncomfortable with an air of androgyny emanating from Constantine that reminds him of his ambivalence about his bisexuality.

Other Williams changes to *The Sea Gull* include a subtle reduction of emphasis on the relationship between Constantine and Nina, while *The Notebook of Trigorin* also brings Arkadina and Nina into Williams's gallery of memorable women characters. Like Blanche DuBois, Arkadina's descent centers on her increasingly desperate attempts to maintain an illusion of youthfulness. She claims this is necessary to retain her fading theatrical career, although it is, she believes, her only hope in holding Trigorin, a similarly self-absorbed figure. Williams emphasizes that the artistic life is, by its very nature, a self-absorbed and solitary existence, a point that comes into fuller focus in his variation on Chekhov's Nina. She longs for an artistic life and abandons Constantine's protective love for her to run off with Trigorin and to the stage. Williams implicates Nina more fully in her decision to run off with Trigorin than Chekhov does—she seems to understand the price that must be paid for the realization of her theatrical ambitions far more than Chekhov's more innocent Nina seems to do. In Moscow, Nina begins her career as an actress, gives birth to Trigorin's child, and loses her innocence in every possible way. The final encounter between Constantine and Nina that Chekhov invents is not significantly changed by Williams. However, as a result of earlier changes, Nina is more fully drawn back to the moment she has lost her innocence of the world, and Constantine comes to the sad realization that Nina symbolizes a purity of spirit he has been unable to capture in his writing since her departure. Both have grown as artists, but neither can find fulfillment or personal happiness.

The Notebook of Trigorin premiered in a 12 September–10 October 1981 production at the Playhouse Theatre in Vancouver, British Colombia, Canada, under the direction of Roger Hodgman. Williams and all involved were dissatisfied with this version, and he continued to revise the play through a 1982 Los Angeles run of the Vancouver production. Following Williams's death in 1983, little attention was paid to the play in part because Williams's literary executor, Maria St. Just (**Maria Britneva**), withheld a play that she believed was a desecration of the Chekhov original. Despite this, a 14 December 1992 staged reading of the play was given at Lincoln Center, with Marsha Mason, George Grizzard, and Kate Burton heading the cast. Following St. Just's death in 1994, director Stephen Hollis mounted a 5 September–4 October 1996 production at the Cincinnati Playhouse in the Park with Lynn Redgrave heading the cast. Though critics were divided on the merits of Williams's adaptation, all of them praised Redgrave's performance. See also **Gender**.

Further Reading

Demaline, Jackie. "Playwright's Demons Overwhelm *Trigorin*." *Cincinnati Enquirer* 7 September 1996: C12.

Fisher, James. "Tennessee Williams's *The Notebook of Trigorin*: Adapting Chekhov's *The Sea Gull* into Dramatic Autobiography." *Text & Performance* 21 (April 2000): 81–99.

Grossberg, Michael. "Cincinnati Playhouse Nails Williams's Twist on Chekhov Play." *Columbus Dispatch* 12 September 1996: 12.

Gunn, Drewey Wayne. " 'More Than Just a Little Chekhovian': *The Sea Gull* as a Source for the Characters in *The Glass Menagerie*." *Modern Drama* 33.3 (September 1990): 313–321.

Hale, Allean. Introduction to *The Notebook of Trigorin: A Free Adaptation of Anton Chekhov's "The Sea Gull,"* ed. Allean Hale. New York: New Directions, 1997. ix–xx.

White, Bob. "*Notebook* Production a Winner." *Oxford Press*, 12 September 1996: 8.

James Fisher

Now the Cats with Jewelled Claws.
Now the Cats with Jewelled Claws (1970) is a two-scene black comedy overloaded with Williams's camp humor, juxtaposing the outrageous with violence that erupts in and from daily life, as in the mayhem at the nursing home in *This Is the Peaceable Kingdom*. Two middle-aged women, Madge and Bea (a more sinister version of Flora and Bessie in *A Perfect Analysis Given by a Parrot*), lunch at a restaurant, run by a gay, aging manager with dentures and dyed hair, and engage in a catty conversation about after-Christmas sales, marital infidelity, vacations, each other's looks, food, and urban life. Amid the banal, comic terror lurks. Tellingly, Bea uses a long hatpin to jab shoppers who get in her way; "panic purchasers" stampede anyone in their path; and massacres break out in bedrooms when people are not allowed to watch their favorite television programs. Absurdly, when Bea and Madge leave the restaurant, they end up kicking and punching each other. Sick jokes, faux allusions ("the tea house of the winter moon" [323]), and insults in the mode of Lenny Bruce and Mort Sahl pepper their ridiculous conversation. In a parodic echo of Blanche DuBois's plight, Bea tells Madge she has a voice like a fire siren. Moments of camp exhibitionism also absurdly break out when Bea exposes her thighs and pantyhose; the manager unexpectedly does a vulgar, Dionysian dance; each entrance by the pregnant waitress is signaled with an arpeggio; and the second biker arranges for fellatio with the gay, toothless manager in the restroom.

Multiplying the absurd and the violent, Williams introduces two gay bikers (about 20 years old) from the Mystic Rose cycle club (which dares to claim Christ as one of their own), proving again that the symbolism of the rose remained prominent in Williams throughout his life. We are asked to compare and contrast the two sets of diners in terms of their questing for love/acceptance, flaunting conventions, and succumbing to violence, even death.

As in so many other plays, *Now the Cats with Jewelled Claws* is filled with allusions to dying and death. Guests in hotel lobbies are sitting corpses. An unseen character, Mr. Black, the personification of death as in Jack in Black in *The Mutilated*, carries a placard announcing his presence outside the restaurant. At the end of *Now the Cats with Jewelled Claws*, one of the bikers has his brains dashed out in front of Geffels Department Store, and his partner is then introduced to his future (death) outside the restaurant lavatory and before the revolving door that the gay manager operates. On the other side of the door lies violence, destruction, death.

Now the Cats with Jewelled Claws is both amusing and eerie, a satire of the conventional world. The title of the play comes from a lyric sung by the manager in the last few moments of the play about cats who slide down from the walls and menace those who see them. The cats are Williams's fetishistic animals, symbolic of the comic terrors in the play as well as those feral bourgeoisie (Madge, Bea) who precipitate and participate in them.

Further Reading

Saddik, Annette. *The Politics of Reputation: The Critical Reception of Tennessee Williams' Later Plays.* Madison, NJ: Fairleigh Dickinson University Press, 1999.

Philip C. Kolin

O

Odets, Clifford (1906–1963). Depression-era playwright Clifford Odets had a major influence on Tennessee Williams. Even before Williams came to New York, Odets was something of a model for the young Tom Williams, whose earliest scripts bear the stamp of the social activist and the documentary realist: *Candles to the Sun* (1935) concerns a miners' strike, and *Not about Nightingales* (1938–1939) is about a prison uprising. Both plays were drawn from headlines and have a distinct socialist/progressive urgency evocative of Odets. *Fugitive Kind* (1936–1938), which blames the hidden poverty and crime in a city like **St. Louis** on the hypocrisy and greed of the capitalist establishment, shows the substantial influence of Odets's radical voice, and *Stairs to the Roof* (1940–1942), an expressionistic fantasy about Ben Murphy's adventures, demands comparison with Odets's *Rocket to the Moon* (1938). Odets's vivid and colorful vernacular poetry and his understanding of what drives people emerged in Williams as well.

Odets was one of the **Group Theatre** members who, having fallen under Harold Clurman's influence, joined the Communist Party. Williams, of course, was never so politically committed, but Odets's focus on social issues did rub off on him. Years after the Group disbanded, Clurman commended Williams and other young writers for sustaining on the American stage the social concerns that Odets advocated in the 1930s. Aside from their political concerns, Odets's plays, like Williams's, also have an intimate, personal quality, depicting lonely characters isolated within a family. Gerald Weales, having pointed out both writers' affection for **Chekhov**, identifies significant parallels between Odets's *Awake and Sing!* and Williams's ***The Glass Menagerie***, especially in the two mothers, Bessie Berger and Amanda Wingfield. While many critics judge Odets an optimistic writer, his plays do reflect a darker side of American life while projecting a belief in the possibility for progress. Williams's plays, particularly his earlier major ones, reflect the same dichotomy: a portrayal of the degradation of the distressed, lost souls he saw as representative of most of our lives—not unlike Frank Elgin in Odets's *Country Girl* (1950)—but always suggesting the possibility of a better world—a Belle Reve or a Musée Mechanique—somewhere else. Odets's hope was an erect concrete place in the future, while Williams's was more to find a dreamscape. But their impulses were not dissimilar.

Odets's early writing efforts at the Group Theatre, where he had gone initially to study acting, led to *Awake and Sing!* (1935), and his ultimate career path was set—and, in a sense, so was Williams's. The successes of Odets's plays for the Group prompted Clurman to establish a department dedicated to finding and developing new writers and plays, leading to the 1938 contest in which Williams was awarded a $100 special prize and which began his association with the Group Theatre. When **Molly Day Thacher**, the Group's playreader, arranged for Williams to observe rehearsals of Odets's *Night Music* (1940), Williams got to watch Clurman direct **Elia Kazan** and to meet Odets. Williams even wrote home in January 1940 that he dated Odets's sister, Florence, once. In an earlier letter, he had been proud to announce that he was referred to in New York as "the Gentile Odets." Ironically, Williams's fate was further entangled with the Group's and Odets's, for Clurman had indicated that he would direct Williams's *Battle of Angels* for the company if *Night Music* were successful. It was not, and shortly afterward the Group Theatre collapsed, leaving Williams without a likely producer for *Battle of Angels*.

Like Williams, Odets was very attached to his mother, Pearl, to whom he dedicated several works and for whom he named one of the noble characters in *Paradise Lost* (1935). Both writers also had troubled relationships with their fathers. Odets's father wanted his son to follow him into the advertising business, much as **Cornelius Coffin Williams** had wanted Tennessee to join him in the shoe factory, but, like Williams, Odets wanted to write poetry. Both fathers had the same reaction to their sons' literary aspirations—anger and rejection. Both writers suffered from depression, but their neuroses drove them to opposite responses: Williams went on "flights" to distant places to escape his demons, but Odets seemed to indulge his, locking himself in his room for days on end, scribbling randomly in his diary. Though he never achieved the renown of Williams, Odets spanned the gulf between the melodramatic post–World War I theater and the mature post–World War II drama that Williams exemplified. It may be said that Odets paved the road from **Eugene O'Neill** to Tennessee Williams.

Further Reading

Brenman-Gibson, Margaret. *Clifford Odets, American Playwright: The Years from 1906 to 1940.* New York: Atheneum, 1981.

Murray, Edward. *Clifford Odets: The Thirties and After.* New York: Ungar, 1968.

Shuman, R. Baird. *Clifford Odets.* Twayne's United States Authors Series. New Haven, CT: College and University Press, 1962.

Weales, Gerald. "Clifford's Children: or, It's a Wise Playwright Who Knows His Own Father." *Studies in American Drama, 1945–Present* 2 (1987): 3–18.

Richard E. Kramer

O'Neill, Eugene Gladstone (1888–1953). American Nobel Prize–winning Eugene O'Neill's influence on Tennessee Williams was profound, both artistically and personally. Williams's interest in O'Neill went back at least to 1928, when a production of O'Neill's *Strange Interlude* was on its way to **St. Louis**. Williams's description of the play focused on its unusual aspects, such as its length and the spoken thoughts of the characters. Eight years later, Williams wrote *April Is the Cruellest Month* (later retitled

Spring Storm), which owes a great deal to *Strange Interlude* in its naturalistic dialogue and the tangled sexual relations. Allusions, too, to O'Neill's life at sea may have been intended in remarks by the protagonist.

Williams had been assigned to read all of O'Neill's plays in a class at Washington University (1936–1937), and he even wrote a term paper analyzing O'Neill's techniques. Earlier, at the University of Missouri (1929–1932), Williams audited Robert Ramsay's course in modern drama, which included O'Neill's *Ile*, *Bound East for Cardiff*, and *In the Zone*. O'Neill had revived interest in and respect for the one-act as a vehicle for young writers, and in 1930 and 1931, Williams entered the university's Annual One-Act Play Contest. In fact, his 1931 entry, *Hot Milk at Three in the Morning*, bears similarities to O'Neill's *Before Breakfast* in portraying a working man trapped in a confining marriage. Williams revised and renamed this one-act as *Moony's Kid Don't Cry*, a title reminiscent of O'Neill's *The Dreamy Kid*. In 1930, the Missouri Workshop, the university's theater group, presented *The Hairy Ape*, and at the end of 1931, *Mourning Becomes Electra* opened in New York accompanied by extraordinary press attention (including a *Time* cover). Eight years later, Williams proposed to his agent a trilogy of southern plays (*Spring Storm*, *Battle of Angels*, and a play he never wrote to have been called "The Aristocrats"), certainly inspired by O'Neill's remarkable production.

In the summer of 1940, Williams vacationed in Provincetown, where O'Neill had gotten his start. The old Wharf Theatre, rebuilt and reopened, was again operating near Captain Jack's Wharf, the restaurant in which Williams and his friends gathered, and it was there that Williams saw a performance of *Diff'rent*. It is possible that in O'Neill's frustrated and puritanical Emma Crosby, who rejected a worthy, but sexually unchaste man only to end up with his even less pure nephew, Williams saw reflections of the spinster Alma Winemiller or the equally repressed Blanche DuBois. Many clear parallels to O'Neill's *Desire under the Elms* surface in Williams's *A Streetcar Named Desire*—in structure, language, themes, and characters. As Alan Ehrlich points out, it is no mere coincidence that both titles include "desire," as the two plays explore the destruction of a family by the introduction of obsessive passion when an outsider enters the claustrophobic world that had existed before and tries to overturn the status quo. Both Williams's Blanche and O'Neill's Abbie are "homeless" when they arrive in their new environments, and both are unbalanced but strong women who had been used to controlling their worlds. In both plays, the writers created unified locales that reinforce the sense of confinement. *A Streetcar Named Desire*'s Stanley and *Desire under the Elms*'s Eben each fight to keep things as they were and turn from resenting the interlopers to a vacillating and uncontrollable attraction/repulsion response. Animal imagery, Ehrlich also observes, is common to both dramas, especially with trapped characters such as Eben and Blanche.

Williams paid homage to the great playwright on numerous occasions. He wrote an appreciation of O'Neill in 1967, noting that he had once written to the older writer in praise of *The Iceman Cometh*—the two men's only direct contact. Williams asserted in an interview with O'Neill biographers Arthur and Barbara Gelb that O'Neill had been the father of the American theater at the opening of the twentieth century. Indeed, if the Provincetown Playhouse had not broken with the commercial trifles then being offered in New York, and had it not started presenting the experimental and innovative works of O'Neill, the American theater might not have been ready for Williams or his contemporaries when they emerged.

Further Reading

Devlin, Albert J., and Nancy Tischler, eds. *The Selected Letters of Tennessee Williams, Volume 1—1920–1945.* New York: New Directions, 2000.

Ehrlich, Alan. "A Streetcar Named Desire under the Elms: A Study of Dramatic Space in *A Streetcar Named Desire* and *Desire under the Elms.*" In *Tennessee Williams: A Tribute*, ed. Jac Tharpe. Jackson: University Press of Mississippi, 1977. 126–136.

Gelb, Arthur, and Barbara Gelb. *O'Neill: Life with Monte Cristo.* New York: Applause, 2000.

Leverich, Lyle. *Tom: The Unknown Tennessee Williams.* New York: Crown, 1955.

Williams, Tennessee. "Concerning Eugene O'Neill." *Performing Arts* [Los Angeles; Ahmanson Theatre, program booklet for *More Stately Mansions*] 12 September–21 October 1967: 9.

Richard E. Kramer

Orpheus Descending. *Orpheus Descending* opened on Broadway on 21 March 1957 in a production directed by Harold Clurman and starring **Maureen Stapleton** as Lady and Cliff Robertson as Val. A drastically revised version of 1940's **Battle of Angels**, *Orpheus Descending* failed to reverse significantly the fate of its predecessor since it closed after only two months. Williams claimed never to have abandoned this project during the 17 intervening years, though serious rewriting apparently began in 1951, with the newly titled *Orpheus Descending* copyrighted in 1955. Williams's preface for the play, "The Past, the Present and the Perhaps," which details its history, appeared in the *New York Times* on 17 March 1957. The publication of *Orpheus Descending* with *Battle of Angels* by New Directions on 5 February 1958 included the original prologue, which was omitted from the Clurman production.

Like *Battle of Angels*, *Orpheus Descending* is set in the Mississippi Delta of the 1940s, specifically a drygoods store in a small town obviously based on Williams's childhood home of **Clarksdale**. True to his word, Williams excised the prologue and epilogue of the previous version and opens this one with a prologue that recalls the former Act One as two local women prepare a homecoming for the terminally ill store owner, Jabe Torrance. Their gossip centers around Jabe's wife, Lady (Myra in *Battle of Angels*), who, as an eighteen-year-old, had married for financial security after her father, known as the Wop, died trying to save his Prohibition-era wine garden on Moon Lake from a fire set by the Mystic Krewe in punishment for the sale of liquor to blacks. Still tormented by her lover's desertion and her consequent abortion, Lady has endured a loveless and childless marriage to a man who, unbeknownst to her until play's end, was the leader of the Klan-like Krewe. Her plans to reopen, symbolically on Easter Sunday, the confectionery adjacent to the store as a re-creation of her father's wine garden incur the disapproval of both her husband and the town.

Also subject to the town's censorship are Carol Cutrere (Cassandra Whiteside in *Battle of Angels*), the younger sister of Lady's former lover, whose prominent family pays her to take her scandalous behavior and liberal views elsewhere; the Conjure Man, a black shaman, who responds to Carol and her request for the Choctaw cry; Val Xavier, a snakeskin-wearing, guitar-toting wanderer, whose appearance seems to be conjured by the cry; and Vee Talbott, the sheriff's wife, whose paintings, as in *Battle of Angels*, reflect her religious visions. Hired and then seduced by Lady, Val attempts to leave, only to be thwarted first by Lady, who

Maureen Stapleton and Cliff Robertson in the 1957 Broadway stage production of *Orpheus Descending*. Springer/Photofest.

is bearing his child, and then by Jabe, who kills his wife and blames the murder on Val. After the town's enraged men turn a blow-torch on Val and the confectionery, only Carol, having traded with the Conjure Man for the snakeskin jacket, escapes, laughing as she exits.

The changes in name, not only of the play but of Lady and Carol, are not merely surface changes; they reflect changes in depth of character and of meaning. Lady is a far more sympathetic and noble woman than Myra and her death, therefore, more tragic. Carol, too, is a more sympathetic character, no longer simply the pretty rebel daughter but a quester made up in prepunk style who again fails to seduce or save Val but does save herself as well as his snakeskin jacket and all it represents. The Conjure Man is no longer a museum caretaker but a mystically

appearing shaman who underscores the racial dimensions of the violence and enhances the mythic dimensions of Val; so, too, does the elimination of the Woman from Waco since the mob is no longer propelled by an outsider and the audience no longer presented the rationale of an actual crime. The fire and the immediacy of Val's death, as opposed to a later-recounted lynching, assume, then, the mythic proportions suggested by the title change.

Orpheus Descending represents a crossroads in Williams's life and work. The Preface attests to his emotional investment in the play as an artistic rendition of his youthful past. Not only his determined revising but also his originally choosing and then leaving unchanged the name Valentine Xavier confirm his personal hopes since Williams derived the name from a paternal relative and considered it as a possible nom de plume. Perhaps this long-standing commitment to the work accounted for his response to the negative reviews of its 1957 reincarnation; exacerbating his depression, this repeat of the past and his father's death are regarded as the impetus for his beginning psychotherapy in that year. Beyond its autobiographical significance, *Orpheus Descending* is important as both a culmination of the themes, characters, and imagery from previous plays and a harbinger of these elements in the plays to come. Williams's intensification of the mythic overtones as well as his insistence on nonrealism in the staging also signals a defining dimension in his drama. In bibliographical terms, *Orpheus Descending* is noteworthy since the playwright's mention in its preface of a predecessor called *Not about Nightingales* prompted Vanessa Redgrave's recent resurrection of this work.

Notwithstanding this keynote position in the Williams canon, the damning reviews of *Orpheus Descending* not only truncated its original run but also foretold its initial assessment by literary critics. The charges of overloading that had been leveled at *Battle of Angels* were certainly not mitigated by its retitled reemergence with an embellished symbolic and mythic structure. Notable Williams critics such as Nancy Tischler and Signi Falk set the tone in finding the play an exercise in excess in which the religious and sexual symbolism emerges as ultimately confusing, if not gratuitous. Robert Bray cites as example of this lack of subtlety the setting in Two River County, an obvious reference to civilization's Tigris and Euphrates origins. The snakeskin jacket, with its pagan and Christian allusions, also provokes critical scorn as it positions Val as an embodiment of not only Orpheus, come to rescue Eurydice (Lady) from Hades (Jabe), but also Christ, come to rescue souls from Hell; moreover, this incarnation of the play broadened the allusions to **D.H. Lawrence** with Val depicted as the unsocialized lover of Lady Chatterley and sexual love presented as a redemptive force. Underlying these allusions is the autobiographical layer with Val as the fugitive artist haunted by the past and hunted by a sexually and religiously repressive society. Until recently, Williams's layering of meaning baffled, if not incensed, most critics of the play.

In 1959, revivals of *Orpheus Descending* were staged in Paris and London as well as in New York at the Grammercy Arts Theatre. A 1960 film adaptation, retitled *The Fugitive Kind* but unrelated to an earlier Williams play of that title, was directed by Sidney Lumet and starred **Anna Magnani** as Lady and **Marlon Brando** as Val. In 1977, the play was revived at the Moscow Central Theatre of the Soviet Army and, in 1988, at the Haymarket Theatre in London. This production by the **Peter Hall** Company, starring Vanessa Redgrave as Lady, moved to Broadway in 1989 and was filmed for a

1990 television viewing. Hall's production accompanied a renewed interest in Williams's play. The favorable response to Peter Hall's 1989 revival in combination with the increasing recognition of a sociopolitical undercurrent in Williams's drama by such critics as Philip Kolin, Robert Bray, and John Clum have served to redeem *Orpheus Descending* from its saga of condemnation. The descent of Val/Orpheus/Christ into the Delta represents a confrontation with the South's original sin and consequent loss of paradisal love. His ambivalence of identity as a once wild, sexually charged being who now seeks purity and security doubtlessly reflects Williams's own ambivalence about not only his sexuality but also the South of his childhood—at once a hotbed of racist/sexist violence and an idyll of remembered innocence.

Though his guitar is as mesmerizing as Orpheus's lyre, the southerner is no more successful than the Greek in overcoming the forces of darkness. As Orpheus disobeys Hades, Val lingers and looks back upon his lover, defying both the husband and the sheriff; the latter, enraged by his wife's worship of Val, has ordered him, in avowedly racist terms, to leave before sundown. As Orpheus is destroyed by the jealous rage of the Maenads, so Val is destroyed by the jealous rage of the men, who collectively turn the blowtorch on him and the converted confectionary. Thus, the fire of bigotry and fear of difference, which had destroyed the Wop and his Eden for lovers, in the end consume Valentine and the re-creation of that Eden by the winemaker's daughter. This final conflagration, however, spares the town's most notable outcasts—the Conjure Man and Carol. A pagan black man (see **Race**) whose Indian cry has called Val into their midst, Uncle Pleasant salvages the snakeskin jacket, affirming the resiliency of sexuality, art, and freedom. Carol's trading of a gold ring for the jacket deepens this affirmation. Unlike the suicidal Cassandra, she exits laughing and swathed in Val's shed skin from this Hell of prejudice and repression—a landscape that Williams held in horror but translated into a transcendent art. See also **Mythology; Religion.**

Further Reading

Bray, Robert. "*Battle of Angels* and *Orpheus Descending*." In *Tennessee Williams: A Guide to Research and Performance*, ed. Philip C. Kolin. Westport, CT: Greenwood, 1998. 22–33.

Clum, John M. "The Sacrificial Stud and the Fugitive Female in *Suddenly Last Summer*, *Orpheus Descending*, and *Sweet Bird of Youth*." In *The Cambridge Companion to Tennessee Williams*, ed. Matthew C. Roudané. Cambridge: Cambridge University Press, 1997. 128–146.

Egan, Rory B. "Orpheus Christus Mississippiensis: Tennessee Williams's Xavier in Hell." *Classical and Modern Literature* 14.1 (Fall 1993): 61–98.

Falk, Signi. *Tennessee Williams*. Rev. ed. Boston: Twayne, 1978.

King, Kimball. "The Rebirth of *Orpheus Descending*." *Tennessee Williams Literary Journal* 1.2 (Winter 1989–1990): 18–33.

Kolin, Philip. "Sleeping with Caliban: The Politics of Race in Tennessee Williams's *Kingdom of Earth*." *Studies in American Drama, 1945–Present* 8.2 (1993): 140–162.

Tischler, Nancy. *Tennessee Williams: Rebellious Puritan*. New York: Citadel, 1961.

Wallace, Jack. "The Image of Theatre in *Orpheus Descending*." *Modern Drama* 27 (1984): 324–335.

Janet V. Haedicke

P

Parrott, Jim (1916–2001). Jim Parrott, who served as the model for Skye in Tennessee Williams's *Vieux Carré*, was a boarder at the **New Orleans** rooming house that became the setting of the play. Williams met Parrott in December 1938, when visiting New Orleans for the first time. Williams soon moved into the same boarding house at 722 Toulouse in the French Quarter. Parrott was a clarinet-playing English teacher who also wanted to be a playwright, and the two developed a friendship that lasted throughout Williams's life.

Wanting to escape Mardi Gras, Williams joined Parrott on a trip to the West Coast to find work in **Hollywood**. According to Lyle Leverich's authorized biography *Tom: The Unknown Tennessee Williams*, the pair encountered several mishaps on their journey to California. Williams and Parrott slept in tents and worked where they could. In fact, Williams relied on Parrott's musical talents to fund part of their trip. While traveling, they met a great variety of individuals, including a family who hitched a ride with them and a Native American woman who ran a campground in Phoenix. Arriving in California several weeks later, Williams checked into the YMCA in Los Angeles, and Parrott headed for his uncle's squab ranch in the country.

During this time, Williams's main support came not from his writing but from temporary jobs and what assistance Parrott and his relatives could provide. On 20 March, Williams learned he was awarded $100 in a prize from the **Group Theatre** play contest for three of his plays in *American Blues*. Williams bought a used bicycle with the money, and he and Parrott headed to Mexico, a place that would repeatedly fire Williams's imagination. They traveled on the historic El Camino Real (the King's Highway) that begins in San Diego and ends at the border. In many ways this trip served as the inspiration for Williams's 1953 play *Camino Real*. Later in the states, Parrott and Williams found work taking care of a small poultry farm, a job that ironically brought Williams close to starvation. They settled in Laguna Beach, where Williams connected with an artist colony. Williams left Parrott to go to Taos, New Mexico, to meet the wife of the late **D.H. Lawrence**.

Williams corresponded with Parrott occasionally but did not see him again until ***Battle of Angels*** failed in Boston in 1940. Desperate to find a refuge, Williams caught a train for Miami, where he met Parrott. Finding Miami unsuitable, Williams allowed Parrott to drive him to Key West. Parrott and Williams then went their separate ways—Williams to write *The Glass Menagerie* and Parrott to serve as a pilot in the Air Transport Command in World War II.

Further Reading

Devlin, Albert J., and Nancy Tischler, eds. *The Selected Letters of Tennessee Williams, Volume 1—1920–1945.* New York: New Directions, 2000.

Leverich, Lyle. *Tom: The Unknown Tennessee Williams.* New York: Crown, 1995.

Williams, Tennessee. *Memoirs.* Garden City, NY: Doubleday, 1975.

Jean Rhodes

A Perfect Analysis Given by a Parrott. A Williams one-act comedy, *A Perfect Analysis Given by a Parrott* was first published in *Esquire* in 1958. It is a satire of some frequent Williams targets—club women, vanity, and the folly of looking for unsuitable beaus—and also features such similarly recurring Williams themes as the absurdity in aging, failed relationships, and waiting for gentlemen callers. Though set in **St. Louis**, *Perfect Analysis Given by a Parrott* contains two characters (Flora and Bessie) and some dialogue included in Williams's 1950 *The Rose Tattoo*.

Aging friends Flora and Bessie banter about weight, dress, hairstyles, and boyfriends (past and present). Both at the edge of 40, a thin Flora worries about skin problems and being prudish, while a more stout Bessie complains of no longer being able to wear a size 16 and not finding enough men to seduce. These ladies, in near-funereal black dresses and long gloves (but sporting bright hats—Flora's is chartreuse and Bessie's magenta), stop at a deserted St. Louis bar to meet some men from the Sons of Mars in Memphis National Convention on a Saturday night. Members of the Women's Auxiliary, Flora and Bessie regularly attend conventions, but for purposes of snagging a date. The empty bar is run by the waiter, a chubby Italian wearing a green apron, whom Flora and Bessie chat with and listen to his story about two Sons of Mars who had come into the bar before the ladies arrived. Then the ladies move on to the antics of some other Sons of Mars who once stripped a girl and sent her out in a taxi (also conveyed in *The Rose Tattoo*). Flora and Bessie continue their discussion of previous boyfriends, and Bessie reveals her philosophy of men, saying she filfills her role in society, even if it is only through one-night stands.

Bessie comments on Flora's uptightness, and Flora reveals that she had her character read by a parrot, who predicted: "You have a sensitive nature, and are frequently misunderstood by your close companions." Like the goat in *Rose Tattoo* or Amanda's glass unicorn in **The Glass Menagerie**, Williams uses the parrot in *A Perfect Analysis Given by a Parrott* as a symbol of foolishness. The parrot's prediction stands as the play's central comic irony: Flora's sensitivity keeps her from getting men, while Bessie's insensitivity attracts men; besides this, Flora's closest companion Bessie really does understand Flora's predicament, but rather than aiding her, Bessie derides Flora just as much as she helps her. The parrot's analysis for Flora may well be Williams's way of revealing, through his drama, his own insecurities about growing older, revealed also in his other late plays such as *This Is the Peaceable Kingdom* and *Lifeboat Drill*. While expressing these insecurities, Williams simultaneously pokes fun at foolish attempts to ascertain the future. Like parrots, Bessie and Flora mimic and mock each other, falsely predicting the other's romantic future. Bessie ridicules Flora's hairdo, upsetting Flora, and as the friends make up, two Sons of Mars enter the bar leapfrogging, tooting toy bugles. The play ends with Flora and Bessie, one on each man's arm, strutting around the table, singing "Mademoiselle from Armentières," an anonymous World War I bar song mocking the ugliest, fattest woman from Armentières (Flora deals with skin problems, Bessie her weight) who tries to date equally repulsive and comical soldiers.

Williams's humor in *A Perfect Analysis Given by a Parrott* contains an undercurrent of sobering, even cutting, reality. Yet it does offer some comic hope at the end by sending the women two men. Flora and Bessie may snap at each other like a pair of past-their-prime queens, exchanging one-liner barbs, as both point out the other's most painful weakness numerous times but always attempt to console each other afterward.

Further Reading

Kolin, Philip C. "Echoes of Reflexivity in Tennessee Williams's 'A Perfect Analysis Given by a Parrott.'" *Notes on Contemporary Literature* 30 (Spring 2000): 7–9.
Londré, Felicia Hardison. *Tennessee Williams.* New York: Ungar, 1983.

J. Marcus Weekley

Period of Adjustment: High Point over a Cavern. A heavy-hearted and serious comedy, *Period of Adjustment* (1958) was Tennessee Williams's first major foray into this comic genre. It was originally published in *Esquire* in December 1960. Williams worked on what he thought was a lighthearted comedy during the time he was finishing one of his darkest plays, *Suddenly Last Summer*. But *Period of Adjustment* did

not completely turn out the way he had expected. To be sure, the result was not a "typical" Williams drama with gory violence, mad characters, wild sex, and assorted grotesqueries. Critics have dismissed *Period of Adjustment* as a poor attempt to capture and critique middle class life and marriage, a failed Williams domestic comedy. Nonetheless, *Period of Adjustment* continued Williams's interrogation of the cries and crises of the human heart, even if they are less tragic, more sentimentalized, in this script. In essence, *Period of Adjustment* represents Williams's own adjustment to a different type of drama and documents his versatility as a playwright.

The plot centers on a surprise visit on Christmas Eve of a newlywed couple on the verge of separating to the home of a couple that has just separated. As in many of Williams's plays, the setting is in the South, in High Point, or Dexter in some versions. Originally, Williams set the play in Memphis but changed names for fear of a lawsuit. The two husbands, George Haverstick and Ralph Bates, are old war buddies. George's new bride, Isabel, is the virginal nurse who attended him for his psychosomatic "shakes" while he was in the hospital. Ralph's wife, Dorothea, has just left him and taken their son with her. By the end of *Period of Adjustment*, both couples are reunited with a hope for prosperity and, perhaps, more children. But before the happy ending, Williams leads us through the cloudier depths of his characters' souls, including sexual dysfunction, role confusion, and illusions.

Williams's accompanying theme of role confusion is evident in many ways. *Period of Adjustment* takes place in a cataclysmic environment, which hearkens back to the frenzied, disheveled setting of **New Orleans** in *A Streetcar Named Desire*. Ralph and Dorothea's home in the High Point/Dexter subdivision is built over a cavern and gradually sinking, hence the subtitle of Williams's comedy. The house, perhaps the major symbol in the play, represents the abyss into which marriage, family, and the crass middle-class are sinking. Moreover, the Freudian imagery of the house being devoured by a cavern is paralleled in the husbands' foolish, confused plans to restore the almost extinct longhorn cattle, whose role in Old West movies is being replaced by shorthorn cattle. George even bluntly expresses his fear of castration by Nurse Isabel. His surname, "Haverstick," is rich with ironic phallic symbolism. But George, according to Arthur Ganz, "has rejected his homosexual nature or at least pretended to a virility he does not possess."

Though the wives are accused of frigidity, Williams's frequent use of icy imagery implies an omnipresent emotional chill within all the characters' lives. Cold weather is a constant and troubling trope throughout the play. The unhappy and unconsummated honeymooners, George and Isabel, travel in a heaterless vehicle, while "White Christmas" plays over the radio. George gives Ralph a gift of iced champagne, perhaps symbolizing their shared bond—a blizzard that resides between both husbands and their wives, freezing desire. The spine of Ralph Bates's character is to take back his manhood and his role, as he understands it, as a husband. The sad spaniel chosen for the Bates home was a compromise between the masculine Doberman pinscher that Ralph wanted and the feminine poodle that Dorothea desired; correspondingly, Ralph is no more satisfied with the asexual canine than he is with Dorothea's feminization of the couple's son. Symbolically, Ralph throws the doll that his son was playing with into the fire. After quitting his job with his father-in-law, Mr. McGillicuddy, and his wife's subsequent abandonment, Ralph plans to move to Hong Kong, a reminder of his manly

glory days as a war hero, and later to raise longhorn cattle with George. When the McGillicuddys try to "take over" his home by gathering the couple's joint property to deliver it to their daughter, Ralph, with George's assistance, defies them. The McGillicuddys are easy Williams's satiric targets—venal, mercenary, bigoted, as seen in the treatment of their black maid Susie, whom Philip C. Kolin regards as a surrogate for Dorothea.

Southern Belle Isabel Haverstick has difficulties switching gears from her motherly care of George as a nurse to attending to his sexual desires as his wife. Her maternal instincts battle with her desire to be mothered herself. Like a little girl, she trivializes and sentimentalizes everything she encounters in the Bates home to a "sweet little" something—house, bedroom, and so on. When she finds an Infant of Prague statue, venerated to bring health, prosperity, and fertility in the bedroom, she identifies with its childlike qualities and, at the same time, reduces the Christ child represented in the statue with her own mothering sympathy. Until the end of the play, she sees herself as the nurse of the hospital she had metonymized into the world. For Williams such a view of the world as hospice makes sense.

George Haverstick, who holds on to his glorious Alamo ancestry, is a Williams dreamer unable to negotiate with Isabel's conflicts. He suffers from psychological tremors, which Ralph attributes to a fear of impotency. In fact, in his tour overseas, George lied about his sexual conquests and, instead of lovemaking, began teaching English to and drinking sake with "Tokyo dolls." Signi Falk labels George and Ralph as two of Williams's "desperate heroes," the misfits who feel trapped in ordinary existence and thus demand comparison with other ill-prepared suitors, such as Mitch in *A Streetcar Named Desire*.

190

Homely Dorothea is torn between her role as her controlling parents' daughter and her role as Ralph's wife and supporter of his dreams. Even her marriage to Ralph was arranged by the McGillicuddys. She also arrived at the marriage bed suffering from psychological tremors. Louise Blackwell rightly sees Dorothea as Ralph's subordinate, and to hold on to his love, she undergoes surgery to make herself more attractive to him. Ralph and Dorothea sleep like siblings in twin beds marked "His" and "Hers" but vow by the end of the play to get a double bed marked "Ours," blending the comic and the serious over Williams's cavern. Both couples are reunited by play's end with Isabel and Dorothea in pink and blue nighties, respectively, perhaps foreshadowing future fertility.

Yet *Period of Adjustment* has a darker side haunted by images of death and uncertainty. For their honeymoon George drives Isabel around in a funeral limousine, recalling the blind Mexican woman in *A Streetcar Named Desire* crying, "Flores para los muertos" where marriage, love, and death ominously commingle. Dorothea painfully suffers from a lack of her own identity. The stucco house, perhaps hiding the flaws of the lives within, sinks even deeper into the cavern. Isabel is still the nurse to the suffering world.

Premiering at Coral Gables's Coconut Grove Playhouse in 1958, *Period* starred James Daly as Ralph, Barbara Baxley as Isabel, Robert Webber as George, and Martine Bartlett as Dorothea. In 1960, Williams rewrote *Period of Adjustment* which became a Broadway hit at the Helen Hayes Theater directed by George Roy Hill, with Rosemary Murphy as Dorothea. Hill also directed the 1962 MGM film version starring Jane Fonda (Isabel), Anthony Franciosa (Ralph Bates), Jim Hutton (George Haverstick), and Lois Nettleton (Dorothea). The British premiere was at the Theatre Royal in Bristol in 1961 and *Period* was subsequently performed in Hamburg (1962) and Athens (1963).

Further Reading

Blackwell, Louise. "Tennessee Williams and the Predicament of Women." In *Tennessee Williams: A Collection of Critical Essays*, ed. Stephen S. Stanton. Englewood Cliffs, NJ: Prentice-Hall, 1977.

Falk, Signi L. *Tennessee Williams*. Rev. ed. Boston: Twayne, 1978.

Ganz, Arthur. "Tennessee Williams: A Desperate Morality." *American Scholar* 31 (Spring 1962): 278–294. Rpt. in *Tennessee Williams: A Collection of Critical Essays*, ed. Stephen S. Stanton. Englewood Cliffs, NJ: Prentice-Hall, 1977. 123–137.

Goldfarb, Alvin. "*Period of Adjustment* and the New Tennessee Williams." In *Tennessee Williams: A Tribute*, ed. Jac Tharpe. Jackson: University Press of Mississippi, 1977. 310–317.

Kolin, Philip C. "The Function of Susie in Tennessee Williams's *Period of Adjustment*." *Notes on Contemporary Literature* 25 (May 1995): 10–11.

Weales, Gerald. "*Period of Adjustment*: High Comedy over a Cavern." *Journal of American Drama and Theatre* 1.1 (1989): 25–38.

Kathleen M. Rossman

Pinter, Harold (1930–). Harold Pinter, English dramatist, significantly influenced the plays of Williams's later period. Pinter's highly influential dramatic style includes slight plots, language that reflects the illogical and repetitive nature of ordinary speech, the unreliability of memory, incommunicability, underlying menace, and characters whose motives and histories remain obscure with no revelation of truth or determined closure. Many of Williams's later plays (1961–1983) reflect this Pinteresque style, focusing on the attempt to express and define experience that can only be conveyed through silence or evoked through fragmented, inarticulate moments of speech in order to access the meaning that lies in the gaps in and between linguistic expression. Williams's experimentation with antireferential language in favor of a minimalistic focus on the underlying action of silence and truncated dialogue is evident in works such as *I Can't Imagine Tomorrow* (1966), *The Gnädiges Fräulein* (1966), *In the Bar of a Tokyo Hotel* (1969), and the much-revised *The Two-Character Play* (1969, 1973, 1976, also known as *Out Cry* in some versions), as well as in several 1981 one-acts, *Lifeboat Drill, Now the Cats with Jewelled Claws*, and *This Is the Peaceable Kingdom*.

A prolific writer, actor, and director, Pinter's first one-acts, *The Room* (1957) and later *The Dumb Waiter* (1957), were followed by his full-length play *The Birthday Party* (1958), which was staged for a one-week run in London and baffled critics in much the same way as Williams's experimental work would throughout the 1960s to 1980s. Pinter came into prominence with his second full-length play, *The Caretaker* (1960), which Williams called "a fabulous work" in a 1962 interview.

In Pinter's plays, words conceal rather than reveal meaning, focusing on what is *not* being said instead of fostering communication. Often the dialogue signifies an act of aggression and a struggle of wills, and the incommunicability in Pinter's work has been explained by critics such as Martin Esslin as an *unwillingness* rather than the more existential *inability* to communicate. However, despite similarities between Pinter and other playwrights of the absurd, such as **Samuel Beckett** and **Edward Albee**, who employ minimalistic dialogue, silences, and pauses to focus on the instability, unreliability, and inadequacy of language as communication, the situations in many of Pinter's plays tend to be more menacing and sinister than those presented by other writers who also explore incommunicability.

While some of Williams's later works such as *The Gnädiges Fräulein, Now the Cats with Jewelled Claws*, or the unpublished *Kirche, Kutchen, und Kinder* contain elements of absurdism, his *Two-Character Play*, for example, is more directly Pinteresque in its menacing tone, contradictions of memory, and awareness of language. The verbal sparring between Ben and Gus in *The Dumb Waiter* regarding the expression "light the kettle" is reflected in the punning overdetermination of language throughout *The Two-Character Play*, as Clare and Felice play with meaning in similar struggles of will. The play's style of dialogue, its acknowledgment that the silence of "prohibited words" can be more powerful than what is spoken, and the setting that includes a "sinister" statue looming over the stage clearly exhibit Pinter's influence.

In several interviews throughout the 1960s Williams praised Pinter, along with Beckett and Albee, for their original and creative visions, admiring their spareness of writing and their ability to explore the subtleties of human relationships through language and silence. In an interview with John Hicks in 1979, Williams called Pinter "the greatest living contemporary playwright," and in 1985 Pinter directed Williams's *Sweet Bird of Youth* (1959). Like Pinter, Beckett, and Albee, Williams left behind the limited conventions of realism and self-consciously played with the implications of language as dramatic action and the subtleties of incommunicability in his later work, often leading critics to dismiss his post-1961 plays as inferior imitations of these playwrights. More recent criticism such as Philip Kolin's collection *Undiscovered Country: The Later Plays* of *Tennessee Williams*, however, has argued against this claim and explored Williams's later works such as *The Gnädiges Fräulein* and *The Two-Character Play* on their own terms as valuable contributions to the tradition of antirealism.

Further Reading

Bloom, Harold, ed. *Harold Pinter*. New York: Chelsea House, 1987.
Esslin, Martin. *The Theatre of the Absurd*. London: Penguin, 1961.
Hicks, John. "Bard of Duncan Street: Scene Four." In *Conversations with Tennessee Williams*, ed. Albert J. Devlin. Jackson: University Press of Mississippi, 1986. 318–324.
Kolin, Philip, ed. *The Undiscovered Country: The Later Plays of Tennessee Williams*. New York: Lang, 2002.
Saddik, Annette. *The Politics of Reputation: The Critical Reception of Tennessee Williams' Later Plays*. Madison, NJ: Fairleigh Dickinson University Press, 1999.

Annette J. Saddik

Piscator, Erwin (1893–1966). One of the leading directors in Berlin in the years following World War I, Erwin Piscator established the concept of epic theater (later taken up by **Bertolt Brecht**). He believed in a didactic, working-class theater devoted to political and economic themes, and—with or without the playwright's permission—he would cut and rearrange a play's scenes to emphasize social issues. He introduced the use of film, projections, and mechanized set pieces such as treadmills as integral parts of both dramaturgy and stage design. The pinnacle of his German career was his 1928 production of *Adventures of the Good Soldier Schweik*. The rise of Hitler caused Piscator to come to America, where he founded the Dramatic Workshop of the **New School for Social Research** in New York City in 1940.

Piscator hired John Gassner to teach a playwriting seminar; Tennessee Williams was one of the first to enroll. Williams's earliest New York productions were under Piscator's auspices at the Workshop. The first, *The Long Goodbye* (1940), did not bode well for the combination of epic theater with Williams's more lyrical, personal style: without Williams's knowledge, the student director wrote and inserted a speech on social consciousness.

In 1942, Piscator announced a production of **Battle of Angels**. He insisted, however, that Williams rewrite the play as epic theater, depicting the South as a fascist state and the protagonists as freedom fighters. Williams made an attempt, including the addition of a dream scene in which a black preacher exhorts Val to take up the work of liberation, but made no more changes after that and refused to further subjugate his vision of the play to Piscator's. Piscator did not stage the play.

Still, Piscator considered having Williams adapt Mark Twain's *Life on the Mississippi*, and the Workshop produced another Williams one-act, *This Property Is Condemned* (1942). That year Williams was a production assistant on Piscator's epic theater adaptation of *War and Peace*, which employed projections and film, and was deeply impressed by its cinematic style.

Piscator returned to Germany in 1955 and settled in West Berlin, where, until his death, he continued to employ elements of his style on a wide variety of plays. He would claim credit for weaning Williams off the traditional three-act form in favor of a more fluid form of construction. Indeed, it is possible that one source of the projections Williams called for in **The Glass Menagerie** was Piscator's epic theater.

Further Reading

Innes, C.D. *Erwin Piscator's Political Theatre.* London: Cambridge University Press, 1972.

Willet, John. *The Theatre of Erwin Piscator.* New York: Holmes & Meier, 1979.

Michael Paller

Plastic Theater. Plastic theater, a concept that Tennessee Williams introduces in his production notes to *The Glass Menagerie* (1945), describes his ideal theater, which makes use of all the stage's resources—lighting, sound, music, movement, sets, and props—to generate a theatrical experience greater than realism. Though Williams never publicly discussed plastic theater again, from *Glass Menagerie* on, his plays are highly theatrical: his language is lyrical and poetic; his settings, "painterly" and "sculptural"; and his dramaturgy, cinematic. His scenic descriptions draw on the world of art, and his use of sound and light is symbolic and evocative, not realistic. In *Camino Real* (1953) and many later plays, for example, Williams exploits styles like expressionism, the subjective expression of the artist's inner experiences; surrealism, the expression of the subconscious through fantastic imagery and the incongruous juxtaposition of subjects; and absurdism, the use of fantasy and irrationality to dramatize the absurdity of the human condition in an irrational world. What makes Williams's theater remarkable is that he disregarded realistic theater at a time when realism was the dominant style on American stages.

There seems to be a connection between Williams's plastic theater and "plasticity" as defined by Hans Hofmann, a prominent and respected painter and teacher in New York whom Williams knew in the early 1940s. Hofmann defines plasticity as the communication of a three-dimensional experience in the two-dimensional medium of a painting, an effect that derives from the tension between the separate elements of the painting—form, line, color, space, and so on. The tension creates the sensation that the painting breathes, even seems to move. Williams married the language of Hofmann with ideas he was already formulating about theater to create the term "plastic theater."

This may be the origin of Williams's term for "plastic theater," but he also developed the concept from various sources from his early years, including at the University of Iowa (1937–1938), where he gained practical experience in all aspects of production. In **Erwin Piscator**'s Dramatic Workshop at the **New School for Social Research**, in 1940, he learned about expressionist techniques that included the use of projections and film. Williams's experience working for MGM in 1943 also contributed to his formulation of a plastic theater. Another source for Williams's nonrealistic ideas was **Eugene O'Neill's** plays that he read, saw, and studied.

Providing further background on Williams's plastic theater is the New Stagecraft's "plastic stage" as described in Kenneth Macgowan's *The Theatre of Tomorrow* (1921) which focused on a three-dimensional stage—constructed scenery instead of two-dimensional painted scenery. On this analogy, Williams, already working with three-dimensional settings, wanted a multidimensional theater, integrating all the resources of the stage so that elements traditionally added by the director and designers would be an equal part of the playwright's creative process. The tension among these disparate arts created the plasticity of the theatrical experience so that the audience has an experience beyond the mere image of actual life. Williams's plastic theater is *theatrical*, not strictly *literary*.

Hope Davis, Fiesta Ensemble, and Ethan Hawke in Tennessee Williams's *Camino Real*, directed by Nicholas Martin, on the Williamstown Theatre Festival's Main Stage, 1999. Photo by Richard Feldman. Photo courtesy of the Williamstown Theatre Festival.

Further Reading

Cheney, Sheldon. *Expressionism in Art*. New York: Liveright Publishing Corporation, 1948.

Hofmann, Hans. "Plastic Creation." *The League* [The Art Students' League of New York, NYC] 5.2 (Winter 1932–1933): 11–15, 21–23.

———. *The Search for the Real and Other Essays*. Ed. Sara T. Weeks and Bartlett H. Hayes, Jr. Andover, MA: Addison Gallery of American Art, 1948. Rpt. Cambridge: MIT Press, 1967.

Kramer, Richard E. " 'The Sculptural Drama': Tennessee Williams's Plastic Theatre." *Tennessee Williams Annual Review* 5 (2002).

Neumann, Claus-Peter. "Tennessee Williams's Plastic Theatre: *Camino Real.*" *Journal of American Drama and Theatre* 6.2–3 (Spring–Fall 1994): 93–111.

Richard E. Kramer

Poems. Tennessee Williams wrote and published poetry throughout his life. An anthology of 1944 (*Five Young American Poets*, Third Series) gathered a number of his early poems, at a time when he was not yet well known as a playwright. Later he produced two volumes of verse: *In the Winter of Cities*, published in 1956, and *Androgyne, Mon Amour*, published in 1977. Other poems appeared in periodicals but were not collected until the edition of Williams's *Collected Poems* (2002), where they are joined by posthumous publications and lyrics from the fiction, plays, and films.

There are three periods in Williams's career as a poet: early, middle, and late. The early period began with his adolescence in the 1920s and lasted until 1936. Throughout this period, which should be regarded as an apprenticeship, he published under his given name "Thomas Lanier Williams" (or "Tom Williams"). The middle period continued from 1936 through 1964—the year when Williams's first volume of poetry was reissued in paperback, just as the most successful phase in his theatrical career was drawing to a close. A third, late period lasted from 1964 until the author's death in 1983. Though these are rough divisions, they correspond to transitional moments in Williams's artistic career and are concurrent with changes in his poetry's emphasis, scope, and technique.

Formally, the verses of the first period demonstrate Williams's competence in conventional techniques and forms, especially the sonnet; in theme and tone they reflect the influence of popular romantic models, from John Keats to Sara Teasdale and Edna St. Vincent Millay. However, between 1935 and 1936 Williams wrote and published "Two Metaphysical Sonnets," suggesting a new interest in the style of John Donne and the other "metaphysical poets" whose reputations had been revived by T. S. Eliot and the early New Critics. At around the same time, Williams began to acquaint himself with the work of modernist poets including Eliot and, more momentously, **Hart Crane**.

The encounter with poetic modernism inaugurated Williams's middle period; its effects emerged in his verse as early as October 1936, when he was writing drafts of a poem that appeared the following April as "Inheritors." Also published in 1937 were such formally adventurous poems as "Swimmer and Fish Group" and "Sacre du Printemps," their titles, respectively, evoking abstract painting and the seminal work of musical modernist Igor Stravinsky. By 1939 Williams was taking these experiments still further in "Tenor Sax Taking the Breaks," which featured an imitation of jazz effects with its precedents in Crane's "Cutty Sark" and (more remotely) in Eliot's *The Waste Land*. Throughout the 1940s, 1950s, and 1960s, Williams continued to write poetry in both traditional and free forms, mingling romantic with modern influences. Many poems of this middle period show the impact of Crane's obscurity and indirection, while avoiding his verbal archaisms and harsher constructions in favor of a more colloquial voice. Simple, tender love poems and playful doggerel, such as the lyrics in dialect from *Blue Mountain Ballads* (which **Paul Bowles** set to music), contrast with ambitious pastiches of personal imagery and recollection and with vividly realized visions tinged by the surreal, the fantastic, or the melodramatic. The latter often tantalize the reader with half-realized narrative scenarios, as in "Intimations," or with private symbolism, as in "Lament for the Moths"; here the poet supplies no key to the central extended metaphor of beauty's sensitivity and tragic fate, leaving its interpretation to the reader (who may, however, be assisted by a familiarity with Williams's plays and stories).

Williams's late period is set apart by a growing predilection toward confession and autobiography. The abstraction and symbolism of his earlier verse give way to a more literalistic transcription of the poet's past and present impressions. In texts such as "Events Proceed" and "Tangier: The Speechless Summer," Williams seems to serve up his private thoughts nearly raw, intimating an attraction to the aims and methods of Beat writing. An extreme instance is the prose poem titled "What's Next on the Agenda, Mr. Williams?"—an exhibitionistic mixture of recollection, rumination, and ranting that resembles a Beat narrative and the New Journalism. Unlike poets of the "confessional" school, Williams was not competing for laurels within the poetic profession so much as resorting to an alternative means of expression, one that offered him some relief from a theatrical world that he found increasingly inhospitable.

Nevertheless, Williams's dramatic skill is integral to his more successful poems. A large number are in effect monologues, even though Williams often frames them as narratives; examples include "Tuesday's Child," "The Road," "Young Men Waking at Daybreak," "Counsel," "Evening," "Night Visit," "Wolf's Hour," and "The Color of a House." The voices speaking here do not always seem as sharply defined as those of characters in a play or in Robert Browning's dramatic monologues (one of which, "My Last Duchess," was the basis for an early and unpublished Williams play). In many of the late poems, the speaking voice is often recognizably that of the poet himself—or, rather, of the character that he tended to project to himself and others, while he labored under the burdens of his later life and declining career.

Among Williams's dominant themes are eroticism and sexuality, time and memory, and the heroism of the poetic imagination, all found in his plays. In many early poems, such as "October Song" and "Sonnet for Pygmalion," Williams seems to express feelings that are erotic yet wistful, contrasting a stereotypical, idealized projection of love with the losses inflicted by time and human frailty. However, a few of these texts convey an impulse to confront, and even defiantly to embrace, the more transiently physical aspects of desire, such as "Ave Atque Vale," a lyric recalling the "decadent" tendencies of late romanticism. Later, more and more of Williams's verse would reflect the craving for sensual gratification that he found affirmed and celebrated in the writings of **D.H. Lawrence**, and that competes in many of his plays with a conflicting yearning for a transcendent, spiritual love.

This intense apprehension of sexual desire appears in the surreal imagery of "The Legend," which borrows its title from Crane while imitating Lawrence's proselike freedom of form. Outdoors, in the heat of an Indian summer, a female character initiates sex with a male figure whose response is reluctant and indeed seemingly involuntary, dictated by physical impulses. As fancifully yet more gently, "Death Is High" depicts the strife between erotic love and a disembodied, pure consciousness that is associated with death. Mutability as such—apart from its effects upon lovers—is prominent in poems that mix Williams's own childhood memories with lyrical fantasy, such as "In Jack-O'Lantern's Weather" and "Recuerdo."

In the published poems of Williams's early

period, erotic experience is figured in heterosexual terms, at least on those occasions when pairs of lovers are given genders. Only in unpublished manuscripts do we find evidence that Williams may already have sought to give a queer inflection to his verse at this time. For instance, there is an unpublished, alternate version of the poem "The Changeling" (approximately datable to the late 1930s) in which the speaker's vocabulary indicates a homosexual (see **Gender and Sexuality**) rather than a heterosexual affair. Other relatively early poems that address homosexuality in unambiguous, though not graphic terms—such as "I Think the Strange, the Crazed, the Queer" (begun by 1941)—would appear in print only much later. By 1944, Williams had begun to publish poems depicting encounters that may readily be understood as having occurred between men. Yet these allusions could be deliberately covert, and layered with metaphysical conceits, as in "The Siege" (begun by 1941). The speakers in "Testa Dell' Effebo" and "San Sebastiano de Sodoma," poems written and published between 1948 and 1950, linger over representations of young men in a poignantly sensuous fashion. To the initiated, such subjects (especially that of Saint Sebastian) were immediately recognizable as icons of a queer sensibility. During the 1950s and 1960s, Williams published poems that ambiguously implied his homosexuality through the speaker's designation of a male beloved, as in "Which Is My Little Boy?" and "Life Story," or else through the choice of an identifiably queer perspective, as in "The Interior of the Pocket" and "Photograph and Pearls." In his late verse Williams exploited a wider range of possibilities for the public expression of his sexuality, whether in a camped-up style ("Miss Puma, Miss Who?") or through open and undisguised reflection ("Androgyne, Mon Amour," "The Rented Room," "The Blond Mediterraneans: A Litany").

Poets in Williams's work occupy a social position that is at once accursed—like that of criminals or scapegoats, or, at the time, that of homosexuals—yet also redemptive, like that of Christ. In his story "The Poet," Williams portrays poetry as a Dionysian art. The poet's power is one of enchantment but is also associated with transgression and death. This combination testifies to Williams's preoccupation with the story of Orpheus, the archetypal poet of Greek myth, and generally to his faith in the cult of inspiration and irrationalism (see **Mythology**). Williams's predilection for poetry written in a romantic, bohemian spirit is articulated in two essays that he published together as a "Preface" in 1944. It may also be seen in poems, such as "The Dangerous Painters," where he depicts the artist's vocation.

Much of Williams's drama and fiction exhibits a strong fascination and identification with the figure of the poet. Williams wrote plays about Crane and Lawrence; he also nearly wrote one inspired by the life of **Vachel Lindsay**. Sebastian Venable, the absent protagonist whose memory haunts the play *Suddenly Last Summer*, is a poet. So is the aged Nonno in *The Night of the Iguana*. So of course is Lord Byron, who expounds on poetry's nature in *Camino Real* after delivering his grotesque recollections of the death of Percy Bysshe Shelley.

Some of Williams's plays feature his own verses, including those that he ascribes to Nonno, "How calmly does the orange branch," as well as the lyrics to a song that Val Xavier sings twice in *Orpheus Descending* ("Heavenly Grass"). In early, unpublished drafts of *Suddenly Last Summer* (though not in the published text), Williams included a version of his own poem "San Sebastiano de Sodoma" and attributed it to Sebastian Venable. Elsewhere in his plays, characters quote the work of actual poets of the past: Teasdale in *Spring Storm*, Keats in *Not about Nightingales*, William Blake in *Summer and Smoke*. A line by Eliot is invoked in *Camino Real*. As epigraphs to the published texts of his plays, Williams employed quotations from poets including Dante Alighieri, Rainer Maria Rilke, John Perse, and Dylan Thomas, as well as his perennial favorite, Crane.

Williams's poetry has found its ardent admirers. A few poems, including "The Beanstalk Country," have been anthologized. The prominence of gay male themes in much of Williams's verse invites readers to situate it in the long and distinguished tradition of poetry by nonheterosexual American men, from Walt Whitman to Crane to later authors including Allen Ginsberg and Frank O'Hara. Finally, scholars of Williams have traced the interaction between his writing of verse and of plays, discovering connections that are more particular and concretely suggestive than the generally "lyrical" quality that many critics observe in his dramatic writing.

Further Reading

Adler, Thomas. "Tennessee Williams's Poetry: Intertext and Metatext." *Tennessee Williams Annual Review* 1 (1998): 63–72.

Ower, John. "Erotic Mythology in the Poetry of Tennessee Williams." In *Tennessee Williams: A Tribute*, ed. Jac Tharpe. Jackson: University Press of Mississippi, 1977. 609–623.

Parker, Brian. "Tennessee Williams and the Legends of St. Sebastian." *University of Toronto Quarterly* 69.3 (Summer 2000): 634–659.

Williams, Tennessee. *The Collected Poems.* Ed. David Roessel and Nicholas Moschovakis. New York: New Directions, 2002.

———. "The Poet." In his *Collected Stories.* New York: New Directions, 1985. 246–251.

———. "Preface to My Poems." In his *Where I Live: Selected Essays*, ed. Christine R. Day and Bob Woods. New York: New Directions, 1978. 1–6.

Nicholas R. Moschovakis

Politics. In his autobiographical essay "Facts about Me," Williams wrote of "the social consciousness which I think has marked most of my writing," declaring, "I have no acquaintance with political and social dialectics. If you ask what my politics are, I am a Humanitarian" (60). He had firmly held political beliefs, ranging from his support of socialist Norman Thomas in the 1930s to his opposition to the Vietnam War in the 1970s, but he rarely participated in political actions or made public statements of his convictions. Because of this, and despite recent discussion of his political views by biographer Lyle Leverich and a growing number of critics (Adler, Balakian, Bigsby, Hale, Kolin, Kullman, Schlatter), Williams is often called an apolitical playwright by critics and historians.

Actually, Williams wrote a substantial amount about political issues. Like many young playwrights beginning their careers in the 1930s, he began by writing socially conscious plays with a strongly leftist political orientation, such as *Candles to the Sun* (1937), a play about striking Alabama coal miners; *Not about Nightingales* (1938–1998), a play about prisoners in a southern penitentiary; and the first version of *Fugitive Kind* (1937), which is set in the lobby of a depression-era flophouse. Traces of the 1930s playwright remain in Tom's poetic references to the hopelessness engendered by the Great Depression in *The Glass Menagerie* (1944). Critics have also pointed to Williams's treatment of political issues involving class (Bray), race and ethnicity (Kolin, Adler), and sexuality (Savran, Bruhm) in his work.

During the cold war period that was the backdrop for most of his career, however, Williams's political consciousness appeared most often under the cover of political allegory or fantasy. Kolin (" 'a play about terrible birds' ") has recently read Williams's *The Gnädiges Fräulein* (1966), along with Alfred Hitchcock's *The Birds*, as "cultural scripts of fear" about "the lunacy and dread of nuclear attack in the 1960's." But before then *Camino Real* (1953) was composed in an eclectic literary mode, ranging from a thinly veiled political allegory of the excesses of McCarthyism to the most idealistic romantic fantasy. *Camino Real* reflects many of the cultural anxieties of the McCarthy era in which it was written. It treats the individual citizen as the impotent victim of an oppressive, seemingly all-powerful regime, which retains its power through surveillance, secrecy, confinement, and anonymous acts of repression and force. Its emphasis on the oppression of the people and the suppression of the call for brotherly solidarity had an immediate application amid the McCarthyist attack on leftist thinking in the American theater of 1953.

Another important subtext is the repression of homosexuality and the oppression of homosexuals, a subject that had immediate importance for Williams as a gay man, as well as timely political importance in the United States of the 1950s, where homosexuals were one of the targets of congressional investigations by Senator Joseph McCarthy and other crusaders against "un-American activities." When *Camino Real* was produced in 1953, it was literally dangerous for Williams to be be identified as a gay man, and it was nearly impossible to treat homosexuality in a Broadway play, except as deviance or disease. Except for the minor character Baron de Charlus, who is quietly killed and taken away by the Streetcleaners after making an assignation with someone in

the Ritz Men Only, the subject of homosexuality is not treated overtly in *Camino Real*. Within what Eve Kosofsky Sedgwick has called the epistemology of the closet, however, the oppression of the homosexual emerges as central to Williams's representation of this existential nightmare of life in the 1950s. The very image of the "Survivor" dying with the word "Hermano" (brother) on his lips and Kilroy's ultimate departure from the *Camino Real* with Don Quixote and Sancho Panza suggest a symbolic opposition to the persecution of the "love that dare not speak its name," but within the allegorical fantasy of the play, this is as clearly as Williams states it.

In 1966, when Williams published his novella *The Knightly Quest*, the political situation in the United States had changed a good deal. The power of McCarthy and of the House Un-American Activities Committee was greatly eroded by the Senate's formal censure of McCarthy in 1954 and by various legal decisions that limited the power of congressional committees. Within this cultural matrix, it was possible for a writer like Williams to address the issues that most concerned him more directly, particularly in fiction. *The Knightly Quest*, a novella that has been described as "part farce, part science fiction, part satire" (Sklepowich 537), is a much more overt treatment of the conjunction of homosexuality and McCarthyist politics than *Camino Real*, while it may be seen as elaborating on the metaphors that Williams had developed in that play.

The Knightly Quest is about the return of Gewinner Pearce to his hometown in the South. The town is dominated by two symbolic structures, the Pearce's house, "a gray stone building that had a resemblance, probably more deliberate than accidental, to something in the nature of an ancient Saracen castle brought up to date" (8), and "The Project," the site of the secret and menacing industry based on "the development of some marvelously mysterious weapon of annihilation" (8–9), that has come to dominate the town. In the early 1960s, Williams's representation of political hope as residing in Don Quixote resonated with the Camelot imagery that had been woven around the presidency of the recently assassinated John F. Kennedy. What was different, of course, was the element of madness that Williams suggested was essential to the country's savior. Williams also connects the divine madness in the romantic vision to the love between Don Quixote and Sancho Panza, with homoerotic overtones.

The Project unites the United States' two major cultural anxieties of the cold war era, the fear of weapons of mass destruction and the fear of subversion by American communists, or what J. Edgar Hoover called "the enemy within," that was countered by the government's increased emphasis on surveillance and a general social pressure to conform to various cultural norms of behavior. Gewinner's brother Braden, who is also the Project's director, boasts to his wife that it will soon be possible for him to "possess and control the whole planet by pressing a button connected with a wire . . . and the whole fucking thing would either be blown to bits or fall under the absolute dominion of the Project" (57).

Williams's depiction of the town and the Project is satirical, humorous, and grotesque. His dystopian fantasy is both entertaining and disturbingly familiar. The real interest of the novella, however, comes in the conjunction of Gewinner Pearce's romantic ideals with the existential nightmare of surveillance, control, and anxiety that is the town. The chivalric overtones of the quest become even more evident when it is considered as a battle between the forces of good and evil. The outcome is distinctly quixotic, as the Project is blown up, and,

presumably, the planet with it, by a bomb planted by Gewinner and two other "don't-fit-inners," who escape on a spaceship called "the Ark of Space—a reassuring touch of romanticism," as the narrator notes. Like Kilroy, who joins the romantic quest of Don Quixote and Sancho Panza by simply going on from the Camino Real, these three nonconformists escape from the cold war hell of the Project by embracing a mad romantic quest. It is only through breaking with reality, Williams suggests, that there can be any happy resolution for the don't-fit-inners of the cold war era.

In *The Red Devil Battery Sign* (1975), Williams suggests a different avenue of escape. This play, set during the Vietnam War, also ends in a kind of mad dissociation, but it is not that of romantic fantasy. The Red Devil Battery Company is the menacing embodiment of the military-industrial complex. The play's protagonist, a character called only Woman Downtown, is being held prisoner in a hotel in Dallas (the site of the Kennedy assassination) and possesses incriminating documents, a result of her having had access to the "design for surrendering a democracy to rule by power conspiracy" (53), and she lives under constant threat from this force. In *Red Devil Battery Sign*, Williams opposes anxiety over the potential destruction of human civilization with an emphatic affirmation of humanity. Two human emotions—compassion and love—affirm redemptive human relationships in opposition to the dehumanization of the Red Devil Battery monsters. In this case, however, Williams does not suggest that an escape into the romantic quest for love is powerful enough to set in opposition to these forces. In the end, Williams brings together the Woman and Wolf, the leader of a wild gang of youths that has taken possession of the Hollow beyond the city, who takes the Woman in his arms and looks into

Politics

her eyes, as *"she recognizes or senses something rightly appointed as her final fate"*
(93). She goes off with the gang, accepting
the leader's statement that she is "Sister of
Wolf" (94). In a moment of Brechtian confrontation, the separation between stage and
audience dissolves completely; as explosions
are heard in the background *"the denizens
of the Hollow all advance, eyes wide, looking out at us who have failed or betrayed
them"* (94) and the Woman *"throws back
her head and utters the lost but defiant outcry of the she wolf"* (94).

This seeming affirmation of the end of civilization and reversion to the primitive or animal element within human nature seems
completely at odds with the chivalric quests
that the protagonists of *Camino Real* and
The Knightly Quest take up. In its affirmation of the most elemental human traits,
however, it may be as romantic as either of
the others. Williams proposes that the Wild
Child may be the alternative to the self-
destruction of civilized society. In going back
to the Hollow and becoming mother to this
contemporary version of J.M. Barrie's "lost
boys," the Woman who is also the sister of
the Wolf has the chance to participate in a
kind of origin myth for a new humanity. The
new family is an instance of the brother-
sister dyad that Williams often uses, as in
The Two-Character Play, to represent the
imagination of the artist. While Kilroy hits
the open road with Don Quixote to escape
the oppressive cold war regime and Gewinner joins an interplanetary excursion to a
more highly evolved society, the Woman
joins with her brother the Wolf to form a
new social organization, perhaps to found a
new species, which, in the eyes of a self-
described Humanitarian, might turn out to
be better than a humankind that has failed
at humanity. See also **Collected Stories**;
Where I Live.

202

Further Reading

Adler, Thomas P. "Culture, Power, and the (En)gendering of Community: Tennessee Williams and Politics." *Mississippi Quarterly* 48.4 (Fall 1995): 649–665.

Balakian, Janet. "*Camino Real*: Williams's Allegory about the Fifties." In *The Cambridge Companion to Tennessee Williams*, ed. Matthew C. Roudané. Cambridge: Cambridge University Press, 1997. 67–94.

Bigsby, C.W.E. *A Critical Introduction to Twentieth-Century American Drama*. Vol. 2: *Williams, Miller, Albee*. Cambridge: Cambridge University Press, 1984.

Bray, Robert. "*A Streetcar Named Desire*: The Political and Historical Subtext." In *Confronting Tennessee Williams's "A Streetcar Named Desire": Essays in Cultural Pluralism*, ed. Philip C. Kolin. Westport, CT: Greenwood, 1993. 183–197.

Bruhm, Steve. "Blackmailed by Sex: Tennessee Williams and the Economics of Desire." *Modern Drama* 34 (1991): 528–537.

Hale, Allean. "Tom Williams, Proletarian Playwright." *Tennessee Williams Annual Review* 1 (1998): 13–22.

Kolin, Philip. "Sleeping with Caliban: The Politics of Race in Tennessee Williams's *Kingdom of Earth*." *Studies in American Drama, 1945–Present* 8.2 (1993): 140–162.

———. " 'a play about terrible birds': Tennessee Williams's *The Gnädiges Fräulein* and Alfred Hitchcock's *The Birds*." *South Atlantic Review* 66 (Winter 2001): 1–22.

Kullman, Colby H. "Rule by Power: 'Big Daddyism' in the World of Tennessee Williams's Plays." *Mississippi Quarterly* 48.4 (1995): 667–676.

Savran, David. *Communists, Cowboys, and Queers: The Politics of Masculinity in the Work of Arthur Miller and Tennessee Williams*. Minneapolis: University of Minnesota Press, 1992.

Schlatter, James. "*Red Devil Battery Sign*: An Approach to a Mytho-Political Theatre." *Tennessee Williams Annual Review* 1 (1998): 93–101.

Sedgwick, Eve Kosofsky. *Epistemology of the Closet*. Berkeley: University of California Press, 1990.

Sklepowich, Edward A. "In Pursuit of the Lyric Quarry: The Image of the Homosexual in Tennessee Williams' Prose Fiction." In *Tennessee Williams: A Tribute*, ed. Jac Tharpe. Jackson: University Press of Mississippi, 1977. 525–544.

Brenda Murphy

R

Race. Though the representation of race and race relations in Williams is not as prominent as in the works of his fellow Mississippians **William Faulkner** and Eudora Welty, race is nonetheless a significant part of Williams's cultural heritage as a southerner and a reflection of his sympathetic views of the Other. Raised in the Deep South at the beginning of the twentieth century, Williams accompanied his maternal grandfather, the Reverend **Walter Dakin**, on his parish rounds and saw firsthand the condition of blacks in the Mississippi Delta, circa 1915 to 1930. Williams was also a world traveler who enjoyed visits to Cuba, Italy, Spain, Africa, and later in his life, Japan. A keen observer of both racial stereotypes and taboos, Williams from the earliest part of his career reveled in writing about the mysteries of a non-Western culture (e.g., Egypt in "Vengeance of Nitocris" [1928]). Race in Williams also reflects the playwright's own anxieties and triumphs over his indeterminate sexual and political identity. As Williams himself once confessed, "I always thought I was black" (Rasky), and he told his agent to withdraw *A Streetcar Named Desire* from production in South Africa if the theater excluded blacks. Blacks, Hispanics, Italians, and members of other ethnic groups are found throughout Williams's plays and fiction as important symbolic characters and as analogues and extensions of some of Williams's protagonists. In many ways, Williams was a radical in his portrayal of race and civil (human) rights and readily admitted that all his plays had a social consciousness. He was always a champion of the oppressed, of the underdog, the Other.

A strong African American presence exerts itself in several of Williams's works, most notably *A Streetcar Named Desire* and *Baby Doll*. George Crandell and Rachel Van Duyvenbode argue that Stanley Kowalski, for example, exhibits many black features that are incorporated into his white identity to foreground the theme of miscegenation. Not uncoincidentally, too, does Stanley live in **New Orleans**, where brown fingers play intoxicating music and where the races easily intermingle. That is, of course, except for white-skinned Blanche who admonishes her sister Stella that men like Stanley are only good for fulfilling her erotic desires, not propagating the race of white property owners from which she and Stella were so proudly descended.

While attending the University of Missouri in 1929–1932, Williams was asked to write essays about "Negro Life," and from this period came his short story "Big Black: A Mississippi Idyll," which won Fifth Place in the Mahon Story Contest at Missouri. This early story invests in the muscular and sexualized Big Black, a construction laborer who is tempted to rape a white girl while she crosses a stream, the tragic agony of a man caught between desire and punishment, a familiar Williams predicament. The story foregrounds the conflict between desire and death. Not a stereotypical portrait of "Negro Life," this key racial document in the canon shows Williams transcending conventional racial categories to create something challenging, even shocking. "Big Black" demands comparison with the film *King Kong* (which was released within a year of Williams's story) that also blends poignant physical racial details with emotional sympathy for the plight of the Other.

In another Williams's short story, "Desire and the Black Masseur" (1946), a nameless, large "Negro masseur" pummels, murders, and then cannibalizes the body of a timid white clerk Anthony Burns in an act infused with religious rituals of atonement and baptism. Within the grotesque narrative, Williams sexualizes the racial taboo and the guilty desire of a homosexual. Psychodynamically, the masseur represented for Williams both the fear of and attraction toward the black Other, the eroticized dark-skinned male, with whom coupling was forbidden sexually and racially. The strong black masseur can also signify the desired union that Burns, the fragmentary self, seeks. In either case, Williams created a black character whose polyvalent identity and meaning defied traditional depictions of "a Negro."

Another black character mediating Williams's views on race appears in "The Last of My Solid Gold Watches," a one-act play published in 1942 and subsequently included in *Twenty-seven Wagons Full of Cotton*. This nameless porter, who works at the hotel where the old white drummer Mr. Charlie Colton dies, has often been regarded as just another example of a black servant, a minor role in Williams. Although he does not say much, like many of the black servants in Williams (e.g., Lacey and Sookey in *Cat on a Hot Tin Roof*; Fly in *Sweet Bird of Youth*; or Susie in *Period of Adjustment*), it is misleading to interpret these characters' silence as succumbing to white autonomy. As the slave narratives of the nineteenth-century illustrate, silences were often the black Other's only rhetoric of resistance. On a deeper symbolic level, the old porter suggests Eliakim, the gatekeeper of the temple doors, and the Angel of Death "come for to carry" Mr. Charlie home. (Williams offers yet another sympathetic porter in "Portrait of a Madonna.") Alone among those who inhabit the world of "The Last of My Solid Gold Watches," the porter offers Mr. Charlie solicitude, dignity, and salvation. In this way, Williams valorizes the timeless black experience over the callow, white world represented by the establishment that Mr. Charlie tries to serve and also by the new drummer, Charlie Harper, who mocks him. Once again, Williams pushes beyond the stereotype of an otherwise racially marginalized black character to express his views about the dignity and status of blacks in an otherwise patriarchal, racially dichotomous South.

Williams was outraged by racial prejudice and injustice. His indignation is dramatically recorded in *Battle of Angels* (1940) and continued in *Orpheus Descending* (1957).

Though the only person of color whom we see in *Battle of Angels* and *Orpheus Descending* is Uncle Pleasant, an "ancient Negro" conjureman who makes charms and intones chants, Williams nonetheless weaves the fate of oppressed black characters into the lives of his protagonists to underscore the ravages of prejudice. As *Battle of Angels* opens, a black prisoner has just escaped from Sheriff Talbott's jail, and the Sheriff and his posse of Klansmen-like deputies unleash yelping dogs to pursue and trap him. The black man's fate is assured—death; his cultural paranoia is fulfilled. A similar fate is reserved for Val Xavier, Williams's quintessential outsider who dares to break away from the prison of conformity and injustice in Two River County. By symbolically linking the two fugitives, Williams deepens Val's tragedy as the Other even as he expresses sympathy for the plight of blacks. At the end of both *Battle of Angels* and *Orpheus Descending*, Val is burned to death by Jabe Torrance, just as Lady's father, Papa Romano (a "Wop from the old country"—another outsider), had been years ago by Torrance and the Mystic Krewe (read: Klu Klux Klan) for selling liquor to blacks, in yet another Williams linkage to publicize the sins and suffering of racial prejudice. The most bigoted characters in *Battle of Angels/Orpheus Descending*, for example, Jabe Torrance and Sheriff Talbott, are the most despised by Williams. When they set fire to the wine garden with Val in it, their "*faces [are] lit by it like the faces of demons.*" Similarly in *Sweet Bird of Youth* Williams's criticism of racist politics is clearly evident in his portrait of Boss Finley and his corrupt, bigoted beliefs and tactics.

When Williams revised *Battle of Angels* to create *Orpheus Descending*, he added a more contemporary instance of racial atrocity. Carol Cutrere, the town kook and reformer in Two River Country, made speeches, went on protest marches, and pushed for help for the "colored majority" of the county who suffered from pellagra, economic slavery, and starvation. Williams then added in *Orpheus Descending* a reference to the Willie McGee case, the most famous trial of a black man since the Scottsboro Boys in the 1930s, to the list of racial evils Carol outlines. Accused of improper relations with a white woman, McGee was sentenced to death by an all-white jury whose decision without much deliberation evoked world outrage, rallying many important figures to the cause of racial justice. In Carol's voice we hear Williams's.

The black characters in *Baby Doll*, Williams's controversial 1956 screenplay, seemingly and perfunctorily function as laborers, servants, singers, and so on, but they also act as a mocking chorus commenting on the foibles and ultimate downfall of another of Williams's bigoted characters, Archie Lee Meighan, the owner of a cotton gin who burns down his competitor's facility—the Syndicate Plantation—to monopolize the local market. Directed by **Elia Kazan**, who shared and perhaps exacerbated Williams's ire over southern bigotry, the black characters in *Baby Doll* openly undercut Archie's position as white landowner, thereby reflecting the imminent presence and mounting power of the civil rights movement that Williams and Kazan wholeheartedly supported. The black characters are radically made superior and more knowledgeable than Archie. Yet even more subversive of white privilege and its hold on the South is Williams's juxtaposing another outsider, the Sicilian Silva Vacarro (Archie's business rival and amorous contender for Baby Doll), with the black characters. In terms of *Baby Doll* as a black/white color film, Vacarro always wears black to solidify his association with the racial underdog; accordingly, Vacarro's dark skin casts him as a most potent and cross-racial rival for the white woman Baby Doll. Black residents even perform a jazz satire to lampoon Archie as a cuckold. In addition, the blacks and Vacarro forge a bond of solidarity, as they help him put out the fire Archie started at the Syndicate gin. Vacarro thus merges with them as the victim of the white power structure that, as in *Orpheus Descending*, used fire, lynchings, and economic enslavement to perpetuate dominance. Seen in terms of Williams's strong opposition to racial prejudice, then, *Baby Doll* incorporates radical ideas about race into a comic tale about a foolish, middle-aged man (Archie) desiring sexual control over a young white woman (Baby Doll).

Perhaps the most complex use of a black character in Williams's canon is Chicken Ravenstock in *Kingdom of Earth* (1967), the only person of color to occupy a leading (central) role in a Williams play. A "wood's colt" (half-white, half black), Chicken disruptively resists notions about racial stereotypes, triumphantly putting them to the test against his tubercular, transvestite half brother Lot. Like *Baby Doll*, *Kingdom of Earth* interrogates racial ideologies, making Chicken more honest and honorable than his white half brother. Accordingly, Chicken is far preferable to the racist community of the Delta where his white father and half brother have been empowered. Uncovering Lot's plans to cheat him out of his share of the property, Chicken ultimately inherits through the two institutions that historically excluded blacks from power—owning property and marrying outside their race (for example, a white woman). In Williams's racialized script, Chicken covenants with the white Myrtle whom Lot brought to the plantation as a bogus wife and pliable witness to undermine Chicken. As Chicken saves Myrtle from the rising flood waters of the Mississippi River, *Kingdom of Earth* concludes

with a new and healthier social/sexual order for Williams.

Along with an African American presence, Spanish-speaking characters and settings also allowed Williams to advance radical ideas on ethnicity and race. As he did with black characters, Williams portrayed Hispanics as outsiders whose sexuality and desire signified the primitivism and indeterminacy he valorized. Biographically, one of Williams's first lovers was a boisterous, pugilistic man named **Pancho Rodriguez y Gonzales**. A Hispanicized influence commingles with an Africanist one throughout Williams's canon, from Mex in *Not about Nightingales* (1935) to Pablo Gonzales and the blind Mexican woman in *A Streetcar Named Desire* (1947), to Papa and Rosa Gonzales in *Summer and Smoke* (1948), to the cannibalistic boys of Cabeza de Lobo in *Suddenly Last Summer* (1958), to the Costa Verde Hotel in *The Night of the Iguana* (1961), to King Del Rey in *The Red Devil Battery Sign* (1975), Williams's most fully developed and sympathetic Hispanic figure. These Hispanic characters mirrored Williams's resistance to orthodoxy. Comparisons between Stanley and Pablo Gonzales in *A Streetcar Named Desire* celebrated Williams's hybridicity by further complicating Stanley's Otherness. In *Summer and Smoke*, Papa Gonzales, who oversees gambling and cockfighting, and his Flamenco-clad daughter Rosa (a Hispanicized rose) symbolize the rebelliousness that Dr. John Buchanan both courts and fears. The Gonzales world of the volatile Moon Lake threatens the staid society of the white Glorious Hill, Mississippi, providing Williams with another opportunity to assault the barriers imposed by an Anglo-Saxon rigidity.

But Williams's use of Hispanic characters and locations is multivalent. The Hispanic world of **Camino Real** may be the most politicized space in the Williams canon. Revealing the dangers of a right-wing Central American dictatorship depicted in *Camino Real*, Williams in effect satirized the oppressions in America (for example, McCarthy witch hunts) that closely resembled those of Tierra Caliente in this 1953 play. Like his dispossessed hero Kilroy, Williams was the vulnerable, fugitive-artist hunted down for his protests on behalf of freedom for the idiosyncratic. *Suddenly Last Summer* offers some similar geographic displacements; Cabeza de Lobo with its nonwhite, urchin boys, represents the place of crucifixion for homoerotic behavior, Sebastian Veneable's or Williams's. Set against the backdrop of the Watergate era, the nightmarish rule of the Red Devil oligarchy is valiantly opposed by King Del Rey, a Hispanic musician-hero who lyrically clings to love, fulfilling a tenet of Williams's own belief system, by trying to save Woman Downtown.

Finally, one of the most well-documented celebrations of race in Williams can be found in the black and multiracial productions of his plays. *The Glass Menagerie* and *A Streetcar Named Desire* both have a long and powerful history of being successfully (re)interpreted by black actors and directors who have deconstructed normative white values demonstrating a continuing and far-reaching African American presence in many of Williams's scripts. See also **Collected Stories**; **Film Adaptations**; **Southern Culture and Literature**.

Further Reading

Crandell, George. "Misrepresentation and Miscegenation: Reading the Racialized Discourse of Tennessee Williams's *A Streetcar Named Desire*." *Modern Drama* 40 (Fall 1997): 337–346.

Kolin, Philip. "Black and Multi-Racial Productions of Tennessee Williams's *The Glass Menagerie*." *Journal of Dramatic Theory and Criticism* 9 (Spring 1995): 97–128.

———. "Civil Rights and the Black Presence in *Baby Doll*." *Literature/Film Quarterly* 24 (1996): 2–11.

———. "Compañero Tenn: The Hispanic Presence in the Plays of Tennessee Williams." *Tennessee Williams Annual Review* 2 (1999): 35–52.

———. " 'Night, Mistuh Charlie': The Porter in Tennessee Williams's 'The Last of My Solid Gold Watches' and the Kairos of Negritude." *Mississippi Quarterly* 47 (Spring 1994): 215–220.

———. "Sleeping with Caliban: The Politics of Race in Tennessee Williams's *Kingdom of Earth*." *Studies in American Drama, 1945–Present* 8.2 (1993): 140–162.

———. "Tennessee Williams's 'Big Black: A Mississippi Idyll' and Race Relations, 1932." *REAL* 20.2 (1995): 8–12.

———. *Williams: "A Streetcar Named Desire."* Plays in Production. Cambridge: Cambridge University Press, 2000.

———. "Williams in Ebony: Black and Multi-Cultural Productions of *A Streetcar Named Desire*." *Black American Literature Forum* 25 (Spring 1991): 147–181.

Rasky, Harry. *Tennessee Williams: A Portrait in Laughter and Lamentation*. New York: Dodd, Mead, 1986.

Saddik, Annette. "The (Un)Represented Fragmentation of the Body in Tennessee Williams's 'Desire and the Black Masseur' and *Suddenly Last Summer*." *Modern Drama* 41 (1998): 347–354.

Van Duyvenbode, Rachel. "Darkness Made Visible: Miscegenation, Masquerade, and the Signified Racial Other in Tennessee Williams' *Baby Doll* and *A Streetcar Named Desire*." *Journal of American Studies* 35 (August 2001): 203–215.

Philip C. Kolin

The Red Devil Battery Sign. *The Red Devil Battery Sign* (1975) is one of Williams's most political plays. Set against the Dallas backdrop of the Kennedy assassination, the play is filled with the turbulence of the 1960s and 1970s—the atrocities of the Vietnam War; National Guard troops trying to maintain order; CIA/FBI "crewcuts" spying on dissidents; silencing and kidnapping Martha Mitchell; and the murder of columnist Dorothy Kilgallen. The leading culprit is the Red Devil Corporation, bureaucratic powers who exercise demonic control through hidden wealth and assassination and who prop up corrupt regimes. *Red Devil Battery Sign* expressed Williams's opposition to the Vietnam War, the bullyism of mind-controlling, totalitarian governments, and his perennial distrust of Big Brotherism. Interviewed at the Boston premiere (18 June 1975), he proclaimed that he was more of a political playwright than **Arthur Miller**. Aside from *Camino Real*, *Red Devil Battery Sign* may in fact be one of Williams's most satiric plays about America. In light of America's involvement in Korea and then in Vietnam, Williams portrayed his country as "the death merchant of the world" (*Where I Live*, 292). Linda Dorff rightly considers *Red Devil Battery Sign* one of Williams's apocalyptic plays.

Williams's inspiration for *Red Devil Battery Sign* originated with a novella he began in 1946, finished in 1965, and published in 1966 called "The Knightly Quest." The story evolved into a script that Williams revised and rewrote at least four times in as many years between its premiere in 1975 and its production by the Vancouver Playhouse in 1980. By the time *Red Devil Battery Sign* arrived in Vancouver, it had been trimmed by at least another 20 percent and was far less cumbersome.

The themes *The Red Devil Battery Sign* investigates are well known to Williams's audiences—a tortured, broken society where money talks, hopes are unfulfilled, and where civilization loses its battle with barbarism. He argued that only when civilization disintegrates and savagery rules do the

wealthy give up their power. Thomas Adler observes that in *Red Devil Battery Sign* Williams was dealing with "not just destruction of art or illusion . . . but of Western culture and civilization itself" (178). But the redemptive power of love makes a brief but significant appearance with King and Woman Downtown and Perla and McCabe. Running through *Red Devil Battery Sign* are other Williams themes expressed through ironic dualities developed in this world of *Catch-22* irrationality—love versus destruction, order versus chaos, culprits versus victims, gentleness versus violence, human beings versus robots, the material versus the spiritual.

Programmed to be anything but human, the main characters in *Red Devil Battery Sign* assert their humanity as they search for moral values through liquor and drugs, political corruption, and corporate "rip-offs." They can be divided into hell-hollering dog packs, Red Devil Battery Monsters, and those who strive for love. Amid the menacing towers of the urban metropolis at night, wolflike denizens lead a revolution from the wasteland of the Hollow. Like the landscapes they inhabit, characters can be bleak, desolate, and nefarious. Even the lovers—King, Woman—have to confront an intense existential loneliness, yet Williams nonetheless celebrates their ability to be human and their need for compassion and acceptance.

By birth, education, and marriage, Woman Downtown is a privileged member of society but has been controlled throughout her life. Among her guardians are the black-bead-clinking "religious" spinster tutor of her childhood; the "jailers" of the Institute for Rebirth (a private institution for disturbed children); the smiling patrolman behind the estate walls of her husband's hacienda; the electroshock therapist at Paradise Meadows Nursing Home; and the crewcuts, house detective, manager, bartender, and "doctor" of the Yellow Rose Hotel. As the daughter of an influential southern senator and the wife of the president of the Red Devil Battery Sign Corporation, she is imprisoned in the Dallas hotel because she knows too much and threatens to disclose her damaging evidence to a congressional committee.

Searching for love, she encounters King Del Ray, the leader of a Mariachi band, "King's Men." Having come close to achieving the American dream when his band and lead singer, his daughter, La Niña, get bookings at the best clubs in Mexico and America, King "flowers" a brain tumor, looses his kingdom, and becomes an invalid dependent on his wife, Perla. Only his love for Woman Downtown awakens him and gives him meaning. When King's tumor kills him, and Woman Downtown's guardian godfather, Judge Collister, is murdered, she descends into the ghoulish wasteland outside the city to join Wolf and the other revolutionary youngsters of the Hollow as "Sister of Wolf," "Mother of all." Amid the sound of an explosion and the glare of a white flare exposing the desolate landscape, she shouts a defiant outcry as the she-wolf in Williams's apocalyptic nightmare.

Three supporting cast members essential to Williams's *Red Devil Battery Sign* include Perla, La Niña (his daughter), and McCabe (his daughter's lover). Like Woman Downtown and King, they try to overcome loneliness while searching for meaning through love. Heroically at times, these characters resist being made invisible and mechanized by the Red Devil that sweeps over the play. Perla fights against being an unappreciated wife; La Niña fears being a depressed expectant mother rejected by her parents; and McCabe wants to be more than as a well-trained, "buttoned-down" gangster.

The major symbol of the play is the grinning Red Devil Battery sign shining through the window of Woman Downtown's penthouse at the Yellow Rose Hotel. This flashing light symbolizes a phantasmagoric hell-mouth (a frequent icon in medieval and early modern drama and the sign of the devil), the demonic conspiracy of the Red Devil Monsters. Bent on world domination by replacing democracies with totalitarian regimes, the Red Devil Corporation turns its operatives into smiling, inhuman robots. Discovering biographical significance in the symbol, Ronald Hayman explains that Williams's heightened sense of paranoia was induced by using a favorite drug of his, Seconal, appropriately and popularly termed "red devils" (221). The various landscapes in the play are also highly symbolic. The Yellow Hotel, with its crewcut guards, is possibly an asylum with shock treatments reserved for anyone who disagrees with establishment policy, a perennial Williams dread. The infernal wasteland of the Hollow stands for urban decay and chaos, the apocalyptic setting for the battle between Wolf and the Red Devil monsters. Williams further increases the tensions in *Red Devil Battery Sign* by symbolically contrasting music, roses, fresh linen, silk gowns, and clean air with the harsh realities of brain tumors, physical violence, and broken relationships.

Directed by Edwin Sherin, with Anthony Quinn as King and Claire Bloom as Woman Downtown, *The Red Devil Battery Sign* premiered at Boston's Shubert Theatre on 18 June 1975 and ran less than two weeks until 28 June. In August, it moved to Broadway's Broadhurst Theatre. Though Quinn received outstanding reviews, some critics thought Bloom was not right for the part. Seven months later, a considerably revised *Red Devil Battery Sign* opened at the English Theatre in Vienna on 17 January 1976, directed by Franz Schafranek, and starred

Keith Baxter as King, Ruth Brinkmann as Woman Downtown, and **Maria Britneva (Lady St. Just)** as Perla. In June 1977 a revised version of the Vienna production arrived at London's Roundhouse, which moved to London's Phoenix Theatre from 7–23 July 1977. The Vancouver Playhouse's production of *Red Devil Battery Sign* ran from 18 October until 15 November 1980. In 1976, the Encyclopedia Britannica Education Corporation and Signet Producers released the film *Tennessee Williams: Theatre in Progress*, recording the history of the first production of *Red Devil Battery Sign* (along with interviews with Williams and Quinn) from initial readings to rehearsals to opening night in Boston.

Further Reading

Adler, Thomas. *American Drama, 1940–1960: A Critical History*. New York: Twayne, 1994.

Dorff, Linda. "Babylon Now: Tennessee Williams's Apocalypses." *Theater* 29.1 (1999): 114–123.

Gross, Robert F. "The Gnostic Politics of the Red Devil Battery Sign." In *The Undiscovered Country: The Later Plays of Tennessee Williams*, ed. Philip C. Kolin. New York: Lang, 2002. 125–141.

Hayman, Ronald. *Tennessee Williams: Everyone Else Is an Audience*. New Haven, CT: Yale University Press, 1993.

Kahn, Sy. "*The Red Devil Battery Sign*: Williams's Götterdämmerung in Vienna." In *Tennessee Williams: A Tribute*, ed. Jac Tharpe. Jackson: University Press of Mississippi, 1977. 362–371.

Kullman, Colby. "Rule by Power: 'Big Daddyism' in the World of Tennessee Williams's Plays." *Mississippi Quarterly* 48 (Fall 1995): 667–676.

Schlatter, James. "*Red Devil Battery Sign*: An Approach to Mytho-Political Theatre." *Tennessee Williams Annual Review* 1 (1998): 93–102.

Williams, Tennessee. *Where I Live: Selected Essays*, ed. Christine R. Day and Bob Woods. New York: New Directions, 1978.

Colby H. Kullman

Religion. Religion plays a significant role in Tennessee Williams's works. Like Alma Winemiller in *Summer and Smoke*, Williams was no stranger to rectories. He was born in the parish house in Columbus, Mississippi, where his maternal grandfather **Walter Dakin** was the Episcopal priest; as a young boy, he lived for a period in the rectory of St. George's Church in **Clarksdale, Mississippi,** and as a young man he stayed in another parsonage in Memphis on a visit to his grandparents. Late in his life, at the instigation of his brother **Dakin,** the playwright converted—apparently only nominally—to Roman Catholicism at Our Lady Star of the Sea Church in **Key West.** When he died, he wanted, like the poet **Hart Crane** whose works he loved, to be buried at sea—an end that Blanche in *A Streetcar Named Desire* also wishes for and that Fred in *The Night of the Iguana* actually attains—but again his brother intervened, arranging a Requiem Mass at the cathedral basilica, followed by burial in **St. Louis,** a city Williams never much liked.

Men of the cloth of various denominations appear for over 30 years in Williams's plays, though they are never as gentle, endearing, and beloved as the dramatist's own grandfather. More often than not, they are heavily criticized, even caricatured for mouthing empty platitudes and being hypocritically un-Christian: for cowering in the face of evil authority (the Reverend in *Not about Nightingales*); for worrying only about propriety and public image (the American Gothic-like Reverend Winemiller); for being greedy and materialistic (the southern grotesque Reverend Tooker in *Cat on a Hot Tin Roof*). The Priest in *The Rose Tattoo*, who urges Serafina to reaffirm life rather than idolatrously worship the ashes of her dead husband, and the closeted homosexual Lutheran minister, whose repression forces him to shun physical connection in the story "One Arm," are presented more sympathetically. The most detailed portrait of a clergyman comes in the defrocked minister, T. Lawrence Shannon, in *The Night of the Iguana*, who became obsessed—like the evangelical preacher in "Desire and the Black Masseur" or Increase Tutweiler in another story, "The Yellow Bird"—by an unrelenting and punishing God of vengeance.

Sometimes, the action in a Williams play will occur on a major feast day of the liturgical year. Both **Period of Adjustment** and "The Mutilated," for example, are set on Christmas Eve, while *Orpheus Descending* occurs on Holy Saturday, that limbo day between the despair of death and the hope of resurrection, with the lighting of the vigil candle replaced by the torching of the garden taverna that had been constructed to recreate a lost paradise of racial tolerance long ago defiled by bigotry. *Sweet Bird of Youth*, with its palm trees, cathedral bells, and choir singing the "Alleluia Chorus," takes place on Easter Sunday evening—that time of the disciples' doubt—and is filled with strains of "lamentation" and ends with a penitential castration. Having the Gentleman Caller's visit in *The Glass Menagerie* occur on a Friday might seem insignificant, were it not for the legend on the screen, "Annunciation," proclaiming the long-hoped-for arrival of the savior; but Jim, rather than saving Laura, plunges her deeper into a life of loneliness where, her candles blown out, she now knows she will never again experience what she had, however briefly, through Jim's kiss. Character names, such as Anthony Burns in "Black Masseur,"

Valentine Xavier in *Orpheus Descending*, Sebastian Venable in **Suddenly Last Summer**, or Celeste Delacroix Griffin in "Mutilated," also carry religious connotations, as does that of Christopher Flanders, the comforting Angel of Death in **The Milk Train Doesn't Stop Here Anymore**. Williams was descended from the family that claimed St. Francis Xavier.

Place, too, in Williams's plays often holds biblical analogues or religious associations. In *Nightingales*, the inferno where prisoners are tortured—ironically called Klondike—is a "suburb of hell," while in **Kingdom of Earth** the mythic deluge comes again in the encroaching floodwaters of the Mississippi. The Mexican hilltop in *The Night of the Iguana*, site of Shannon's agonized dark night of the soul and of his "painless crucifixion" lashed to a hammock, may recall both Gethsemane and Golgotha. And Monk's Place, the beachfront saloon in **Small Craft Warnings**, is, as its name suggests, a sanctuary to which the emotionally and spiritually bereft can retreat. But for the way in which Williams's religious proclivities can adumbrate his handling of stage space, **Summer and Smoke** affords probably the clearest indication. The stage setting is reminiscent of an allegorically conceived altarpiece in the form of a triptych: the Victorian Gothic rectory on one side; the doctor's office with its anatomy chart on the other; with a fountain in the form of a stone angel named "Eternity" in the center—all against a cyclorama backdrop of a sky that is the Renaissance blue of religious art. In this modern morality, spirit or soul (the English translation of Alma's name) will do battle with body or matter. If the repressed Alma speaks initially of the soaring Gothic cathedral spires as symbolizing one's aspirations to divinity (failing to recognize their phallic connotations), she comes ultimately to turn away from unfeeling stone and embrace a humanity that must, rather than deny sexuality, integrate it as one of God's "little mercies" and a potentially grace-filled act.

Iconographic images, particularly of Christ or his Blessed Mother, occur with some frequency in Williams's dramas as well. Above the bar at Monk's in *Small Craft* is displayed a large sailfish—the traditional symbol for Christ; and the bar becomes, if not a church, at least a kind of sacred place, a locus where the lost can come and, in a series of spotlighted monologues, go to confession (the original one-act on which the play expands was, in fact, called "*Confessional*"). In reality Monk ministers to the others, and at the end, Violet ascends the stairs to take a cleansing shower, with Monk emphasizing the need to wash her feet. If Lucretia Collins in "Portrait of a Madonna" (see *Twenty-seven Wagons Full of Cotton and Other One-Act Plays*) suffers from the delusion that she was violated and made pregnant, Blanche in *A Streetcar Named Desire* actually leaves the stage as a violated Madonna, dressed in the della Robbia blue of the Renaissance; her mention of dying from eating tainted grapes may be, in fact, an explicit allusion to Mignarb's well-known painting the *Madonna of the Grapes*. At the end of the same play, Williams leaves viewers with an image of what might be seen as an unholy family, with the lustful Stanley groping inside the blouse of Stella who holds the babe in swaddling clothes and erases the sin she knows Stanley committed against her and Blanche. In *The Rose Tattoo*, Serafina burns a vigil light before a small shrine to a gold-starred, blue-robed Virgin, only to blow out the candle when she discovers that Mary did not protect the innocence of those living within her house. And in "Mutilated," with its roses, candles, incense, and bells, after Trinket forgives Celeste, the pain in her breast miraculously disappears, and they sense the presence of Our Lady, even imagining that they touch the hem of her gown.

Sometimes these images form part of larger ritual patterns that occur in several of Williams's works. The ritual may simply be a meal, a kind of secular communion, oftentimes tellingly interrupted, as is the case in both *The Glass Menagerie* and *A Streetcar Named Desire*. At other times, the pattern is worked out more elaborately. Occasionally, the Christian liturgy is inverted in a kind of black mass culminating in cannibalism that signifies a predatory world, as in "Desire and the Black Masseur" and *Suddenly Last Summer*. In the first, Williams places the story's climax at the end of the Lenten season, so that Burns's death—counterpointed by a fundamentalist church service—becomes a strange rite of atonement that forcefully indicts an overly puritanical emphasis on guilt and punishment. In the latter, the white-clad homosexual Sebastian—one of whose poems his mother had earlier "elevated" as if it were the Eucharist—himself becomes the sacrificial victim as the hoard of young boys attack and devour him. If *Night of the Iguana* hints at an almost Eastern mysticism where the kimono-clad Hannah, appearing calm as a Buddha, soothes Shannon with a cup of sedative tea, "Mutilated" not only refers to the Babe suckling at Mary's breast as the ultimate sign of giving but also includes a kind of secularized communion service, with its bread and its offering of wine and its reference to a meal of "kindness," all alluding to the Last Supper.

The God who is worshipped in Williams's plays appears in many different guises, depending on the "alphabet blocks" with which characters choose to write His name. If the ritual is a perversed one, as it is in *Suddenly Last Summer*, it may be because a character has used the "wrong . . . blocks" to spell God's name, resulting, like Sebastian's own, in a severely distorted image of the deity. Traveling in the Encantada Islands, Sebastian—looking for God—had once witnessed flocks of giant birds tearing open and eating the newly hatched sea turtles; taking this as a kind of epiphany or revelation, in his misreading he constructs a personal notion of the godhead as some horribly savage, ferocious monster. In this Manichean "world of light and shadow," the darkness is made somehow "luminous," while the Melvillean white (here of Sebastian's clothing) becomes dark. In *Sweet Bird of Youth*, if the demagogic politician Boss Finley claims to possess a prophetic voice when he preaches white supremacy, the Heckler who challenges him professes belief in a God who remains silent, speechless, leaving mankind to do His work; while in *Small Craft Warnings*, when the new "messiah" is stillborn in a trailer park with a star shining overhead, Doc claims to find proof of human absurdity in the face of a dark and mysterious deity. In *The Night of the Iguana*, Shannon has devised a notion of God as a petulant "senile delinquent," distant and demanding, an "oblivious majesty" shown forth in displays of thunder and lightning. His God is so devoid of saving grace that Shannon attempts to tear the gold cross, sign of Christian love and forgiveness, from around his neck. Like other excessively guilt-wracked heroes and heroines in Williams—Blanche in *A Streetcar Named Desire* for failing Allan, Brick in *Cat on a Hot Tin Roof* for hanging up on Skipper, Chance in *Sweet Bird of Youth* for corrupting Heavenly—he needs someone to restore his sense of dignity and self-worth, to reignite his belief in his ability to respond humanely to another that will make him feel worthy of acceptance, so that (in Blanche's words) "there's God . . . so quickly."

The clearest exposition of Williams's belief system is, in fact, found in *The Night of the Iguana* in two narratives, one in prose and the other in poetry, that lead up to and follow from a decisive, redemptive action on Shannon's part. In the first, the spinster portrait painter Hannah Jelkes, who has the "ethereal" look of the medieval saint, tells Shannon about being out in a rowboat with a man who requested a piece of her underclothing that he could fondle; seeing in the man a "depth of loneliness" such as she had never before experienced, she consented. While Shannon names this action "dirty," Hannah insists that it was, indeed, a "love act" to set aside her own moral qualms and respond nonjudgmentally and compassionately to the other person in time of need since "Nothing human disgusts [her], unless it's unkind, violent." Hannah then asks Shannon to go out to "one of God's creatures" in need by untying the iguana. Only when he does this can her grandfather, the aged Nonno, complete the poem over which he has been struggling. And when he recites the poem, it is about the reality of living after the fall, in the ruined Eden of the present, fully aware of loss and yet refusing to allow oneself to become so consumed by guilt and a lack of faith in having been redeemed that positive action becomes impossible. For Williams, it might be said that hell is the self, while God is the other, and so to deny the other is to deny God. Hannah inspires Shannon to act, and his action allows Nonno to create. And significantly, the alphabet blocks that spell Shannon's name contain all the letters needed to spell the names of the other two.

In Williams, ethics is not unconnected to love and creativity. That Williams's ethical system is also an erotic one becomes clear from Hannah's response to the underwear fetishist, which suggests that acts only become good or bad insofar as they respond, or fail to respond, unselfishly to another, without using or abusing the other person. At times, physical sexuality—coming together to assuage human loneliness, as in *Summer and Smoke* or *The Rose Tattoo* or

Small Craft Warnings—is invested with a religious dimension, even a sacramental transcendence. In his early lyric "Poem for Paul," later expanded as the song of the Carollers in "The Mutilated," Williams made this link explicit, beseeching that those who are misfits and outcasts—all those marginalized as Other—will have some mercy given to them and not be rejected, as Blanche rejects Allan and as Mitch, in turn, leaves her, or as Brick recoils from Skipper.

In Williams, a moral identity is tied to his aesthetic credo as well, for it is the artist who helps individuals come to understand how it is that they can be God to the other. Sometimes, as is true of the troubled Vee Talbot in *Orpheus Descending*, the artist is actually a seer, a visionary inspired by some divine presence who recognizes that nothing is outside the realm of the artist's transformative power. More often, the artist is the truth-bringer, who through narrating a story—however offputting or terrible it might initially seem—prods another to ethical action, as do Catheriene Holly in *Suddenly Last Summer* or Hannah Jelkes in *The Night of the Iguana*. Occasionally, the artist is linked explicitly with the deity, as is Nonno in completing his final poem. He affirms that it "is finished"—echoing the *consummatum est* of Christ on the cross—and Hannah proclaims it "good"—as God did of his own work after each day of Creation. Little wonder that Williams himself, compassionate moral symbolist that he was, affirmed in his **Memoirs**: "the passion to create is all that we know of God."

Further Reading

Bredeson, Kate. "Sometimes Cloudy, Sometimes Clear: God, Religion, and the Williams Passion Play." *Tennessee Williams Literary Journal* 5.1 (Spring 2003): 71–79.

Fritscher, John J. "Some Attitudes and a Posture: Religious Metaphors and Ritual in Tennessee Williams' Query of the American God." *Modern Drama* 13:2 (1970): 201–215.

Kolin, Philip C. " 'having lost the ability to say: "My God!" ' The Theology of Tennessee Williams's *Small Craft Warnings*." In *The Undiscovered Country: The Later Plays of Tennessee Williams*, ed. Philip C. Kolin. New York: Lang, 2002. 107–124.

Leverich, Lyle. *Tom: The Unknown Tennessee Williams*. New York: Crown, 1995.

Phillips, Gene D. "Tennessee Williams and the Jesuits." *America* 25 June 1977: 564–565.

Thomas P. Adler

The Remarkable Rooming-House of Mme. Le Monde. *The Remarkable Rooming-House of Mme. Le Monde* is a brief but bizarre late Tennessee Williams one-act play. It was presumably written in 1982 when Williams gave rights to publisher George Bixby of Albondocani Press, who released the play in October 1984 in a limited edition of 176 copies. In *Le Monde*, Williams presents a house of horrors whose residents include not only the "gimp" Mint, but the proprietor, Mme. Le Monde, who is as malevolent as Medusa. Her son, Boy, who isn't even worthy of a name, and Hall, the all-too-unwelcome house guest from Mint's schooldays at Scrotum-upon-Swansea, finish the torrid lineup of monstrous characters whose acts prove to be even more grotesque. From large hooks hanging from the ceiling, the partially clothed Mint desperately clenches his fists around the cold metal rings, his only mode of mobility, in the attic of Mme. Le Monde's boarding house. This pitiful figure is dependent on others who are nonchalant about the sexual and moral indiscretions foisted upon him.

Yet he is the most redeemable character in Williams's play. The other characters in *Le Monde* are violent, narcissistic, and devoid of emotional depth outside of satisfying their own desires. Mint represents an individual without any ego; he has succumbed to his disability, a mysterious one, which arose after his mother went to an asylum (Williams's own fear). The loss of his mother seems to have crippled not only Mint's legs but his soul as well. This loss can be the only satisfying explanation of Mint's lack of defense against sexual molestation by Mme. Le Monde's Boy, neglect by his mother, and the torments Mint receives from Hall, who visits Mint after a sexual escapade with Mme. Le Monde herself. Hall selfishly eats all of Mint's tea and biscuits, only to complain about the small quantity and mold on them. He then refuses to assist Mint in his rings, and when he finally does, Hall places him as far away as possible within the tiny attic apartment where the play takes place. While Hall might be considered the opposite of Mint, his insecurities nonetheless join him with "the gimp" to expose Hall as a rapist, a corrupt salesman, and a user who is satiated only by groping for power. However, Hall's authority pales in contrast to that of his concubine, Mme. Le Monde. His personality reflects all characteristics of the id, the self-indulgent, irresponsible, and pleasure-seeking components of Freud's famed triad.

Mme. Le Monde plays the sadistic part of the superego. As her name implies, she is "the world" and her rules dominate the play. Her fiery red hair symbolizes Satan's own fury. With an almost comical jerk, she kills her son, after he rapes Mint, then squashes "the gimp," leading to his death while Hall looks on, awaiting his own demise. In a *coup de théâtre*, Madame pushes Hall down the stairs, similar to those found in carnivals that slant to become a slide, leading to the bowels of her rooming house. While laden with horrific sexual symbolism, *Le Monde* nonetheless offers humor through Williams's witty play on words and on **music**; for example, when Hall is consuming

Tennessee Williams, 1980. Photo by John Schneider, used courtesy of New Directions Publishing Corp.

Mint's meager rations, the tune "Tea for Two" plays in the background. The event is hardly the civilized tea that the song proclaims.

Typical of Williams, each character no doubt represents some historical (or symbolic) figure, including the author himself. Like so many of his later works, *Le Monde* provided Williams with a catharsis; his play was his secret weapon to annihilate the Mme. Le Mondes, Halls, and Boys that existed within his own world. In fact, **Maria Britneva (Lady St. Just)** has been seen as a model for Mme. Le Monde, though Williams could have been satirizing other people in his life who caused him misery, leaving him, like Mint, a sympathetic but pathetic character who had never received the attention he so deserves. *The Remarkable Rooming-House of Mme. Le Monde* has never been preformed, and because of its limited exposure, this play of guilty pleasures is not likely to be staged very soon.

Further Reading

Adler, Alfred. *The Individual Psychology of Alfred Adler*. New York: Perrenial, 1964.

Freud, S. *The Ego and the Id*. New York: Norton, 1964.

Kristin J. Kolin

The Roman Spring of Mrs. Stone. Tennessee Williams's imagistically ornate novella *The Roman Spring of Mrs. Stone* (1950), about an aging actress who flees from a disastrous performance into the arms of a handsome young gigolo, might be seen as a precursor of his 1959 play **Sweet Bird of Youth**. Thematically, both works explore a concern central to Williams: the decay of physical beauty and the diminishment of artistic power with the passing of time. In *The Roman Spring of Mrs. Stone*, Karen Stone's whole life, both professional and personal, has been performative, from assuming stage roles like Juliet, too young for her age, to denying emotional needs under a mask of detachment. Even her marriage, built on fear of pregnancy, settled into being more a mother-and-child than a husband-and-wife relationship. After Mr. Stone's death, she arrives in Rome and enters into a liaison with the narcissistic Paolo—though her gaze often fixes as well upon the disreputable-looking stalker loitering outside her apartment. Voyeuristic looking becomes a recurrent motif, and a series of mirrors that reflect either beauty or its loss become key symbols. The atmosphere of the novella is indolent, languorous. Blue-skied Rome is an almost baroque city of fountains and stones, indicative of fertility and sterility, and of cathedral domes and pagan obelisks, suggesting the opposing pulls of religious sensibility and potentially brutal sensuality. The wealthy women of Mrs. Stone's social circle are seen as rapacious birds of prey, with the power to buy and control.

And yet Williams finally treats Karen Stone with poignancy and compassion in a prose style virtually shorn of dialogue and one that approaches stream-of-consciousness. Karen Stone has recently found out that her life demands coming to terms with losses more troubling than just decreasing beauty in the face of time's onslaught. She has given up any pretensions of ever having been a great artist rather than just a competent actress. The onset of menopause means she will never bear a child—though, ironically, it has also unlocked long-repressed physical desires. What she must face most squarely is a fearful sense of drifting, of a purposeless movement toward emptiness and an existential void. When she throws her apartment key down to the solitary exhibitionist and consents to an assignation with him, she signals her rejection of nothingness and consciously acts to stop that sense of drift. Just as Alma Winemiller's decision to go off with the salesman at the end of **Summer and Smoke** (1948) might be seen not as a descent into profligacy but, rather, as a necessary solace—an antidote to human need and an affirmation of sexuality as a part of being fully human—Mrs. Stone's action gives evidence to a desperate endurance beyond awareness of time and loss. Both the seasonal (March) setting and the title Williams gives his novella attest to the possibility of regeneration of a sort—a last-ditch embrace of life in defiance of a condition of near death.

The film version of *The Roman Spring of Mrs. Stone*, directed by Jose Quintero with a luminous performance by **Vivien Leigh**, was released in 1961, and a British television version, starring Helen Mirren, appeared in 2003.

Further Reading

Draya, Ren. "The Fiction of Tennessee Williams." In *Tennessee Williams: A Tribute*, ed. Jac Tharpe. Jackson: University Press of Mississippi, 1977. 647–662.

Fisher, James. " 'An Almost Posthumous Existence': Performance, Gender, and Sexuality in *The Roman Spring of Mrs. Stone*." *Southern Quarterly* 38 (Fall 1999): 45–57.

Gérard, Albert. "The Eagle and the Star: Symbolic Motifs in *The Roman Spring of Mrs. Stone*." English *Studies* 36 (August 1955): 145–153.

Thomas P. Adler

The Rose Tattoo. *The Rose Tattoo* (1950–1951) was Tennessee Williams's first full-length comedy and is generally recognized as his most optimistic play, a Dionysian celebration of sexuality that seems to reverse the pattern of his earlier tragedies. It is more complex than just this, however, in both tone and technique; and its complicating elements look forward to *Camino Real* and to plays written at the end of his career. Williams began work on *The Rose Tattoo* in the fall of 1948 and over the next three years developed it through at least six full-length drafts, laboring to balance tragedy with farce and finding special difficulty in arriving at an appropriate conclusion.

A major influence was **Elia Kazan**, who made two important suggestions: that early scenes in which the husband Rosario appeared be omitted and, more questionably, that Williams revise to make the play a comic-grotesque mass in praise of the "male force." Williams hoped that **Irene Selznick** would produce, Kazan direct, and the Italian actress **Anna Magnani** play the part of Serafina, which had been written especially for her, but when all three fell through (for different reasons), he turned to a group of artists associated with New York's Actors Studio. Cheryl Crawford, of **Group Theatre** fame, became producer. Daniel Mann, fresh from success with **William Inge**'s *Come Back, Little Sheba*, directed. The designer was Boris Aronson, with Williams's ac-

claimed collaborator **Jo Mielziner** suggesting the embankment that rises behind Serafina's house. The roles of Serafina and Alvaro were created by a very young **Maureen Stapleton** and **Eli Wallach**, initiating a connection with Williams's drama that would continue for many years.

A revised text of the first production was assembled by Williams's friend **Paul Bigelow**, restoring many of the performance cuts; and this was published by both New Directions and Dramatists Play Service in 1951 and reprinted in volume 2 of *The Theatre of Tennessee Williams* (1971). *The Rose Tattoo* is thus one of the few major plays by Williams to reach print in only one version. These editions are all prefaced by one of Williams's best essays, "The Timeless World of a Play."

The plot of the The *Rose Tattoo* is rooted in symbolism. A Sicilian immigrant called Serafina delle Rose believes that, when she conceives, a stigmata of her husband Rosario's rose tattoo appears on her breast. She is asked by a nightclub hostess called Estelle Hohengarten to sew a red silk shirt for a lover who, unbeknownst to Serafina, is Rosario himself; and this sexual betrayal is emphasized by the invasion of her yard by a nosey neighbor's goat. Rosario is killed while smuggling, and in defiance of her priest, Serafina insists on a cremation so that she can keep his ashes at home. Three years later, she has become a slattern and is reluctant to let her daughter Rosa attend high school graduation because the girl has fallen in love with a sailor. Serafina's farcical attempts to don a corset for the ceremony are interrupted by two man-hunting floozies who maliciously disclose Rosario's affair. She beats them away, then implores a "sign" from the statue of the Madonna. This takes the form of Rosa bringing home Jack, but Serafina gives the sailor a hard time, making him swear before the Madonna to respect

Maureen Stapleton and Eli Wallach in the 1951 Broadway stage production of *The Rose Tattoo*. Springer/Photofest.

her daughter's innocence. When they leave for a picnic, she finds she has forgotten to give Rosa the wristwatch that was to be her graduation present.

Having failed to bully the priest into betraying Rosario's confessions, Serafina again implores the Madonna for a sign. This time it takes the form of Alvaro Mangiacavallo, a Sicilian truck driver who takes refuge with her from unprovoked attacks by a redneck traveling salesman. As they cautiously get to know each other, Serafina realizes that his body is like her husband's despite his foolish face and crass behavior, and she lends him the red shirt to wear while she repairs his jacket. At this point, the goat invades the yard again, and it is Alvaro who captures it.

Serafina is struggling out of her corset when Alvaro arrives to return the shirt, reeking of rose hair oil and boasting of a new rose tattoo. A grotesque sex chase follows until Alvaro hears about Rosario and Estelle. He phones Estelle directly, so Serafina must finally admit her husband's infidelity. She smashes his funeral urn, blows out the Madonna's votive light, and invites Alvaro to complete their "conversation."

Returning at dawn, Rosa resents Jack's sexual restraint. She arranges an assignation with him later at a hotel, then falls asleep half naked on the sofa. A hung-over Alvaro discovers her there, wakes her by braying "Che bella" like the goat outside, and is chased away by Serafina for assaulting her daughter. Rosa assures her mother that he never touched her but angrily storms off to join Jack, again forgetting the watch that significantly now has stopped. Rosario's ashes have flown away too; Alvaro calls from the distance; neighbors mockingly pass the red shirt uphill toward him; and Serafina, believing she has seen the rose stigmata again and must therefore be pregnant, rushes away to join him.

Williams's sister **Rose** haunts *The Rose Tattoo*, not only in the name "Rosa" and the pervasive rose symbolism but also in such situations as the child gathering lightning bugs, a puritanical mother's tyranny over her daughter's dating, and the scene of Alvaro's intrusion on the sleeping girl, which seems to reflect Rose Williams's accusations against her father (who may also be satirized in the traveling salesman). Even more important is Williams's delightful discovery of Italy, his fascination with Anna Magnani, and especially his experience of Sicily with his partner, the ex-truck driver **Frank Merlo**, to whom the play is dedicated "in return for Sicily" and whose nickname "Little Horse" (eat a horse) becomes Alvaro's surname "Mangiacavallo."

Working drafts reveal a debt to **García Lorca**'s Spanish plays; and it also seems likely that Williams would have known Giovanni Verga's sardonic stories of Sicilian peasant life, since **D.H. Lawrence**, one of Williams's most prominent influences, published translations of them and wrote essays in their praise. An even more probable influence is the great dramatist Luigi Pirandello, who also wrote Sicilian short stories, including one called "The Rose" about the sexual desperation of a young widow in a prurient Sicilian village. The parallels are not detailed enough for this to be a "source," but Pirandello's direct influence is evident in the ideas of Williams's second essay about the play.

"The Meaning of *The Rose Tattoo*" was first published in *Vogue* on 15 March 1951 but actually was written as early as April 1950, midway through the process of revision. Williams begins it by saying that *The Rose Tattoo* celebrates "the Dionysian element in human life"; and it is this that most critics have fastened on. He goes on to qualify this statement, however, in two important ways. He says that the Dionysian experience "must not be confused with mere sexuality" but at its purest is manifest by the flight of birds (Alvaro's "rondinella felice") and by children at play; and importantly, that it can also be found in the playwright's own freedom to experiment. "The Timeless World of a Play" was published originally in the *New York Times* on 14 March 1951 to herald *The Rose Tattoo*'s opening on Broadway and was subsequently chosen by Williams to preface the play's publication. Both of its main arguments derive from Pirandello: the idea that art and passion try to impose stasis on the flux of time (as in the play's symbolic wristwatch), the outcome of which is necessarily "tragic"—a word reiterated throughout the essay; and Williams's decision that the only way to combine such tragic stasis with realistic flux is by exploring the "grotesque." This is Pirandello's term for a style that fuses tragedy and comedy

throughout, not only qualifying the form, as in tragicomedy, but also making the comic element uneasily self-conscious. The hallmark of this style in Pirandello is sardonic laughter, which is close to Williams's own black sense of humor that he called his personal alternative to tears. Both essays are reprinted in the collection *Where I Live* (1978), and misled perhaps by the publication dates, critics have tended to focus on the Dionysian statement of the first essay but neglect the significance of its successor. However, a combination of Williams's determination to experiment and his stated focus on the grotesque may clarify some of the problems that critics have found in the play.

For instance, plot structure: By omitting the original Rosario scenes, Williams created a problem of exposition that he solved clumsily by the three-year gap in Act One and Estelle's confession over the telephone in Act Three, which the audience is somehow supposed to overhear. Moreover, there are many extra characters—the doctor, the school mistress, the traveling salesman, even the two floozies (imported from a separate one-act called *A Perfect Analysis Given by a Parrot*), who are not essential to the plot but serve rather to establish the alien American environment in which the Sicilian community has to orient itself.

This is a clue to Williams's essentially *spatial* rather than linear concept of unity in the play, which can also be seen in his heavy doubling of effects. Serafina claims to have seen the rose stigmata twice; she asks the Madonna for signs twice; the goat invades her yard twice; she twice beats people away with her broom; there are two comic corset scenes; Rosa and Jack return to the darkened house twice; Rosa locked in is balanced by Rosa locked out; and so on. There are too many such doublings to be accidental; and their effect is to cut right across the linear plot. A related effect is achieved by Williams's experiment with a double chorus: Life-affirming children, whose games reflect the action symbolically, are opposed to their censorious, black-garbed mothers, whose life-denying aspects are internalized by Serafina's tailors dummies, two of whom, dressed as bride and widow, seem perpetually at variance.

The latter relates to the play's most important breakthrough, a reliance on symbols that anticipates Williams's claim that "symbols are nothing but the natural speech of drama" in his next play *Camino Real*. The goat and wristwatch have already been touched on. The former is related to the priest's accusation that Serafina has become an animal, which she reiterates herself when she decides to accept Alvaro, and also to the piggy bank that Alvaro shakes and Rosa smashes; and the passing of time emblematized by the wristwatch is extrapolated in train whistles (twice) and a minor leitmotif of "numbers" and is opposed by the insistence of both Serafina and Rosa that true passion is always for the first time. Williams manages to give nearly every detail a symbolic value, including elaborate noises offstage: Alvaro's eight-ton truck contrasted to Rosario's ten-ton vehicle, their loads of phallic bananas, the broken spectacles through which Serafina regards Alvaro, her constricting corsets, "graduation day" and Rosa's prize of a *Digest of Knowledge*, and so on. But overwhelmingly there are roses, traditional symbol both of physical and spiritual passion, with ashes as their opposite, and the ruby vigil light, the red silk shirt, and the children's scarlet kite as their symbolic extensions. A standard complaint is that Williams has overdone this rose symbolism, but this exaggeration was certainly intentional. It can be seen as a grotesque distancing device, anticipating the technique of such later plays as *The Gnädiges Fräulein*.

Certainly, Williams did not wish Serafina's final choice to be seen merely as a surrender to sexual need and the "male force." It is partly a defiant response to her neighbors' mockery but is mostly motivated by her belief that she has once more conceived. Williams explained it as a victory of the life force itself, beyond the ambiguities of its limited human instruments; and his experiments with the grotesque were meant to enforce such a perspective.

The Rose Tattoo opened at the Erlanger Theater in Chicago on 29 December 1950 and transferred to the Martin Beck Theatre in New York on 3 February 1951. It ran on Broadway for 133 performances to mixed but generally favorable reviews and garnered Tony Awards for the play itself, for design, for Stapleton, and for Wallach. Mann also directed a 1955 film version for Paramount Studios in a rather botched adaptation by Williams and a **Hollywood** writer called Irving Kantor. This bowed to 1950s cinema morality by not having Alvaro and Serafina sleep together, which made nonsense of the end but was redeemed by a magnificently tempestuous interpretation of Serafina by Anna Magnani, who won an Oscar for her performance, and an intensely comic performance by Burt Lancaster as Alvaro. Especially noteworthy revivals have been a 1966 production in New York with Maureen Stapleton recapitulating her performance as Serafina and the director, Milton Katselas, highlighting the play's exaggerated folk elements in a way that Williams preferred to the original's emphasis on realism, and a very successful London production in 1991 directed by **Peter Hall** in which much attention was given to the play's symbolic "soundscape." See also **Mythology**.

Further Reading

Gronbeck-Tedesco, John. "On *The Rose Tattoo*." in *Tennessee Williams: A Casebook*, ed. Robert F. Gross. New York: Routledge, 2002. 63–78.

Hewes, Henry. "Theater—Off the Leash." *Saturday Review* 26 November 1966: 60.

Kolin, Philip C. " 'Sentiment and Humor in Equal Measure': Comic Forms in *The Rose Tattoo*." In *Tennessee Williams: A Tribute*, ed. Jac Tharpe. Jackson: University Press of Mississippi, 1977. 214–231.

Parker, Brian. "Multiple Endings for *The Rose Tattoo*." *Tennessee Williams Annual Review* 2 (1999): 53–68.

Starnes, Leland. "The Grotesque Children of *The Rose Tattoo*." *Modern Drama* 12 (1970): 357–369.

Styan, John L. *The Dark Comedy: The Development of Modern Comi-Tragedy*. Cambridge: Cambridge University Press, 1968. 49–51.

Brian Parker

Saroyan, William (1908–1981). William Saroyan was the leading American avant-garde playwright of the late 1930s and 1940s and both a theatrical and a political model for the young Tennessee Williams. Saroyan achieved theatrical success with *My Heart's in the Highlands* (1939), produced by the Theatre Guild and the **Group Theatre**. His next play, *The Time of Your Life* (1939), won the Pulitzer Prize (which he declined). Saroyan also wrote novels, essays, and short stories. Significantly, at the beginning of his career Williams submitted short stories to the same magazine, *Story*, that had published Saroyan's breakthrough piece "The Daring Young Man on the Flying Trapeze," but the magazine did not accept Williams's pieces.

Saroyan created strongly individualistic characters struggling to maintain their integrity, and their eccentricities, in the face of society's pressure. That these themes appealed to the young socialist-leaning Williams is demonstrated in *Fugitive Kind* (1937), with its denizen characters marginalized by an oppressive society—artists, the unemployed, and the hunted gangster Terry Meighan, who fights for survival against long odds. Saroyan's influence also seems clear in Williams's *Stairs to the Roof* (1940), with its "little people" in conflict with an overwhelming system, its powerful element of fantasy, and even in a character called The Girl. Allean Hale points out resemblances to Saroyan's style in *Stairs to the Roof* but considers Williams superior in developing characterization.

Williams read Saroyan's work while at the **New School for Social Research** in 1940 and wrote to Saroyan, who replied that he had noticed the announcement of the planned production of Williams's **The Long Goodbye**. In 1941 Williams wrote Saroyan again, congratulating him on the quality of his wildly theatrical play *Jim Dandy*. In response Saroyan commiserated with Williams that the failure of **Battle of Angels** demonstrated the theater's inability to support any but the most routine plays. But the relationship was not mutually complimentary. Williams, the incessant rewriter, recorded in his **journal** (1942) his irritation at Saroyan's impetuous, headlong way of writing and told his family that, after he finally met Saroyan in 1943, he found him "likeable enough" but felt a distance between himself and the boisterous and iconoclastic Saroyan.

Saroyan and **Clifford Odets** may be the two poles of Williams's early development as a playwright, with Odets's focus on social issues (e.g., **Candles to the Sun** was strongly influenced by Odets) and Saroyan's championing the worth of the individual against corrupt society (as represented by the evil cop Blick in *The Time of Your Life*). Like Saroyan, Williams presents social issues through strong individual personalities, as early as *Not about Nightingales* (1938), with its complex characterization of the warden Boss Whalen who is sentimental about himself yet he burns men to death. *The Glass Menagerie* evokes Saroyan's influence in Williams's heightened realism of language and the longings and dreams of his characters. Leverich considers *Jim Dandy* an influence on *Camino Real*. Late in Williams's career, **Small Craft Warnings**, which demands comparison with *The Iceman Cometh*, may also be read as Williams's answer to *The Time of Your Life*. The parallels between *Small Craft* and *Time* indicate Williams's bleaker vision: Tom transports Kitty to safety, but Monk can only send Violet upstairs; Kit Carson leaves the bar in order to kill the brutal Blick, but Doc, intending to assist at a birth, leaves to participate in not one but two unmerited deaths.

Williams recognized a kindred spirit in Saroyan and responded enthusiastically to his call that if the world is to change, it must change from the inside out, beginning with the human heart, like the flowers Don Quixote imagines in *Camino Real* pushing through the rocks.

Further Reading

Leverich, Lyle. *Tom: The Unknown Tennessee Williams*. New York: Crown, 1995.

Williams, Tennessee. *Stairs to the Roof*. Ed. with an introduction by Allean Hale. New York: New Directions, 2000.

Kirk Woodward

Saxon, Lyle (1891–1946). A writer and editor at the center of the literary scene in **New Orleans**, Lyle Saxon befriended the young Tom Williams when he first arrived in the city in December 1938. Saxon served as a reporter for the New Orleans *Times-Picayune* from 1918 to 1926, and from 1935 to 1942 he was the director of the Federal Writers Project in Louisiana, responsible for preparing the state guide to Louisiana and the city guide to New Orleans. He had hoped to hire the aspiring Williams, but the job never materialized. Known as "Mr. New Orleans," Saxon was zealously devoted to preserving Louisiana's heritage, protecting its historic places, and promoting its literature. He wrote a history of the infamous pirate who helped save New Orleans in the War of 1812, *Jean Lafitte the Pirate* (1930); another on *Fabulous New Orleans* (1928); a novel, *Children of Strangers* (1937); and several award-winning stories. Together with Robert Tallant, Saxon helped edit and contributed to the journal *Gumbo Ya-Ya*, which recorded, and thus preserved, Louisiana folklore.

Williams could not have met a more supportive admirer or colleague than Saxon. As he had with other artists, Saxon encouraged Williams in his writing and fostered his love for the city that would become the playwright's "spiritual home." A distinguished-looking southern gentleman, Saxon was actively involved in the New Orleans gay community and through him Williams was introduced to the bohemian life of the city. See also **Gender and Sexuality**.

Further Reading

Harvey, Cathy Chance. *The Life and Selected Letters of Lyle Saxon*. Gretna, LA: Pelican Publications, 2003.

Thomas, James W. *Lyle Saxon: A Critical Biography*. Birmingham, AL: Summa Publications, 1991.

Philip C. Kolin

Selznick, Irene (1907–1990). Irene Selznick was the producer of *A Streetcar Named Desire*. She was the daughter of movie mogul Louis G. Mayer, head of the Metro-Goldwyn-Mayer Corp., and the ex-wife of David O. Selznick, the producer of *Gone with the Wind*. Without her financial commitment ($25,000) and strong encouragement, Williams's play might never have been produced. Selznick played an active role in almost every part of the production process. She was successful in persuading **Elia Kazan**, the most sought-after director at the time, to direct *A Streetcar Named Desire*. Given her **Hollywood** connections, Selznick originally wanted to cast Bette Davis for the part of Blanche and John Garfield or Burt Lancaster for Stanley, but seeing **Jessica Tandy** and **Marlon Brando**, she easily changed her mind. She hired the costume designer Lucinda Ballard and the scenographer **Jo Mielziner**. The rest was history as Selznick was highly instrumental in making *A Streetcar Named Desire* a world success. Like Kazan and Williams, Selznick fought the censors who threatened to destroy the artistic integrity of Williams's script. Anticipating that *A Streetcar Named Desire* was destined for film production, she hired Lillian Hellman to work on a "shooting script" that might satisfy the censor's concern over Allan Grey's homosexuality (see **Gender and Sexuality**; Hollywood), but the Hellman rewrite was never used.

Further Reading

Selznick, Irene. *A Private View*. New York: Knopf, 1983.

Tischler, Nancy. "Sanitizing *A Streetcar Named Desire*." *Louisiana Literature* 14 (Fall 1999): 48–56.

Maureen Curley

Sexuality. See Gender and Sexuality.

Small Craft Warnings. *Small Craft Warnings* was Williams's most commercially successful post–*The Night of the Iguana* play, running off Broadway for 200 performances in 1972, while few of his other plays in his last three decades ever made it that far or often closed after a few days once there. Emerging from Williams's one-act play *Confessional*, *Small Craft Warnings*, through three acts, poignantly reflects familiar Williams themes and characters. As the meteorological metaphor in Williams's title indicates, the characters in *Small Craft Warnings*—"drifters and misfits"—are small vessels tossed adrift on the troubled seas of life, much as their creator was. Like Williams, too, the characters in *Small Craft Warnings* feel abused and abandoned, searching for a haven from loneliness and soiled desires. Tellingly, for the first time in his life on the professional stage Williams acted in one of his own plays, taking the role of Doc, the drunken and drug-abusing physician whose mistakes haunt him as much as Williams's perceived failures in the theater followed him. In *Small Craft Warnings*, then, Williams entered the script of his own life.

But the play is far more important than a venting of Williams's chimeras. Though criticized for its lack of plot, meager humor, and overt symbolism, *Small Craft Warnings* raises some of Williams's most searching questions on life, death, human relation-

A 1993 production of *Small Craft Warnings* at the University of Houston. Courtesy of Sidney Berger, School of Theatre, University of Houston.

ships, and the presence of God. These ideas are vital to the conversations/confessions in the play, almost all of which take place at Monk's bar on the Pacific California coast, a setting that recalls the bars Williams frequented in the 1940s. *Small Craft Warnings* also demands comparison with other "bar" plays such as Harry Hope's in **Eugene O'Neill**'s *The Iceman Cometh* or Johnny's Bar in Charles Gordone's *No Place to be Somebody* (1969), places where patrons attempt to find intoxication from rejection, false hope, and the consequences of illusions. The sounds of the ocean, radio forecasts about rough weather, and an engulfing fog contribute to the symbolic status of Monk's as a safe haven, a stage for confession and refuge. In fact, the eponymous Monk serves

as a priest/monk guarding his patrons from further abuses (physical and psychological) as they confess their crimes of the heart. A central symbolic element of the play is the spotlight confessional that many of the characters enter to deliver monologues about their identities, dreams, and wearied failures. Emphasizing the sacramental, a large fish (replete with Christian symbolism) hangs over Monk's bar.

Gathering on this one night of revelations at Monk's are his local patrons plus two visitors. Unquestionably, the two most important characters in *Small Craft Warnings* are Leona and Violet, faithful members of Monk's community and carefully balanced portraits of two types of Williams's women—the overbearing and the vulnerable. Leona is the former; Violet, the latter. One of Williams's most memorable female characters in the 1970s, Leona Dawson is the life force of *Small Craft Warnings*. A beautician who befriends stranded young men (gay and straight), Leona has a quick, termagant-like temper she unleashes on her unfaithful soon-to-be-former boyfriend Bill whom she catches cheating with Violet at Monk's. In a repeated bit of stage business, Leona strikes out at those who challenge her by hitting them with her sailor cap and bearing her fists. This night at Monk's is unduly difficult for Leona, since she is commemorating the death day of her gay brother Haley (as distant and disappearing as the comet) whom she apotheosizes as an angel because of his musical talent. Stricken with pneumonia, he was the epitome of beauty for Leona and yet another example in the Williams canon of the erased, absent homosexual, for example, Allan Grey in *A Streetcar Named Desire*, Skipper in *Cat on a Hot Tin Roof*, and Sebastian Venable in *Suddenly Last Summer* (see **Gender and Sexuality**). Boisterous, quarrelsome, but always sincere, Leona has faith in God, looks to the beauty of the sky, and showers maternal solicitude on those in need.

Violet was the beneficiary of Leona's care until she angered her by plying her trade—masturbating men under the tables at Monk's—with Bill, a typically Williamesque blend of the erotic and the grotesque. Weaker and completely dependent on the kindness of strangers and friends alike, Violet is the play's nymph. Likened to a water lily, an apt metaphor for her vulnerable, weepy state, Violet is the voice of lamentation at Monk's. She lives above an arcade in a flat without a bathroom, is seldom clean, and flees to the ladies' room at Monk's to escape the avenging Leona. A fallen woman in the lineage of Williams's Bertha (*Hello from Bertha*), Violet is ultimately delivered by Monk, who invites her upstairs to his apartment for a bath, food, and sexual/personal safety, one of the most hopeful conclusions in a Williams play.

Another regular at Monk's is Doc, who leaves to take care of a woman (ironically residing in Treasure Isle) in labor. Boozed and drugged up, he ends up killing her and her child, whose corpse he puts in a shoebox and sends out to sea to conceal his crime. Leona reports him, but Doc escapes. The stench of the human condition is on his hands; the descriptions of Doc's relationships are sordid, oozing with bodily decay. God (see **Religion**) for Doc is an uninterested coal miner, symbolic for this Williams character who travels the dark side of human existence. In his confession, Doc appears as one of the most forlorn portraits of Williams. Also among the bar regulars are Bill McCorkle, Leona's parasitical and unfaithful boyfriend, who has no confession to make. Steve, another patron, is a short-order cook who tries to care for Violet and is happy to receive any attention from the opposite sex.

Two new arrivals at Monk's are the jaded, gay screenwriter Quentin accompanied by Bobby, a young boy from Iowa whom he just picked up down the beach. Quentin is the first openly acknowledged gay character in Williams's plays and has often been regarded as a reflection of Williams. The most skeptical character in the play, Quentin claims he cannot see or hear God and then describes the gay life as one of isolation and disappointment. Bobby, on the other hand, is a young gay whose idealism is high; he is awed by the works of nature, such as the Pacific Ocean. Though he arrives with Quentin, Bobby does not leave with him; the screenwriter fittingly exits alone into his hopeless world. Significantly, most of Monk's guests move on, searching for the contact with another human being, the same motive that propelled Williams in his peripatetic existence.

The production history of *Small Craft Warnings* reflects in part the play's dramatic symbolism. It opened on 2 April 1972 (Easter Sunday night) at the Truck and Warehouse Theatre, directed by Richard Altman, and then substantially revised and lightened by Williams, moved uptown to the New Theatre where Candy Darling, a famous drag queen, played Violet. In 1973 Elaine Stritch was highly acclaimed as Leona in the London premiere at the Hampstead Theatre Club. Another British production took place in May 1995 at the Library Theatre in Manchester. Capturing Williams's tavern atmosphere perfectly, *Small Craft Warnings* was staged in 1976 at Morgan's Old New York Bar and Grill where the patrons were both part of the audience and the ambience of the play. The Steppenwolf Theatre in Chicago staged *Small Craft Warnings* in 1996, and in November 1997 Rick Corley brought the play to Moscow's Sovmerenik Theatre for its Russian premiere. In 2001, the Jean Cocteau Repertory in New York staged a penetrating production of *Small Craft Warnings*.

Further Reading

Kolin, Philip C. " 'Having lost the ability to say: "My God!" ' The Theology of Tennessee Williams's *Small Craft Warnings*." In *The Undiscovered Country: The Later Plays of Tennessee Williams*, ed. Philip C. Kolin. New York: Lang, 2002. 107–124.

MacNicholas, John. "Williams' Power of the Keys." In *Tennessee Williams: A Tribute*, ed. Jac Tharpe. Jackson: University Press of Mississippi, 1997. 581–606.

Smith, Marc Chalon. "*Small Craft Warnings*: Characters Set Adrift." *Los Angeles Times* 19 March 1991: F3.

Spoto, Donald. *The Kindness of Strangers: The Life of Tennessee Williams*. Boston: Little, Brown, 1985.

"Tennessee Williams Acting in 'Warnings.' " *Variety* 7 June 1972: 1, 60.

Wardle, Irving. "Miss Stritch Shines as the Bar Room Wit." *London Times* 30 January 1973: 9.

Philip C. Kolin

Something Cloudy, Something Clear. One of Tennessee Williams's last dramatic works, *Something Cloudy, Something Clear* was completed in 1981 and proved to be one of his most autobiographical plays. A "memory play," it is the logical counterpart to Williams's first dramatic success, *The Glass Menagerie*, but it can be fully appreciated on its own terms. It is, perhaps, the finest and most characteristic (and, at the same time, original) work of Williams's last decade. In *Something Cloudy, Something Clear*, *The Glass Menagerie*'s Tom Wingfield is transformed into August, a young, aspiring playwright seeking his first break; *Something Cloudy, Something Clear* is, like *The Glass Menagerie*, deceptively simple in its structure but richly lyrical in its language and complex in theme, character development, and dramatic devices.

Unraveling his past and present, Williams weaves a tapestry of images of life and death, a meditation on love and art. August, the central character and Williams's alter ego, is spending the summer of 1940 on Cape Cod, a period in which Williams languished uneasily on the brink of creative success and during which he fully accepted his homosexuality. *Something Cloudy, Something Clear* makes clear that Williams viewed the summer of 1940 as the fork in the road for him. He left his earlier life behind and moved into a future in which artistic triumph, failure, and personal tragedy awaited him. The play's heart can be located in Williams's impassioned need to confront his memories (both comforting and painful), to identify the junctures when choices made placed him on the road to his present—in this case, circa 1980—and that inevitably shadow loves and losses gone by. In *Something Cloudy, Something Clear*, August becomes enamored of Kip Kiernan, a handsome young man spending the summer on the beach with a fragile beauty, Clare. Kip, recovering from unsuccessful surgery for a brain tumor, and Clare, suffering from diabetes, are both doomed beings. Ultimately realizing this, August finds in himself powerful feelings for both as he becomes deeply entangled in their lives and as he struggles to realize himself as an artist.

Something Cloudy, Something Clear is a variation on recurring autobiographical themes of Williams's dramatic accomplishment. Other elements emerge most obviously in the inclusion of figures from Williams's past (a childhood sweetheart **Hazel Kramer**, mercurial actress **Tallulah Bankhead**, and **Frank Merlo**, Williams's longtime lover whose lingering death cast a dark cloud over the final 20 years of Williams's life). Other characters are provided fictional names but are based on actual people, including Maurice and Celeste Fiddler (the real-life producers **Lawrence Langner** and Armina Marshall with whom Williams fought) and Caroline Wales (Miriam Hopkins, star of Williams's early ill-fated play *Battle of Angels*). Only one of the play's main characters, Clare, is wholly fictional; she is a fragile heroine reminiscent of Laura in *The Glass Menagerie* or Alma in *Summer and Smoke*.

On the most obvious level, the play's title refers to a cataract on one of August's eyes (the cloudy one), a recurrent health problem for Williams. But the title is less obvious in the double exposure of the play's structure: August is seen both as he *was* and as he *is*. The wiser, somewhat more compassionate August observes his callow youthful self, a being at times clouded by impetuousness and selfishness. Abrupt switches in perspective permit Williams to focus on two key ideas also suggested by the title—what his characters refer to as life's "exigencies of desperation" (the cloudy) and "negotiation of terms" (the clear). The play splinters and freezes time, a commodity; August ruefully notes that everyone seems to want more of it despite its short supply. A characteristically lyrical work, *Something Cloudy, Something Clear* is, like most of the plays Williams completed in the last decade of his life, a chamber piece—considerably smaller in scale than his earlier works of an almost operatic scale (*A Streetcar Named Desire*, *Camino Real*, etc.) but no less imbued with their major attributes and stylistic characteristics. *Something Cloudy, Something Clear* is, at various turns, delicate, heartbreaking, poetic, and its characters are complexly drawn and memorable. Critics argued that Williams was either attempting some sort of self-serving, self-justification or that he felt he was far too harsh in his self-portrait. Perhaps Williams was attempting to do what **Eugene O'Neill** had done in his most elegiac works, *Long Day's Journey into Night* and *A Moon for the Misbegotten*—to pay a debt to, to forgive his dead lover Kip, and, at the same time, to find forgiveness for his own sins.

The passing of time, a recurrent Williams theme, is central to *Something Cloudy, Something Clear*. The play's fractured time scheme is enhanced by the dreamlike environment Williams creates, as he makes clear by his description of the setting that has "the spectral quality of a time and place from deep in the past." This description could easily apply to *The Glass Menagerie*. Williams also underscores the potency of dreams and illusions in other ways in *Something Cloudy,*

Charles E. Polly as August in the 1997 Eastenders Repertory Company production of *Something Cloudy, Something Clear* in San Francisco. Directed by Susan E. Evans.

Something Clear: Clare escapes into her dreams and speaks directly of them as the only true sources of knowledge. *Something Cloudy, Something Clear*'s unique time structure permits an instantaneous movement from past to present—a thorough, simply accomplished conflation of the concepts of time and location permitting exploration of a range of themes with conciseness and directness. The double exposure of time extends to the characters themselves—August is at once seen as man/artist, young/old, and understanding/uncomprehending, while other characters represent heterosexual/homosexual, strong/weak, aesthetic/prosaic, and compassionate/brutal aspects. It is also through August that Williams most effectively accomplishes the feat of exploding

time. As Williams notes, only he, the author, looks at the characters from a perspective 40 years later.

August's ruminations on theater and the struggles of the artist seem at first a decidedly secondary concern, but the contradictory combination of pride and insecurity Williams had in his accomplishments as a playwright is a major dramatic force, as are his struggles against pressures to compromise his work. The Fiddlers, an avaricious couple who want to option August's work without paying much for it, obviously represent the commercialization of art. August speaks of his difficulties in maintaining autonomy as an artist in a commercialized theater, but the play also provides an interlude in which he finds himself in an argument with the flamboyant Tallulah Bankhead, representing the tumult and frustrations of Williams's theatrical adventures. He spurns the theater's (and Bankhead's) excess, its commercialism, and its inherent falseness (as represented by Bankhead's notoriously camp performance of Blanche DuBois in a 1956 New York revival of *A Streetcar Named Desire*). However, he is also drawn to it, and despite his anger at Bankhead for what he regards as a gross caricature of his most famous character, he speaks lovingly of her. Clare and Kip are purer spirits able to recognize the value of art they cannot create—they do not want to sell it or see it compromised; they require it to lift them out of reality. Williams's art sustained his life on many levels, but it finally proved inadequate. Clare seems to be speaking for Williams when she sadly notes that most of the human family live on only about half of their dreams, while others have even less to sustain them. However, Williams does not leave it at that. At one point, listening to music emanating from August's silver Victrola, Williams has Kip exclaim on the power of art—that, like dreams, it can be clarifying but only to those able to recognize its true worth.

Something Cloudy, Something Clear was first produced by New York's Jean Cocteau Repertory on 24 August 1981 with Williams's blessing, directed by Eve Adamson and starring Craig Smith as August. The production met with critical apathy, as have rare subsequent productions, including the first significant New York revival in September 2001 by the New York Art Theatre at the Theatre of St. Clement's, directed by Anatole Fourmantchouk. *Something Cloudy, Something Clear* remains one of Williams's least-produced full-length plays despite its obvious and clarifying connections as one of his most autobiographical works. See also **Gender and Sexuality**; *Memoirs*.

Further Reading

Clum, John M. "*Something Cloudy, Something Clear*: Homophobic Discourse in Tennessee Williams." *South Atlantic Quarterly* 88 (1989): 161–179.

Fisher, James. " 'In My Leftover Heart': Confessional Autobiography in Tennessee Williams's *Something Cloudy, Something Clear*." In *The Undiscovered Country: The Later Plays of Tennessee Williams*, ed. Philip C. Kolin. New York: Lang, 2002. 194–206.

Kakutani, Michiko. "Tennessee Williams: 'I Keep Writing. Sometimes I Am Pleased.' " *New York Times* 13 August 1981: C17.

Kolin, Philip C. "*Something Cloudy, Something Clear*: Tennessee Williams's Postmodern Memory Play." *Journal of Dramatic Theory and Criticism* 12 (Spring 1998): 35–55.

Mann, Bruce J. "Memories and Muses: *Vieux Carré* and *Something Cloudy, Something Clear*." In *Tennessee Williams: A Casebook*, ed. Robert F. Gross. New York: Routledge, 2002. 139–152.

Novick, Julius. "Review: *Something Cloudy, Something Clear*." *Backstage* 26 October 2001: 43.

James Fisher

Southern Culture and Literature. Born a southerner (in Columbus, Mississippi) and having lived his formative years in the South, Williams was culturally and spiritually rooted in the South. On his father's side, he was descended from a southern aristocrat, a Tennessee governor, and on his mother's from an Episcopal priest who, though born in Ohio, graduated from Sewanee, the University of the South. Williams repeatedly wrote about the South as both literal place and mythological landscape (see **Mythology**). The places, times, characters, and themes of the South infused his work as they did his life. His favorite southern city was **New Orleans**, which he christened as his "spiritual" home. The tension that exists between a southerner's dream of an idyllic life and the harsh reality of having to live it breathes energy into all of Williams's art. The grace and poetry of southern life became some of his principal subjects.

Scholars of southern literature consider Tennessee Williams to be the region's leading playwright, followed by Lillian Hellman, Paul Green, and Horton Foote. Before Williams, Paul Green, who in the 1920s wrote folk plays, was the South's first truly significant twentieth-century playwright. Williams as southern playwright displays well-defined characteristic of regional language and symbol. As in **Faulkner** and Welty, he explores the psychological and familial burdens of the past, both those of the Old and the New South. Amanda's memories in *The Glass Menagerie* of gentlemen callers and jonquils, Blanche's nostalgia in *A Streetcar Named Desire* over the antebellum plantation world of Belle Reve ("beautiful dream"), and the lost world of Alma's innocence in *Summer and Smoke* are haunting sources of great conflict in these characters' lives. The hot-headed *chevalier*, the poor upstart white, and the African American are recognizable stereotypes in southern literature that Williams further incorporated into his plays and fiction. Big Daddy in *Cat on a Hot Tin Roof* (1955), who claims to own "thirty thousand acres of the richest land this side of the valley Nile," the trashy Archie Lee Meighan in *Baby Doll*, and Chicken Ravenstock in *Kingdom of Earth* are examples of some varied southern character types in Williams. Big Daddy, in fact, is closer to Faulkner's Sutpen from *Absalom, Absalom!* than to other plantation owners in Faulkner, but he is always the pragmatist.

Deep religious fervor, a love of the land, and family traditions are also potent factors in southern literature, all abundantly present in Williams. Like the majority of southern

playwrights, he also attempted to incorporate the more lyrical aspects of southern speech in his dramatic dialogues. Williams's poetically charged dialogues, his imaginative embellishment of naturalistic situations, and his expressionistic staging techniques reflect his southernness. These qualities plus a gift for depicting picturesque settings—New Orleans, the Delta, or the Mississippi Gulf Coast—together with a subliminal distrust of the South's pride in its questionable homogeneity further establish Williams as a southern playwright.

Between 1944 and 1961, Williams wrote his arguably most famous plays, many of which were set in the South and most all of which were made into films, vastly increasing their influence on American popular culture. *The Glass Menagerie* (1944) evokes Amanda's girlhood memories of Blue Mountain, Mississippi; *A Streetcar Named Desire* mythologizes New Orleans as a place of sexualized enchantment and Poe-esque lurid dreams; *Summer and Smoke* captures both the rectitude and seething passion of Glorious Hill, Mississippi; *The Rose Tattoo* evokes the hot-blooded residents of the Mississippi Gulf Coast; and *Cat on a Hot Tin Roof*, **Orpheus Descending**, and *Kingdom of Earth* capture the myths and landscapes of the Delta of Williams's youth. But *Battle of Angels*/*Orpheus Descending* may embody most clearly the southernness of Williams's dramatic universe with its portraits of life in Two River County, Mississippi, the Williams equivalent of Faulkner's Yoknapatawpha County. These Williams plays describe rural southern life, characters, themes, and myths, while *Suddenly Last Summer* begins and ends in the polite society of New Orleans's Garden District with excursions into the Cabeza de Lobo. In fact, judging by just the locations of his Pulitzer Prize–winning plays, Williams was a highly regarded southern writer who blended the scandalous and the aristocratic. His plays gave voice to the romantic dreams upon which so much Southern literature is based.

Williams, however, both evoked and interrogated southern literary stereotypes. The evils of racism are explored in *Battle of Angels/Orpheus Descending* (1940/1957) and *Sweet Bird of Youth* (1959) in particular. A patriarchal society, dedicated to worshipping a deceased elite, joins with a more updated money-hungry, pleasure-seeking culture to create a southern symbolic torture chamber for the sensitive or idealistic individual such as Val Xavier in *Orpheus Descending*. Still we might conclude that the penchant of Blanche DuBois for "magic" over realism mirrors her creator's preferences. But such a clear-cut association and endorsement are wrong. What Williams succeeds in doing is to convey the magnetic appeal of southern cultural myths as he deconstructs them in play after play. Amanda's jonquils yellowing with the antiquity of her natural Blue Mountains in *The Glass Menagerie* do not bloom in her St. Louis tenement. Blanche's beaux, like Belle Reve, are part of a world of fading fictions.

Many perversions and distortions of human behavior attributed by Williams were the stock in trade of southern writers. Rigid gender stereotypes were a well-defined part of the southern landscape. The nearly schizophrenic division between strong sexual needs and a chaste public image, which both Lucretia Collins in *Portrait of a Madonna* and Blanche DuBois in *A Streetcar Named Desire* try to maintain, is not a conflict shared by male characters who are free to boast of their sexuality (Val in *Orpheus Descending*, Stanley in *A Streetcar Named Desire*, Big Daddy in *Cat on a Hot Tin Roof*, etc.). In fact, the veneration of the male as "stud" and progenitor and the codification of physical bravery and strength, leadership, and aggressiveness are carried to such

an extreme that certain male characters in Williams's plays seem to surrender their masculinity rather than compete with the southern macho prototypes they have witnessed at close hand. The puerile, alcoholic, and possibly homosexual Brick, Blanche's suicidal young husband, and Sebastian Venable in *Suddenly Last Summer* are prepared to reject life itself if it requires assuming a dominating sexuality. In fact, the traditional southern hero is absent in Williams's repertory. The courageous, heterosexual southern hero, progenitor of dynasties and paternalistic defender of the weak, can be a daunting figure to an insecure male with ambivalent sexuality, who is resentful of authority and lacks physical courage, ambition, and the desire to dominate others. This may account for Williams's suspicion about the traditional hero and the icon he presents.

The hypocrisy of a society that denies a woman's sexuality (as decried in many southern works such as Kate Chopin's *Awakening*) was also anathema to Williams. Lucretia, Blanche, Carol in *Orpheus Descending*, and Catherine Venable in *Suddenly Last Summer* (1958), Maggie the Cat, Alma in *Summer and Smoke* (1948), and Hannah in *The Night of the Iguana* (1964) are misled by the discriminatory double standard into hating themselves for showing the libidinal urges considered healthy in men.

The power of Williams's dramaturgy presents a daunting legacy for his successors. The late Preston Jones, Marsha Norman, and Beth Henley all owe a debt to Tennessee Williams as they continue his exploration of southern value systems and conflicts. Jones, a Texan, and Norman, a Kentuckian, belong to border states, ones certainly not associated with the antebellum South but that nonetheless shared certain cultural assumptions with Williams's South. Henley is a

Mississippian and hence unquestionably belongs to that group of literary stalwarts produced by the Magnolia State in the twentieth century. Though not directly influenced by Williams, Horton Foote (born only five years after Williams) does share themes with Williams of individuals seeking their own identity in the presence of a monolithic, patriarchal southern culture. See also **Clarksdale, Mississippi; Film Adaptations; Gender and Sexuality; Race;** *Twenty-seven Wagons Full of Cotton and Other One-Act Plays.*

Further Reading

Devlin, Albert J., ed. *Conversations with Tennessee Williams.* Jackson: University Press of Mississippi, 1986.

Holditch, Kenneth, and Richard Freeman Leavitt. *Tennessee Williams and the South.* Jackson: University Press of Mississippi, 2002.

King, Kimball. "Tennessee Williams: A Southern Writer." *Mississippi Quarterly* 48 (Fall 1995): 627–648.

Watson, Charles S. *The History of Southern Drama.* Lexington: University Press of Kentucky, 1997.

Kimball King

Spring Storm. *Spring Storm* is one of Williams's apprentice plays, along with *Not about Nightingales*, *Stairs to the Roof*, and *Candles to the Sun*. He wrote *Spring Storm* in 1937–1938 for a drama workshop led by Professor **Edward Charles Mabie** at the University of Iowa and had hoped it would be staged at the university, but Mabie found the play unacceptable because of its strong sexual content and lack of depression-era social messages. Through his association with **Willard Holland**, the director of the **Mummers** who had left **St. Louis** for **Hollywood**, Williams thought *Spring Storm* might be accepted as a screenplay, but that possibility fell through, too. Nor did the Mummers ever stage it; and so *Spring Storm* remained un-

produced until its world premiere by the Actors Repertory of Texas on 10 November 1999. A month later, Marin Theatre of Mill Valley, California, also staged *Spring Storm* on 7–12 December 1999.

Spring Storm bears the early hallmarks of Williams's themes and style. It is set in Port Tyler, Mississippi, a small Delta town resembling **Clarksdale**, where Williams grew up. The play contains references to many Clarksdale-area landmarks—St. George's Church (where Williams's grandfather **Walter Dakin** served as pastor), Moon Lake, Friar's Point—which also show up in *A Streetcar Named Desire*, *Summer and Smoke*, and *Orpheus Descending*. *Spring Storm* also captures the world of other Williams's small southern towns with their pretentious families and their aristocratic ancestors, attempts at southern chivalry, gentlemen callers, gossip, eccentric characters, and of course, scandal. Most characteristic of Williams's later works, too, is the frank expression of sexual desire, especially on the part of the women who reveal in *Spring Storm* their sexual urges and whom Williams portrayed in their most vulnerable and intimate moments.

A well-made, three-act play, *Spring Storm* also documents Williams's indebtedness to Chekhovian (see **Chekhov, Anton**) plots. The play is orchestrated around two sexual triangles featuring two men—Arthur Shannon (a sensitive poet who is the son of a banker) and Dick Miles (an impoverished but intelligent depression-era hero who works for the government building levees)—and two women—Heavenly Critchfield (a social climber and party-loving debutante) and Hertha Nielsen (a librarian called "the Story Lady," whose ancestors are branded as immigrants). As *Spring Storm* begins, Arthur loves Heavenly who loves Dick, while Hertha loves Arthur and Dick as well. But aspiring to a higher social position, Heavenly transfers her affection to Arthur, whom she tries to seduce by appearing naked in a moonlit scene, prompting Professor Mabie to dismiss the play with these words, "We all have to paint our nudes." Unashamedly, Heavenly tells her mother that she even had premarital sex. Unbuttoning her desires, Hertha confesses her love for Arthur, who rebuffs her, which results in Hertha committing suicide. *Spring Storm* ends with Arthur leaving town to avoid disgrace. Dick also forsakes Port Tyler and Heavenly, leaving her sitting on her front porch, waiting for one of the men to return. But like Laura in **The Glass Menagerie**, Heavenly is destined to be alone as a porch maiden the rest of her life.

The profiles of many of Williams's most famous characters can be traced in these four characters. Dick Miles suggests Val Xavier from *Orpheus Descending*, and Heavenly resembles an early Carol Cutrere from the same play. As a victim of sexual repression and a doomed romance, Hertha looks forward to Alma Winemiller from *Summer and Smoke*. The unathletic and timid poet Arthur brings to mind an early Tom Williams who also escaped to avoid disgrace occasioned by his sexual desires.

While *Spring Storm* may be melodramatic and awkward in places, this early Williams play nonetheless creatively uses symbols (Williams's trademark) everywhere—roses, jonquils, lanterns, fountains, liquor, **music**, storms, and the psychic changes they portend. *Spring Storm* is also a highly poetic play imbued with lyrical arias and even intersperses a poem in Act Three, Scene Two, when an emboldened Hertha dares to read a sexually objectional verse to Mrs. Kramer, who objects to having the book in the library her son would use. (This name also echoes the Kramer family that disapproved of Tom Williams courting their granddaughter Hazel.) Significantly, too, *Spring Storm* is

the only apprentice play set in the South, which alone makes it a valuable barometer of Williams's inspiration and a beacon of where such motivations would lead him over the next 40 years. See also **Southern Culture and Literature.**

Further Reading

Friesen, Lauren. "We All Have to Paint Our Nudes: The Iconography of Sexual Longing in *Spring Storm*." In *A Tennessee Williams Casebook*, ed. Robert F. Gross. New York: Routledge, 2002. 5–12.

Hale, Allean. "Early Williams: The Making of a Playwright." In *The Cambridge Companion to Tennessee Williams*, ed. Matthew C. Roudané. Cambridge: Cambridge University Press, 1997. 11–29.

Williams, Tennessee. *Spring Storm*. Ed. Dan Isaac. New York: New Directions, 1999.

Maureen Curley

Stairs to the Roof. *Stairs to the Roof* is unique as the only known boy-girl romantic comedy Williams ever wrote. Composed in 1940, when at 29 he had just changed his name to "Tennessee," it was not produced until 1945, as a tryout at the Pasadena Playbox, with full production at the Playhouse there in 1947. Seven of 12 reviews were favorable, calling the play impassioned, poetic, provocative, although expressing puzzlement at its "new style." Revived in November 2000 as "a play for the Millennium," honoring Williams's description, *Stairs to the Roof* was given a 21st Century Premiere by the Krannert Center for the Performing Arts, University of Illinois, Urbana. A three-day symposium involving distinguished Williams scholars followed. In October 2001 *Stairs to the Roof* had a British premiere at the Chichester Festival to glowing reviews from eight London papers. "This is enchanted theatre," reported the *Evening Standard* (10 October), while the 21 October

Sunday Telegraph wrote that "the show captures the infectious joy of a phenomenally gifted young writer beginning to discover what he could do."

Stairs is Williams's fifth long play, far more sophisticated in craftsmanship than the four that preceded it. It shows the influence of being written in New York, where in 1940 he enrolled in the **New School for Social Research** to study under John Gassner and had his first exposure to the Broadway stage. Penniless, hoping for a commercial success, he typed on the title page "Written for stage or screen with Burgess Meredith in mind." From the first, Williams dared to write for a leading star. He called the play a catharsis for his "season in hell," 1933–1935 of the depression, which he spent in a shoe factory typing orders eight hours a day. Dedicating his "social play" to all the little wage earners of the world, he hoped it might become the great American drama.

It concerns Benjamin Murphy, a lowly clerk who stages a one-man rebellion against the monotony of his eight-to-five job and all the dehumanizing forces of a mechanized society. Escape is the play's theme, and his begins when he discovers secret stairs to the factory roof where he can view broader horizons. When his boss finds Ben writing poetry into his order book, he threatens to fire him. Just as Ben is faced with returning jobless to the wrath of a nagging wife, he meets The Girl, a secretary in the factory who feels equally boxed in by her job. The two embark on a series of fantastic adventures that include meeting Mr. E, a godlike figure who offers them the chance to populate a better world. Most of the action takes place in Forest Park, **St. Louis**, not far from the setting of Williams's future *The Glass Menagerie*. In fact, this could be an extension of Act One of that play, dramatizing Tom's speech: "Look, Mother, do you think I'm *crazy* about the *warehouse*?"

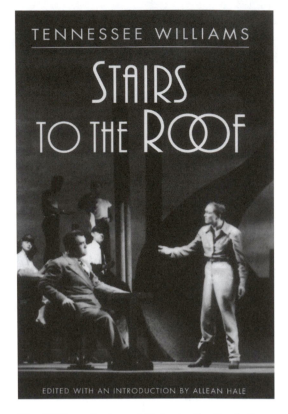

The 1947 production of *Stairs to the Roof*. Cover design used by permission of New Directions Publishing Corp.

Williams's last "apprentice" play, this shows his debt to *The Adding Machine* by Elmer Rice in its scenes of officeworkers typing in unison like automatons and its portrayal of the company stockholders as mechanized as robots. The huge clock on the wall is a dominant symbol; when The Girl finally rebels, she throws away her boss's clock. Of key significance are Williams's stage directions. Advanced for the day in their demand for metatheatrical techniques such as changing scenes through lighting and using **music** throughout, they demonstrate his manifesto against realism. The style is mainly expressionistic, each of the 14 scenes dissolving into the next, as in a film; also cinematic are the projections of skyscrapers called for in the script. Enlarging on these directions to stress the play's futuristic feeling, at Krannert theater the entire set—from skyscrapers to woodland scenes—was computer generated, using the most advanced technology. The Chichester production was altogether expressionistic, even "Kafkaesque," using a transparent glass screen to enclose the officeworkers, thus suggesting a box as the controlling image, while the main action occurred in front and was reflected in the glass. In both productions the play explodes into space-age fantasy when the lovers fly off to inhabit a new star.

Stairs to the Roof has more kinship to the 1953 fantasy *Camino Real* than to any other Williams play; its soapbox speech on brotherhood is virtually repeated in *Camino Real*. Williams finished *Stairs to the Roof* in December 1941, just after Pearl Harbor, to find that as World War II erupted there was no market for a play with a utopian ending. He never saw his play. By the time it was produced, his other St. Louis drama, *The Glass Menagerie*, was on its way to becoming a classic and he was about to launch *A Streetcar Named Desire*.

Further Reading

Billington, Michael. *The Guardian* 12 October 2001.
———. *Theatre Record* 8–12 October 2001.
Hale, Allean. "A Play for Tomorrow." Introduction to *Stairs to the Roof* by Tennessee Williams. New York: New Directions, 2000. ix–xix.
Newmark, Judith. "Early Williams Play Reveals a Different Tennessee." *St. Louis Post-Dispatch* 8 November 2000, sec. E: 1.

Allean Hale

Stapleton, Maureen (1925–   ). One of the premier actresses associated with Williams's plays, (Lois) Maureen Stapleton was born in Troy, New York, where five theaters fed her almost insatiable addiction to the movies—and where one of those theaters would eventually be renamed in her honor. After moving to New York City at age 17, she studied acting, first under Herbert Berghof at the **New School for Social Research** and then with Mira Rostova, finally becoming associated with the Actors Studio. Stapleton's long and fruitful connection with Williams began in 1951 when she won a Tony Award for her acting in *The Rose Tattoo*. Williams had originally written the part of Serafina Delle Rose for the Italian film star **Anna Magnani**, but she had difficulties with English and was unable to commit to a lengthy run. And so Williams, as he reports in his *Memoirs*, supported the young Stapleton for the role because he found her "brilliant in characterization." Although Magnani was given the part on film, Stapleton later starred in two New York revivals of *The Rose Tattoo*, in 1966 and in 1973. Reviewers responded just as favorably to her performances after they had seen the less restrained Magnani in the film as they had when she originated the role.

Stapleton went on to become a close friend of Tennessee (they called each other "Paw" and "Maw"), once ministering to him after an accidental overdose, and an even closer friend of his longtime lover, **Frank Merlo**. Williams wrote an unproduced television play, *Stopped Rocking*, for her; and she acted in his *Twenty-seven Wagons Full of Cotton*. Two years later, in 1957, she starred in *Orpheus Descending* (a rewrite of the ill-fated *Battle of Angels*) as Lady Torrance—another role originally intended for Magnani, who once again got the part in the film version titled *The Fugitive Kind*, while Stapleton had to be satisfied with a minor role. But in 1965, she would star as Amanda Wingfield in the twentieth anniversary production of *The Glass Me-*

nagerie, and in 1976 as Big Mama in an adaptation for television of *Cat on a Hot Tin Roof*, with Laurence Olivier. Stapleton, who finds it "easier" to work in movies than on the stage, received a Best Supporting Actress Oscar for her characterization of Emma Goldman in Warren Beatty's *Reds*, as well as an Oscar nomination for Woody Allen's *Interiors* and an Emmy nomination for *The Queen of the Stardust Ballroom*. A commonsense actress who claims that her main job is "to keep the audience awake," Stapleton has also appeared on stage in works by **Miller** and Hellman, as well as in Neil Simon's *The Gingerbread Lady*, for which she won a second Tony Award.

Further Reading

Stapleton, Maureen, and Jane Scovell. *A Hell of a Life: An Autobiography*. New York: Simon & Schuster, 1995.

Thomas P. Adler

St. Just, Lady. See Britneva, Maria (Lady St. Just).

St. Louis. Tennessee Williams, famed as a southern playwright, could as justifiably be called a Missouri writer. Although only *The Glass Menagerie* is recognized as a St. Louis play, much of his work actually derived from his 21 years in St. Louis—his longest residency in any one place. He wrote at least 14 plays set in St. Louis against 8 set in **New Orleans**, which claims him. "The Poker Night" scene that was the genesis of *A Streetcar Named Desire* was actually a St. Louis memory. Although he declared a lifelong hatred for St. Louis, it was there he spent the formative years that made him a playwright, and to that city he often returned for his characters and background.

In July 1918 at age seven Tom was brought from **Clarksdale, Mississippi**, to St. Louis to live with a father he scarcely knew. Left behind were the grandparents who had reared him and his sister Rose, who was more like his twin. In Clarksdale, a cotton town of 6,000, he had had an agrarian childhood; in St. Louis, he was thrust into the huge public Field school, where he was teased for his southern accent and excluded from play because of his limp, resulting from diphtheria. Home, which had been a sunny rectory, was now the dark apartment at 4633 Westminster Place. Tom was chiefly influenced in his attitude toward St. Louis by his mother **Edwina**. As the Episcopal rector's daughter, she had enjoyed social prestige; in the fifth largest city of the United States, she was nobody. She impressed on her children that in St. Louis only status mattered and that they could not hope to attend the private schools where wealthier children were enrolled at birth. Williams later wrote: "That name, public school, kept stabbing at my guts." The sense of being an outsider would become a dominant theme in his writing.

To his father, **Cornelius Williams**, St. Louis was the city of opportunity where he would have a managerial job in the largest shoe company in the world. St. Louis had an outstanding school system, two universities, fine libraries, a famed Symphony Orchestra, a splendid Art Museum. Forest Park, larger than Central Park in New York, had one of the earliest natural habitat zoos and was building the largest outdoor theater in the United States, the Municipal Opera, where Tom would first encounter stage performances including music, dance, scenic effects and lighting, the total theatrical experience that would influence his own plays. His early play *Stairs to the Roof* is laid in Forest Park. The zoo gave him a metaphor for his household as a menagerie, each member caught in a separate cage. St. Louis also had more motion picture theaters per capita than in New

York City, and in his frequent escape to the movies, Tom absorbed the cinematic techniques used in his plays some 20 years before he worked at MGM in **Hollywood**.

In reality, Cornelius Williams made a good salary, but as the frustrated Edwina held back affection, he held back money. Their new life together became an extended warfare. Cornelius, lusty and boisterous, took his disappointment out in drinking; Edwina, aggressively puritanical, resorted to scolding. She would use Tom as her confidant; "C.C." would retaliate by calling Tom "Miss Nancy." Caught between father and mother, the boy felt trapped. Escape became the motivation that formed a theme for his plays. His enrollment in Ben Blewett Junior High School at age 13 was the first step in the escape. St. Louis had pioneered the junior high school movement, and Blewett, only seven years old, was a national model. It occupied a city block and was run like a small city. With a sizable ethnic mix, it emphasized citizenship, student government, and activities for any skill, from orchestra to team sports, and offered 30 clubs, from French to Office Practice, expecting each student to participate in at least one. Fierce competition between the 42 home rooms also encouraged student activity. Tom found his medium in the school newspaper. At 13 his first story "Isolated," written on a secondhand typewriter his mother bought him, was published in the 1924 Blewett *Junior Life*; in November 1925, his poem "Nature's Thanksgiving," appeared, followed in January 1926 by "Old Things," an experiment in free verse. The 1925 yearbook devoted an entire page to a poem, "Demon Smoke," by Thomas Williams, ninth grade—his first exercise in social protest and his first paid work. It won a $5 prize from the St. Louis Smoke Abatement League. (St. Louis, whose factories were fueled by coke, was arguably the smokiest city in the United States.) The

prize opened the possibility that he could make money by writing and thus win his father's respect. Among the 37 students in his home room, Tom was identified as "our literary boy." Blewett is remembered in Williams's play *A Lovely Sunday for Creve Coeur.*

During his brief term at Soldan High School, at 15 his film review of "Stella Dallas" was published. The real importance of Soldan was as a background for Laura's memories in *The Glass Menagerie*, although the experiences attributed to her in the play actually happened to Tom. It was doubtless he, not his sister, who limped down the auditorium aisle. Abnormally shy, Tom noted with envy Edward Meisenbach, who had 14 entries under his name in the yearbook and was the tallest boy in class pictures where Tom was the shortest. Meisenbach, who did indeed star in the school's Gilbert and Sullivan opera, furnished half of the composite portrait of Jim, *The Glass Menagerie*'s "Gentleman Caller." For the rest of his portrait Williams would use a college fraternity brother, Jim Connor, who was Catholic and endowed with Irish charm. The Soldan experience ended with Tom taking **Hazel Kramer** to the graduation dance on the river steamer *J.S.* and his resolution to marry her. Hazel would appear in various forms in future plays, from "Heavenly" in *Spring Storm* to "La Niña" in *The Red Devil Battery Sign*.

A move to Enright Avenue in September 1926 put Tom in University City High School. Here at 16, he won a contest in *Smart Set* magazine for his answer to the question, "Can a Good Wife Be a Good Sport?" His reply, in the May 1927 issue, purported to be from the wronged husband, citing "my own unhappy marital experiences." In 1928 his horror story "The Vengeance of Nitocris," published in *Weird Tales*, earned $35. At 17, after his grand-

239

father took him on an extensive European tour, he wrote 10 travel articles, which, published in the *U City Pep*, spurred his ambition to become a journalist. The apartment at 6454 Enright was where the actual events of *The Glass Menagerie* took place. No tenement, it was one of several blocks of similar red brick apartments, which Williams saw as a "hive." The building is gone, but the alley is still there, as are numerous similar apartments. A block away on Delmar Boulevard is the Tivoli, one of the many movie houses to which Tom escaped from his work at the shoe factory on 15th and Delmar.

The depression and his Missouri residency dictated that Tom go to the University of Missouri at Columbia, rather than to the University of the South at Sewanee, his grandfather's choice. Missouri had the oldest and best School of Journalism in the country. Although he went prepared to become a journalist, Missouri University was where Tom became a playwright. In 1929 the school offered exceptional opportunities for creative writers, with contests in Poetry, the Essay, the Story, and Playwriting, each with a prize of $50. At 19 Tom wrote his first play, *Beauty Is the Word*, which won sixth honorable mention. His entries in essay and fiction won honors as well, and his second play, *Hot Milk at Three in the Morning*, revised as *Moony's Kid Don't Cry*, would be published nationally in Mayorga's *Best One-Act Plays of 1940*. A playwriting course at Missouri was his first exposure to dramatic literature, especially Strindberg and **O'Neill**. Reading *Miss Julie* and seeing an expressionistic performance of *The Hairy Ape* may have been recalled when he wrote *A Streetcar Named Desire*. From the University of Missouri he drew several of his most important characters, fraternity brothers Harold Mitchell, who became "Mitch" in *A Streetcar Named Desire*, and Jim Connor, who became O'Conner in *The Glass Menagerie*.

Names of other "brothers" entered his work: Moise, Venable, Dobyne—and the college atmosphere of "Ole Miss" in **Cat on a Hot Tin Roof** may have come from "Old Mizzou" instead. Tom's writing progress was interrupted in his junior year when his father, a military school graduate, took him out of school for failing ROTC and put him to work in the shoe factory, typing orders eight hours a day. Although he hated the work so that he later subtracted those three years from his age, he met there a Polish worker named Kowalski who would become the best-known male character in American drama.

Released from the factory by a nervous breakdown in 1935, Tom entered Washington University in St. Louis, where he studied playwriting under Prof. William Carson and met **Clark Mills (McBurney)**, the university poet, who introduced him to the college literary groups and to a group of radical writers connected with *The Anvil, the Magazine of Proletarian Fiction*. Their influence, and the factory experience, fostered the social protest of his early plays. Williams, Mills, and classmate William Jay Smith formed a self-promoting "St. Louis Poets Workshop," Tom publishing more than 30 poems in two years. His first published story, "Twenty-seven Wagons Full of Cotton" (see **Twenty-seven Wagons Full of Cotton**) appeared in *Manuscript* in 1936, and in the summer of 1937 he and Clark set up a "literary factory" in Clark Mill's basement, where Williams produced numerous stories, poems, and plays. In February 1936, seeing **Alla Nazimova** in *Ghosts* was the final determinate in his becoming a playwright. Having his first long play, **Candles to the Sun**, produced by the St. Louis **Mummers** in March 1937 to favorable reviews cemented this ambition. The Mummers, and especially their director, **Willard Holland**, gave him valuable experience in the mechanics of writing and rewriting for actual production. His second play, *Fugitive Kind*, written for them, was produced the same year. As the only produced playwright in Carson's annual play contest, Williams expected to win. When his entry *Me, Vasha!* was derided by fellow students as melodrama, he quit Washington University. They could not know that the mad heroine in the play was a revealing portrait of his sister, who was retreating into schizophrenia at the time. Rose would inhabit many of his plays, from *The Glass Menagerie* to *The Two-Character Play/Out Cry*. Her madness impelled him to the lifetime of compulsive writing that he felt kept him from going insane as well.

If Williams had not moved to St. Louis, he would not have gone to the University of Iowa, then the Midwestern mecca for playwrights. Here he studied under **Edward Charles Mabie**, a director of the Works Progress Administration's (WPA) Federal Theatre, and E.C. Conkle, whose *Prologue to Glory* was currently a Broadway success. Tom read the required body of theater literature, 40 plays a semester, from Maeterlinck to O'Neill. He was exposed to international trends in theater, learned the elements of stagecraft and the discipline of turning out a dramatic sketch every week, with the reward of seeing his best work produced. *Spring Storm* and *Not about Nightingales* evolved from his Iowa experience. Iowa put great emphasis on "regionalism," and Tom's southernism was unique there. Fable has it that fellow students, noting his accent but ignorant of his Mississippi origin, first called him "Tennessee." True or not, it seems that Iowa was the determinant in Williams becoming the Southern playwright. Upon graduating in August 1938, jobless at 27, he returned to St. Louis for his last stay, and in the family attic at 42 Aberdeen Place he began *Battle of Angels*, which would ultimately be produced by the Theatre Guild

of New York. It was in St. Louis, May 1939, that he received word that the four short plays titled **American Blues** by "Tennessee Williams"—his first use of the name—had won a $100 prize from the **Group Theatre**. This caught the attention of **Audrey Wood**, the agent who would propel him to Broadway, fame, and his physical escape from St. Louis. Mentally, he never left. St. Louis was the site of his family trauma, the basic subject for many of his 70 or more plays. It was there that the worst experiences of his life took place: his sister's tragedy and his own confinement in Barnes Hospital's psychiatric ward in 1969. Before he died, he confessed that the St. Louis years were "like the irritant in the oyster shell." They had made him a writer. See also **Poems; Southern Culture and Literature; Williams, Thomas Lanier, III ("Tennessee")**.

Further Reading

Ben Blewett Junior High School. Junior Life Yearbooks, 1923, 1924, 1925. Missouri Historical Library, Columbia, Missouri.

Hale, Allean. "Tennessee Williams's St. Louis Blues." *Mississippi Quarterly* 48 (Fall 1995): 609–626.

Leverich, Lyle. *Tom: The Unknown Tennessee Williams*. New York: Crown, 1995. 46–64.

"Saint Louis." *Missouri, A Guide to the "Show Me" State*. New York: Duell, Sloan & Pearce, 1941. 423–434.

"Saint Louis." *The How and Why Library*. Chicago: F. E. Compton & Co., 1921. 4.

The Scrip. Soldan High School Yearbooks, 1927, 1928, 1929. St. Louis Public Library.

Allean Hale

Stopped Rocking and Other Screenplays. *Stopped Rocking and Other Screenplays*, first published as a collection in 1984, includes four scripts that cannot be dated precisely. *The Loss of a Teardrop Diamond* and *All Gaul Is Divided* were probably writ-

241

ten in the 1950s, *One-Arm* dates back to the 1960s, and *Stopped Rocking* belongs to the mid-1970s. *One-Arm* is directly based on the 1948 short story; *All Gaul Is Divided* is a longer and earlier version of Williams's late play *A Lovely Sunday for Creve Coeur*, while the other two screenplays are original (not based on any Williams plays). In these screenplays, which have not received the critical attention they deserve, Williams developed probing cinematic techniques by which character development is assimilated to scenic landscapes and foregrounded through telling dialogues. Symbolic vignettes also serve to deepen character. Interestingly, the four screenplays in this volume incorporate the motifs and autobiographical elements also present in Williams's plays. Yet while **Baby Doll**, another Williams screenplay, profited from using Hollywood's cinematic conventions, *Stopped Rocking*'s themes of nervous breakdown and madness, sexual delinquency and prostitution, were not amenable to Hollywood's mores. The anarchic defiance of bourgeois codes in the collection did not meet the requirements of a conventional Hollywood treatment.

All Gaul Is Divided begins inside a **St. Louis** high school classroom in the late 1920s, during "the last week of school." The protagonist, Jenny, a beautiful 30-plus spinster, teaches high school until she has a nervous breakdown due to her inability to reconcile her romantic idealism with the unconscious demands of her sexuality, as revealed through her overwhelming attraction to the high school's gym teacher, Harry Steed. Jenny's naïveté is particularly signaled by her attraction to Harry (a failed golf pro whose social pretensions have motivated him to become a stud for rich widows in the tradition of Chance Wayne or Chris Flanders). She is ultimately forced to resign or modify her expectations when the social avenues represented by scheming colleagues

Lucinda Keener and Harry Steed are delusive. Jenny seeks compensation for her failed attempt at love at a three-way picnic with the Bodenhafers and, presumably, a relationship with a prosaic widower, Buddy. Her neurotic behavior suggests Alma in **Summer and Smoke** and Blanche in **A Streetcar Named Desire**.

In the next screenplay, *The Loss of a Teardrop Diamond*, a fatefully named young socialite Fisher Willow—"Fishie" to her detractors—attempts to break into Memphis society to accommodate her rich relatives and thereby secure her inheritance. Yet losing the diamond threatens her chances. Fisher enlists the aid of a family employee, the idealistic Jimmy Dobyne, to be fitted for a tuxedo to suitably accompany her. Fisher's acceptance of Jimmy's father's alcoholism and the stigma of his mother's institutionalization can be traced to a shared sense of "pride" (her father destroys the south end of the levee and floods his land for profit, so that she is socially stigmatized). Jimmy agrees to aid her in recapturing her fallen status and play escort. The loss of the earring becomes the central focus when, at Julie Fensternmaker's Halloween ball, Fisher loses a $5,000 piece of jewelry borrowed after much cajoling from her wealthy socialite Aunt Cornelia. *The Loss of a Teardrop Diamond* is essentially a high-spirited social drama in juxtaposing vital characters such as Fisher with grotesque caricatures such as Aunt Cornelia. Such connections can be emphasized through montage, abstract shifts in perspective, and the development of a consistent and developing point of view as Fisher's character becomes the camera's central focus.

One-Arm (also the title of a collection of Williams's fiction) features an "off-camera" narrative voice-over that omnisciently relays the details of the life and execution of a handicapped male hustler named Ollie, beginning with flashbacks to a drunk driving accident in which Ollie was the sole survivor, minus one arm. Ollie becomes embroiled in the murder of a porn impresario (who wants to exploit Ollie's mutilation in a pornographic film) and is ultimately executed for his crime. While on death row, he receives thousands of letters from johns and contacts made during his itinerant existence and, perversely, insists on answering as many as he can. A nameless divinity student confesses to his analyst that reading about Ollie's plight in the newspaper has aroused homoerotic dreams of bestiality in which Ollie becomes a golden panther who licks him clean. The student visits Ollie in jail, but when Ollie finally claims his right to his own satisfaction after years as a prostitute, poignantly requesting a massage through the prison bars, the student flees. The somewhat arbitrary narrative voice concludes with a description of Ollie in which he is likened to a broken Apollo. Throughout the script, Ollie wears a skivvy shirt and dungarees, a costume that, as the production notes stipulate, clings as classically to his body as the clothes of antique sculpture. *One-Arm*'s dramatization of the experiences of down-and-outs in various settings yet once more reveals Williams's pained concern about the universality of human degradation through attention to sordid urban detail.

Institutionalized for the last five years, Janet in *Stopped Rocking* must come to terms with the dissolution of her marriage to the chiseled, blonde Olaf—nicknamed "Stone Man" by his unfaithful live-in lover and colleague, the predatory and alluring Alicia— and subsequent transfer from the asylum to a state-funded institution under the direction of the rigid Dr. Cash. Williams ably orchestrates the themes of memory translated to the screen (for example, Ollie's flashbacks), desire (motivating the plot schemas), psychic repression and collapse (Jenny and Janet),

and professional obtuseness (Sister Grim and Dr. Cash). However, Janet hopes for a reconciliation, and when this is impossible, she takes Thorazine for her nervous condition at Olaf's urging (according to the **Memoirs**, generic Seconal remained Williams's own drug of choice; see also **Drugs**).

Stopped Rocking alternates themes of kinetic force and vitality in which Janet asserts her claims to life and love with scenes of stasis and passive resistance as she ultimately relinquishes these prerogatives; thus, any cinematic conversion of this script would stress the absence of movement in characters (such as Sister Grim, and even Olaf, with his stony face and static gestures and the kinetic charge of Jan's frenzied vitality). Symbolic landscapes might be utilized to suggest such psychic tension through foregrounding the agonistic elements in the struggle between fixity, on the one hand, and movement, on the other. As an insecure, defenseless woman under the control of a domineering man, Janet in *Stopped Rocking* resembles Blanche DuBois. Thus, the camera dissolve indicating the utterly peaceful relapse at the close of the title script extends the range of resonances and echoes in a retrospective recapitulation of the cruel suppression of Janet's vital force.

The screenplays collected in *Stopped Rocking* mine the principal thematic and stylistic resources of Williams canon while heightening the cinematic. Psychological notation and character development are boldly conceived visually, as Williams draws on the entire range of stage devices and techniques and extends their application to the medium of cinema. A deft interweaving of detachment and empathy is achieved through comprehensive and precise montage; Williams's screenplays indicate how distant panning shots might alternate with close-ups, an effect especially evident in the treatment of the protagonists in the collection. Secondary characters and foils are given a wider purview through being kept at a greater distance from the camera lens. Looming close-ups would here serve to accentuate details of dress and emblematic objects; for example, Steed's virile accoutrements, Olaf's rigid gesture and expressions, and Alicia's predatory, seductive attire. Camera angles and fades are especially effective in creating a poetic and ironic poignancy or fragility of mood, as with the close-ups of Jenny's ravaged dress during the closing number "Blossom Time." See also **Film Adaptations; Hollywood.**

Further Reading

Lux, Mary F. "Tenn among the Lotus Eaters: Drugs in the Life and Fiction of Tennessee Williams." *Southern Quarterly* 48 (Fall 1999): 117–243.

Phillips, Gene D. *The Films of Tennessee Williams.* Philadelphia: Art Alliance, 1980.

Williams, Tennessee. *Stopped Rocking and Other Screenplays.* New York: New Directions, 1984.

Yacowar, Maurice. *Tennessee Williams and Film.* New York: Ungar, 1977.

Christina Hunter

A Streetcar Named Desire. *A Streetcar Named Desire*, perhaps Williams's most influential play, premiered in 1947, just three years after **The Glass Menagerie**. An immediate success, *A Streetcar Named Desire* earned a Pulitzer Prize and Donaldson and Drama Critics' Circle Awards and became an icon in American (and world) theater and a film classic when the script was adapted for Warner Brothers in 1951. The American Theatre Critics Association voted *A Streetcar Named Desire* the most important play of the twentieth century, beating out **Arthur Miller**'s *Death of Salesman* and **Eugene O'Neill**'s *Long Day's Journey into Night*, and the American Film Institute honored it as one of the top 50 American films of all time. *A Streetcar Named Desire* is a crucible of Williams's themes, his most haunting characters—Blanche DuBois, Stanley Kowalski (with his cry "Stella"), Mitch, and Stella—as well as a cluster of his signature symbols. Written in haunting, lyrical prose, *A Streetcar Named Desire* is saturated with the ethos of **New Orleans**, Williams's spiritual home where the play is set.

A Streetcar Named Desire reflects Williams's tortured, fractured biography. Blanche and Stanley embody the two sides of the playwright's androgynous nature. Like Blanche, Williams saw himself as the fugitive artist, a victim of rejection and hysteria. Following Blanche, Williams was a frenetic traveler in search of refuge. Her eventual devolution into madness was one of Williams's greatest lifelong fears, but her passion for beauty in art, music, and literature were also Williams's lifelong passions. Yet Williams was also present in Blanche's executioner, Stanley Kowalski. Inscribing himself into Stanley, Williams mirrored himself as a sexual predator, insatiable in questing for and gratifying appetite. Stanley suggests the rough homosexual trade Williams (and his Stanley-like lover **Pancho Rodriguez y Gonzales** at the time he wrote *A Streetcar Named Desire*) was accustomed to in the 1940s, as his autobiographical, retrospective portrait of August attests in **Something Cloudy, Something Clear.** John Clum and David Savran both locate Williams's submerged homoeroticism in the heterosexual dynamics of *A Streetcar Named Desire*.

Beyond doubt, *A Streetcar Named Desire* mines a variety of recurrent Williams themes. According to Williams himself, *A Streetcar Named Desire* was a tragedy because of misunderstanding resulting from a lack of communication where neither Stanley nor Blanche was the heavy. Numerous critics, however, echo director **Elia Kazan**'s interpretation, expressed in his *Notebook* (required reading on *A Streetcar Named Desire*), that the play depicted the powerful clash between the Old South's charm, agrarian economy, and gentility (symbolized by Blanche) and the new and brutal industrial social order Stanley represents. Significally, when Kazan directed *A Streetcar Named Desire* for film, he added a scene (not in Williams's play) in the factory where Stanley and Mitch worked with pounding dynamos whirling away in the background. Blanche's and Stanley's respective geographies reflect the political and social themes Kazan foregrounded. Blanche arrogantly valorizes the decaying world of the Old South, with its manners and civility, the romantic Delta landscape of Amanda Wingfield's gentleman callers with their bouquets of jonquils. That beautiful world—and its loss—is signaled in the symbolic name of the DuBois estate— Belle Reve, or beautiful dream. This world turned into a nightmare for Blanche when her male ancestors squandered the plantation through their debauchery, leaving only a small plot reserved for the family graveyard. Contrasting with the locale of Blanche's beautiful dream is Stanley's squalid Elysian Fields apartment, filled with the garish, the broken, the ruined. Stanley's violent New Orleans landscape symbolizes the struggle of the working classes, seeking escape through liquor, gambling, and sex. Prostitutes roll drunks, fights erupt everywhere, and vibrant neon colors cast a lurid light over blues bars and streets.

A Streetcar Named Desire explores other prominent themes in the Williams cannon, most notably desire, which, in its many manifestations, may be the most generative idea in the play. Williams charted new sexual territory in the American theater by exploring female sexuality, homosexuality, and sexual politics. *A Streetcar Named Desire* mapped a wife's fantasies (at the end of Scene Three

and the beginning of Scene Four), foregrounded a single woman's taboos (as in Scene Six), and celebrated exposed male flesh (aptly portrayed by **Marlon Brando**'s naked chest). Blanche's nymphomania, Stella's graphic passion for Stanley, and Stanley's satyriasis earned *A Streetcar Named Desire* immense notoriety, some of it from condemning censors. Another central theme is **madness**, explicitly depicted in Blanche's hallucinations and schizophrenic frenzy; her unmooring from reality echoes Williams's own sister **Rose**'s nervous breakdown. Blanche's nerves are at fever pitch from the start of *A Streetcar Named Desire*; Stanley has only to screech like a cat to make her jump. Theologically, *A Streetcar Named Desire* profoundly addresses Christian beliefs about grace and redemption. Stanley's French Quarter has been read as the land of the living dead, a ghoulish underworld, a hell from which Blanche emerges, in search of grace, purified through madness and likened to martyrs and to the Blessed Mother. Other themes prominent in *A Streetcar Named Desire* include illusion versus reality, role-playing, dysfunctional family conflicts, loss, the plight of artists, time as the cruel enemy, and women's tragic plight in a male-dominated world.

Acting out Williams's ideas, the characters in *A Streetcar Named Desire* have colorful pasts. Blanche DuBois is frequently regarded as Williams's most daring creation. Certainly, she speaks some of his most quoted—and parodied—lines about kindness, strangers, and long afternoons in New Orleans. She is a rich amalgam of contraries and multiple identities. At heart, Blanche is a faded Southern Belle, an aging woman who longs for a man to rescue and nourish her. Williams had earlier written about the southern "porch maiden" in *Spring Storm* (1938) and continued to be pulled toward this familiar social and literary type, through such characters as Amanda in *The Glass Me-nagerie*, Alma in **Summer and Smoke**, and decrepit variations including Lucretia Collins in "Portrait of a Madonna" or the Spinster in "Lord Byron's Love Letter." Blanche surely has much in common with other women characters who have suffered for their Old South values of gentility. According to Kenneth Holditch, Blanche demands comparison with Edna Pontellier, the doomed romantic idealist in Kate Chopin's novel *Awakening*. It was not coincidental that **Vivien Leigh**, who played Scarlett O'Hara in *Gone with the Wind*, was cast as Blanche in the 1951 *A Streetcar Named Desire* film, though Blanche was nowhere near as agile or shrewd as Scarlett. As the representative of a decaying genteel tradition, Blanche enshrines the beautiful and the spiritual. Even her name, meaning "white wood" in French, suggests purity and a noble heart, but it also evokes **Chekhov**'s *Cherry Orchard* where another aristocratic lady—Mme. Ranevskaya—is evicted from her ancestral estate.

Blanche is, however, a consummate role player, an actor who takes many parts in *A Streetcar Named Desire*. In the early scenes, she is a sex kitten spraying perfume and asking Stanley to button her dress and light her cigarette, two sexually provocative acts. But, simultaneously, she is the artist/poet, the guardian of literature (she teaches Poe, Whitman, Hawthorne) and the arts. With Stella she prides herself on being a confidante and a solicitous sister. Before Mitch, she plays a prudish schoolmarm protecting her unsullied chastity. She cannot abide a crude remark or the intrusion of glaring reality in her world of make-believe. To create magic, she buys a colored Chinese lantern to cover the naked light bulb in Stanley's apartment. Unquestionably the major symbol in *A Streetcar Named Desire*, this prop reflects Blanche's own ambiguity, signifying her

From left: Jessica Tandy, as Blanche; Kim Hunter, as Stella; and Marlon Brando, as Stanley in the 1947 Broadway production of *A Streetcar Named Desire*. Photography Collection, Harry Ransom Humanities Research Center, The University of Texas at Austin.

"vulnerability" as well as her artistic recreation of time, as Thomas P. Adler has claimed. In Scenes Eight and Nine, Blanche sizzles as the woman scorned, bitterly denouncing accusations against her honesty. Falling further into madness, she becomes a Cleopatra dressed in a Mardi Gras ball gown and rhinestone tiara in Scene Ten, shortly before Stanley rapes her.

For many readers, Blanche is a tragic heroine whose attempts to survive are endangered by Stanley's aggression and Mitch's ineffectuality. Her sympathizers focus on her suffering. She is victimized by misogyny—from Stanley; Mitch; her male ancestors; Shaw, the salesman friend of Stanley; Kiefaber, the merchant in Laurel who besmirched her name; and Mr. Graves, the principal who fired her. Like her creator, Blanche suffers from the physical ravages of mental anguish. She is a neurasthenic personality, afflicted with paranoia and, ultimately, schizophrenia. For this reason she takes hot baths, secluding herself in the bathroom, a feminine enclave, a hiding place from Stanley. Throughout *A Streetcar Named Desire* Blanche is associated with water, as if she can be cured as well as transformed through healing ablutions. Yet Blanche has also been linked to doomed damsels of **mythology** such as Philomela, who was raped, as Blanche was, by her brother-in-law; Eurydice who was sealed in the kingdom of the dead never to be rescued by her husband Orpheus, just as Blanche cannot be redeemed by Allan Grey, her first husband, by Mitch, who abandons his desire to marry her, or by Shep Huntleigh, the Texas millionaire, whom, in her delusion, she believes will take her away from her New Orleans inferno and ply her with diamonds.

But Blanche has attracted a host of detractors who deny her the status of a tragic figure and, instead, zero in on her decadence and duplicity, claiming she has deceived and lied in her heart. When *A Streetcar Named Desire* was first performed in England, critics branded her a tart, or whore, because of her brazen nymphomania and accompanying brazen costume (she wore a red wrapper or housecoat, signifying passion). Her aristocratic airs and inflated language further multiply treacheries for the anti-Blanche faction. Indebted to Michel Foucault, William Kleb, for example, argued that Blanche is a disease infecting Stanley's sexually healthy, procreative household and that Stella escaped Belle Reve so she would not end up like her older sister. In truth, Blanche does attempt to break up Stanley's home and to disrupt his conjugal powers. She has also been cast as the figure of death, the white goddess of doom, as Lionel Kelly maintains,

while Calvin Bedient denounces her as the "Mona Lisa of dread."

Stanley Kowalski is Williams's quintessential stud—the "gaudy seed bearer." So indelible was Marlon Brando's representation of Stanley on Broadway and in film that actors playing the part are almost always judged by his characterization and mannerisms, for example, a muscular, naked chest, Vesuvian passion, and intimidating tough guy talk. Everything about Stanley exudes male sexuality and points to **D.H. Lawrence**'s strong influence on Williams's championing the unabashed representation of sexual prowess. Stanley's signature costume is the sweaty T-shirt. Always the hunter, Stanley opens the play by tossing a blood-stained package of meat to Stella. Food is the register of his conquests; he constantly feeds his face or drinks liquor. In Scene Ten, he shakes a bottle of beer and sprays the room with it, an unmistakable phallic symbol of his triumph over Stella and a harbinger of his raping Blanche. His name matches his clamorous behavior (*Stanley* = Old English for "stone"; *Kowalski* = Polish for "blacksmith"). He loves to bowl, and the *Streetcar Named Desire* film shows Stanley in the noisy, brawling world of the bowling alley. Not surprisingly, Stanley is the captain of his bowling team. Loud, brash, vulgar, Stanley fulminates with rancor. He gets into fights with his friends, his neighbors, his wife, Blanche, the people at work. Violence surrounds him.

But above all, Stanley is the ultimate gambler; he wants to win at all costs and is not afraid of taking chances. He was lucky in World War II, surviving the major and dangerous Salerno campaign. He loves card games, especially poker, and in Scenes Three and Eleven, Stanley and his friends are seated around the kitchen table playing cards, quarreling, and maneuvering. In many ways, Stanley recalls Williams's own liquor-

247

swilling, card-playing, pugnacious father, **Cornelius Coffin Williams**. Gambling imagery pervades the play, particularly in Stanley's domestic sphere, where Blanche is dealt a losing hand. He is the winning patriarch whose home is his bastion. Stanley's heroes reflect his gaming, macho values; he quotes Huey P. Long who preached that every man was a king in Louisiana. Stanley further invokes the Napoleonic code, insisting on his right to his wife's (and her family's) possessions, fearing that Blanche has squandered them. If Blanche lives in a fantasy world of romantic beaux and Varsouvianas, Stanley, too, inhabits a world of illusion where red silk pajamas and colored lights trope his sexual conquests. Stanley does have a loving, tender side, but raping Blanche and lying about it are unerasably heinous crimes.

Stella (whose name translates as "star") is a pivotal figure in the *Streetcar Named Desire* world, the prize possession over whom Stanley and Blanche fight to gain control. Unlike her older sister, Stella is not shackled to Belle Reve, which she leaves for Stanley's sexual protection and her pleasures. Her pregnancy is a visible sign of her victory over the past and her devotion to the present. Williams links Stella with even more symbols of satiety—food, liquor, glamour magazines. Some critics have faulted her for abandoning the aesthetic values her sister espouses and wonder how Stella could have ever been a DuBois. But she is an adapter, a survivor. She is at home in Elysian Fields, sharing domestic secrets with and listening to her neighbor Eunice's advice. Throughout the play she persists as Blanche's comforter and advocate, until the last scene when she valorizes Stanley's view of reality over her sister's. Convinced that if she believed Blanche's story, her marriage would end, Stella succumbs to her husband's caress. Likable, kind, and perhaps too forgiving, Stella is both winner and loser.

Mitch is yet another of Williams's unsuitable suitors. Different from Stanley's other friends, Pablo or Steve, Mitch is sensitive and less crude. He is worried about a dying mother and, in his attachment to her, he is satirized by Stanley's crowd as a mama's boy. He fears lonesomeness. Mitch is oafish and uncertain and talks about his weight, his height, and how much he sweats. Symbolically assigned to the spare parts department at Stanley's plant, he is easy prey for Blanche's traps, but in the end he, like she, loses the opportunity for love. His foolish attempt to rape her contrasts with Stanley's brutal success. At the end of the play, Mitch is reduced to monosyllables and weeps as Blanche walks past him without a word on her way to the madhouse. Mitch is sentenced to a type of death, too, because of his own failed romantic dreams, too.

The plot of *A Streetcar Named Desire* is highly symbolic, almost mythic. Though earlier critics faulted Williams for its allegedly episodic structure, *A Streetcar Named Desire* begins promisingly in the spring when Blanche arrives hoping she has found sanctuary with her sister, and possibly a husband in Mitch, but ends in the fall as Blanche, hallucinatory and violated, is carted off to the asylum. John Mood insightfully concludes that the key to Williams's plot is inscribed in the directions Blanche receives at the beginning of the play to find Stella and Stanley's home. The doomed voyager, she travels from Desire (sex, life, hope) to Cemeteries (rape and psychic death in the nightmarish world of Stanley's French Quarter) to Elysian Fields (the land of total forgetfulness).

Carefully structured, the action in *A Streetcar Named Desire* unfolds through a series of analogues, contrasts, echoes, a finely orchestrated network of structural and verbal parallels. Between Scene One and Scene Ten, Blanche constantly plots to escape Stanley, convince Mitch of her pristine eligibility for marriage, and win her sister away from Stanley. Her initial flirtatiousness with Stanley in Scene Two turns to fear in Scene Three. In this crucial scene—"The Poker Night" (one of the original titles Williams considered for *A Streetcar Named Desire*)—Blanche meets Mitch, witnesses Stanley's harrowing domestic violence, and laments her sister's return to an apish husband. This early scene is a microcosm of much of the action in *A Streetcar Named Desire*, where no matter how many stratagems Blanche devises for self-protection, she ultimately remains the outsider, the Other. Her courtship tactics with Mitch, insisting on proper and pristine gentlemanly conduct from him, boldly contrast with the saturnalian outbursts of the Kowalskis and their neighbors, the Hubbles, in Scene Five. The Hubbles provide a satyr play within *A Streetcar Named Desire*, comically contrasting with Stanley and Stella's lovemaking, according to Gilbert Debusscher.

Scene Five shows Blanche flirting with the newspaper boy who collects for the *Evening Star*, another Williams's image of fire, **mythology**, and romanticism. Characteristically, Blanche attempts to seduce the young man through a register of sexual allusions but stops short, no doubt recalling how similar actions led to her dismissal as a teacher. In Williams's brilliant juxtaposition of exits and entrances, the paperboy leaves as the bumbling Mitch enters, whom a whimsically satiric Blanche greets as her "Rosenkavalier," or romantic hero. In Scene Six, which might be titled "The Party's Over," Blanche and Mitch return from their date at Lake Pontchartrain, a fizzled night symbolized by Mitch holding a statue of Mae West (the burlesque queen) upside down, further portraying him as a sexual bungler. Hearing the two most significant sounds in the play— the Varsouviana and the gun shot ending the waltz—Blanche is transported back to her

tortured past. She then confides in Mitch that her young husband, Allan Grey, shot himself at Moon Lake Casino (a perennial Williamsesque site for both fluid desire and sharp danger) after she found him with another man. Structurally, the rhapsodic promise of the waltz, played at gala balls, contrasts with the sleazy, hot blues trumpet from the Four Deuces, Stanley's bar. The unseen Allan Grey, an erased gay man possibly representing the suppressed young homosexual Tom Williams, demands comparison with Mitch's dead girlfriend who gave him a cigarette case with the lovelorn message that she would love him better after death.

Behind the scenes (Five through Seven), Stanley has been investigating Blanche's past, learning that she had been putting on false airs and is notorious in Laurel, from where she was evicted from the shoddy Flamingo Hotel. At Blanche's ill-fated birthday party in Scene Eight, she is stood up by Mitch, whom Stanley has warned not to marry her. In another violent display, Stanley intimidates Blanche and Stella and, terrifyingly, clears the table by shoving dishes and food to the floor. He then gives Blanche a birthday present, a one-way ticket back to Laurel, her greatest fear. In this scene, Williams uses a frequent plot device, the failed dinner, present in *The Glass Menagerie*, **Baby Doll**, and **Small Craft Warnings**. Events move swiftly after the doomed party. Blanche's madness deepens, as she hears more voices, further strains of the Varsouviana, and unanchors even farther from reality. An angry Mitch, unshaven and surly, comes to Stanley's in Scene Nine, finding Blanche alone since Stanley has taken Stella to the hospital to have her baby; she attempts to placate him with Southern Comfort, a sweet liqueur, but when he tries to rape her, she screams "Fire," echoing the street vendor's cry of "Red Hot," at the end of Scene Two (immediately before the fiery poker game in Scene Three). At this point, her impending doom is signaled by the visit of the blind Mexican woman selling flowers for the dead, a figure symbolizing blind fate as well as All Souls Day funerary customs, as Henry Schvey notes.

When Stanley returns in Scene Ten to await the birth of his son who, ironically, is born on Blanche's birthday, 15 September, he waves his red silk pajamas in victory and decides to have some "madhouse" with Blanche. The final action—Scene Eleven—opens with the card players (as in Scene Three), while Eunice and Stella behind the portieres (the stage curtains for Blanche's final exit) ready a delusional Blanche for her last performance, the journey to the asylum. Williams links Blanche to the Madonna, the quintessential suffering queen, through water imagery, grapes, and a Della Robbia blue dress, a contrast from the virginal white she wore at the beginning of the play. Her ideal beau, Shep Huntleigh (with his idyllic sounding name), never shows up. *A Streetcar Named Desire* ends as the doctor, dressed in black, a figure of death as well as the stranger who offers Blanche kindness, escorts her through the room of sober players.

In terms of the play's exploration of the multivalent meanings of desire, neither Stanley nor Blanche is completely victorious. Blanche's story in Scene Eleven does have the last word by following and framing Stanley's malicious history in the deeds of Scenes Nine/Ten, as June Schlueter recognized. But though Blanche departs with dignity, Stella accepts her husband's narrative, who comforts her by putting his hand in her blouse. In the 1951 *A Streetcar Named Desire* film, however, censors rejected Williams's ending since it allowed Stanley to get away with rape and, instead, insisted that Stella leave Stanley as a punishment for his crime. Accordingly, Stella runs up the stairs to Eunice's again, as she did at the end of Scene

Three, vowing never to return to him, an ending of which Williams dissapproved.

A Streetcar Named Desire boasts an illustrious stage history. The play premiered on 3 December 1947 on Broadway at the Ethel Barrymore Theatre and ran for 856 performances. A creation of one of the most impressive collaborations in the theater, *A Streetcar Named Desire* was directed by Elia Kazan, designed by **Jo Mielziner**, and starred Marlon Brando as Stanley, **Jessica Tandy** as Blanche, **Kim Hunter** as Stella, and **Karl Malden** as Mitch. Except for Tandy, the cast members were relative newcomers who began their careers, thanks to *A Streetcar Named Desire*, with numerous awards. Also contributing to the play's success was Alex North's sleazy jazz score and Lucinda Ballard's symbolic costuming. A spin-off from the Broadway production, two road companies took *A Streetcar Named Desire* on tour with Ralph Meeker and Judith Evelyn as Stanley and Blanche in one and Anthony Quinn and Uta Hagen, who succeeded Tandy on Broadway in 1949, in the other.

A smash hit, *A Streetcar Named Desire* premiered on numerous world stages from 1948 to 1951, including Mexico City in 1948; Sweden in 1949 in a production directed by Ingmar Bergman; in Rome in 1949 where Franco Zeffirelli designed the set and Luchino Visconti directed; in Paris in 1949 where Jean Cocteau added black dancers naked from the waist up, to suggest New Orleans eroticism; in London in 1949 with Sir Laurence Olivier directing his wife Vivien Leigh, who would star in the Warner Brothers film; and in Tokyo in 1951. Williams's script was adapted and translated into various cultural signifiers as his haunting description of New Orleans mythologized the city around the globe.

In 1973, *A Streetcar Named Desire* celebrated its twenty-fifth anniversary with bicoastal productions in New York and Los

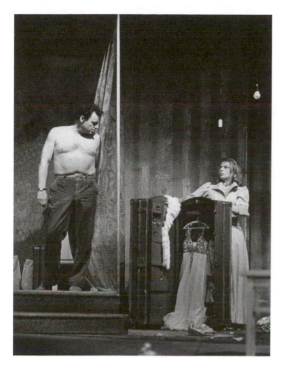

A 1975 East German production of *A Streetcar Named Desire*, directed by Hans Michael Richter, at the Leipziger Theatre, Leipzig, Germany. © 1975 by Helga Wallmüller. Used by permission of Helga Wallmüller.

Angeles. Ellis Rabb directed Rosemary Harris as Blanche, James Farentino as Stanley, Patricia Conolly as Stella, and Philip Bosco as Mitch in the New York production, which critics faulted for its lack of intimacy and because Harris lacked vulnerability and Farentino failed to exude Brando's passion and seductive charm. James Bridges's direction of the Los Angeles *Streetcar Named Desire* in 1973 disappointed critics who claimed that **Hollywood** glamour and realism interfered with Williams's expressionism. Moreover, Jon Voight's new interpretation of Stanley was too tame and too tender, and Faye Dunaway's Blanche was not hysterical enough and too humorous.

Twice *A Streetcar Named Desire* has been made into a teleplay. On 4 March 1984, ABC TV aired a *A Streetcar Named Desire* directed by John Erman and starring Ann-Margret (Williams's choice before he died in 1983) as Blanche, Treat Williams as Stanley, Randy Quaid as Mitch, and Beverly D'Angelo as Stella. Unsurprisingly, the production reflected television violence. Ann-Margret's Blanche was very different from Jessica Tandy's or Uta Hagen's; she was less aristocratic and much more aggressive and sexual. Lacking Brando's charisma, Treat Williams was an exceptionally brutal Stanley; an aerial view of the rape (Scene Ten) is one of the most horrifying and graphic in the history of the play. Randy Quaid portrayed a very convincing Mitch, lumbering awkward, but sincere. A second teleplay of *A Streetcar Named Desire* was broadcast on 29 October 1995 on CBS's *Playhouse 90* staring Jessica Lange and Alec Baldwin, who reprised their roles from their Broadway performances of *A Streetcar Named Desire* in 1992. Less physical than either Brando or Williams, Baldwin showed audiences a subtle, even more crafty, Stanley; Jessica Lange's Blanche was more Baldwin's match in her retorts than Tandy, Leigh, or Ann-Margret had been. John Goodman's Mitch and Diane Lane's Stella also offered some new interpretive twists to their characters. See also **Film Adaptations; Mythology;** *A Streetcar Named Desire* **as Opera.**

Further Reading

Adler, Thomas P. "*A Streetcar Named Desire*": *The Moth and the Lantern*. Boston: Twayne, 1990.

Bedient, Clavin. " 'These Are Lives That Desire Does Not Sustain': *A Streetcar Named Desire*." In *Confronting Tennessee Williams's "A Streetcar Named Desire": Essays in Critical Pluralism*, ed. Philip C. Kolin. Westport, CT: Greenwood, 1993. 45–58.

Clum, John. *Acting Gay: Male Homosexuality in*

American Drama. New York: Columbia University Press, 1992.

Debusscher, Gilbert. "Trois images de la modernité chez Tennessee Williams: Un microanalyse d' *Un Tramway Nommé desire*." *Journal of Dramatic Theory and Criticism* 3 (Fall 1988): 143–156.

Holditch, Kenneth. "The Broken World of Romanticism, Realism, and Naturalism in *A Streetcar Named Desire*." In Confronting *Tennessee Williams's "A Streetcar Named Desire": Essays in Critical Pluralism*, ed. Philip C. Kolin. Westport, CT: Greenwood, 1993. 147–166.

Kelly, Lionel. "The White Goddess, Ethnicity and the Politics of Desire." In *Confronting Tennessee Williams's "A Streetcar Named Desire": Essays in Critical Pluralism*, ed. Philip C. Kolin. Westport, CT: Greenwood, 1993. 121–132.

Kleb, William. "Marginalia: *A Streetcar Named Desire*, Williams, and Foucault." In *Confronting Tennessee Williams's "A Streetcar Named Desire": Essays in Critical Pluralism*, ed. Philip C. Kolin. Westport, CT: Greenwood, 1993. 27–44.

Kolin, Philip C. *Williams: "A Streetcar Named Desire."* Plays in Production. Cambridge: Cambridge University Press, 2000.

Mood, John. "The Structure of *A Streetcar Named Desire*." *Ball State University Forum* 14 (Summer 1973): 9–10.

Murphy, Brenda. *Tennessee Williams and Elia Kazan: A Collaboration in the Theatre*. Cambridge: Cambridge University Press, 1992.

Savran, David. *Communists, Cowboys,* and *Queers: The Politics of Masculinity in the Work of Arthur Miller and Tennessee Williams*. Minneapolis: University of Minnesota Press, 1992.

Schlueter, June. " 'We've had this date with each other from the beginning': Reading toward Closure in *A Streetcar Named Desire*." In *Confronting Tennessee Williams's "A Streetcar Named Desire": Essays in Critical Pluralism*, ed. Philip C. Kolin. Westport, CT: Greenwood, 1993. 71–82.

Schvey, Henry. "Madonna at the Poker Night: Pictorial Elements in *A Streetcar Named Desire*." In *From Cooper to Philip Roth*, ed. J. Bakker and D.R.M. Wilkinson. Amsterdam: Rodopi, 1980. 71–77.

Philip C. Kolin and Maureen Curley

A Streetcar Named Desire as Opera. André Previn and Philip Littell's operatic adaptation of *A Streetcar Named Desire* coincided with a renaissance in the American lyric drama. Even as the recording industry was scaling back its classical division, opera companies were expanding their seasons, their repertories, and perhaps most surprising, their audiences.

The operatically scored *A Streetcar Named Desire* premiered at the War Memorial Opera House in San Francisco in September 1998; it was the most prominent—and easily promoted—contribution to the late 1990s rebirth of American opera. Previn, born in Berlin, was a **Hollywood** composer and arranger whose migration to classical music and marriage to Mia Farrow made him a celebrity. For his operatic debut, *A Streetcar Named Desire*, he and producer Lotfi Mansouri assembled a notable cast: Renee Fleming as Blanche, Rodney Gilfry as Stanley, and Elizabeth Futrel as Stella.

The first cast of a new opera, for better or worse, makes history. Fleming, a physical contrast to her mothlike predecessors, **Jessica Tandy** and **Vivien Leigh**, nicely communicated her character's false gentility; though her occasionally "soft" diction worked against certain aspects of the character, the sheer beauty of her voice enriched the role. Baritone Rodney Gilfry was buff, and for some of the performance barechested. He had no arias—but testosterone to spare, which raised the opera's temperature even as it tended to flatten the character.

Futrel's supple voice and strong presence made her Stella as memorable as any stage actor's. The premiere was recorded and nationally televised, then released on CD (DGG) and video (Image Entertainment). Productions followed in the United States (among other places, San Diego, **New Orleans**, and Austin) as well as in Wales, Australia, and Germany.

Rather like David Selznick's *Gone with the Wind*, Previn and Littell's *A Streetcar Named Desire* persuades audiences that they are seeing the original. Theirs was no mean feat since the Williams estate barred excessive tampering with the play, and leaving room for musical development, the libretto used less than 50 percent of Williams's dialogue. Littell and Previn retained the play's memorable (and most-quoted) moments, like Stanley's bellowing—in speech, not song—for Stella. For the most part, though, they rethought the drama as lyric theater. The morning after Stanley's attack on Stella, she sings a lyric that expresses the allure of Stanley and his colored lights. The dramatization of Stanley's rape occurs in the orchestra, not on the stage, at least not literally. As the music conveys the menace, the set appears to come apart. (Designer Michael Yeargan's work for San Francisco may be seen on video.) The fractured house evokes the sexual assault and, more important, Blanche's psyche: one part genteel southern woman, one part fraud, Blanche has been ripped apart and her emotional collapse made imminent.

Previn's *A Streetcar Named Desire* is not a "numbers" opera; that said, it does contain several arias. Near the end, Blanche sings the genuinely touching "I Can Smell the Sea Air," which demonstrates Previn's ability not only to ingratiate but also to develop a character in **music**. The composer creates an even more touching moment for

Mitch, sung by Anthony Dean Griffey at the premiere; talking with Blanche after their date, Stanley's friend conveys his shyness, his vulnerability, and his impossible attraction to a woman he hardly knows. Several critics were nonetheless unkind to the music; despite dense orchestrations à la Richard Strauss, they said, the music served chiefly as carpeting for the characters' speeches. One wonders, would *Streetcar* the musical (with solos, duets, even ensembles, composed by a man trained in Hollywood) have been more effective than *Streetcar* the opera? Previn himself had second thoughts: in 2001 he thinned the orchestration and reportedly cut 30 minutes from the running time for the Pittsburgh Symphony's "fully staged concert version" of the work.

Whatever its flaws, *Streetcar* the opera reminds audiences that Blanche, not Stanley, lies at the heart of the drama. Previn had of course seen the Warner Brothers' 1951 film and heard Alex North's music for the play and film; the opera, especially its conclusion, he insisted, would be different. North had made the tone of the final curtain music victorious. In the final moments of the opera, however, a hush falls as Blanche leaves with the doctor and the matron. Moreover, she says her famous exit line, "I have always depended on the kindness of strangers," to the audience rather than any character on stage. Williams considered *A Streetcar Named Desire* a tragedy. So did Previn, and as Blanche looks at us, at once faraway and painfully close, so perhaps do we.

Further Reading

Hamlin, Jesse. "Taking *Streetcar* to the Opera." *San Francisco Chronicle*, "Datebook," 6 September 1998: 3.

Kolin, Philip C. *Williams: "A Streetcar Named Desire."* Plays in Production. Cambridge: Cambridge University Press, 2000.

"Notes for *A Streetcar Named Desire*. Librettist

Philip Littell." *Opera News* (September 1998): 40.

Schiff, David. "We Want Magic." *Atlantic Monthly* September 1999: 92–96.

Leonard J. Leff

Suddenly Last Summer. Originally paired with *Something Unspoken* on a double bill titled *Garden District*, *Suddenly Last Summer* is one of Williams's darkest theatrical visions in its depiction of a frighteningly predatory universe. With elements of **mythology** and mysticism, *Suddenly Last Summer* is one of Williams's masterworks, and it is among his most frequently produced plays.

Themes from earlier Williams plays are woven into this otherwise unique portrait of family tragedy, mental illness, and homosexuality set in a florid, Gothic image of the **New Orleans** of Williams's fertile imagination. In the primeval garden of the rotting Venable estate in the summer of 1936, *Suddenly Last Summer* begins in the aftermath of the violent and mysterious death of the young poet Sebastian Venable. Sebastian's imperious mother, Violet, attempts to convince young Dr. Cukrowicz of Lion's View Sanitorium to perform a lobotomy on her distraught niece, Catherine Holly, who has witnessed Sebastian's horrific death. Mrs. Venable, a deeply disturbed and controlling woman, romanticizes her relationship with her son and does not want Catherine's version of Sebastian's death—or his secret life as a homosexual—to prevail over her deification of her son. Despite Mrs. Venable's need to vanquish her foe and her interference with Cukrowicz, the doctor encourages Catherine to confront her blocked memory of Sebastian's final hours during which, she hysterically recounts, he met a grotesquely ritualized death at the hands of a mob of predatory youths he had sexually abused.

Ironically, Sebastian is devoured by his promiscuous sexual appetites in a bleak world where only the most efficient predators survive.

Suddenly Last Summer is among Williams's most autobiographical works, exposing, as he himself once explained, the emotional trauma of his life. Under Dr. **Lawrence Kubie**, Williams's years in psychoanalysis were intended to control his anxieties about his artistic struggles and to "cure" him of his homosexual desires. Instead, as *Suddenly Last Summer* suggests, Williams's time in psychoanalysis served only to increase a deeply held distrust of doctors and his fear of the still-primitive quality of medical technology. In *Suddenly Last Summer*, Williams's sympathetic Dr. Cukrowicz seems to be a caring doctor (if also a somewhat ambivalent one), but he is under significant pressure from his superiors to perform a lobotomy on Catherine at the insistence of Mrs. Venable, in a situation fictionalizing the tragedy of Williams's sister **Rose**, who spent her life institutionalized following an ill-advised bilateral lobotomy that Williams's mother, **Edwina Dakin Williams**, insisted on in response to Rose's emotional turmoil. Complex issues regarding mental illness figure prominently and somewhat ironically in this play as the seemingly sane Mrs. Venable demands treatment for the seemingly disturbed Catherine. As Catherine's account of Sebastian's horrifying end is slowly revealed, Mrs. Venable's tenuous hold on reality snaps, and Catherine seems to be purged of the disturbing memories that have caused her apparent emotional breakdown. Numerous critics, including Jacqueline O'Connor and Steven Bruhm, have discussed mental illness in the play.

Suddenly Last Summer may be an unfair indictment of Williams's mother, but there is

A Citizens' Theatre, Glasgow, Scotland, production of *Suddenly, Last Summer*. Directed and designed by Philip Prowse, with Aleksander Mikic (left) and Ellen Sheean (right). Photographed by Richard Campbell. Courtesy of Citizens' Theatre, Glasgow.

little doubt that Mrs. Venable, the true villain of the play, is culpable of plotting to lobotomize Catherine (just as Williams believed his mother was the force behind his sister's misguided surgery) and for raising a son who is a depraved megalomaniac. *Suddenly Last Summer* offers perhaps his most severe condemnation of Edwina Dakin Williams in a grim portrayal lacking the humor that balances his depiction of her in *The Glass Menagerie*. Other critics have pointed to the play's ritualized death—a bizarre blasphemous Eucharist—of the jaded Sebastian as a self-exorcism for Williams, who sees himself in this promiscuous, homosexual poet. If *The Glass Menagerie* and **Something Cloudy, Something Clear** are more obvious autobiographical fictions, *Suddenly Last Summer* is an emotional autobiography set into a Victorian melodrama. Williams's depiction stresses the deep personal and professional scars resulting from the traumatic experiences of his life, including the dominance of his powerful mother, his sister's tragedy, his own flaws, his artistic frustrations, and his struggle with his sexuality.

The play is also a philosophical rumination on mythology and religious beliefs, the condition (and significance) of the artist in society, of sexual and psychological perversion (in which homosexual desire seems connected to violence), and as an assault on the brutality of a Darwinian modern world. Other studies relate *Suddenly Last Summer* to mid-twentieth-century U.S. politics, with Mrs. Venable representing the forces of fascism (an embodiment of the dictators of Europe and South America) in her savage ruthlessness. Dr. Cukrowicz's seeming acquiescence to Mrs. Venable mirrors the actions of those who observed (instead of actively resisted) Senator Joseph McCarthy's "witch hunt" against alleged communists in American society and government institutions (see **Politics**). As a conflicted homosexual, Williams was certainly sensitive to the fact that McCarthy equated homosexuality with treason. Certainly the play's view of the martyred Sebastian is more complex. The implied subversive politics of *Suddenly Last Summer*, not recognized by critics in its original production, has gained currency in late-twentieth-century scholarship, as the political undertones of Williams's plays have been more fully explored. In the sexual politics of *Suddenly Last Summer*, Williams seems influenced to some extent by Lillian Hellman's *The Children's Hour* where the lie that is told is more damning than the sexual transgression. Mrs. Venable's deceptive depiction of Sebastian and her raising him in a decadent luxury condemns her in Williams's eyes.

A variety of influences—literary and autobiographical—can be found in *Suddenly Last Summer*, from Herman Melville to **Hart Crane** to Williams himself. Melville's "Norfolk Isle and the Chola Widow," dealing to some extent with the notion of the relativity of good and evil, aided Williams in his depiction of Catherine's emotional di-

lemma. As Robert Gross points out, aspects of Crane's life and image as the "poet wanderer" gave Williams a model for Sebastian and the overall tone of this Gothic melodrama. Christian imagery, such as that surrounding the martyrdom of St. Sebastian, also pervades the play, particularly in the character of Sebastian who can be seen as both martyr and rapacious predator. Sebastian is also a nearly allegorical Christlike (or anti-Christlike) figure driven by Mrs. Venable, the defender of Sebastian's artistic goals, while the sensual Catherine embodies sexual desire—from straight and gay love to such perversions as incest and rape. Sebastian's search for God in the Galapagos Islands—where he imagines himself as a sacrifice to a cruel God, as Catherine explains, underscores Williams's daemonic vision of God and man. The attempts by Sebastian and his mother to mask his pederasty are doubtless shaped by Williams's experiences as a gay man in a social environment in which remaining closeted was an unspoken requirement. Mrs. Venable's idealization of her son and her relationship with him, which borders on incest, willfully ignores the obvious fact that Sebastian used his mother as bait for young men. When Mrs. Venable ages to the point that she is no longer an alluring figure, Sebastian cynically turns to Catherine whom he plans to exploit for the same purpose. Despite all this, Mrs. Venable strains to provide a sympathetic image of her son to Cukrowicz, but it is Catherine's critical description of Sebastian that comes nearer the mark, even if a level of sympathy is evinced by her description of his grisly murder.

Several of Williams's earlier plays have also left their imprint on *Suddenly Last Summer*. Grotesque elements and imagery of the natural world connect *Suddenly Last Summer* with Williams's **Camino Real** as well as in its religious (see **Religion**) and literary aspects. Sebastian connects to the sensitive poet, a figure present in virtually all of Williams's dramas (from Tom of *The Glass Menagerie* to Val Xavier of *Orpheus Descending* and Chance Wayne of *Sweet Bird of Youth*), although Williams, usually sympathetic to this oft-employed figure, shows us a poet as a victimizer, despite the fact that Sebastian dies a victim himself. Sebastian's character also connects *Suddenly Last Summer* to several Williams's plays that explore the gap between the spirit and the flesh, but none more so than *The Night of the Iguana* in which the defrocked Reverend Shannon falls into alcoholism and pursuing nymphets to blot out his failure to find God, as well as his own prodigious failings.

Sebastian Venable emerges as a significant character despite the fact that he does not actually appear in the play, but it is Mrs. Venable who may be *Suddenly Last Summer*'s most unforgettable character—a monstrous, grotesque manipulator who relishes the power of her wealth, while her Venus flytrap devours insects as she attempts to devour those around her. Katharine Hepburn and Maggie Smith have interpreted the role on stage and screen to critical favor. The superficially genteel Mrs. Venable, imperious, aggressive, and ruthless, is a hideous variation on an array of Williams's aging women, including Amanda Wingfield of *The Glass Menagerie*, Blanche DuBois of *A Streetcar Named Desire*, Big Mama of *Cat on a Hot Tin Roof*, and Alexandra del Lago of *Sweet Bird of Youth*, among others. The least agreeable aspects of Mrs. Venable tie her closely to at least one non-dramatic Williams woman, Karen Stone, the predatory actress of his 1950 novella *The Roman Spring of Mrs. Stone*, a character in whom Williams mixes vulnerable characteristics with the cruel, selfish will of Mrs. Venable. Karen also represents the decline of the artist seen in Sebastian as well as other Williams char-

acters including Alexandra del Lago and his reinvention of Boris Trigorin in *The Notebook of Trigorin*, his adaptation of Chekhov's *The Sea Gull*, completed near the end of his life.

The predatory bird imagery pervading *The Roman Spring of Mrs. Stone* anticipates many of the horrifying symbols drawn from the natural world in *Suddenly Last Summer*. The decayed Venable mansion reflects the deterioration of Violet's mental state which in turn is mirrored in the primeval garden of carnivorous plants and choking vines. This garden is a reverse Eden—a steamy tropical realm with blood glistening on the leaves of the exotic plants—that is closer to Hell than Heaven. It is a Darwinian universe in which predator and prey coexist before the inevitable devouring of both, most vividly described in Catherine's account of Sebastian's destruction. Animal sounds screech and hiss in this prehistoric landscape as Mrs. Venable's prize Venus flytrap, which she feeds with dead flies, serves as this central symbol underscoring the deadly seductiveness of Mrs. Venable, obscured only by a thin veneer of southern mannerliness. The Venus flytrap may also provide an allusion to the horrific medical experiments and tortures of Hitler's Nazis as well as a more general metaphor for the predatory world Catherine describes. Numerous animal symbols drawn from a hostile natural world also emphasize Williams's key themes, the most powerful of which may be the description of the turtle hatchlings of the Encantadas. When hatched, these vulnerable infants race toward the sea but are instead assaulted by flesh-eating birds who turn them over to reveal their soft underbellies. Their connection to Mrs. Venable's raising of her son is obvious, but the symbol resonates in other parts of the play. For example, Catherine's description of one turtle running away in the wrong direction parallels Sebastian's wrong choices and Mrs.

Venable's plot to have Cukrowicz perform a lobotomy on Catherine seems like the human equivalent of the plant's lethal stratagems. His prior escape into a Buddhist monastery suggests a softness in him—as well as a desire for atonement or salvation—that is of little use in this brutal world. Moreover, Sebastian's exploitation of Catherine as the attraction for his victims finds him preying on her softness.

Suddenly Last Summer was critically applauded in its New York premiere on 7 January 1958 at the York Theatre as part of the *Garden District* double-bill with *Something Unspoken*. Some critics found its unrelenting depiction of a cannibalistic cosmos and the play's more lurid elements shocking, as they did in September 1958 when the play was first produced in London at the Art Theatre (the play was first staged in France in 1965). In 1959, in an expanded screenplay coauthored by Williams and **Gore Vidal**, *Suddenly Last Summer* was filmed under the direction of Joseph Mankiewicz. A notable 1994 Hartford Stage Company production, directed by JoAnne Akalaitis, was acclaimed by critics, and it was followed by a 1995 revival as part of the *Garden District* double-bill with *Something Unspoken* at New York's Circle in the Square featuring Elizabeth Ashley. This production won only mixed reviews, but an earlier 1993 television version starring Maggie Smith, Natasha Richardson, and Rob Lowe was highly praised.

Further Reading

Armato, Philip M. "Tennessee Williams' Meditations on Life and Death in *Suddenly Last Summer*, *The Night of the Iguana*, and *The Milk Train Doesn't Stop Here Anymore*." In *Tennessee Williams: A Tribute*, ed. Jac Tharpe. Jackson: University Press of Mississippi, 1977. 558–570.

Bruhm, Steven. "Blackmailed by Sex: Tennessee Williams and the Economics of Desire." *Modern Drama* 34 (December 1991): 528–537.

Clum, John M. "The Sacrificial Stud and the Fugitive Female in *Suddenly Last Summer*, *Orpheus Descending*, and *Sweet Bird of Youth*." In *The Cambridge Companion to Tennessee Williams*, ed. Matthew C. Roudané. Cambridge: Cambridge University Press, 1997. 128–146.

Colanzi, Rita M. "Tennessee Williams's Revision of *Suddenly Last Summer*." *Journal of Modern Literature* 16.4 (Spring 1990): 651–653.

Ford, Marilyn Claire. "*Suddenly Last Summer*." In *Tennessee Williams: A Guide to Research and Performance*, ed. Philip C. Kolin. Westport, CT: Greenwood, 1998.

Gross, Robert F. "Consuming Hart: Sublimity and Gay *Poetics* in *Suddenly Last Summer*." *Theatre Journal* 47 (1995): 229–251.

Hurley, Paul J. "*Suddenly Last Summer* as 'Morality Play.'" *Modern Drama* 8 (1966): 392–402.

O'Connor, Jacqueline. *Dramatizing Dementia: Madness in the Plays* of Tennessee Williams. Bowling Green, OH: Bowling Green State University Popular Press, 1997.

Parker, Brian. "A Tentative Stemma for Drafts and Revisions of *Suddenly Last Summer*." *Modern Drama* 41 (Summer 1998): 303–326.

Saddik, Annette J. "The (Un) Represented Fragmentation of Body in Tennessee Williams's 'Desire and the Black Masseur' and *Suddenly Last Summer*." *Modern Drama* 41 (Fall 1998): 347–354.

James Fisher

Summer and Smoke. First performed in 1947, *Summer and Smoke* derives from "The Yellow Bird," a short story that was published that same year and introduces Alma Tutwiler as the spinster daughter of a small-town southern minister. The struggle between darkness and light, spirituality and the senses, and love and lust was familiar territory for Williams who rewrote the story of Alma (renamed Winemiller for the plays) once again as *The Eccentricities of a Nightingale* (1964). Williams began *Summer and Smoke*, originally titled *A Chart of Anatomy*, in **St. Louis** as early as February or March 1944 and worked on the script in Mexico, **New Orleans**, Taos, New Mexico, and Nantucket Island between then and 1946.

Containing elements of Williams's life, *Summer and Smoke* echoes **Edwina Dakin Williams**'s tales of her youth in Port Gibson and Natchez, Mississippi. In 1916, the year in which the play is set, Edwina and her children were living with her parents, Reverend **Walter Dakin** and **Rosina Otte Dakin**, in **Clarksdale, Mississippi,** fictionalized in the play as Glorious Hill. Like Reverend Winemiller, Reverend Dakin was an Episcopal minister, and like Alma, Williams grew up at the rectory. Dakin's father had been a small-town doctor like Dr. John Buchanan, and Rosina Otte Dakin had taught piano and voice like Alma, who is called "The Nightingale of the Delta." There were Tutwilers in Clarksdale, as well as other surnames from Williams's life in *Summer and Smoke*: Williams's own first love was **Hazel Kramer;** the name of the salesman is Archie Kramer; and Rosa Gonzales shares her first name with Williams's sister **Rose** and his grandmother, and her last name with Williams's hot-tempered lover in the 1940s, **Pancho Rodriguez y Gonzales.** Both Mrs. Winemiller and Alma manifest characteristics of Williams's sister and mother. The older woman is drawn from the later, clearly disturbed Rose, but Edwina Williams's depiction of her daughter's overreaction to illness echoes Alma's. Edwina Williams, herself called a nightingale, had a streak of Puritanism like Alma. Williams also insisted that he was Alma himself and was haunted

by her while the hedonistic John is a portrait of Williams's father **Cornelius**, who preferred carousing to domesticity and who, in fact, lost part of his ear in a fight over a card game much as John is knifed in a drunken fight while gambling at Moon Lake with Papa Gonzales.

Like other heroines—Blanche from *A Streetcar Named Desire* and Matilda from *You Touched Me!*—Alma is attracted to the thing that will destroy her—a passion for her neighbor, John Buchanan, Jr., the wild young doctor. Alma is the southern gentlewoman, the Puritan; her name is Spanish for "soul." Glorious Hill distrusts and misunderstands her, seeing her as the outsider reaching for something spiritual. John, who clearly represents the body, reality, and the present, is the primitive, elemental, Lawrentian hero of the body. He retreats to his medical practice, the anatomy chart in his office representing his devotion to the physical. His dalliance with dance-hall girl Rosa Gonzales—an escapade that results in two episodes of violence—and finally his engagement to the vital and beautiful Nellie Ewell, one of Alma's former pupils, further shows his attraction to the flesh. Pitted against John's sensual nature, Alma is in an emotional battle. She goes to John's office to offer herself to him but learns he has come over to her spiritual beliefs.

Many other characters in *Summer and Smoke* are also highly symbolic. The two fathers represent mainstream society—Reverend Winemiller, the church; Dr. Buchanan, Sr., the social establishment—which victimizes the outcasts. Alma's literary circle that meets at the rectory, Roger Doremus, Mrs. Bassett, Vernon, and Rosemary, are her fellow outcasts. These misfits contrast with the brawling and gambling Latins like Papa Gonzales and his daughter Rosa, who represent "elemental" and wild humanity. Nellie symbolizes unspoiled vitality for

Williams, while John and Papa Gonzales, who ultimately shoots John's father to death in a drunken rage, may be the male counterparts to Nellie and Rosa. Moon Lake Casino, an emblematic world of gaming, drinking, and sexual escapades, is a familiar Williams locale from other plays like *A Streetcar Named Desire*.

Williams called *Summer and Smoke* a synthetic drama because it presents subjective experience through a unifying symbol. The most prominent is the stone angel, called Eternity, embodying the cold spirituality that separates the houses of John and Alma. It bridges the world of the spirit, symbolized by the rectory, and the body, represented by the doctor's office. The anatomy chart hanging in Dr. Buchanan's office, the importance of which is suggested by the play's original working title, clearly depicts the physical and represents science. Together with these two visual icons of soul and body, Eternity forms a triptych. The angel, which is a fountain, also symbolizes the two sides of Alma: cold stone and life-giving water. Fire is another signature Williams symbol found in abundance in the works of D.H. Lawrence; it is Promethean—a dangerous gift of sexual passion and purification. Aptly, fireworks are seen at the beginning of *Summer and Smoke* and become a recurring emblem of sexual climax and also illumination, expansiveness, and an upward, spiritual impulse. Ironically, Alma talks of the Gothic cathedral, a representation of phallic power and spiritual aspirations. The nightingale, a recurrent symbol (for instance, **Not about Nightingales**), is a night bird (significantly there are no dawn scenes in the play) that is doomed when caged and is Williams's private code word for sexual climax. Finally, the play is symbolically divided into summer and winter, representing fire and ice, the two aspects of Alma, and her passage from a time of blossoming promise to decay—a

progression that haunted Williams all his life.

Most critics condemned Williams for recovering in *Summer and Smoke* the ground he covered previously in **The Glass Menagerie** and *A Streetcar Named Desire*. Reviewers in 1948 found it less dynamic and powerful than *A Streetcar Named Desire* and less moving and magical than *The Glass Menagerie*. Alma was regarded as a pale precursor to Blanche and a wan successor to Laura. Critics charged, too, that the overall point of *Summer and Smoke* was too obvious, with schematic characters representing superficial traits making a simplistic statement. The play's symmetry, too, was attacked as too obvious. Some critics accused Williams of composing an elementary psychology lecture, not a play, because of its symbols. Yet Williams did not intend *Summer and Smoke* to be a totally realistic drama but rather dramatic poetry, as his production notes reveal. Many critics, such as Signi Falk, have called *Summer and Smoke* a tone poem.

Summer and Smoke has been labeled a morality play or a parable of good versus evil, reinforcing the Puritan-Cavalier dichotomy of Williams's heritage. But the play also deals with illusion versus reality and past versus present, as reflected in the title, taken from a line in **Hart Crane**'s poem "Emblems of Conduct." Exploring *Summer and Smoke* from a Freudian point of view, W. David Sievers, for example, suggests that Alma's neurosis results from sexual repression, and she loses John because she becomes his mother image. Other Freudian themes include children contending with controlling parents and the repercussions of inhibited sexuality. In his Jungian analysis, Richard Henry Spero sees *Summer and Smoke* as a journey to self-knowledge in which the would-be lovers are opposites in a struggle toward a superior consciousness.

Mary McDonnell and Harry Hamlin in the Roundabout Theatre Company's 1996 production of *Summer and Smoke*. Photo by Joan Marcus. Used by permission of the Roundabout Theatre.

Summer and Smoke had a successful Dallas premiere directed by **Margo Jones** for her Theatre '47 at the Gulf Oil Theatre in Dallas on 8 July 1947 with Katherine Balfour as Alma and Tod Andrews as John; Jack Warden was the waiter at the Moon Lake Casino. Because *A Streetcar Named Desire* was already playing on Broadway that December, however, *Summer and Smoke* did not open in New York's Music Box Theatre until 6 October 1948, when critics compared the play to *A Streetcar Named Desire* and *The Glass Menagerie*. The production closed on 1 January 1949 after 100 performances.

In 1950, a tour of *Summer and Smoke* starring Dorothy McGuire and John Ireland covered the western United States. On 22 November 1951, the London premiere directed by Peter Glenville opened, and on 24 April 1952, off-Broadway was born as a venue for serious theater when Circle in the Square restaged *Summer and Smoke*, starring Geraldine Page. Running for 356 performances, the revival, directed by José Quintero, was lavishly praised. Two years later, Washington's Arena Stage produced a popular *Summer and Smoke* (9 February–21 March) directed by Alan Schneider with George Grizzard and Frances Sternhagen (Mrs. Winemiller). In July 1986, Christopher Reeve and Laila Robins portrayed the would-be lovers at the Williamstown (Massachusetts) Theatre Festival, and two years later, Marshall Mason directed Reeve for the Center Theatre Group in Los Angeles, opposite Christine Lahti (11 February–1 April).

Summer and Smoke was the first major Williams play, and the only one during his lifetime, to be set to song. Composed by Lee Hoiby with a libretto by **Lanford Wilson**, the opera was debuted on 19 June 1971 by the St. Paul Opera Association. On 23 June 1982, television's Public Broadcasting System aired the 1980 Chicago production.

Further Reading

Adler, Thomas P. "Before the Fall—and After: *Summer and Smoke* and *The Night of the Iguana*." In *The Cambridge Companion to Tennessee Williams*, ed. Matthew C. Roudané. Cambridge: Cambridge University Press, 1997. 114–127.

Brandt, George. "Cinematic Structure in the Work of Tennessee Williams." In *American Theatre*, ed. John Russell Brown and Bernard Harris. London: Edward Arnold, 1967. 163–187.

Falk, Signi. *Tennessee Williams*. Boston: Twayne Publishers, 1978.

Gross, Robert F. "Tracing Lines of Flight in *Summer and Smoke* and *The Milk Train Doesn't Stop Here Anymore*." In *Tennes-*

see *Williams*: *A Casebook*, ed. Robert F. Gross. New York: Routledge, 2002. 91–106.

Sievers, W. David. *Freud on Broadway: A History of Psychoanalysis and the American Drama*. New York: Hermitage, 1970.

Spero, Richard Henry. "The Jungian World of Tennessee Williams." Ph.D. dissertation, University of Wisconsin, 1970.

Williams, Tennessee. "Questions without Answers." *New York Times* 3 October 1948, sec. 2: 1, 3.

Richard E. Kramer

Sweet Bird of Youth. *Sweet Bird of Youth* (1959) is one of Williams's self-described "violent" plays and one of the most torrid and gruesome plays in the canon. *Sweet Bird of Youth* focuses on castration—physical, emotional, and psychological. At its core, the play reflects Williams's own preoccupying concern with the castrating effects of time, the implacable enemy of both the playwright and his creations. Thematically, Williams was not only interested in exploring the issue of tangible loss such as the inescapable aging of the body; he was also exploring loss caused by self-betrayal due to corruption of the mind, body, and spirit. *Sweet Bird of Youth* can thus be seen as an intimate portrait of Williams's inner life. The play also brings to light the damaging effects caused by intense competition brought to bear by a capitalist and racist society, affecting Williams the playwright.

Williams wrote the play during some of his most psychologically troubled years. This full-length *Sweet Bird of Youth* emerges from two shorter plays—*Sweet Bird of Youth* (featuring Chance and Princess) and *The Pink Bedroom*, featuring what was to become the Boss Finley plot line and the essence of the second act. The earliest version of the play was staged in 1956 in Coral Ga-bles, Florida, but, in typical Williams fashion, between this time and the Broadway opening in 1959 the play underwent many revisions, which Brenda Murphy has carefully documented. Essentially, *Sweet Bird of Youth* began as a two-character play focusing on the troubled relationship between Chance and Princess, encompassing what are now the first and third acts of the play. Working with **Elia Kazan**, Williams added a plethora of new characters and a subplot concerning Boss Finley's political power and the castration of a black man from *The Pink Bedroom*.

The plot of *Sweet Bird of Youth* centers on the return of Chance Wayne to his hometown, St. Cloud, on the Gulf Coast on Easter Sunday, a symbolic place and a symbolic time. Upon his arrival, Chance has in tow the aging movie star named Alexandra del Lago, who is referred to as Princess Kosmonopolis. He returns to find the love of his life, Heavenly Finley, who, in his absence, suffered through a hysterectomy at the age of 15 after she contracted syphilis from Chance. His reception in town is contradictory: some remember him as the bright young man of promise but the Finley family hates him and pushes him to leave. The metaphor in Williams's title is thus central to the play's construction because the main characters are in desperate flight—the Princess is seeking refuge from **Hollywood** and from what she thinks will be horrible reviews of her latest film. Inwardly, she tries to escape personal demons through various debaucheries such as casual sex, heavy drinking, and **drugs**, all escapes well known by Williams himself. Chance has a big dream—he imagines not only marrying Heavenly but taking her with him back to Hollywood to star in films together, thus fleeing the small southern town that stifles their love. Heavenly's father, Boss Finley, seeks revenge for what Chance did to his

Geraldine Page and Paul Newman in *Sweet Bird of Youth*, directed by Elia Kazan, 1959. Springer/Photofest.

daughter and vows to castrate Wayne, should he stay in town. But Chance is determined to leave with Heavenly and sees his best opportunity to escape when the Princess is on the phone talking with a Hollywood columnist (who in the film version is Walter Winchell) and learns she was wrong about her movie; it was a smash hit. Chance begs the Princess to tell the columnist about two bright discoveries, emerging stars—Heavenly and himself. But she completely ignores his pleas. Devastated, he loses his will to continue the flight. The Princess seemingly regains her confidence, though in the stage directions Williams stresses that she knows her life will not be one success after another. He notes that they are both "castrated" but in different ways. Though Alexandra begs Chance to come with her, he chooses not to and, in a surprise ending, accepts the fate planned for him by Boss Finley and his son, Tom Junior, a pernicious tool of his father. A subplot concerning Boss Finley's political career as a bigoted demagogue reveals Williams's continuing diatribe against racism in the South. Together with *Orpheus Descending* and *Kingdom of Earth, Sweet Bird of Youth* explores the lurid and despicable aspects of southern culture Williams could not tolerate.

Williams was heavily influenced by the European symbolists. Not surprisingly, *Sweet Bird of Youth* abounds with symbolism of three kinds: classical/mythological (see **Mythology**), Christian, and Freudian. Many critics found *Sweet Bird of Youth* beautiful and convincing, comparing it with the timelessness of a Greek myth. From the classical world, we can find parallels between Chance and Adonis, two beautiful youths linked with fertility and self-destruction. Alexandra del Lago has been compared to Aphrodite; her name "Alexandra" has its roots in the classical world with Alexander the Great but also to Cassandra, the self-destructive seer from *The Illiad*. Even her alias, the Princess Kosmonopolis, roughly signifies in Greek the state or nature of the Universe. Appropriately, St. Cloud and the Gulf Coast have mythological roots linking the play to the Mediterranean world as well as, ironically, to an imaginary paradise of love and hope. From the start of the play, Williams notes a "vaguely Moorish" atmosphere in the hotel, where the grove of Royal Palm trees outside the Royal Palms Hotel suggests metaphorically and the Island of Cyprus, giving the illusion of an island of escape and solitude, a place of exile. Christian symbolism also abounds. The play is set on Easter Sunday, a day clearly reflective of hope and resurrection, but also evokes the grisly horrors of Good Friday and the death of Christ. Yet Chance is an unsuccessful savior in *Sweet Bird of Youth*. Boss Finley emphasizes that he was symbolically crucified by being burned in effigy on Good Friday. Finally, a host of Freudian symbols include an image of Chance climbing a giant beanstalk (a phallic reference) as well as several scenes between Chance and the Princess that suggest an Oedipal interpretation of the action. Some critics believed that Williams overloaded *Sweet Bird of Youth* by using so much symbolism.

But Williams combined his signature symbolism with gritty realism and the driving force of inevitability driving the characters to make *Sweet Bird of Youth* gut-wrenchingly honest theater. He puts sexuality frankly on the theatrical landscape, with female lust and the ramifications of promiscuous sex on display. Chance's role and reputation in the sexual politics of *Sweet Bird of Youth* have been much discussed. Is he a self-serving gigolo or Heavenly's devoted lover? His sexuality, like other elements in *Sweet Bird of Youth*, is open to charges of mendacity and venality. The Princess is also sexually a strong player. For example, she is able to enjoy playing with Chance as if he were a sexual object without any real negative consequences. Heavenly, by contrast, not only suffers from the physical effects of the hysterectomy but must face the shame that comes from having her father, brother, and many other people in St. Cloud know about it. While not especially lurid or thematically risky today, *Sweet Bird of Youth* startled audiences in the 1950s, both in the theater and in its film version.

While *A Streetcar Named Desire*, *The Glass Menagerie*, and *Cat on a Hot Tin Roof* are universally regarded as Williams's best plays, *Sweet Bird of Youth* seems to fall in the second tier of his works. A major complaint is that Williams's characters, especially Princess, are reminiscent of Norma Desmond in Billy Wilder's *Sunset Boulevard* which make use of the over-the-hill movie star and the kept male counterpart. The characters are too much like Williams's other famous creations. Like Blanche, Chance's main goal is to recapture the feeling of youthful love which was lost, and, like her again (and apparently Williams himself) he endeavors to escape his pain through casual sex, drugs, and booze. For some critics, Boss Finley shares too many characteristics with Big Daddy from *Cat on a Hot Tin*

Roof. Heavenly, conversely, is often viewed as an underdeveloped, cameo role instead of a more fully realized character. A cadre of contradictory terms have been used to describe the play as a whole—brash, sentimental, symbolic, and mythic, yet Williams combines these diverse elements in *Sweet Bird of Youth* for grand theater.

A smash hit, *Sweet Bird of Youth* premiered on Broadway in 1959 at the Martin Beck Theatre and ran for 375 performances, starring Paul Newman (as Chance) and Geraldine Page (as the Princess), who reprised their Broadway parts for the film version of the play in 1961. The play was directed by Elia Kazan and designed by Jo Mielziner who brought success to many earlier Williams plays. The 1975 New York revival directed by Michael Kahn, starring Christopher Walken as Chance and Irene Wolf as the Princess, was more favorably reviewed than the premiere. Perhaps the most successful revival, however, came in the 1994 production staged by the British National Theatre. Reminiscent of Page's performance, Claire Higgins captured the essence of both sides of the Princess. Higgins could be as bold and over the top as Norma Desmond in the final moments of *Sunset Boulevard* or as insecure and shattered as Blanche in her weakest moments in *A Streetcar Named Desire.* The success of the play for audiences has hinged on the ability of the actress playing the "Princess" Alexandra del Lago to bring out her multidimensional character. Many actresses have powerfully interpreted the role, including Lauren Bacall in London and Joanne Woodward in Toronto. See also **Race; Religion; Southern Culture and Literature.**

Further Reading

Boxill, Roger. *Tennessee Williams.* New York: St. Martin's, 1987.

Clum, John. "The Sacrificial Stud and the Fugitive Female in *Suddenly Last Summer, Orpheus Descending, and Sweet Bird of Youth.*" In *The Cambridge Companion to Tennessee Williams,* ed. Matthew C. Roudané. Cambridge: Cambridge University Press, 1997. 128–146.

Colanzi, Rita. "Caged Birds: Bad Faith in Tennessee Williams's Drama." *Modern Drama* 35 (1992): 461–465.

Dukore, Bernard F. "American Abelard: A Footnote to *Sweet Bird of Youth.*" *College English* 26 (May 1965): 630–634.

Hays, Peter L. "Tennessee Williams's Use of Myth in *Sweet Bird of Youth.*" *Educational Theatre Journal* 18 (October 1966): 255–258.

Murphy, Brenda. *Tennessee Williams and Elia Kazan: A Collaboration in the Theatre.* Cambridge: Cambridge University Press, 1992.

Thompson, Judith J. *Tennessee Williams' Plays: Memory, Myth and Symbol.* Rev. ed. New York: Lang, 2002.

John Rindo

T

Tandy, Jessica (1909–1994). Jessica Tandy was born in London, England, as Jessie Alice Tandy. She was the first Blanche DuBois in the Broadway premiere of Tennessee Williams's *A Streetcar Named Desire* (1947). Williams first met Tandy in January 1947 when her husband, actor-director **Hume Cronyn**, directed Tandy in a production of Williams's *Portrait of a Madonna*, a one-act drama in which the main character, Lucretia Collins, sees a former lover in a hallucination that leads to her being sent to a mental institution (see *Twenty-seven Wagons Full of Cotton and Other One-Act Plays*). Along with *A Streetcar Named Desire* director, **Elia Kazan**, Williams saw Tandy in the Cronyn-directed production of *Madonna*, a small play many scholars regard as the seedling from which *A Streetcar Named Desire* sprang. By all accounts, Tandy's performance caused them to drop their plans of casting either Katharine Cornell or **Tallulah Bankhead** as Blanche.

Tandy's interpretation of Blanche, under Kazan's guidance, emphasized, as she later told writer Marguerite Steen, Blanche's "intricate and complex background—her in-domitable spirit—her innate tenderness and honesty—her untruthfulness or manipulating truth—her inevitable tragedy." Tandy's patrician and intelligent Blanche won her generally enthusiastic reviews (although dissenters complained that her performance was excessive and too theatrical), and she performed the role for over a year and a half, becoming, as Harry Rasky writes, the Blanche against which all future Blanches would be judged. Later notable Blanches, Uta Hagen, Rosemary Harris, Ann-Margret, and Jessica Lange, among others, all brought their unique qualities to the play, but none managed to capture the dignity and fragility most critics describe in Tandy's performance. The critics especially praised Tandy's ability to give Blanche's descent into madness a nobility, that her mastery of Blanche's neuroses and hysteria was at once clinically real and theatrically majestic, and that she imbued the character with a memorable fragility against which **Marlon Brando**'s Stanley Kowalski could register with particular effectiveness. Regarding Blanche's nymphomania, critics uniformly agreed that Tandy's innate poise kept this aspect of the character from falling into caricature or vulgarity, managing the difficult task of being seductive without being scandalous. Tandy refused to pose as the sexualized Blanche found in **Thomas Hart Benton**'s painting of *A Streetcar Named Desire*.

A Streetcar Named Desire won Tandy acclaim and stage stardom, but she was passed over for the role when the 1951 film was made because she had only had comparatively minor success in supporting roles in movies prior to this time. She was not thought of as a screen actress, and producers felt she had no box office appeal. While her *Streetcar Named Desire* stage co-stars, Brando, **Karl Malden**, and **Kim Hunter**, carried their roles over to the screen, English actress **Vivien Leigh**, who won her second Academy Award for her performance, replaced Tandy.

Despite the inevitable disappointment of being left out of the film, Tandy later played Blanche on television in 1955 and appeared in other Williams roles, including Marguerite Gautier in **Camino Real** in a 1970 New York revival featuring Al Pacino as Kilroy. Tandy's Marguerite profited from her strong sense of the theatrical and the fragility inherent in her Blanche DuBois. Tandy also appeared in a short-lived 1983 revival of *The Glass Menagerie*, playing Amanda Wingfield, a role she had recorded for Caedmon Records in 1964 with Montgomery Clift, Julie Harris, and David Wayne in support. She performed one of Blanche DuBois's speeches from *A Streetcar Named Desire* in a 1973 television documentary about Williams called *Tennessee Williams' South*, and in 1977 Tandy and Cronyn appeared in a series of scenes from Williams's plays on a CBC-TV (Canada) special, *Many Faces of Love*. They later performed this Williams "concert recital" on television. Along with a 1948 television performance of *Portrait of a Madonna*, Cronyn again directed Tandy in

this Williams one-act classic as part of a bill of one-acts titled *Triple Play* for a successful national tour in the summer of 1958.

Overlooked for the role of Blanche DuBois on screen, near the end of her life she became one of **Hollywood**'s most beloved character actresses, appearing most significantly in *Driving Miss Daisy* (1989), for which, at age 80, she became the oldest recipient ever of an Academy Award for Best Actress. Appropriately, Tandy won this award by playing an elderly southern woman who might easily be imagined as a distant cousin of Blanche DuBois.

Further Reading

Barranger, M.S. *Jessica Tandy: A Bio-Bibliography*. Westport, CT: Greenwood, 1991.
Kolin, Philip C. *Williams: "A Streetcar Named Desire."* Plays in Production. Cambridge: Cambridge University Press, 2000.
Rasky, Harry. *Tennessee Williams: A Portrait in Laughter and Lamentation*. New York: Dodd, 1986.
Spector, Susan. "Alternative Visions of Blanche DuBois: Uta Hagen and Jessica Tandy." *Modern Drama* 32 (1989): 545–561.
Steen, Marguerite. *A Pride of Terry's: A Family Saga*. Westport, CT: Greenwood, 1978.

James Fisher

Taylor, Laurette (1884–1946). Once touted by Stanislavsky as the greatest of America's actresses, Laurette Taylor came out of retirement to score a triumphant comeback in the role of Amanda Wingfield in *The Glass Menagerie*. Born Laurette Cooney, she achieved stardom in 1912 in *Peg O'My Heart*, written by her husband J. Hartley Manners—whose death in 1928 caused her to retreat from the stage. George Jean Nathan suggested her for the part of Amanda in a vehicle that Taylor called "a beautiful—a wonderful—a great play!" Despite difficulty with learning her lines, with adopting a southern accent, with alcoholism, and with the onslaught of the cancer that would shortly take her life, Taylor gave an incandescent performance that became legendary, earning her 24 curtain calls on opening night in New York. Her reviews so outshone those of **Eddie Dowling**, her costar and director, that it created backstage friction. Taylor famously taunted **Edwina Williams**, the playwright's mother, over how she liked seeing herself portrayed on stage as "a fool," and she reportedly found Tennessee's father, **Cornelius**, "dull." But in his letters, Williams himself affectionately called Taylor "a grand old girl," while in his *Memoirs* he praised her "heroic perseverance" and "magnificent art." Hailing her performance as "incredibly luminous, electrifying," he felt that as an actress she ranked with Sarah Bernhardt and Eleonora Duse.

Further Reading

Leverich, Lyle. *Tom: The Unknown Tennessee Williams.* New York: Crown, 1995.

Thomas P. Adler

Tennessee Williams/New Orleans Literary Festival. The Tennessee Williams/New Orleans Literary Festival was founded in 1986 by a group of New Orleanians who shared a desire to celebrate and showcase this region's rich cultural heritage, particularly the special bond between **New Orleans** and Tennessee Williams, who considered the city his spiritual home. It brings writers and performers to New Orleans and provides educational programs for the general public. Activities offered at the Festival include master classes, theater performances, readings, celebrity interviews, literary panel discussions, the Tennessee Williams Scholars' Conference, a book fair, walking tours, and more. The five-day event occurs in March each year, with the bulk of activities taking place in the city's fabled French Quarter. Le Petit Théâtre du Vieux Carré, the third-oldest community theater in the United States, serves as the Festival headquarters. Additional Festival sites include the Cabildo of the Louisiana State Museum, the Historic New Orleans Collection, and the Palm Court Jazz Café.

From an ambitious start with 500 audience members enjoying a two-day program, attendance has increased more than 10-fold, and programming has expanded to five days and nights. The seventeenth annual event in 2003 attained a new attendance record of over 10,000 audience members. *USA Today* has described the Festival as "one of the most important literary festivals in the country." There are three principal components: literary programming, theatrical presentations, and special events.

The literary component has two main activities: panel discussions that provide a public forum on a diverse array of topics, and master classes with more intensive workshop sessions with a notable author or literary expert. The panel discussion "I Remember Tennessee" is a recurring feature of every Festival and has included biographer Lyle Leverich, friend and collaborator Donald Windham, **Dakin Williams**, and **Kim Hunter** (Stella in *A Streetcar Named Desire*'s Broadway premiere and 1951 film). More than two dozen panels are presented each season, a number of which are devoted to Williams's life, work, influence, and performance.

The theater component is, logically enough, powerfully focused on the Williams legacy. The Festival produces one—and more recently, two—full production of a Williams play each year, including major plays such as *Sweet Bird of Youth*, *A Streetcar Named Desire*, and *The Night of the Iguana*, as well as lesser-known works such as *Tiger Tail*, *Small Craft Warnings*, and his seldom-seen one-acts, such as *The Travelling Companion*. These plays are augmented by coproductions of other works by Williams presented as staged readings and featuring the participation of notable actors, including **Eli Wallach**, Anne Jackson, Alec Baldwin, and Elizabeth Ashley.

The Tennessee Williams Scholars' Conference is an integral part of this Festival honoring the playwright and exploring his ideas, dramatic techniques, and influences. Inaugurated at the Festival's tenth anniversary, the Scholars' Conference provides an opportunity for leading literary critics and biographers to exchange information and take part in discussions on the work of America's greatest playwright.

Further Reading

Cappel, Cherry. "18th Annual Tennessee Williams/New Orleans Literary Festival." www.tennesseewilliams.net.

Donovan, Sharon. "Stella, Streetcars, and Scholars." *Southern Accents* (March 1999): 24–32.

Lou Anne Morehouse

Texts. The state of Tennessee Williams's texts, including both unpublished papers and published works, can be explained in large part by two characteristic features of Williams's writing process: (1) Williams never though of a work as finished; and (2) Williams frequently worked on more than one writing project at a time. Thus, similarities among characters or thematic parallels can often be traced to texts on which Williams was working at approximately the same time. Since Williams also wrote short stories, novels, poetry, and essays, the genesis of some plays can be traced to works in a different genre. Among some of the more famous examples, *The Glass Menagerie* began as a short story called "Portrait of a Girl in Glass"; *Summer and Smoke* began as "The Yellow Bird." "Two on a Party" was the fictional basis for *Sweet Bird of Youth*, just as a story called "The Night of the Iguana" became a play with the same title. "The Knightly Quest," a novella, eventually became *The Red Devil Battery Sign*.

Throughout Williams's career the pattern of simultaneous composition and repeated revision occurs again and again. Conceived originally as part of a trilogy of plays, *Battle of Angels* resembles in theme and/or characterization other dramas on which Williams was working at the time. In the series of three plays that Williams imagined as part of a southern trilogy, *Battle of Angels* was to follow both *Spring Storm* (written in 1937 but not published until 1999) and *The Aristocrats* (the name for an idea that would later become *A Streetcar Named Desire*). Over a period of 17 years, Williams continued to revise the play, culminating with the Broadway production of the play, revised and retitled as *Orpheus Descending*. Other plays, such as *Summer and Smoke*, *Camino Real*, and *The Two-Character Play (Out Cry)*, underwent similar transformations. At the same time that Williams was writing *Summer and Smoke*, for example, he was also drafting *A Streetcar Named Desire*. In the wake of *A Streetcar Named Desire*'s phenomenal success in 1947, however, *Summer and Smoke* failed to live up to the high expectations set by Williams's most successful play. Thinking that he had indeed failed with *Summer and Smoke*, Williams continued to revise it. More than 20 years later, it would reappear—staged in 1976 at the Arena Theatre (Buffalo, New York)—as *The Eccentricities of a Nightingale*.

Unlike *Battle of Angels* and *Summer and Smoke*, *Camino Real* began as a shorter work, "Ten Blocks on the Camino Real," and was expanded (to 16 blocks) for its Broadway debut in 1953. Similar to these earlier plays, however, it failed to find its audience and closed after a brief run, a failure than Williams might better have anticipated.

When Williams showed the shorter version of the play to his agent, **Audrey Wood**, she advised Williams to put the play away—for a long time—and recommended against its publication. Acting against her apparently better judgment, Williams not only published "Ten Blocks on the Camino Real" (in a collection of short plays called *American Blues*, 1948) but also insisted on revising the work for production.

With other works Williams was equally persistent. Following the unsuccessful production of *The Two-Character Play* at the Hampstead Theatre Club in London in 1967, Williams rewrote the play as *Out Cry*. It would be performed in Chicago in 1971 and then in New York in 1973 before Williams would revert to the earlier title for a New York production in 1975. These transformations are reflected also in three different published versions of the play: *The Two-Character Play* (1969), *Out Cry* (1973), and again as *The Two-Character Play* (1979), all published by New Directions.

In some cases, the published record of transformation represents a small portion of the changes Williams may have made to a particular dramatic work, as the case of *The Red Devil Battery Sign* illustrates. Although *The Red Devil Battery Sign* is published in two editions, at least four different versions of the script exist, each corresponding to a different production of the play. *The Red Devil Battery Sign* was first performed in June 1975 at the Shubert Theatre in Boston. Williams then revised the script for a January 1976 production at Vienna's English Theatre. Two other performances, a 1977 production at the London Roundhouse Theatre and a 1980 production at the Vancouver Playhouse Theatre, also incorporate changes that Williams made to the script. Many of the reviews and critical assessments of the play thus often refer to material (e.g.,

references to the assassination of John F. Kennedy) that is not included in published editions of the play.

The physical record of this writing process, the result of more than four decades of persistent composition and revision, is a huge assortment of papers, many of them organized just as Williams left them on the drafting room floor—unnumbered, undated, and haphazardly assembled. For the 10 years immediately following the death of Tennessee Williams, Maria St. Just (**Maria Britneva**), executrix of the Williams estate, limited scholars' access to materials and restricted the publication of unpublished materials. During that time, only *The Red Devil Battery Sign* (1988) and a short play called **The Chalky White Substance** (1991) were published. Since St. Just's death in 1993, restrictions on access to Williams's papers have been eased, and six previously unpublished plays have been edited for publication: **Something Cloudy, Something Clear** (1995); **The Notebook of Trigorin** (1997), an adaptation of **Anton Chekhov**'s *The Seagull*; *Not about* **Nightingales** (1998); **Spring Storm** (1999); **Stairs to the Roof** (2000); and **Fugitive Kind** (2001), and another *Candles to the Sun* is forthcoming.

In addition to these posthumous play publications, Williams's work in other genres is now beginning to appear in print. Albert Devlin and Nancy Tischler plan to publish more than 1,200 letters in *The Selected Letters of Tennessee Williams* (in two volumes). The publication of Williams's private **journals** (Yale 2003), like the publication of his **correspondence**, will add to the growing interest in Williams's biography and the genesis of his dramatic work. Moreover, scholarly work, such as Brian Parker's pioneering effort to trace the development of plays such as *The Rose Tattoo* and *The Night of the Iguana* (by organizing and describing the extant unpublished typescripts) promises to facilitate the study of Williams and to shed additional light on the more familiar published texts.

Williams's major dramatic works were usually published in separate editions soon after the Broadway or first major production of the play. A separately published English edition (at least for the major plays) usually followed the first American edition. In 1956 Secker & Warburg succeeded John Lehmann as Williams's publisher in Great Britain.

The history of Williams's publications in the United States and abroad is one index of the playwright's popularity. The success of *The Glass Menagerie*, for example, is indicated by its publication in many editions. First published by Random House (1945), it has since been published by John Lehmann (1948), the Dramatists Play Service (1948 and 1957), Secker & Warburg (1956), New Directions (1970), and the New American Library (1987). It has also been published in English-language editions and in translations abroad. As an indication of its international appeal, *The Glass Menagerie* has been translated into more than 25 different languages.

Just as the typescripts of Williams's plays reveal a startling number of alterations, Williams's published works appear in many variant forms. The English edition of *The Glass Menagerie*, for instance, includes more than 1,100 changes from the first American edition. Williams saw the first London production of the play as an opportunity to revise the text, and many of these changes are incorporated into the John Lehmann edition.

The publication of *A Streetcar Named Desire* illustrates another consequence of the variable nature of stage production and the attempt to preserve the text of the production in print. Wanting to capitalize on the success of *A Streetcar Named Desire* at the box office, James Laughlin rushed to get the text of the play into print soon after its opening night on Broadway on 3 December

1947. By 22 December 1947, 5,080 copies of *A Streetcar Named Desire* went on sale. In his haste, Laughlin relied on an early script of the play that was subsequently revised. As a result, the first printing of *A Streetcar Named Desire* published by New Directions includes errors that were corrected in subsequent printings of the play (the second and the third). It was not until the fifth printing of the play, released more than two months after opening night, that New Directions published a version of *A Streetcar Named Desire* that more nearly reflected the play as it was staged on Broadway (the fifth printing incorporates 91 substantive changes to the text).

Of the many plays that include textual variation, **Cat on a Hot Tin Roof** may be the one most widely known for its controversial revisions. Similar to other plays in the Williams canon, *Cat on a Hot Tin Roof* began as a short story called "Three Players of a Summer Game." In the spring of 1954, Williams then reimagined the story as a full-length play and began to revise it. After completing one version of the play, Williams shared the script with director **Elia Kazan**, who had previously directed both *A Streetcar Named Desire* and *Camino Real*. At the same time that Kazan was enthusiastic about the prospect of directing another Williams play, he suggested three major changes to the text that Williams willingly incorporated. Specifically, Kazan suggested first that the character Big Daddy reappear in the third act of the play (in Williams's original version, Big Daddy exits at the end of the second act, never to return); second, Kazan recommended that Brick undergo a transformation in character; and third, he thought that Maggie should be made more sympathetic to the audience. Although Williams agreed to the changes, he nevertheless doubted the wisdom of Kazan's advice. In a move that surprised the director, Williams published both the Broadway version of the third act and his original version (in a single New Directions edition). In a note of explanation, sandwiched between the two third acts, Williams claimed that he embraced only the third of Kazan's suggestions wholeheartedly and that he preferred his original script.

Apart from these changes to *Cat on a Hot Tin Roof*, Williams would continue to revise the text. The "acting edition" published by the Dramatists Play Service, for example, includes a passage about "mendacity" that is absent from other published editions of the play. When *Cat on a Hot Tin Roof* was revived in 1974, staged first at the American Shakespeare Theatre in Stratford, Connecticut, and then at the ANTA Theatre in New York, Williams created a hybrid of the original and Broadway versions of the third act. The 1975 New Directions edition thus includes 174 substantive changes to the text.

Just as the publication history of Williams's work provides insight into the creative process, it also offers readers an index to the fluctuating popularity of the author's work. In the 1960s, for example, New Directions published some of Williams's plays in smaller numbers. For instance, only 4,000 copies of **The Milk Train Doesn't Stop Here Anymore** (1964) were printed (without a second printing). Similarly, **Kingdom of Earth** (1968) appeared in only one printing of 4,000 copies (of which 1,175 were destroyed). With over 10,000 copies in print, **Small Craft Warnings** (1972) and **Vieux Carré** (1979) may be numbered among the more successful works by Williams during the later part of his career.

Just as Williams frequently revised his dramatic work, he also revised his fiction, poetry, and nonfiction, although instances of textual variation in these published texts are fewer in number than in the plays. Even so,

the fictional texts are of special interest because of their sometimes controversial subject matter. Sensitive to the content of his first collection of stories, *One Arm* (1949), Williams requested that copies be sold by subscription rather than by general display.

Apart from the regularly issued plays, poems, and short stories, other works by Williams have been published and sold in special editions, limited to a small number of copies. These editions include, for example, *Grand* (1964), *It Happened the Day the Sun Rose* (1981), **The Remarkable Rooming-House of Mme. Le Monde** (1984), and *Steps Must Be Gentle* (1980).

Other Williams texts are of interest because of accidental errors overlooked by the publishers. *American Blues* (1948), the first collection of plays by Williams to be published by the Dramatists Play Service, is exceptional because it was printed with Williams's name misspelled "Tennesse" on the front cover. **Period of Adjustment** (1960) was altered soon after publication because the publisher feared that it contained libelous material. The second printing, appearing just two weeks after the first printing, changes the setting of the play from Memphis to a fictional town called Dixon. Apparently unknown to the publisher, one appearance of "Memphis" is unchanged in the second printing.

As these many examples illustrate, the textual history of Williams's typescripts and published texts is complicated by multiple versions that scholars are just now beginning to study in systematic fashion. As of yet, there is no scholarly edition of the works of Tennessee Williams. The best available collections now include *The Theatre of Tennessee Williams* (New Directions, 1971–1992) and the compilation published in 2000 by the Library of America, edited by Mel Gussow and Kenneth Holditch—*Tennessee Wil-*

liams: *Plays 1937–1955* and *Tennessee Williams: Plays 1957–1980*. See also **Collected Stories**; **Journals**; **Poems**.

Further Reading

Crandell, George W. *Tennessee Williams: A Descriptive Bibliography*. Pittsburgh: University of Pittsburgh Press, 1995.

Parker, Brian. "Documentary Sources for *Camino Real*." *Tennessee Williams Annual Review* 1 (1998): 41–52.

———. "A Preliminary Stemma for Drafts and Revisions of Tennessee Williams's *Cat on a Hot Tin Roof* (1955)." *Publications of the Bibliographical Society of America* 90 (1996): 475–496.

———. "A Provisional Stemma for Drafts, Alternatives, and Revision of Tennessee Williams's *The Rose Tattoo* (1951)." *Modern Drama* 40 (1997): 279–294.

———. "A Tentative Stemma for Drafts and Revisions of Tennessee Williams's *Suddenly Last Summer* (1958)." *Modern Drama* 41 (1998): 303–326.

George W. Crandell

Thacher, Molly Day (1906–1963). Molly Day Thacher entered Williams's life at a pivotal moment, providing him both with confidence and with his first and vital agent. After graduation from Vassar and two years at the Yale Drama School, Thacher moved to New York and married director **Elia Kazan** in 1932. She edited the magazine *New Theatre*, wrote plays, and was a playreader for the Theatre Guild (where she championed Robert Anderson's *Tea and Sympathy*) and headed the **Group Theatre**'s Play Department and later the Playwrighting Division of the Actors Studio.

In 1938, the Group Theatre announced a contest for playwrights aged 25 and under. Williams was 27 at the time, but figuring he could subtract his years spent in factory work, he entered anyway, submitting *Fugi-*

tive Kind, **Candles to the Sun**, **Spring Storm**, and **Not about Nightingales**, and a collection of one-act plays titled **American Blues**. In 1939 Thacher, who judged the contest along with Harold Clurman and Irwin Shaw, sent Williams a hundred dollar prize and a special citation for *American Blues*. The prize affirmed Williams's confidence in his own talent and marked the beginning of his journey toward success in New York. Thacher had lobbied the Group Theatre's treasurer, Kermit Bloomgarden, to create a special award in recognition of Williams's potential.

Thacher then recommended Williams to her friend, agent **Audrey Wood**, and after some delay Williams signed with Wood, initiating their long and productive relationship. Thacher also lobbied the Theatre Guild to present **Battle of Angels** in 1940. When Williams, impressed by Elia Kazan's direction of *All My Sons*, wanted him to direct *A Streetcar Named Desire*, Thacher persuaded her reluctant husband to agree, with sensational results. Thacher was not enthusiastic about **Camino Real**, suggesting that Williams cut 45 minutes out of the play, but she successfully intervened between her husband and Williams when tempers flared over revisions. In his **Memoirs** Williams relates how Kazan and Thacher visited him after his spectacular blowup at the first reading of **Sweet Bird of Youth** in early January 1959 and again on 24 September 1963, just after **Frank Merlo**'s death. Only weeks passed before Williams attended the funeral of Thacher, who died of a stroke at the age of 56.

Further Reading

Leverich, Lyle. *Tom: The Unknown Tennessee Williams*. New York: Crown, 1995.

"Molly Day Thacher." Obituary. *New York Times* 15 December 1963: D18.

Williams, Tennessee. *Memoirs*. New York: Doubleday, 1975.

Kirk Woodward

This Is (An Entertainment). *This Is (An Entertainment)* is Williams's undeniably and absurdly exuberant comedy in which he explores issues of identity and power, seen through the prism of sexual allure. Williams wrote the bulk of the play between 1974 and 1976, making it contemporaneous with *The Red Devil Battery Sign* and *Clothes for a Summer Hotel*. Like these plays, *This Is* is a product of Williams's search for a style more plastic (see **Plastic Theater**), theatrical, and less realistic than the work that had made him famous in the 1940s to 1950s. Indeed, *This Is* goes far beyond most of Williams's full-length plays in the extent to which it acknowledges its own theatrically, making constant use of direct address, knowing asides, and frequent references to itself as a play. The leading character, The Countess, refers to the plays's texts as "the jokebook."

This Is takes place in the Grande Hotel Splendide, located in an unnamed middle-European country under siege by a revolutionary army. The hotel is crumbling and faded, linking it to the earlier *The Two-Character Play* and the later *A House Not Meant to Stand* and even *Vieux Carré*. Williams's continuing interest in decaying settings may be viewed as a comment on the condition of cold war America or, more expressionistically, on his own debilitated mental and physical state.

The hotel is populated by a group of ancient, feeble aristocrats caught up in a violent situation beyond their understanding or control (reminiscent of the romantics in *Camino Real*). Principal among these are the Countess and her husband, Count Rechy, an arms manufacturer grown rich providing saturation and cluster-bombs to a great power embroiled in an Asian war. The action consists of the Count and Countess's debates on how to evade the approaching enemy forces, punctuated by the Countess's sexual adventures with her chauffeur, a bellhop, and the guerrilla general himself. The Countess and the Count try on numerous costumes in which they may plausibly escape the hotel; the Count's tend to be various women's outfits, from a black Spanish mantilla to a chambermaid's uniform. The Countess, meanwhile, dressed in a black leather dominatrix outfit, menaces the bellhop with a whip. *This Is* might be summed up as an image of two selfish adults obsessed with sex, appearances, and power who, at a time of impending doom, misplace and then quickly forget about their two children.

The play bears a curious resemblance to Jean Genet's 1948 play *Splendid's*. It, too, is set in a palatial hotel called Splendid's, which has been seized by a gang of mobsters who, holed up on an upper floor, are themselves surrounded by the police. Where Genet's play, however, focuses on the desperation of the criminals and never shows us the guests, Williams is interested in the plight of the hotel's occupants and does not bring the guerrilla leader on until the last act. Both plays are interrupted by radio announcements—in *This Is* of the approach of the guerrilla forces and in *Splendid's* of the police force's attempts to storm the hotel—and both are regularly disrupted by bursts of offstage machine-gun fire.

Did Williams know the Genet play? *Splendid's* was neither published nor produced in his lifetime, and there is no evidence that Williams ever met Genet. He was a fan of the French writer, however, and was acquainted with Genet's American translator, Bernard Frechtman. In the late 1950s, Frechtman and Williams discussed possible English titles for Genet's *Les Negres*; and so it is possible that Frechtman may have described *Splendid's* to him, as well.

This Is received only one major production in the twentieth century, which was its premiere at the American Conservatory Theatre in San Francisco in January 1976, directed by Allen Fletcher. The draft that Williams submitted to the theater for rehearsal was reasonably tight. However, throughout rehearsals and even following the opening, Williams provided an almost daily stream of additions, until the performing text was at least twice as long as the original. Audiences were confused and the critics hostile. Stanley Eichelbaum in the *San Francisco Examiner* was representative when he concluded that "apart from a few shimmering moments, 'This Is' leaves considerable doubt that it is salvageable." Linda Dorff found *This Is* to be an intentionally outrageous work that uses material from cartoons, camp, and other media to interrogate and to satirize theater as well.

Further Reading

Dorff, Linda. "Theatricalist Cartoons: Tennessee Williams's Late Outrageous Plays." *Tennessee Williams Annual Review* 2 (1999): 13–34.

Eichelbaum, Stanley. "But Tennessee, Is This an Entertainment?" *San Francisco Examiner* 21 January 1976: 32.

Williams, Tennessee. *This Is (An Entertainment)*. Revised, April 1978. Tennessee Williams Papers. Rare Book and Manuscript Library, Columbia University.

Michael Paller

This Is the Peaceable Kingdom. *This Is the Peaceable Kingdom, or Good Luck God* is a late short play exhibiting Williams's "bizarre humor" concentrating on the geriatric tantrums he explored in *Lifeboat Drill* and *The Frosted Glass Coffin*. Set in a nursing home in Queens during a spring 1978 strike, the action culminates when the residents—black and white—revolt, causing pandemonium; they use their crutches as weapons, assault staff members, beat and nearly strip a socialite do-gooder come to bring them food, and turn the nursing home into a war zone. In fact, Williams comically likens the incident to a prison riot, with police entering with tear gas, news reporters flashing their cameras, and inmates ducking for safety. Amid the mocking irony of events Williams includes an unseen Voice that, throughout the play, announces that this is indeed the Peaceable Kingdom with love for all.

This seriocomic revolt, though, accounts for no more than 15 percent of the play. Most of *This Is the Peaceable Kingdom* is taken up with a continuing dialogue between two grown children—Bernice (about 60) and her Hebrew-teaching brother Saul—who squabble about the care their mother—Mrs. Shapiro—receives at the home. These children are concerned about her worsening condition and meretricious care, including having the private duty nurse flush two sets of their mother's dentures down the toilet. As Bernice force-feeds her nearly comatose mother, who occasionally manages to blurt out syllables resembling Yiddish, she attacks Saul for having ever suggested this home. In turn, Saul accuses Bernice of being as senile as the residents. Like the residents, Saul experiences his own trauma, having a petit mal seizure and then a near heart attack. In the middle of the riot, Mrs. Shapiro dies, and Bernice absurdly ties a big bow around her head to keep the old woman's toothless mouth shut. As a counterpoint to Bernice and Saul's jibing conversation, two of the residents—Ralston and Lucrettia—exchange comments about the deplorable condition of the patients' treatment, the ethnic rivalry between Christians and Jews, and their own imminent demise. In what is the topic sentence for this play, and for many other late

Williams works as well, Lucrettia fears that human dignity is lost at "the point where decent existence is ended and indecent existence begins" (335).

Mrs. Shapiro's condition, which clearly is at the point of indecent existence, becomes the focal point for the revolt, or at least the emotional rallying point of the play. Toothless, blind, deaf, and reduced to a vegetable, she and those like her in the home motivate the residents who can navigate to rebel. In the process, Williams excoriates, through his satire, familiar targets in his canon. One of the most obvious is the club woman—the chauffeured socialite from the Gov. Dinwoddie Chapter of the Colonial Dames of America—who condescendingly and bigotedly (she dislikes the black residents) brings small cellophane-wrapped packages of food but disdains to have much contact with the residents. She represents all those snooty women's clubs that Williams saw inflating already pompous individuals.

Another Williams target in this play is officious institutionalism. The home, the matron, the Voice insisting on peace but promoting callous treatment—all underscore the institutionalism that Williams denounced and dreaded. Religious and ethnic prejudice (see **Race**) also comes in for attack as Lucrettia boasts about her Christianity in stereotyping the Shapiros, and they likewise categorize and stigmatize Christianity by insultingly calling her a "goyim" and demanding that their mother be transferred to a Jewish nursing home, sadly situated in Spanish Harlem, a dangerous place, as they point out. The language and actions of the black residents are also criticized by several white characters. Finally, Williams's ultimate trompe l'oeil is to have Ralston proclaim to Lucrettia that he is God as he miraculously wheels her back to her room in amazement that he can walk. In the tradition of Par Lagervist's *The Sybl*, Williams comically suggests that God may also be a resident in a nursing home, and He, not the system, is the only one to care for the residents, both the quick and dead. See also **Religion**.

Further Reading

Saddik, Annette. *The Politics of Reputation: The Critical Reception of Tennessee Williams' Later Plays*. Madison, NJ: Fairleigh Dickinson University Press, 1999.

Philip C. Kolin

Tiger Tail. See *Baby Doll.*

Todd, Fred W., Tennessee Williams Collection. The Fred W. Todd Tennessee Williams Collection was recently acquired by the Historic **New Orleans** Collection. In 1956, as a student at Stephen F. Austin State University, Fred Todd purchased the Signet paperback edition of *Baby Doll* at a drugstore in Nacogdoches, Texas. Although he was an admirer of Williams's work, he had no idea that this seemingly insignificant purchase would be the beginning of a lifetime pursuit to document the life and career of Tennessee Williams. Through the years Todd collected materials on other Southern writers, such as **Truman Capote**, Eudora Welty, and Flannery O'Connor, but he eventually sold these collections in order to continue to build his Tennessee Williams Collection, one of the finest private collections on an American playwright. Rare book and manuscript dealers such as Andreas Brown of New York's Gotham Book Mart and the late Marguerite A. Cohn of House of Books, Ltd. were instrumental in uncovering new treasures for Todd to acquire.

The Collection's strength is in the diversity of material collected and the fact that Todd did not focus on Williams as an isolated individual but sought to document the personal and professional worlds that surrounded him. The collection is divided into

16 separate series—manuscripts (see **Manuscript Collections**), **correspondence**, photographs, playbills, periodicals, play scripts, cinema material, translations, legal and financial documents, family papers, Williams's separate publications, contributions to books, recordings/**music**, biographies, books about the theater, and literary criticism.

The cinema material includes posters, lobby cards, and photographs, including **Vivien Leigh**'s personal collection of film contacts from *A Streetcar Named Desire* and a photo album from the filming of *The Roman Spring of Mrs. Stone*, presented to Leigh by the studio. The manuscripts series include drafts of plays, poetry (see **Poems**), short stories, and essays. Some notable items include *Personal Film Story Treatment of "The Gentleman Caller"* and manuscript pages from *A Streetcar Named Desire*. The correspondence series contains both personal and professional letters to and from Williams, as well as related correspondence such as a group of letters from Williams's friend **Marion Black Vaccaro** to her family discussing her travels with Williams. Also of interest are a letter by Williams to the producers of the first film version of *The Glass Menagerie*, in which he is strongly critical of the movie, and a 1941 letter from Williams to **William Saroyan**, in which he expresses frustration with his writing career but optimism for the future.

The book collections are outstanding and include pristine examples of first editions, many of which are signed by Williams or have a notable provenance. A highlight of the contributions series is the 1925 Ben Blewett Junior High School yearbook that contains Williams's poem "Demon Smoke." Among the items in the separate publications is a copy of *I Rise In Flame, Cried the Phoenix* inscribed to **Audrey Wood**. It is 1 of only 10 copies printed on Umbria hand-made paper. Picking highlights from the many thousands of items in the Todd Collection is an exercise in subjectivity, but it is safe to say that there is something to intrigue anyone with an interest in Williams's life and career. See also **Texts**.

Further Reading

"Historic New Orleans Collection" www.hnoc. org.

Mark Cave

The Travelling Companion. *The Travelling Companion* is a one-act Williams play, written in 1982 and first staged in 1996 at New York's Center Stage as part of a double bill with *The Chalky White Substance*. Written shortly before Williams's death, it is—like *Something Cloudy, Something Clear* (1981)—both nakedly autobiographical and frankly uncloseted in its treatment of its protagonist's homosexuality. Vieu, an aging writer, is even referred to as "Tenn" in one handwritten amendment to the 21-page manuscript. Set in a New York hotel room, the play's two scenes depict Vieu's uncertain relationship with his young, recently acquired "traveling companion," Beau. Having picked him up in what he believed to be a gay bar in San Francisco, Vieu assumes that the studlike Beau fully understands what is expected of him. Beau, however, sees his role as that of a valet and refuses to sleep in the same bed as Vieu. Insisting on his heterosexuality, he threatens to create a disturbance in the hotel if he is not provided with a separate cot. It is only after he has drunk extensively and popped several quaaludes that Beau loosens up enough to reassess the situation—offering to stay on a while longer if Vieu buys him a new guitar.

The Travelling Companion contains echoes of several earlier Williams plays. Beau, whose old guitar needs to be "redeemed"

The Travelling Companion. Tyree Giroux (left) as Vieu, Anthony Cran (right) as Beau. Menagerie Theatre Company at Phoenix Arts Centre, Leicester, England, 1998. Directed by Paul Bourne. Photo courtesy of Paul Bourne.

from hock, recalls Valentine Xavier, the fallen angel of *Orpheus Descending*, while Vieu is strongly reminiscent of Alexandra del Lago in *Sweet Bird of Youth*. Like her, he needs breathing apparatus and a handsome young companion to survive. The chief interest of *The Travelling Companion* is in its reframing of these familiar tropes in an openly homoerotic scenario. Yet Vieu is treated brutally rather than sympathetically by Williams, an old man locked into the outdated gay disguise of "fatherly" patron to a beautiful boy, and his mental state disintegrates rapidly. Vieu's itinerant lifestyle, moving from hotel to airplane to hotel, has left him unsure even of which country he is in (Beau has to remind him that this is New York, not London), and in his rambling

speeches, his string of former companions seem to blur together in his mind. Williams's depiction of this character again makes use of the fractured sentence structure common to many of his later plays, and in this instance, the device is used to underline Vieu's distracted state of mind—he tends to talk in allusive fragments rather than coherent sentences.

Since Beau tends to talk simply in coarse monosyllables, these two voices achieve little real communication. A further consequence is that the "reality" of their past history and present situation remains undecidable; each one seems to be in denial, to some degree, and so neither man's perspective can necessarily be trusted. (Was it a gay bar or not? Is Beau the injured "innocent," or a gay man who, when sober, kids himself he's straight? Have they, perhaps, been through all this before?) The play's use of such "subjective realism" is complemented by Williams's instructions for atmospheric lighting, and for the sparing use of the unseen guitar, whose notes punctuate the action at key moments. This short, deceptively simple play powerfully evokes an image of two lost souls, both dependent in different ways on the all-too-conditional kindness of strangers. See also **Drugs; Gender and Sexuality.**

Further Reading

Williams, Tennessee. "*The Travelling Companion.*" *Christopher Street* 58 (November–December 1981): 32–40.

Stephen J. Bottoms

Twenty-seven Wagons Full of Cotton and Other One-Act Plays. The first collection of Williams's 13 one-act plays, *Twenty-seven Wagons Full of Cotton and Other One-Act Plays* was originally published in 1945. In addition to the original 13 plays, 3 others were included in volume 6 of *The Theatre of Tennessee Williams.* As with many of his short stories, writing one-act plays often provided Williams with earlier testing ground for full-length works such as **The Glass Menagerie, Cat on a Hot Tin Roof,** or **Baby Doll.** Reflecting his own nomadic nature and his experiences in **New Orleans** and **St. Louis** especially, many plays in *Twenty-seven Wagons Full of Cotton and Other One-Act Plays* are set in boarding houses and concern the alienation of the individual, the plight of the outsider, and reconciling the inner spirit with the flesh.

Twenty-seven Wagons Full of Cotton, the play for which the collection is titled, finds a southern cotton gin owner in conflict with an Italian immigrant and was the earlier version of *Baby Doll.* Jake Meighan treats his wife, Flora, like a child; and even though

they have been married several months, the couple has not yet consummated their relationship. Flora still sleeps in a baby crib. Silva Vaccaro, the Sicilian outsider, runs the rival gin, which is burned down. When Meighan indirectly informs Flora that he burned down the competitor's gin, he swears her to secrecy. But Vaccaro seduces Flora, an innocent who is fooled by the charm of the Sicilian (an early prototype of Stanley Kowalski in **A Streetcar Named Desire** and Rosario in **The Rose Tattoo**), enabling him to avenge the arson and prove that his masculinity is superior to that of Jake, the insider and southerner. The outsider thus hoodwinks the insider and triumphs over Jake's arrogance and destructive behavior. This play foregrounds such major Williams themes as the Old versus the New South, men versus women, and the flesh versus the spirit. Of all Tennessee Williams's one-act plays, *Twenty-seven Wagons Full of Cotton* has received the most critical attention as well as the most productions.

The Purification draws on such American classics as Edgar Allan Poe's "The Fall of the House of Usher" and Herman Melville's *Pierre* by focusing on an incestuous relationship between a brother and sister. The only verse drama Williams wrote, "The Purification," is set in a courtroom where the brother, referred to in the play only as the Son, is on trial for his taboo actions and hence must receive purification. The sister is dead, though her spirit appears in the play several times. A Chorus comments on the action while another man defends himself for breaking the couple apart. Critics have compared the play to another one in the collection, *Auto-Da-Fé,* as well as to **The Two-Character Play** and *The Glass Menagerie.* Largely indebted to **Federico García Lorca**'s work, *The Purification* explores the problem of reconciling taboo desires (incest, homosexuality) with social and spiritual inclinations, and offers an early example of the familiar Williams brother/sister dyad.

Originally produced in New York in 1947, *The Lady of Larkspur Lotion* is a comedy set in a French Quarter boarding house that Williams would later use in **Vieux Carré**. The title of the one-act play refers to a common cure for body lice, which the pretentious but fragile Mrs. Hardwicke-Moore uses for nail polish remover—or so she claims to her landlady, Mrs. Wire. After Mrs. Hardwicke-Moore complains about the cockroaches in her room, the landlady accuses her of being a prostitute and demands late rent money. Another tenant, referred to in the play simply as "The Writer" and a vagrant, defends Mrs. Hardwicke-Moore. The play anticipates the outcasts and artists in Williams's longer plays, especially *Vieu Carré* and **Something Cloudy, Something Clear.** The joke on which the title is based reinforces the difficulty that Mrs. Hardwicke-Moore experiences in accepting the truth of her own decadent profession and lifestyle.

The Last of My Solid Gold Watches chronicles the last days of the old drummer Mr. Charlie, who realizes selling shoes is no longer as easy as it once was. The title refers to Mr. Charlie's pocket watch, a symbol of his business success and his more hopeful past. He encounters a younger salesman, Harper, and an African American porter, whom Philip C. Kolin identifies as the kindly heavenly doorkeeper Eliakim. As a robust figure who likes to tell stories, Mr. Charlie reflects both Williams's father Cornelius and Big Daddy in *Cat on a Hot Tin Roof*. Williams dedicated this Delta play to actor Sidney Greenstreet. This one-act deserves comparison with Eudora Welty's short story "The Death of the Traveling Salesman."

In *Portrait of a Madonna*, spinster Lucretia Collins imagines a ghost impregnates her and thus anticipates the mad characters common in Williams's plays. *Portrait of a Madonna* emphasizes the fragility of the Old South and the inevitable change that threatens it. Ultimately, the reclusive Miss Collins is taken away to a mental institution, and the hotel workers who send her away comment on the southern ideals by which she abided. Her sexual repression and severe Christian upbringing precipitated her madness. Miss Collins may be an earlier version of Blanche DuBois in *A Streetcar Named Desire* and Alma in **Summer and Smoke**, but the similarities between Laura in *The Glass Menagerie* and Miss Collins are also plausible, as well as those with the female characters in Williams's short story "Completed."

One of the most carefully structured plays in the collection, *Auto-Da-Fé* (literally, "act of faith," in an Inquisitorial purge) is a study of sexual repression and religious conflict found throughout in Williams's fiction as well. A young, unmarried man, Eloi, shares quarters with his mother, Madame Duvenet, and a tenant, whom Eloi suspects spies on him. The young man's paranoia increases when his mother learns that he is distraught over a "pornographic" photograph of a naked younger and older man that he receives through his job as a postal worker. When Eloi confronts the young man in the photograph at his home and suggests that he is perverted, the young man hints that Eloi is hiding something about and/or from himself. Through a tissue of Biblical allusions, Williams reveals that Eloi struggles with sodomy. Like Amanda Wingfield's fears about her son Tom, Madame Duvenet is aware that her son is hiding something—even from himself. To avoid confronting his homosexuality, Eloi burns the house down. Thus, the title of this short play is ironic—rather than any genuine act of spiritual purification, the fire is an attempt to hide the truth from himself, his mother, and the tenant.

Also set in the French Quarter, *Lord Byron's Love Letter* takes place during Mardi Gras where the Spinster and the Old Woman fool tourists into thinking they possess a love letter written by Lord Byron near the end of his life while fighting for the Greeks against the Turks. A matron, accompanied by her husband, is especially interested in hearing the letter read, more for the power of Byron's celebrity status than in sincere appreciation of his life and works. Unfortunately, the inebriated husband is so enthralled in Mardi Gras activities that he and his wife leave before giving a donation to the two women, a central irony in the play. *Lord Byron's Love Letter* foregrounds the clash between the romantic past and crass reality and also expresses the lack of appreciation for the artist figure in society—twin themes Williams often explores. This play evokes the romantic memories by which Amanda in *Glass Menagerie* and Blanche DuBois in *A Streetcar Named Desire* live and perish.

Another boarding house play—*The Strangest Kind of Romance*—is set in a thinly disguised St. Louis. It concentrates on the odd but comforting relationship between lonely, weak Little Man and his cat; he is more interested in his landlady's maternal protection than in her sexual advances. The protagonist may be read as a closeted gay man and his relationship with the cat a figurative way for Williams to trope gay subjectivity. The play addresses the plight of the proletariat—an issue in *The Glass Menagerie* and *Not about Nightingales*. Little Man works in a factory until he can barely survive and the landlady kicks him out. Her father-in-law, the Old Man, who represents Walt Whitman, chastises her for her mistreatment of him as well as the lonely man. Another boarder, the Boxer, bullies Little Man and anticipates Stanley Kowlaski's abuse of Blanche. Even though the cat, Nitchevo, named by a former Russian tenant, runs

away, the play ends happily as Little Man and his cat are reunited.

Anticipating the brother and sister relationship in *The Glass Menagerie*, **Small Craft Warnings**, and *The Two-Character Play*, *The Long Goodbye* is a memory play focusing on a brother Joe, and Silva, a friend, as the former moves out of the apartment that Joe, his sister Myra, and their mother have shared. Unlike the extended flashbacks and framing in *The Glass Menagerie*, Williams employs another cinematographic technique—moving throughout the play from past to present and past again. While the moving men remove the furniture, Joe recalls conversations he had had with Myra, his beloved sister, and his mother before she killed herself. Myra presumably is a fallen woman—leading her brother to the difficult reality of lost idealism. Again reflecting Williams's political interests in the 1930s, Silva represents the socialist, encouraging Joe, a writer, to become active in the movement against capitalism, and criticizes Joe for being morbidly fixated on his past. Reminiscent of the fiction of F. Scott Fitzgerald, this play expresses many conventional Williams themes—failure of romantic idealism, the troubled family, and the inability to move beyond the past—he treated in such early plays as **Fugitive Kind** and **Spring Storm**.

Hello from Bertha centers on the failing spirit of Bertha, a destitute prostitute in an East St. Louis boarding house who is threatened with eviction to a madhouse. Goldie, a fellow worker, cannot convince Bertha to leave her bed so that the other girls may use the room. Bertha cannot get over her ill-fated affair with Charlie, nor can she accept the fact that her call girl days are over. Hoping to be rescued from her destitute state, Bertha is similar, as Philip C. Kolin argues, to Blanche DuBois in her hope that she will be rescued by her ideal man. Many other

Tennessee Williams, circa 1948. Photo by Angus McBean, used courtesy of New Directions Publishing Corp.

Williams themes surface in *Hello From Bertha*, among them the symbolic St. Louis setting Williams detested, the tragic disappointments of a faded woman (as in **The Mutilated**), and the boarding house as metaphor for the cruel world.

This Property Is Condemned is set on a railroad embankment in the rural South where the young boy Tom meets Willie, a school dropout from a poor family whose mother and sister have died. Willie has inherited the reputation of her sister, Alva, for being too friendly with strange men visiting the town via the railroad. Her house is condemned, but she still lives there, fighting for subsistence and hoping to be delivered by one of her gentleman callers, again familiar Williams tropes and settings. Roger Boxill maintains that the condemned property is

like Belle Reve—lost and forlorn. Londré identifies in this play a "lyrical effect of decadence." *Talk to Me Like the Rain and Let Me Listen*, also exploring troubled relationships, is set in Manhattan. To emphasize a couple's alienation from each other in the city, Williams scripts the voices of children playing and singing offstage. Yet the couple is out of luck and dreams of a better future with little hope of connecting with one another.

The final play in the original collection, *Something Unspoken*, again underscores the failure of connection, the Old versus the New South, and issues of sexual repression. A southern matriarch, Miss Cornelia Scott, and her longtime companion, Miss Grace Lancaster, have shared their lives for 15 years. But Cornelia, a member of the Daughters of the Confederacy, is losing control of the organization and refuses to attend the election meeting, though, much like Amanda Wingfield selling magazine subscriptions, she wants to remain in control by having her friends talk with her on the telephone and spy on her younger colleagues who want to vote her out. Ironically, Cornelia decides to utter "something unspoken" to Grace about their relationship with each other—her affection for Grace. But Grace, unwilling to face the reality of their love for one another, cannot accept Cornelia's declaration of love. Nevertheless, Grace does appreciate the 15 roses she received from Cornelia celebrating their years together. In *Something Unspoken*, Williams experiments with the power of silence and voice in framing one's identity and admitting homosexuality. Sharing similarities with Lillian Hellman's *The Children's Hour*, the play anticipates Williams's short story "Happy August the Tenth."

Among the three plays added to the original *Twenty-seven Wagons Full of Cotton* collection, *The Long Day Cut Short, or the*

Unsatisfactory Supper is an earlier version of *Baby Doll*. In this play, Archie Lee and Baby Doll argue with each other over the plight of Aunt Rose, who had become a burden to her entire family. When she fails to produce a satisfactory supper, Archie Lee tells her to live with other relatives. But Baby Doll, Aunt Rose's niece, attempts to spare her feelings; Archie Lee, similar to the hard-hearted, callous Jake in *Twenty-seven Wagons Full of Cotton*, treats her unkindly. Contemplating where she will go, Aunt Rose works in the rose bushes around the house. What Archie Lee needs is a good dose of humanity, not a good meal—something that Aunt Rose painfully understands. This play, which can stand by itself as a theater piece without the rest of *Baby Doll* or *Tiger Tail*, concentrates on social outcasts—a maiden aunt with nowhere to go and nothing to do except cook and garden for her relatives and who demands comparison with Laura in *The Glass Menagerie* and Blanche in *A Streetcar Named Desire*.

In *Steps Must Be Gentle*, first published in 1982, Williams imagines a conversation between the dead **Hart Crane** and his mother Grace. Reflecting on his own difficulties with his mother **Edwina**, Williams portrays the problem of communication between family members whose expectations and realities conflict. Grace cannot accept the "rightness" of Crane's homosexuality, and Hart cannot accept the unforgiving nature of his mother. The expressionistic *Steps Must Be Gentle* revisits the suicide of Hart Crane at sea, yet another example of the fate of artists in society. Grace pleads with her son to understand her plight, since she tried to make her son's artistic reputation last by arranging for his work to be taken seriously and to protect his name. Yet neither Grace not Hart is able to move outside of ego (both possess a martyr complex) to understand the other's

space. Like her son, Grace dies in obscurity, serving her last days as a scrubwoman.

Closing volume 6 in *The Theatre of Tennessee Williams* is *The Demolition Downtown*, an experimental, futuristic piece concerned with the rise of a totalitarian government in the United States. The Laneses and the Kaneses, two couples who live next door to one another in an urban apartment building, contemplate the problematic nature of living in a postapocalyptic world. Hoping to run away from the new government, the husbands devise an escape plan while the wives determine that, for their survival, it is best to cooperate, at least superficially, with the leadership of the new government and mask their genuine contempt. The demolition around them symbolizes the failure of the previous regime to protect humanity. Containing fragmented and incomplete lines, Williams's style here suggests the gradual deterioration of language to communicate and humanize (compare *The Two-Character Play*). Comparable to *Talk to Me Like the Rain and Let Me Listen*, this play addresses alienation within urban life and lack of communication among partners.

Throughout the original *Twenty-seven Wagons Full of Cotton* collection and the reprinted three plays as well, Williams writes about the isolation of the individual, the problem of human identity, the dehumanization of the human spirit, and the plight of family. While not as developed or polished as his major works, these one-act plays nonetheless offer an excellent introduction to Williams's major themes and character types. With this collection Williams established himself as the champion of the fugitive and outcast. And, most important of all, *Twenty-seven Wagons Full of Cotton* showed the world the talent and promise of the young Tennessee Williams who, in Jessica Tandy's words, "mastered the art of the one-act play" (quoted in Steen 178).

Further Reading

Boxill, Roger. *Tennessee Williams*. New York: St. Martin's, 1987.

Hale, Allean. "Early Williams: The Making of a Playwright." In *The Cambridge Companion to Tennessee Williams*, ed. Matthew C. Roudané. Cambridge: Cambridge University Press, 1997. 11–28.

Kolin, Philip C. " 'Hello from Bertha' as a Source for *A Streetcar Named Desire*." *Notes on Contemporary Literature* 27 (January 1997): 6–7.

———. " 'Night, Mistuh Charlie': The Porter in Tennessee Williams's 'The Last of My Solid Gold Watches' and the Kairos of Negritude." *Mississippi Quarterly* 47 (Spring 1994): 215–220.

Londré, Felicia. *Tennessee Williams*. New York: Ungar, 1979.

O'Connor, Jacqueline. " 'Living in this little hotel': Boarders or Borders in Tennessee Williams Early Short Plays." *Tennessee Williams Annual Review* 3 (2000): 101–115.

Preshaw, Peggy W. "The Paradoxical Southern World of Tennessee Williams." In *Tennessee Williams: A Tribute*, ed. Jac Tharpe. Jackson: University Press of Mississippi, 1977. 5–29.

Scheick, William J. " 'An Intercourse Not Well Designed': Talk and Touch in the Plays of Tennessee Williams." In *Tennessee Williams: A Tribute*, ed. Jac Tharpe. Jackson: University Press of Mississippi, 1977. 763–773.

Shackelford, D. Dean. " 'The Ghost of a Man': The Quest for Self-Acceptance in Early Williams." *Tennessee Williams Annual Review* 4 (2001): 49–58.

Steen, Mike. *A Look at Tennessee Williams*. New York: Hawthorne, 1969.

Dean Shackelford

The Two-Character Play/Out Cry. Williams may have begun thinking about and working on *The Two-Character Play*, later revised as *Out Cry* and then again as *The Two-Character Play*, as early as 1959. "Williams often referred to *The Two-Character Play* and *Out Cry* as among his most important work and his most personal" (Londré 94). These plays are clearly among the most complex and controversial as well. The obvious connections among all versions of this play and Williams's masterwork **The Glass Menagerie**, as well as other overtly autobiographical Williams plays, though, are plainly evident. From the start to the end of his career, Williams was obsessed by the brother-sister relationship. The play's brother and sister, Felice and Clare, may represent, as some critics claim, Williams's conflicted responses to what he viewed as the madness of modern society, the struggle to understand another being, the isolation of the individual, and the illusory and transitory nature of existence. Felice embodies a Beckettian (see **Beckett, Samuel**) determination to go on in the face of the absurdities of existence and human tragedy while Clare represents another in the gallery of Williams portraits of romantic, fragile beings who face the very real possibility of disintegrating under the weight of life's confusions and pressures.

All versions of *The Two-Character Play* and *Out Cry* deal most centrally with fear, as two actors, Felice and Clare, playing a brother and sister, confuse their roles with reality. The two actors enact a tale of siblings living together in the home where their father has committed suicide after murdering their mother, while at the same time, the fears and frictions between the acting duo are revealed as it becomes apparent that they are trapped in an old theater. The 1979 version of the play especially emphasizes the exploration of fear, but many other themes emerge as well. At times, Felice and Clare seem to be simply somewhat older versions of Tom and Laura from *The Glass Menagerie*. Felice's beleaguered solicitousness toward the emotionally fragile Clare is the most obvious manifestation of this, as well as the "memory" qualities inherent in the play-within-the-play structure. Williams also allows the characters to explore the role of the artist in society, the internal struggles of the individual to fully understand the self and others, the notion that multiple personas exist within an individual, the impact of parental failings on children, the nature of madness and sanity, the fear of isolation, the moral conundrums of living in the real world (as opposed to an imaginary or romanticized one)—as well as Williams's frequent impulse to view the drama as autobiography and, in this case, perhaps as therapy. Beyond question, *The Two-Character Play* in all of its manifestations is a significant part of the autobiographical continuum of Williams's drama.

Williams, in fact, described *The Two-Character Play* as the most difficult work he had written up to that time, an "interior landscape" that reflected the deep depression he fell into in the 1960s during what is often described as Williams's dark age. The play's siblings represent Williams and his sister **Rose**, the offspring of damaged and damaging parents, and the major chords of the play deal with two shadowy corners of Williams's life—his close relationship with his mentally unstable sister and his need of the stage (in its capacity as a lyrical, illusory world) as a defense against unhappy realities. Williams's career-long exploration of the nature of theater is also central to this play, first in its exploration of the Pirandellian struggle between the real and the imaginary—and, most obviously, in the play's ideas about madness and sanity. If, as some scholars suggest, Williams was offering a statement about the relationship of an artist to his society, it was a deeply personal statement that is only a part of this multilayered play. Williams's theater is, in effect, a jail from which neither the artist nor his characters can escape. Studying the set of *Out Cry* with its "stairs [that] go nowhere, they stop in space," Felicia Londré identifies a key related them: "The incompleteness of this staircase, like the incompleteness of the entire setting for the play-within-the-play, recalls Williams's obsessions as an artist . . . fear of incompletion" (103).

On another level, Felice and Clare represent different aspects of Williams's own persona, with Felice as survivor and Clare as victim. Some critics have described the play as Williams's attempt to illuminate the human struggle of reconciling distinctly separate and often contradictory personas coexisting within one person. Those critics who condemned the play simply dismissed it, claiming that Williams was using the stage for therapy. However, Williams went beyond himself in attempting to dramatize his own psychological dilemmas. Other aspects of the play illuminate his characters' fear of captivity—they are trapped in the theater, trapped in the family dysfunction of the play-within-the-play's characters, and trapped in their own psychological and emotional struggles, or, like Val Xavier in *Orpheus Descending*, trapped inside the solitary confinement of their own flesh.

The structure of *The Two-Character Play* and *Out Cry* in its various versions is circular, as the characters unwind bits of their story while continually returning to the fear and sense of entrapment they feel. Williams artfully and effectively achieves a claustrophic quality as the circles seem to grow small and tighter around the two characters. Abandoned by their cast mates and crew, the play they enact stumbles, and the confusion is mirrored in the relationship of Felice and Clare, both in the play-within-the-play and outside it. Hence it becomes increasingly difficult to separate the actor and the character as Williams attempts to crystallize the feelings of disorientation and confusion in his bruised and unhappy characters as the play's circles close. Yet Williams foregrounded in *The Two Character Play/Out Cry* key postmodern issues of reflexivity and minimalization.

The demons of Williams's life are boldly evident in *The Two-Character Play* and *Out Cry*—family dysfunction, his sister's precarious hold on sanity (and her tragic lobotomy), sexuality, the value of art, and perhaps most centrally, the need for compassion for the world's fragile and sensitive beings and the related need for a romanticized view of life. These themes dominate as they frequently do in Williams's most characteristic works.

The Two-Character Play was first staged in December 1967 at London's Hampstead Theatre in a production directed by James Roose-Evans and starring Peter Wyngarde and Mary Ure. Critics were uniformly dismissive. In 1971, revised with the new title *Out Cry*, the play was produced at London's Ivanhoe Theatre under **George Keathley**'s direction, featuring Donald Madden and Eileen Herlie. The actors won praise, but the play did not. Revised again, but still titled *Out Cry*, the play was produced at New York's Lyceum Theatre in 1973. This Broadway production featured Michael York and Cara Duff-MacCormick under Peter Glenville's direction and with scenic design by **Jo Mielziner**, but these formidable talents did not succeed in making the play successful. It was not well received by critics and managed to eke out only a short run. The Broadway revision of *Out Cry* featured Williams's most significant change. In the original version of *The Two-Character Play*, Felice and Clare were middle-aged, but in *Out Cry* they are made considerably younger. The last version of *The Two-Char-acter Play* was published by New Directions in 1979 and might well be considered the definitive version of this play—or, at least, Williams's last attempt to revise it. In it, he has more sharply focused the play's themes and clarified its sketchy, ambiguous style.

Following Williams's death, *The Two-Character Play* continued to have a modest production life. In 1995, the Theatre Marigny in **New Orleans** presented *The Two-Character Play* featuring Linda Westbrook and William Heard, under Heard's direction. In 1997, a production of *The Two-Character Play* at the Peabody House Theatre near Boston, Massachusetts met with the usual critical apathy. A December 1999 production at the Boston Center for the Arts, under the title *Out Cry*, was praised as a spirited reconsideration of the play. Aside from these and a few other productions, *The Two-Character Play* and *Out Cry* are rarely staged.

Further Reading

Adler, Thomas P. "The Dialogue of Incompletion: Language in Tennessee Williams's Later Plays." *Quarterly Journal of Speech* 61 (February 1975): 48–58.

Colt, Jay Leo. "Dancing in Red Hot Shoes." *Tennessee Williams Review* 3.2 (1982): 6–8.

Devlin, Albert J. "The Later Career of Tennessee Williams." *Tennessee Williams Literary Journal* 1.2 (Winter 1989–1990): 7–17.

Kahn, Sy M. "Listening to *Out Cry*: Bird of Paradox in a Gilded Cage." In *New Essays on American Drama*, ed. Gilbert Debusscher and Henry I. Schvey. Amsterdam: Rodopi, 1989. 41–62.

Londré, Felicia. "The Two-Character Out Cry and Break Out." In *The Undiscovered Country: The Later Plays of Tennessee Williams*, ed. Philip C. Kolin. New York: Lang, 2002. 93–106.

Nikolopoulou, Kalliopi. " 'Le Jeu Suprême': Some Mallarmean Echoes in Tennessee

Williams's *Out Cry.*" In *Tennessee Williams: A Casebook*, ed. Robert F. Gross. New York: Routledge, 2002. 121–138.

Pagan, Nicholas O. "Tennessee Williams's Out Cry in the *The Two-Character Play.*" *Notes on Mississippi Writers* 24.2 (1992): 67–79.

Stamper, Rexford. "*The Two-Character Play*: Psychic Individuation." In *Tennessee Williams: A Tribute*, ed. Jac Tharpe. Jackson: University Press of Mississippi, 1977. 354–361.

James Fisher

V

Vaccaro, Marion Black (1906–1975). One of Tennessee Williams's oldest and most valued friends, Marion Black Vaccaro was the daughter of an Episcopal priest, and she filled a place in Williams's life that might have been occupied by his sister **Rose**, had her mental health not failed her. The relationship with Vaccaro began early in the playwright's career and lasted until her death in 1975. Williams dedicated one of his major plays, *Orpheus Descending*, to her. After *Battle of Angels* folded, Williams recuperated and revised the play in **Key West**, Florida, in January 1941, where he found a much-needed refuge in a small cabin behind the Tradewinds boarding house run by Marion's mother, Clara Atwood Black.

A colorful character, Vaccaro attended Smith College on a scholarship, where she pursued her poetry writing and earned a degree in education. Prior to marrying Regis Vaccaro, she earned a living as a tutor to Patricia Ziegfeld, the daughter of Florenz Ziegfeld, Jr., the famed showman. She moved in elite social circles, befriending both Billie Burke, the actress and wife of Florenz Ziegfeld, and Diana Barrymore of the Hollywood Barrymores. Her husband Regis was from a wealthy **New Orleans** family and the principal heir to the Standard Fruit Company fortune. Marion's combination of worldliness, social acumen, and family involvement in the Episcopal Church made her an attractive companion for the struggling young playwright who shared a similar family background.

Thanks to Vaccaro, Williams joined an enclave of artists who provided support and encouragement. By day, he revised his failed play, but by night he and Vaccaro would take in the local nightlife at Sloppy Joe's Bar on Whitehead Street in Key West, Ernest Hemingway's former hangout. When the pair grew bored with Key West, they would embark for Cuba. In pre-Castro Cuba, they took advantage of the exotic nightlife, which in the 1940s offered the liminal world Williams craved. While there with Vaccaro, Williams met such notable literary figures as Ernest Hemingway, Jean-Paul Sartre, and Simone de Beauvoir. Williams considered Vaccaro an accomplished poet and managed to get Sartre to read examples of her work during one of their visits to Cuba.

Since Vaccaro's husband was the worst alcoholic Williams knew, the couple's lifestyle was compatible in some ways to Williams's, whose father was an alcoholic. Yet the painful impact of Regis's alcoholism drove Vaccaro and her mother to seek Williams's assistance in getting him out of town. On his way out of the Keys, Williams stayed at Vaccaro's farm near Brunswick, Georgia, and visited it in April 1941. While there, he noted in his **journal** that he had a new idea in mind for a play called *A Woman's Love for a Drunkard: Regis and Marion*. While this play was never written, elements did appear in **Cat on a Hot Tin Roof**. In fact, Maggie finds herself in a situation not unlike Marion's—having to endure the difficulties of marriage to an alcoholic (Brick) to maintain a secure position in life. Williams used the name Vacarro (spelled slightly differently) for the shrewd Sicilian in **Baby Doll** (1956) who outsmarts Archie Lee Meighan, the owner of a rival cotton gin.

Heading for New York in May, Williams lost contact with Vaccaro, but he renewed his friendship with her in New Orleans in 1946. By this time, Vaccaro was widowed, and she and her mother took up residence in the elegant Pontalba Apartments adjacent to Jackson Square in the French Quarter. When a touring company of *The Glass Menagerie* came to town, Vaccaro threw a lavish party for them. It was with Vaccaro that Williams devised a plan to move his sister Rose to Coral Gables, where Vaccaro settled with her mother. Having been under psychiatric care for years and after a lobotomy, Rose required constant companionship, and Williams hoped he could provide her with a comfortable life by moving her and a private nurse to Coconut Grove. Though Vaccaro encouraged Williams and secured a home for him, his dream for Rose was never realized.

In the 1950s and 1960s Williams and Vaccaro again were traveling companions, going to Tangier or the Greek Island of Rhodes. Williams outlived Vaccaro, who died in 1970, but stayed in contact with her surviving brother George, who gave Williams a portrait of Vaccaro that hung in his Key West bedroom, depicting her as she looked in 1941. See **Correspondence**.

Further Reading

Develin, Albert J., and Nancy M. Tischler, eds. *The Selected Letters of Tennessee Williams, Volume 1—1920–1945*. New York: New Directions, 2000.

Leverich, Lyle. *Tom: The Unknown Tennessee Williams*. New York: Crown, 1995.

Spoto, Donald. *The Kindness of Strangers: The Life of Tennessee Williams*. Boston: Little, Brown, 1985.

Williams, Tennessee. *Memoirs*. Garden City, NY: Doubleday, 1975.

Jean Rhodes

Vidal, Gore (1925–). Gore Vidal, novelist and social commentator, established a lifelong friendship (or love-hate relationship) with Williams. Vidal and Williams first met in the American Academy in Rome in March 1948. In Paris that same year Vidal acted as translator for Williams and Jean Cocteau, who staged the first French production of **A Streetcar Named Desire** at the Théâtre Edouard VII in October 1949. Williams and Vidal had different points of view on art but were not rivals in the same genres. In 1949, Vidal had just published a bestselling novel, *The Season of Comfort*, while Williams, in the 1940s, was America's greatest playwright. Vidal, a WASP (white Anglo-Saxon Protestant), and Williams, the southern Puritan, did not have a creative symbiosis such as the "Literary Factory" Williams established with **Clark Mills (McBurney)**, nor did they always praise each other, but they inspired each other by exchanging ideas and critiques. It was Vidal who called Williams (with its sexual connotations) and often, even more playfully and ironically, "The Glorious Bird," referring to Shelly's "Hymn to Intellectual Beauty" and parodying Shelley's "amorous birds." Such an epithet was fitting not only for the playwright but also for his work where birds fly everywhere—the "legless birds" in *Battle of Angels*, Stanley Kowalski as "a richly feathered male bird," carnivorous birds swooping in *Suddenly Last Summer*, the cocaloony birds in *The Gnädiges Fräulein*, and even the title of *Sweet Bird of Youth*.

When "the Bird" was a highflyer in the late 1950s, Vidal served as coauthor of the script for Joseph L. Mankiewicz's screen version of *Suddenly Last Summer*. Though Vidal and Williams had agreed not to satirize each other in their works, the decadent Sebastian Venable may be a portrait of a Vidalian-like artist. On the other hand, Vidal created a mysterious phantomlike film director named "Mr. Williams" in his 1974 novel *Myron*. Still in the "golden age" of their Shelley-Byron–like liaison in the early 1960s, Vidal savored and endured the eccentricities of Williams, the narcissistic poet, with patience and irony, appreciating Williams's grotesque humor, his haunting imagery, and his creative flights into art.

After Williams's mental and physical breakdown in the mid-1960s, they grew estranged, and their feud reached its climax in 1976 when Vidal reviewed Williams's *Memoirs*, mocking the playwright's sex life and his hypochondria, exposing his limited vocabulary, and disparaging his late plays. "The Bird" held Vidal responsible for displacing *Memoirs* from the bestseller list of the *New York Times*. Earlier tremors in the relationship may have been brought to the surface, for when Williams asked Vidal to revise his story "Rubio y Morena" (in 1948), he accused Vidal of "removing my *style*, which is all that I have."

But by 1985, some two years after Williams's death, Vidal proved to be a true and fair friend in his assessment of Williams's work, lauding Williams's political consciousness in his 1965 novella "The Knightly Quest," defending Williams against charges by conservatives, hailing him for establishing the male as a sex object on stage, and creating the best women characters in the modern theater. Vidal's last tribute to Williams's genius came in his preface to *Collected Stories* (1985), honoring Williams as a restless and gifted writer who "could not possess his own life until he had written about it."

Further Reading

Kaplan, Fred. *Gore Vidal: A Biography*. New York: Anchor, 2000.
Spoto, Donald. *The Kindness of Strangers: The Life of Tennessee Williams*. Boston: Little, Brown, 1985.
Stanton, Bob. *Views from a Window: Conversations* with *Gore Vidal*. New York: Lyle Stuart, 1980.

Thomas Molzahn

Vieux Carré. *Vieux Carré*, which opened in 1977, may be Tennessee Williams's most faithful re-creation of the atmosphere and decadent charm of the French Quarter in **New Orleans**. The play dramatizes Williams's experiences when he first came to New Orleans in December 1938, shortly after completing his degree from the University of Iowa. At 27 he was what we would now call a "nontraditional student," and his postgraduate "education" in the French Quarter was anything but traditional for this impressionistic young writer. In his letters (see **Correspondence**) and **journals** from this initial period in New Orleans, he describes the French Quarter as an exotic wonderland, a place where he feels almost completely liberated from the constraints of conventional society. And in *Vieux Carré* the author's thinly disguised self, the Writer, similarly finds a freedom that was denied in the stultifying environment of his former home.

Although the boarding house at 722 Rue Toulouse, the setting for *Vieux Carré*, was not the very first place Williams actually lived in New Orleans, nor the place of his longest residence, it was the site that remained with him almost all of his life and is arguably the address that we most closely associate with his stay in New Orleans. This boarding house, with its cast of eccentric inhabitants, exposed Williams to behavior and customs that he had never encountered before. As the Writer (Williams) tells Mrs. Wire, the landlady, "I ought to pay you—tuition!" His "matriculation" at 722 Toulouse only lasted a few weeks, but the events that transpired there remained with him virtually his entire life, as the boarding house served as a repository for memories and impressions that would furnish him a wealth of material for both his fiction and drama.

Vieux Carré was begun during Williams's actual residence at 722 Toulouse in 1939, but the play was not produced until 1977. The original working title was *Vieux Carré, or Dead Planet, the Moon*. In the intervening years, Williams published the one-act play *The Lady of Larkspur Lotion*, and the short story "The Angel in the Alcove" containing thematic elements found in *Vieux Carré*. In addition, Williams reworked *Vieux Carré* during the 1960s and 1970s in two one-act plays as *Broken Glass in the Morning, or Skylight* and *I Never Get Dressed Till after Dark on Sundays* that he fused in 1977 into a play-within-a-play structure that he intended to present on Broadway. After considerable negotiations among the actors, director, and producer, Williams abandoned the experimental structure and substituted the memory-framing device that had worked so well with **The Glass Menagerie**. But problems continued with the production. He ex-

722 Rue Toulouse, circa 1938. Courtesy The Historic New Orleans Collection, Museum/Research Center.

tensively revised the play with suggestions from director Keith Hack, and the play enjoyed more successful runs in London the following year. Even at the time of his death Williams was reworking *Vieux Carré* for production on the West Side of Manhattan.

The play's main ingredients are staples in Williams's repertoire. Grace under destitution, the compensatory value of the imagination in confronting the "real" world, the necessity of communication, the lingering effect of the past and consequent suffering from previous losses, and the uncertainty of the future are all themes that Williams deals with in other plays as well. In addition, the atmospheric underpinnings of the boarding house and the environment of the Quarter are as important as any character in the play. With *Vieux Carré* Williams seemed determined to join **Faulkner**, Sherwood Anderson, and other famous writers in bringing the French Quarter to life for the entire world to see.

When the 28-year-old Writer arrives at the boarding house, he is unwillingly "adopted" by the landlady Mrs. Wire. Although he forms associations with some of her other boarders, he remains essentially an observer rather than a participant. He is physically attracted to Tye McCool who works as a barker at a Strip joint and who resembles Stanley Kowalski in his overpowering sexuality. But the Writer's apparent soul mate is Jane, Tye's girlfriend, dying of leukemia and seeking escape in sex with Tye. The Writer's reluctance to forge emotional bonds is conditioned by his function as an alienated artist and his reluctance to seek permanence in this transient community. He is also discovering his own homosexuality and learns about life and death from Nightingale, a gay artist dying from tuberculosis. As the Nightingale tells him, "That little opacity on your left eye pupil could mean a like thing happening to your heart."

In its final form, *Vieux Carré* is a memory play; that is, the events are related through the nostalgic eyes of the Writer, or Williams when he first visited New Orleans, some 35 years before the play would be produced. As with Tom Wingfield in *The Glass Menagerie*, the Writer briefly introduces the dramatic situation and then reappears in the action himself, with occasional asides to the audience. As with Tom's final departure, too, the Writer concludes the play outside of the time scheme that transpires during the play with poetic musings about the "Echoes" from the "fading but remembered" voices. Unlike *The Glass Menagerie*, however, with its tightly structured tension involving the Wingfield family, the characters and situations of the boarding house are less united and cohesive—a problem that has led

to many reviewers chiding Williams for his lack of unity in the drama, a familiar complaint against Williams's other late plays.

But, as Lyle Leverich has reminded us, Williams did not simply try to recreate the past but rather rewrote of "the impressions of things past" (447). Thus one should not regard the play as merely a retelling of Williams's first experiences in New Orleans. There are several different tableaux in the play: the Nightingale and the Writer, Jane and Tye, Misses Carrie and Maude, and the Writer and Sky, the drifter with whom he runs away. The voyeuristic landlady, Mrs. Wire (whose name was actually Mrs. Anderson), tries to regulate all of these relationships, but the boarders often find means to subvert her machinations. In addition, there is a Chaplinesque court scene that takes place outside of the rooming house, offering comic relief and another view of life within "the city that care forgot." Despite all the stage business and complicated relationships among and between the characters, the Writer, as observer/recorder, does serve as a unifying principle, and one wonders just why some object to the play as lacking coherence or continuity. In many respects *Vieux Carré* is a picaresque drama, and the Writer is the picaro. The play has the same episodic structure, autobiographical groundings, confessional expression, low-life characters, and vividness of detail so characteristic of the picaresque novel. Moreover, the picaro/Writer becomes acquainted with all the characters while avoiding their pitfalls as he makes his escape down the road in search of another adventure. Whether or not Williams had the picaresque mode in mind when he rewrote *Vieux Carré*, the influence of the genre is undeniable. Besides, at one point Williams said that he would never write another drama so meticulously conforming to unity as he did with *Cat on a Hot Tin Roof*. Always the experimenter, perhaps the picaresque was yet another style that intrigued Williams and engaged his artistic effort.

As with *The Glass Menagerie*, *Vieux Carré* develops patterns of confinement and escape. In fact, in one sense the Writer has fled the Wingfield household only to reemerge at the rooming house at 722 Toulouse. When asked by interviewer Mike Wallace what first brought him to New Orleans, Williams said, **"St. Louis."** And when Mrs. Wire tells the Writer that she looks upon him as an adopted son, he replies, "Mrs. Wire, I didn't escape from one mother to look for another." Suspended between his role as an objective narrator and an emotionally invested participant, the Writer remains on the threshold of commitment throughout the play. He begrudgingly acquiesces to the Nightingale's advances, occasionally serves as a surrogate son for Mrs. Wire, and becomes Jane's confidant. However, he chooses to leave all of these relationships behind as he crosses over to the "cacophony" of the future. Although he closes the door on this part of his past, he cannot escape the lasting impression that these ghosts, "fading but remembered," have made upon him. Bruce Mann has argued that "Williams enters into the characters of Jane, Nightingale, and Mrs. Ware but finds himself in a nightmare, experiencing again and again the shattering self-division of his identity crisis that has left him isolated and bereft of sanctuary" (142). Ultimately, though, this final scene, with its emphasis on those whom the Writer is destined to remember, is reminiscent of Tom's inability to purge his memory of his beloved sister Laura.

In *Vieux Carré* almost everyone is trapped by circumstances seemingly beyond their control. Sometimes the sense of confinement is spatial, sometimes it is temporal, and frequently it is represented by emotionally binding ties. Most of the other characters also seek escape from the orbit of the boarding house either through alcohol and drugs or by the willful avoidance of reality through illusion. For example, Nursie, Mrs. Wire's domestic help, has apparently long suffered under the landlady's rule, and at the beginning of the play she says, "It's time for me to retire." In scene eight she says, "I come here to tell you I quit." Yet she remains through the course of the play, and one senses that the only way she'll leave is when she collapses and dies in the house.

Mary Maude and Miss Carrie, the two bag ladies, or crones, as Williams liked to call these characters, escape to the locked darkness of their room and emerge only when they smell Mrs. Wire's gumbo on the stove. Moreover, they escape their pathetic existence by fabricating invitations to Garden District dinner parties hosted at Miss Carrie's cousin's house. Jane, who is "Tyed" to her obnoxious but irresistible lover, cannot avoid the leukemia that is killing her, so she tries to find momentary pleasure through the escape offered by the physical side of this warped relationship. Jane cryptically says that she "quit my former connection" in New York for New Orleans, and she becomes the only boarder who seems to form any emotional partnership with the Writer. During the final scene, as Jane and the Writer play a game of chess, each is actually more concerned with the moves that they will make apropos of their future. Jane deludes herself by describing her elaborate travel plans, but apparently only the Writer will be traveling far from the confinement of 722 Toulouse. Whatever the case, the implication is that these personalities have formed such an impression in the mind of the Writer that their "ghosts" will remain with him and be a permanent part of his "mental landscape" (Mann 143) however far in time and

space he travels away from the Vieux Carré.
See also **Collected Stories**.

Further Reading

Bray, Robert. Introduction to *Vieux Carré* by
Tennessee Williams. New York: New Directions, 2000.

———. "*Vieux Carré*: Transferring 'a Story of
Mood.' " In *The Undiscovered Country:
The Later Plays of Tennessee Williams*, ed.
Philip C. Kolin. New York: Lang, 2002.
142–154.

Dorff, Linda. " 'All Very [Not!] Pirandello': Radical Theatrics in the Evolution of *Vieux
Carré*." *Tennessee Williams Annual Review* 3 (2000): 13–33.

Leverich, Lyle. *Tom: The Unknown Tennessee
Williams*. New York: Crown, 1995.

Mann, Bruce N. "Memories and Muses: *Vieux
Carré* and *Something Cloudy, Something
Clear*." In *Tennessee Williams: A Case-
book*, ed. Robert F. Gross. New York:
Routledge, 2002. 139–152.

Robert Bray

W

Wallach, Eli (1915–). Eli Wallach was one of a group of actors whose career got started and skyrocketed by acting in a Tennessee Williams script. Like **Maureen Stapleton**, **Marlon Brando**, and **Karl Malden**, Wallach studied at the Actors Studio in New York where he played in *American Blues*. In 1948, Wallach met his wife, Anne Jackson, when the two of them acted in an off-Broadway production of *This Property Is Condemned*. Wallach played Alvaro Mangiacavalo in the 1951 Broadway premiere of *The Rose Tattoo* opposite Maureen Stapleton's Serafina delle Rosa. Praised for his ability to combine robust comedy with tearful sympathy, Wallach won several awards, including a Tony and the Drama Critics Award. In 1953, he took the role of Kilroy in Williams's highly experimental and short-lived *Camino Real*. Wallach's good looks and sincerity earned him the critics' respect as he skillfully interpreted Kilroy as the all-American boy.

Wallach made his film debut in another Williams play, *Baby Doll*, in 1956. Playing Silva Vacarro, a hot-blooded Latin, Wallach brought his unique gifts to the role. His dark looks, seductively low voice, silver-tipped tongue, and roué's charm nicely complemented Carroll Baker's blonde sensuality. Wallach's shrewd maneuvering contrasted with Karl Malden's portrayal of Archie Lee Meighan's aging, voyeuristic antics. *Baby Doll* was one of Wallach's, and Williams's, most controversial films. Working with director **Elia Kazan**, Wallach regarded *Baby Doll* as one of his most important film experiences.

In May 1999, Wallach and Jackson won kudos for their "Tennessee Williams Remembered" at the Circle in the Square Theatre presenting a potpourri of scenes from Williams's plays, including some in which Wallach acted, lines from Williams's letters (see **Correspondence**), and their own fond recollections of the playwright who had a central influence on their careers. But "Tennessee Williams Remembered" was not only a tribute to the playwright but a reflection of the collaboration in the theater between Williams and the actors who loved him.

Further Reading

Black, David, with Eli Wallach. *The Actor's Audition.* New York: Vintage, 1990.

Bryer, J., and R. Davison, eds. *The Actor's Art: Conversations with Contemporary American Stage Performers.* New Brunswick, NJ: Rutgers University Press, 2001.

Philip C. Kolin

Where I Live. *Where I Live* (1978) is the only published collection of Williams's nonfiction containing, almost exclusively, previously published articles from newspapers and magazines, forewords and prefaces, and book reviews that Williams wrote over a 30-year period. These pieces cover topics ranging from biographical sketches ("Facts about Me") to manifestos of Williams's aesthetic principles, to explanations and justifications for his plays. These prose pieces deserve comparison with Williams's **correspondence** and **journals**.

Opening with "Preface to My Poems," Williams is a youthful author pursuing a dramatic career, but his style and interests, though, clearly anticipate his more mature prose in his use of humor and self-mockery, his emphasis on the artist's value to society, his weaving in autobiographical elements, his informal and almost casual style, and his sincere homage to other writers (e.g., **Hart Crane** and Walt Whitman). The following essay, "Something Wild," further introduces and articulates Williams's artistic vision in light of his early career in **St. Louis** with the **Mummers**. Given his own uncertainties, he aptly describes art as a form of "anarchy" and disorder. Even though Williams feared the rise of totalitarianism and the dominance of bourgeois American values, he was optimistic about the artist's place in society.

Among the most well-known essays in *Where I Live* is "On a Streetcar Named Success," in which Williams questions whether the success of a legitimate playwright is a blessing and he fears that he will grow complacent and self-satisfied by receiving it. A more playful piece is "Questions without Answers" (1948), jammed with Williams's humor, addressing the problems artists face in explaining their works. In this essay Williams grows impatient with those attempting to experience vicariously his inner life as he projects his constructed self-image as mask, a valuable insight he gives audiences into his works. Similarly, in a later essay "The World I Live In" (1957), Williams conducts a self-interview, responding to charges that his plays are too harsh by emphasizing that writing serves a therapeutic role in his life and that violence and tension are everywhere. Desiring to inspire audiences to explore their own identities, he cautions them about a world filled with mendacity, the subject of *Cat on a Hot Tin Roof*, *Camino Real*, and many other Williams's plays. Perhaps the best statement of Williams's aesthetic principles is "A Writer's Quest for a Parnassus" (1950), concentrating on his quest to be a writer within an unappreciative American culture. While San Francisco and **New Orleans** were the most romantic of American cities for Williams, he did not consider the United States to be the ideal place for authors because McCarthyism endangered art. Preferring Rome and Paris, Williams regrets a growing nationalism (calling it "evil") that separates rather than unites people, thus providing a wonderful gloss on *Camino Real*. Williams early and later in his career tied aesthetics to politics in these essays.

Among the several book reviews in *Where I Live*, Williams's assessment of his friend **Paul Bowles**'s *The Delicate Prey and Other Stories* is especially valuable as an aperture into Williams's thoughts about writing. He admits that while the spiritual alienation within Bowles's world may be shocking, the collection avoids sentimentality and evokes the spirit of the times. In another laudatory review, "If the Writing Is Honest," Williams assesses **William Inge's** *The Dark at the Top of the Stairs*, later reprinted as the preface to Inge's published play. Another friend whose work Williams honored in print was **Carson McCullers**. In fact, he wrote the introduction to her *Reflections in a Golden Eye*, concentrating on the problematic role that the grotesque—the "Gothic" in Southern fiction—played in the reception of her work. Echoing Flannery O'Connor, McCullers for Williams captured the mystery of the human spirit and the awfulness of the modern world through her powerful symbolism. In his "Biography of Carson McCullers" (1961) Williams turned to her last novel, *Clock without Hands*.

Of special interest in *Where I Live* are Williams's essays about his own plays. "The Timeless World of a Play" (1951), often reprinted, gives perhaps the best explanation of his understanding of tragedy and how the tragic writer for Williams mobilizes the audience's fears to ultimately valorize human dignity. Influenced by Aristotelian and other classical notions of tragedy, Williams defended **Arthur Miller's** *Death of a Salesman* as a valuable artistic statement about the human condition. Williams's views in this essay can be readily applied to *A Streetcar Named Desire*. In "The Meaning of *The Rose Tattoo*" (1951) he explains the Dionysian principles at work in the play: Serafina's husband, Rosario, symbolizes Dionysus and becomes a catalyst for her own understanding of self; Rosario's, an "absent presence" reinforcing the life principle she has lost. In his "Foreword to *Camino Real*," (1953), Williams denies the play's obscurity and labels it an allegory of our times, hoping to boost the play's box office success. This article, like many in *Where I Live*, reflects the struggle Williams found in his career between his art and popular/commercial success. In his crucial essay "Afterword to

Camino Real," which was first published with the text of the play, Williams theorized more fully about his organic view of art. Another article dealing with *Camino Real*, "Reflections on a Revival of a Controversial Fantasy," from the 15 May 1960 *New York Times*, argues that two speeches by Don Quixote are central to the play.

Several pieces in *Where I Live* address *Cat on a Hot Tin Roof*, including "Critic Says 'Evasion,' Writer Says 'Mystery' " (1955), as Williams confronts the homophobia surrounding Brick and claims that ambiguity and fragmentation lie at the heart of the character, anticipating so much contemporary criticism of the play. Similarly, "Person-to-Person" (1955) expresses Williams's desire to say something to people by transcending reality and "personal lyricism." Reflecting his discontent over the Broadway version of *Cat on a Hot Tin Roof*, "Author and Director: A Delicate Situation," originally published in *Playbill*, skewers overly intrusive directors (i.e., **Elia Kazan**) who distort the artist's vision. Although Williams acknowledges the collaborative nature of theater, he asserts that a director must recognize that the writer understands the play better than anyone else, a refrain made by **Edward Albee**. In "The Past, the Present, and the Perhaps" (1957), later used as a foreword to **Orpheus Descending**, Williams chronicles his years as a struggling playwright and his quest for success, focusing on **Battle of Angels** and *Orpheus Descending* and also his earlier plays, including **Spring Storm** and **Not about Nightingales**. Williams seems optimistic about the future (he calls it the "perhaps"). Appearing in the *New York Herald* just before **The Night of the Iguana** opened in 1961, "A Summer of Discovery" gives Williams's self-description as an "unregenerate romantic" and chronicles his longings after success in a time of world crisis. This essay traces the roots of the play during Williams's visit to Mexico in 1940 and again underscores that the origins of Williams's work are rooted in his own experience. In "Tennessee Williams Presents His POV" he discusses the difficulty of writing adult drama in a repressed era. Provoked by gossip columnists who condemn his works, Williams identifies the characteristics of contemporary American plays and celebrates the dramatic tradition of **Bertolt Brecht** and William Shakespeare.

As the collection closes, Williams focuses primarily on places, his friends and food. "Five Fiery Ladies," from *Life* (1961), praises **Vivien Leigh**, **Anna Magnani**, Elizabeth Taylor, Katherine Hepburn, and Geraldine Page—who starred in his plays—with his strongest affection going to Anna Magnani. "T. Williams's View of **Tallulah Bankhead**" offers witty insights into Williams's troubled relationship because of Bankhead's "tiger" strength. With "Too Personal?"—an introduction to *Small Craft Warnings*—Williams again acknowledges his romantic theory of art, the role of the artist, and the audience. "Homage to **Key West**" (1973) reveals his affection for this artist colony/home, while "The Pleasures of the Table" (1978) rhapsodically describes his love of Italian food and his favorite Italian restaurants throughout the world. The final essay, "The Misunderstanding and Fears of an Artist's Revolt" (1978), reiterates Williams's idea that art is a revolutionary medium and affirms his idealistic aesthetic principles. All in all, *Where I Live* provides a guided tour of Williams's world of ideas, people, and places. See also **Poems; Southern Culture and Literature.**

Further Reading

Shackelford, Dean. "The Transformation of Experience: The Aesthetics and Themes of Tennessee Williams's Nonfiction." *Southern Quarterly* 38 (Fall 1999): 104–116.
Williams, Tennessee. *Where I Live: Selected Essays*. Ed. Christine R. Day and Bob Woods. New York: New Directions, 1978.

Dean Shackelford

Williams, Cornelius Coffin (1879–1957). Cornelius Coffin Williams, also known as C.C., was Tennessee Williams's father. His ancestry impressed the genteel Dakin family when he began courting Edwina in 1906. His father, Thomas Lanier Williams II, for whom Tennessee (Thomas Lanier Williams III) was named, had a very respectable career of public service as state railroad commissioner and candidate (albeit unsuccessful) for governor of Tennessee. Though C.C. was considerably less proud of their achievements, the Williams family tree also contained two poets: Tristram Coffin and Sidney Lanier, the former resurfacing as the poet Nonno (Jonathan Coffin) in *The Night of the Iguana* and the latter having his last name joined with Williams's. C.C.'s maternal lineage was equally illustrious, thanks to ties to the pioneering Nantucket Coffins.

While C.C.'s pedigree was nearly impeccable, his performance as a husband and father was not. He had left his study of law at the University of Tennessee after two years to join the army during the Spanish-American War. He left military service with a restless spirit and a penchant for heavy drinking, gambling, and womanizing. Whether he discovered these tastes or merely developed them in the army is moot. More certain is that none of these characteristics would prove assets for a stable marriage and family life. While he worked as a traveling salesman, first for the Knoxville clothier Claiborne, Tate, and Cowan, and later for the International Shoe Company, Cornelius could indulge himself without censure from Edwina. After being promoted to a managerial position in the International Shoe Company in **St. Louis**—a job that prompted the uprooting of his wife and children from their pleasant life in the company of his in-laws in Mississippi—he was forced into a more conventional matrimonial situation.

Tennessee Williams and his sister **Rose** remembered hearing their mother's screams of protest escaping from the bedroom when their father made unwanted sexual advances toward her. If Edwina was, as she has been accused, ruthless in withholding marital affections from C.C., he was equally vindictive in his treatment of Rose and his elder son Tom. While he favored his more masculine-acting younger son **Dakin**, Cornelius derided the unmanly tendencies developing in Tom, referring to him as "Miss Nancy." When Tom's literary talents began to blossom at the University of Missouri, C.C. took no pride in these, blinded as he was by Tom's repeated failures in the ROTC program. Eventually he yanked his son from campus life, replanting him in the International Shoe Company.

Though the clash of his parents' sensibilities led to domestic turmoil and indelible psychological scars on all three Williams children, allusions to C.C.—both blatant and covert—cover the landscape of Williams's work, though not as regularly as do references to his mother and sister. Williams often sought solace in his writing when his father denied him his love. And since his father never seemed to value his son's literary pursuits, it was perhaps the most poetic form of revenge Williams could exact. (Ironically, Williams once owned a bulldog he christened Cornelius.) The most explicit satire of Williams's father occurs in *The Glass Menagerie* (1944), an autobiographical memory play, where a photograph of an ab-

sent father hanging in the living room looms over the drama both literally and figuratively. Tom, an aspiring writer and the play's narrator, longs to escape a stultifying job at the International Shoe Company as well as a soul-crushing family life with his mother and fragile sister. While C.C. did not abandon the family permanently, his travels, his behavior, and his disposition resulted in a metaphorical absence.

Shades of Cornelius might also be seen in Stanley Kowalski's violent temper, drinking, and card playing in *A Streetcar Named Desire. The Last of My Solid Gold Watches* (1946) contains an appearance of Williams's father in Charlie Colton, another C.C. and traveling shoe salesman from Mississippi. Angered by the depiction of the traveling father, C.C. wrote an angry letter to literary agent **Audrey Wood** threatening to sue his son and the publishers if he was depicted in any other works. The ultimatum was not strictly heeded because in *Period of Adjustment* (1957–1958), Ralph's military background and attitude toward what he perceives as sissy tendencies in a boy mirrors C.C.'s opinion of his own son. Cornelius may also be satirized, as Philip Kolin argues, in a late Williams's story, "Completed" (1974), where a Cornelius Dunphy attacks his daughter Ella (the name of C.C.'s sister and Rose and Tennessee's aunt) for her ageless virginity. Aunt Ella becomes her niece Rosemary's (Rose Williams) caretaker. *Will Mr. Merriwether Return from Memphis?* (1969) also includes a reference to C.C. through the figure of another absent husband Cornelius Waddles, as does *Moise and the World of Reason* (1975) with its relative named Coffin. Additionally, in one of Williams's late plays, *A House Not Meant to Stand* (1980), a drunk named Cornelius is a central character, though his political aspi-

---

rations approximate his grandfather's ambitions rather than his father's.

Memories of C.C. continued to hound Williams until the end of his career, especially in a late autobiographical short story titled "The Man in the Overstuffed Chair" (1982), where Williams describes his fearful life with his father but concludes with C.C.'s final acceptance of him. The chair, the title and the story's chief symbol, is fat, sad, and absorbs all the family's troubles, a poetic translation of C.C. for Williams. Though Williams may never have completely healed from the injuries inflicted by his pugnacious father, theater audiences around the world have reaped their dramatic consequences. See also *Collected Stories*; *Twenty-seven Wagons Full of Cotton and Other One-Act Plays*.

Further Reading

Hayman, Ronald. *Tennessee Williams: Everyone Else Is an Audience*. New Haven, CT: Yale University Press, 1993.

Kolin, Philip. "It's Not Life with Auntie Mame: Tennessee Williams's 'Completed.' " *Tennessee Williams Literary Journal* 5 (Spring 2003): 80–83.

Leverich, Lyle. *Tom: The Unknown Tennessee Williams*. New York: Crown, 1995.

Spoto, Donald. *The Kindness of Strangers: The Life of Tennessee Williams*. Boston: Little, Brown, 1985.

Williams, Tennessee. "The Man in the Overstuffed Chair." In *Antaneus: The Autobiographical Eye*, ed. Daniel Halpern. New York: Ecco Press, 1982. 281–292.

Leslie Atkins Durham

Williams, Edwina Estelle Dakin (1884–1980). Edwina Williams was the dramatist's mother and the model for Amanda Wingfield in *The Glass Menagerie*. She was born in Marysville, Ohio, the only child of **Walter Edwin Dakin**, a teacher who later would become an Episcopal priest, and **Rosina Otte Dakin**, a musician who gave private lessons. When Edwina was a scholarship student at Harcourt Place Seminary, a finishing school in Gambier, Ohio, she played a southern girl in a theatricale; after the family moved south, she continued to live out the role, refashioning herself as a Southern Belle. On 2 June 1907, she married the playwright's father, **Cornelius Coffin Williams**, in the rectory of St. Paul's Church in Columbus, Mississippi. On the road a great deal, he turned out to be something of a gambler, drinker, and womanizer; when he was home, his wife claims that "a vise of anger" gripped the house—so perhaps she felt justified in coming between Tom and his father. Edwina's vindictiveness toward Cornelius threads through much of her memoir, *Remember Me to Tom*, where she justifies her performative construction of reality as a way of ensuring that "things [were] not as bad as they seemed." This denial carried over into her maintaining the facade of a happy marraige until she finally demanded that Cornelius leave, as well as into her apparent obliviousness about her son's homosexuality.

Tennessee's attitude toward his mother mixed admiration with criticism. Although he regarded her as "indomitable" and "a lady" of some verbal eloquence, at the same time he saw her as oftentimes "fatally wrong." Beset by health problems that necessitated several surgeries, she tended to be garrulous, overbearing, and domineering; possessive of her children, she exhibited a strain of moral, even puritanical, superiority. Her memoir includes a generous sampling of Tennessee's very early prose and poetry, as well as somewhat tortured entries from his diaries. Although sometimes disturbed or shocked by the content of her son's plays and stories, she finally turned a blind eye to the "savage acts" that Tennessee, in one of his letters, reports she called "ugly" and "indecent," in order to praise his discerning and compassionate works for their "truth" and "beauty." She saw her son's commitment to his vocation as a writer as his way "to escape madness and death."

Aspects of Edwina's character are apparent in several of Williams's most compelling female characters. Although she claimed not to recognize herself in Amanda, she is clearly there in the memory of jonquils and gentlemen callers, in the membership in the Daughters of the American Revolution (DAR), and in the nagging of the son over his fondness for the works of **D.H. Lawrence.** She is present as well in the nostalgia for a cultured past and the hysteria of Blanche in *A Streetcar Named Desire*; in the disdain for the physical of Alma in *Summer and Smoke*, who lived—as Edwina did for much of the time before moving to **St. Louis**—in a rectory shadowed by the church; and perhaps most resonantly in Violet Venable, who orders a lobotomy to quiet the ravings of her niece in *Suddenly Last Summer*, just as Edwina had sanctioned the operation on her daughter and Tennessee's beloved sister Rose. After bouts of increasing senility, Edwina—to whom Williams had signed over half the financial proceeds of *The Glass Menagerie*—died three years before her son.

Further Reading

Leverich, Lyle. *Tom: The Unknown Tennessee Williams*. New York: Crown, 1995.

Williams, Edwina Dakin [as told to Lucy Freeman]. *Remember Me to Tom*. New York: Putnam, 1963.

Thomas P. Adler

Williams, Rose Isabel (1909–1996). The eldest sibling of Tennessee Williams, Rose Williams and her tragic life were the sources of some of his most potent imagery and characters. The name "Rose" appears throughout the Williams canon. The young Tom Williams was enchanted with her beauty and exuberance, and Rose assumed the role of teacher and leader to her shy, bookish brother with ease. The two were so close that they were nicknamed "the couple" by their nurse, Ozzie, and they clung to each even more closely when, in 1918, the Williams family moved from **Clarksdale, Mississippi**, to **St. Louis**, Missouri, a city that both children found confusing and frightening.

The psychological context of the Williams family—its unstable mix of rage, sexual repression, and mental illness on both sides—affected Tom and Rose differently. Tom discovered an outlet for his anxieties in his prose and poetry; but Rose was not blessed with artistic talent. Until she was a teenager, her life was normal. By the time she was 14, however, changes in her personality became noticeable. She became subject to severe mood changes and a barely suppressed hysteria. Her interest in her brother was replaced by a natural attraction to boys her own age—an attraction, however, that would fall victim to her mother's hatred of all things sexual. In 1925, Edwina Williams decided the best way to deal with Rose's increasing rebelliousness was to send her away and enrolled her in All Saints' College in Vicksburg, Mississippi. School did not improve Rose's condition, and her parents removed her from All Saints in 1927, deciding she would have her "coming out" that fall, instead, in Knoxville, Tennessee, to be arranged by her father's sisters, Aunts Ella and Isabelle. No serious offers of either courtship or marriage followed, and she returned to St. Louis sullen and depressed.

Increasingly, she fought with her parents; without a completed education or job skills, she was stranded in the increasingly tense Williams home. She began seeing a psychiatrist, who diagnosed her problems as fear of sex, but treatment—by this psychiatrist and by subsequent ones—did not help. Finally, in 1937, the family committed Rose to St. Vincent's, a Catholic sanitarium near St. Louis, where she was diagnosed with "dementia praecox," or schizophrenia. The family soon transferred her to the State Hospital in Farmington. There, a series of insulin treatments were administered without success. Her condition remained unchanged for six years, and in 1943, her mother authorized the superintendent at Farmington to perform a lobotomy. For unknown reasons, Williams, his mother, and brother **Dakin** would all write later that the operation had occurred in 1937 and that it was one of the first to be performed in the country. Although the surgery had a calming effect and restored some of Rose's wit and vitality, it did not banish her delusions or in any way cure her. She would remain institutionalized for the rest of her life. After the success of *The Glass Menagerie*, Williams made sure that Rose always had the best care. He visited her frequently and took her on trips to New York City and **Key West**. He created a trust that ensured her care would continue after his death.

It is only to be expected that Rose, who, Williams wrote, provided the deepest love of his life, would also be the source of much of his most fruitful, constructive material. Rose is most associated in the popular imagination with Laura, the fragile young woman devoted to her glass menagerie in Williams's first major success. She can also be clearly seen as the inspiration for the doomed Catharine Holly, similarly threatened with a lobotomy by her Aunt Violet in *Suddenly Last Summer* (1958). These portraits are, however, anomalies. Only in *The Glass Menagerie* (1944) is the picture of Rose so simple, while *Suddenly Last Summer* depicts her as an innocent victim of scheming relations.

Rose Williams, age 21, with a friend, Park Austin, 1930. Courtesy of Allean Hale.

There are a great many other likeness of Rose in Williams's work, not all of them equally flattering or sympathetic. While Williams never ceased loving and caring for her, his feelings were complex and often contradictory, and it was the rare Williams play that did not display some aspect of them. In two early one-acts—*The Long Goodbye* (1940) and *The Purification* (1940)—a sister is portrayed in terms of sexual restlessness, a desire to escape, and even incest. Feelings such as these, sometimes central, sometimes tangential, but always intense, are to be found in well over the majority of Williams's plays. Other feelings associated with images of Rose throughout his work often center around guilt over an unspecified, perhaps imagined, crime (varying from a sexual transgression to guilt over using her tragic life as material, to the "crime" of having survived threats to his sanity as Rose succumbed).

Williams's skill in handling the many facets of his feelings for Rose vary from the subtle and well modulated, as in *This Property Is Condemned* (c. 1942) and *Talk to Me Like the Rain and Let Me Listen* (c. 1950), to the decidedly unsubtle and overwhelming *The Rose Tattoo* (1950) and distorting-mirror baroque of *The Two-Character Play* (1967) and *Out Cry* (**1971**), to the accusatory *Clothes for a Summer Hotel* (1980) and the forgiving, elegiac *Something Cloudy, Something Clear* (1981). She is also present through the sister Rosemary who visits her Aunt Ella in Williams's short story "Completed" (1974). Although Williams's feelings about his sister range from uncomplicated devotion to physical desire to guilt, resentment, and a final understanding and forgiveness, there is no discernible pattern to the way these emotions occur from play to play. Their development is neither direct nor progressive, and some of the plays present several emotional reactions at once.

However one may choose to interpret the various guises of Rose throughout Williams's canon, her constant presence in her brother's work is undeniable. Just as in *The Glass Menagerie* Tom is never able to bid Laura good-bye, no matter how far from home he travels, Williams's career can be seen as an attempt to say farewell to Rose—in play after play, story after story. See also *Twenty-seven Wagons Full of Cotton and Other One-Act Plays*.

Further Reading

Devlin, Albert J., and Nancy M. Tischler, eds. *The Selected Letters of Tennessee Williams, Volume 1—1920–1945*. New York: New Directions, 2000.

Kolin, Philip C. "It's Not Life with Auntie Mame: Tennessee Williams's 'Completed.' " *Tennessee Williams Literary Journal* 5 (Spring 2003): 80–83.
Paller, Michael. "The Escape that Failed: Tennessee and Rose Williams." In *Magical Muse: Millennial Essays on Tennessee Williams*, ed. Ralph F. Voss. Tuscaloosa: University of Alabama Press, 2002. 70–90.
Williams, Edwina Dakin [as told to Lucy Freeman]. *Remember Me to Tom*. New York: Putnam, 1963.

Michael Paller

Williams, Thomas Lanier, III ("Tennessee") (1911–1983). Tennessee Williams was born on 26 March 1911 in Columbus, Mississippi, where his mother **Edwina Estelle Dakin Williams** was living with her parents, **Walter Edwin** and **Rosina Otte Dakin**, both Ohioans who adapted to life in the South. Reverend Walter Dakin was rector of St. Paul's Episcopal Church, and Edwina remained there because her husband **Cornelius Coffin Williams** ("C.C.") was so frequently on the road, mostly as a traveling salesman. During her teen years as a Southern Belle in Port Gibson and then Columbus, Mississippi, Edwina had enjoyed the attentions of numerous gentlemen callers, and it was her reminiscences that were later evoked through Amanda Wingfield in *The Glass Menagerie*. Like the absent husband in that play, C.C. was working for a telephone company when he came through Columbus and began to court the rector's daughter. The marriage—on 3 June 1907—joined two very different personalities. There was a streak of Puritanism in the small-town, society-conscious Edwina, while C.C. had already begun to indulge his proclivities for drinking, poker playing, and womanizing. His distinguished Knoxville family counted poets Tristram Coffin and Sidney Lanier among its ancestors, as well as the

Tennessee political leader Thomas Lanier Williams II, for whom Tom was named.

C.C. and Edwina's first child, **Rose Isabel Williams**, was born on 17 November 1909, only 16 months before Tom's birth; brother and sister would always remain close. Over the next few years Reverend Dakin moved the family to Nashville, Tennessee (1913), Canton (1915), and **Clarksdale, Mississippi** (1916); Reverend and Mrs. Dakin settled in Memphis after his retirement in the 1930s. Rose and Tom enjoyed their idyllic southern childhoods, their imaginations stimulated by the spellbinding stories told by their African American nanny Ozzie. In 1916 five-year-old Tom suffered nearly fatal diphtheria; the long convalescence fostered his introspective and literary inclinations.

In 1918 when C.C. became a manager at the International Shoe Company in **St. Louis**, Edwina and the children made the traumatic transition to life in a smaller household in a big city apart from her parents. The regular presence at home of the overbearing father made life miserable for Rose and Tom, who bonded more closely than ever. Their younger brother **Walter Dakin Williams** was born on 21 February 1919. The Williamses lived in various apartment buildings over the years, and although none seems to have been quite as dreary as the tenement setting of *The Glass Menagerie*, the emotional landscape in the home was harrowing. Nor did school provide much respite for young Tom. Eugene Field School in St. Louis so overwhelmed the sensitive boy that he was allowed to return to his grandparents in Clarksdale for schooling in 1920. St. Louis's nationally recognized Ben Blewett Junior High did nurture his penchant for writing (an interest that was galvanized at age 12 when his mother bought him a typewriter) through publication of several pieces in the school newspaper. Ever shy, at Soldan High School and University

Young Tom Williams at Ben Blewitt Junior High School, St. Louis, 1924. Courtesy of Allean Hale.

City High School, he continued to focus on writing and kept his circle of friends small: his sister Rose, **Hazel Kramer** (whom he befriended when he was 11 and she was 9 and whom he would always remember as his first love), and Esmeralda Mayes. Tom's high school years saw his earliest commercially published pieces, including "Can a Good Wife Be a Good Sport?" in *Smart Set* (May 1927), followed by "The Vengeance of Nitocris" in *Weird Tales* (August 1928).

A European tour with his Grandfather Dakin in summer 1928 intensified 17-year-old Tom's intellectual ferment. Before sailing from New York, they attended the original 1927 production of Jerome Kern's *Show Boat*. The Episcopal parishioners on the tour included some colorful figures who would later appear as eccentric characters in Williams's plays, while his dapper grandfather would be the prototype for the poet Nonno in *The Night of the Iguana*. The group's itinerary took them to Paris, Nice, Milan, Venice, Rome, Sorrento, Montreux, Cologne, Amsterdam, and London, and inspired Tom to write nine travel articles for his high school newspaper. In Paris, Tom suffered an apparently spontaneous bout of mental turmoil, which—as described in his *Memoirs*—seems uncannily similar to the intellectual torment visited upon Leo Tolstoy during and after his night at Arzamas.

Tom attended the University of Missouri in Columbia from 1929 to 1932. There he majored in journalism, pledged **Alpha Tau Omega** fraternity, and entered playwriting competitions (twice winning honorable mention). When he failed ROTC, however, his father abruptly took him out of school and put him to work at the International Shoe Company. Like Tom in *The Glass Menagerie*, he dusted shoes, did clerical work, and hated the job. He found his escape at the movies and in devoting evenings and weekends to his writing. Deeply depressed after Hazel Kramer's marriage to another man, Tom was granted a summer respite at his grandparents' home in Memphis in 1935. That summer was noteworthy for two reasons: his first produced play and his voracious reading of the works of **Anton Chekhov**. The play in four scenes, *Cairo! Shanghai! Bombay!*, was presented on 12 July 1935 on a backyard stage by a neighborhood group calling itself The Garden Players.

The late 1930s brought new impetus to Williams's formation as a writer: studies at Washington University in St. Louis and at the University of Iowa (from which he earned his B.A. in English in 1938); seeing **Alla Nazimova** on tour in Ibsen's *Ghosts* in 1936; production of two of his full-length plays, *Candles to the Sun* and *Fugitive Kind*, in 1937 by the amateur **Mummers** drama club in St. Louis, along with the encouragement of the group's director **Willard Holland**; and friendship with two other as-piring writers, **Clark Mills (McBurney)** and William Jay Smith. Giving mutual encouragement, the three called themselves a "Literary Factory."

Tom's adoption of the pen name "Tennessee" can be traced to his 1939 submission of three plays grouped under the title *American Blues* to the **Group Theatre** playwriting competition for writers under 25. He mailed the manuscript from his grandparents' home in Memphis, Tennessee, affixing the memorable name while falsifying his birthdate to qualify. Both the name and the birth year stuck, the latter causing long-term confusion in various records, many of which still list 1914 as his year of birth. The inaccuracy became a source of embarrassment to Williams, who prided himself on honesty in his public and private discourse.

Tennessee Williams's first of many sojourns in **New Orleans** lasted about two months (December 1938 to February 1939), after which he and his friend **Jim Parrott** traveled to California, taking odd jobs, with a side trip to Mexico, much bolstered by his $100 Group Theatre prize. He signed with agent **Audrey Wood**, who helped him apply for a Rockefeller Foundation grant, and with that $1,000 he settled briefly in New York in 1940. Summer in Provincetown on Cape Cod proved most memorable for his affair with a Canadian dancer, **Kip Kiernan**, whom Williams always remembered as his first serious male love. Tom had dated women in college and had hoped to marry Hazel Kramer but came to terms with his homosexuality at 28. Although he made no effort to conceal his sexual orientation in adulthood, many were shocked at his forthright "coming out" on national television in 1970 when David Frost's interview culminated in a question about "things like the homosexuality" and Williams replied: "I don't want to be involved in some sort of scandal, but I've covered the waterfront."

Fall of 1940 brought the Theatre Guild's Boston premiere of Williams's *Battle of Angels*, which was marred by a smoke machine that belched fumes and black clouds at an already-hostile audience (Boston was not the ideal place for tryouts of a play conflating religion and sexuality). Although not taken to New York as hoped, the play continued to occupy Williams with revisions for many years, including a major revision called *Orpheus Descending* (1957) and the film *The Fugitive Kind* (1960), not to be confused with the 1937 play *Fugitive Kind*. During his nomadic existence of the next few years, Williams wrote a steady stream of plays, some—like *Not about Nightingales* (written 1939, produced 1998)—to remain virtually unknown until after his death. He sustained himself during the early 1940s with a series of odd jobs: teletype operator, waiter, shoe salesman, elevator operator, and movie usher. Long-standing problems with his eyes necessitated in 1941 the first of several cataract operations.

One professional who took an interest in Williams's early work was the Texas director **Margaret (Margo) Jones**, who had seen *Battle of Angels* and asked **Audrey Wood** to show her everything else by Williams. It was Jones's initiative that got productions of *You Touched Me!* (based upon a **D.H. Lawrence** story and written with his friend **Donald Windham**) in Cleveland and at Pasadena Playhouse in 1943. That year, during a stint as a contract writer at MGM (see **Hollywood**), Williams drafted a play then titled *The Gentleman Caller*. Jones served as codirector, with producer-director **Eddie Dowling** (who had also played Tom), on that play, retitled *The Glass Menagerie*. One of Williams's most autobiographical plays, it evokes the unhappy St. Louis years and may also be read as both tribute and apology to his sister Rose, who had undergone a pre-

Tom and Rose Williams, circa 1930. Courtesy of Dakin Williams family collection.

frontal lobotomy as treatment for schizophrenia in 1943. Indeed, Rose inspired much of Williams's writing throughout his career—including *Summer and Smoke* (1947), *The Rose Tattoo* (1950), *Suddenly Last Summer* (1959), *Out Cry* (1971), and *The Two-Character Play* (1973)—and he always felt that his ability to have her well cared for was his great accomplishment in life. In January 1944 the death of his beloved Grandmother Dakin ("Grand"), whose unwavering support over the years had often included gifts of money, was another serious blow to the Williams family.

The Glass Menagerie opened in Chicago during an ice storm in December 1944 and—thanks to the unstinting support of Chicago critics Claudia Cassidy and Ashton Stevens, both of whom used their influence to urge the public to see the production by the promising new playwright—survived the opening week's poor attendance, enabling the show to move to Broadway in March 1945. The risky casting of **Laurette Taylor**, who had long been absent from the stage, paid off in what is regarded as a legendary performance.

With his second Broadway production, *A Streetcar Named Desire*, Williams swept the awards for 1947 and embarked upon his years of success by taking a trip to Europe. He began his 14-year liaison with **Frank Merlo**, with whom he traveled in North Africa the following year. They settled in a house on **Key West**, where Williams could write, paint, and swim whenever he was not in rehearsal in New York or on location with the many films made of his plays in the 1950s and 1960s. He also published novels, collections of stories and **poems**. **Elia Kazan**, who had directed *A Streetcar Named Desire*, remained an important artistic associate. Notably, Kazan directed *Cat on a Hot Tin Roof* (1955) and *Sweet Bird of Youth* (1959), as well as the underappreciated *Camino Real* (1953). Brenda Murphy's *Tennessee Williams and Elia Kazan* documents that collaboration.

With *Camino Real*, Williams seemed finally to push the theatergoing public past its limit of tolerance for theatrical experimentation; the critics panned it as confusing as well as heavy-handed in its deployment of symbols or poetic stage devices to issue a call for brotherhood. Yet such tendencies in form and content were always present in Williams's plays. Although *The Glass Menagerie* is beloved as a lyrical coming-of-age play, it departs from traditional realism in its use of a narrator who moves in and out of memory scenes; the stage directions also call for screens on which epigraphs would be projected in Brechtian (see **Brecht, Bertolt**)

fashion. Williams's social conscience also informs this play, while other early plays like *Not about Nightingales* are far less subtle in their reference to problems faced by society's misfits and outcasts. Williams's moviegoing habit may have contributed to his cinematic sense of structure. If *Camino Real* was Williams's most experimental work to reach Broadway, it is interesting that it came so close in time to his most perfectly crafted play, *Cat on a Hot Tin Roof*, which is so tightly constructed that the stage time is unbroken real time. After the social upheavals of the 1960s and in his own life, Williams could only go forward by exploring new dramatic techniques, and this led to his sense of being victimized by critics.

The compulsion to write was the constant factor in Williams's life, both before and after the national recognition he earned at 33. None of the setbacks he experienced—illnesses, eye operations, personal relationships, critical hostility—ever disrupted his daily routine of writing on whichever of his works-in-progress came to hand. "Could you live without writing, baby?" he asked an interviewer. "I couldn't" (*Paris Review* 81 [Fall 1981]: 166). Nevertheless, the 1957 death of his father, with whom he had reconciled, took an emotional toll. He began psychoanalysis that year.

The Night of the Iguana (1961) was the last of Williams's plays to reach a wide audience. His next Broadway play, **The Milk Train Doesn't Stop Here Anymore** (1963), achieved only 69 performances; *Slapstick Tragedy*'s run (1966) was even shorter, only 7 performances. Meanwhile, Frank Merlo's death from cancer in 1963 after a period of difficulties in their relationship left Williams deeply depressed. Williams was subsequently to look back on the 1960s as his "Stoned Age," a period of especially heavy dependence on medications and alcohol. He would never miss a day of writing, although the quality sometimes led him to destroy what he had done. His restlessness impelled a life of frequent travel abroad. During his stays at his home in Key West, he also became a serious painter (see **Art**).

Obsessed with his sister Rose, whom he occasionally brought from her sanitarium to visit him in New York or Key West, Williams wrote the brother-sister play that he would continue revising for many years. *The Two-Character Play* premiered in London in 1967. A version titled *Out Cry* did well at Chicago's Ivanhoe Theatre under **George Keathley**'s direction in 1971, although Williams's emotional turmoil at that time led him to end his long association with agent Audrey Wood. Further revised and retitled *The Two-Character Play*, it reached New York in 1975. Other plays of the period included *Kingdom of Earth* (1968) and *In the Bar of a Tokyo Hotel* (1969). Williams made his acting debut as Doc in the off-Broadway premiere of his own play *Small Craft Warnings* (1972). Meanwhile he was also writing his disjointedly confessional *Memoirs* (1975).

When Williams reached the nadir of his physical and emotional resilience in 1969, his brother Dakin first orchestrated his brief conversion to Catholicism and then his three-month commitment to the mental ward of Barnes Hospital in St. Louis. Because confinement had always been one of Williams's worst fears, as exemplified in its thematic recurrence throughout his canon, Williams found it difficult to forgive his brother. His last years were spent in travel and continued playwriting: *Vieux Carré* (1977), *The Red Devil Battery Sign* (1977), *A Lovely Sunday for Creve Coeur* (1979), *Tiger Tail* (1978), *Clothes for a Summer Hotel* (1980), *Something Cloudy, Something Clear* (1981), and *A House Not Meant to Stand* (1982). Among these, two are strongly autobiographical. *Vieux Carré* re-

Tennessee Williams, 1972. Photo by Bruce Paulson. Used courtesy of New Directions Publishing Corp.

calls his early sojourns as a struggling artist in New Orleans, and *Something Cloudy, Something Clear* draws upon Williams's Cape Cod summer with Kip in 1940.

Tennessee Williams was found dead in his room at the Elysee Hotel in New York, on 25 February 1983, apparently asphyxiated from having accidentally swallowed the plastic cap of a medicine bottle. Although Williams had asked that he be cremated and the ashes scattered on the water close to where **Hart Crane** had leaped to his death from a ship north of Havana, he was buried in Mt. Calvary Cemetery in St. Louis. The proceeds from his $10 million estate were reserved for the support of his sister Rose. After her death in September 1996, the remainder of his estate went to the University of the South in Sewanee, Tennessee.

In addition to his plays, Williams wrote

novels, short stories, poetry, and a steady stream of letters. He won two Pulitzer prizes (*A Streetcar Named Desire* and *Cat on a Hot Tin Roof*) and four New York Drama Critics' Circle Awards (for the foregoing as well as *The Glass Menagerie* and *The Night of the Iguana*).

Following his death there was a period during which Williams's work was neglected by both academic critics and the stage; the eclipse might be at least partially attributed to the control exercised by a trustee of his literary estate, Lady Maria St. Just, who had befriended Williams in London in 1948 when she was **Maria Britneva**. Her influence over Williams when he was alive and her power over his posthumous reputation is chronicled by John Lahr in "The Lady and Tennessee." Her death in February 1994 seemed to open the floodgates, so that plays that had long languished in manuscript could be published, including *The Notebook of Trigorin* (a 1981 adaptation of Chekhov's *The Seagull*) and very early works: *Fugitive Kind* (1937), *Candles to the Sun* (1937), *Spring Storm* (1938), *Not about Nightingales* (1939), and *Stairs to the Roof* (1941). Others are to be expected. See also **Awards and Honors; Correspondence; Drugs; Journals; Madness; Poems; Politics; Race; Southern Literature and Culture.**

Further Reading

Bigsby, C.W.E. *A Critical Introduction to Twentieth-Century American Drama*. Vol. 2: *Williams, Miller, Albee*. Cambridge: Cambridge University Press, 1984.

Devlin, Albert J., ed. *Conversations with Tennessee Williams*. Jackson: University Press of Mississippi, 1986.

———, and Nancy M. Tischler, eds. *The Selected Letters of Tennessee Williams, Volume 1—1920–1945*. New York: New Directions, 2000.

Hale, Allean. "Early Williams: The Making of a Playwright." In *The Cambridge Companion to Tennessee Williams*, ed. Matthew C. Roudané. Cambridge: Cambridge University Press, 1997. 11–28.

———. "Tennessee Williams's St. Louis Blues." *Mississippi Quarterly* 48 (Fall 1995): 609–625.

Kolin, Philip C., ed. *The Undiscovered Country: The Later Plays of Tennessee Williams*. New York: Lang, 2002.

Lahr, John. "The Lady and Tennessee." *The New Yorker* 19 December 1994: 77–97.

Leverich, Lyle. *Tom: The Unknown Tennessee Williams*. New York: Crown, 1995.

Murphy, Brenda. *Tennessee Williams and Elia Kazan: A Collaboration in the Theatre*. Cambridge: Cambridge University Press, 1992.

Rader, Dotson. "The Art of Theater V: Tennessee Williams." *The Paris Review* 81 (Fall 1981): 144–196.

Spoto, Donald. *The Kindness of Strangers: The Life of Tennessee Williams*. Boston: Little, Brown, 1985.

Van Antwerp, Margaret A., and Sally Johns, eds. *Dictionary of Literary Biography Documentary Series*. Vol. 4: *Tennessee Williams*. Detroit: Gale, 1984.

Williams, Tennessee. *Memoirs*. Garden City, NY: Doubleday, 1975.

Felicia Hardison Londré

Williams, Walter Dakin (1919–). The second son of **Edwina** and **Cornelius**, Walter Dakin Williams was named after his maternal grandfather but enjoyed favored-son status in the eyes of his father. Unlike Tennessee, who always fancied himself a son of the South and cultivated the accent to prove it, Dakin inherited little of his mother's southern affectation and regards himself as more a midwesterner than a southerner. Though they were born eight years apart, and for the most part held little in common beyond their sibling ties, Dakin has come to regard himself as the "professional brother" of whom he calls "the world's greatest playwright."

Dakin Williams, 1998. Courtesy of the Tennessee Williams Festival.

As a child, Dakin was more extroverted and athletic than his older brother and consequently more adept at socializing, an "indomitable enthusiast," as Tennessee called him. He excelled in high school academics at University City High School in **St. Louis** and after graduation received his bachelor's and law degrees from Washington University. From there he pursued an M.B.A. at Harvard until he was drafted during World War II. While in the air force, Dakin served overseas in Burma and was recalled during the Korean War. He gained national attention in the 1960s and 1970s, in his unsuccessful attempts first as a gubernatorial candidate, then as a senatorial candidate in the State of Illinois. He even had a truncated run as a presidential candidate (on the "Love Everyone" platform).

Contrary to many published reports, Da-

kin and Tennessee enjoyed a close relationship for many of their adult years. He was Tennessee's unofficial attorney/accountant and negotiated several theater and movie productions for his brother. The most famous schism occurred in 1969, when Dakin had Tennessee committed to Barnes Hospital in St. Louis. At this time Tennessee was experiencing a paranoic breakdown as a result of his drug and alcohol intake, and Dakin most probably saved his life by hospitalizing and detoxifying his brother. Tennessee, however, regarded this forced hospitalization as an act of betrayal, and the relationship remained strained until 1982. Shortly before Tennessee died, Dakin maintains that the two brothers were reaching a rapproachment and that mysterious forces had Tennessee murdered because the playwright was considering changing his will to leave Dakin substantially more than the mere $25,000 that he had originally bequeathed to him. When Tennessee died in February 1983, Dakin buried him in St. Louis, even though Tennessee had requested to have his body thrown into the Caribbean close to where the poet **Hart Crane** had jumped overboard. Tennessee's remains were placed next to those of his mother and sister at Calvary Cemetery in St. Louis.

Even though Edwina and **Rose** are memorialized in *The Glass Menagerie*, Tennessee excluded Dakin in his most autobiographical play. But possibly Gooper in *Cat on a Hot Tin Roof* is modeled loosely on Dakin. And Cornelius McCorkle, in the unpublished *A House Not Meant to Stand*, may suggest Dakin as well as his father and Tennessee's father, Cornelius Coffin Williams.

Frequently attending the **Tennessee Williams/New Orleans Literary Festival**, Dakin continues to celebrate his brother's legacy by reading his work and commenting on the autobiographical connections. He has written several books relevant to his relationship with his brother.

Further Reading

Williams, Dakin. *The Bar Bizarre*. Key West: Sunrise Publishing, 1980.

———. *His Brother's Keeper: The Life and Murder of Tennessee Williams*. Collinsville, IL: Dakin's Corner Press, 1983.

———, with James O'Connor Sargent. *The Satanic Verses*. Memphis: EEI Publishing Co., 1997.

Williams, Dakin, and Shepherd Mead. *Tennessee Williams: An Intimate Biography*. New York: Arbor House, 1983.

———, and W.R. Stewart. *Nails of Protest*. Vanity Publisher, USA, 1996.

Robert Bray

Will Mr. Merriwether Return from Memphis? Tennessee Williams's little-known two-act comedy *Will Mr. Merriwether Return from Memphis?* was first published as a "Found Text" in the *Missouri Review* (1997), though its exact date of composition is uncertain. The plot revolves around various séances with apparitions received by two southern widows, Mrs. Louise McBride, who has been pining for the return of her boarder, a drummer named Merriwether, and her quirky neighbor, Nora Waddles, whose drunken, philandering husband comes back as a rag-time dancing apparition. Visiting the women is a cast of lovelorn, mostly historical, apparitions, including Madame du Barry, Eleanor of Aquitaine, Vincent van Gogh, and Arthur Rimbaud and his sister, who distract the widows as well as confess the frustration of their desires. Adding to the whimsy of the plot are three slapstick crones called the Eumenides; "fantastical" characters such as Mrs. Eldridge, who, with a lacquered face, draws the youth out of the black men; and a gay French instructor, dismissed because of his indiscretions, who teaches Louise's nymphal daughter Gloria. The characters' confessions, a frequent Williams device, thus occur on both sides of the grave. By poking holes in the failed romantic dreams, a staple of many of his plays from **The Glass Menagerie** to **Summer and Smoke** to **The Night of the Iguana**, Williams joins the sexually sacrosanct apparitions to their mortal auditors.

Mr. Merriwether is a mélange of putative sources, including George Peele's *Old Wives Tale* (with the wandering knight Eumendies), *A Midsummer Night's Dream*, Strindberg's *Ghost Sonata*, and Williams's lurid, early fiction, for example, "The Vengeance of Nitocris" and the "Big Black: A Mississippi Idyll" (see **Collected Stories**). *Merriwether* is hilarious in places, scandalous in others, but packed with Williams's characteristic themes and techniques. Essentially, the play is a bittersweet romp, demonstrating Williams's skill at writing fantasies, and deserves comparison with such early work as **Stairs to the Roof** (1938) and a later one such as **The Gnädiges Fräulein** (1967). The apparitions in Merriwether need to be compared with Williams's other ghosts in **Clothes for a Summer Hotel** and *Steps Must Be Gentle: A Dramatic Reading for Two Performers*. *Merriwether* captures Williams's preoccupation with investigating but rarely capturing desire. Paradoxically, Louise is caught by and yet emancipated by desire. On the one hand, she warns her daughter about the dangers of "earthly fire" that can ignite a lady's skirt yet, on the other hand, she rejoices at her drummer's return as a sexual spectre entering through her window with a daisy in his mouth. Merriwether combines Williams's humor with his pathos.

Further Reading

"Found Text." *Will Mr. Merriwether Return from Memphis? Missouri Review* 22.2 (1997): 83–131.

Philip C. Kolin

Wilson, Lanford (1937–). Lanford Wilson is a contemporary gay playwright from Missouri who had been heavily influenced by Williams. Wilson himself admitted that he owed his vocation to Williams. When he was a struggling, young writer working on a short story, he realized that the story was really a play because of its resemblance to *The Glass Menagerie*. In *Home Free* (1963), Wilson borrowed Williams's cast of sister and brother from *The Glass Menagerie* but stretches their dependency and love into the realm of incest, complete with the horror of a sister made pregnant by her brother. Wilson moved to a more open treatment of homosexuality in *Lady Bright* in which a lonely "queen" uses the telephone to mask and display her desperation, as Amanda did in *The Glass Menagerie*. His *Balm in Gilead* (1965) dramatizes the world of losers, prostitutes, and desperate survivors familiar in such Williams's plays as *Camino Real, Sweet Bird of Youth*, and *The Night of the Iguana*. Some critics recognized Wilson as Williams's heir because of their common search for transcendence and their insistence that it be sought in human, passionate experience.

Wilson made an explicit homage to Williams when he wrote the libretto for the operatic version of *Summer and Smoke* in 1971. Composer Lee Hoiby had decided to make an opera of *Summer and Smoke*, but he discovered Wilson's affinity to Williams, seeing Wilson's *The Rimers of Eldritch* (1966), and was impressed by the similar **music** of his language. Williams was pleased with Wilson's adaptation, which reduced the 120 pages of script to a 35-page libretto without sacrificing the tone or intent of *Summer and Smoke*. Williams and Wilson worked together to create a television script in 1974 when Wilson wrote the script of a story idea that Williams had supplied. *The Migrants* starred Cloris Leachman and a very young Ron Howard as the 16-year-old Lyle. An updating of Steinbeck's *The Grapes of Wrath*, this show followed a migrant laboring family from Florida to New Jersey and back again through desperate situations and backbreaking work. The script was credited to Wilson, and in the final moments of the show the teenage lovers escape the labor camp and are speeding in an old car toward Cincinnati, where they hope to find work and a better life. With no real plan, the ending sounds the Williamsesque eternal hope as the young boy insists that he will think of something. With his hit play *The Hot-l Baltimore* (1973) Wilson moved fully into the realm that Williams invoked most memorably in *Caminio Real*—a world of losers who refuse to lie down and die. His simple one-act play *Brontosaurus* (1977) also concludes with a reprise of the famous ending of *The Glass Menagerie* where Laura lights and then blows out a single candle.

Tantalizing as these specific echoes are, Wilson's worldview provides the most pervasive evidence of Williams's influence. Although over the years Wilson made many stylistic experiments, including direct addresses to the audience and the use of mixed media in his shows, he has never lost the existential loneliness that he found in Williams's characters. Both writers are interested in the blurring of illusion and reality and the interconnection of life and the theater. Although Wilson may add layers of irony and black comedy, he adheres to their shared tragic vision. However, he seldom invokes as memorably as Williams has the failure of communication, the disappointment of desire, and the hollow glory of human speech in a silent universe.

Further Reading

Barnett, Gene A. *Lanford Wilson*. Boston: Twayne, 1987.

Bryer, Jackson R., ed. *Lanford Wilson: A Casebook*. New York: Garland, 1994.

Norma Jenckes

Windham, Donald (1920–   ). An essayist, playwright, novelist, short story writer, and biographer, Donald Windham was Tennessee Williams's intermittent companion and collaborator in writing *You Touched Me!* (1943). Born and raised in Atlanta, Windham recalled his early years in *Emblems of Conduct: An Autobiography of Childhood* (1964). He left Atlanta in 1940 for New York City, where, after a brief stint as managing editor of *Dance Index*, Windham developed his creative writing skills.

At a party in January 1940, Windham met Williams, who was looking forward to the Theatre Guild's production of *Battle of Angels*. That spring, after Windham showed Williams his partially completed play script based on **D.H. Lawrence**'s short story "You Touched Me," Williams readily assented to collaborate with Windham, a gesture that recalls his only other, and earlier, coauthorship with Dorothy Shapiro on *Cairo! Shanghai! Bombay!* (1935). While readying *You Touched Me!* for production, first at the Cleveland Playhouse in October 1943 and then at New York's Booth Theatre in the fall of 1945, Williams increasingly assumed a proprietary role in the writing and staging of the play. Ostensibly a romantic comedy about the sensual awakening of Matilda, the play unmistakably bears Williams's imprint in the conception of the plot—the effect that a stultifying Puritanism has in inhibiting understanding and sympathy. Williams's struggle for artistic control generated tensions that were eventually to mar his relationship with Windham and foreshadowed problems in his collaboration with **Elia Kazan**.

A writer/director conflict again surfaced in the Windham/Williams relationship when Williams, who directed Windham's *The Starless Air* (1953), at the Houston's Playhouse Theatre, started altering lines and inserting new speeches; one speech about mendacity was used nearly word for word in *Cat on a Hot Tin Roof*. Despite their reaching a compromise, this conflict contributed to the erosion of their friendship and eventual estrangement. The play never had a New York performance. Windham's next significant publication, *The Hero Continues* (1960), took a direction that was to engage him thematically in much of his subsequent work, particularly his memoirs. Drawing partially on Tennessee Williams's career, this short novel depicts the ruinous effect that celebrity status has on the ironically named protagonist, Dennis Freeman, as he pursues success on Broadway. Williams's response was lukewarm; the generally flattering depiction of Freeman, so Williams concluded, was inadvertent. He concluded that Windham was using the book as a vehicle to release long-suppressed hostilities toward him.

Windham's *Tennessee Williams' Letters to Donald Windham, 1940–1965* (1977) generated a noisy brawl over whether or not Williams had granted Windham copyright to the letters. After a spate of charges and countercharges, along with bitter side taking between champions of each of the parties, Williams dropped a threatened lawsuit when an earlier agreement he had signed giving Windham rights to the letters was declared legally binding. The vehemence over the letters was far greater than the book's immediate critical reception; reviewers generally took pleasure in citing Williams's catty wit but lamented the lack of more important matters—backstage stories or Williams's thoughts about the theater. The letters focus on their collaboration that led up to the production of *You Touched Me!*, including some random, succinct statements Williams made about his "blue devils," namely, his bouts with depression. Otherwise, shared references to the world of theater or mutual friends are too random and gossipy to represent the milieus in which both men moved. But what is especially valuable is Williams's letter detailing the structural problems he perceived in **Sweet Bird of Youth** or another letter where Williams, touchingly though grudgingly, acknowledges the pain his hated father suffered.

Sandy Campbell, Windham's intimate companion, published limited editions of some of Windham's more recent autobiographical memoirs, notably *As If . . . A Personal View of Tennessee Williams* (1985). A pastiche of impressions, anecdotes, "snapshots," and "parentheses" about Williams, *As If* reveals the ambiguous and contradictory elements in the playwright's behavior. The title sums up Windham's conclusion—Williams's skill in giving others the impression of identifying with them, of being vulnerable, engaged, and disarmingly honest, was counterfeit, was simply "as if." Dismissing Williams's *Memoirs* (1975) and the essays collected in *Where I Live* (1978) as misleading, Windham instead mines Williams's plays (notably **The Night of the Iguana** and **The Rose Tattoo**) and his fiction (**The Roman Spring of Mrs. Stone**, "One Arm," "Hard Candy," and **Moise and the World of Reason**) for passages displaying Williams's dramatized self-portraits and his fiery dynamics with his family. Though not accurate biography, the letters about the royalty distribution of *You Touched Me!* or the quarrel over the publication of Windham's *Letters* are worthwhile. Windham's primary interest in these, however, is self-vindication. Windham's *As If* and *Footnote to a Friendship: A Memoir of Truman Capote* (1983), issued together as *Lost Friendships: A Memoir of Truman Capote,*

Tennessee Williams, and Others (1987), were regarded either as vehicles for evening up old grudges or as compassionate and remarkably tactful portraits of artists bedeviled by drugs, alcohol, and celebrity.

Further Reading

Brustein, Robert. "The Perfect Friend." *New York Times Book Review* 20 November 1977: 9.

Devlin, Albert J., and Nancy M. Tischler, eds. *Selected Letters of Tennessee Williams, Volume 1—1920–1945.* New York: New Directions, 2000.

Kellner, Bruce. "Donald Windham." In *Contemporary Gay American Novelists: A Bio-Bibliographical Sourcebook.* Westport, CT: Greenwood, 1993. 401–407.

———. *Donald Windham: A Bio-Bibliography.* Westport, CT: Greenwood, 1991.

Rascoe, Burton. "*You Touched Me!* A First Rate Comedy." *New York World Telegram* 26 September 1945: 34.

Arthur Wrobel

Wood, Audrey (1905–1985). Tennessee Williams's first agent and close friend for 32 years, Audrey Wood was arguably the most famous literary agent in New York from the founding of the Liebling-Wood Agency in 1937 through the 1970s, when Wood was head of the drama department of International Creative Management (ICM). Not only was she an agent for playwrights like **William Inge** and Preston Jones, but she represented Williams's novelist friends such as **Carson McCullers** and **Truman Capote**. Her judgment was highly regarded.

Williams was introduced to Wood when he entered **American Blues** in the **Group Theatre** play contest in 1938. Although he did not win first prize, his collection of plays caught the attention of Group playreader **Molly Day Thacher**, who persuaded the company to award him a special prize of

$100. When Thacher wrote Williams in California about the award, she suggested Wood as a good agent. Thacher also called Wood and recommended Williams, sending his *American Blues* as an introduction. Several days later, Wood wrote Williams and encouraged him to come to New York. Too unsure of himself to venture all the way to New York on speculation, he sent Wood some plays and the story "The Field of Blue Children," which touched Wood deeply. Williams and Wood continued to correspond as he worked his way across the continent. In early September 1939, he hitchhiked into New York and, still disheveled from the road, went directly to the Liebling-Wood agency.

Wood was a no-nonsense, all-business, shrewd, and dedicated agent for her clients. Williams's tattered initial appearance and his diffidence, however, appealed to Wood, and she, her husband, and Thacher began to look after this apparently vulnerable and lost southern youth, out of place in New York and without resources beyond the remains of the Group's $100. Wood advised Williams in all aspects of his life, not just his budding career as a dramatist, and found herself acting as surrogate mother to her lost southern boy. For all his mood swings, his paranoia, and his hypochondria, Williams awakened in Wood a maternal response that may have rivaled that of **Edwina Williams** herself. Wood encouraged Williams to study the theater business and attend plays, and she urged the young writer to enroll in the Playwrights Seminar taught by Theresa Helburn and John Gassner at the **New School for Social Research** in the fall of 1940. She also suggested he spend the summer that year at Provincetown, Massachusetts, the site of Williams's *Something Cloudy, Something Clear,* among other works. In 1943, Wood got her young client his first real salaried job

as a writer—working for Metro-Goldwyn-Mayer (see **Hollywood**) as a screenwriter. The job led directly to his first New York hit, *The Glass Menagerie.*

Indeed, from its very conception *The Glass Menagerie* was in large the result of Wood's faith in and support of Williams and his immense promise. From securing Williams the MGM job during which he wrote the screenplay for *The Gentleman Caller,* which evolved into *The Glass Menagerie*; through guiding him through the revisions; through sending the final draft to **Eddie Dowling,** who ultimately produced and directed it; through serving as nursemaid and protector to Dowling's novice financial backer, Louis J. Singer, and to Williams's overprotective mother during rehearsals and early tryouts; through defending the script against a proprietary claim by MGM; though shepherding the playwright to and through the White House reception for the cast; to making the deal for the 1950 Warner Brothers film—Wood was midwife to her client's first successful theatrical achievement.

Wood loyally and enthusiastically represented Williams, seeing him through the debacle of *Battle of Angels* in 1940, Williams's first professional failure, as well as the triumphs of *The Glass Menagerie* (1945)—six years after she first began to represent him—and *A Streetcar Named Desire* (1947). She also represented him for *Camino Real* (1953), *Cat on a Hot Tin Roof* (1955), *Kingdom of Earth* (*The Seven Descents of Myrtle*) (1968), and *The Two-Character Play/Out Cry* (1971) and gave him dramaturgical advice on the numerous drafts and revisions of each of his scripts with encouraging, constructive, knowledgeable guidance on such matters as cutting speeches, expanding scenes, and developing characters.

Tennessee Williams and Audrey Wood, date unknown. Harry Ransom Humanities Research Center, The University of Texas at Austin.

In his early years, Wood managed Williams's money, banking his salary from MGM and the early royalties from *The Glass Menagerie* and doling out a small allowance to him. She negotiated the deals for many of his stage productions, the publication of his plays and novels, and the film adaptations of *The Glass Menagerie*, *A Streetcar Named Desire*, and **Suddenly Last Summer**. Wood also made the arrangements for **Anna Magnani** to appear in the film version of **The Rose Tattoo**, helped persuade a reluctant Margaret Leighton to accept the part of Hannah Jelkes in *The Night of the Iguana*, and finally convinced an unwilling Geraldine Page to sign her contract for **Sweet Bird of Youth** on the first day of rehearsals. It was Wood who, with producer **Irene Selznick**, selected **Elia Kazan** to direct *A Streetcar Named Desire* and helped change his mind when he demurred, and in so doing helped to make American theatre history.

Over the years, in truth, Wood advised Williams and influenced all his career decisions—and many of his personal ones—

though he ultimately made them himself. Williams's thorny and changeable nature, exacerbated by his health, drug, and alcohol problems, finally made him resent and distrust Wood's influence, and their relationship dissolved acrimoniously in July 1971. Williams and Wood remained estranged until Edwina Williams's death in 1980, when Wood broke the silence. A debilitating stroke in 1981 ended Wood's career in the theater; she died in 1985.

Further Reading

Devlin, Albert J., and Nancy M. Tischler, eds. *The Selected Letters of Tennessee Williams, Volume 1—1920–1945.* New York: New Directions, 2000.

Leverich, Lyle. *Tom: The Unknown Tennessee Williams.* New York: Crown, 1995.

Wood, Audrey, with Max Wilk. *Represented by Audrey Wood.* Garden City, NY: Doubleday, 1981.

Richard E. Kramer

Y

You Touched Me! Frequently overlooked by scholars and critics, *You Touched Me!*, a comedy based on the **D.H. Lawrence** short story of the same name, was Tennessee Williams's sole dramatic collaboration, except for a very small part that Dorothy Shapiro contributed to *Cairo! Shanghai! Bombay!* Working with his friend and writer **Donald Windham**, Williams actually completed work on *You Touched Me!* prior to the opening of *The Glass Menagerie*, the play that catapulted him to the front rank of American dramatists in the mid-1940s.

After tryouts in Cleveland and Pasadena, *You Touched Me!*, under Guthrie Mc-Clintic's direction, opened on Broadway at the Booth Theatre on 25 September 1945. It was not well received, and the triumphant opening of *The Glass Menagerie* only a few months earlier added to critical disappointment. The more insightful critics recognized thematic connections with *The Glass Menagerie* despite the fact that *You Touched Me!* was billed as a romantic comedy, but most also felt that the Williams-Windham collaboration was a decided step backward for Williams.

Although its setting is changed to the present, *You Touched Me!* mirrors the events of the original story by Lawrence, who had a seminal influence on Williams. The play focuses on the attempt of a World War II flyer, Hadrian (played in the original production by a young Montgomery Clift), to get his childhood friend, Matilda, away from the influence of her narrow-minded, rigidly conservative Aunt Emmie. Hadrian is assisted in his machinations by Matilda's father, an alcoholic ex-sea captain, Cornelius Rockley (Edmund Gwenn in the Broadway production), a man defeated by life who is able to find a touch of redemption through his hope for Matilda's escape. Emmie, who schemes to marry her rector as an enhancement to her moral superiority in the stifling mid-western small town in which the play is set, attempts to control Matilda and, as Rockley bitterly complains, to turn her into a lifeless piece of clay. Emmie ultimately fails in this as well as her periodic attempts to reform the Captain when Matilda runs away with Hadrian.

Williams's contributions are unmistakable in the play's romanticism and in its lyrical pleas for compassion. Matilda, a sensitive spirit, is a somewhat more resolute and capable character than *The Glass Menagerie*'s Laura, but the connections are obvious. Encounters between Emmie and Matilda are reminiscent of those between Laura and her domineering mother, Amanda, in *The Glass Menagerie*, but the strength of *You Touched Me!* lies in the delicately written scenes between Hadrian, who attempts to grasp her fears, and Matilda, who is tentatively drawn to Hadrian's passion for living. Critics described the play as a fable, but most found it a misfire, stressing that its poetic realism was somewhat uneasily mated with comedy that, at times, bordered on farce. Many reviewers applauded the play's insistence on touching and being touched by others as well as the sympathy for the fragile hopes human beings share which is essential in this tragic and lonely world.

Although *You Touched Me!* had a brief life on summer theater and college stages, it is rarely produced and seems an artifact of an earlier era of American plays that Williams otherwise rejected as he led American drama into a new era of innovation and seriousness.

The rocky friendship between Williams and Windham continued into the 1960s, culminating in the late 1970s with Windham's publication of his 25-year **correspondence** with Williams, a collection of letters some critics felt damaged Williams's reputation.

Further Reading

Fedder, Norman J. *The Influence of D.H. Lawrence on Tennessee Williams.* The Hague: Mouton, 1966.

Weales, Gerald. "Tennessee Williams Borrows a Little Shaw." *Shaw Review* 8.2 (May 1965): 63–64.

Windham, Donald. *Lost Friendships: A Memoir of Truman Capote, Tennessee Williams, and Others.* New York: William Morrow, 1983.

———, ed. *Tennessee Williams' Letters to Donald Windham, 1940–1965.* New York: Holt, 1977.

James Fisher

Bibliography of Primary Sources

Works are arranged chronologically.

COLLECTIONS OF THE PLAYS

The Theatre of Tennessee Williams. 8 vols. New York: New Directions, 1971–1992.

Tennessee Williams: Plays 1937–1955. Ed. Mel Gussow and Kenneth Holditch. New York: Library of America, 2000.

Tennessee Williams: Plays 1957–1980. Ed. Mel Gussow and Kenneth Holditch. New York: Library of America, 2000.

INDIVIDUAL PLAYS

Battle of Angels. New York: New Directions, 1945.

Twenty-seven Wagons Full of Cotton and Other One-Act Plays. Norfolk, CT: New Directions, 1945; London: Grey Walls, 1947. Contains *Twenty-seven Wagons Full of Cotton: A Mississippi Delta Comedy*; *The Purification*; *The Lady of Larkspur Lotion*; *The Last of My Solid Gold Watches*; *Portrait of a Madonna*; *Auto-Da-Fé: A Tragedy in One Act*; *Lord Byron's Love Letter*; *The Strangest Kind of Romance: A Lyric Play in Four Scenes*; *The Long Goodbye*; *Hello from Bertha*. The expanded 1953 edition from New Directions includes three additional later plays not in the 1945 edition: *This Property Is Condemned*; *Talk to Me Like the Rain and Let Me Listen*; and *Something Unspoken*.

A Streetcar Named Desire. New York: New Directions, 1947.

You Touched Me! With Donald Windham. New York: French, 1947.

American Blues: Five Short Plays. New York: Dramatists Play Service, 1948. Contains *Moony's Kid Don't Cry*; *The Dark Room*; *The Case of the Crushed Petunias: A Lyrical Fantasy*; *The Long Stay Cut Short, or The Unsatisfactory Supper*; and *Ten Blocks on the Camino Real*.

Summer and Smoke. New York: New Directions, 1948.

I Rise in Flame, Cried the Phoenix. New York: New Directions, 1951.

The Rose Tattoo. New York: New Directions, 1951.

Camino Real. Norfolk, CT: New Directions, 1953.

Cat on a Hot Tin Roof. New York: New Directions, 1955. Rev. ed., New York: New Directions, 1975.

Bibliography of Primary Sources

Baby Doll. New York: New Directions, 1956.

Orpheus Descending [with *Battle of Angels*]. New York: New Directions, 1958.

Suddenly Last Summer. New York: New Directions, 1958.

Garden District. London: Secker & Warburg, 1959.

Sweet Bird of Youth. New York: New Directions, 1959.

Period of Adjustment. New York: New Directions, 1960.

The Night of the Iguana. New York: New Directions, 1962.

The Eccentricities of a Nightingale and *Summer and Smoke.* New York: New Directions, 1964.

Grand. New York: House of Books, 1964.

The Milk Train Doesn't Stop Here Anymore. New York: New Directions, 1964.

Kingdom of Earth (The Seven Descents of Myrtle). New York: New Directions, 1968.

In the Bar of a Tokyo Hotel. New York: New Dramatists Play Service, 1969.

The Two-Character Play. New York: New Directions, 1969.

Dragon Country: A Book of Plays. New York: New Directions, 1970. Contains *In the Bar of a Tokyo Hotel*; *I Rise in Flame, Cried the Phoenix*; *The Mutilated*; *I Can't Imagine Tomorrow*; *Confessional*; *The Frosted Glass Coffin*; *The Gnädiges Fräulein*; and *A Perfect Analysis Given by a Parrot.*

Small Craft Warnings. New York: New Directions, 1972.

Out Cry. New York: New Directions, 1973.

This Is (An Entertainment). Unpublished. San Francisco, performed 1976.

Kirche, Kutchen, und Kinder. Unpublished. New York, performed 1979.

Vieux Carré. New York: New Directions, 1979.

A Lovely Sunday for Creve Coeur. New York: New Directions, 1980.

Steps Must Be Gentle. New York: Targ Editions, 1980.

Clothes for a Summer Hotel: A Ghost Play. New York: New Directions, 1981.

The Travelling Companion. Christopher Street 58 (1981): 32–40.

The Remarkable Rooming-House of Mme. Le Monde. New York: Albondocani Press, 1984.

Stopped Rocking and Other Screenplays. New York: New Directions, 1984. Contains *Stopped Rocking*; *All Gaul Is Divided*; *The Loss of a Teardrop Diamond*; and *One Arm.*

The Red Devil Battery Sign. New York: New Directions, 1988.

Tiger Tail [with *Baby Doll*]. New York: New Directions, 1991.

Something Cloudy, Something Clear. New York: New Directions, 1995.

The Notebook of Trigorin: A Free Adaptation of Anton Chekhov's "The Sea Gull." New York: New Directions, 1997.

Will Mr. Merriwether Return from Memphis? Missouri Review 22.2 (1997): 89–131.

Not about Nightingales. New York: New Directions, 1998.

Spring Storm. New York: New Directions, 1999.

Stairs to the Roof: A Prayer for the Wild of Heart That Are Kept in Cages. New York: New Directions, 2000.

Fugitive Kind. New York: New Directions, 2001.

Candles to the Sun. New York: New Directions (forthcoming).

COLLECTION OF FICTION

Collected Stories. With an introduction by Gore Vidal. New York: New Directions, 1985.

FICTION

One Arm and Other Stories. New York: New Directions, 1948. Contains "One Arm," "The Malediction," "The Poet," "Chronicle of a Demise," "Desire and the Black Masseur," "Portrait of a Girl in Glass," "The Important Thing," "The Angel in the Alcove," "The Field of Blue Children," "The Night of the Iguana," and "The Yellow Bird."

The Roman Spring of Mrs. Stone. New York: New Directions, 1950.

Hard Candy: A Book of Stories. New York: New Directions, 1954. Contains "Three Players of a Summer Game," "Two on a Party," "The Resemblance between a Violin Case and a Coffin," "Hard Candy," "Rubio y Morena," "The Mattress by the Tomato Patch," "The Coming of Something to the Widow Holly," "The Vine," and "The Mysteries of the Joy Rio."

Three Players of a Summer Game and Other Stories. Harmondsworth, England: Penguin Books, 1965. Contains "Three Players of a Summer Game," "The Important Thing," "One Arm," "Portrait of a Girl in Glass," "The Coming of Something to the Widow Holly," "Two in a Party," "The Yellow Bird," "The Field of Blue Children," The Malediction," "The Angel in the Alcove," "The Resemblance between a Violin Case and a Coffin," and "The Night of the Iguana."

The Knightly Quest and Other Stories. New York: New Directions, 1966. Contains "The Knightly Quest," "Mama's Old Stucco House," "Man Bring This Up Road," "The Kingdom of Earth," and "Grand."

The Knightly Quest: A Novella and Twelve Short Stories. London: Secker and Warburg, 1968. Contains "The Knightly Quest," "The Poet," "Chronicle of a Demise," "Desire and the Black Masseur," "Hard Candy," "Rubio y Morena," "The Mattress by the Tomato Patch," "The Vine," "The Mysteries of the Joy Rio," "Mama's

Old Stucco House," "Man Bring This Up Road," "The Kingdom of Earth," and "Grand."

Eight Mortal Ladies Possessed: A Book of Stories. New York: New Directions, 1974. Contains "Happy August the Tenth," "The Inventory at Fontana Bella," "Miss Coynte of Greene," "Sabbatha and Solitude," "Completed," and "Oriflamme."

Moise and the World of Reason. New York: Simon and Schuster, 1975.

It Happened the Day the Sun Rose. Los Angeles: Sylvester & Orphanos, 1981.

ESSAYS

Where I Live: Selected Essays. Ed. Christine R. Day and Bob Woods. New York: New Directions, 1978.

POETRY

In the Winter of Cities: Poems. Norfolk, CT: New Directions, 1964.

Androgyne, Mon Amour: Poems. New York: New Directions, 1977.

NONFICTION

Memoirs. New York: Doubleday, 1975.

The Collected Poems of Tennessee Williams. Ed. David Roessel and Nicholas Moschovakis. New York: New Directions, 2002.

Bibliography of Secondary Sources

LETTERS, INTERVIEWS, JOURNALS

Devlin, Albert J., ed. *Conversations with Tennessee Williams*. Jackson: University Press of Mississippi, 1986.

———, and Nancy M. Tischler, eds. *The Selected Letters of Tennessee Williams, Volume 1—1920–1945*. New York: New Directions, 2000.

Fox, Peggy L., and Thomas Keith, eds. *Tennessee Williams and James Laughlin: Selected Letters*. New York: Norton, forthcoming.

St. Just, Maria. *Five O'Clock Angel: Letters of Tennessee Williams to Maria St. Just, 1948–1982*. New York: Knopf, 1990.

Thornton, Margaret, ed. *The Journals of Tennessee Williams*. New Haven, CT: Yale University Press, 2004.

Windham, Donald, ed. *Tennessee Williams' Letters to Donald Windham, 1940–1965*. New York: Holt, 1977.

BIBLIOGRAPHIES

Crandell, George W. *Tennessee Williams: A Descriptive Bibliography*. Pittsburgh: University of Pittsburgh Press, 1995.

Gunn, Drewey Wayne. *Tennessee Williams: A Bibliography*. 2nd ed. Metuchen, NJ: Scarecrow, 1991.

Kolin, Philip C. *Tennessee Williams: A Guide to Research and Performance*. Westport, CT: Greenwood, 1998.

McCann, John S. *The Critical Reputation of Tennessee Williams: A Reference Guide*. Boston: G.K. Hall, 1983.

BIOGRAPHIES

Hayman, Ronald. *Tennessee Williams: Everyone Else Is an Audience*. New Haven, CT: Yale University Press, 1993.

Holditch, Kenneth, and Richard Freeman Leavitt. *Tennessee Williams and the South*. Jackson: University Press of Mississippi, 2002.

Leavitt, Richard, ed. *The World of Tennessee Williams*. New York: Putnam, 1978.

Leverich, Lyle. *Tom: The Unknown Tennessee Williams*. New York: Crown, 1995.

Maxwell, Gilbert. *Tennessee Williams and Friends*. Cleveland, OH: World, 1965.

Nelson, Benjamin. *Tennessee Williams: The Man and His Work*. New York: Oblensky, 1961.

Pagan, Nicholas. *Rethinking Literary Biography: A Postmodern Approach to Tennessee Williams*. Rutherford, NJ: Fairleigh Dickinson University Press, 1993.

Rader, Dotson. *Tennessee: Cry of the Heart: An Intimate Memoir of Tennessee Williams.* Garden City, NY: Doubleday, 1985.

Rasky, Harry. *Tennessee Williams: A Portrait in Laughter and Lamentation.* New York: Dodd, 1986.

Smith, Bruce. *Costly Performances. Tennessee Williams: The Last Stage.* New York: Paragon, 1990.

Spoto, Donald. *The Kindness of Strangers: The Life of Tennessee Williams.* Boston: Little, Brown, 1985.

Steen, Mike. *A Look at Tennessee Williams.* New York: Hawthorn, 1969.

Van Antwerp, Margaret A., and Sally Johns, eds. *Dictionary of Literary Biography Documentary Series.* Vol. 4: *Tennessee Williams.* Detroit: Gale, 1984.

Williams, Dakin, and Shepherd Mead. *Tennessee Williams: An Intimate Biography.* New York: Arbor House, 1983.

Williams, Edwina Dakin [as told to Lucy Freeman]. *Remember Me to Tom.* New York: Putnam, 1963.

Windham, Donald. *Lost Friendships: A Memoir, Truman Capote, Tennessee Williams and Others.* New York: Morrow, 1987.

Wood, Audrey, with Max Wilk. *Represented by Audrey Wood.* Garden City, NY: Doubleday, 1981.

CRITICISM

Adler, Thomas P. *American Drama, 1940–1960: A Critical History.* New York: Twayne, 1994.

———. *Mirror on the Stage: The Pulitzer Plays as an Approach to American Drama.* West Lafayette, IN: Purdue University Press, 1987.

———. *"A Streetcar Named Desire": The Moth and the Lantern.* Boston: Twayne, 1990.

Bigsby, C.W.E. *A Critical Introduction to Twentieth-Century American Drama.* Vol. 2: *Williams, Miller, Albee.* Cambridge: Cambridge University Press, 1984.

———. *Modern American Drama, 1945–2000.* Cambridge: Cambridge University Press, 2000.

Bloom, Harold, ed. *"The Glass Menagerie": Modern Critical Interpretations.* New York: Chelsea House, 1988.

———. *"A Streetcar Named Desire": Modern Critical Interpretations.* New York: Chelsea House, 1988.

———. *Tennessee Williams: Modern Critical Views.* New York: Chelsea House, 1988.

Boxill, Roger. *Tennessee Williams.* London: Macmillan, 1987.

Crandell, George W., ed. *The Critical Response to Tennessee Williams.* Westport, CT: Greenwood, 1996.

Debusscher, Gilbert, and Henry I. Schvey, eds. *New Essays on American Drama.* Amsterdam: Rodopi, 1989.

Falk, Signi L. *Tennessee Williams.* Rev. ed. Boston: Twayne, 1978.

Fedder, Norman J. *The Influence of D.H. Lawrence on Tennessee Williams.* The Hague: Mouton, 1966.

Fleche, Anne. *Mimetic Disillusion: Eugene O'Neill, Tennessee Williams, and U.S. Dramatic Realism.* Tuscaloosa: University of Alabama Press, 1997.

Griffin, Alice. *Understanding Tennessee Williams.* Columbia: University of South Carolina Press, 1995.

Gross, Robert F., ed. *Tennessee Williams: A Casebook.* New York: Routledge, 2002.

Hauptmann, Robert. *The Pathological Vision: Jean Genet, Louis-Ferdinand Celine, and Tennessee Williams.* New York: Lang, 1984.

Hirsch, Foster. *A Portrait of the Artist: The Plays of Tennessee Williams.* Port Washington, NY: Kennikat, 1979.

Hurrell, John D., ed. *Two Modern American Tragedies: Reviews and Criticism of "Death of a Salesman" and "A Streetcar Named Desire."* New York: Scribner, 1961.

Jackson, Esther Merle. *The Broken World of Tennessee Williams.* Madison: University of Wisconsin Press, 1965.

Kolin, Philip C. *Williams: "A Streetcar Named Desire."* Plays in Production. Cambridge: Cambridge University Press, 2000.

————, ed. *Confronting Tennessee Williams's "A Streetcar Named Desire": Essays in Critical Pluralism.* Westport, CT: Greenwood, 1993.

————, ed. *Tennessee Williams: A Guide to Research and Performance.* Westport, CT: Greenwood, 1998.

————, ed. *The Undiscovered Country: The Later Plays of Tennessee Williams.* New York: Lang, 2002.

Londré, Felicia Hardison. *Tennessee Williams.* New York: Ungar, 1979.

Miller, Jordan Y., ed. *Twentieth Century Interpretations of "A Streetcar Named Desire": A Collection of Critical Essays.* Englewood Cliffs, NJ: Prentice-Hall, 1971.

Murphy, Brenda. *Tennessee Williams and Elia Kazan: A Collaboration in the Theatre.* Cambridge: Cambridge University Press, 1992.

O'Connor, Jacqueline. *Dramatizing Dementia: Madness in the Plays of Tennessee Williams.* Bowling Green, OH: Bowling Green State University Popular Press, 1997.

Parker, Dorothy, ed. *Essays on Modern American Drama: Williams, Miller, Albee, and Shepard.* Toronto: University of Toronto Press, 1987.

Parker, R.B., ed. *"The Glass Menagerie": A Collection of Critical Essays.* Englewood Cliffs, NJ: Prentice-Hall, 1983.

Phillips, Gene D. *The Films of Tennessee Williams.* Philadelphia: Arts Alliance, 1980.

Robinson, Marc. *The Other American Drama.* Cambridge: Cambridge University Press, 1994.

Roudané, Matthew C. *The Cambridge Companion to Tennessee Williams.* Cambridge: Cambridge University Press, 1997.

Saddik, Annette. *The Politics of Reputation: The Critical Reception of Tennessee Williams' Later Plays.* Madison, NJ: Fairleigh Dickinson University Press, 1999.

Savran, David. *Communists, Cowboys, and Queers: The Politics of Masculinity in the Work of Arthur Miller and Tennessee Williams.* Minneapolis: University of Minnesota Press, 1992.

Schlueter, June, ed. *Dramatic Closure: Reading the End.* Rutherford, NJ: Fairleigh Dickinson University Press, 1995.

Shaland, Irene. *Tennessee Williams on the Soviet Stage.* Lanham, MD: University Press of America, 1987.

Sievers, W. David. *Freud on Broadway: A History of Psychoanalysis and the American Drama.* New York: Hermitage, 1955.

Stanton, Stephen S., ed. *Tennessee Williams: A Collection of Critical Essays.* Englewood Cliffs, NJ: Prentice-Hall, 1977.

Tharpe, Jac, ed. *Tennessee Williams: A Tribute.* Jackson: University Press of Mississippi, 1977.

Thompson, Judith J. *Tennessee Williams' Plays: Memory, Myth, and Symbol.* Rev. ed. New York: Lang, 2002.

Tischler, Nancy M. *Tennessee Williams: Rebellious Puritan.* New York: Citadel Press, 1961.

Vannatta, Dennis. *Tennessee Williams: A Study of the Short Fiction.* Boston: Twayne, 1988.

Voss, Ralph, F., ed. *The Magical Muse: Millennial Essays on Tennessee Williams.* Tuscaloosa: University of Alabama Press, 2002.

Yacowar, Maurice. *Tennessee Williams and Film.* New York: Ungar, 1977.

Index

Note: Page numbers for each main entry are in **bold** type. Topics directly related to Tennessee Williams, such as the names of specific plays and other works, are found under "Williams, Tennessee," and not in the main sequence of the index.

Index

338

About the Editor and Contributors

PHILIP C. KOLIN, professor of English at the University of Southern Mississippi, has published 25 books. He is the founding coeditor of *Studies in American Drama, 1945–Present* and has published widely on Williams. Among his books are *American Playwrights since 1945*, *Confronting Tennessee Williams's "A Streetcar Named Desire": Essays in Critical Pluralism*, *Tennessee Williams: A Guide to Research and Performance*, *Williams: "A Streetcar Named Desire"* (in the Cambridge University Press Plays in Production Series), and *The Undiscovered Country: The Later Plays of Tennessee Williams*. Kolin has also edited special issues of the following journals on Williams—*Mississippi Quarterly*, *Southern Quarterly*, and *Studies in American Drama, 1945–Present*. His essays on Williams have appeared in *Missouri Review*, *Theatre History Studies*, *American Drama*, *Modern Drama*, *Tennessee Williams Literary Journal*, *Tennessee Williams Annual Review*, *Journal of Dramatic Theory and Criticism*, *Theatre Survey*, *American Drama*, *Centennial Review*, *Popular Culture Review*, *Literature/Film Quarterly*, *Resources for American Literary Studies*, and *Magical Muse: The Theatre of Tennessee Williams*. Kolin is also the theater reviews editor for the *Tennessee Williams Annual Review* and the general editor for the Routledge Shakespeare Criticism Series. He has also published books on Edward Albee, David Rabe, Shakespeare, and (forthcoming) Adrienne Kennedy. His *Successful Writing at Work* is now in its seventh edition. Kolin has published two books of poetry as well—*Roses for Sharron* and *Deep Wonder*, which won an award from the Catholic Press Association.

THOMAS P. ADLER is professor of English at Purdue University. His numerous publications on modern and American and British playwrights include *"A Streetcar Named Desire": The Moth and the Lantern* and two chapters on Williams in his book *American Drama, 1940–1960: A Critical History*. He also authored *Mirror on the Stage: The Pulitzer Plays as an Approach to American Drama*. His many articles on Williams and other contemporary playwrights have appeared in *Modern Drama*, *Theatre*

Journal, Mississippi Quarterly, and other publications.

SIDNEY BERGER is John and Rebecca Moores Professor and Director of the School of Theatre, University of Houston. Berger is also the founder and producing director of the Houston Shakespeare Festival and the Children's Theatre Festival. Recently inducted into the College of Fellows of the American Theatre at the Kennedy Center, Berger has extensive professional directing experience, including productions at the Alley Theatre, where he served as an associate artist, Theatre under the Stars, and at Stages Repertory Theatre. Among his publications are *The Theatre Team* and *The Playwright versus the Director*, both coedited with Jeane Luere.

STEPHEN J. BOTTOMS is a senior lecturer in theater studies at the University of Glasgow, Scotland. He is the editor of Methuen's recent student edition of *The Glass Menagerie* and author of *The Theatre of Sam Shepard* and *Albee: Who's Afraid of Virginia Woolf?*, both from Cambridge University Press. He also edited *The Cambridge Companion to Edward Albee.*

ROBERT BRAY, professor of English at Middle Tennessee State University, is the founding editor of the *Tennessee Williams Annual Review* and the founding director of the Tennessee Williams Scholars' Conference, held each March in New Orleans. He has contributed an essay on Williams and politics for *Confronting Tennessee Williams's "A Streetcar Named Desire": Essays in Critical Pluralism* and two chapters to *Tennessee Williams: A Guide to Research and Performance*. His most recent work includes articles in the *Historic New Orleans Quarterly* as well as the introductions to

New Directions editions of *The Glass Menagerie* and *Vieux Carré*.

JACKSON R. BRYER is professor of English at the University of Maryland and coeditor of *Resources for American Literary Study*. He has published more than 30 books on American authors. He has also edited Eugene O'Neill's letters for Yale University Press. His essay " 'Entitled to Write about Her Life': Tennessee Williams and F. Scott and Zelda Fitzgerald" was published in *Magical Muse: Millennial Essays on Tennessee Williams*. He is the director of the Scholar's Conference for the Annual William Inge Theatre Festival.

MARK CAVE is manuscripts librarian at the Historic New Orleans Collection, which is the home of the Fred W. Todd Tennessee Williams Collection. He has worked at cataloging this immense collection and facilitating access to it.

MARK EDWARD CLARK is associate professor of classics at the University of Southern Mississippi. His publications on classics and the classical tradition have appeared in such journals as *Museum Helveticum, Philologus, Rheinisches Museum, Illinois Classical Studies, Classical World, Numen*, and *Bulletin for the History of Medicine*. Clark continues to work on the influence of classics upon Williams and other southern writers.

JOHN M. CLUM is professor of theater studies and English and chair of the Department of Theater Studies at Duke University. His essays on Tennessee Williams have appeared in *Modern Drama* and *The Cambridge Companion to Tennessee Williams*, as well as in his book *Acting Gay: Male Homosexuality in Modern Drama*. He is also the author of *Something for the Boys: Musical Theater and Gay Culture* and *"He's All Man": Learning Masculinity, Gayness and Love from American Movies*. His play *Randy's House* has been produced all over the United States.

GEORGE W. CRANDELL serves as head of the English Department at Auburn University. He is the author of *Tennessee Williams: A Descriptive Bibliography* and editor of *The Critical Response to Tennessee Williams*. He has contributed to *Tennessee Williams: A Guide to Research and Performance* and *Magical Muse: Millennial Essays on Tennessee Williams*. His essay " 'I Can't Imagine Tomorrow': Tennessee Williams and Representations of Time in *Clothes for a Summer Hotel*" was published in *The Undiscovered Country: The Later Plays of Tennessee Williams*. His numerous articles have appeared in *Modern Drama*, *Mississippi Quarterly*, *Southern Quarterly*, and other publications.

MAUREEN CURLEY has published in a variety of academic areas. She has written on Yeats for the *Yeats Eliot Review*, on Adrienne Kennedy for the *Bulletin of Bibliography*, on Anne Sexton for *Notes on Contemporary Literature*, and on Sylvia Plath and Langston Hughes for *The Explicator*. She has also published an essay on the influence of business models on teacher education in *School and Community*. Her poetry has appeared in *Silver Wings*. Most recently, she has prepared a writing guide for Houghton Mifflin as well as contributed several Tech Notes to the seventh edition of *Successful Writing at Work*. With Philip C. Kolin, she is coeditor of *Lilies: A Journal of Sacramental Poetry*. Curley is also at work on a collection of short stories tentatively entitled *The Shared Closet*.

ALBERT J. DEVLIN is professor of English at the University of Missouri, Columbia, specializing in modern and southern American literature. He has authored and edited books on Eudora Welty (*Eudora Welty's Chronicle: A Story of Mississippi Life*, and *Welty: A Life in Literature*) and Tennessee Williams (*Conversations with Tennessee Williams*). He served as consultant for the Tennessee Williams film project, *Lion of the American Stage* (PBS, 1995) and, with Nancy Tischler, edited the Williams estate-authorized edition *The Selected Letters of Tennessee Williams, Volume 1—1920–1945* and the forthcoming second volume. He has contributed an essay on *Cat on a Hot Tin Roof* to *The Cambridge Companion to Tennessee Williams* and on the significance of the year 1939 in Williams's life in *Magical Muse: Millennial Essays on Tennessee Williams*. His articles have appeared in the *Tennessee Williams Literary Journal* and elsewhere.

CARLOS L. DEWS is associate professor of English at Columbus State University and founding director of the Carson McCullers Center for Writers and Musicians. He is the editor of *Illumination and Night Glare: The Unfinished Autobiography of Carson McCullers* and the editor of the Library of America's edition of McCullers's complete novels. He is at work on a book about the friendship of Carson McCullers and Tennessee Williams.

LESLIE ATKINS DURHAM is an assistant professor of theater arts at Boise State University. Her writing on Gertrude Stein has recently appeared in the *Journal of Dramatic Theory and Criticism* and in *Text and Performance Quarterly*. She is currently completing a book-length study on productions of Gertrude Stein's work. Her directing credits include work by Tennessee Williams,

Paula Vogel, Maria Irene Fornes, Sam Shepard, and Samuel Beckett.

PENNY FARFAN is associate professor of drama at the University of Calgary in Canada and has published articles in such journals as *Text and Performance Quarterly*, *Theatre Journal*, *Canadian Theatre Review*, *Modern Drama*, *Woolf Studies Annual*, *American Drama*, and *Inversions*. She has also served as the book review editor for *Modern Drama*. Her research focuses on women and performance in the late nineteenth and early twentieth centuries and on contemporary feminist drama.

JAMES FISHER, professor of theater at Wabash College, is the author of several books, including *The Theater of Tony Kushner: Living Past Hope*. He has published numerous articles and reviews, including essays on the plays of Tennessee Williams in *Mississippi Quarterly* and *Text and Presentation* and in *Tennessee Williams: A Guide to Research and Performance*. His essay " 'In My Leftover Heart': Confessional Autobiography in Tennessee Williams's *Something Cloudy, Something Clear*" was published in *The Undiscovered Country: The Later Plays of Tennessee Williams*.

VERNA FOSTER teaches modern drama, Shakespeare, and dramatic theory at Loyola University of Chicago. She has published numerous essays on Renaissance and modern drama, especially tragicomedy, on which topic she has completed a book-length study. Her most recent publications include an essay on *A Streetcar Named Desire* as tragicomedy in *American Drama* and an essay on *A Lovely Sunday for Creve Coeur* for *The Undiscovered Country: The Later Plays of Tennessee Williams*.

JOHN GRONBECK-TEDESCO is associate dean of the College of Liberal Arts and Sciences at the University of Kansas and the editor of the *Journal of Dramatic Theory and Criticism*. He has published essays on Williams and other contemporary playwrights in *Publications of the Mississippi Philological Association*, *Mississippi Quarterly*, and *Studies in American Drama, 1945–Present*. His essay on *The Rose Tattoo* was included in *Tennessee Williams: A Casebook*, and another essay, "Morality, Ethics and the Failure of Love in Shakespeare's *Othello*," appeared in *Othello: New Critical Essays*.

JANET V. HAEDICKE is professor of English at the University of Louisiana at Monroe. She has published numerous articles on Williams as well as on such contemporary American playwrights as Mamet, Henley, and Shepard. She has recently assumed Co-editorship of the *Tennessee Williams Literary Journal*.

ALLEAN HALE, Tennessee Williams specialist in the Theater Department at the University of Illinois at Urbana, has published or presented more than 50 articles on the playwright and has been a consultant on five PBS documentaries. She has edited four Williams plays for New Directions, including *Not about Nightingales*, *Fugitive Kind*, and *Stairs to the Roof*, and is on the editorial board of the *Tennessee Williams Annual Review*. Her essay "*Gnädiges Fräulein*: Tennessee Williams's Clown Show" was published in *The Undiscovered Country: The Later Plays of Tennessee Williams*, and her "Early Williams: The Making of a Playwright" appeared in *The Cambridge Companion to Tennessee Williams*. Her "*In the Bar of a Tokyo Hotel*: Breaking the Code" is included in *Magical Muse: Millennial Essays on Tennessee Williams*.

CATHY HENDERSON is the curator of exhibitions at the Harry Ransom Humanities Research Center, University of Texas at Austin, the principal repository of Tennessee Williams papers. She has curated exhibitions on "Tennessee Williams in New Orleans," "Twentieth-century American Playwrights," and postwar British theater. She has been a panelist at the Tennessee Williams New Orleans Literary Festival and contributed a chapter to *Tennessee Williams: A Guide to Research and Performance* on *I Rise in Flame, Cried the Phoenix*.

DEANA HOLIFIELD teaches at Pearl River Community College and is doing research on Gothic elements in nineteenth- and twentieth-century literature, as well as preparing a study of the southern Gothic in Williams's plays. She has published previously on communication technologies and writing.

CHRISTINA HUNTER has prepared "A Tennessee Williams Bibliography, 1998–2001" for the *Tennessee Williams Annual Review*. She has presented papers at the Tennessee Williams Scholars Conference and at the Florida State University Film and Literature Conference. She is currently working on a study of Williams's apprentice plays.

NORMA JENCKES teaches drama and playwriting at the University of Cincinnati where she also is the director of the Helen Weinberger Center for the Study of Drama and Playwriting. She is the founding and continuing editor of a scholarly journal, *American Drama*, and has published on Albee, Williams, O'Neill, Lawton, Miller, and Odets. She has published widely on George Bernard Shaw, British and Irish drama, and American playwrights. Her essays on studying *Camino Real* and *Clothes for a Summer Hotel* were published in *The Undiscovered Country: The Later Plays of Tennessee Williams*. She also edited *New Readings in American Drama: Something's Happening Here*.

THOMAS KEITH is an editor at New Directions Publishing Corporation in New York City where he has been involved in the publication of a dozen Tennessee Williams titles. Along with Peggy Fox, he is the coeditor of *The Selected Letters of Tennessee Williams and James Laughlin* and contributed "*A House Not Meant to Stand*—Tennessee's Haunted Last Laugh" to *The Undiscovered Country: The Later Plays of Tennessee Williams*.

KIMBALL KING is professor of English at the University of North Carolina at Chapel Hill and coeditor of *Southern Literary Journal* as well as the general editor for the Routledge Casebooks on Modern Drama Texts Series. He is the author of numerous articles on southern writers, and he contributed an essay on Williams and southern literature for a special issue of the *Mississippi Quarterly* devoted to Tennessee Williams.

KRISTIN J. KOLIN is a national certified counselor with a master's degree in counseling from Wake Forest University and is currently working as a rehabilitation counselor in Charlotte, North Carolina. Her previous Williams work includes a charcoal drawing that appeared in a special issue of *The Southern Quarterly* in 1999. She has made a presentation on the principles of mindbody counseling at the National Conference of the American Counseling Association and is doing research on logotherapy.

SUSAN KOPRINCE is a professor of English at the University of North Dakota. Her publications include *Understanding Neil Simon* and articles on Tennessee Williams's unseen characters, William Inge, Zoe Atkins, Edith Wharton, and others.

RICHARD E. KRAMER, an actor, director, theater and writing teacher, dramaturg/literary manager, reviewer, researcher, and former editor of two theater newsletters, has participated in panels for the East Central Theatre Conference, the Modern Language Association, and the Mid-American Theatre Conference. His work appears in *The Cambridge Guide to World Theatre*, *The Cambridge Guide to American Theatre*, *Speaking on Stage*, and *Tennessee Williams: A Guide to Research and Performance*, as well as in such journals as *Drama Review*, *Studies in American Drama, 1945–Present*, *Journal of American Drama and Theatre*, *Theatre History Studies*, and the online edition of the *Tennessee Williams Annual Review*.

FRANCIS X. KUHN is associate professor and chair of the Department of Theatre and Dance at the University of Southern Mississippi. A professional stage director, Kuhn has directed works by Tennessee Williams for both regional and academic theaters. He has published on Eugene O'Neill, and his essay " 'My Cue to Fight': Stage Violence in *Othello*" was recently published in *Othello: New Critical Essays*.

COLBY H. KULLMAN, professor of English at the University of Mississippi, is editor of the two-volume *Theatre Companies of the World* and coeditor (with Philip C. Kolin) of *Studies in American Drama, 1945–Present*. He coedited *Speaking on Stage: Interviews with Contemporary American Playwrights* (with Philip C. Kolin). He is on the National Advisory Boards of the Mississippi Delta Tennessee Williams Festival, the William Inge Theatre Festival, and Alaska's Last

Frontier Theatre Festival. For the past 10 years, he has given tours of Tennessee Williams's Mississippi Delta. He has published articles on Tennessee Williams in *Mississippi Quarterly*, *Southern Quarterly*, and *Tennessee Williams: A Guide to Research and Performance*. His interview with Arthur Miller appeared in *Michigan Quarterly Review*.

LEONARD J. LEFF has taught film history and screenwriting at Oklahoma State University. With Jerold Simmons he has authored *The Dame in the Kimono* on the archival production history of *A Streetcar Named Desire* and other films made from American plays. His essay "And Transfer to Cemetery: The Streetcars Named Desire" appeared in *Film Quarterly*, and another essay on the racial politics of *Gone with the Wind* was published in *The Best American Movie Writing 2001*.

FELICIA HARDISON LONDRÉ is Curators' Professor of Theatre at the University of Missouri, Kansas City, and dramaturg for Missouri Repertory Theatre, Nebraska Shakespeare Festival, and the Heart of American Shakespeare Festival. In 1993 she was visiting foreign professor at Hosei University in Tokyo, and in 1995 she held the Women's Chair in Humanistic Studies at Marquette University. Her first book was *Tennessee Williams*. Since then her books include *Tom Stoppard*, *Federico García Lorca*, and *The History of North American Theater: The United States, Canada, and Mexico from Pre-Columbian Times to the Present*, a book in progress, with Daniel J. Watermeier. She currently serves on nine editorial boards and is vice-president of the American Theatre and Drama Society. Her essay "*A Streetcar Named Desire* Running Fifty Years" was published in *The Cambridge Companion to Tennessee Williams*, and an essay on *The Two-Character Play* appears in *The Undis-*

covered Country: The Later Plays of Tennes-see Williams. She has also written for opera.

MARY FRANCES LUX, professor of medical technology at the University of Southern Mississippi, has published an essay titled "Tenn in the Land of the Lotus Eaters" for the *Southern Quarterly* and presented "Tennessee Williams: Drug Use in His Life and Fiction" at the Third Annual Meeting of the Southern Association for the History of Science and Medicine. Continuing her interest in medicine and drama, she also published " 'Work on My Medicine': Physiologies and Anatomies in *Othello*" in *Othello: New Critical Essays.*

LINDA ELKINS McDANIEL, who teaches at William Carey College in Hattiesburg, Mississippi, is the author of a number of essays that have appeared in collections on southern authors, such as Styron and Poe in *Poe and Our Time* and William Gilmore Simms in *Long Years of Neglect.* Her publications on William Faulkner include articles in *Mississippi Quarterly* and *Notes on Mississippi Writers* and a book-length study, *William Faulkner's* Flags in the Dust. *Annotations to the Novel.*

THOMAS MOLZAHN, who works at the University of Cologne, is a journalist and coeditor of the cultural magazine *Hagen.* His research interests focus on Thomas Mann's influence on Tennessee Williams. He has published articles on E.T.A. Hoffman, Thomas Mann, and Theodor Storm.

LOU ANNE MOREHOUSE has served as Executive Director of the Tennessee Williams Literary Festival and was responsible for coordinating many of its events.

NICHOLAS R. MOSCHOVAKIS, an independent scholar, is the coeditor with David

Roessel of *The Collected Poems of Tennes-see Williams* for New Directions. He has also edited and coedited several previously unpublished texts by Williams (most recently for *Hudson Review* and *Michigan Quarterly Review*) and is currently at work on an edition of Williams's unpublished early one-acts. He contributed "Representing Othello: Early Modern Jury Trials and the Equitable Judgments of Tragedy" to *Othello: New Critical Essays* and has published articles in *Shakespeare Quarterly* and *Milton Quarterly.*

BRENDA MURPHY is professor of English at the University of Connecticut. She has published extensively on Williams and modern drama. Among her books are *Tennessee Williams and Elia Kazan: A Collaboration in the Theatre*; *O'Neill: "Long Day's Journey into Night"*; *Congressional Theatre: Dramatizing McCarthyism on Stage, Film, and Television*; *Miller: "Death of a Salesman"*; *American Realism and American Drama, 1880–1940*; *Cambridge Studies in American Literature and Culture*; and with George Monteiro, *John Hay—Howell's Letters.* She has edited *The Cambridge Companion to American Women Playwrights* and *A Realist in the American Theatre: Selected Drama Criticism of William Dean Howells.*

JACQUELINE O'CONNOR is an assistant professor of English at Boise State University, where she teaches drama and American literature. She is the author of *Dramatizing Dementia: Madness in the Plays of Tennessee Williams* and of several articles on boarding house representations in Williams's plays. She contributed two essays to *The Cambridge Companion to Tennessee Williams.* Her other publications include essays on playwrights David Rabe, Anna Cora Mowatt, Ntozake Shange, and Luis Valdez.

MICHAEL PALLER teaches theater history and American drama and criticism at the State University of New York at Purchase. He has been consulting dramaturg for the Roundabout Theatre Company and literary manager and dramaturg at George Street Playhouse. He has also been consulting dramaturg for the Manhattan Theatre Company in New York and the Long Wharf Theatre in New Haven. His essay on *The Milk Train Doesn't Stop Here Anymore* appears in *The Undiscovered Country: The Later Plays of Tennessee Williams*. He has also written on the image of Rose Williams in Williams's plays for *Magical Muse: Millennial Essays on Tennessee Williams* and has published numerous articles.

BRIAN PARKER, Distinguished Professor Emeritus of English at the Trinity College of the University of Toronto, has served as founding director of the Graduate Drama Centre, head of Graduate English Studies, and vice-provost of Trinity College. He has published numerous works on Williams and textural scholarship for *Tennessee Williams Annual Review, Papers of the Bibliographic Society of America*, and *Modern Drama*. His articles on *The Rose Tattoo, The Night of the Iguana*, and other Williams plays are providing the textual history for these scripts. He has edited a collection of critical essays on *The Glass Menagerie* and has also edited several Renaissance plays.

GENE D. PHILLIPS, S.J. teaches literature and film history at Loyola University of Chicago. He is the author of *The Films of Tennessee Williams* and has contributed essays on the plays and films of Tennessee Williams to *Confronting Tennessee Williams's "A Streetcar Named Desire": Essays in Critical Pluralism, The Encyclopedia of Stage Plays into Film, Video Versions: Film Adaptations of Plays on Video*, and *The Undiscovered*

Country: The Later Plays of Tennessee Williams as well as to the *Tennessee Williams Literary Review*. He has also written books on Alfred Hitchcock and Stanley Kubrick.

W. DOUGLAS POWERS is assistant professor of theater at Susquehanna University and is also a professional actor and director. His publications, including an article on Williams's contemporary Lynn Riggs and a forthcoming book on a masked Cherokee ritual. He has primarily done research on American Indian drama.

JEAN RHODES is a professor of literature at Middle Tennessee State University in Murfreesboro, Tennessee. Her interests include the playwright's biography and letters, examination of dramaturgical issues and his early plays and late novels. Her research has resulted in presentations at the Tennessee Williams Scholars' Conference in New Orleans, Louisiana, and the International Image and Imagery Conference in St. Catharine's, Ontario.

JOHN RINDO is an associate professor of theater at the University of Puget Sound in Tacoma, Washington. In 1989 he won a National Award at the Kennedy Center in Washington, D.C. for his direction of *Tracers*, a play about veterans who had served in the Vietnam War. He has directed over 30 productions, specializing in Shakespeare, Williams, and especially musical theater. Currently he is working on a book about the nature of stage direction titled *Exits: Pursued by a Bear* (a title taken from Shakespeare's *The Winter's Tale*). Rindo plans to direct the National Theatre's version of Williams's *Sweet Bird of Youth* as soon as the production rights become available.

KATHLEEN M. ROSSMAN is a freelance writer and editor, currently living in northern Colorado. Her articles have appeared in *Studies in American Drama, 1945–Present* and *Mississippi Folklore Register*.

TERRI SMITH RUCKEL teaches writing at Louisiana State University. She has contributed " 'A Giggling, Silly Bitchy Voluptuary': Tennessee Williams *Memoirs* as Apologia Pro Vita Sua" to the special Tennessee Williams issue of *Southern Quarterly*. Her essay "*Ut Pictura Poesis, Ut Poesis Pictura*: The Painterly Texture of Tennessee Williams's *In the Bar of a Tokyo Hotel*" was published in *The Undiscovered Country: The Later Plays of Tennessee Williams*. She is currently completing a project that studies intersections of gender, race, and "southern sexuality" in contemporary southern women's writings. She is a frequent reviewer for *World Literature Today*.

ANNETTE J. SADDIK is an assistant professor of English at New York City College of Technology (CUNY), where she teaches twentieth-century drama, literature, and writing. Her publications on Williams include a book on the later work, *The Politics of Reputation: The Critical Reception of Tennessee Williams's Later Plays*, as well as articles in *Modern Drama* and *Theatre Journal*. Her essay "The Inexpressible Regret of All Her Regrets: Tennessee Williams's Later Plays as Artaudian Theatre of Cruelty" was published in *The Undiscovered Country: The Later Plays of Tennessee Williams*.

DEAN SHACKELFORD was associate professor of English at Southeast Missouri State University, where he taught classes in film, drama, and twentieth-century American literature until his untimely death in 2003. He also served as director of undergraduate studies in English. His publications have appeared in *Southern Quarterly*, *Modern Drama*, *Mississippi Quarterly*, and *The*

Flannery O'Connor Bulletin. His work primarily dealt with southern writers, including Tennessee Williams, Flannery O'Connor, Harper Lee, and on a "queer" approach to Williams and the religious dimensions of his work.

SUSAN SWARTWOUT is associate professor, director of the University Press, and editor of *Big Muddy: Journal of the Mississippi River Valley* at Southeast Missouri State University. Her writing has been published in many literary journals, in anthologies, and in two poetry collections. Her essay on Katherine Anne Porter's *Hacienda* was published in *Value and Vision in American Literature*. She has recently published a book with Longman titled *A Student's Guide to Getting Published*.

MARGARET BRADHAM THORNTON is the editor of *The Journals of Tennessee Williams* published by Yale University Press in 2004. In addition to her work on Williams, she has written on Jean Rhys and Barbara Pym.

RALPH F. VOSS, professor of English at the University of Alabama, has edited *Magical Muse: Millennial Essays on Tennessee Williams*. He has also published *A Life of William Inge: The Strains of Triumph*, and *Elements of Practical Writing* and coauthored *The Heath Guide to College Writing* (with Michael L. Keene). He is a member of the National Advisory Boards for the William Inge Festival and the Mississippi Delta Tennessee Williams Festival.

J. MARCUS WEEKLEY is currently completing his Ph.D. in English at Texas Tech University. A poet, he has published poems in numerous literary quarterlies. He has also published on technical communication issues.

JÜRGEN C. WOLTER is professor of English at Bergische Universität, Wuppertal, Germany, where he teaches American literature. He has published two books on antebellum American drama and theater and articles on a number of American writers such as Eugene O'Neill, Tennessee Williams, Arthur Kopit, David Mamet, Sam Shepard, Zora Neale Hurston, William Faulkner, and Toni Morrison.

KIRK WOODWARD has taught acting, playwrighting, and creative dramatics. A staff producer for Twelve Miles West, he has also been president of the Attic Ensemble, producing partner for the LPC Company (plays for children), and managing director of Stage Left, Inc. Author of over 20 produced plays, he has directed plays by Williams, Pinter, and Shakespeare.

ARTHUR WROBEL is professor of English at the University of Kentucky, where he was the editor for the scholarly journal *AN&Q* for many years. He has written on several nineteenth- and twentieth-century American authors, particularly Melville.